Envisioning an English Empire

EARLY AMERICAN STUDIES
Daniel K. Richter and Kathleen M. Brown, Series Editors

Exploring neglected aspects of our colonial, revolutionary, and early national history and culture, Early American Studies reinterprets familiar themes and events in fresh ways. Interdisciplinary in character, and with a special emphasis on the period from about 1600 to 1850, the series is published in partnership with the McNeil Center for Early American Studies.

A complete list of books in the series is available from the publisher.

Envisioning an English Empire

Jamestown and the Making of the North Atlantic World

EDITED BY ROBERT APPELBAUM
AND JOHN WOOD SWEET

PENN

University of Pennsylvania Press

Philadelphia

Copyright © 2005 University of Pennsylvania Press
All rights reserved
Printed in the United States of America on acid-free paper

10 9 8 7 6 5 4 3 2 1

Published by
University of Pennsylvania Press
Philadelphia, Pennsylvania 19104-4011

Library of Congress Cataloging-in-Publication Data

Envisioning an English empire : Jamestown and the making of the North Atlantic world / edited by Robert Appelbaum and John Wood Sweet.
   p. cm.—(Early American studies)
  ISBN 0-8122-3853-2 (alk. paper)—ISBN 0-8122-1903-1 (pbk. : alk. paper)
  Includes bibliographical references and index.
   1. Smith, John, 1580–1631. 2. Jamestown (Va.)—History. 3. Great Britain—Colonies—America—History—17th century. I. Appelbaum, Robert, 1952–. II. Sweet, John Wood, 1966–. III. Series
F234.J3 J3255 2005
973.2'1—dc22   2004058847

Contents

Foreword   xi
  Karen Ordahl Kupperman

Introduction: Sea Changes   1
  John Wood Sweet

Part I. Reading Encounters

1. The Conquest of Eden: Possession and Dominion in Early Virginia   25
   James Horn

2. Powhatans Abroad: Virginia Indians in England   49
   Alden T. Vaughan

3. John Smith Maps Virginia: Knowledge, Rhetoric, and Politics   68
   Lisa Blansett

4. The Politics of Pathos: Richard Frethorne's Letters Home   92
   Emily Rose

Part II. The World Stage

5. The Specter of Spain in John Smith's Colonial Writing   111
   Eric Griffin

6. The White Othello: Turkey and Virginia in John Smith's *True Travels*   135
   Pompa Banerjee

7. England, Morocco, and Global Geopolitical Upheaval   152
   Susan Iwanisziw

8. Irish Colonies and the Americas   172
   Andrew Hadfield

Part III. American Metamorphosis

9. Hunger in Early Virginia: Indians and English Facing Off over Excess, Want, and Need   195
    Robert Appelbaum

10. Between "Plain Wilderness" and "Goodly Corn Fields": Representing Land Use in Early Virginia   217
    Jess Edwards

11. Settling with Slavery: Human Bondage in the Early Anglo-Atlantic World   236
    Michael J. Guasco

12. "We All Smoke Here": Behn's *The Widdow Ranter* and the Invention of American Identity   254
    Peter C. Herman

Conclusion: Jamestown and Its North Atlantic World   275
    Constance Jordan

Notes   289

Bibliography   325

List of Contributors   357

Index   359

Acknowledgments   369

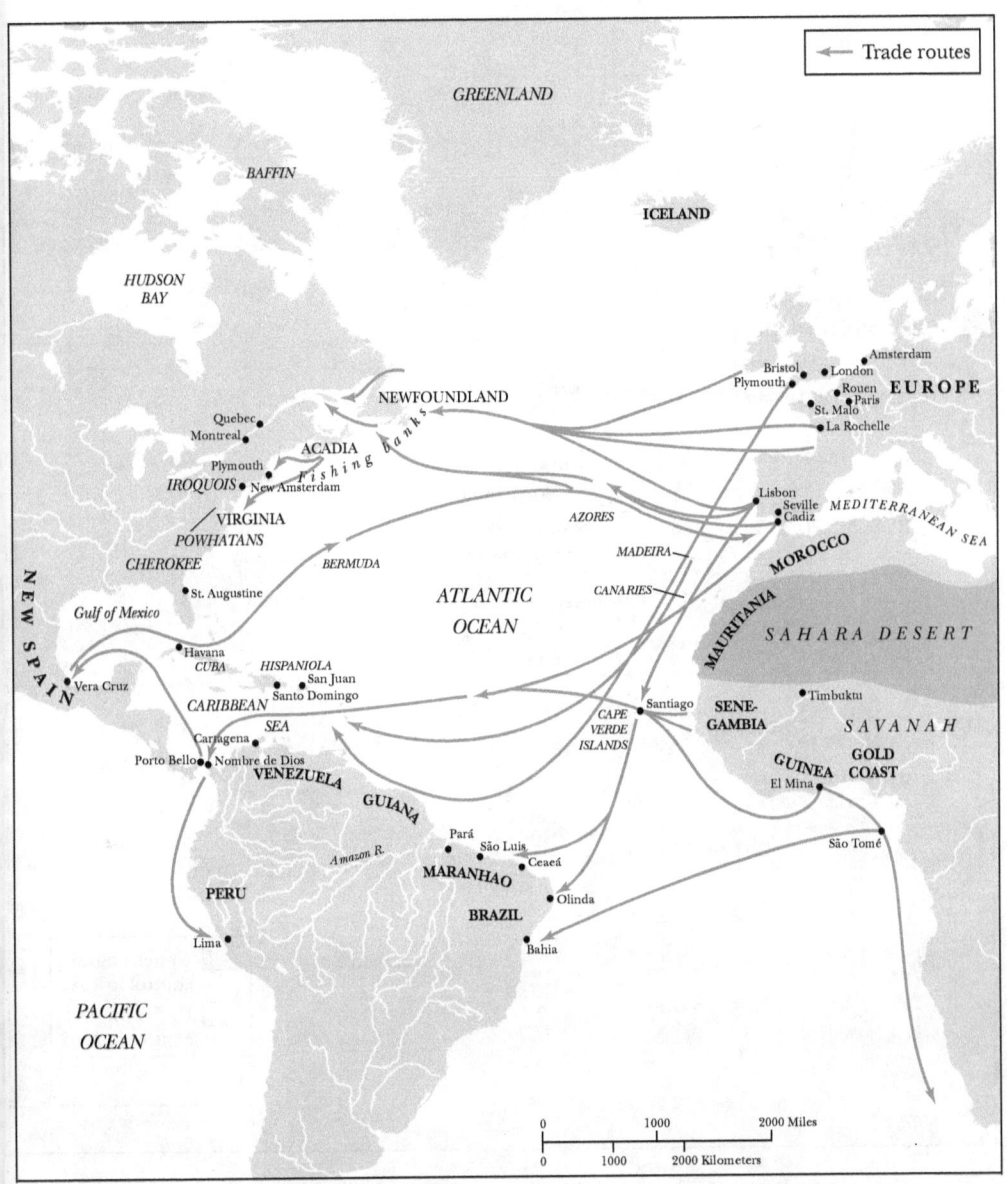

Map 1. The North Atlantic World: principal trade routes, ca. 1630. Sources: Meinig, *The Shaping of America*, map 8; Gleach, *Powhatan's World*, fig. 1; Kwamelna-Poh et al., *African History in Maps*, map 6.

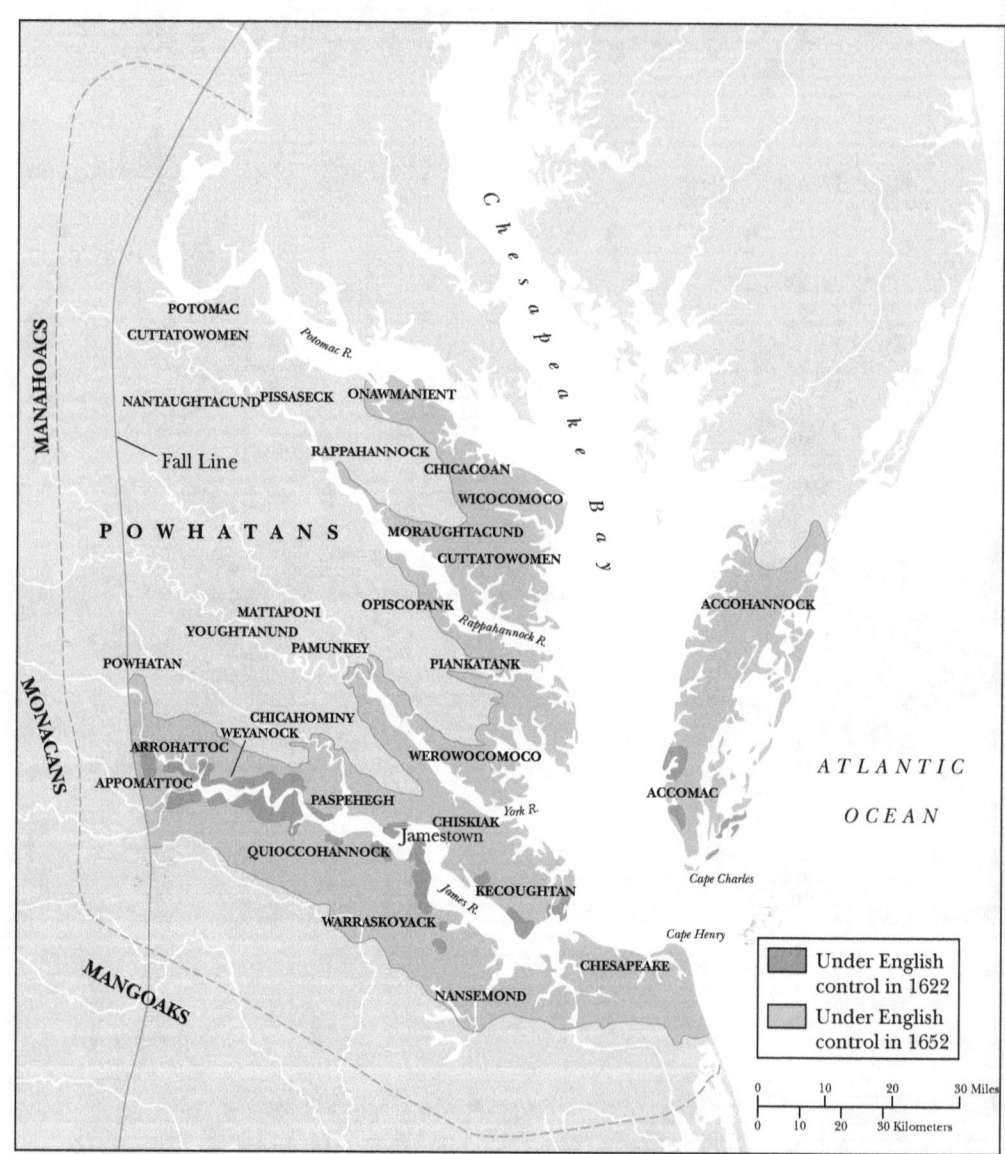

Map 2. Powhatan territory and the Virginia colony, 1607–1652. Sources: Gleach, *Powhatan's World*, fig. 2; Nugent, *Cavaliers and Pioneers*, 1611, 1622, 1652; Billings, *The Old Dominion*.

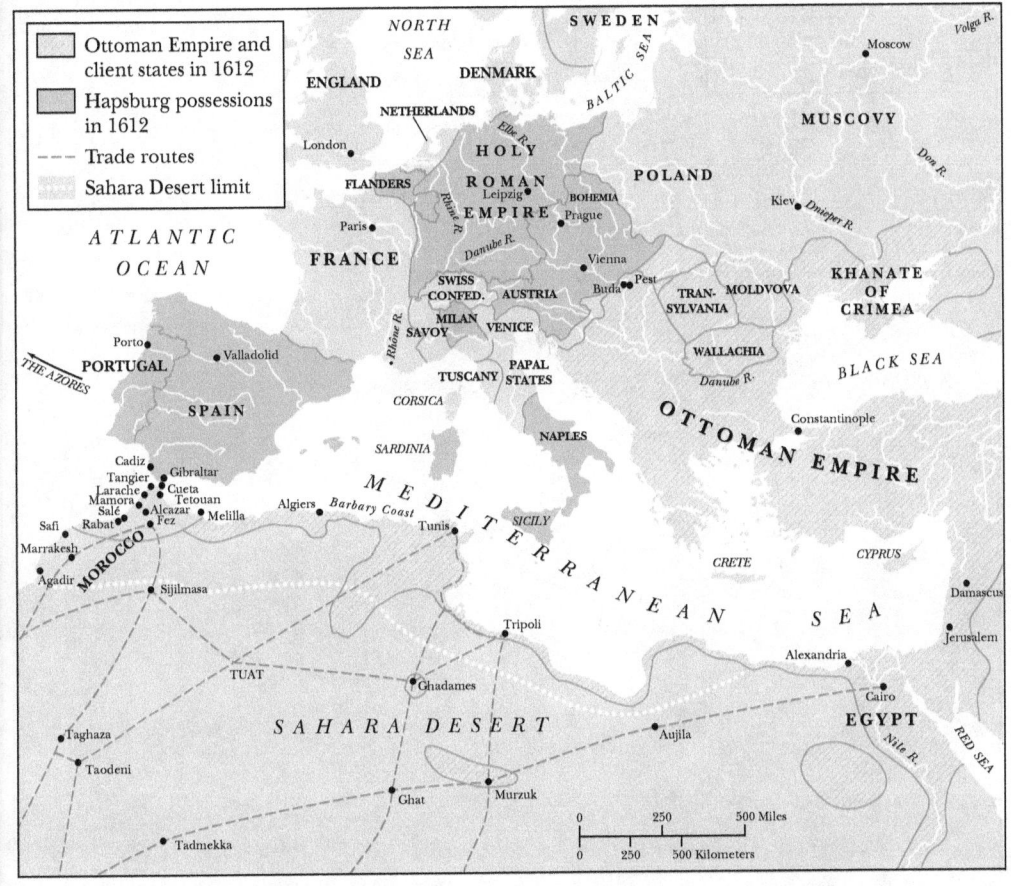

Map 3. The Mediterranean world, ca. 1612. Sources: Pitcher, *Historical Geography*, map 23; Kwamena-Poh et al., *African History in Maps*, map 6.

Map 4. Great Britain: principal English and Scottish plantations in Ireland, 1556–1700. Source: Canny, *Origins of Empire*, maps 6.1, 6.2.

Foreword

KAREN ORDAHL KUPPERMAN

In recent decades, study of Jamestown became stuck in a narrow focus on the events of the early colony. Conflict between its larger-than-life leaders and the fate of its less-than-worthy rank and file took center stage and the questions of which leader was right or whether anyone was telling the truth loomed large. But a larger context is needed now. The history of Jamestown and the beginnings of English settlement in America is better served when we view it in an Atlantic frame. It is better served, too, when we take advantage of the renewed focus on the early colonial period current among many disciplines, and bring together literary specialists, historians, and archaeologists to pool knowledge and perspectives.

Rather than isolating Jamestown's founding as the beginning of American history, the Atlantic perspective provides a more realistic context for English thinking about overseas ventures. It aims to understand the place of colonies as contemporaries did. The first question then becomes "Why 1607?" American enterprises must be set first within European history, and for the English they began within the great opposition to Roman Catholic Spain as the ultimate other. Pacification of Roman Catholic Ireland through colonization was an old theme, and England's safety was the principal concern there. Richard Hakluyt, the great Elizabethan promoter of American ventures, spread the Black Legend of Spanish rapaciousness supported and excused by Rome. Ralegh's failed colony of Roanoke, first conceptualized as part of that resistance to Spain, preceded Jamestown, as did the Spanish settlement of St. Augustine in Florida, whose settlement in the 1560s was the true beginning of permanent European settlement within the future United States.

The Old Atlantic World contained many others, and many English in America had had previous experience in Europe and the Mediterranean. The earliest plantations in all regions were led and to a great extent populated by men who had served in the armies of the religious wars in Europe; Virginia colony secretary John Pory praised "that university of warre, the low Countries."[1] Others, like the Pilgrims who founded Plymouth colony, had lived in exile there.

In the wake of the founding of the Levant Company and the entrance of

English merchants into eastern trades, many American venturers had traveled in the rich east and some, like George Sandys, who later became the Virginia Company's treasurer in Virginia, had published books about their experiences. Sandys's best-selling account appeared as *A Relation of a Journey Begun An: Dom: 1610. Foure Bookes Containing a description of the Turkish Empire, of Ægypt, of the Holy Land, of the Remote parts of Italy and Ilands adjoyning* (London, 1615), and it went through many editions; facing the title page was a portrait of the author identifying him as "George Sandes Poet & Traveller." John Smith was one who had not only lived within the Ottoman Empire, but had been by his own account enslaved there as a war captive. Others had been captured by and ransomed from the feared Barbary pirates of North Africa. So bold had these pirates become that a few English were even seized from villages on the west coast of England. What this means is that when English writers compared American Indian clothing or rituals to Irish habits or Muslim worship and beliefs, they were both showing their own sophistication and conveying an understanding that their readers would recognize.

Some transatlantic voyagers had also had experience or knowledge of African regions south of the area they called Barbary. John Pory, who reported on the first meeting of the Virginia Assembly in 1619 as colony secretary, had earlier published his translation and adaptation of the history of Africa written by the man we know as Leo Africanus with Pory's additions from other sources. Pory wrote on his title page that the main part of the book was "written in Arabicke and Italian by Iohn Leo a More, borne in Granada, and brought up in Barbarie."[2] A few English ships had ventured to the coast of West Africa and seen the early shape of the trade in enslaved Africans.

All this prior experience shaped the mental context of colonization; the texts from American experience were often written by people who had known other societies and cultural contexts in the Old World, and had in many cases been exposed to more advanced and opulent societies than their own. The date 1607 grew out of English history, in policy changes in the aftermath of the end of the Tudor regime at the death of Elizabeth I and the accession of the Stuarts with James I in 1603. It also signaled a new level of both competence and economic organization that made it possible for England to compete for the first time on the Atlantic stage. Expertise came in part from experience abroad. Competence was not complete, however, and the English colonies all imported experts from continental Europe—mineralogists, glassmakers, textile specialists. Every colony was also dependent on American Indian knowledge and largess. By 1619 and possibly before, Virginia had residents who had come directly from Africa.[3] Thus every venture was Atlantic in both background and personnel.

The Indian polities that allowed English settlement also had an Atlantic context. Although their trade networks centered on the great internal waterways in the American continent, the coastal Algonquians had repeated experience of European ships throughout the sixteenth century. They also had direct knowledge of Europe through voyagers such as Squanto from New England and Paquiquineo, the Virginia Pamunkey man usually known to us by his Spanish name Don Luís de Velasco, who had lived in Europe. Some American groups actively sought roles in the Atlantic trades and initiated Europeans into the possibilities they saw. Before such crops as tobacco were established, most of the trades were conducted in Indian-produced commodities.

Considering Jamestown in an Atlantic frame allows us to transcend particular issues and to examine the colony's course in something like the way contemporaries would have done. Instead of viewing Jamestown as an isolated point in history, an Atlantic approach also leads us to acknowledge the virtually simultaneous foundation of Quebec and Santa Fe and to understand the widespread renewed commitment in Europe to an American presence as the seventeenth century opened. Jamestown's Atlantic context involved contact and exchange between and among colonies all along the coast, and national differences in Europe did not dictate relationships in America.

The enterprise of viewing Jamestown in an Atlantic frame is immeasurably enhanced by new interest in American enterprises possessed by literary scholars, archaeologists, ethnohistorians, and art historians. For historians the application of the techniques of textual analysis employed by students of literature to the texts of encounter and colonization has been wholly beneficial. The range of questions we ask of those texts, and how we contextualize them, has been extended immeasurably.

Changing views of Captain John Smith's story of his own life offer a good example of the transformative effect of new techniques from a variety of disciplines. Earlier models of textual analysis, applied by historians in the nineteenth century, had led to the charge that Smith lied when he wrote of his captivity and rescue by Pocahontas, seeking to cash in on her celebrity when she was in London. Scholars focused on internal consistency between Smith's various works, and he failed that test. More recently, work emanating from a whole host of disciplines has led to reconsideration of Smith's story. The earliest and most surprising of these reconsiderations came from students of early modern Transylvania and Hungary, who found Smith's description of his service there before he went to Virginia, told in his autobiographical *The True Travels, Adventures, and Observations of Captaine John Smith* (London, 1630), to be a valuable and accurate resource for their studies in a source-poor field.[4] Having participated in the fight of Protestant Dutch seeking freedom from the Roman Catholic Spanish Hapsburgs, Smith had gone on to serve in the Hapsburg armies resisting Ottoman encroachment on eastern Europe. He wrote that he "was desirous to see more of the world, and trie his fortune against the Turkes, both lamenting and repenting to have seene so many Christians slaughter one another."⁵

Ethnohistorians and archaeologists have also contributed perspectives that make us understand Smith and other writers in a new light, one that appreciates their achievement. For example, all early English observers wrote that American Indian polities were hierarchically organized with a hereditary elite and strong chiefs. Such reports have often been dismissed as the myopic reports of culture-bound English who were unable to understand societies very different from their own. But archaeologists are now finding burials and other remains that confirm the accuracy of those early observations; hereditary elites apparently did exist broadly across indigenous American polities.⁶ And ethnohistorians have argued that the event in which Smith believed Pocahontas had saved his life may have been an induction or adoption into Powhatan society, a symbolic death and rebirth such as young men went through as they reached adulthood. Shortly after the ceremony Powhatan told Smith that he would henceforth regard him as a son, and Pocahontas called him father when they met in England, perhaps indicating their understanding of his new status.⁷

Archaeologists working with environmental scientists have also given us a new understanding of the most fundamental context of the creation of the Atlantic world. The extreme cold of the Little Ice Age, including the very cold winter of 1607–8, conditioned the experience of all colonization and sea-borne ventures. Evidence of a period of sustained cold throughout the northern hemisphere from reports, pictures, and other "proxy evidence" has now been confirmed by detailed analysis of ocean and lake bed cores.⁸ Very recent work in dendrochronology has also demonstrated that the Chesapeake region was in the throes of unprecedented drought conditions when the English arrived. All this new evidence makes us see the developing relationship between newcomers and Americans, especially the effect of the colonists' insistent demands for food, very differently. Historians have admired the cleverness of Powhatan and his ability to outwit the English in bargaining. Powhatan, "this subtil Salvage," exasperated Smith, "valuing a basket of corne more pretious then a basket of copper, saying he could eate his corne, but not his copper." Smith also wrote that "Men maie thinke it strange there should be this stir for a little corne, but had it been gold with more ease we might have got it." Our new knowledge of the extreme drought conditions places these statements in a completely different light; Powhatan was not merely sparring with colonial leaders but protecting his people's meager food supplies in a time of great stress.⁹

At the same time literary studies allow us to go beyond the simple truth/falsehood dichotomy in reading Smith's biography. We can now understand how Smith was fashioning a self in his literary works, as he presented his own exploits and his analysis of the colonial scene. Smith's great work, the *Generall Historie,* was published in 1624, ten years after his last trip to

America, and his autobiography, *The True Travels, Adventures, and Observations of Captaine John Smith*, was published in 1630 in the last year of his life. The early seventeenth-century London literary world saw many dramas, poems, and prose works in which English venturers faced exotic foes and some experienced captivity and even forced conversion. Some, such as *The famous historye of the life and death of Captaine Thomas Stukeley* (London, 1605) or Richard Daborne's *A Christian Turn'd Turke: or, The Tragicall Lives and Deaths of the Two Famous Pyrates, Ward and Dansiker* (London, 1612) took off from the published life stories of actual people, English and Fleming, who became renegades. Philip Massinger's very popular *The Renegado, or The Gentleman of Venice* (1624) featured a Turkish princess named Donusa whose slave named Carazie was an English eunuch; Carazie told his mistress that he "was made lighter by two stone weight, at least, to be fit to serve you!" John Fletcher's *The Island Princess*, written in 1620–21, was set in the Moluccas and the hero, a Portuguese venturer, resisted forced conversion to Islam so steadfastly that his princess was won for Christianity, as was Donusa in *The Renegado*.[10]

As Jean Howard points out, many of these plays center on men who, like Smith and unlike Othello, were not born to elite heroic roles, but who took on such leading roles in novel exotic locations. The new Atlantic scene made possible a kind of advancement unavailable at home. Smith first wrote of his rescue by Pocahontas in 1624, and he told the story of his early life and his exploits in eastern Europe culminating in captivity in the Ottoman Empire in 1630. Like Carazie in *The Renegado*, he was the slave of a noble woman in Constantinople; he wrote that he made his violent escape when he was sent to be trained as a janissary. Rather than assuming that he simply made up these stories, an interpretation made much less plausible by recent research on the background of these events, it seems reasonable to argue that Smith saw the dramatic possibilities in his own story and presented those remembered events from decades earlier in a form that would draw the attention of the world he then inhabited.

All the disciplines whose research makes possible a renewed interest in the texts of the early modern Atlantic have in common the seriousness with which they take their sources and the generators of those sources. The first requirement for all of us is to examine the sources fully and carefully rather than to mine them for pithy quotes. The second is, having placed the sources under the microscope, to open them out and place them in the broadest possible context. Scholars must try to know as much as the creators of their sources knew and must try not to make easy assumptions about their motivations, justifications, and evasions. We must seek first to comprehend the choices they made and the institutions they created as contemporaries understood them rather than in terms of their meanings to later generations. The result of such interdisciplinarity is a far richer picture of the past—and one that contemporaries might recognize.

Introduction
Sea Changes

JOHN WOOD SWEET

One of the stranger exports of early Virginia was a new English translation of Ovid's *Metamorphoses*, published in London in 1626.[1] It was the work of the colony's erstwhile treasurer, George Sandys, who insisted in his preface that he did it in his spare time, presumably by candlelight.[2] Sandys had come to Virginia with an ambitious vision of the colony's future: he was to oversee its transformation from a disorderly, tobacco-crazed outpost into a stable, populous, and productive extension of the mother country. Perhaps his time was better spent in this work of scholarship and poetry: it is a fine translation, still in print almost four hundred years later. In any case, during his tenure the affairs of the Virginia colony were transformed by a series of disasters that he could probably have done little to control. Early in the morning of March 22, 1622, only six months after he arrived, the colony was nearly wiped out by a well-coordinated attack of an alliance of local natives that simultaneously slaughtered settlers at their outposts along Chesapeake Bay and the James River. In the months to come, many of the survivors who regrouped at Jamestown—and hundreds of new settlers sent to fortify the colony—died of disease and starvation. The Virginia Company of London, the joint-stock company that sponsored the colossally expensive venture, already weakened by disputes over the colony's future, faced bankruptcy. And Parliament launched an investigation that threatened the company with the loss of its royal charter.

So perhaps we should not blame Sandys, thousands of miles from home, in this crude, beleaguered colony, for being a bit obsessed with Ovid and the heritage of classical civility he represented—looking back to the celebrated legacy of the Roman empire, which had reshaped the world around the Mediterranean, as the English ventured into a dangerous, enticing New World that was then taking shape around the shores of the Atlantic. Perhaps he identified with Ovid, who had been sent by Augustus away from Rome and into exile in a remote province. And perhaps, in his enthusiasm for the English venture in Virginia, Sandys missed some of Ovid's ironic tone and his running critique of Roman imperialism.[3] In any case, it would be wrong to dismiss Sandys's interest in the legacy of the Roman empire as an escapist fantasy. For many English political leaders and promoters of overseas colonization, an idealized view of ancient Rome helped them envision—and justify—what they wanted to do in America.

Nowadays, we often imagine that the Virginia settlers were motivated almost exclusively by a drive for profit, but—as we are reminded by Sandys's obsession with Ovid, by conflicts within the company, and by crucial role played by the region's natives—the visions of those involved in the Virginia venture were actually much more complicated, ambitious, and contested. The purpose of this volume is to better understand the various visions that shaped early Virginia—and, more broadly, to rethink our basic assumptions about the relationships between ideas and actions, between ideology and interests, between events and the contexts that gave them meaning.

The idea for this collaboration grew out of a set of discussions at the National Endowment for the Humanities Summer Institute on Jamestown in the Atlantic World sponsored by the Folger Shakespeare Library and directed by Karen Ordahl Kupperman.[4] Robert Appelbaum and I emerged from those discussions convinced that we need to redraw the "map" of the early Atlantic world in two basic ways. In recent years, scholars have begun to recognize that European colonies in North America can be better understood in terms of an emerging Atlantic world; but we felt that Anglo-American historians need to remember that this world included Europe and the Mediterranean, as well as Africa and the Americas. Consequently, we sought out experts in who could help us understand the networks, alliances, and rivalries that encompassed not only England and the Powhatan chiefdom, but also Spain, France, the West Indies, Ireland, Morocco, and Turkey. In addition, we were convinced that Jamestown should be understood not simply as a historical event in the customary sense, but also as a literary phenomenon. For it was largely by way of the written word that participants defined their positions in this emerging world. Bringing together the perspectives of both historians and literary scholars, this collection attempts to understand thought and action in Jamestown and the emerging North Atlantic world by exploring a wide range of surviving texts—the books adventurers read, the manuscripts they left behind, the printed works they produced—and reading them as both historical records and literary productions.

The texts that document early Virginia reveal a complex, dynamic world—a world of relationships transformed by wide-ranging and rapidly expanding economic networks, and a world largely defined by representations intended to explain, to understand, and to deceive. The early settlers and leaders of the venture, it becomes clear, were motivated by religious, nationalistic, and intellectual—as well as economic—ambitions. Native leaders evaluated the benefits of tolerating these interlopers and the risks of openly opposing them within the context of their own complex calculations about building alliances, projecting authority, and controlling trade. Powhatan, the paramount chief who dominated the region, had interests to protect not just in the area immediately around Jamestown but also across a territory that encompassed much of the Chesapeake Bay watershed and in trading routes that extended hundreds of miles into the interior of the continent.[5] Similarly, English promoters of overseas colonies had much wider horizons than is often assumed. They thought of the colonial venture in broad international contexts: in terms of rivalry with Spain, the ongoing fight between Christendom and the Turks, complex diplomacy with North Africans, and renewed efforts to colonize Ireland. Ultimately the original expectations of native peoples, settlers, and other interested parties were overrun by experiences both predictable and unforeseen. Intentionally or not, they all participated in the creation of a new Atlantic World that transformed life in Europe, Africa, and the Americas. New networks of trade, cultural exchange, and political power confronted peoples on both sides of the Atlantic with new possibilities, changing how they could think about themselves, the relationships they could establish with others, and the kinds of futures they could envision.

Back in 1607, when the first Jamestown settlers landed on the shores of Chesapeake Bay, their crude outpost survived because nobody saw it as worth the trouble of wiping out. Partly that's because they lied about their intentions. Shortly after the settlers arrived, Powhatan, the leader of a regional paramount chiefdom, had them brought before him and demanded to know why they had come into his country. The settlers explained that they had only landed temporarily to repair ships damaged by Spanish aggression and bad weather. At least that is the story Capt. John Smith told in a narrative of the colony's first year that was published in London as *A True Relation* . . . (1609).[6] The formal instructions the colonists brought with them—in a sealed box, not to be opened until after they arrived—made it clear that the settlement was intended from the start to be permanent, populous, and profitable. The adventurers were to establish an English colony in the Americas that would set the stage for a challenge to Spain's Catholic empire. They were to win over the local natives, preferably by "reducing" them to civility and converting them to Christianity. And they were to make the entire enterprise pay not just by serving as a base for piratical raids on the Spanish treasure fleets but by finding gold, by discovering other merchantable commodities, or by locating the westerly route to the trading centers of Asia that Columbus had set out to find over a century earlier.[7]

This initial vision of the Virginia venture was wildly unrealistic: indeed, the early adventurers may have deceived themselves more than they fooled anyone in Powhatan's chiefdom. The views of the local natives were shaped by years of experience managing occasional European interlopers. For decades, the Chesapeake had been visited by mariners from Portugal, Spain, France, and England—who generally looked around, traded a bit, and left—without seeing much reason to return. Officials of the Spanish empire, masters of the Caribbean and Central America, had been keeping an eye on North America. Largely to prevent other European powers from establishing a foothold in Florida that might allow them to disrupt the flow of silver and gold from the Gulf of Mexico, the Spanish had established the first permanent European settlement in what is now the United States at San Augustín, Florida, in 1565. Several years later, in 1570, they went so far as to sponsor a Jesuit outpost on the shores of the Chesapeake. They brought with them a local Indian, usually known by his Spanish name, Don Luis de Velasco. He had spent the previous decade traveling widely in the Caribbean colonies and in Europe after being taken from his homeland by a party of Spanish explorers. In returning Don Luis home, the missionaries hoped he would teach his people the Castilian language, Spanish customs, and the Catholic faith. Instead, he promptly moved away from the mission, rejoined his multiple wives, and resumed his native customs. Predictably, the Jesuits objected. In any case, the conflict of cultures was soon settled when local natives effectively wiped the mission out. This was enough to discourage the Spanish, who found little of inherent interest in these cold climes and mainly sought to serve notice to the French, who were exploring the northern regions of the St. Lawrence riverway.[8]

In the wake of the Spanish came the English, who in the 1580s sought to establish a foothold on the North American seaboard between Spanish possessions to the south and French claims to the north. The Roanoke venture, like a number of other English settlements attempted further north in subsequent decades, failed without much help from the local natives. In fact, the outpost survived as long as it did only to the extent that the local natives furnished them with food and military protection. The tiny band of settlers left there in 1587 to hold the fort were not so much lost as they were abandoned when the Spanish Armada of 1588 prevented Sir Walter Ralegh from sending them supplies and a new complement of settlers. Some of the settlers abandoned there may have made their way up to Chesapeake Bay and made new lives for themselves living among the local Natives—though the Jamestown settlers never succeeded in tracking them down.[9] While these European interlopers could be troublesome, they also offered local natives potential benefits: they arrived with attractive trade goods, they had different technology and know-how that might be exploited, and they might be recruited as allies in local and regional struggles for power. In any case, none of these colonial ventures could have left the local natives with the impression that these Europeans posed much of a threat . . . at that point.

Looking back on the early years of the Virginia venture, some four hundred years after the fact, our own vision is inevitably distorted. Incomplete sources, a welter of historical associations, and the limits of our own imaginations inevitably cloud and color our views. Some historians of the United States have seen Jamestown as the origin of representative government, republican ideals, and widespread economic opportunity in America. Others have seen it as the origin of the Old South's plantation system—with the conquest and dispossession of native peoples, the enslavement of Africans, and the hegemony of a small elite of planters at its center. British historians tend to see Jamestown at the origins of England's overseas empire, which in subsequent centuries reached global dimensions. Until recently literary scholars tended to overlook events in Jamestown, since they viewed such historical phenomena as, at best, tangential to the great works of art they studied. Nowadays, literary scholars influenced by postcolonial theory often see the literature relating to events in Jamestown as an early symptom of England's grand imperialist project. But in its early years, Jamestown was none of these things—neither irrelevant nor the center of metropolitan attention. The English were not pioneers in the Atlantic: they were latecomers, following in the wake of the Spanish, the Portuguese, the French, and the Dutch. The settlement at Jamestown—however puffed up its prospects were in contemporary propaganda—was for its first two decades disastrously disappointing: most of the settlers who went there quickly died, most of the money invested in the venture was lost, and the colony itself was soon overshadowed by England's expanding Atlantic interests.

Nonetheless, Jamestown offers a particularly revealing window into the dynamic social and cultural world of which it was a part and into the developing interconnections that made the Atlantic into a new world of its own. The large number of texts published about Jamestown in its early years is in part a reflection of the nature of the enterprise itself: as a private joint-stock company, the colony had to attract investments. So, instead of simply bending the ears of a few at court, the Virginia Company had to rally interest from a much wider range of merchants, gentry, and large numbers of people with more modest means. In addition, because Jamestown involved such huge investments and because it came so early in the history of English overseas ventures, it attracted the interest of those at the center of power at the English court, including James I himself, as well as the most brilliant of England's literary figures, such as William Shakespeare. Jamestown thus provides a unique opportunity to explore the complex phenomenon that constitutes the theme of this volume: the "envisioning" of English empire.

When Robert Appelbaum and I first began our own exploration of the texts and contexts of Jamestown and the making of the North Atlantic World, we thought there would be a sharp divide between literary scholars and historians. And to some extent that expectation has been borne out.

Historians tend to place more emphasis on trying to determine what actually happened and why. Literary scholars tend to be more interested in complexities of language and meaning within texts in order to reflect upon "what happened" in terms of broader ideological impulses and imaginative interpretations. But, generally, we found that we shared common concerns and faced common problems: the representations of the colonial experience that are to be found in the historical records and texts of the experiment are multisided, and the texts that we must interpret are complex and often contradictory. George Sandys, for instance, left several different kinds of documentation, including not only his translation of Ovid but also reams of business correspondence, and together these texts leave us with a complex image of the man: laboring in practical ways to transform the colony's economy, to fulfill a specific vision of its future, while laboring to translate an ancient text of a classical empire with ambiguous parallels to his own adventures. We must read the texts critically, carefully, and at times suspiciously in order to understand either what happened or what it meant.

In the years after 1607, as the early English adventurers and the natives of the Chesapeake region assessed their prospects, they inevitably looked in three directions at once: they looked inward to their own societies and immediate ambitions, they looked outward to others, and they looked forward in time. This three-part perspective has been followed in the organization of this volume. We begin, in "Reading Encounters," by looking inward, examining the conditions of the initial encounters between the Jamestown settlers and the Powhatans and the relations of both with those in power in London. Then, in "The World Stage," we look outward, and explore the broad international contexts that gave meaning and defined the horizons of the English in this period—relations with Spain, with the Turks, with North Africa, and with Ireland. Finally, in "American Metamorphosis," we turn to the ways in which the visions of both settlers and Natives were transformed over time by their experiences. We consider colonial conflicts and exchanges over cultures of food, new ideologies of property and slavery, and changing perceptions of colonial identity at the time of Bacon's Rebellion in the 1670s. What results is a multidisciplinary and multifaceted view of the Jamestown experience as a whole, from the early plans and ideological inventions that would feed into the enterprise, to the eventual perception that, for better or worse, what had begun as a military outpost had ended up as the starting point for a new kind of society.

Reading Encounters

It would be wrong to say that Captain John Smith simply made up the famous story about how he was rescued from the wrath of Powhatan by the intercession of his fair daughter Pocahontas. Certainly, there are grounds for suspicion: after a relatively short stint at Jamestown, early Virginia's most celebrated adventurer spent of the rest of his career writing about his adventures, analyzing the development of the colony, and giving advice to other Anglo-American adventurers. And the stories he told about his time in Virginia evolved over time. The Pocahontas story does not appear in the history of the colony he published in 1612, after he was ousted from his position of leadership by his fellow settlers, survived an attempted assassination, and decided to returned to England. In fact, he first alluded to Pocahontas as his savior only ten years later, after she—renamed Rebecca, reborn as a Christian, and married to John Rolfe—had traveled to London and made a sensation at the royal court.[10] Was Smith trying to rehabilitate his tarnished reputation by claiming the sensational Indian princess as the agent of salvation God sent him? No doubt. But the problem is not that simple. Smith was as much a man of letters as a man of action—and in his narratives of events it is often difficult to separate his efforts to turn stories to his own ends from his (perhaps unconscious) efforts to understand himself and his place in the new world he helped to create.

The short, stout, pugnacious Captain Smith may well have given the first group of colonists their best leadership and the authorities of the Virginia Company the best practical advice they ever received, and his accounts of his experience in Virginia may even be the most accurate and penetrating of all the "True Reports" that were written at the time. But when he talked about himself his mind was filled with visions of chivalry, exoticism, amorous adventurism, and romantic self-inflation. Indeed, if we are to follow his many autobiographical writings, it appears that Pocahontas was not the first fair maiden to rescue him—she was, at best, the third. The fanciful vision Smith projected of himself and his adventures abroad was as much a part of who he was and how he envisioned the colonial enterprise as his hard-nosed, militant practicality. Yet, in any case, Smith's understanding—and shifting representations—of the incident is only one part of the story of what actually happened. As Native American historians have recently demonstrated, Smith seems to have entirely misunderstood how Powhatan and Pocahontas viewed the incident. Very likely, this brash interloper was never slated for execution. Rather, his near-death experience was part of a ritual of adoption intended to bring him within Powhatan's fold—and under Powhatan's authority.[11]

As the Jamestown adventurers and the Natives of coastal Virginia came together, their interactions were profoundly shaped by their perceptions and representations of themselves and each other. Looking back on these events, we face twin challenges: How did these groups "read" each other? And, how can we can "read" them through the incomplete, inconsistent, and otherwise invented texts they left behind? Sources here are largely narratives, reports, and letters home. The task of discovering "what actually happened" and "what it meant" is not easy. Documents of various kinds are limited: it is not always obvious when we as readers should be skeptical, when credulous, or when we should put aside questions of literal meaning and should focus instead on a text's rhetorical strategies or tone, or follow its allusions and explore its intellectual contexts. Always, our preconceptions shape what we are inclined to believe: for generations historians assumed that early travelers were exaggerating when they talked about seeing wondrously large fish and shellfish in the waters off North America. But modern biologists suggest that in fact before Europeans began overfishing the Atlantic seaboard, the inhabitants of the oceans really were both more numerous—and much larger.[12] Whether focusing on organizers of the Virginia venture, local rulers like Powhatan, or English indentured servants, the essays address the same basic questions: How did each envision their interactions with each other? How did these expectations shape their experiences? What were the causes and circumstances of their visions of the encounter? What were the consequences? The answers are sometimes surprising.

Literally envisioning the lay of the land around them—both physically and politically—was a major challenge for the early Jamestown settlers, a challenge Lisa Blansett explores in "John Smith Maps Virginia." Soon after setting up a fortified outpost on a scrubby, low-lying peninsula in a brackish section of the James River, Captain John Smith undertook an ambitious expedition to chart the lay of the land and its inhabitants. Traveling mostly in small boats, they covered almost two thousand miles in subsequent months, following the bay's lacy coastline and meandering rivers—generally stopping when the land began to rise toward the Appalachian mountains and they hit whitewater. For Atlantic-oriented settlers, this "fall line" would prove an enduring geographic marker dividing the flat, coastal "tidewater" that could be reached by boats and the hilly piedmont that required arduous trekking overland. Smith's ability to organize what he learned into a visual map of the landscape rested on his mastery of specific technologies and techniques, which he associated with the superiority of European culture. In a complex interplay of the powers of representation, the ability to envision a landscape according to certain conventions allowed Europeans to project ownership of it, to imagine mastery of it. Yet, as Blansett emphasizes, Smith was less in control than he liked to imagine. At each stop along the way, Smith relied upon information from the locals—when he wasn't fighting with them—about who they were, what their relationships were to other natives, and what else lay out of sight. In the end, Smith's elaborate, influential *Map of Virginia* (1612) is not just a sign of the triumph of European technology surveying new dominions, as Smith liked to think, but a record of the ineluctable interconnectedness of colonizer and colonized.

How, then, did the early settlers and the natives of the region envision their relationships with each other? During his various exploratory excursions, Smith learned that the all the land surrounding the site where the Jamestown adventurers had settled was controlled by a paramount chiefdom under the authority of Powhatan. Despite the rosy predictions of early colonial promoters that the local natives would flock to the settlers and willingly work for them, embrace English civility, and convert to Christianity, the early settlers found that once on the ground conflict, domination, and ultimately conquest were never far from their minds. Thinking perhaps of the model of the Spanish conquistadors, who had achieved stunning military victories by turning subject peoples against powerful native empires, the early settlers looked for local tribes who might rebel against Powhatan—or for groups outside his mantle who might be recruited as allies. Powhatan, the early Virginians learned, held a firm grip on the region. The Indian "emperor," for his part, was curious about these English interlopers, their goals, and the land they had left behind. In "Powhatans Abroad," Alden Vaughan reminds us that when Powhatan and his people looked east to better understand the English interlopers, they were not simply passive spectators. Indeed, a number of Powhatan Indians traveled to England. They left home with widely different expectations and had very different experiences abroad. Some were dispatched by colonists to serve as novelty acts for English entertainment and to help the Virginia Company raise money and attract settlers. More significantly, others were sent by Powhatan on missions of diplomacy and reconnaissance. For a time, Powhatan was able to sustain the hope that he might, by developing new machineries of intelligence and diplomacy, foster mutually beneficial relations with the English and develop a truly bicultural society.

Conflict between the two parties often seems to have been inevitable, since the English settlers came with the intention of taking possession of expanding swaths of Indian land, a determination that even disastrous setbacks and steadfast resistance failed to dampen. Although the settlers were vastly outnumbered and relied upon the natives for much of their sustenance, their behavior was often quite bellicose. Indeed, they often attempted to subdue the much more powerful native population by strategically employing terror tactics. On several occasions settlers used brutal violence against natives they were able to capture (generally women and children) in efforts to terrorize those too powerful or skilled to fight directly. Yet, as James Horn emphasizes in "The Conquest of Eden," the conflicts in this period between the region's Natives and the English were not simply about land. Both the natives and the English had the tools and traditions of conciliation for resolving disputes over territory and, in any case, the first tip of land the English chose for themselves was a scrubby peninsula that the local natives had little use for. Rather, what the English and Natives competed over primarily was their rival world views and ambitions. If the English thought of absorbing the natives into an English polity governed by a British monarch, James I, and operated as a Christian nation, the region's natives thought of absorbing the English into their own great political system, presided over by the paramount chieftain Powhatan, and operated according to their own customs and beliefs.

If relations with the region's inhabitants turned out less rosy than predicted by early promoters of the Virginia venture, the effort to make the colony survive—much less turn a profit—turned out to be much more difficult than anyone initially envisioned. In addition to intermittent warfare, the colony was plagued by persistent disease, starvation, and poor discipline. And nowhere did the settlers find gold or any other source of easy wealth. Smith, licking his wounds back in England, wrote accounts of the colony's difficult early years that, although clearly exaggerated, have been extraordinarily influential in shaping historical understandings of early Virginia. With withering sarcasm, Smith laid the blame mainly on the settlers the company initially sent to Jamestown: idle gentlemen who disdained honest work and lazy rabble obsessed with the lure for quick, easy wealth. "There was no talke, no hope, no worke, but dig gold, wash gold, refine gold, loade gold," Smith complained. Having met with only ingratitude after all his efforts to keep the colonists focused on housing, defending, and, above all, feeding themselves, Smith could not resist pointing out that all these gold-seekers ever found was "guilded durt."[13]

By the end of Jamestown's difficult first decade, many of those involved in the venture had lost faith in the original vision of the colony and were divided over plans for its future. Colonists on the ground had recently begun growing West Indian tobacco and were scrambling to take advantage of Virginia's first really marketable source of profit. This set in motion a tumultuous grab for land and control of labor within the colony. But nobody in London liked this outcome. One group of aristocratic investors wanted to give up on trying to grow or discover wealth, and use the colony instead as a base for piratical raids on the Spanish treasure fleets. Another group of merchants wanted to create a more mixed and diverse economy—making the colony more like England. In a portentous grab for power, the faction headed by Sir Edwin Sandys (George's elder brother) took over control of the company in 1619. Sir Edwin was determined to make the colony work as a mixed economy and sent over thousands of settlers, his younger brother to manage its affairs on the ground, and instructions to build iron works, grow silk, manufacture glass, and so on. Despite the obvious obstacles, this vision may have met with more success than historians often recognize.[14] In part, the 1622 attack can be seen as a result of Opechancanough's (Powhatan's successor) realization that the colony was growing rapidly and would sooner or later threaten his people's way of life.

In the aftermath of this attack, the colony faced a harrowing year—the surviving colonists waged a brutal war and many of those who did not die fighting fell sick or succumbed to malnutrition. And, in London, the Virginia Company faced a flood of bad publicity. One attempt to reassure prospective settlers was a strikingly upbeat broadside published in London, which was attributed to an unnamed colonist and dated March 1623. No longer, the broadside argued, were settlers hamstrung by misguided meekness toward the region's natives. Instead, they were bent on vengeance. Among those now taking up arms was the colony's treasurer-translator, George Sandys:

Stout Master George Sands upon a night
   did bravely venture forth
And mong'st the Savage murtherers,
   did form a deed of worth.
For finding many by a fire,
   to death their lives they pay:
Set fire to a Town of theirs,
   and bravely came away.

This brutal military campaign had forced the region's surviving natives to flee. Virginia would grow prosperous as the deer and turkey multiplied and corn grew, as iron and lumber works were reestablished, as forts were completed protecting the colony from naval attacks from foreign powers, and as women arrived to grace the overwhelmingly male settlement. Without a trace of irony, the bloodthirsty broadside concluded that there was now reason to hope that "faire *Virginia*" would now "prove plentifull by peace."[15]

Meanwhile, a dramatically different vision of the struggling colony came from the pen of a young settler named Richard Frethorne in the form of a private letter written in the spring of 1623 to his parents back home in England—the subject of Emily Rose's essay, "The Politics of Pathos." Nowadays, this letter is one of the most widely read accounts of early Virginia. It is commonly assigned classroom reading, soliciting our sympathy across the centuries—a fascinating and gruesome record of the life of an indentured servant living near Jamestown in the aftermath of the 1622 war. The letter is powerful and pessimistic: Frethorne tells his parents that he is miserable, sick, and starving. Virginia is nothing like he expected. He begs his parents to arrange for him to return home—or at least to send him some food. This, of course, is the opposite of the image those in control of the company wanted to project. Yet, as Rose reveals, it was music to the ears of those opposing the company's current management. This letter was never simply a naive, heartfelt letter home by an ordinary settler: it may have started out, and it certainly became, a pawn in high-stakes, backroom rivalries within the Virginia Company, in Parliament, and at the royal court. In the halls of power, then as now, the assertion of authority and the orchestration of influence was linked to the ability to control images and project visions.

The World Stage

When Christopher Columbus came to London seeking funding for his transatlantic venture, the English king turned him away—and it was not for almost a century that influential Englishmen began to think of this decision as a mistake. After 1492, the English monarch did send John Cabot to find a northerly route across the Atlantic to the trading centers of the Orient, but he found no passage through the northern American landmass and nothing of much interest along the coast except for the rich fisheries in the Gulf of Maine. For much of the next century, the leaders of England were preoccupied by internal dynastic struggles and religious wars, and the British Isles remained largely isolated from the world overseas, despite efforts to establish trading relations with Spain and the development of an important fishery in the Newfoundland banks.[16] It was only around the 1580s that the horizons of English leaders, merchants, intellectuals, and adventurers began to broaden. Stunned by the enormous wealth Catholic Spain was reaping from its new American colonies—and threatened by Spain's enormous military power—Protestant England looked for new opportunities for trade and empire. Among the forces pushing for change were the two Richard Hakluyts, a young man and his uncle of the same name, who began an ambitious editorial undertaking, publishing long-forgotten as well as new accounts of English overseas travel and exploration. The shelves of works they compiled, commissioned, and published stand as an enduring monument to their determination to provide practical knowledge, legitimation, and encouragement to English overseas ventures.[17]

What then was the relationship between England's expanding political and economic horizons and the origins of the Virginia venture? England's venture in Virginia was profoundly shaped by England's self-conscious role within a broadly envisioned and closely intertwined international scene. At the time, most English people interested in overseas ventures did not consider North America a particularly promising prospect. Instead, merchants began to greatly expand overseas trade—with the African Coast, with the Levant, with Russia, and in the Indian Ocean. Following the examples of the Portuguese and Dutch, they sought to cut out middlemen in Europe and the Middle East and find more direct and profitable routes to trading centers in Asia.[18] Politicians and militant Protestants focused on the dual threats of Spain, which was waging a long and brutal war in the attempt to subdue the largely Protestant Low Countries, and the Ottoman Empire, the great Muslim power of the Middle east which was attempting to conquer the Holy Roman Empire from the east. And people interested in colonial ventures looked first to Ireland, where the Protestant English sought to subdue the Catholic natives and establish profitable plantations. Indeed, during the early seventeenth century, far more British settlers went to Ireland than ventured across the Atlantic.[19]

Among these separate ventures, there were many clear personal interconnections. John Smith, for instance, had traveled widely before he set sail for Virginia: as a very young man he joined the fight in the Low Countries against the Spanish and within a few years ended up in Hungary fighting the Turks. Later, looking back on his life, he implied that these European experiences led directly to his contributions to the project of American colonization: "The Warres in *Europe, Asia,* and *Affrica* taught me how to subdue the wilde Salvages in *Virginia.*"[20] Similarly, Sir Walter Ralegh, who sponsored the Roanoke venture, was but one of many early promoters of American ventures who were also involved with early attempts at colonization in Ireland. But, as Andrew Hadfield cautions in his essay "Irish Colonies and the Americas," the links between Irish colonization and North America become less clear upon closer examination. After the failure of Roanoke, Ralegh continued to manage extensive estates in Ireland, but gave up on North America. Instead, he set his transatlantic sights on Guiana—the uncharted territory above Portuguese claims in Brazil and the Spanish presence to the northwest—where he hoped to find the legendary El Dorado, another great golden American empire. As he put it, it was not Seville oranges that had made the king of Spain wealthy and powerful: "It is his Indian gold."[21] His expedition failed and its most tangible legacy was the account he published, *The Discoverie of the Large, Rich and Bewtiful Empyre of Guiana* (London, 1596). Yet, while neither Ralegh nor any other English adventurers found the gold they hoped for, English outposts in the West Indies were soon beginning to produce profitable crops—including tobacco—years before the Jamestown venture was envisioned.[22] Indeed, by the 1620s, England's islands in the Caribbean successfully emulated the older Spanish model of colonial plantation agriculture—and attracting far more British settlers and returning far greater profits than Virginia.

So, instead of attempting to trace personal and institutional ties between the Virginia venture and other English activities at the time, we focus on the common intellectual and political problems confronted by the English in a variety of overseas contexts. As the Spanish expanded their American empire and amassed enormous wealth in the sixteenth century, the English struggled to make sense of their success and develop their own ideas about the nature of colonialism and its legitimacy. Turkey also provided a crucial frame of reference for English people looking abroad at this time: some Englishmen, like the young John Smith, even traveled to Hungary to join the ongoing war between the Muslim Ottoman Empire and the Christian Holy Roman Empire. Similarly, the issue of formation of racial prejudice is illuminated by looking at England's unlikely alliance with Morocco in the early seventeenth century—and the images of North Africa that alliance brought to the English theatre. Finally, we turn to the attempts of the English to intellectually justify their brutal conquest and campaigns of terror against the Irish in their attempts to "civilize" and resettle that region.

When the English saw the Spanish amass vast colonies and huge wealth, they liked to speak of these Catholic conquistadores as barbarously cruel to native peoples and enslaved Africans. To be sure, the early years of European empire were so grim and their human costs so high that the English had little need to exaggerate.[23] So few Caribbean natives survived the aftermath of Columbus's arrival that within a few decades Spanish colonists attempting to grow sugar there began importing enslaved African laborers. And in the wake of Cortéz's and Pizarro's conquests, as much as 90 percent of local populations died. But the so-called "Black Legend," as Eric Griffin reveals in his essay, "The Specter of Spain in John Smith's Colonial Writing," was more complex and powerful than simply loathing of the Spanish or sympathy with colonized peoples. The bitter animosity of the English toward the Spanish, with whom they had for a long time been officially at war, was motivated in large part by envy. The English set themselves apart from Spanish imperialists and the "Black Legend" partly as a imaginative byway through which they might ultimately succeed as imperialists even better than the Spanish.

Young John Smith could stomach only so much anti-Spanish and anti-Catholic violence. In the year 1600, at the ripe old age of twenty, he gave up the fight against the Spanish in the Low Countries, "both lamenting and repenting to have seen so many Christians slaughter one another." Instead he decided to "trie his fortune against the Turkes."[24] Pompa Bannerjee discusses this in her surprising essay, "The White Othello." Smith's writings about his adventures in Turkey—which included beheading three men whom be bested in duels, being left for dead on the battlefield, and being enslaved—provide an illuminating counterpoint to his histories of Virginia and other writings. Significantly, before returning to England, Smith traveled across Europe to the shores of North Africa. He was always a man of the Mediterranean and North Atlantic worlds, and never simply an Englishman obsessed with Virginia.

Relations between England and Morocco, as well as other parts of the Muslim world, were much more important than our traditional focus on European countries and their New World encounters may lead us to suspect. Susan Iwanisziw focuses our attention on this crucial diplomatic and cultural nexus in "England, Morocco, and Global Geopolitical Upheaval." If the Spanish were England's enemies because of Spain's militant Roman Catholicism, the Moroccans were England's allies, in spite of their "heathen" religion, and even in spite of differences that later generations would look upon as insuperable divisions of race.[25] The contexts of international political alliances and cross-culturally minded structures of feeling had a great impact on colonialist desire. Morocco was frequently represented on the English stage in this period. Examining these plays, Iwanisziw shows how unresolved notions of friendship and affiliation, of valor and sexual desire, of alliance, race, and miscegenation, underlay the English emerging colonial mentality.

A similarly fresh perspective on early Virginia emerges when we consider

England's single greatest colonial possession throughout this period: Ireland. Ireland has long been seen as the great incubator of English colonialist plans for America, and so in some sense it was. But as Andrew Hadfield demonstrates in "Irish Colonies and the Americas," parallel after parallel traditionally drawn between Ireland and the Americas in terms of England's "Westward Enterprise" can be seen to fall by the wayside. Ireland and America were not alike. What colonial adventurers in both places shared was a single body of thought upon which they all drew—a colonialist ideology inspired by histories of ancient Rome. The argument was basically that in conquering less civilized societies like Anglo-Saxon Britain, the Romans had improved them, uplifting them from a primitive state to one that was more advanced. This is what the Romans had said they were doing—they called it *translatio imperii*, a phrase that refers to the ideal of extending Roman civility from one place to another through the process of imperial conquest, settlement, and dominion. Of course, at the time, this argument was not always convincing to the victims of Roman aggression.[26]

So it is striking that over a thousand years later this self-gratulatory view of Roman imperialism became widely accepted by educated English people.[27] In large part, this view of history became attractive to them because it provided a useful way of viewing themselves and their relationships with foreigners. First, it explained why the English were superior to other Britannic peoples whom the Romans had not managed to conquer and who, therefore, had never benefited from Roman rule. Thus, the Celtic Scots and Irish had remained primitive while the English advanced. Second, this ideology allowed the English to imagine that they had now inherited the mantle of the Romans—and thus had a right, even a kind of obligation, to conquer and civilize more primitive peoples, such as the Irish or the American Indians. Of course, this nostalgic vision of Roman imperialism also had a brutal edge. As one early Virginia adventurer, William Strachey, put it: "Were not wee our selves made and not borne civill in our Progenitors dayes? and were not Caesars Britaines as brutish as Virginians? The Romane swords were best teachers of civilitie to this & other countries neere us."[28]

American Metamorphosis

America was full of unexpected transformations. In fact, the expression "sea change" was coined by William Shakespeare in his play *The Tempest*, which was in part inspired by accounts of the wreck of a ship sent to resupply Jamestown in late 1609. Blown off course by a gale, the flagship of the flotilla ended up jammed between two rocks off the coast of "Devill's Isle" in the Bermudas. Some died, but the others managed to get ashore, where they found a perfectly habitable island populated mostly by hogs left there by Spanish explorers decades earlier. The Jamestown group eventually built new boats that got them to their destination in Virginia, and both printed and manuscript accounts of their remarkable adventure soon came to Shakespeare's attention. In the play, a survivor of the shipwreck makes it ashore, while another character looks on and sings a mysterious song about the apparent death of the survivor's father:

Full fathom five thy father lies;
Of his bones are coral made;
Those are pearls that were his eyes:
Nothing of him that doth fade,
But doth suffer a sea-change
Into something rich and strange.[29]

Ultimately neither the English colonists nor the Powhatans ever found what they were looking for in Virginia: their interactions created a strange new world. The advocates of the Roman ideology of *translatio imperii* thought they were transplanting their culture from one place to another, bringing English civility and the true faith to the both the wild Irish and the wild Indians, but in retrospect it is clear that the colonial enterprise entailed an exchange and transformation in culture among the English as well as among the Powhatans.

The metamorphoses wrought by the conflicts, exchanges, and disappointments of early Virginia were not only political and economic but also cultural and ideological. Consider, for example, the complex colonial dynamics of food. In the wake of Columbus's 1492 voyage, the exchange of food crops and livestock transformed diets, agricultural practices, and landscapes on both sides of the Atlantic. Crops like maize, potatoes, and beans quickly became staples in Europe, and domestic livestock like pigs, sheep, and cows quickly began to transform American landscapes and farming practices.[30] At Jamestown, the exchange of food played an even more crucial role than the parties involved initially anticipated. The first adventurers greatly underestimated how much food they would need to bring with them, and as a result they were almost immediately dependent on the local natives for sustenance. For years to come, the Virginia settlers failed to grow enough food to sustain themselves. Many of the first armed conflicts between the Natives and the English interlopers stemmed from the settlers' continuing, desperate demand for food.

Yet the conflict over food involved more than competition for survival. As Robert Appelbaum reveals in "Hunger in Early Virginia," food was also a *cultural* artifact, rich with symbolic associations, and it ultimately became a crucial symbol of the cultural and social differences between settlers and natives. In this clash of cultures, the conflict was generally expressed not in what people thought and felt so much as in what they did when they were hungry, and even in how they experienced the demands of hunger. At home, the mercantile, protocapitalist English had erected a vast sociocultural apparatus to forestall the experience of deprivation and the extreme hunger it caused; the natives seemed to follow another system, and indeed to be neither too concerned from day to day where their next meal would come from nor too upset when, for want of supplies, extreme hunger set in. The irony, of course, is that the English colonists, so obsessed with providing themselves with a steady diet, proved in Virginia's early years such abysmal failures at feeding themselves. And yet the natives who fed them, with their annual seasons of want and seasons of plenty, seemed to the colonists utterly savage and wild.

Of course, the crop that ultimately saved the Virginia colony was not a food but rather a drug: a fragrant, tropical strain of tobacco. Tobacco quickly became the staple crop that defined Virginia's colonial economy, and it also became a prominent symbol of colonial identity. When the English playwright Aphra Behn reworked contemporary accounts of Bacon's Rebellion (1675–76) into a play about the nature of the Virginia colony, she employed frequent references to tobacco and to smoking. In his essay, "We All Smoke Here," Peter Herman sees what may be an idea first articulated by Behn: that the colonists were creating a culture of their own on the Virginia lowlands. Behn's own ambivalence about political developments in England at the time of the Glorious Revolution (1688) seems to have engendered a complex but ultimately wistful and admiring look at developments in Jamestown during the time of the Rebellion. In the eyes of the play's central character, a cosmopolitan widow frustrated with the constraints of English political culture and social conventions, Virginia appears as a fantastic alternative: an idealized vision of a freer, more liberating new world.

English rights and liberties were indeed central concerns in the colonial world, though developments in Virginia were hardly as rosy as Behn imagined from the other side of the Atlantic. No colonial cultural transformations were more important than changes in English ideologies of land ownership and the control of labor. These are central themes of *The Tempest*—in which a European refugee takes possession of Caliban's island and then enslaves him. Caliban complains:

This island's mine, by Sycorax my mother,
Which thou takest from me

* * *

               All the charms
Of Sycorax, toads, beetles, bats, light on you!
For I am all the subjects that you have,
Which first was mine own king: and here you sty me
In this hard rock, whiles you do keep from me
The rest o' the island.[31]

Caliban's outraged sense of injustice, magnified by betrayal, has powerful echoes with the events of early Virginia, in which the Powhatan Indians had good reason to feel that they had been deceived, betrayed, and brutalized by the English interlopers. Indeed, the play was first published—in the great Folio Edition of Shakespeare's complete plays—only a short time after news of Opechancanough's devastating attack had arrived in London.

That land was a critical issue in colonial society is obvious, and in recent years historians have developed much better understandings of the cultural differences between English and Indian land tenure systems. As the London minister Robert Gray posed the question in *A Good Speed to Virginia* (1609): "by what right or warrant we can enter into the land of these Savages, take away their rightful inheritance from them, and plant ourselves in their place, being unwronged or unprovoked by them?" Of course, the transfer of land to the English was not just about military power and diplomacy, but also about divergent/convergent understandings of the nature of ownership itself. Gray, for instance, anticipated the theories John Locke developed later in the century by arguing that the Indians of North America should be considered like "wild beasts" who not only failed to take advantage of the landscape and natural bounty that God had granted them but had to be exterminated if they stood in the way of English efforts to improve this "vacant" land.[32]

In "Between 'Plain Wilderness' and 'Goodly Corn Fields,'" Jess Edwards takes a long look at the history of English notions of property in relation to colonialism in Virginia. From the start of the Jamestown venture, English observers and adventurers on the ground voiced a range of opinions about the morality and legality of expropriating Indian territory. In general, scruples were increasingly pushed aside after the massacre of 1622, when the English adopted more of a policy of extermination and expulsion. Virginia governor Sir Francis Wyatt reported after the attack: "Our first work is the expulsion of the Salvages to gaine the free range of the countrey for encrease of Cattle, swine &c which will more then restore us, for it is infinitely better to have no heathen among us, who at best were but thornes in our sides, then to be at peace and league with them."[33] If this was revising history, then that in a way is appropriate—for the ideological battle to justify dispossessing American Indians ultimately involved reimagining America as a wilderness, a virginal continent, either not inhabited by native peoples or not used by them.[34]

The effort of the English to impose their view of land ownership was no doubt a power-grab that was consequential for the region's natives. But Edwards reminds us that control of land was under fierce conflict at home as well. One of the great events of the seventeenth century, which both determined and was determined by the experience of the American colonies, was the transformation in English property relations. Edwards reveals how principles and methods for knowing and controlling land developed in response to colonial needs and opportunities. We learn too how changing notions of property in the homeland, where traditional use-based feudal relations were rapidly giving way to capitalist contract-based relations, facilitated the parceling up of Powhatan lands into presumably legal estates, the ownership of which could be justified by the doctrine of "improvement." The great spokesman for this transformation was the philosopher John Locke, who was also the great spokesman for constitutional liberties—as well as a member of the council of the Royal African Company, which monopolized English slave-trading ventures. In the long run, one of the byproducts of the Roman-inspired *translatio imperii* was a sea change in the concept of liberty. The change, however, would proceed in two opposite directions: on the one hand, toward the Lockean concept of self-determination and the constitutional principles that needed to be established in order to guarantee it; on the other hand, toward the plantation owner's concept of chattel slavery, of the rights of the self-determined Lockean to deny all the rights of self-determination to others, based again on the principle of private ownership and "improvement."

Another major theme of *The Tempest* is slavery: Prospero not only holds the native Caliban in servitude to do his menial work, he also forces the sprite Ariel to do his bidding. And historians often look to early Virginia to understand the origins of the slave regime of the Old South. In recent decades we have learned a great deal about this process—and come to appreciate that the institutionalization of "modern" plantation slavery in Virginia would come only at the end of the seventeenth century. During the early seventeenth century most laborers in the colonies were English indentured servants, and the number of Africans was small and their status less rigid that it would be later. Historians have long argued over the nature of this transformation—whether racial prejudice or economic interests were the driving forces—but this debate tends to make a fetish of the Virginia experience.

Focusing narrowly on Virginia is misleading for two reasons. Most obviously, Virginia did not invent plantation slavery in the Americas. Slavery and staple-crop plantations were already a familiar feature of the Atlantic world long before Jamestown was first envisioned. Cash-crop plantations worked by enslaved Africans were established by the Spanish in the Caribbean only a few years after 1492; and these Caribbean plantations, in turn, largely followed models developed in the fifteenth century by the Portuguese and others in Madeira, in the Canaries, and, before that, in the Mediterranean. The nexus of sugar and other staple crops and enslaved laborers—often from the Guinea Coast of Africa—was already well established before any of the twenty-odd Angolans who arrived in Jamestown in 1619 were even born.[35] Perhaps historians of colonial North America downplay these precedents because they tend to undermine the image of the United States as autonomous, making free choices, and setting precedents. But the early Virginia experience was, in fact, largely about trying to replicate the more successful patterns already established by the Iberian Atlantic empires.

Surprisingly, though, there may be more than we have imagined about

American slavery's English background. As Michael Guasco reveals in his essay, "Settling with Slavery," this form of bondage was more familiar in England than we commonly remember. Slavery held a range of meanings for English people at the opening of the seventeenth century. Well before the idea of plantation slavery took hold of the English imagination, the English had a great number of uses for slavery, both in principle and in practice. Slavery was a part of the intellectual framework of English life; many English had actually found themselves enslaved at the hands of foreign enemies, and practices of bondage, if not of slavery per se, played a big role in early colonization. Nevertheless, as Guasco suggests, America's "peculiar institution" was hardly foreordained. Many of the early colonists were opponents of bondage and slavery, and Africans, eventually the great victims of the peculiar institutionalization, were by no means singled out in the early years of Virginia as an unfit, detestable, or "slavish" people.

* * *

A "double Stranger," Sandys called his translation of Ovid when he arrived back in London after several years in Virginia: "Sprung from the Stocke of the ancient Romanes; but bred in the New-World." Sandys did not reflect explicitly about how his understanding of *The Metamorphoses* shaped his understanding of America. It is not clear whether he took at face value the ending of the poem, which celebrates Julius Caesar for completing the project set in motion by Aeneas—making the old outpost of Latium into a worldwide empire. At the end, Jove speaks in praise of Caesar's successor, Augustus:

Hee shall the habitable Earth command;
And stretch his Empire over sea and land.
Peace given to Earth; he shall convert his care
To civill Rule, just Lawes; and by his faire
Example Vertue guide.[36]

Of course, this same Augustus was the man who had sent Ovid himself into exile, and it seems unlikely that he was writing here without a veil of irony and bitterness.

Did Sandys reflect on this implicit commentary about the discrepancy between ideals and actions, between visions and events? We don't know. But Sandys certainly did reflect upon how his experiences in Virginia changed his understanding of this ancient text. After the initial publication of his translation in 1626, Sandys continued to work on the project, producing a slightly refined, lavishly illustrated, and extensively annotated second edition in 1632, which included comments on the text inspired by his observations in Virginia and stories he heard there. His commentary makes clear his appreciation for Ovid's view of the unpredictability of human affairs—a world where intentions were often overruled by fate, and even the wills of the gods could be turned to disastrous account.[37] In this sense, too, Sandys's experience is emblematic of broader colonial developments.

None of the visions of Virginia espoused by either English adventurers or native leaders were ever realized. If their visions shaped events, events were never entirely under their control. Sandys's intervention in Virginia failed. Instead of developing a mixed, English, economy with a variety of profitable products, the settlers remained focused on tobacco. After supplies reaching London rose and prices crashed, tobacco cultivation increased even as the kinds of economic opportunities it could sustain changed. By the 1670s, 5 percent of crown revenue came from taxes on Virginia tobacco. Meanwhile, the colonial society grew increasingly dominated by a small number of large planters. Eventually, it became a slave society. In the midst of this fitful transition, Jamestown itself—the starting point of the Virginia colony—was itself dramatically transformed. At the end of the violent insurrection known as Bacon's Rebellion in the 1670s, Jamestown was burned to the ground. And it never regained its former status. The rapidly expanding colony required a new capital, further west, and the center of colonial power shifted to Williamsburg.

At the end of this volume, in her concluding essay, "Jamestown and Its North Atlantic World," Constance Jordan reflects on this vain yet vital attempt to envision change and to control it—by turning to one of the classical touchstones for early modern proponents of overseas colonization, Virgil's *Aeneid*. The view of historical change Virgil developed in the *Aeneid*, an epic recounting Rome's mythic origins, is significantly different from Ovid's. The changes that occupy Ovid in the *Metamorphoses* are often fantastic and outlandish, and human affairs are ruled as much by accident as by intention. Sandys's translation conveys this sense of fatalism: "What was before, is not, what was not, is: / All in a moment change from that to this." However, Jordan emphasizes, this was not the way most of the first English proponents of colonialism saw their role in history. The *Aeneid* epitomized the classical theme of *translatio imperii*—the Roman ideal of "translating" empire from one land and culture to another. English advocates of the Virginia venture often saw themselves in a similar, heroic mode, driven by destiny. The great irony of this ambitious imperial vision was its fate always to be incomplete, compromised, transformed. If another world was in the making when the English adventurers embarked upon the colonization of Jamestown, other worlds were being lost: past worlds were being destroyed and possible worlds were being precluded. Nobody in early Virginia lived to see the kind of world they had initially envisioned.

Part I
Reading Encounters

Chapter 1
The Conquest of Eden
Possession and Dominion in Early Virginia

JAMES HORN

> *After good deliberation, hee [Wahunsonacock] began to describe mee the Countreys beyond the Falles, with many of the rest . . . Nations upon the toppe of the heade of the Bay . . . the Southerly Countries also . . . [and] a countrie called Anone, where they have an abundance of Brasse, and houses walled as ours. I requited his discourse, seeing what pride hee had in his great and spacious Dominions, seeing that all hee knew were under his Territories.*
>
> —John Smith

> *The land which we have searched out is a very good land, [and] if the Lord love us, he will bring our people to it, and will give it us for a possession.*
>
> —Robert Johnson

By the early 1580s, few promoters of colonization—whether statesmen, merchants, or scholars—seriously doubted England's right to take possession of those parts of the Americas uninhabited by Christians. Sir George Peckham invoked the "Law of Nations," which sanctioned trade between Christians and "Infidels or Savages," the "Law of Armes" which allowed the taking of foreign lands by force, and the Law of God, which enjoined Christian rulers to settle those lands "for the establishment of God's worde" to justify English claims. In ancient times and "since the nativitie of Christ," he pointed out, "mightie and puissant Emperours and Kings have performed the like, I say to plant, possesse, and subdue." Spain's exclusive claims to the New World—by virtue of first discovery and papal donation—were explicitly rejected. Elizabeth I did not understand why she or any "Princes subjects should be debarred from the Indies, which she could not perswade herself the Spaniard had any just Title to by the Bishop of Rome's Donation." With laudable pragmatism if shaky geography, Richard Grenville advocated the establishment of English colonies in South

America on the grounds that "since the Portugall hath attained one parte of the newe founde worlde to the Este, the Spaniarde an other to the weste, the Frenche the thirde to the northe: nowe the fourthe to the southe is by gods providence lefte for Englande."[1]

The voyages of Martin Frobisher to Terra Incognita in search of a northwest passage and gold between 1576 and 1578 and Sir Humphrey Gilbert's ill-fated attempt to establish plantations in Newfoundland and along the northern seaboard conjured up what seemed to be a very real possibility of the English becoming the dominant power in the North Atlantic. John Dee, the Hermetic magus who influenced a generation of mariners and explorers, believed an *Imperium britannicum* was imminent. Claiming America for the English on the grounds of discovery and conquest by the Welsh prince, Owen Madoc, the legendary King Arthur centuries before, and voyages of John and Sebastian Cabot in the reign of Henry VII, he set out the queen's right to take possession of "foreyn Regions": By the "same Order that other Christian Princes do now adayes make Conquests uppon the heathen people, we allso have to procede herein: both to Recover the Premisses, and likewise by Conquest to enlarge the Bownds of the foresayd Title Royall." Richard Hakluyt the younger, the greatest propagandist of his age, was perplexed that "since the first discoverie of America (which is nowe full fourscore and tenne yeeres), after so great conquests and plantings by the Spaniardes and Portingales there, that wee of Englande could never have the grace to set fast footing in such fertill and temperate places as are left us yet unpossessed of them." Founding colonies would be a clear signal of England's intent to stake a claim to American lands and seas as other European powers had done, and not to be shut out of the New World by the Spanish or anyone else. The crown's dominions would be enlarged, the treasury's coffers filled, and national honor satisfied. The "plantinge of twoo or three strong fortes upon some goodd havens" on the mainland between Florida and Cape Breton would provide convenient bases for fleets of privateers operating in American waters, eventually weakening Spanish power in the Old World as well as the New. Finally, as the most forward-looking writers such as Christopher Carleill, Peckham, and the two Richard Hakluyts pointed out, colonies would promote valuable commerce and long-term prosperity, as well as social and economic well being at home.[2]

But while the English had little doubt about the justice of their rights to establish colonies or the long-term benefits they would bring, there was less certainty about how those rights would be realized and how English settlers would be received by native populations. If first discovery was vital to claims of possession so too was the fact of occupation. It is unlikely Spain and Portugal would have been able to hold onto their colonies for long without settling and developing them, and it was precisely those regions of the Americas largely uninhabited by the Spanish that other colonizing powers eventually seized upon. Rituals of possession—the unfurling of flags, solemn declarations, the erection of crosses and monuments—pronounced formal title to the land, but ultimately occupation and the capacity to defend settlements from internal and external aggressors proved to be the crucial test for all colonizers.[3] In this sense, the founding of England's first permanent colony in America, Virginia, and the protracted struggle between the English and indigenous peoples that ensued, is of particular interest. English justifications for conquest and possession were not simply worked out in abstract but were significantly influenced by the experience of contact, notably by the hostilities that stigmatized Anglo-Indian relations at Roanoke and Jamestown.[4]

England's First Virginia

English settlement of Virginia began not on the James River but a hundred miles to the south at Roanoke Island, on the Outer Banks of modern North Carolina. Following the death of Sir Humphrey Gilbert on the high seas in September 1583 returning from Newfoundland, the mantle of chief sponsor of England's colonizing efforts fell on the broad shoulders of the queen's new favorite, Walter Ralegh. Letters patent issued by Elizabeth in the spring of 1584 empowered him to "discover search fynde out and viewe such remote heathen and barbarous landes Contries and territories not actually possessed of any Christian Prynce and inhabited by Christian people" and to "holde occupy and enioye . . . forever all the soyle of all such landes Countreys and territories so to be discovered or possessed." The wording was conventional, derived from the patent granted by Henry VII to John Cabot before the voyage of 1497, which in turn was based on papal injunctions, such as the bull *Inter Caetera* issued by Alexander VI in 1493, the principal legal justification for Spanish claims to the New World. As we have seen, the English did not subscribe to the exclusionary intent of the Alexandrine bulls, but they adopted without question the centuries-old dictum that newly discovered "savage" or "heathen" lands could be legitimately possessed and settled by Christians.[5]

The decision to plant a colony at Roanoke was probably determined by Dee's understanding of the geography of the American coast, as illustrated by his map of 1580, and Simon Fernandes, the Portuguese master mariner in Ralegh's service who had explored the region some years earlier with the Spanish. Even so, much of the mid-Atlantic seaboard remained a mystery. While writers and propagandists had built up a growing body of knowledge about America in general during the previous three decades, and sporadic privateering expeditions had added more detailed information about the Caribbean and Spanish Main, relatively little was known about the mainland north of Spanish settlements. Ralegh could have had only a very rough idea about the extent or potential of the lands he now formally possessed, and consequently his first decision was to dispatch two small vessels under Philip Amadas and Arthur Barlowe, guided by Fernandes, to reconnoiter the region and find a location suitable for settlement.

Arriving off the Outer Banks in early July 1584, after a week or so sailing along the coast, Fernandes eventually discovered an entrance into the inner "Sea" where Amadas and Barlowe formally took possession of the region "in the right of the Queenes most excellent Maiestie" and their master, Ralegh. Barlowe's account, carefully edited for publicity purposes, revealed a land ripe for occupation. On the island of Hatarask, there were "many goodly woods, full of Deere, Conies, Hares, and Fowle, even in the midst of Summer." The forests were not like those of Muscovy and Bohemia, "barren and fruitlesse," but contained "the highest and reddest Cedars of the world" as well as "many other [trees] of excellent smell, and qualitie." After a few days on the island they encountered a group of local Indians, described as a "very handsome, and goodly people, and in their behaviour as mannerly, and civill, as any of Europe." The king of the local tribe (Secotans) was called Wingina and, Barlowe observed, was "greatly obeyed, and his brothers, and children reveranced."[6] Here was Eden, a land of plenty where the "earth bringeth foorth all things in abondance, as in the first creation, without toile or labour." In a phrase reminiscent of Peter Martyr, the great Milanese scholar who had written an influential account of America half a century before, the Indians were described as a "very handsome, and goodly people, . . . most gentle, loving, and faithfull, void of all guile, and treason, . . . such as lived after the manner of the golden age." Besides emphasizing the Indians' simple way of life, Barlowe was careful to detail their weaponry and methods of warfare, themes developed in Thomas Hariot's more elaborate description published a few years later. He, like Barlowe, believed the Indians "in respect of troubling our inhabiting and planting," posed little threat, and was hopeful that "through discreet dealing and governement" would be brought to "the trueth, and consequently to honour, obey, feare and love us."[7]

Effective as it may have been as a piece of propaganda, Barlowe's account was highly misleading in providing a realistic assessment of the difficulties of establishing a settlement in the Outer Banks. The shallow waters of the sounds and treacherous waters offshore were wholly unsuitable for ocean-going vessels, which were forced to anchor a couple of miles off the coast exposed to the fury of Atlantic storms. As a potential harbor for privateering fleets a worse location could hardly be imagined. His depiction of the natural bounty of the region, a land of milk and honey where little effort was needed to subsist, was merely a conventional reworking of the age-old fantasy of Arcadia, which had little to do with the practicalities of provisioning a colony and creating self-sufficiency in foodstuffs. Finally, his view of simple and pliant Indians who would not only assist English colonists in establishing themselves but, in time, would provide a docile labor force, ignored evidence all around him of warlike and independent peoples who would fight tenaciously to defend their lands. Successful in raising interest and financial backing in England, Barlowe's account left the first colonists dangerously unprepared for the conditions they would encounter and ultimately contributed to the disasters that followed.

It is hardly surprising, therefore, that within six months of the arrival of a colonizing expedition under the command of Ralph Lane the following year relations with local tribes had broken down, mainly as a result of English aggression. The Secotans, Lane reported, were convinced the settlers were "fully bent to destroy them . . . [and] they had the like meaning towards us." Hariot was told of a prophecy "that there were more of our generation [English] yet to come, to kill theirs and take their places." The collapse of the Roanoke colony and the hostilities that scarred Anglo-Indian relations left an enduring legacy. Menatonon, chief of the Chowanocs, informed Lane of a powerful king who lived in the north on a great bay, who "had trafficke with white men" but who was "loth to suffer any strangers to enter into his Countrey."[8] This was Wahunsonacock, paramount chief of the Powhatans, at that moment consolidating his territories to the north in Virginia, and it is more than likely news of the violent and unpredictable behavior of the English had come to his ears. For their part, the English remained convinced of the potential bounty of "the maine of Virginea" and of the imperative to possess it. Richard Hakluyt believed the conquest of Virginia could be accomplished with far less difficulty than the subjugation of the "warrelike" Irish. A well-armed force would be quite capable of overcoming "such stubborne Savages as shall refuse obedience to her Majestie." Events at Roanoke revealed that the Indians were far removed from the innocent and peace-loving peoples characterized by Barlowe. To English eyes, the treachery and hostility of local tribes, ("betrayed by our owne Savages," said Lane) together with their obstinate resistance to civilized ways, rendered them a more intractable presence than had been anticipated.[9] It was a lesson taken seriously by the Jamestown colonists twenty years later.

"Fatall Possession": The Founding of Jamestown

By the time the English attempted once again to establish permanent settlements in America, the entire complexion of European colonization had changed. During the 1580s and 1590s, scores of English privateers had set out to plunder Spanish treasure fleets on the high seas or mount daring assaults on Spain's rich possessions in the West Indies and along the Main. Most were modest ventures made up of one or two ships in consort but some, such as Drake's voyages of 1585 and 1595, were full-scale military expeditions involving large fleets and several thousand men. Never before had English shipping been so common in American waters, and as a result increasing numbers of mariners and merchants acquired invaluable knowledge of transatlantic crossings, Caribbean islands, and the American coast. At the same time efforts to plant colonies continued, encouraged in part by the seemingly tenuous hold of the Spanish over much of their American empire and by the persistent vision of finding gold and other precious minerals or at the very least establishing a trade in the valuable natural commodities of the region. Ralegh's exploration of the Orinoco to the "rich and beawtifull Empire of Guiana" in search of the golden city of El Dorado was believed practical because that part of the Main was virtually uninhabited by Spanish settlers or "any Christian man, but onely the Caribes, Indians, and salvages." He played for high stakes and dreamt of English colonies in Guiana comparable in wealth to Mexico and Peru, of an English New World (a New Britannia) that would eventually rival Spain's in riches and power, but justly governed by a virtuous English monarch avoiding the cruelty and tyranny of the Spanish conquista. Even when tales of the fabulous Indian civilization of Manoa proved worthless, the English continued exploring the area from the Orinoco to the Amazon (known as the Wild Coast), owing to the emergence of the area as a major producer of tobacco, which by the 1590s and early 1600s was becoming increasingly popular in Europe and commanded high prices.[10]

The Wild Coast marked the southernmost limit of English voyages in this period, but at the same time West Country and London merchants, backed by influential statesmen such as Lord Burghley, the Lord Treasurer, were renewing their interests in the far north, initially the Gulf of St. Lawrence and its valuable fisheries where the French and Basques were establishing themselves, and subsequently along the coast of Maine and New England. In the late 1590s, the failure of an unlikely scheme to plant a colony of Puritan dissenters in the Magdalen Islands on "Ramea" (Amherst Island) in the Gulf persuaded English investors to look further south where they would avoid direct competition with the French. Voyages between 1602 and 1605, involving explorations of Penobscot Bay and nearby islands, Cape Cod, and the coastline as far as Narragansett Bay, were followed by enthusiastic descriptions of the natural fertility of the land, waters teeming with fish (in greater plenty than was found off Newfoundland), and the friendliness of local Indians.[11] But perhaps more important than individual discoveries themselves was the broader implication of the voyages. By the opening years of the seventeenth century it was becoming clear that if Spanish warships remained a threat along much of the coast from Florida to South Carolina, and the French were tightening their grip on the St. Lawrence, then to have any real chance of success English colonizing projects would necessarily have to be located somewhere along the nine hundred miles from Cape Fear to Nova Scotia. New England represented one possibility; the other was the Chesapeake.

The succession of James I to the throne in 1603 marked an important change in foreign policy. Having little desire to continue the war against Spain, he quickly negotiated a peace treaty ending the plunder of Spanish shipping and possessions. But although condemning piracy in the Atlantic and Caribbean, James had no intention of renouncing English claims to the American mainland north of Florida and lent his tacit support to a number of schemes to establish colonies along the northeastern seaboard. West Country merchants were anxious to exploit the fish, oil, furs, and timber of New England, while their London counterparts, with connections in the Mediterranean and Levant, were keen to promote colonies that would produce commodities traditionally imported from southern Europe—citrus fruits, wine, olives, raisins, sugar, dyestuffs, salt, and rice—as well as the kinds of industrial crops that were being intensively cultivated on marginal lands around London and elsewhere in southern and central England. By the royal charter of April 10, 1606, the North American coast was divided into two spheres of interest: the Plymouth group (which also represented merchants and financiers from Bristol, Exeter, and smaller outports) was permitted to settle lands in latitudes between 38 and 45 degrees, namely New England, while the London group was allowed to establish colonies in the south between 34 and 41 degrees, from North Carolina to the Chesapeake.[12]

Leaving shortly before Christmas 1606, the expedition financed by the London Company set out for the Chesapeake Bay under the command of the experienced mariner Christopher Newport. After a leisurely crossing, the *Susan Constant, Godspeed,* and *Discovery,* carrying about 144 adventurers and crew, rounded the Virginia capes and entered the Chesapeake Bay in late April 1607. Most of the first "settlers" in fact went not to settle but to establish a beachhead, explore the land, search for a river passage to the South Sea, and with luck find gold or silver mines ("To get the pearl and gold"). The majority signed on with the hope of returning home within a year or two, preferably rich. Although the men were instructed to sow wheat and other crops "for Victual" to promote self-sufficiency, the colony was not planned as an agricultural community, and no women or children were taken along to create the conditions for family life. That would come later once the colony was secured, but in the meantime the primary task of the first expedition was to rediscover the Chesapeake, take possession for the English, and survey its resources.[13]

The colonists were impressed by their first view of the land. George Percy wrote with unrestrained delight of the "faire meddowes and goodly tall Trees, with such Fresh-waters running through the woods, as I was almost ravished at the sight thereof." To give thanks for their safe arrival and to mark the country as now belonging to the English, Newport's men named Cape Henry in honor of the king's eldest son and erected a cross there. First contacts with the Indians were mixed. A small landing party sent to scout the area around the cape was attacked by "Savages creeping upon all foure, from the Hills like Beares, with their Bowes in their mouthes," who according to George Percy, "charged us very desperately" and wounded a couple of men before retiring into the woods "with a great noise." A few days later, however, the colonists were entertained by the Indians of Kecoughtan and were welcomed also by the Paspaheghs and "Rapahannas" (Quiyoughcohannocks). The English soon learned that different tribes had very different responses towards them.[14]

During the next two weeks the settlers explored the lower reaches of the James River, searching for a suitable site to establish themselves. George Percy favored a point of land (named by the English "Archers Hope") on the creek where forty years earlier Spanish Jesuits had landed before crossing to the York River, but the eventual site chosen was further upriver on Jamestown Island, "in Paspihas Countrey," about sixty miles from the coast. Newport was anxious to begin exploring the region and a week after their arrival left the newly established colony with twenty-three men on a voyage of discovery up the James River, determined not to return before finding the "head of this Ryver, the Laake mentyoned by others heretofore, the Sea againe, the Mountaynes Apalatsi, or some issue."[15] The expedition represented a belated continuation of the reconnaissance of the bay begun by John White and Thomas Hariot, who had set out from Roanoke in the winter of 1585. White and Hariot had scouted the lands of the lower reaches of the James along its southern shore to the Nansemond, and Newport now intended to carry the exploration of the James to its conclusion in the interior. All along the river the Englishmen were met by friendly tribes apparently eager to trade and Newport learned much from them, notably the existence of a great king, Powhatan (Wahunsonacock), and lands to the west where Powhatan's enemies, the Monacans, lived in the mountains of "Quirank." The falls, "by reason of the Rockes and Isles," however, rendered any further progress up the river impossible and effectively put an end to the hope of quick and easy access to the lands beyond.

Nevertheless, from Newport's point of view the voyage had been a success, despite the disappointment of failing to find a passage to the western sea. The English now had a good idea of the extent of the river and had learned something about the peoples who lived along it. The river ran by estimation 160 miles "into the mayne land between two fertile and fragrant bankes," was between a quarter and two miles wide, and could be navigated by ocean-going shipping most of its length up to the falls. On either side, the country abounded with fair trees, wild fruits, and game, and according to Gabriel Archer, the river teemed with "multitudes of fish, bankes of oysters, and many great crabbs better in tast than ours." At the confluence of the James and Chickahominy, they had discovered the lands of the "Pamaunche" (Pamunkey), rich in "Copper and pearle," where the people wore copper ornaments in the ears, around their necks, "and in broad plates on their heades," and where the king had a "Chaine of pearle" worth at least £300 to £400. Finally, during the many feasts and entertainments on the voyage they established cordial relations with Indians on both sides of the river, including a bond of friendship with the "greate kyng Pawatah" himself.[16]

Having explored further up the river than any previous European, Newport was anxious to mark the achievement with a symbolic monument—setting up a cross with the inscription "Jacobus Rex. 1607." at the falls—which would serve as a clear signal to other Europeans (but not to the Indians) that the English now claimed possession of all the lands from the entrance of the bay to the mountains. The ritual was accompanied by a solemn prayer for the king's and the settlers' "prosperous succes," followed by a "greate showte" proclaiming James sovereign. When their Indian guide, Nauirans, grew uneasy at the English celebration, Newport told him "that the two Armes of the Crosse signifyed kyng Powatah and himselfe, the fastening of it in the myddest was their united Leaug [league], and the shoute the reverence he dyd to Pawatah which cheered Nauirans not a litle."[17]

Yet appearances were not what they seemed. The limits of understanding gave each side ample opportunity to deceive the other and both took full advantage. To the English, the exploration of the James and the cataloguing of its peoples and natural resources represented essential preliminaries to taking possession of the region. Surveying, measuring, recording were integral to building up knowledge of the land, assessing its potential use and profit, and gauging the military strength of its inhabitants. Equally important was naming (identifying) the natural features and tribes encountered along the way, in some cases adapting Algonquian terms (accommodated to English pronunciation), in others adopting the names of the royal family, prominent lords, and the explorers themselves. Not only the did the imperative of Anglicizing the landscape create recognizable markers and bounds instrumental in the construction of a mental image of the region, it also endowed a strange and sometimes threatening place with a degree of familiarity and provided a comforting reminder of the close links maintained with England across the ocean. Newport had no compunction about misleading the Indians about their true intentions and the meaning of the cross at the falls. Following instructions from the London council not to offend "the naturals," he deliberately encouraged the impression that his men were more interested in trade than in occupying the land. The London Company recommended that the settlers avoid antagonizing the Indians before the colony was established and able to produce all its own food. Perhaps with the experience of Roanoke in mind, the company's leaders accepted that the colony might well be dependent on the goodwill of local peoples initially, not only for food supplies but also for information about the region and trade.

For their part, the Powhatan Indians deliberately misled Newport about the identity of "Pawatah," who was in fact one of Wahunsonacock's sons, Parahunt, not the great king himself, and further deceived him by blaming the Chesapeakes for the attack on the English at Cape Henry whereas tribes loyal to the Powhatans were responsible. The generous hospitality extended to the English at the falls and elsewhere during the voyage was merely a subterfuge to keep them upriver long enough for an alliance of five tribes, numbering about two hundred warriors, to launch "a very furious Assault" on the unsuspecting colonists at Jamestown. The attack was beaten off after an hour of intense fighting, largely owing to the murderous effect on the Indians of small shot fired from the ships' cannon.[18] Indecisive in military terms, the assault on Jamestown in late May was nonetheless highly significant. English hopes that their arrival in the Chesapeake Bay would be unopposed or even welcomed by local Indians were dashed and it was now clear they had settled in the midst of a powerful alliance.

If the attack on Jamestown had been a temporary setback, nevertheless the English were in an optimistic mood by the time Newport sailed for England toward the end of June. With a touch of exaggeration, the colonists' leaders wrote to the London Company of a land that would eventually "Flowe with milke and honey," in the form of all sorts of natural products, and hinted at greater discoveries yet to be made in the mountains where perhaps gold was to be found. Archer wrote enthusiastically, "we can by our industry and plantacion of comodious marchandize make oyles wynes soape ashes, . . . Iron [and] copper," cultivate sugar canes, olives, hemp, flax, hops, and fruits. He concluded, "I know not what can be expected from a common wealth that either this land affordes not or may soone yeeld."[19]

But while in the summer of 1607 the colony's potential seemed boundless, the reality over the next few years proved very different. A deadly combination of disease, Indian attacks, and famine ravaged the settlement and brought the colony to the edge of extinction.

In the first flush of optimism after landing, John Smith described Jamestown as "a verie fit place for the erecting of a great cittie," but aside from considerations of defense the choice could hardly have been worse.[20] The best lands along the river had been occupied for centuries by local tribes, while the site they had chosen was waste ground used by the Paspaheghs for hunting. Large areas of swamp and marshland (natural breeding grounds for swarms of biting insects) rendered half the island uninhabitable and were unsuitable for tillage. The absence of freshwater springs meant that drinking water had to be drawn from brackish wells dug by the settlers or from the river, which in the summer became increasingly saline and polluted. Unknown to the colonists, they had arrived during a severe drought that would make the problem of finding fresh water all the more difficult. Six weeks after Newport sailed for England the terrible roll call began: "The sixt of August there died John Asbie of the bloudie Flixe

[flux]. The ninth day died George Flowre of the swelling. The tenth day died William Bruster Gentleman, of a wound given by the Savages, and was buried the eleventh day. The fourteenth day, Jerome Alikock Ancient, died of a wound, the same day Francis Midwinter, Edward Moris Corporall died suddenly." On August 22 the colony suffered its greatest loss with the death of Bartholomew Gosnold, perhaps the only man who could have held the fractious leaders together. And so through the end of August into September, George Percy wrote, "Our men were destroyed with cruell diseases as Swellings, Flixes, Burning Fevers, and by warres . . . many times three or foure in a night, in the morning their bodies trailed out of their Cabines like Dogges to be buried. . . . There were never Englishmen left in a forreigne Countrey in such miserie as wee were in this new discovered Virginia," he continued in a bitter indictment of the London Company. "Thus we lived for the space of five monenths in this miserable distresse, not having five able men to man our Bulwarkes upon any occasion," and so weakened by disease "the living were scarce able to bury the dead." Percy was mistaken in his assumption that "meere famine" was the principal cause of sickness and death. Rather than starvation, the major killer was polluted river water, "full of slime and filth," which led variously to salt poisoning, dysentery, and typhoid. An epidemic swept the settlement leaving half the 104 men and boys dead before the end of September. By the onset of winter fewer than forty survived.[21]

Smith's Epic

It was against this background of dire necessity that John Smith began trading with the Indians for provisions, first downriver to the large settlement of Kecoughtan and then upriver to the fertile lands along the Chickahominy, where in late December he was captured by the Pamunkey chief, Opechancanough (Figure 1.1). Following several weeks of marches and countermarches back and forth across the frozen landscape between the Pamunkey and Rappahannock Rivers, he was eventually brought into the presence of Wahunsonacock at his capital, Werowocomoco, and received with great ceremony. Smith was the first Englishman to meet the "Emperour" and was impressed by the old man's "grave and Majesticall countenance," which, he freely admitted, "drave me into admiration to see such a state in a naked Salvage." In the *True Relation*, written immediately after the event, he recalled the "great king" told him of the many peoples of the region and lands beyond, including "a fierce Nation that did eate men" and nations to the north, "under his territories," where a year before they had killed a hundred in battle. "Many Kingdomes hee described mee to the heade of the Bay," Smith continued, "which seemed to bee a mightie River, issuing from mightie Mountaines betwixt two Seas." He concluded, "I requited his discourse, seeing what pride hee had in his

Figure 1.1. "C[aptain] Smith taketh the King of Pamaunkee prisoner, 1608." Detail from the plate "Ould Virginia," engraving by Robert Vaughan in John Smith, *Generall Historie* (London, 1624). Courtesy of the John Carter Brown Library, Brown University. This image represents Smith as considerably shorter than Powhatan's war-chief, Opechancanough, whose hair-lock he grasps in a gesture of dominance. The previous year, it had been Opechancanough who had taken Smith prisoner.

great and spacious Dominions." Following an oration along similar lines, wherein Smith recounted the nations subject to his great king (James I) whom he styled "King of all the waters," Wahunsonacock invited him to "forsake Paspahegh [James Fort], and to live with him upon his River, [in] a Countrie called Capahowsicke." The offer was not intended to apply to Smith alone, as the following phrase makes clear: "he promised to give me Corne, Venison, or what I wanted to feede us, Hatchets and Copper wee should make him, and none should disturb us." Smith and all the settlers would be guaranteed food and safety if they acknowledged Wahunsonacock as their lord and became a subordinate tribe of his chiefdom.[22]

Years later back in England, Smith wrote a considerably more detailed account of the event that included the significant addition of his last-minute reprieve from death by the dramatic intervention of the king's favorite daughter, Pocahontas. Writing in the third person, Smith described what happened:

> At his [Smith's] entrance before the King, all the people gave a great shout. The Queene of Appamatuck was appointed to bring him water to wash his hands, and another brought him a bunch of feathers instead of a Towell to dry them: having feasted him after their best barbarous manner they could, a long consultation was held, but the conclusion was, two great stones were brought before Powhatan [Wahunsonacock]: then as many as could lay hands on him dragged him to them, and thereon laid his head, and being ready with their clubs to beate out his braines, Pocahontas the Kings dearest daughter, when no intreaty could prevaile, got his head in her armes, and laid her owne upon his to save him from death: whereat the Emperour was contented he should live to make him hatchets, and her bells, beads, and copper.

Destined to take on mythic proportions as a symbol of the transcendent power of love over racial hatred, the truth of Smith's story remains obscure despite the huge volume of writing and controversy it has generated. What is clear from both versions, however, is that Wahunsonacock considered the possibility of sparing the lives of the English by absorbing them into his dominions as a separate people occupying a new tribal territory carved out from the underpopulated lands along the north bank of the lower York. Whether or not he was sincere is as uncertain as Smith's salvation by Pocahontas, but it is likely that, as the colonists' numbers rapidly dwindled during the summer, so his view of them changed: instead of seeing them as a threat he decided the settlers might be of use by providing him with English weapons and copper. With this in mind, he required that Smith send him "two great gunnes" and "a gryndstone" (for sharpening knives and swords) to seal their accord. With abundant English copper to bribe allies and firearms to destroy his enemies there would be no limit to his conquests.[23]

Smith's return to the fort in early January 1608 after a month's absence must have seemed little short of miraculous to his compatriots, who had long since given him up as lost. Not only had he survived unscathed, he brought news of his meeting with Wahunsonacock, a respite from hostilities, and the Indians' promise to supply the starving English with provisions. Taking advantage of the newly established peace, several months later Smith undertook two explorations of the bay that would form the basis of one of the most important achievements of the period: his map and description of Virginia (Figure 1.2). On the first voyage, Smith and fourteen men coasted the Eastern Shore before following the bay northwards for about a hundred miles. After spending a couple of weeks exploring the Potomac, they returned to Jamestown where they arrived on July 21, with the happy news of their discoveries and the hope ("by the Salvages relation") that the bay stretched far to the west to meet the South Sea.[24] Smith did not remain long at the fort but left a few days later to complete his discovery of the bay. On the first expedition he had heard from the Kuskarawoacks of a mighty nation further north called the "Massawomekes" and decided to find them. Accordingly, the expedition made their way to the headwaters of the bay, where they met seven or eight canoes full of Indians they later learned were Massawomecks who spoke a strange language. After exchanging gifts the Indians left and were not seen again, so Smith set course for the Eastern Shore, where they were entertained for several days in the "pallizadoed towne" of the Tockwoughs. There, they were visited by sixty "gyant-like" Susquehannocks, mortal enemies of the Massawomecks, who came with gifts of venison, tobacco pipes, targets (wooden shields), bows, and arrows. The Susquehannocks pleaded with Smith to become "their Governour and Protector, promising their aydes, victualls, or what they had to be his, if he would stay with them, to defend and revenge them of the Massawomeks," but Smith refused and after learning about a great lake "or the river of Canada" beyond the mountains left them at Tockwough, "sorrowing our departure."

Having explored the inlets and rivers of the upper bay, Smith and his men returned down the bay to the Patuxent River and then continued on to the Rappahannock River. Sailing their barge as far into the freshes as possible, "there setting up crosses, and graving our names in the trees," they were suddenly attacked by about a hundred Indians who they learned from a wounded captive were Mannahoacs. From him, further information was gleaned about the peoples and lands of the interior. His people were ruled by the kings of Hasinninga, Stegora, Tauxuntania, and Shakahonea, and their allies, the Monacans, lived close by in the mountains and along the rivers. He knew of the Massawomecks, who, he told Smith, "did dwell upon a great water, and had many boats, and so many men that they made warre with all the world." Asked why they had attacked them, he answered, "they heard we were a people come from under the world, to take their world from them." On the final stage of the journey, the company reconnoitered the Piankatank River and then sailed to the south bank of the

Figure 1.2. John Smith's *Map of Virginia*, the tenth and final state of the engraving (1631), currently bound into a copy of Smith's *Generall Historie* (London, 1624). Courtesy of the John Carter Brown Library, Brown University. Unlike modern maps, the top of the page is oriented to the west, not the north. The map shows native villages and chiefdoms as well as new, English place names. The Maltese crosses delineate the boundary between areas Smith and other Englishmen had seen themselves and places they knew only through native informants. This detail shows the area closest to "James' towne" (labeled in large print toward the upper left). Smith's map was originally published in 1612 from a large copper plate engraved by William Hole in Oxford. Over the next two decades, Smith reused the map in other publications and, taking advantage of the malleability of the copper plate, repeatedly updated it, adding new place names as they became available (such as "Washeborne" in the foreground and "Sparkes point" at the mouth of the Potomoc).

James to "the country of the Chisapeack," where entering the Nansemond River, they were attacked by a combined force of several hundred "Chisapeacks" and Nansemonds. Fending off their attackers and threatening to destroy all the canoes they captured, Smith and his men were able to come to terms with their enemies and the following day returned to Jamestown with as much corn as they could carry, thus completing in six weeks a journey that had taken them to the furthest reaches of the bay.[25]

Smith and his men were acutely aware of the epic proportions of their two voyages, which were subsequently likened in their writings to famous Spanish discoveries and great feats of exploration in times past. In *The Generall Historie*, for example, Smith asked: "peruse the Spanish Decades; the Relations of Master Hackluit, and tell me how many ever with such small meanes as a Barge of 2 tuns, sometimes with seaven, eight, or nine, or but at most, twelve or sixteene men, did ever discover so many fayre and navigable Rivers, subject so many severall Kings, people, and Nations, to obedience, and contribution, with so little bloudshed."[26] To ensure their own immortality Smith and his men named (or renamed) the lands and rivers they passed after themselves: the "Sasquesahanocks river we called Smiths falles; the next poynt to Tockwhogh, Pisings poynt; the next it poynt Bourne. Powells Isles and Smals poynt is by the river Bolus; and the little Bay at the head Profits poole; Watkins, Reads, and Momfords poynts are on each side of Limbo; Ward, Cantrell, and Sicklemore, betwixt Patawomek and Pamaunkee, after the names of the discoverers." The highest mountain they could see to the north, "Peregrines mount," and "Willowbyes river" were named for Lord Willoughby, lord of the manor where Smith was born. The only casualty of the voyage, Richard Fetherstone, was buried in "Fetherstons bay," and honored by "a volly of shot." Where they stopped on their journey or went inland, they left written messages or sometimes brass crosses in holes in trees "to signifie to any, Englishmen had beene there."[27] Whereas Newport and his company had earlier given names to prominent features and the peoples only along the James River, Smith and his men wrote their names across the entire Chesapeake region.

Smith exaggerated when he later wrote he had subjected thirty-five Indian kings to the obedience of the English, but there is little doubt that during the voyages he increasingly took upon himself the role of a plenipotentiary. Time and time again, in a series of encounters that followed a strikingly similar pattern, Smith and his men forced initially hostile tribes to obey the English and sue for peace. Members of the first expedition recalled how "our Captaine ever observed this order to demand their bowes and arrowes, swordes, mantells and furrs, with some childe or two for hostage, whereby we could quickly perceive, when they intended any villany." Far up the Rappahannock River after a sharp engagement with the Mannahoacs, Smith demanded that their four chiefs surrender their bows and arrows "and then the great King of our [the English] world would be their friend, whose men we were." A ceremony took place "upon a low Moorish poynt of Land," where the chiefs and English exchanged gifts, which was followed by much celebration, singing, and dancing by "foure or five hundred of our merry Mannahocks." Downriver, Smith took on the role of a regional peacemaker in an encounter with the bellicose Rappahannocks, whose chief was also assured of the friendship of King James in return for peace with the English and neighboring tribes. Once again, an exchange of gifts followed by singing and dancing sealed the new accord, this time by six or seven hundred Indians.[28]

Smith's map, published in 1612 as *A Map of Virginia. With a Description of the Countrey*, presented to the eye the "way of the mountaines and current of the rivers, with their severall turnings, bayes, shoules, Isles, Inlets, and creekes, the breadth of the waters, the distances of places and such like." This first attempt to visualize the Chesapeake in detail was hugely influential on cartographic representations of the region for the next seventy years. No one else was able to provide anywhere near such a comprehensive picture of the bay and its peoples. It was a remarkable achievement, surpassing in detail and practical significance, if not aesthetic quality, even the wonderful watercolor maps of Roanoke and the mid-Atlantic coast drawn by John White. Smith gave expression to the sheer expanse of the Chesapeake (approaching a third of the land area of England), the magisterial bay and broad waterways, the myriad creeks and islands, and the numerous tribes and diversity of native peoples. Here was no small island, cramped strip of coast, or minor river valley but an entire country, the bounds of which even Smith had been unable to compass. While at the time of his two voyages the English occupied only tiny Jamestown Island, his map effectively staked England's claim to the whole region, by right of discovery and conquest, and by virtue of English presence in name if not in person.[29]

Smith's achievements, however, were more apparent to later generations than to his own contemporaries, who had more immediate concerns. The English now had a good idea of the extensiveness of the lands they claimed to possess, but unlike the Spanish in Central and South America they had discovered little of real worth in their new world: no gold, silver, or precious minerals, no convenient access to the Orient, and no advanced Indian civilizations that could be readily plundered. In telling language, the unfavorable comparison with Spanish exploits was recognized by the adventurers themselves:

> It was the Spanyards good hap to happen in those parts where were infinite numbers of people, who had manured the ground with that providence, it affoorded victualls at all times. And time had brought them to that perfection, they had the use of gold and silver, and the most of such commodities as those Countries affoorded: so that what the Spanyard got was chiefly the spoyle and pillage of those Countrey people, and not the labours of their own hands. . . . But we chanced in a Land even as God made it, where we found onely an idle, improvident, scattered people,

ignorant of the knowledge of gold or silver, or any commodities, and carelesse of any thing but from hand to mouth, except ba[u]bles of no worth; nothing to incourage us, but what accidentally we found Nature afforded.[30]

As prospects of quick riches faded it would be Hakluyt's vision, not the example of Spanish conquistadors, that would guide colonists' efforts to produce suitable commodities for sale in England, and for this they needed to occupy the land.

War and Retribution

Shortly after taking charge of the colony in September 1608 following instructions from the Virginia Company, Smith journeyed to Werowocomoco to inform Wahunsonacock that King James had sent him presents to be delivered at Jamestown. In fact, the company had sent gifts to be employed as props (and bribes) at the "coronation" of the Powhatan chief, a ritual intended to confirm their recognition of Wahunsonacock's status among his own peoples while at the same time symbolizing his submission and allegiance to James I. Just as Okisko, king of the "Weopomiok," had yielded himself "servant, and homager, to the great Weroanza of England [Elizabeth I]." in the final days of the first Roanoke colony, so Wahunsonacock was called upon to play the part of a local lord under the authority of the English king and his envoys in Virginia.[31] Barely nine months before, during Smith's captivity, the great chief had offered to support and protect the colonists if they submitted to his rule; now the English had brazenly turned the tables. Wahunsonacock, however, was reluctant to play the role assigned to him. Replying to Smith's invitation to come to Jamestown, he responded: "If your king have sent me presents, I also am a king, and this my land, 8 daies I will stay [at Werowocomoco] to receave them. Your father [Newport] is to come to me, not I to him." Accordingly, Newport and Smith accompanied by fifty men made their way to the Powhatan capital where the gifts—a bason, ewer, bed, and bedclothes—were put on display. The coronation itself proved a farce. Wahunsonacock would only consent to wear the "scarlet cloake and apparel" brought by the English for the purpose after being assured they would do him no harm, but even worse he refused to kneel to receive his crown, "neither knowing the majestie, nor meaning of a Crowne, nor bending of the knee. . . ." After "many perswasions, examples, and instructions, as tired them all," Newport, "by leaning hard" on the king's shoulders managed to get him to stoop a little "and put the Crowne on his head." In his honor, the English fired a volley which caused "the king [to] start up in a horrible feare," but seeing all was well he thanked the English and "gave his old shoes and his mantle [cloak] to Captain Newport."[32]

Smith, a relentless critic of Newport and company policy, had been highly skeptical of the "strange coronation," because the colonists in his opinion had the king's favor "much better, onlie for a poore peece of Copper," whereas "this stately kind of soliciting made him so much overvalue himselfe, that he respected us as much as nothing at all." But Wahunsonacock was far more astute than either Smith or Newport gave him credit. The coronation had cost him nothing. He had made the English come to him, accepted their gifts, and in return given them merely some old clothing, (their value presumably residing in the fact they had been close to the royal body). He had confirmed his prestige in the eyes of his own people by inverting the meaning of the ritual: it was he who received the acclamation and homage of the English, not the other way round. Smith was doubtless right in his observation that Wahunsonacock did not understand the symbolism of the crown or the act of receiving it. But more accurately, the Powhatan king did not accept the *English* meaning of the ritual, just as (apparently) the English completely misunderstood the significance the Indians attached to the event.[33]

From both sides' point of view, the coronation was yet another example of charade masking intent. Newport was no Virginia king-maker. The crown had been proffered not in recognition of Wahunsonacock's title to royalty but to confirm the Indians' status as vassals of the English. For his part, the Powhatan chief had already decided to rid himself of the troublesome intruders by cutting off food supplies. Several reasons prompted his decision. Whatever he thought about the chances of the small English contingent surviving long or of the potential value of the trade in European goods, particularly weapons, his overriding concern must have been for the security of his territories and his own position as chief of chiefs. The arrival of more settlers in 1608 may have convinced him that the English posed more of a threat than a benefit. "Many do informe me," he told Smith in the fall, "your comming is not for trade, but to invade my people and Possesse my Country."[34] Under these circumstances it was imperative to take action against the newcomers, and that such action be seen as a warning to any petty chiefs who might have considered siding with the English against him. The nature and recent development of his empire largely dictated his course of action. He could not tolerate a powerful independent people planting themselves in the midst of his lands, and the combination of war, threats, and fear that held together his dominions determined that if the English could not be controlled they must be confronted.

About the same time, the Virginia Company came to a similar conclusion. If the Indians would not accept English rule by persuasion they would have to be subdued by force. A new charter endowed the colony's governor with near absolute powers, and the company began recruiting veteran officers from campaigns in Ireland and the Netherlands to take charge of affairs, men such as Sir Thomas Gates, Lord De La Warr, and Sir Thomas Dale. The decision had not been taken lightly, and followed an intense debate among company members about how to justify military action and the importance of avoiding the bloody excesses that characterized the Spanish. As the project of colonization took on a militant Protestant tone, so it became more closely linked in the English mind to an evangelical crusade. Conversion must follow conquest. "Our intrusion into their possession shall tend to their great good," Robert Johnson believed, "our comming hither is to plant our selves in their countrie: yet not to supplant and root them out, but to bring them from their base condition to farre better." Robert Gray put the matter more bluntly. Christian kings may lawfully make war on savage peoples providing the ultimate objective was to reclaim them from their barbarous ways. "Those people are vanquished," he wrote in a memorable turn of phrase, "to their unspeakable profite and gaine."[35]

A force of nine ships carrying some 500 men commanded by Gates and Sir George Somers was dispatched from London in May of 1609. Gates was instructed by the Virginia Company to take Wahunsonacock prisoner or render him a "tributary," and to require his chiefs to acknowledge no other lord but James I. Priests and chiefs were to be removed from the people and taken into custody, and the young brought up in the manners and religion of the English. Thereby, it was anticipated that the "people will easily obey you and become in time civill and Christian." The company further advised that the colonists abandon fair trade and get food from the Indians by force, since "they will never feede you but for feare."[36] Hostilities broke out shortly after the arrival of the "third supply," six of the original nine ships carrying about 250 settlers (the remainder of the fleet had been shipwrecked on Bermuda and would not arrive in Virginia for another ten months). Food shortages at Jamestown persuaded Smith to disperse some of the colonists downriver near the Nansemonds' village at the entrance of the James and others upriver near the falls, where he established his men in the fortified village of Powhatan. English aggression in stealing corn, attacking villagers, and burning their houses led to swift revenge by Indian warriors, forcing the settlers to return to the ill-provisioned Jamestown after sustaining heavy losses. Having confined the English to the fort, and deciding against a frontal assault, Wahunsonacock's warriors sealed off the island in an attempt to starve the English into submission. During the siege of Jamestown from November 1609 to May 1610 about half the garrison died of disease and malnutrition, were killed as they tried to escape, or were slain after putting "themselves into the Indians handes, though our enemies."[37]

These were among the most harrowing times of Virginia's troubled early history, exceeding even the horrors of the settlers' first summer. Once again, it was George Percy who recorded the "worlde of miseries" they endured. To satisfy their "Crewell hunger," he wrote, they ate their horses and dogs, vermin around the fort such as rats and mice, and when these ran out even their boot leather. In desperation, some went beyond the palisade into the woods in search of "Serpents and snakes, and to digge the earthe for wylde and unknowne Rootes where many . . . weare Cutt off and slayne by the Salvages." But worse was to come as weeks turned into months. Percy recalled, "And now famin begineinge to Looke gastely and pale in every face thatt notheinge was spared to mainteyne Lyfe and to doe those things which seame incredible As to digge up dead corpses outt of graves and to eate them and some have Licked upp the Bloode which hathe fallen from their weake fellowes." To prevent the colony falling into complete disorder, martial law was enacted. Anyone caught stealing from the common store was executed; a man who murdered his wife and ate her was tortured to extract a confession and then dealt with similarly.[38]

When Gates arrived in May 1610 the "sixty" survivors were in such a terrible condition "itt was Lamentable to behowlde them." Many, through extreme hunger, "Looked Lyke Anotamies [anatomies] Cryeinge owtt we are starved We are starved." One Hugh Price, "In A furious distracted moode did come openly into the markett place Blaspheameinge exclameinge and cryeinge owtt that there was noe god. Alledgeinge that if there were A god he wolde nott suffer his creatures whom he had made and framed to indure those miseries." The palisades of the fort had been torn down, entrances left open, and houses "rent up and burnt" for firewood. William Strachey observed "the Indian killed as fast without," if men went beyond the fort, "as Famine and Pestilence did within." In "this desolation and misery," Gates considered he had no other choice but to abandon the colony. After burying their cannon "before the Fort gate" (an indication that abandonment was seen as temporary), the English left Jamestown at midday on June 7 and sailed downriver to Hog Island. Having arrived three years earlier to the sound of trumpets, the English marked their departure by the somber beat of the drum and a volley of small shot.[39]

The following day, however, a remarkable turnabout occurred. Continuing down the James River, Gates and his small flotilla were met by an advance party of the new governor, Thomas West, Lord De La Warr, who had recently entered the bay with three ships and 150 colonists, two-thirds of whom were soldiers. De La Warr's arrival saved the English colony and in the long run proved decisive in the war against the Powhatans. Taking the offensive for the first time in nearly a year, the English organized themselves into military companies and conducted a series of devastating and brutal raids on neighboring Kecoughtans, Paspaheghs, Chickahominies, and Warrascoyacks, during which they adopted a scorched earth policy reminiscent of campaigns in Ireland in the 1590s and put to the sword men, women, and children. Villages were burned to the ground, "Temples and Idolls" destroyed, and ripening corn carried away. The following year, between April and August 1611, another six hundred colonists arrived with a "greatt store of Armour, Municyon[,] victewalls," and other provisions, enabling English commanders to continue their destructive raids on tribes all along the James River from its mouth to the falls.[40]

No decisive battle marked the end of the war, but English success in establishing themselves upriver at Henrico, downriver near the Indian town of Kecoughtan, as well as on Jamestown Island was abundantly clear to Wahunsonacock by 1614. Refusing to surrender formally, he had nevertheless come to accept that his warriors were incapable of dislodging the invaders from his lands. For their part, the English considered the victory theirs. They had successfully fended off the Powhatan threat and consolidated their hold on the colony. They had also entered into alliances with tribes on the Eastern Shore and concluded articles of peace with the powerful Chickahominies, who adopted the English king as their overlord. A pamphlet of 1616 confidently asserted that the colonists were "by the Natives liking and consent, in actuall possession of a great part of the Countrey."[41] The marriage of Wahunsonacock's favorite daughter, Pocahontas, to an English gentleman, John Rolfe, in April 1614 symbolized the new accord between the two peoples, who now (seemingly) lived side by side in harmony and friendship as one nation.

But the question remained: whose nation? Wahunsonacock had tacitly agreed to live in peace with the English but had not relinquished his title to the region nor acknowledged James I his king, and if a number of tribes had transferred their allegiance to the English during the war, nevertheless the core of his empire remained intact. Seduced by their own propaganda, which lauded the praises of the new colony, and enjoying the fruits of prosperity as a result of the adoption of tobacco cultivation, the English were completely duped by the great king's effective successor, Opechancanough, and lulled into a fatal sense of false security. The great uprising of March 22, 1622 left 347 settlers dead, about a quarter of the entire colony, and was a defining moment in Anglo-Indian relations in early America. It removed any moral obligation from the English (in their view) to continue their self-imposed labor of bringing civility and Christianity to the Indian.[42] English policy did not change significantly after 1622, in the sense that the second Anglo-Powhatan war was in many respects a continuation of the first, but any hopes that the two peoples could live together in peace were utterly confounded by what propagandist Edward Waterhouse called the "barbarous Massacre." By "this last butchery," Samuel Purchas fulminated, the Indians "made both of them and their Country wholly English." They could be cleared from the land in the knowledge that "having little of Humanitie" they had given up their right to be treated like humans. "Our first worke," governor Sir Francis Wyatt wrote from Virginia in 1623 or 1624, "is expulsion of the Salvages to gaine the free range of the countrey for encrease of Cattle, swine &c which will more then restore us, for it is infinitely better to have no heathen among us, who at best were but thornes in our sides, then to be at peace and league with them." To English eyes, the uprising fully justified the dispossession of the Indians. As Waterhouse argued: "our hands which before were tied with gentlenesse and faire usage, are now set at liberty by the treacherous violence of the Savages . . . so that we, who hitherto have had possession of no more ground then their waste . . . may now by right of Warre, and law of Nations, invade the Country, and destroy them who sought to destroy us." The subjugation of the Indians as a conquered people was taken for granted and their removal from English lands proceeded with gathering pace through the 1620s and 1630s. A final desperate act of resistance led by Opechancanough was mounted in 1644, but the country had already been lost and with it the Powhatan empire.[43]

Conquest and Dominion

The twin imperatives of conquest and dominion are of importance in explaining Anglo-Indian encounters in early America, influencing English policy toward colonization, and shaping Indians' attitudes to the strangers who had come into their lands not just to trade but to settle. From this point of view, the descent into violence that characterizes relations at Roanoke and in the Chesapeake was not just the inevitable outcome of English aggression toward peoples they considered culturally inferior, a consequence of the breakdown of trade, or an expression of the Indians' defensive reactions to European invaders. Negotiations and eventually hostilities were structured on both sides by a powerful sense of territory and sovereignty.[44] In Virginia, colonists encountered an aggressive and skilful chief who at least initially may have entertained the possibility of absorbing the English settlers into his domains. If Wahunsonacock believed the colonists' stories of a great king across the water, he evidently did not consider that settlers should necessarily remain subject to such a distant authority, any more than he could conceive of English claims to his lands or their expectation he should conform himself to English governorship. He had told John Smith at the mock coronation that he was already a king and the lands surrounding them were his. But when he reminded Smith that he was one of his chiefs, Smith told him: "you must knowe as I have but one God, I honour but one king [James I]; and I live here not as your subject, but as your friend." Sovereignty was indivisible; there could be no compromise.[45]

This was the crux of the matter. Neither Smith nor any other English leader could transfer his allegiance to an Indian king, any more than Wahunsonacock could accept the sovereignty of the English monarch. Since neither side was capable of comprehending the basis of the other's claims, arguments and counter-arguments were soon overtaken by violence, war, and the forcible dispossession of Indians hostile to the English.

Smith was astute in his observation that the Indians "were our enemies, whom we neither knew nor understood," but equally the Powhatans had no means of understanding the English compulsion to claim Virginia as their own. In these circumstances, a bloody struggle for possession was inevitable.

Chapter 2
Powhatans Abroad
Virginia Indians in England

ALDEN T. VAUGHAN

In the summer of 1603, an English expedition brought two or three natives of Powhatan's domain to London, where in September the captive "Virginians" paddled a canoe on the Thames before a rapt audience. That event inaugurated—several years before Captain John Smith and his companions secured a foothold in Virginia—the human exchange between Powhatan's Tsenacommacah ("densely inhabited land") and King James's England.[1] Although the movement of peoples would in the long run be dominated by thousands of English men and women making permanent homes in Virginia rather than two dozen Powhatans residing temporarily in England, the thinner eastward current would play a significant, if unheralded, part in the Atlantic world's cultural interaction.

The captives of 1603 are notable not only for their chronological primacy but for having been taken to England by force. Most of the subsequent eastward voyagers before the demise of the Virginia Colony as a corporate enterprise went willingly, the surviving records suggest, either as envoys of Chief Powhatan or as temporary guests of the Virginia Company of London. The few but important Indians in the first category served Tsenacommacah by scouting the English colonists' homeland for information about its people and resources. The second and larger category consisted of Virginia Company recruits for English schooling and conversion to Christianity. A notable exception to the two paradigms was Pocahontas, the Powhatan princess whose presence in England demonstrated the colony's missionary potential. Regardless of the circumstances behind their transatlantic travels, Indians in England before 1624 gave thousands of English people a first-hand impression of American natives and, through them, some inkling of Powhatan culture.

The Virginians who exhibited their skills on the Thames in 1603 are a hazy initial episode in the story of Tsenacommacah's inhabitants abroad. The precise circumstances of their seizure are unknown; their voyage and initial reception in England are undocumented; and, after a moment's fame on the Thames, they drop from sight.[2] The sole record of their English experience is Sir Robert Cecil's list of "rewardes" for services rendered to his London household, which shows payments of four and five shillings during the first week of September 1603 "to the virginians"; the actual disbursement was probably by Sir Walter Cope, who seems to have supervised the Indians in London. Another five shillings were "geven by Myles [surely a Cecil employee] to ii watermen that brought the cannowe to my Lords howse" on the Strand, and twelve pence "to a payre of ores[men] that waited on the Virginians when they rowed with ther Cannow."[3] No further evidence illuminates Tsenacommacah's first migrants to England.

What these Virginians observed in their London stay can only be surmised, but there are grounds for informed guesses. Nearly a score of American natives had been in England during the previous two decades, all of them apparently persuaded, or forced, to leave their homelands to serve their hosts' pragmatic purposes. Leaving aside the eight or so who arrived before 1577 (information on them is sparse; half died within a month), the Indians in England between that date and 1603 were interrogated about their homelands, indoctrinated in English customs, taught the English language, and sent back with new expeditions as interpreters, guides, and liaisons to their own and neighboring peoples. From the experiences of these American natives, and by extrapolating from the evidence on five Abenakis from the "northern parts of Virginia" (renamed New England in 1616) who arrived in 1605, the expectations for Cope's Virginians of 1603 can be readily surmised.[4]

The most exemplary early American visitor, from England's perspective, was Manteo of Croatan Island, who learned English in London from the linguistically talented Thomas Hariot in 1584–85, then served as interpreter, guide, and diplomat for the first Roanoke Island outpost in 1585–86. After another journey to England in 1586–87, Manteo returned to Roanoke with the "lost" colony of 1587 and probably shared its fate. Manteo's companion of 1584–85, the Roanoke native Wanchese, vehemently opposed English settlements after completing his transatlantic round trip, but he was a notable exception in the pre-1603 roster of Indian intermediaries.[5] The two other Indians from the Carolina coast who were in England in the 1580s seem to have assisted the English. Towaye probably accompanied Manteo on his second trip to England and definitely returned with him to Roanoke in 1587, perhaps as a second interpreter. The other Indian, seized by Sir Richard Grenville in 1586, was likely preparing to accompany Grenville's aborted relief expedition to Roanoke in 1588 when he succumbed to disease.[6] English-trained Indians had not saved the Roanoke outposts from disaster, but they had been valuable to the colonial enterprise.

Sir Walter Ralegh's explorations in the Orinoco River valley in the 1590s reinforced the point. The ten or so natives of Trinidad and Guiana taken to England by his agents in 1594 and 1596, and by Ralegh himself in 1595, became interpreters of varying proficiency, their linguistic skills contingent, most likely, on the duration of their stays abroad. John Provost of Trinidad, for example, served Ralegh's nephew Sir John Gilbert "many yeeres" in England and in the late sixteenth and early seventeenth centuries was a reliable interpreter and guide in Guiana to several English scouting parties and to at least one incipient English outpost. He also persuaded wary Guianan natives that the English, unlike the slave-raiding Spanish, should be welcomed as peaceful and potentially useful visitors.[7] Surely Sir Robert Cecil had similar roles in mind for the Virginians who plied the Thames in 1603.

Why none of those Indians were aboard the *Susan Constant, Godspeed,* or *Discovery* when Christopher Newport's little fleet sailed from London in December 1606 is unknown but easily imagined. The South Americans, even if willing, would have been irrelevant in Tsenacommacah's unfamiliar geographic and linguistic setting. Cope's Virginians most likely had not survived the plague of 1603, which killed thousands of Londoners that summer and frightened many of the gentry and nobility into temporary exile. (King James left London in early August; Lord Cecil was miles away when the Indians lodged at his house.[8]) If the Virginians somehow survived the plague and subsequent diseases, they may have returned to the Chesapeake on an unrecorded voyage between 1603 and 1606. In the latter year, the Virginia Company of London's counterpart for the settlement of the area north of the Hudson River assigned several captive New England Algonquians, seized in 1605, to its two scouting expeditions and other Indians to a colonizing expedition in 1607. A Spanish fleet captured the two Indians who sailed on the first of those voyages, but their compatriots on the second and third performed the intended roles moderately well at the short-lived Sagadahoc Colony in Maine.[9] The absence of one or more Indian guides on Christopher Newport's fleet of 1606–7 is therefore surprising and can only mean that no qualified Virginian was available. Jamestown's troubled early history would illustrate, by their absence, the usefulness of cultural intermediaries.

Powhatan's Envoys

In early 1608, a few weeks after Powhatan's famous first confrontation with John Smith, the sachem dispatched his envoy Namontack "to King James his land, to see him and his country, and to returne me the true report thereof."[10] Smith described Namontack as the chief's "trustie servant, and one of a shrewd subtill capacitie," although he was often referred to—figuratively in some accounts, literally in others—as the chief's son. As a hostage to Namontack's safe return, the Powhatans received from Captain

Christopher Newport a linguistically ironic swap: for the "savage" (in English parlance) Namontack they acquired a thirteen-year-old English lad named Thomas Savage, introduced to Powhatan as Newport's son.[11] He would spend the next three years with the Virginia Algonquians, learning their language, observing their customs, and endearing himself to Chief Powhatan. After Savage's return to Jamestown in about 1611, he translated for the colony often and well until his death in the early 1630s.[12] Thus the paramount chief of Tsenacommacah and the leader of the English outpost each used a surrogate son to glean information about the other's customs, resources, and intentions.

At this early stage of English colonization, Powhatan had no reason to fear for Tsenacommacah's future. The hundred or so colonists at Jamestown seemed unlikely to survive: always short of food, badly sheltered, and scarcely able to defend their small enclave, despite their thunderous weapons, gigantic (to Indian eyes) vessels, and self-assumed cultural superiority. By the time Namontack reached Jamestown in early March 1608, fire had destroyed most of its crude buildings, "which being but thatched with reeds," remembered one of the colonists, "the fire was so fierce as it burnt their Pallisado's, (though eight or ten yards distant) with their Armes, bedding, apparell, and much private provision." In the ensuing weeks of bitter cold and extreme shortage of food, half the colonists died.[13] Long before Namontack boarded Newport's ship, he must have expected to be unimpressed by England.

In London, Powhatan's first appointed envoy to Whitehall made quite a stir. The Venetian ambassador informed his government that a leading inhabitant of Virginia had arrived "to treat with the King." Pedro de Zuniga, Spain's ambassador to England, notified Philip III that "Newport brought a lad who they say is the son of an emperor of those lands" who had been instructed "that when he sees the King he is not to take off his hat, and other things of this sort." Zuniga was "amused by the way they [English authorities] honour him, for I hold it for surer that he must be a very ordinary person."[14] Such European preoccupation with Namontack's social status is telling. If the Venetian and Spanish ambassadors reported accurately the English perceptions of this Tsenacommacah native, his billing as the son of an emperor made him mildly important; what his hosts might learn from him about the American environment or Powhatan culture seemed to matter very little. Namontack was not, to be sure, the first Indian in England, nor even the only one there (in 1608 he shared the exotic limelight with a few natives of New England and several of Trinidad and Guiana), but he was the first voluntary envoy from the area of England's sole existing outpost. English authorities *should* have cared.

No accounts survive of Namontack's activities abroad. He must have seen London's notable sights and perhaps glimpsed other parts of England. That he had an audience with King James is doubtful, absent any record of the event, though he may have spotted the monarch in a passing carriage, and he surely met officials of the Virginia Company of London. That Powhatan's envoy was topical is nonetheless evident from the character in Ben Jonson's *Epicoene* (1609), who drew a "map or portrait" of Namentack when he was there.[15] Of greater importance for the Powhatans, Namontack must have made extensive mental notes on the English capital—its teeming population compared to Tsenacommacah's, its multistoried buildings, its innumerable ships, its pomp and ostentatious wealth; but also its gagging odors, littered streets, and widespread, sometimes lethal poverty. Namontack surely carried home an ambivalent description of Captain Newport's nation. In any event, the envoy's stay lasted only four months. Newport sailed from England in mid-July 1608 with Namontack aboard and reached Jamestown in late September.[16] A few weeks later, John Smith visited Powhatan at Werowocomoco and "redelivered him *Namontack* he had sent for *England*."[17]

Back in Tsenacommacah, Namontack spoke favorably of his experience. Francis Magnel, an Irishman who spent eight months in Virginia, reported that "The Emperor [Powhatan] sent one of his sons to England, where they treated him well, and sent him back to his land. The Emperor . . . and his people were very happy over what he told them about the good reception and entertainment he found in England."[18] And Namontack was sufficiently trusting of English customs to play a crucial role in Newport's "coronation" of Powhatan as King James's Virginian vassal—a role the supreme sachem of Tsenacommacah had no intention of playing. A suspicious Powhatan acceded to the ceremony only when "perswaded by *Namontack* they would not hurt him." Weeks later, Namontack helped the hungry colonists obtain several hogsheads of corn despite Tsenacommacah's renewed hostility to the English intruders.[19] From that point on, Powhatan's first envoy to England is primarily notable for the uncertainty of his fate and for his embodiment of the evidential confusion that shrouds early Indian transatlantic travel.

Despite Smith's assurance that he "redelivered" Namontack in the autumn of 1608 and sure signs that Namontack was at Tsenacommacah later that autumn, he seems to have disappeared. In 1614 Powhatan complained to secretary of the colony Ralph Hamor that after Namontack went to England in exchange for Thomas Savage, he "as yet is not returned, though many ships have arrived here from thence, since that time, how ye have delt with him I know not."[20] Smith later provided a possible explanation. In his *Generall Historie of Virginia, New-England, and the Summer Isles* (1624), Smith ended a brief, second-hand narrative of *Sea Venture*'s wreck on Bermuda in 1609 with a grim scenario: "There were two Salvages also sent from *Virginia* by Captain *Smith*, the one called *Namuntack*, the other *Matchumps*, but some such differences fell betweene them, that *Matchumps* slew *Namuntack*, and having made a hole to bury him, because it was too short, he cut of[f] his legs and laid them by him, which murder he concealed till he was in *Virginia*."[21] A year after the publication of Smith's history, the Reverend Samuel Purchas corroborated the story. In reprinting an early Virginia assertion that among the Powhatan Indians "Murther is scarsly heard of," Purchas added a marginal note: "Yet *Namantack* in his returne was killed in *Bermuda* by another Savage his fellow."[22]

Perhaps Smith and Purchas were right. Newport departed Virginia on his third trip to England in December 1608 and probably arrived before mid-January 1609.[23] If Namontack accompanied him a second time and Matchumps went with them, the two Powhatans could have boarded *Sea Venture* in early June 1609 and, along with all passengers and crew, survived its crash off the Bermuda coast in late July. Matchumps had abundant opportunity to kill Namontack during the ten months in which Admiral George Somers directed the building of two small ships for the final leg to Jamestown. But undermining the plausibility of an Indian versus Indian crime on Bermuda in 1609 is the absence of any reference to Namontack or Matchumps, either by name or ethnicity, in the many contemporaneous accounts of *Sea Venture*'s wreck and its aftermath. Some chroniclers might have considered two Indians of slight importance; for English writers and readers, the central message of England's tempestuous rediscovery of Bermuda was God's merciful rescue of one hundred and fifty terrified souls on an island paradise that was widely reputed to be the "Isle of Devils." But why would one of the survivors, the learned William Strachey, whose very long letter of 1610 to an anonymous "Excellent Lady" abounds with the Bermuda episode's people and events, have overlooked the presence of two Virginia natives on an archipelago which almost miraculously had no natives of its own? And would Strachey not have mentioned Namontack's conspicuous absence when the survivors sailed on to Jamestown in 1610, while relating that two Englishmen, one a murderer, were left behind? Such omissions seem improbable by an author whose *Historie of Travell into Virginia Britania*, written no more than two years after he and the other Bermuda survivors reached Virginia, mentions both Matchumps and Namontack, with no hint of an altercation between them or of the latter's demise.[24]

The soundest surmise from the scraps of conflicting evidence on Powhatan's first envoy to England may be that in 1608 Namontack spent about four months in England, where he was well treated and returned home with useful information; that during the next few months he assisted in Powhatan's coronation and served as a guide and interpreter to the colonists. He then probably went to England a second time, perhaps in late 1608—possibly a year or two later—and had not returned to Tsenacommacah by 1614. He may have been killed by Matchumps on Bermuda in 1609 (despite no mention in the reports) or slain by Matchumps at a later date on the Bermuda Islands or elsewhere, with Smith entering a garbled report at the end of his account of the *Sea Venture* episode and Purchas uncritically adopting Smith's explanation. But whatever his fate, Namontack is the first envoy from North America to observe England and report his findings to the indigenous side of the incipient British empire.[25]

A few more Powhatans followed Namontack's path to England before 1616, although the intermittent Anglo-Indian wars allowed scant opportunity for ambassadorial visits, and the circumstances of most Indian travels are unclear. In 1610, for example, Strachey mentioned Powhatan's displeasure with Jamestown's leaders for not giving him a coach and horses, "for hee had understood by the *Indians* which were in *England*, how such was the state of great *Werowances*, and Lords in *England*, to ride and visit other great men." In addition to Namontack, Powhatan's informants could have been Powhatan's brother-in-law Matchumps, who, according to Strachey, "was sometyme in England," and Kainta, son of a local chief, captured by the English during one of the internecine wars, and "sent now [ca. July 1610] into *England*, untill the ships arrive here againe the next Spring."[26] Nothing further is known about Kainta's travels or his presumed return to Virginia after about eight months abroad. Why colonial officials sent this captive to England is unknown. He must have been there too briefly to master the English language, though he probably learned enough to be useful to Powhatan; he could have been exposed to intensive questioning and indoctrination; and eight months was surely long enough for any American visitor to observe that the aristocracy traveled by horse and carriage. Or perhaps Kainta was primarily a curiosity, a symbol of the colony's power to seize and transport a "savage" prince—another Virginian on display.

The "Indian College"

By the time Kainta arrived in England, the linguistic training of Indians abroad no longer retained the urgency it had held at Roanoke and Guiana. In Virginia, Thomas Savage and several other colonists were now adept at the Powhatan language and presumably more loyal to colonial interests than Indians educated in England were likely to be. But the conversion and education of the Powhatans and their neighbors was another matter. The colony had few clergymen and no schools and thus no practical way to fulfill the Virginia Company of London's obligation to "bring the infidels and salvages, lyving in those partes, to humane civilitie." A pamphlet addressed to the Virginia Company insisted that it is "not the nature of men, but the education of men, which make[s] them barbarous and uncivill"; if you "chaunge the education of men . . . you shall see that their nature will be greatly rectified and corrected."[27] The best place to instill civility and Christianity, English imperialists believed, was England, though it was worth a try in Virginia.

A plan to indoctrinate Indians in England was underway by the early summer of 1609. Shortly before Sir Thomas Gates boarded the *Sea Venture*, the London Company advised him to "procure . . . some convenient nomber of their Children to be brought up in your language, and manners." After Gates was presumed to have been lost at sea, the company sent Sir Thomas West, Lord De La Warr, to administer the colony; if Indian leaders "shalbe willfull and obstinate," he was to seize Indian shamans and "send over some three or foure of them into England [so that] we may endevour theire Conversion here."[28] Although intermittent war with the Powhatans prevented the full implementation of those instructions, a trickle of potential Indian converts across the Atlantic began about 1610. Kainta may have been the first.

Once again, the particulars are obscure. The earliest recruit, if not Kainta, was probably "one *Nanawack*, a youth sent over by the *Lo. De Laware*, when hee was Governour there," according to a pamphlet of 1630, harking back to De La Warr governorship in 1610–11. If conversion was the goal for Nanawack, it failed initially, for "living here a yeare or two in houses where hee heard not much of Religion, but saw and heard many times examples of drinking, swearing, and like evills, [he] remained as hee was a meere Pagan." A change of venue made all the difference. With the boy "removed into a godly family, hee was strangely altered, grew to understand the principles of Religion, learned to reade, delighted in the Scriptures, Sermons, Prayers, and other Christian duties, wonderfully bewailed the state of his Countrymen, especially his brethren; and gave such testimonies of his love to the truth, that hee was thought fit to be baptised." As often happened to Indians abroad in the seventeenth century, death intervened. His hosts were nonetheless impressed by the depth of Nanawack's faith, for he "left behinde such testimonies of his desire of Gods favour, that it mooved such godly Christians as knew him, to conceive well of his condition."[29]

The London Company's long-range plan was to enroll Powhatans at a school and college in Virginia, where academic studies would complement the training in religion and manners. A colony law of August 1619 directed each town and plantation to "obtaine unto themselves by just meanes" several Indian youths for exposure to "true Religion & civile course of life. Of which children the most towardly boyes in witt & graces of nature [are] to be brought up . . . in the firste Elements of litterature, so as to be fitted for the Colledge intended for them." College education would, of course, extend beyond English literature to Latin and Greek, as would a preparatory school's lessons, if a prominent English educational reformer had his way. John Brinsley advocated high quality grammar schools as the antidote to the "inhumanitie" exhibited by "manie of the Irish, the Virgineans, and all other barbarous nations," in accordance with Ovid's judgment that "Right learning of ingenous Arts, / The savage frames to civill parts." But not until 1620 would the company have sufficient funds to begin either an Indian school or a college.³⁰

In the meantime, several Powhatans followed in Kainta's and Nanawack's footsteps. In 1617 Samuel Purchas observed that the sponsors of Virginia's intended Indian college had "brought thence children of both sexes here to be taught our language and letters, which may prove profitable instruments in this [educational and missionary] designe." Just who those Indian children were—their names, ages, dates, and circumstances of migration—is unknown. They must have been few in number, given most Indian parents' reluctance to part with their children and the paucity of references in the surviving records to Indian youths in England. Two burial records for a London parish in 1613 may pertain to such visitors: entries for October 28 and November 4 read identically: "A Virginian, out of Sir Thomas Smithes howse."³¹ While "Virginian" in 1613 could still refer to an Indian from anywhere along the eastern coast of North America between Florida and Canada, none outside of the Virginia Company of London's territory—that is, the Virginia Colony and its environs—would likely have been living at the home of the company's president. Perhaps the two Indians who died in 1613 were adult Virginians whose arrival in London is undocumented; one may have been Nanawack. The most plausible explanation is that they were two of the anonymous youths sent to England by Lord De La Warr and his successors for schooling and conversion.

Two young males from Tsenacommacah, probably part of the missionary/educational contingent, had their likenesses widely distributed in Jacobean England. In early 1615, the Virginia Company issued "A Declaration for the certaine time of drawing of the great standing Lottery," a moderately successful bid to raise funds for the corporation's general expenses and especially its missionary work (Figure 2.1). This large broadside featured two full-length drawings of Virginia Indians: on the upper left corner is Eiakintomino, facing to his left and holding a bow and arrows, wearing a fringed mantle and purse, with a turtle near his left foot. On the upper right hand corner, Matahan has a similar pose, garment, accoutrements, and turtle, but he faces to his right and has a slightly different feathered ornament in his hair. The first four lines of a poem which supposedly expressed the Virginians' Christian longings are near Eiakintomino's feet, the other four lines near Matahan's. The whole text reflects English expectations of imminent Indian conversion to Anglicanism and a current English penchant for comparing the Indians' presumed lack of civility to the ancient Britons' before the Roman conquest.³²

Although there is no proof that Eiakintomino and Matahan posed in England—adaptations of illustrations by John White and others proliferated for centuries without the artists seeing an Indian—there is reason to believe that these Indians were in London in 1615 or earlier. Almost con-

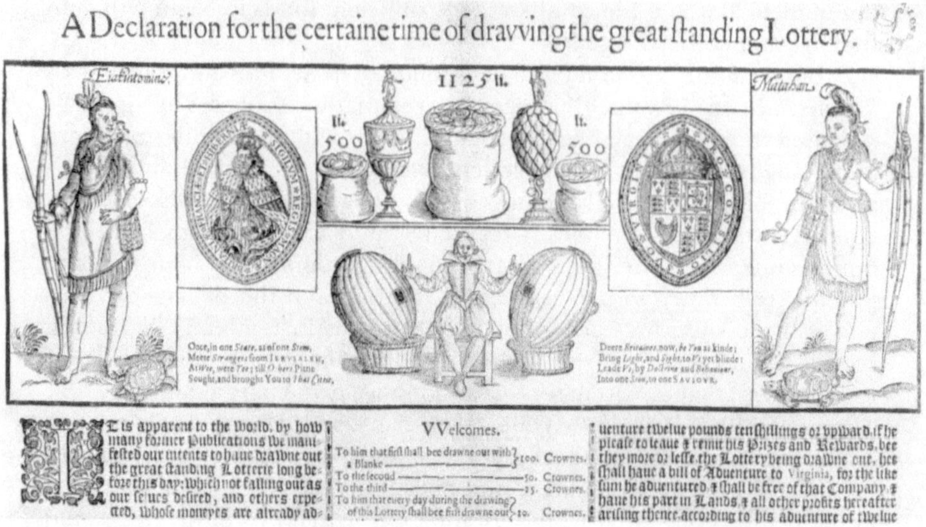

Figure 2.1. The Virginia Company of London, "The Great Standing Lottery," broadside (London, 1615), detail. Courtesy of the Society of Antiquaries of London. This larger broadside advertised a lottery to raise money for the Virginia Company and features portraits of two Virginia natives: Eikintomino on the left and Matahan on the right. The text promotes the idea that the Virginia colony will benefit the region's natives: they are depicted as eager to convert to English ways and adopt the English religion. The verse at the men's feet reminds readers that the English themselves were at one time pagans, and begs them to "Bring *Light* and *Sight* to *Us* yet blinde."

temporary with the lottery broadside is the Dutch artist Michael van Meer's full-length watercolor portrait of Eiakintomino in St. James Park, flanked by five large fauna. The handwritten Dutch caption identifies the scene as "A young man from the Virginias" and, elsewhere on the picture, "These Indian birds and animals [in fact, they are European rather than "Indian"], together with the young man, were to be seen in 1615, 1616 in St James Park or zoo which is [illegible] near Westminster before the city of London."[33] No evidence survives about Eiakintomino's and Matahan's fate.

Their lives in England must have overlapped with several youths in the delegation of Powhatans, featuring Pocahontas, assembled by Sir Thomas Dale in 1616. Tomocomo (a.k.a. Uttamatomakkin, Tomakin), Pocahontas's brother-in-law and her most prominent native companion on the great promotional visit of 1616–17, lamented to Samuel Purchas that he was himself too old to learn a new religion, "bidding us teach the boies and girles (which were brought over from thence)." Tomocomo may have referred to Indians who had been sent earlier, but other potential students surely accompanied him to England. In June 1616 a Londoner noted that Dale "hathe brought divers men and women of that countrye *to be educated here.*"³⁴

Another Englishman estimated that "ten or twelve old and younge of that countrie" arrived with Pocahontas. A London parish record suggests that one male member died about two months after their arrival in England, for on August 6, 1616, "A Virginian, called Abraham, [was] buried out of Sr. Thomas Smithes." Another Powhatan apparently lived for several years with George Thorpe, a member of Parliament and sometime councilor to James I, who in 1620 would become Virginia's supervisor of the prospective Indian college; before his departure for that assignment, Thorpe mentioned a document "written [as amanuensis] by the virginian boy of mee George Thorpe." The youth must have been in England for at least a year, probably much longer, to have mastered English well enough to write a legible copy of a complex text. He is almost surely the "Georgius Thorpe" who was baptized at St. Martin in the Fields on September 10, 1619, and whose burial was recorded seventeen days later as "Georgius Thorp, homo Virginiae." Another Powhatan who may have come to England and remained past 1617 is Tomocomo's wife and Pocahontas's sister, Matachanna, who could have been caring for the Rolfes' young son Thomas and may herself, like the youngster, have been too ill to return to Tsenacommacah in 1617. Perhaps she returned to Virginia a year or two later; there is no known burial in England, and her very presence in England is conjectural.³⁵

Clear evidence survives that two, perhaps three, female Powhatans remained in England for several years after Pocahontas's death. In May 1620 the Virginia Company noted that "one of the maides w[hi]ch Sr Thomas Dale brought from Virginia . . . who some times dwelt a servant w[i]th a Mercer in Cheapside is nowe verie weake of a Consumption"; the company paid for her medications.³⁶ Six months later, two young women in the company's care, Mary and Elizabeth (no surnames or Indian names are recorded), were indigent, and Mary—perhaps the unnamed consumptive—was ill. The company tried "to place them in good services where they may learne some trade to live by hereafter," but such efforts were fruitless, probably because the women lacked appropriate skills or proficiency in English, perhaps because English prejudice curtailed their opportunities. In any case, the company soon cut its losses by sending both maids to Bermuda, where women were in short supply, to be married "with such as shall accept of them."³⁷

The Virginia Company bore the costs of passage and all necessities for the "two Virginian virgins" and the four boys who served them: clothing, bedding, soap, starch, food, and drink for bodily comfort; bibles and psalters for spiritual comfort. The women carried also the company's request that Governor Nathaniel Butler use "his care and authoritie" to find "honest English husbands" (which Butler thought "a harder task in this place than they wer aware of") and to arrange for their postnuptial employment: "after some staye in the Ilands," the company proposed, the Indians "might be transported home to their sauvage parents in Virginia (who wer ther no lese than petie kinges), and so be happely a meanes of their conversion." John Smith echoed that sentiment a few years later: "After they were converted and had children," he hoped, "they might be sent to their Countrey [Tsenacommacah] and kindred to civilize them." The Virginia Company's missionary hopes persevered.[38]

One of the Powhatan women, probably Mary, died at sea, but the other reached Bermuda and, less than a year later, fulfilled one of the Virginia Company's intentions. In the spring of 1622 she was "married to as fitt and agreeable an husband as the place would afford," reported Governor Butler, who entertained more than one hundred guests at a lavish reception. Butler's generosity was motivated partly by the hope "that the staungers at their returne to Virginia might find reason to carry a good testimony with them of the wellfare and plenty of this plantation."[39] Although Butler did not identify the strangers from Virginia, the implication is that two or more Powhatans had attended the wedding.

The records are unfortunately silent on what proselytizing efforts Elizabeth (if she was the survivor) may have made in Tsenacommacah or even if she left Bermuda. With the Virginia Colony entering a decade of brutal Indian-English warfare after the Powhatan uprising of March 1622, a Christian Indian and her English husband would have been unlikely immigrants.

Pocahontas in England

Pocahontas was, potentially, Powhatan's most effective envoy to England. True, Tomocomo was Powhatan's designated reporter in the group that accompanied his daughter, and she had not seen her father for nearly four years, yet when Pocahontas reached England in 1616 she could gain entry where Tomocomo could not. Her fluent English, conversion to Christianity, marriage to an Englishman, and adoption of "civilized" clothing made her acceptable to London society (Figure 2.2). And she was a Powhatan *princess*, welcomed by English nobles and gentry for her high birth as well as her personal charm. With her continuing fondness for her father and her adherence to a vision of Virginia that extended, rather than displaced, her natal society, Pocahontas would probably have shared her observations with Powhatan. The pity is that Tsenacommacah's most effective ambassador to the Court of St. James did not live to tell the paramount chief a word of what she had seen and heard in eight busy months—more useful information about England and the English, probably, than everything

Figure 2.2. Pocahontas in 1616: "Matoaka alias Rebecca daughter to the mighty Prince Powhattan Emperor of Virginia," drawn from life by Simon van de Passe. Courtesy of the John Carter Brown Library, Brown University. This engraving—and a copy of it in which Pocahontas's features have been slightly Europeanized—circulated in 1617, and were included in copies of John Smith's *Generall Historie* (1624).

gleaned by Namontack, Tomocomo, and the other Virginians who visited England between 1608 and 1617.

From the English perspective, Pocahontas was in London primarily to promote the Virginia Company, its missionary program, and the feasibility of English "civility," even intermarriage, for Tsenacommacah's people. She epitomized England's social aspirations for America. The Virginia Company therefore treated her more prominently and lavishly than it did any of her companions, and to some extent it reaped the expected rewards. Historians and anthropologists have long debated Pocahontas's precise role in England and—especially and most intriguingly—what the experience meant to her, but there is no doubt that from a public relations standpoint, the months before she took ill were unprecedented for an indigenous American visitor.[40] Yet despite the far greater attention paid to the Powhatan princess than to any of her predecessors in England, the monopoly of English writings in the surviving sources—although sometimes purporting to quote or paraphrase Indian voices—makes any reconstruction of the events and assessment of their meaning an exercise in cautious probability at best.

This much is documented. While the other members of Dale's delegation were distributed to households throughout London, the Rolfes (and perhaps Tomocomo) lodged initially in an old hostelry and former theatre at the bottom of Ludgate Hill, the Bell Savage Inn (another linguistic irony), owned originally by a family named Savage, though not, apparently, closely related to the Virginia Colony's Thomas Savage.[41] There the Powhatan princess received a variety of English visitors and ventured forth to see London's sights and meet its luminaries. The most notable excursions were undoubtedly to attend the royal family. Next in importance, and better recorded, was a visit to Lambeth Palace, across the Thames from Westminster, where the Reverend Dr. John King, Bishop of London, "entertained her with festivall state and pompe," according to Samuel Purchas, who was also a guest, "beyond what I have seene in his great hospitalitie afforded to other Ladies." Purchas noted that Pocahontas was patronized by "divers particular persons of Honor, in their hopefull zeale by her to advance Christianitie." That motive explains the Bishop of London's enthusiasm: his and his successors' clerical jurisdiction—from the founding of Virginia until the Revolution of 1776—included all of English America. If the bishop meant seriously to promote the gospel in the infant British empire, he had best begin with the person John Smith described to Queen Anne as "the first Christian ever of that Nation, the first *Virginian* ever spake *English*, or had a childe in mariage by an *Englishman*."[42] If "that Nation" meant Tsenacommacah, the first and third statements are true; but unless Smith meant *fluent* English, the second is surely false, in light of Namontack, Matchumps, and other Powhatans who had crossed the Atlantic and must have learned passable English, perhaps with Thomas Hariot's help. But hyperbole aside, Smith's point is sound: Pocahontas was by far the best evidence yet that the colonization of eastern North America might lead to an integrated but predominantly Christian community and a culturally English society. The bishop did his part to honor England's most prestigious religious and social convert.

By the time Pocahontas's triumphal visit neared its completion, the Virginia Company was preparing her next contribution to the conversion of Virginia's natives. On March 19, 1617, the company voted a special award to John Rolfe of one hundred pounds from its missionary funds,

> uppon promise made by the said Mr: Rolfe in behalfe of him self and the said Ladye, his wife, that bothe by their godlye and vertuous example in their perticuler persons and famelye, as also by all other good meanes of perswasions and inducemts, they would imploy their best endevours to the winning of that People to the knowledge of God, and embraceing of true religion.[43]

Armed with this new charge, the Rolfes joined Samuel Argall, Tomocomo, and a perhaps a few more of the Powhatan delegation aboard the *George* for the arduous voyage home. With Pocahontas's death at Gravesend a few days later, the missionary enterprise lost what Purchas hailed as "the first fruits of *Virginian* conversion." Because no other native of Tsenacommacah could match Pocahontas's social stature and achievements, the Virginia Company's interest in bringing other Indians to England waned rapidly, especially when the boys and girls who accompanied Pocahontas failed to fulfill the company's high hopes. In 1622 Sir Edwin Sandys, Sir Thomas Smyth's successor as head of the Virginia Company, discouraged the transportation of more Indians to England for education because "he feared (upon experience of those brought by Sr Tho: Dale)" that the enterprise "might be farr from the Christian worke intended."[44]

The failure of Tsenacommacah's boys and girls to absorb English religion and customs did not preclude Powhatan and his successors from sending individual envoys to England, but Tomocomo's experience boded poorly for his category of Indian traveler. At first, Tomocomo had drawn almost as much attention as his sister-in-law, although for antithetical reasons. Whereas Pocahontas was substantially anglicized and therefore admired in England for what she had become, Tomocomo was blatantly and proudly Indian, shunning English religion, English clothing, even English hair styles. Although the sources are not specific on the garb he affected in London, it was probably little more than a breech clout, mantle, and moccasins; and, as we know from Samuel Purchas, the right side of Tomocomo's head was shaved clean while the left side sported a "Devill-lock" several feet long.[45] Tomocomo was a powerful, dramatic presence.

Smith, who had known Tomocomo in Virginia, encountered him again in London in early 1617. Smith thought the meeting was "by chance," but Tomocomo insisted that Powhatan had ordered him to find Smith, who was "to shew him our God, the King, Queene, and Prince, I [Smith] so much had told them of." Smith's response was brief and unsatisfactory to Tomocomo: "Concerning God, I told him the best I could, the King I heard he had seene, and the rest hee should see when he would"—that is, whenever Tomocomo wanted to. But Tomocomo refused to believe he had seen King James until Smith (who had surely heard of their attendance at a royal masque) explained the circumstances. "Then he replyed very sadly," Smith recalled, "You gave *Powhatan* a white Dog, which *Powhatan* fed as himselfe, but your King gave me nothing, and I am better than your white Dog."[46]

If Tomocomo barely recognized King James, he surely got to know Samuel Purchas, B.D., pastor of St. Martin's by Ludgate, who tried to enlighten Powhatan's envoy about Anglican Christianity, with an unnamed employee of Sir Thomas Dale as interpreter—perhaps an Indian, more likely Thomas Savage or another bilingual colonist. "With this Savage," Purchas recalled of Tomocomo, "I have often conversed at my good friends Master Doctor *Goldstone* [Theodore Gulstone], where he was a frequent guest." Purchas's description of those conversations is brief but intriguing. They were not, as one might expect, didactic monologues by Purchas and Gulstone on Anglican theology and English culture; rather, Tomocomo did his share of showing and telling. "I have both seen him sing and dance his diabolicall measures," Purchas observed, "and heard him discourse of his Countrey and Religion." On the latter subject, Purchas had only disdain for the Indian's views. Tomocomo, he concluded, was "a blasphmer of what he knew not, and preferring his God to ours, because he [i.e., the Powhatans' god] taught them (by his owne so appearing) to weare their Devill-lock at the left eare." Tomocomo, Purchas protested, "beleeved that this *Okee* or Devil had taught them their husbandry, etc."[47]

While Tomocomo was unpersuaded by England's theology, he had to be impressed by its population, which numbered two to three million compared to Tsenacommacah's ten to fifteen thousand. Powhatan had asked him "to see and signifie the truth of the multitudes," and Tomocomo dutifully notched the numbers on a stick en route from Plymouth to London, "But his arithmetike soone failed." Purchas reported that Tomocomo was "no lesse amaze[d] . . . at the sight of so much Corne and Trees . . . , the *Virginians* imagining that defect thereof" in England had caused the migration to America.[48] Like other Indian visitors to England before him, Tomocomo must have told a disappointed Powhatan that the English, despite their many shortcomings by Indian standards, were numerous beyond belief and that their natural resources exceeded Tsenacommacah's. It was a grim message for Indian leaders who expected England to be as sparse and inept as its early American outposts suggested.

Partly, perhaps, because Tomocomo was disturbed by England's boundless population and potential power, but more likely because he felt slighted by King James and patronized by the Reverend Purchas, Powhatan's envoy carried home a jaundiced view of his hosts. Upon his return to Tsenacommacah in May 1617, he lambasted the whole nation. "Tomakin rails agt Engld[,] English people and particularly his best friend Tho: Dale," Governor Samuel Argall observed, though he added that "all his reports are disproved before opachanko [Opechancanough] & his Great men" to the end that "Tomakin is disgraced."[49] Unless Argall indulged in wishful thinking, it appears that some of Tomocomo's well-traveled compatriots—possibly Matchumps, Kainta, or members of the Pocahontas party—contradicted his stories.[50] Tomocomo would be Tsenacommacah's last envoy to England.

The Failure of Diplomacy

During nearly two decades of Powhatan visits to England, thousands of English men, women, and children gawked at the strangers from across the ocean. By and large, English viewers paid dutiful attention to Lady Rebecca Rolfe for her social standing and the royal family's imprimatur and especially for her embrace of Protestant Christianity, the English language, and English customs; she was, in Purchas's words, "accordingly respected." Londoners stared in awe, very likely, at Namontack, Kainta, and Tomocomo, who had high status at home and were surely escorted by officials of the Virginia Company, themselves men of some prominence. But English treatment of the boys and girls who lived in private homes, walked London's streets, and struggled with the Anglican catechism and the Jacobean classical curriculum was probably insensitive, perhaps callous, even malicious, which might account for the Powhatan children's failure to impress Edwin Sandys. In some instances, natives of Tsenacommacah may have followed the footsteps of the captives of 1603 as sights to be ogled or, like Martha's Vineyard's Epenow a decade later, be "shewed up and downe *London* for money as a wonder."[51]

Which is not to say that England learned nothing from the visitors. Assuming that the twenty or more Indians from Tsenacommacah were representative of their tribesmen in physique and physiognomy, the English public saw people quite similar to themselves in size and general appearance, not the monsters or sharp-toothed cannibals of many fanciful reports from the New World. The English public also learned that the Indians' dark color was largely a veneer. Reverend William Crashaw's sermon of early 1609 explained that "a *Virginean*, that was with us here in *England* [probably Namontack], . . . was little more blacke or tawnie," after wearing English clothes for awhile, "then one of ours would be if he should goe naked in the South of *England*."[52] Virginians, English observers must have concluded, were eminently suitable to "civility," for despite Tomocomo's alarming costume and immense pony tail, Pocahontas—and most if not all other Indians in England—appeared regularly in adopted English attire and accepted, superficially at least, English norms of behavior. And along with the living examples of native America before their eyes, English readers had corroborating testimony in the descriptive accounts of Indians and their cultures, sometimes partly about the Indians in England, by a host of English writers: John Smith, Samuel Purchas, James Rosier, John Brereton, Ferdinando Gorges, and many, many more, and numerous illustrations, original or derivative, by John White, Jacques le Moyne de Morgues, the de Bry family, and others. The English people did not become fully informed about American natives by such publications nor by the Indians' physical presence, of course, but many Londoners surely became less ignorant, possibly less prejudiced, by learning how truly human they were. Crashaw insisted, "the same God made them as well as us, of as good matter as he made us, gave them as perfect and good soules and bodies as to us and the same Mesiah & saviour is sent to them." Indians, in short, are "*our brethren.*"[53]

Crashaw was speaking, of course, as a clergyman. For England's secular proponents of American colonization, visiting Indians, whether they came willingly or not, had other uses. Except for some passages in the writings of Purchas and Smith, few accounts survive of how information about America was gleaned from the Powhatans, but evidence exists on how Englishmen during the same era probed other Indian visitors' minds. James Rosier, who described five Abenakis brought from coastal Maine in 1605 is a prime example; he had many conversations, by sign language and rudimentary spoken words, in which he learned much geographic and ethnographic knowledge about coastal Maine. For the Indians, ironically, such conversations often backfired. Of the three Abenakis who lodged in his home, Sir Ferdinando Gorges remembered, "the longer I conversed with them, the better hope they gave me of those parts where they did inhabit, as proper for our uses, especially when I found what goodly Rivers, stately Islands, and safe harbours those parts abounded with."[54] The Abenaki homeland would soon suffer from English incursions and imported diseases.

Indians from Maine, Virginia, or elsewhere also gleaned information about England, and every visitor who survived his stay abroad no doubt carried home an abundance of useful observations. The difference between Indian and English intelligence-gathering was in its purpose: imperial, in England's case; protective, in the Indians'. Although England's vision of an American empire was still in the future, the movement for colonies and converts was gaining momentum, stimulated in part by the presence of Indians in England.

Powhatan contributed to the flow of visitors by sending Namontack in 1608, John Smith reported, "to know our strength and Countries condition." Namontack probably acquired a general sense of both matters—

England's military "strength" as represented by castles and cannons, uniformed men and armed ships; England's "condition" as reflected in swarming people and bustling commerce, as well as undercurrents of economic, religious, and political unrest. Namontack's "true report" to Powhatan must have made the chief more suspicious of English intentions and more skeptical about cordial cohabitation in the Virginia tidewater. Eight years later, Powhatan's charge to Tomocomo was essentially the same as to Namontack: find the truth and report it faithfully to me. In the interval between the first and last envoys, "some others which had been heere in former times," Purchas noted in 1617, citing Thomas Dale as his source, "being more silly, which having seene little else then this Citie [London], have reported much of the Houses, and Men, but thought we had small store of Corne or Trees."[55] Such selective reporting may explain why Tomocomo tried to record the population on a stick.

The disquieting facts collected by Powhatan's envoys surely impressed and discouraged the chief and his successors—his brother Opitchapam briefly, then their brother Opechancanough—for many years. England had too many emigrants lusting for land, too many ocean-going vessels designed for commerce or war, too many firearms, and too many idle soldiers ready for new mayhem. By 1617, when Tomocomo returned to Tsenacommacah, the colony's booming tobacco crops had created insatiable demands for more farm land, with devastating effects on tribal holdings and on Anglo-Indian relations. By then, Powhatan had perhaps grasped the full import of England's restless population and perceived the colony's determination to wrest Tsenacommacah from Indian control. Had he fully comprehended that dismal prospect a few years earlier, he might have rephrased his lament of 1614 to Ralph Hamor. "I am now olde," he told Hamor, "and would gladly end my daies in peace, so as if the English offer me injury, my country is large enough, I will remove my selfe farther from you."[56] Although peace prevailed when Powhatan died in July 1618, it would last fewer than four more years. By hindsight, it seems clear that the death of his favorite daughter and Tsenacommacah's most eminent envoy to England had already undermined the prospects—if they ever seriously existed—for a truly bicultural society on the American side of the seventeenth century's Atlantic world.

Chapter 3
John Smith Maps Virginia
Knowledge, Rhetoric, and Politics

LISA BLANSETT

Having completed a veritable Odyssean itinerary from Turkey to Virginia, John Smith returned to England and began work publishing his many travels, shaping an oeuvre that in his own mind established him as an epic hero.[1] The nightmare of Jamestown was a recent trauma for Smith, who had been effectively stripped of his commission and expelled by Captain Gabriel Archer at the behest of an ill-informed Virginia Company council. He had stood his ground until official documents arrived to remove him from power, but accidentally injuring himself in a gunpowder explosion, he soon departed. Preceding him to England were a number of notes, letters, sketches, and joint-authored missives to his employers, the Virginia Company. Among those documents were materials that became *The True Relation*, "sent to a friend" in 1608.[2] Not authorized for publication by Smith, *The True Relation* was nevertheless printed and entered into Stationer's Register that year. The book's popularity enhanced Smith's standing until chatter impugning his reputation began to circulate beyond company members. Four years later, a description and map of the Virginia colony were published as a single book in Oxford, but never entered into the official documentation of works in print. The absence of *A Map of Virginia* from the Register effectively removed it from official book history.

Despite its lack of official sanction, the engraved map's popularity made it widely circulated as a separate document and as an illustrative companion to several books beyond the 1612 work, from Smith's *Generall Historie* to Samuel Purchas's *Pilgrimes* and into twenty-seven different adaptations and reproductions. In addition to its popularity the map owes its wide dissemination to the printing press and to the work of the image's engraver, William Hole. The copper plate Hole etched was changed several times for a total of ten different map states. At each acid wash and re-etching, more details were added, including geographic information added after further exploration (states 5, 6, 8, 9), Smith's arms, crest, and motto (3 and 4), and a coordinate frame showing a grid of latitude and longitude degrees.[3]

Although the first three states are the only versions proper to the 1612 *Map of Virginia*, later states—usually the tenth—can now be found bound into copies of the book.[4] Early bound-in maps, including Smith's, often fall prey to the knife—sometimes rare book dealers or collectors remove plates from a book to sell separately; other times, they cobble together parts of more than one copy to assemble a "complete" volume.

Smith's apparently close collaboration with the engraver suggests a desire to fashion the image that would represent his work and, perhaps more importantly, to translate his experience directly into a visual representation. He had been incensed and baffled by official criticism and the ostracism he was subjected to, and in response he devoted himself to redacting his unpublished materials and revising some of the details from those already published. This labor ultimately conferred upon him the honor he so desired—most of that praise has been bestowed posthumously and from the American side of the pond. From the time he left Virginia (1609) until his death (1631), he mined the veritable treasure trove of observations and artifacts he had collected, and shaped them into the many texts by which we remember him and his vision of the Virginia colony's first years.

As a whole, Smith's oeuvre reveals an energetic, even obsessive, manager who diligently gathered facts and figures, narrated dramatic events and trifling incidents, recorded cultural practices, and enforced a political structure predicated on worth, not birth. While most of the early settlers came with a narrowly established profession or title, Smith demonstrated a broad range of aptitudes and skills, both manual and intellectual. His talent and experience gave him the wherewithal to imagine new ways of collecting and organizing information and of experimenting with political and social organization. His innovations would contribute to the English engagement with cultural difference; his ambitious plans for colonial success and his strategic adaptations to rapidly changing conditions would offer alternative models of order (and the opportunity for a continuously running performance of "I told you so" ex post facto). The combined image and text of his *Map of Virginia* reveal not only the intentions and agendas of both Smith and his culture, but also suggest the inconsistencies and multivalent significance of the Jamestown experiment.

The residues of these intentions and agendas, inconsistencies, and meanings adhere to and shape the texts that record Smith's experiments. As a representation, the map has absorbed a number of the personal, social, and political issues at stake for Smith and for Virginia. The overall relationship of the map to the territory—the image to reality—is itself complex, as present readers find this map both familiar and strange in the way that it stands for what we imagine to be "Virginia." In this way, readers do not expect this map be accurate, an allowance that simultaneously permits factors external to the map—the age of the map, its history—to influence meaning. The cartographic document itself offers numerous opportunities for interpretation in terms of individual parts and how those discrete parts comment on, speak to, or critique others in the map's meaningful assemblage. Beyond the boundaries of the page, the map suggests a genealogy of its material production, including contemporary aesthetic values and scientific technologies. Within the frame, the map makes visible some of the effects of colonial contact. The artifact becomes more than ink inscribed on paper; it is an archive, the import of which can be read in the map.[5]

What's in a Map?

As Smith's long subtitle promises, the full text of the *Map of Virginia* is a description of *the Country, the Commodities, People, Government and Religion. Written by Captaine Smith, sometimes Governour of the Country. Whereunto is annexed the proceedings of those Colonies, since their first departure from England, with the discourses, orations, and relations of the salvages, and the accidents that befell them in all their journeys and discoveries, etc.* This text covers a number of matters that twenty-first century readers would recognize as political, physical, and economic geography, along with anthropology, history, theology, and social criticism—criticism of both native and English ways. The "annex'd mappe" was tipped into the book as a companion. The map's original size was 12 by 16 inches, folded to fit within the relatively large, quarto-sized volume. Two maps, then, one in written document, one as cartographic image, comprise the *Map of Virginia*.[6]

Alone, the cartographic image (Fig. 3.1) presents a detailed view of an area designated as "Virginia," with representations of flora and fauna, hills and rivers, indigenous villages and colonial outposts. Oriented with North on the right, the landmass fills most of the sheet and is filled with about two hundred place names and a number of conventional icons signifying both nature and culture (trees and towns). "The Virginia Sea" holds a ship, a compass rose, and a lone sea creature. At the top left corner, there is a miniature image identified as Powhatan. A caption under the image of Powhatan advises that the emperor "held this state and fashion" when Smith was his prisoner. To the right of Powhatan, an ornate, partially scrolled banner dominates the top, with "Massaomecks" written directly above it and small structures dotting the shore along a partial crescent of water. To the right of the banner, a legend translates the icons—a Maltese cross and two structures—as representing the limits of western exploration, the supplementation of native reports, and the royal versus common houses inhabited by Native Americans. Below the banner rests the obligatory English royal seal with monarchical motto. Directly across the map on its vertical axis from the royal seal, a large surveyor's compass and the map's scale are depicted. The map is dominated on the right by the "Susquehannock Bowman," who is sutured into the image as though standing on the landscape—or on a stage—with his legs' shadows cast on the surface.

The many details and illustrations were brought together—to the point of merged images in some cases—by engraver William Hole.[7] The technology of engraving makes reproduction relatively simple (requiring only ink, a roller or press, and paper), and it allows for a number of revisions and additions. The engraved map's popularity as a separate document permitted it to be stitched into a number of other books, from Smith's *Generall Historie* to Samuel Purchas's *Pilgrimes*, and into twenty-seven different adaptations and reproductions. In all, the map was printed in ten different states (versions) until the plate was retired in 1632. At each acid wash and re-etching, more details were added, including reports of further exploration.

The map's portability has allowed it to acquire significance on a number of different registers. To the early modern English, the map announced naval superiority, presented economic opportunities, and proclaimed the triumph of truth over fantasy. Real men had gone to explore and settle a faraway landscape, returning months or years later with plausible but still awe-inspiring tales. The map, as an index of power and as a manifestation of desires fulfilled and deferred, served as a powerful tool of an expansionist agenda: the map's effects could help decimate a culture, annihilate its people, and transform ecology. Even as the English settlers repeatedly failed at the relentless challenges in Jamestown, the map served as an emblem of abstract and hence undefeatable notions of power and control. The map's symbolic territorial and cultural appropriations represented the larger ideological project in which a past could be overcome and a future could be imagined. As such, the map posited the inevitability—the very destiny—of the colonial agenda.

Smith's map functions on many levels, however. On one level, a causal relationship between representation and meaning limits the map to functioning as a mirror held up to nature, a cultural artifact rendering the face of the real. On other levels, however, Smith can be seen to be analyzing as well as representing its subject matter, and in this respect to be devoted to examining the knowledge, beliefs, morality, laws, and habits of the natives. And on still another level, Smith can be seem to be concerned with what is now referred to as "material culture," including in his descriptions such objects as tools, crops, habitations, and personal ornaments. Smith might be said to be concerned with Indian "culture" as a whole, on all its levels, and his representational and classificatory strategies may be seen to owe something to the idea of culture in a much earlier sense of the word's etymology. With roots in the Latin *colere*, the word originally encompasses "inhabit, cultivate, protect, honour with worship."[8] From that classical form, a branch of meaning develops out of *cultivate* to become *culture* as denotative of husbandry, and similarly as the root of *agriculture*. It was only

Figure 3.1. John Smith's *Map of Virginia* (1631). Courtesy of the John Carter Brown Library, Brown University. The large, detailed map includes not just geographical information but also a number of symbols and ornaments, such as the image of "Emperor" Powhatan on the upper left and the Susquehannock man on the right.

Over time, Smith added not only place names but also other features like the grid around the border showing latitude and longitude and his coat of arms, with the motto "vincere est vivere"—to conquer is to live.

later, in the eighteenth century, that the notion of "culture" would come to be associated predominantly with urban as opposed to rural life.[9] Smith's map is located at a time when the concept of culture is in flux, in which culture in its mainly rural context is in the process of being reshaped through contact with other forms of relationships between human and nature. Smith's map-making strategies can be seen both to reflect those concerns and to push the concept toward a hegemonic but complex relationship with the culture of an Other.

The Upstart Geographer

When John Smith disembarked at Jamestown in 1607, though bound in chains he was determined to make a success of his mission to the New World. His appointment by the Virginia Company did not have many privileges or perquisites attached to it, and he had been confined since docking in the Caribbean island of St. Nevis on charges of plotting mutiny. Despite serious conflicts with some of his shipmates, however, Smith was among the men most experienced in travel; he had learned the rudiments of other languages by ear, fought in foreign wars, killed before he was killed, been decorated for his martial valor, escaped incarceration, wandered through Russia, and survived innumerable situations that few could have endured. He came equipped with a complete library of navigational texts, charts, and measurement tables, along with the latest theories of successful navigation and, apparently, a very nice compass dial.[10] Freed from incarceration and exonerated, his experience and savvy as a traveler superceding his reputation as a troublemaker, he was soon admitted to a reconnaissance party led by Captain Christopher Newport. The party of some twenty-odd men left Jamestown in answer to the Virginia Company's directive to employ themselves "for two months in the discovery of the river above you, and in the country about you."[11] The first expedition traveled up the James River in May 1607 searching for an outlet to the long-imagined Northwest "passage to the other sea," the "South sea" (or Western Sea or East India Sea).[12] Of course, that particular goal would prove illusory, but the party documented its route, sounding fathoms to determine how far inland navigable depths could be found.[13] At roughly mile thirty-three of the journey, Gabriel Archer described "spying" a canoe with eight men, whom the English convinced to approach. The ensuing conversation was held in an ad hoc sign language during which "one seemed to understand our intention and off'red with his foot to describe the river to us. So I gave him a pen and paper, showing first the use, and he laid out the whole river from the Chesseian Bay to the end of it, so far as passage was for boats."[14] This description marks the first topographical knowledge of Virginia dispensed "by relation."

At the sites where the expedition stopped, whether in response to threatened violence, impassable topography, injury, want of victuals, or other situations, the party would leave a marker. As Smith reports in his *True Relation,* "we returned to the fals, leaving a mariner in pawn with the Indians for a guide of theirs, hee that they honoured for King followed us by the river (further he would not goe) so there we erected a *crosse.*"[15] George Percy (who would later label Smith perfidious and pompous), adds the details of what seems to have been an abbreviated ritual of possession: "wee set up a *Crosse* at the head of this River, naming it Kings River, where we proclaimed James King of England to have the most right unto it."[16] On the map, these episodes and sites are symbolized by "Maltese Crosses"; the map's legend glosses the crosses as indicating "to the crosses hath bin discover'd" on one side and "what beyond is by relation" on the other. The erected crosses constitute a symbolic act that is reminiscent of the Spanish practice of reading of the *Requirimento,* a speech act establishing dominion upon its recitation (regardless whether any of those subject to that domination would hear or understand the performance). Yet, the English were rather less formal in their linguistic appropriations; at that moment they were primarily interested in trade and commerce, not dominion. Whereas popes and monarchs had furnished Portuguese and Spanish conquest, a mercantile venture had initiated the Virginia project. Indeed, "Spanish colonialism produced the census, British colonialism the map."[17] The English crosses seem to beget a perfunctory act of fealty to earthly and celestial sovereigns. In the context of the quest for the next great market, however, the sign accrues alternative meanings. In short, the cross can be seen as a place-holder—a directional sign on an imagined throughway to the other side (and the other sea). As such, the markers create imaginary narratives that signify a starting point for subsequent expeditions, and that are rooted in an idea of comprehensive knowledge as the product of serial efforts. Such a substitution of a comprehensive narrative rather that a isolated (and decontextualized) symbol also parallels the structural lines of Smith's own pursuit of an identity rooted in accumulated experience as a compensation for the static sign of aristocratic birth he did not possess. While the Portuguese and Spanish markers symbolize the end of the line (even if that line would expand later) and contain inhabitants within the fold, Anglo crosses point outward in the direction of mercantile expansion.[18]

Smith ventured from the fold of Jamestown on frequent reconnaissance sorties. His travels in and around the colony covered some three thousand miles—by report—as he and his group recorded each shoal and every inlet of the Chesapeake Bay and its estuaries.[19] Indeed, Smith enforced a policy of exploration in hope of improving the physically and psychologically woeful conditions inside the fort. He sent settlers into the environs to gather food and information, or to live with an indigenous group, by which he meant to encourage mobility and self-reliance while also obtaining important first-hand information. As he gathered information about Virginia, he slowly developed a new vision of colonial success. He came to realize that the company's plan of taking Virginia's raw materials in exchange for supplying the goods necessary for the survival of its laborers (colonists) left the colony vulnerable. The incipient metropolitan-colonial system in effect remapped the world by imagining the distant outpost as proximate in the flow of goods and money. The geographical realities of a spatial division of labor, however, isolated Virginia. In practical terms, the system produced long periods between deliveries of goods to the colony, and those deliveries were insufficient to meet the necessities of colonial life. Moreover, they kept settlers mindful of England rather than of the need to adapt to a "land . . . as good as this book doth report it."[20] Smith's response to the Virginia Company's economic structure (and the pressures applied in the instructions it sent) emerged gradually; each adaptation he made can be seen to have coalesced into a model that he could claim kept settlers fed and industrious during his tenure as president.[21] A way of seeing and being in the world that he called "experience" became his ruling principle.

At first, Smith worked within the framework established by the Virginia Company for a good return on its investment. The primary purpose of his early sorties was first, to map a more efficient flow of goods and money to an established, valuable market; and, second, to catalog the goods and services that might be developed in a new market. The details he records in his early records situate the collected knowledge in a taxonomy of commodities and profits.[22] Under the heading "Of such things which are naturall in Virginia and how they use them," Smith's descriptions in the *Map of Virginia* reveal his investment in the raw-goods model the Company had invested in. The extensive catalogs of natural resources primarily list commodities that can be extracted from the environment.[23] On the map, this market of plenty is articulated in the bountiful details that fill the topography; the numerous types of trees, for instance, indicate a wealth of choices. The small hunter on the far left of the territory also invokes the idea of appropriation rather than cultivation, and the hint of a body of water at the map's top right quadrant reminds the viewer of the search for the ultimate fetishized commodity, gold.

Early failures—of trade based on shipping raw materials, of finding a passage to the East, and of sustaining colonists on what they could find or barter for—created a foundation for Smith's adaptive strategies. As president of Virginia, he focused his energies on a kind of immersion program that created a decentralized plantation model of self-sustaining agricultural enterprises and the development of small industries. The entire community had to participate in this venture, a point he makes clear as he simultaneously admonishes and encourages his charges to participate in the collective endeavor or starve. His experience became his philosophy of government, as articulated in his memoir of New England, a later venture.

There, he fully links land, labor, virtue, and the pursuit of happiness in epideictic rhetoric that echoes Roman senators: "Who can desire more content, that hath small meanes; or but only his merit to advance his fortune, then to tread, and plant that ground he hath purchased by hazard of his life? If he have but the taste of virtue, and magnanimitie, what to such a mind can bee more pleasant, then planting and building a foundation for his Posteritie, gotte from the rude earth, by Gods blessing and his own industrie, without any prejudice to any."[24] Still, a good Anglo-Saxon chieftain would lead his men into battle rather than strategizing from an outpost, a military creed to which Smith subscribes.

The passage reads as a prophetic manifesto of American expansionist ideology, and yet it is important to note that such terms as "purchased by hazard of his life," do not constitute a proto-Lockean paradigm.[25] A prehistory of alienable property and possessive individualism might be imagined for the Jamestown settlers, but Smith's vocabulary references an Anglo-Saxon structure of local chieftains whose retainers (as a group called the *comitatus*) earn property and protection through their pledge to preserve the lord's life at the hazard of their own. The "ring-giver" model of government, moreover, gives Smith alternating roles. He is the loyal thane, foreign minister to an English government, the ring-giver who names a river after Powhatan and represents the emperor and a substitute thane (the Susquehannock bowman) on his map.[26]

The embedded vision of property as a symbol of fealty rather than a labor of acquired possession and alienable property exists on a fluctuating scale throughout Smith's works. In his writings and as an underpinning to the map, he inhabits several different land-dependent roles. The relationship of property to status—to identity in Renaissance England—is written into Smith's pronouncement. He refashions experience as compensation for social status in such a way that he can imagine a site-specific ecology of economics, settlement, and social structure, a development plan that he continued to promote long after leaving.

Smith plays the experience card repeatedly in exhortations of his fitness to run the Virginia colonies. As a response to the question of worth, the word "experience" figures on several different but related registers. Using Spenser's *Faerie Queene* (1596) to mark contemporary usage, we find that the word would mean to test, as in to test one's loyalty or to demonstrate some prowess or courage.[27] At the same time, the word could connote an experiment that demonstrates "truth"; an affective response; and finally, knowledge itself.[28] The denotative and connotative come into simultaneous play as the term moves metonymically from the subject of knowledge to the object of knowledge to knowledge itself, the reaction to knowledge, and a quality of character and measure of personal worth. I have tested, I have proven, I have gained, I possess, I am experienced. In this way, Smith is able to envision his own being as a process of becoming in his desire to mitigate the effects of the social class into which he had been thrust. Yet it is his social status that finally plays the trump card. Appointed experimentally by the company, he is scheduled for redundancy in early 1607 because, as Smith complains, disenchanted gallants have returned with unfavorable reviews of the enterprise and its government. The tropes of experience Smith deploys allow him repeatedly to recapitulate his worth and to dispute the charges.

Through his strategies of inquiry in Virginia, Smith moves from the tentative and conditional (to try) to unrestrictive (I am) valences of "experience." Given Smith's "rudimentary education," his interests and his research methods reveal an intuitively sophisticated approach to cultural difference.[29] He indexes and translates "native" words "because many doe desire to knowe the maner of their language."[30] He catalogs wild and cultivated biota; he identifies "valuable" commodities by the dozen, from fish soup to walnuts.[31] In his collecting, he does not just observe from afar: he asks local inhabitants to tell him about the land, the culture, the politics, the beliefs. He ventures far from camp to navigate and record river routes, to note rock formations, to speculate on what lies just over the hill, and to wonder how he might make the whole place "work" as a society. He is in the water, on the ground, in the trenches. His approach to knowledge and his desire for comprehensive accounts lead him to a methodology based on witnessed phenomena, accumulated facts, and the written record.

To gentlemanly contemporaries, his methods seemed rather yeoman-like; that is to say, his social superiors considered his attitudes and approaches to be common or churlish. By way of response, Smith repeatedly admonishes the ruling classes for their idleness, against which he poses his dicta on manual labor in Jamestown. Not interested in the finer points of gentlemanly leisure, he focuses on a practical rather than learnedly theoretical approach to seeing, knowing, and understanding. Outside the learned community for Smith was Willoughby, Lincolnshire, where his father was a farmer and husbandman.[32] In Renaissance England, the husbandman, also called estate steward, and sometimes overseer,[33] was responsible for a statistical analysis of an estate, for archiving family papers, for, in essence, describing the estate in its current form as annual (or thereabouts) reiteration of the estate's history and manorial prestige. His expertise was both juridical and practical, and in the capacity of the latter he was consulted on the distribution of livestock in pastures, of crop selection (and rotation), and "improvements" to the estate. After completing his inventory indoors, the husbandman "was to butt and bound the Manor as a whole, together with its individual parcels or premises."[34] Their records were "a reliable source of information about place-names, roads and other topographical detail."[35] His work became the official record of the property and was required by statute—a practice that dated to Roman land management—to include a measure in acres of "improved" lands (arable, meadow, pasture), and to assign a monetary value to those parcels.

Smith's approach to documenting Virginia echoes some of the methods found in early sixteenth-century "handbooks," like those described in John Fitzherbert's companion set, *Boke of Surveyeng* and *Boke of Husbandry*. In addition to differentiating types of property (improved, common, etc.), Fitzherbert advocates a "task-time" measurement that calculates area as a sum of how long the field takes to plow; the valuation then assigned was not absolute or standardized, but based on the details of the work and associated with local values and equivalences. This sort of embodied, or experiential collection of data was superseded late in the century by precise protocols for exacting measurement and valuation tables. By way of comparison, Thomas Hariot, a mathematician of St. Mary's, Oxford, and tutor to Sir Walter Raleigh's progeny, surveyed Virginia in territory, in commodity, and in culture with an analytical framework for ordering what he saw. Beginning with two general areas, "of the commodities and of the nature and manner of the naturall inhabitants," Hariot compartmentalizes the "merchantable commodities" while Smith is oriented around topography, physical geography, economic geography, political and cultural geographies.[36] The latter's prose descriptions, in fact, follow a pattern of movement rather than abstracted analytical categories. As an organizing trope, peregrination gives the reader a functionally parallel experience of encounter and discovery. At the same time, such a structure emphasizes an embodied experience, as Smith evokes the feel of a warm climate, the sight of a giant human, the scents and tastes he found in Virginia. Not the Oxford-trained scholar, Smith instead has, like the husbandman, "butted and bound" the land, implicitly (and nostalgically) suggesting an integrated, local economy of cooperative (and occasionally collective) labor, rather than a purely commercial model.

The Cartographic Crucible

Smith's multiple roles and wide-ranging expertise as navigator, explorer, writer, and cartographer merge in the map of Virginia. Each element of Smith's map connects him to a long history of mapmaking and to the intersecting colonial desires represented in a collage of historical moments, technological advances, aesthetic choices, and social formations. As collage, the features seem separate, for what has a surveying instrument to do with the image of a bowman? The trees, hills, and men juxtapose scrolls, crests, and Latin mottos. Together, however, the separate pieces begin to speak across the gaps, suggesting particular points of contact between approaches to topography and to the human inhabitants contained within the map.

In generic terms, the map is chorographic, that is to say, its representations of local particularities take precedence over a relation of part (colony) to whole (Britain/Europe/Old World/whole world) or, put another way, can be seen as the difference between the local and the global.[37] In Smith's map, the balance of emphasis and effect fluctuates constantly within the bounds of a map's completeness and its assumed comprehensiveness. The map's representations of science and technology infiltrate readings of the natural phenomena, while the natural phenomena revise the status of science and technology. Entering into this balance are later revisions and additions made to the map based on new information or new desires, which, in turn, changed nuances of meaning. At the same time those additions suggest the contradictory status of cartography by revealing that maps are not absolute and stable; rather, maps are changeable, unstable, and subject to a number of conflicting needs and power structures at odds. That which is represented as being true and accurate must also be dependent on a running supply of fresh information to retain the illusion of such a totality. Ironically, then, the map is a representation of knowledge accrued over time even while it must establish its own credibility based on its timeless truths.

The addition of the conventional graticule, the framing scale that marks latitude and longitude, was among later additions to the map; it was added in the fourth state of the engraving.[38] At that time, another addition was made, the addition of Smith's motto, *Vincere est Vivere*, "to conquer is to live." The historical coincidence of these additions reveals an embedded significance as the Latin motto's martial and territorial claims are framed by that cartographic convention that best signifies possession in terms of its technological import and as a result of its scientifico-aesthetic containment within the measure of an entire globe. In this way, the map of Virginia both becomes a local survey in its "butt and bound" technology while it also acquires a place in a world system through the homogenizing influence of geographic measure and cartographic convention.

The several objects, techniques, and effects of technology depicted in the map suggest the superior, rational methods of measurement, in the case of the surveyor's compass, while the compass rose invokes the mariner's "art" of careful observation, mathematical computation, and the assumed absolute nature of cardinal direction.[39] The effective sum of these features is an assurance of truth through the trope of reproducibility; in other words, this map is true because it could be used by other travelers to witness the wonders themselves and, in the circular logic of a map cartography, also prove the map true by its instrumental efficacy and by the presence of the new traveler.

The map's scientific reproducibility is challenged, however, as humans are individually unique, despite universalizing imperatives. Smith depicts several human subjects from minute hunters to diminutive chieftain to imposing bowman. In their making, these figures function as part of the "particularizing" methods Smith developed. He reports eyewitness encounters with the indigenous peoples and local landscapes. Although scrupulously particular, a number of visual caveats seep in: the tiny hunters are lifted from de Bry's engraving of Virginia, which had been placed much further south inland of North Carolina's Roanoke; the figure of Powhatan is a pictorial merger of funereal architecture; the bowman was once a slightly more respectable "werowance" in Hariot's descriptions, and the figure is given a new tribal identity by Smith as Susquehannock "bowman." The effects of these transformations register as depictions of relative insignificance tempered by fear of being overcome, suggestions of an organized system of "troops," who have the particular role of "bowman." At the same time, the difference between de Bry's engravings and Hole's compilation of them suggests a generalized image of the Native American. Like the adage "if you've seen one, you've seen them all," the conflation of local culture groups is figured by a metonymic device: What appears to be the result of induction—from particular to general—is a substitution of a known entity for an unknown totality. As a totalizing and homogenizing artifact, the map effaces a number of the groups (subgroups, tangential groups, and oppositional groups) cited in the text, even as the map transliterates indigenous names.[40] The scrupulous particularity of more than two hundred "native names" and his limited sample of the local lexicon indicate an ambivalent approach to difference and otherness, and ultimately contribute to a map that cannot homogenize or contain the many cultural cross-currents.

The first maps that can be said to include America would seem to have been drawn from a mariner's dream rather than from observation. The lack of geographical evidence would be replaced with fantastical figures, sea monsters, mermaids, chubby-cheeked winds puffing zephyrous energy into sails for smooth sailing or driving the vessel into the proverbial watery grave. The iconography bespeaks the enormous scale of what the West did not know, its ignorance inscribed on the blank landscapes as *terra incognita*. The simultaneous emergence of printed travel accounts and improved technology enabled more ships to take to the seas with a minutely-more-than-scant hope of returning to spin a mariner's yarn or two about *nova orbs*. The fifteenth century saw the state begin sponsoring seafaring expeditions with the stipulation of sole claim for all discoveries territorial and material, and perhaps a discretionary reward for the man at the helm. As the Portuguese and Spanish fitted boats and dreamed of golden cities, other countries began to get wind of the projects and the rumors of wealth or eternal youth or fascinatingly grotesque humans or objects unseen and unproved. The map of Virginia's iconography, composition, and its relationship with the accompanying description, indicate that a hint of the fantastical wafts through the map.

Smith combines the spatial imagination of a husbandman/surveyor with that of a pilot or coastline navigator The relationship of the man who measures space and the man who measures water is described by John Dee in his "Preface" to *Elements of Euclid* (1570): "Geographie" is one of the skills "growen" of "knowledge Geometricall," and as such is one of the "Derivative . . . Sciences, and Artes Mathematical" coequal with "geodesie, or Land Measuring;" "Chorographie," "an underling, and a twig, of Geographie," and "Hydrographie [which] deliuereth to our knowledge, on Globe or in Plaine, the perfect Analogicall decription of the Ocean coastes, through the whole world."[41] Dee represents the relationships among mathematics, geography, and cartography or platt-making on a "groundplat" that itself demonstrates a "geometrization of knowledge," an epistemic shift in theories and practices of quantification, perspective, and property.[42]

The map uses two different cartographic projections, planometric (from above) and bird's eye view (from an elevated, but not perpendicular sight line). It thus makes visible two different ways of imagining space, one that flattens a globe, the other that endeavors to create the illusion of three-dimensionality in its depictions of foregrounds and backgrounds, of corporeal curves and facial depths. The composition or arrangement of features rises from the sea where the ship has anchored (lower left) to represent movement with a predominantly diagonal emphasis from the mouth of the Chesapeake toward the Susquehannock warrior. Above the warrior, moreover, the preposition "to" signifies a spatial process: *from* one point *to* another. Also included in the legend above the bowman is "discovery," also a loaded term that signifies a narrative of movement from the unknown to the known, particularly as comprised of a series of actions invested in learning. Knowledge is presented as accretive, dependent on discovery. Yet, on the other hand, the knowledge of this map is also problematized. Within the bounds of the map is a relentless syncopation of different world views that reside within and yet strain against Western representational strategies.

The map's residual references to long-past social practices are tempered by other features of the map that allude to different traditions and dissimilar goals. In the "nautical" apparatus the reader finds significant re-presentations of nautical charts reimagined in a new context. The nautical or "Portolan" chart establishes a mode of travel, while land surveying establishes ownership.[43] The coastline navigator might use extant pilots (records of coastal features like reefs and shoals made by observation and, mostly, trial and error) to reproduce successful landings, or he might carefully plumb the depths on approach and log the findings for those who follow. The pilot's primary role is ensuring a safe landing with a comprehensive record of largely unseen (underwater) hazards. The nautical courses, and possible hazards, are referenced by the large compass rose, the mad marine life, and the vessel under full sail. In this map, however, the importance of the pilot's records is shifted from comprehensive record for safe landing (a kind of public service) to a comprehensive record that demonstrates the labor, ingenuity, and dogged determination of a particular captain. The seaworthy technology of the mariner represents travel and thus superiority, but this claim seems to belong as much to an individual as it does to a larger cultural, economic, and scientific project. The sum effect is a narrative in little: I came, I saw, I measured. The circulation of metonyms also suggests comprehensiveness: a journey ends on the map (and thus references the sea beyond), and yet must have also commenced on the map; the contours bespeak the task of mapping.

Smith's map is the most comprehensive and detailed depiction of Virginia of its time. The map included in Thomas Hariot's *Briefe and True Report of the New Found Land of Virginia* shows a Virginia further south (which is in fact now largely North Carolina). Immediately following de Bry's map in the text is his engraving of "The Arrival of the Englishman" (Figure 3.2), an image that suggests in more concrete detail the generalized (internalized, normativized) narrative of arriving. The more explicit narrative of de Bry's engraving can be read within a history of "arrival myths"—a trope that Raphael Samuel situates as a subset of myths of origin, or what anthropologists often call "creation myths."[44] The arrival in de Bry's version refers to a prehistory of failure—sunken ships—suggesting the limits of technology and foreshadowing the doom many of the settlers would meet with. But the narrative of arrival is collapsed into a single symbolic moment on Smith's map. A single ship approaches the coast; no invocation of loss troubles the moment. The single ship safely sailing into port functions as a testament to Smith's personal triumphs of piloting and recording the coastal depths well as adding enormous geographical and cultural detail to the more sparsely populated de Bry engraving.

The simultaneous registers of ways of seeing, ways of narrating, and ways of classifying find a particularly salient projection in the dominating bowman. This out-of-scale figure on the right side of the map is nearly identical to the engraving of "Weroan or great Lorde of Virginia" included in Hariot's study. Both figures adopt the same contraposto stance, both are wrapped in a fringed skin, both hold bows in their right hands. The *Map of Virginia*'s bowman, however, becomes a model of vigor and vitality in the fashion of classical Greek and Roman statues. His aesthetic resemblance to more familiar Western representations of the male body afford him a temporary, structural alliance with the heroic figure (Figures 1.2. and 3.3). The Hariot werowan holds an arrow in his right hand, the line of which crosses the bow at the same level as those behind him shoot arrows. He is well equipped for using the weapon, as he also carries a full quiver of arrows. Although he is in the extreme foreground of the landscape, that landscape is itself more menacing, filled with indigenous men either shooting or preparing en masse off to the left. In Smith and Hole's version, the man's identity changes, and he is renamed for his culture group, "Sasquesa-

84   Lisa Blansett

Figure 3.2. "The arrival of the Englishmen in Virginia," engraving by Theodor de Bry after a drawing by John White. Thomas Hariot, *Briefe and True Report* (1590), pl. 2. Courtesy of the John Carter Brown Library, Brown University. This image shows the Roanoke settlers navigating the treacherous passage through the Outer Banks. Part map and part view, the image conjures a history of tragic shipwrecks (five ships sunk are visible from "Hatorasck" to "Trinety Harbor" and points north), and references a seafaring past filled with unknown creatures (monster fish). The reconnaisance vessel sent through the Outer Banks barely misses a shallow on its immediate right as it heads for a small island. Roanoke is represented as already inhabited—with a palisade, three small square enclosures, and several Mercury-like figures running willy-nilly with bows drawn in several directions (including pointed directly at the boat). At the bow of the English vessel stands a figure holding up a cross. In contrast to this image of representing arrival and encounter, Smith's map represents the English presence in Virginia as a fait accompli.

hanoug," rather than his political role. The caption beneath him meanders and fragments at his right foot, noting that he is one of a "Gyant-like people." The giant man supplements his bow with a club on which he leans somewhat more in the manner of a sword-holding gentleman posing for a portrait. The club, moreover, would provide a handy tool for braining the wild pig he has slung over his back. His depiction alludes to yet another familiar English pastime, the hunt, for which the bowman stands in for an attendant huntsman who retrieves the object of the hunt in services to the

Figure 3.3. "A weroan or great Lorde of Virginia," engraving by Theodor de Bry after a drawing by John White. Hariot, *Briefe and True Report* (1590), pl. 3. Courtesy of the John Carter Brown Library, Brown University. Smith and Oxford engraver William Hole borrowed the *Map of Virginia*'s bowman from an engraving Theodore de Bry published in 1590, which in turn was based on a drawing by John White on the scene at Roanoke several years earlier. Through this process of adaptation, the figure was transformed from menacing, even animal-like (note the weroan's tail), into a generous friend bearing food, his well-muscled body foretelling the healthful environment to be found in Virginia. The aesthetic transformation, however, cannot fully erase colonial fears of annihilation articulated in Smith's descriptions defenses and attacks.

gentlemen who kept the blood off their collective hands. The bowman is coopted into the myth of the faithful servant, the good native who brings food for the starving settlers. His inclusion in the map and his renamed status as "Susquehannock Bowman" give Smith temporary credit for a discovery (encounter with a "new" tribe, as signified by the transliteration of their name), while aesthetically resolving the menace of the werowans who raided the settler camps and effacing the symbolic and real violence wreaked upon the bowman's people. At the same time, however, the threat of violence—specifically violence upon the English settlers—persists in the bowman's well-muscled strength and substantial weaponry. He is, after all, a bowman, a martial classification that calls forth his brethren of the same label, an imagined troop found on the field of Smith's past military experience. In prose descriptions, Smith recalls numerous guerrilla incursions and defensive strikes that reinvest the hale and hearty aestheticized vision with more than his looks.

The faithful servant who delivers fresh wild pig calls forth Smith's own designation as werowan. In Smith's typically analogical descriptions, he echoes a ceremony of knighthood, or, rather, an older one of ring-giving. The Anglo-Saxon Weard or Weard-Fader, remembered by the kenning "ring-giver," confers title and privilege to the loyal warrior, with all the privileges pertaining thereto. As Smith promises to render unto Powhatan the Manacam and Pocoughtaonack nations, Powhatan begins a "loud oration" in which "he proclaimed me a werowanes of Powhatan, and that all his subjects should so esteem us, and no man account us strangers nor Paspaheghans, but Powhatans, and that the corn, women, and country should be to us as to his own people."[45] Reminiscent more of the Old English epic *Beowulf* than of later tales of chivalry and courtesy, the rite allows us to see the depiction of the map's bowman as an expression of fear and fascination, of identification and distance. Smith re-presents a myth of origins using local talent, displacing his own fantasies onto the Other. For a moment, then, the bowman substitutes for Smith's own position as steward, surveyor, and even werowan, and yet simultaneously situates him as the dominant figure on the map.[46]

The bowman was not an unknown visual trope. Other contemporary maps include representations of the inhabitants situated in the pictorial territory or scattered around the edges. The convention of depicting representative examples of the local population appears regularly throughout the seventeenth century; the most popular composition type makes a frame out of the corporeal examples depicted in an idealized ethnic or national costume. French, Spanish, Dutch, and English cartographers all used the indigenous human body as a means for claiming authentic facts and for depicting systems of social and racial classification.[47] As Valerie Traub suggests, the systematized representation of difference connotes a normative schema. While I agree that this interpretation of converging maps and bodies depicted on a table of normal and fantastical, I would also suggest that the "exhibition of alterity" she articulates also imagines a temporary space in which beauty (and all the social and moral modifiers are latched onto that category) and otherness coexist. Moreover, the representation functions as the means of disseminating the availability of alternate bodies and practices. The convention continues through the seventeenth century. Concurrently, however, another tradition develops that moves the exemplary figures into yet more aestheticized (and miniaturized) objects inserted into cartouches.

The Return of the Native

The complex cross-fertilization of Native American and Western ways of seeing and being are strikingly distilled into one of the several contemporary texts in which the reader will find Smith's map. Smith's anecdotes from the "contact zone" simultaneously reveal the irretrievable nature of the native experience of colonization and suggest the complex interplay of cultural forces.[48] The extent and nature of this contact zone appears a number of times throughout Smith's work and his compendia of others' tales. The dangers Smith faced and imprisonments recounted in his works are referenced—one obliquely—in the image of Powhatan on the map and its caption. The caption documents Smith's audience with Powhatan. The *True Relation* recounts the ultimate outcome of the relation with Powhatan as a kind of knighthood, for which "with a loud oration he proclaimed me a werowanes of Powhatan, and that all his subjects whould so esteem us, and no man account us strangers nor Paspahegans, but Powhatans." Yet, the image also refers to other contacts between Smith and tribal leaders which were not redolent of Smith's skill as ambassador. The story of Smith's capture figures into several of Smith's publications, the most elaborate and most sensational finding a home in the *General Historie of Virginia*.[49] In terms of this belated retelling, the image on the map alludes to a point after Smith has been conveyed to the village, but does not depict any signs of capture or conversation. Powhatan and his retinue sit inside a structure that appears rough-hewn in comparison to the elaborate banner to its right. Smith's removal to the caption situates him in language, and thus culture, while the indigenes are contained within their own culture, which pales by comparison as it nevertheless assigns a measure of development to them. At another level, the image alludes to de Bry's engraving of a funereal structure and ritual, but is combined with another of a native shaman. The mysteries of death, healing, and power seep into Hole's engraved appropriation. The synthesis of images creates a kind of visual circulation that points the reader to yet another set of images: those found in the *General Historie*. In that pastiche, a map of "Ould Virginia," Smith as Indian tamer (shorter than his victim but wielding the superior technology of a metal knife), the shaman, and in the center framed beneath an arch, a circle of Native Americans gathers with Smith in attendance, sitting next to the pile of sticks that reportedly signifies "England." The narrative that can be fashioned from circulating images adds another dimension to the image in the earlier *Map of Virginia*. John Smith's absence from a pictorial narrative of capture removes him from any suggestion of subordination places him outside the frame. Instead, the man who had temporarily dominated Smith becomes the object of mere curiosity and difference.

The map's image of Powhatan also becomes a point of retroactive resolu-

88   Lisa Blansett

Figure 3.4. Humphrey Cole, Compendium Dial, 1569. Courtesy National Maritime Museum, Greenwich. Captain John Smith probably carried a compass that looked something like this one, which may have been owned by Sir Francis Drake. With its sundial, calendar, compass, and engraved coordinates for celestial and terrestrial sites, this elegant compendium dial was useful for mapping land as well as charting sea voyages. At one point, when captured by Powhatan's men, Smith used such a compass theatrically—first by attempting to impress his captors with a lesson on European technology, the shape of the earth, and the nature of the solar system and then by offering the elaborate compass to Powhatan as a gift.

tion. The retelling of the capture in the later *Generall Historie* refashions the narrative in ways that add intended amplifications but also suggest a number of unintended effects. The extended time of the incarceration, suggesting a longer-term intimacy, enhances Smith's endurance and courage and adds to his authoritative claims of experience.[50] "He demanding for their captain," the story goes, "they showed him Opechancanough, king the Pamaunkee."[51] Smith produces an ivory mariner's compass and demonstrates its mechanisms and representations (Figures 3.4 and 3.5).[52] The natives react appropriately, as "much they marveled at the playing of the fly and needle, which they could see so plainly and yet not touch it because of the glass that covered them."[53] His technological superiority apparently granted, Smith goes on to transform the moment into a lesson on Western cosmography.[54] He establishes the geographical distances and differences

Figure 3.5 "Their conjuration about C[aptain] Smith 1607." Detail from the plate "Ould Virginia," engraving by Robert Vaughan, in John Smith, *Generall Historie* (London, 1624). Courtesy of the John Carter Brown Library, Brown University. During a ritual performed after Smith's capture by Opechancanough in December 1607, Smith receives a lesson in the Powhatan's view of geography. Signifying the cultural and political landscape, the circle encompasses Smith and a small pile of sticks, which represent his homeland.

between populations and racial characteristics; he demonstrates the mimetic relation between representation and the reality of the planet, and promotes himself as charismatic instructor. The deed done, however, the Pamaunkee "nevertheless" tie Smith to a tree and aim their weapons at him. The end seems predetermined. Yet, as the narrative suspense builds around this crisis, a resolution is fashioned: "But the king, holding up the compass in his hand, they all laid down their bows and arrows, and in a triumphant manner led him to [the town of] Orapaks, where he was after their manner kindly feasted and well used."[55] The narrator imagines the king in terms of an extant discourse of papacy, its superstitions, and its representation of the host as the real presence of Christ's body.

How "well used" Smith is becomes disputable as he is held captive—at one point he is conducted to a long-house where "thirty or forty tall fellows did guard him."[56] "Kindly feasted"? Perhaps, but even the narrative suggests that Smith's anxiety prevented him from partaking of such hospitality; the social exchange remains incomplete as the dramatic irony saturates the gap between a feast and a nervous stomach. Despite the unsettled nature of the social situation, the anecdote provides narrative completion to Smith's scientific lessons in the interpretation of "native" signs and practices performed. The critical interpretation of the ritual construction of concentric circles in terms of a primitive (Ptolemaic) map resolves a conflict that cannot be negotiated at the moment. As a belated response, the report's invocation of Smith's observational methodology, his deductive logic, and his reinterpretation of the "signs" within a familiar scientific paradigm allow him to reinvest the anxious experience with his own assumed mastery. As Smith passes the events through this epistemological filter, he transforms the indecipherable practices and alien signs into a legible text for educated English audiences.

The faint trace of Native American agency can be detected in the narrator's inability to see causal relations between the display of the compass and the subsequent restraint of Smith; in fact, the addition of "nevertheless" stresses the incommensurability of the sequence.[57] The British narrator must then try to control the event in its retelling and yet (unwittingly) cede narrative control to that which resists interpretation. It is in the gap between the narrative of the moment of cultural exchange and the myopic interpretive moves in its retelling that we find "what the natives knew" not as a direct reflection of Native American agency, but as a discursive effect.

This narrative represents the meeting between Smith and Opechancanough as a crisis averted through Western ingenuity and seat-of-the-breeches diplomacy. Yet the genius of the scene resides in the palimpsest of colonialism. Smith's use of the compass seems to signify British technological power, and yet the gesture of exchange also reveals a talismanic power. Moreover, Smith's imputation of Paumunkee amazement and admiration emphasizes Smith's own disorientation in the face of the unknown;

he supplies an orienting narrative where the coordinates are unclear. And this cultural disorientation cannot be resolved by the compass. Even as the compass is used to render legible the holder's orientation, the instrument also takes its place as its own opposite. The compass becomes a spectacular tool of negotiation inserted in the gap between the known and the unknown, between familiar and strange. Smith seizes on this moment of the colonial uncanny by transforming his diversionary tactics into a lesson in Western cosmography; as magician he conjures the universal applicability of rationality. The sign of technology and reason, however, effects an almost alchemical transformation in which mimesis is the assumed mode of representation, and the antipodeans become neighbors while the geographical and social distance is minimized in the object.

The return of the native to the text, however, arises from conversions of illegible to legible, the irresolvable for resolved, the anxious for the resolute. The power of the native voice, never fully retrievable from archival documents, finds its way into the colonial text through these contradictions and by way of the provisional textual resolutions. Thus, in this ritual of concentric circles, the island of Britain is represented as a pile of sticks at the edge of the ritual's circles. The English narrator's intention of using the implicit comparison between cosmographies to award technological superiority to the British is ironically transformed by the dead wood stacked for his leader. The irony evident to the early twenty-first century reader also points toward textual readings that suggest the complexity of the processes of mediation, negotiation, accommodation, and opposition. On the eve of the tercentennial of Jamestown's founding, the reader cannot wait for the "Early Modern" Native American to walk upon the stage of Western history. Instead, the reader may reimagine ingenious but subtle forms of resistance, agency used deftly if, ultimately, futilely.

Chapter 4
The Politics of Pathos
Richard Frethorne's Letters Home

EMILY ROSE

In April 1623, young Richard Frethorne wrote a letter to his parents that has become one of the most famous and widely reproduced documents from colonial North America.[1] At the time he wrote, Frethorne was an indentured servant who had recently arrived in the struggling colony of Virginia, and his letter tells of tough times. A year earlier, a devastating attack by the Powhatan confederacy had killed one-third of the English settlers and nearly destroyed the colony. Frethorne reported that that he was going hungry, everyone else was sick and dying, his clothes had been stolen; in short, life in England was infinitely better. He implored his parents to help him return home—or at least to send him some food. Until he arrived in this new world, Frethorne wrote, "[I] thought no head had been able to hold so much water as hath and doth daily flow from mine eyes."

As an eyewitness account of the young Jamestown settlement, the Frethorne letter has been widely cited by historians of early colonial America and frequently used in high school and college classrooms. Little is certain about its author (except that he was a young English Protestant male indentured servant) but more is known, or knowable, about Frethorne than is generally thought. To place the letter in its proper context, one needs to situate it within the course of events on both sides of the Atlantic during the same years and to take account of the historiography of Virginia.

America's most pathetic settler died and was forgotten for several centuries, but in recent decades he has been dramatically revived in the historical imagination. Indeed, Frethorne's changing fortunes reflect broad changes in historical understanding of early colonial Virginia. Excerpts of the letter were first published in 1881, but were ignored for decades. Frethorne's pitiable condition did not fit the heroic mold favored by turn-of-the-century historians such as Alexander Brown and Thomas Wertenbaker.[2] The leading colonial historian of the early twentieth century, Charles Andrews, referred to the letter only in a footnote—and then only to dismiss it as "lugubrious."[3] But since the middle of the twentieth century historians have become less invested in "cavalier" interpretations of the Old South and more interested in the experiences of ordinary settlers. From their perspective, the early Virginia settlers were not sophisticated ideological exiles motivated by high political or spiritual ideals, but rather ambitious servants of humble origins motivated by the pursuit of wealth. Building on earlier work by Oscar Handlin, Bernard Bailyn, and others, Edmund Morgan famously emphasized the varied backgrounds of the early settlers, the intense hardships they faced, and the class conflicts that soon developed.[4] Almost four centuries after the fact, historians finally discovered the sorrowful world of Richard Frethorne. Resurrected by historians, Frethorne has taken on a new life in the contemporary classroom, where in countless commercial document collections, textbooks, and online offerings, his letter provides a short, vivid account of the hardships of Virginia's early settlers.

Surprisingly, few historians have looked closely at Frethorne's letter, attempted to trace the life of its author, or questioned the nature of the document. What were the conditions under which it was written? Who was the letter's intended audience? What purposes might it have served? Perhaps because of its "domestic" character—a private letter to obscure parents—the letter is taken as uncrafted and innocent of the manipulation, bias, and distortion that characterize more public writings about the struggling colony at a time when it was just beginning to produce a vastly profitable staple crop. The Frethorne letter owes its current prominence to the fact that, far from being typical, it is actually one of the few of its kind. Frethorne may be appealing as a representative of ordinary servants during the dramatic early years of the Virginia settlement, but the letters he wrote home—and at least one of his other letters has been preserved—suggest that he himself was not all that typical.

Not many private letters from early emigrants to the New World remain and only a handful appear in print. Most of the letters that have survived are business correspondence, lengthy memos, and reports from one official to another. Those colonial letters that survived were copied and circulated because they contain information of a general character and of economic interest, not the outpourings of personal anguish that would be appreciated only by an author's family. The public and profitable nature of newsletter reporting was well understood in Virginia. Regular newsletters sent by agents in the field quickly evolved in the 1620s into newspapers and weekly *courrantos*. The secretary of the colony beginning in April 1619 was one John Pory whose prime occupation in England had been newsletter writer or "intelligencer."[5] While still in Virginia he engaged friends in London to request a newspaper monopoly for him.[6] Members of the upper classes sent news and information to their benefactors and supporters back home; indentured servants rarely had the means, opportunity, or education to write.

The rare survival of a personal letter from a teenaged servant in Virginia to his parents in England should raise questions about its nature and the reasons it would have been preserved. The Frethorne letter home was not found in the papers of his parents, for no such collection exists. Nor did it turn up in the voluminous business archive of the Virginia Company. Rather, a contemporary copy was preserved in the Manchester Papers, a collection of the Rich family, the earls of Warwick. This fact alone strongly suggests that Frethorne's letter home was duplicated and preserved because someone in their influential circle thought it might prove useful. Why this letter might have seemed valuable in 1623 becomes clear when we examine it more closely, evaluate available evidence about the author's background, compare this text to his other known letter, and consider the role of the earl of Warwick in the proceedings of the Virginia Company in these years.

We can infer with some confidence a good deal about Frethorne's circumstances in England, his experience in Virginia, and the reasons his letters were saved. Frethorne emerges as a less shadowy but also a less typical figure—better off and better educated than other indentured servants. He appears to have come from a well-informed, tobacco-producing area of England, one that suffered economic and social disruption at the time he departed. He had been in the New World just a few months before writing and had many connections to one "faction" in the fight over the future of the company responsible for settling Virginia. The drama of his letter lies in the high-stakes struggle over control of the Virginia Colony that involved Parliament, the king, and some of England's most powerful individuals. The letter was part of a transatlantic propaganda campaign that helped determine the fate of this highly capitalized, royally chartered commercial enterprise that linked settlers in Virginia to England's center of power.

Leaving England

To retrace the history of Richard Frethorne, one can work backward from the date and other comments in the letter to surmise when he arrived in Virginia, when he left England, what his circumstances may have been, and why he might have left.

Frethorne wrote in the early spring of 1623; he had probably arrived in late autumn or winter of 1622 after a trip that usually took two to three months (but could range from five weeks to five months). The company determined that late summer and early fall sailings were healthiest, and, starting in 1620, had arranged for departures to take place at that time of year. In January 1622 officials in Virginia happily reported that all passengers on the last nine ships had arrived hale and hearty in early winter.

Frethorne would have arrived at the same time the following year. We have no idea of his first impressions—the extant letter to his parents was not his first letter home.

The shift in sailing dates from early spring to late summer was a conscious innovation of the Virginia Company, intended to improve the health of the colonists once they arrived. Previously, ships had departed in the spring to take advantage of weather conditions at sea and to coincide with the patterns of the fishing industry and the eastern trade; fall sailings, although far rougher, were better for the well-being of the prospective settlers and the economic needs of the American colony. As Governor Yeardley noted, colonists who arrived in the cool weather of the autumn were better equipped to deal with the new environment than those who fell sick in the hot summer.[7] The rougher but shorter crossing in the northern latitudes was also better for the supplies than was the warm southern crossing, which was slower and more pleasant but caused the beer to sour, the food to rot, and the seeds to die. Having benefited from the faster route across the Atlantic that the company had commissioned Captain Argall to find, Frethorne would have arrived around November or December and written home about four months later, after he had settled in.

It is not clear if, before he left England, Frethorne had word of the devastating Indian attack ("massacre") which took place in March 1622 and nearly destroyed the colony, news of which only reached London in July. From his letter it appears that Frethorne was in the second group of young indentured servants assembled by Irish merchants. At a meeting of the Virginia Company held in April 1622 some Irish "undertakers" proposed to transport 20 or 30 young men at a total cost of eight pounds each with an additional 40 shillings for apparel. If the second group embarked in August, word of the desperate state of the colony may not have filtered down to those settlers already prepared to depart.[8] Alternatively, Frethorne may have sailed on the *Abigail*, a ship originally scheduled to depart England in July but delayed as the company absorbed the bad news: it did not set off until mid-October.[9] It arrived in Virginia on the twentieth of December with the governor's wife and twenty servants bound for the same settlement as Frethorne: Martin's Hundred.

Frethorne was probably a young teenager. The Virginia Company sought youngsters because they were cheaper to settle than adults (who cost £12,10s each to transport) and because they were more likely to respond to the opportunities available in the new world. Usually committed to work for seven years, indentured servants could look forward to owning their own land and tools once their period of service was completed. The availability of indentured servants for domestic labor also made Virginia attractive to women and established families—a significant goal of the company, which was eager to promote long-term settlement. Despite these and other efforts to attract women and families, few came. Frethorne appears to have been a typical Virginia settler in one respect: he was a single, young, unattached man.[10]

Frethorne probably came from the west of England. Boats for the New World sailed from Bristol, and indentured servants were recruited from the west coast of England and the Severn river valley. The western ports and the merchant elite of the cities of Bristol and Gloucester had long had an interest in Atlantic ventures, and Irish entrepreneurs had previously brought Englishmen to the new world from there.[11] The colonists whom Daniel Gookin transported from Ireland in 1621 appear to have come originally from England.[12] The Irish planter Sir William Nuce planned to bring 2,000 people to Virginia, and they too would have come from England rather than Ireland. Thus, in all likelihood, the undertakers indentured teenagers from a traditional area for recruitment, among people and communities familiar with the demands, contracts, and circumstances of the voyage.

Like many other early Virginia colonists, Frethorne may have embarked from the port city of Gloucester. English coastal communities around Gloucester were knowledgeable about the voyage to Virginia and the commercial capabilities of England's various colonies and overseas ventures. Gloucestershire men interested in developing Virginia included John Smyth of Nibley, William Tracy, esquire, and Captain George Thorpe, the deputy for the colony's planned college and a kinsman of Thomas Dale. Smyth, Thorpe, George Yeardley, and others were the founders of Berkeley Hundred, the private plantation documented in the Smyth of Nibley papers now in the New York Public Library.[13] Tracy, Thorpe, and Yeardley moved to Virginia, where Tracy died in 1621, Thorpe was killed in the 1622 attack, and Yeardley became governor. Smyth stayed in England: he was the estate steward, lawyer, and business agent for the Berkeley family.[14] Gloucestershire was also the home of John Berkeley of Beverstone Castle, the English ironmaker sent in 1621 to establish the industry in Virginia, who was also killed in 1622 with all his workers.

It is likely that Richard Frethorne took his unusual surname (not otherwise recorded in Virginia and extremely rare in England) from the parish of Frethorne, nine miles from the city of Gloucester and near the Berkeley holdings. Frethorne, which abuts Berkeley Hundred on two sides, was a small parish, less than six miles around with just 28 families by 1650.[15] One of the parishes on the Severn river which were subject to regular flooding, Frethorne lay in the middle of the narrow part of the Vale of Berkeley that suffered endemic malaria in the seventeenth and eighteenth centuries because it was marshy.[16] John Smith alluded to its "wealth without health." Other writers blamed the vapors rising from the Severn for the fevers or "agues" of the inhabitants, now known to be insect-borne infectious diseases. Although Frethorne was poor and small and there was no village center in the parish, it is recorded as having a school in the late seventeenth century, which might explain how young Richard learned his letters.[17]

Significant changes in the small parish of Frethorne around the time of Richard Frethorne's departure for America may have prompted him to leave home. After centuries of ownership by the Clifford family, who had built a fine house in which to entertain Queen Elizabeth, the manor passed rapidly through different owners in the early seventeenth century. One account suggests that the manor changed families twice in a very brief period.[18] The change of family ownership of the manor of Frethorne—something that was to happen only once in more than two centuries—may have been connected with the trade depression of 1621 (and excessive spending to entertain the monarch). In any case, because of the turnover of the manor, whether within the Clifford family or not, the future may have looked bleak for local families accustomed to a single patron.

The economic and social fabric of the area was decaying in other ways. The river looping around Frethorne had changed course dramatically around 1615, and population in the neighboring parishes had been dropping continuously since the late sixteenth century, even though this was a time of rapidly rising population elsewhere in England.[19] The receding river—always more important than the few roads in the area—left the local *putchers* (baskets to catch fish) dry and empty. Some of the *warths*, land and salt marshes reclaimed from the receding river, were appropriated by the Cliffords; the rest were only successfully defended as common land in 1631. The inhabitants generally relied on the river and maritime trades: there were few husbandmen and agricultural tenants in Frethorne and three-quarters of those held less than 20 acres apiece. The area had poor hard soil, full of fossils.

At just this time there seems to have been a change from copyhold to leasehold tenure, which increased the economic instability and removed traditional security for the copyholder from one generation to the next, engendering new relations between landlord and tenant. Farmers in England generally did not "own" their land, they "held" it from a landowner who originally held it from the crown. Copyhold tenure was the traditional form of landholding and offered various protections to the landholder, unlike the short term leasehold—the end of copyholding marked the end of the feudal system in England. In contrast, colonists in Virginia held their land "in free and common socage" with free and absolute title to their land. Early American colonists did not leave behind an unchanging "merrie old England," but a country that was adopting new financial policies which threatened traditional practices. Uncertainty prevailed at home as well as in Virginia.[20]

Virginia offered the prospect of advancement in a familiar industry. British port cities had an important export trade focused on the Atlantic, and Gloucestershire was also the center of the burgeoning domestic English tobacco trade.[21] The company's agreement to pay a 20 percent tax on their Virginia tobacco exports in exchange for the suppression of domestic tobacco planting indicates that the English industry already offered significant competition for the colony by 1619.[22] Gloucestershire continued to be a major tobacco-producing area throughout the seventeenth century.[23] By 1622 it was clear that tobacco would be the staple crop of the Virginia colony and that rapid profits were possible. It was sensible, therefore, for the undertakers to search for indentured servants from among domestic tobacco producers.

If, indeed, Richard Frethorne came from the Gloucester area, he would have seen or heard of friends and neighbors who invested heavily in or traveled to America, both men of high status and respect in the community and youths packed off by their parents in the hope of their finding a promising future. One may presume that Frethorne faced different circumstances from some maidens in Somerset who ran away from home a few years earlier for fear of being kidnapped and hustled off to Virginia.[24]

By 1622, colonists had been traveling back and forth between Virginia and England for more than a decade and could supply a fair picture of the countryside, the Indians, the products made in the colony, and the work involved in producing them. Some, like Captain John Smith, had returned permanently to England, as did at least eight of the original Berkeley Hundred settlers less than a year after their departure in 1620. Others returned only to bring their wives and families back to Virginia with them or to settle their affairs. Word of mouth and first-hand testimony from those returning to Gloucestershire undercut intensive propaganda from the company. More than any other commercial enterprise of the period, the Virginia Company was aware of the uses to which propaganda could be put. In order to attract settlers and investors, the company issued poems, sermons, translations, financial reports, laws, histories, tracts, broadside advertisements, and ballads at a feverish rate. Complaints to the Privy Council made note of the "cozening ballads" that induced Englishmen to emigrate, while the company complained of criticism from the London stage that demoralized the adventurers. Frethorne probably heard both good and bad of the colony, but even if he knew of the spring attack, he would only have had sketchy details in the summer of 1622 before he left. The original reports from Virginia suggested a hopeful future and these were reinforced by the vigorous publishing campaign. The leaders of the colony wrote to London assuring investors that it would be a "far more safer, happy and flourishing estate than it ever was before."[25]

After the onset of the trade depression of 1621, which hit the cloth counties around Gloucester with particular force, Virginia would have seemed especially attractive to a younger son. A generous harvest in the fall of 1620 resulted in low prices while a bitter winter exacerbated bad times. The cold wet summer that followed produced an exceptionally poor harvest and a severe depression gripped the countryside. Unemployed workers stormed stores to get grain. By early 1622 famine broke out in various pockets of England, the rural depression compounding a business and trade depression brought on by currency manipulations in eastern Europe and by the onset of war on the continent, which threatened English textile exports. Contemporaries reported "many poor people are ready to mutiny for want of work" and officials in Gloucestershire warned "our whole country is greatly impoverished."[26] At the time Frethorne's parents were arranging his passage across the Atlantic, the Privy Council urgently instructed justices of the peace in Gloucestershire and eight other counties to control "tumultuous assemblies" and to enforce the poor law.[27] The colony later reported to the Privy Council that corn was cheaper in Virginia than it was in England in the winter of 1622–23. At the time he left England, Frethorne could have looked forward to working his seven years of indenture and gaining some fertile land for himself in Virginia, a far rosier picture than the restricted opportunities at home.

Living in Virginia

Frethorne started out on the right foot. Whether by prior arrangement in England or by luck, once he arrived in the New World, he was sent or ended up as the servant to the head of Martin's Hundred.[28] Martin's Hundred, an early private plantation ten miles east of Jamestown, was one of the great Virginia success stories by early 1622, "a formidable and finely focused investment."[29] It was the most popular of the private or subsidiary plantations, boasting the largest number of individual investors of any settlement and sufficiently capitalized to claim 20,000 acres of land in Virginia.[30] It was founded in the name of Richard Martin, the Recorder of the City of London, an eminent lawyer whom the company had hired to argue its case before Parliament in 1614. He was posthumously to be memorialized as the spokesman and founder of Virginia ("praeco Virginiae ac parens").[31] Martin, however, died suddenly, even before the first ships landed, and John Wolstenholme then became the moving force: the center of Martin's Hundred, Wolstenholme Towne, was named after him. Wolstenholme was a merchant and tax collector (farmer of the customs) before he became an important colonial entrepreneur.[32] When the company divided into "factions," Wolstenhome, like Pory, sided with the earl of Warwick and Sir Thomas Smith.[33]

Life had been good at Martin's Hundred during the first few years of its existence. Chartered in 1618 during the early years of the tobacco boom, it started off as a relatively prosperous outpost of the expanding Jamestown settlement.[34] Frethorne's master, Governor Harwood, was accustomed to wearing gold thread like that found on the garter tags discovered by archaeologists on the site of the old house.[35] The year before Frethorne arrived the colony was sufficiently prosperous that the Virginia Council ruled that clothing enhanced with gold was to be restricted to the elite, a revival of medieval sumptuary laws intended to preserve class distinctions. Other material finds hint at the success of Martin's Hundred around this time: "part of the gilded spur, table knives encrusted with silver and inlaid with gold, and an elbow section from a suit of armor more elaborate than was possessed by most Virginia colonists—all spoke of wealth."[36] There was pottery from the Rhineland and from Spain, top quality lead-glazed earthenware made in Virginia but of English quality, many glass bottles, and fabric seals from Augsburg. Bits of a cast-iron fireback decorated with the arms of James I were also found, an object that "would only have been brought over by someone having social aspirations."[37]

Even under the best of circumstances, however, Virginia might not have lived up to Frethorne's hopes. He would have heard the good news about Virginia in official company publications circulated throughout England, in popular ballads, public sermons, and in personal communications directed locally to neighbors and friends and based on first-hand experiences. Optimistic letters came back to Gloucestershire from George Thorpe, who had settled at Martin's Hundred, at a site that enjoyed, among other advantages, clear, fresh, drinking water. Thorpe, the first in Virginia to manufacture corn whiskey, wrote that he preferred this liquor to English beer. He pointedly assured his partners in Gloucestershire that rumors about the unhealthiness of Virginia were untrue—and asked his wife to travel to America to join him.[38] Letters like Thorpe's and the similarly upbeat account Peter Arundell wrote a month later may well have been circulated, copied, or their contents reported in the neighborhood.[39] Thorpe was concerned by unrealistic expectations, as he explained to his investors: "I am persuaded that more do die here of the disease of their minds than of their body by having this country overpraised in England and by not knowing that they shall drink water here."[40] Frethorne was one of those disappointed by the water: "For as strong beer in England doth fatten and strengthen them, so water here doth wash and weaken these here," he wrote his parents.[41]

Unlike many apprentices and servants in the New World, Frethorne had a social network of respected mentors and concerned elders. His employer was Governor William Harwood, a Derbyshire man who had arrived in Virginia in August of 1620, probably with family members; he had been born in Barnstaple, the constituency Richard Martin had represented in Parliament. While visiting Jamestown on business Frethorne lodged with John Jackson the gun maker, and he worked with John Jackson the bricklayer at Martin's Hundred—two men who were well-respected in the colony (one was a delegate from Martin's Hundred to the 1619 General Assembly).[42]

The Atlantic world was complex and varied, and early Jamestown was a much more polyglot place than we have been accustomed to imagine. The young Anglican apprentice lived with and relied on fellow colonists of varied backgrounds and religious beliefs—Separatists (English-speaking Puritans from Holland), Walloons (French-speaking Catholics), Huguenots (French Protestants)—all of whom were more welcome in the British colony than were Catholic subjects of the king of Spain. The Virginia Company did not inquire too closely into one's religious beliefs as long as a prospective settler was willing to swear political loyalty. There were more foreigners in the Jamestown society than Frethorne would have met in a small English riverine parish: Poles, French, Italians, Welsh, Irish, Dutch, and Germans. Virginia attracted those who did not fit within the religious and social standards of typical English society. Frethorne worked side by side with black Africans who may have been far more urbanized than he was and who came from a more cohesive cultural group.[43] Not only was the smaller society of colonial Virginia more diverse than that of rural Gloucestershire, the "foreigners" were better educated and sophisticated, world-class specialists in their trades, whether silk-making, metallurgy, tobacco growing, whaling, poetry, or spying. The natives also proved more proficient than the English colonists in such important skills as hunting, planting, and fishing.

The prosperous developments at Martin's Hundred were cut short by the Indian attack in March of 1622, in which more than 300 colonists were killed. Martin's Hundred was the hardest hit of the settlements along the James River: all its buildings were burned, and it was there in a dung heap that the body of a forty-year old "granny" dragged by her Elizabethan style headdress, then scalped by Indians and overlooked by her friends and family for almost 400 years, was recently discovered.[44] Archaeologists conclude that the settlement of Martin's Hundred was temporarily abandoned in the wake of the 1622 attack, but Frethorne's letter suggests that it was not. He refers to the repeated ten-mile trip to Jamestown to unload goods and never mentions transferring permanently from Jamestown back to Martin's Hundred.

The devastating effect of the attack was compounded by the high mortality of the winter of 1622–23, caused by "a load of stinking beer." The colonists who had arrived healthy in the autumn were infected by disease spread by settlers who came later in the winter. Colonists suffered bloody flux (diarrhea, dysentery, or typhoid fever) and possibly malaria along with malnutrition. Many new arrivals were too sick to work; the attack had occurred at the onset of sowing time, and continued fear of the Indians meant that established colonists did not venture out to plant crops.

Frethorne reports that many of those who came with him died. He was witness to a crucial turning point in the colony—not its near destruction, but its swift repopulation. After such significant loss of life the Indians and the Spaniards expected that the colony would be abandoned, as were the colonies of Roanoke, Sagahadoc, and Avalon and as Jamestown itself was abandoned in 1610 after the "Starving Time," just before Lord De la Warr arrived. Roanoke in North Carolina, the first English colony in America, was abandoned (or "disappeared") by 1590 after a second attempt at settlement. The Popham colony of Sagadahoc in Maine (also known as the Northern Virginia or Plymouth Company settlement) was founded at the same time as the Virginia colony but lasted little more than a year. It was abandoned in 1608 for many of the same reasons that made Richard Frethorne want to leave: tenuous relations with the Indians, bad weather, poor economic prospects, low morale, and the opportunity to return home.[45] Calvert, Lord Baltimore, abandoned his colony of Avalon in Newfoundland in 1629 in utter discouragement.[46]

If it was left up to the slow-turning wheels of the English government, the colony of Virginia would have followed the sorry example of these other failed American ventures. After the 1622 disaster, it took many months for the government simply to approve the transport of obsolete arms from the Tower to Virginia where they did little to bolster the colony's defenses. Private enterprise worked more quickly. The Virginia Company avoided disaster and managed to prevent the colony from unraveling by quickly sending hundreds of new servants to repopulate the colony. Although the managers have been blamed for sending too many settlers rather than too few, and although infections brought by the newcomers caused more harm than had the knives and arrows of the natives, the ability of the colony to replenish its population in the years immediately following kept it afloat. It was the arrival of boatloads of hopeful, ambitious boys like Frethorne that saved the venture.

Writing Home

Frethorne wrote in the spring of 1623 against a backdrop of great disappointment just after a bitter winter and following the spread of disease from the *Abigail*, which had arrived in December. Hunger stalked the land. The Virginia settlers had eagerly anticipated the arrival of the *Seaflower* with much-needed supplies, but on March 18, while en route to Virginia, that ship was accidentally blown up (through the incompetence of the captain's son, who was partying while the ship was docked in Bermuda). When Frethorne first wrote his parents, the ship was overdue in Virginia. During this time Frethorne and his fellow settlers faced unanticipated scarcity, fear of Indian retribution, and continued illness. In Jamestown in the same month, a peace treaty was concluded at a party where the English captain poisoned 200 Indians drinking a celebratory toast and his fellow colonists slaughtered another 50.[47]

By the time the letter arrived in England, the health of the colonists was gradually improving and food supplies were more abundant, but when Frethorne was writing the colonists were desperate. Harwood warned his men that within two weeks they would have to go out and scavenge for roots in the woods. It was, however, no "starving time" like the one the colonists had experienced in 1609–10, a time some surviving colonists could recall. A study of tree-ring data suggests that the 1609–10 famine was exacerbated by one of the worst droughts in the Tidewater region in 770 years. Conditions were then slow to improve in the colony and were compounded by cruel government. In their petition to the Privy Council colonists recalled that before 1619, under the administration of Sir Thomas Smith

> the allowance for a man in those times was only eight ounces of meal and half a pint of peas a day, both the one and the other being moldy, rotten, full of cobwebs and maggots, loathsome to man and not fit for beasts; which forced many to fly to the savage enemy for relief, who being again taken, were put to sundry kinds of death, by hanging, shooting, breaking upon the wheel and the like: that others were forced by famine to filch for their bellies; of whom one, for stealing two or three pints of oatmeal had a bodkin thrust through his tongue and was chained to a tree till he starved.[48]

In 1623 there was no inherent difficulty in living off the land. The famine that year was manmade, not dictated by nature: settlers were too frightened of Indian attacks to sow or harvest crops.

Frethorne reached beyond his immediate family in his efforts to return home. A month before he wrote his parents he sent a plaintive letter to a Mr. Bateman in England.[49] A member of the Northwest Passage Company and the East India Company, Robert Bateman was also a Member of Parliament in 1614 and 1621. Just before Frethorne embarked for the New World, the king recommended that Sir John Wolstenholme serve as head of the Company ("treasurer") and Bateman serve as his deputy.[50] Frethorne may have been a poor indentured servant, but he had Bateman's ear and Bateman had the king's. Bateman had received his Virginia Company shares from the earl of Warwick. In April 1623 he was listed along with Wolstenholme as a partisan of the earl and was named to the royal commission that took over the Virginia Company in 1624.[51]

The apprentice "sold by his parents" was not so isolated and friendless as his letter home might suggest. For Richard Frethorne to write directly to Bateman indicates that he had a source of influence and patronage within the Company. Bateman was a member of the London political and financial elite; he represented the capital in Parliament and three of his sons became aldermen of the city.[52] Considering his youth, Frethorne was unlikely to have met Bateman at work or through trade connections, so Bateman was most likely a family friend. Goodman Jackson, who was so kind and helpful to Frethorne in Jamestown, may also have been a friend from England. "Goodman" was a term of respect and placed the gun maker in the higher ranks of the colonists, just below the gentry and members of the wealthy merchant class.[53] Frethorne therefore either made important connections soon after his arrival or could boast useful links with influential leaders that dated from the period of his youth in England. Curiously, the letter to Bateman is far more pious in tone and content than the one to his parents and is full of biblical citations. The two men may have been connected through shared religious sympathies.

Frethorne was better off than many of his fellow servants in Virginia. In addition to anticipating some form of political support and patronage, he could also count on emotional and practical support from his family. When the young indentured servant wrote to his mother and father, he asked after his brothers and sisters. This reference to an intact nuclear family is striking at a time when many other young servants in Virginia lacked influence and family. Many indentured servants journeyed to the New World because they had few prospects and no means of support in the Old. Although Frethorne indicates that his parents had received some funds in return for his indenture, he also indicates that they were not poor. He notes that they distributed charity to beggars and that he expected them to send money for cheese, beef, oil and vinegar, spices, and alcohol or to raise it from friends. He further suggests that this would be a good investment for them, and promises to repay any amount they might send.

There are other indications that Frethorne was not a typical indentured servant. He notes that Goodman Jackson, the gunsmith, was surprised that he was sold as a servant: "He much marvelled that you would send me a servant to the Company; he saith I had been better knocked on the head." The wording suggests that Frethorne was not prepared to be a servant and perhaps had been brought up to expect something better.[54] It is possible that he was sent to the colonies to "make a man of himself"—that his behavior or other circumstances back home had suggested such a step to his parents. Some parents clearly regarded Virginia as an appropriate destination for their obstreperous offspring. "An unruly son of the Lady Finch's whom she sent to Virginia to be trained," for example, according to a letter of Chamberlain, "fell into a quarrel with the watch, and was so hurt he died the next morning."[55] That Frethorne's parents cherished and did not abandon him is indicated in his plaintive "[I] saith that if you love me you will redeem me suddenly, for which I do entreat and beg." To the parents of an unruly and spoiled child or one who had few prospects at home during a national depression, shipping a child to the colonies seemed like a sensible proposition, one that would be the making of a younger son. More conventional plans for their son may have changed with the onset of the depression.

Frethorne was strikingly literate for his age and circumstances. Many people therefore assume that someone else wrote the letter on the servant's behalf, which is possible but would have been costly. Frethorne appears to have been sufficiently educated to write himself and to write often. Ink and paper, however, were hard to come by and must have been imported from England. They may well have been provided to Frethorne by London patrons rather than by his anxious parents. One possibility is that he was given the necessary supplies and encouraged to write a suitably damning account. John Pory, for example, the secretary of the colony, was well equipped with such resources. Had he desired, he could easily have supplied Frethorne with writing materials on one of his trips to Jamestown. From the Manchester archive we learn that Pory's erstwhile employer, the earl of Warwick, was eager to have Frethorne's first-hand testimony about conditions in the colony. Pory was Warwick's man in Virginia and took on delicate and clandestine assignments for the earl both before and after his stay in Virginia. Given this background, it is appropriate to consider the political as well as the personal circumstances that might have drawn Richard Frethorne to Virginia and which may have prompted him to write.

Power Politics

Frethorne's letter home was not preserved because his family cherished heartfelt words from their despondent son. We do not even know whether his parents received it. The letter survives because it was a useful and ultimately successful tool in a struggle to wrest control of the colony from the stockholders of the Virginia Company. The letter was used as propaganda, just as were the printed ballads, sermons, and publications extolling the virtues of the new colony. It is usually assumed that Frethorne's letter was private and confidential, intended only for the eyes of his immediate family. Most extant letters and accounts from the 1610s and 1620s from Virginia, however, were meant to be circulated, and their authors understood that their writings would have a wide readership.

Freethorne's letter had a significant contemporary audience because it was taken from the ship when it docked in London and included in a packet sent to the Privy Council for a hearing in June 1623, two months after he wrote it. Other private letters from Virginia were also found in that collection, summarized and abstracted by Sir Nathaniel Rich, cousin and confidant of Henry Rich, the second earl of Warwick. Warwick's intent was to demonstrate that public and private accounts of the colony contradicted each other. Frethorne's letter, among others, persuaded the government that the colony was mismanaged and that the Virginia Company ought to be dissolved.

Frethorne's plaintive missive was sent to England on the same ship that carried letters from George Sandys to his brothers Samuel and Miles. The intended recipients were both Members of Parliament and substantial investors in the Virginia Company; their younger brother George, the poet, was the colony's treasurer, the eyes and ears in Virginia for his older brother Edwin, the leading executive of the Virginia Company in London.[56] George settled in Virginia with yet another kinsman, the Reverend

David Sandys (who died the following year); as noted above, their niece Margaret was married to the governor of the colony, Francis Wyatt. Mrs. John Ferrar, possibly a relative of Nicholas Ferrar, Edwin Sandys's chief deputy in England, also wrote home about the tough times in Virginia. These letters—Wyatt's, Sandys's, Ferrar's and Frethorne's—were among those confiscated and sent on to the Privy Council. Yet the same month a gentleman from Virginia sent to London an enthusiastic song on the delights of the colony to be sung to the popular tune "All Men be Good Fellows."[57]

The conflicting reports that arrived in England apparently on the same ship, composed in the same weeks, reflect a battle for the heart and soul of the Virginia Company. There was a conflict of interest between the group led by Sir Edwin Sandys and the earl of Southampton supported by the Ferrars and the group led by Henry Rich, earl of Warwick, and his cousin Nathaniel Rich, supported by Sir Thomas Smith and Sir John Wolstenholme. The Sandys-Southampton group had the support in Virginia of the governor and the treasurer (Francis Wyatt and George Sandys), but Warwick had the support of the secretary (John Pory).[58] As soon as the letters arrived in London the fight for control of the company went directly to the Privy Council. When they arrived, Nathaniel Rich recorded in a handwritten note that he had all the letters from Virginia except Frethorne's, "which must be added out of the copy at large."[59] If Rich did not have Frethorne's letter at hand, how did he know the indentured servant would see things his way? One explanation is that he was not waiting to get the letter from Frethorne's parents in England, but already knew what the tenor of its contents would be.

The Riches could have learned about Frethorne from Nathaniel Butler, the governor of Bermuda, a Warwick partisan who had left the island under a cloud in October 1622.[60] On his way back to England Butler stopped for a few months in Virginia during the winter of 1622–23, and on his arrival in London that spring composed a blistering attack on Sir Edwin Sandys and the Virginia Company at the behest of the earl of Warwick, his longtime patron. This attack, the *Unmasking of Virginia*, was the basis for the eventual cancellation of the charter and the dissolution of the company.

Butler went to Virginia with the goal of discrediting the company and colony. The colonists complained to the Privy Council that "his ears were open to nothing but detraction and he only enquired after the factious, of which there were none among us, and how he might gather accusations against those in the government, being as it should seem, sent over for that purpose."[61] Butler had the time, opportunity and desire to seek out young Richard Frethorne and encourage him to write home. Warwick's supporters were not above forging documents and contriving letters in England from individuals known to be living in Virginia. Sir John Bourchier, for example, claimed that a letter Nathaniel Rich delivered to him, allegedly from his daughter Mrs. Whittakers in Virginia, was an obvious forgery, as she and her husband later came to confirm.[62] John Smyth of Nibley knew the practice and wrote to his partners, "I fear the old Virginia trick of surprise of letters (if not counterfeiting them also) is cast upon us by Mr. Woodleefe [the man they had originally picked as governor of Berkeley Hundred]."[63] Warwick's group, in turn, complained that Sandys's group manipulated the official reports from the colony. One should consider the possibility that Frethorne's letter, so ardently sought by Nathaniel Rich and of such timely use, may have been solicited and not merely copied for the Privy Council.

In May, before Frethorne's April letter could have arrived in London, the Privy Council demanded all the books and documents of the Company in England, as well as those arriving on the next ships from Virginia. Back in March, Alderman Robert Johnson, Sir Thomas Smith's son-in-law, had petitioned the crown for an investigation of the Virginia Company. As the investigation progressed that spring, it appears that Warwick was prepared to lay Frethorne's complaints before the Privy Council before they reached his parents. The Riches kept copies of Frethorne's letters, but it is not known what happened to the originals or whether they were ever forwarded to their intended recipients.

Richard Frethorne endured a difficult year in 1623. He was young, scared, cold, hungry, and lonely. His original leader and mates had died and the rest were very sick. He was 3,000 miles from home and he missed his family, his friends, and the comforts of his old life. Malnourished and poorly clothed, he lived under wartime conditions, justly fearful of being scalped by Indians, shot by Spaniards, or robbed and infected by his countrymen.

But he was not a typical indentured servant. He had friends in high places and was able to communicate with them as well as with his family. Frethorne had contractual hopes of better things to come. Those who made it through 1623 found that the situation in Virginia soon improved. The colony expanded and the colonists enjoyed better living conditions. In the 1650s George Alsop, a young English servant in Maryland, wrote to his parents in England: "The indentured servants of this colony which are stigmatized as slaves by the clabber mouth jaws of the vulgar in England, live more like Freemen here than most Mechanic Apprentices in London, wanting for nothing that is convenient or necessary and accordingly are extraordinarily well used and respected."[64]

In the end, Frethorne's letter helped the earl of Warwick and his associates claim victory over the earl of Southampton and his associates. As a result of the hearings before the Privy Council, the company charter was revoked in 1624 and the London investors lost control of the colony and lost the value of their investment. Sir Edwin Sandys and the Ferrars turned their attention to Parliament and the Ferrars subsequently retired to the religious community they established at Little Gidding; Southampton went off to the Continent to fight and soon after died there with his eldest son. Sir Nathaniel Rich was repeatedly reelected to Parliament and later served as deputy governor of the Bermudas; his cousin Henry Rich, the earl of Warwick, continued investing in pirate ships and went on to become chief admiral under Parliament. Margaret Sandys, Lady Wyatt, and her husband Sir Francis Wyatt returned to Virginia, where he served as governor under the royal seal; her uncle George eventually retired to their estate in England and published a translation of Ovid that brought him more fame as a poet than he had enjoyed as a colonial administrator. When Wyatt was asked to serve a second term in Virginia in 1639, he appointed George Sandys as the colony's agent in London. Sir John Wolstenholme remained active in colonial affairs and died in 1639 at the age of 77, having recommended that the company charter be revived.

Despite the letters written by Frethorne and others, government officials took little action and accepted no responsibility for the conditions in Virginia. They continued to negotiate a monopoly on tobacco imports from which the crown could profit, they did not send grain—although they instructed the bankrupt company to do so—and they did not finance supplies, lend money, or send anything more than a few rusty arms from the Tower. The government restricted the marketing of colonial products abroad and denied the company the opportunity to open Virginia to free trade, which would have brought food to the colony from Dutch ships. It continued to press the company to send to Virginia poor felons, the aged and infirm, the diseased, and those unable to work, at the cost of the shareholders rather than the government. Frethorne's letter carefully deflects attention from those responsible for the poor conditions he endured and he lays blame only indirectly.

Richard Frethorne apparently died in Virginia not many months after writing his letter home. The name "Richard Freetharm," appears under Martin's Hundred dead on the list of "The Living and Dead" composed in February 1624.[65] Martin's Hundred, his home, was abandoned and decades later resettled under the name "Carter's Grove."[66] Whatever his parents sent, and whatever consideration Mr. Bateman and the earl of Warwick showed came too late for the hungry apprentice. Since food supplies arrived in the colony shortly after the letter was composed, one can assume that Frethorne died of illness and disappointment, as Thorpe had predicted many would.[67] For some, like Richard Frethorne, "there [was] nothing to be gotten here but sickness and death"; for others, the opportunities outweighed the risks.

Part II
The World Stage

Chapter 5
The Specter of Spain in John Smith's Colonial Writing

ERIC GRIFFIN

By the autumn of 1607 internal divisions were about to bring the Jamestown colony to an abortive end. With the company's stores on the verge of depletion and his superiors debating an early return to England, Captain John Smith was compelled to lead a relief expedition up the Chickahominy, "where hundreds of savages in diverse places stood with their baskets expecting his coming." Reflecting upon the encounter some years later, Smith endowed the event with what might initially appear to be an odd tricultural significance. "The Spaniard never more greedily desired gold than he victual," Smith wrote, "nor his soldiers more to abandon the country than he to keep it."[1]

Smith's diffuse, third-person rhetorical construction reveals a complex international dynamic at work in Virginia, as elsewhere in the emerging North Atlantic world.[2] Indeed, the typology that attends the episode via Smith's third term, "the Spaniard," can tell us much about the anxieties and aspirations of England's colonial adventurers at this early moment of English expansion. For the captain's allusion was a cultural act: with the merest allusion to "the Spaniard" and his reputed "greed," Smith could count upon an instant nod of recognition among an English reading public.[3] Though Spanish avarice was but one of a set of commonplaces that came to comprise the Black Legend of Spanish cruelty,[4] from the late sixteenth century onward there could be found in English public culture a no more potent index of Spain's national character than its legendary "thirst for gold."[5] So broadly disseminated had the tales of Spain's New World atrocities become by the time England's first sustainable American colony was planted at Jamestown that few readers could have failed to register the gravity of Smith's condition.

Yet the ambivalence in Smith's remark bespeaks more than simple Hispanophobia.[6] The apparent revulsion at Spanish avarice he voices in one breath slides seamlessly into Hispanophilic admiration of Spain's New World *conquista* in another. Smith and his English contemporaries were all too aware that at this moment in Atlantic history, "the Spains"—as the united kingdoms of Iberia had come to style themselves since the Portuguese incorporation of 1580—were the only European power that had been able "to keep" any substantial portion of American "country."[7] In Smith's brief reflection, then, we glimpse not only cognizance of Spain's imperial excess, but also a keen awareness of Spain's "golden successe"—as Richard Hakluyt had collectively (and euphemistically) dubbed Iberia's many sixteenth-century triumphs.[8] This ambivalence is not indicative merely of Smith's personal obsessions; neither is it an anomaly of style. Rather, it is characteristic of the conflicted attitude toward Spain that pervades much of the colonial writing of the period.[9]

To examine the cultural formation I refer to as the "specter of Spain" is to gain a sense of how interrelated the English and the Spanish remained at this early moment of North Atlantic colonial activity. When we trace the webs of significance that continued to link the two nations in spite of their storied antagonism we begin to see how much these rivals had in common.[10] At the same time, examining the specter of Spain enables us to interrogate the whiggish historical tendency to view the Virginia experience as standing primarily for "the first representative body, the origin of the American form of government," as Jamestown archaeological site director William Kelso has recently restated the commonplace—a nationalistic emphasis that has often obscured the international context in which the early Jamestown project was caught up.[11]

In what follows I pursue the specter of Spain through several of the more important discursive fields in which the Jamestown experiment was embedded. This essay will thus take up matters of transatlantic exploration and settlement, questions regarding the pacification and Christianization of Virginia's native population, and competing strategies of economic and military involvement. In each of these cultural arenas English colonists viewed the practices of the Spanish as providing measures and models for their own colonial adventures. But in order to get a sense of how thoroughly the specter of Spain haunted England's early colonial project—and thereby grasp what is different about Smith's perspective—it will be necessary to probe the "white" legend of Spain's providential election.[12] For unless we have grasped the attractions of this religiopolitical tradition, we cannot gauge the rhetorical force of the Black Legend of Spanish Cruelty, the propagandistic discourse that helped to furnish the terms by which John Smith, in the manner of so many English colonial writers, sought to advance England's political, religious, and economic interests—not to mention his own.

The Virgin and Her Navigators

The pervasiveness of *La leyenda negra* in the early modern public sphere has become axiomatic. But we have often tended to observe the presence of

Black Legend discourse without reflecting upon the imperial ideology which the Protestant writers who marketed it to such great effect sought to displace. Although the reputation for greed to which Smith alludes had been circulating with accounts of Spain's New World exploits since at least as early as Peter Martyr's *De Orbe Novo Decades* (Alcalá, 1516), during much of the sixteenth century concerns regarding the ethical implications of Spain's colonial activities tended to recede before an appreciation of the magnitude of the conquests the Spanish had achieved.[13] The acknowledged odds and unprecedented circumstances over which the conquistadores prevailed were seen to have required extreme methods. In 1555, the Englishman Richard Eden went so far as to argue that "the Spaniardes as the ministers of grace and liberite [had] browght unto these new [Amerindian] gentiles the victorie of Chrystes death whereby they beinge subdued with the worldely sworde, are nowe made free from the bondage of Sathans tyrannie, by the myghty poure of this triumphante [Spanish] victourer."[14] But while the accomplishments of men like Cortéz, Pizarro, and Balboa, in combination with the seemingly endless shipments of bullion sent homeward from the American mines, were seen to confirm heavenly favor, it was the extension of the boundaries of Christendom—with Spain adding vast territories in America even as Portugal established new colonies in Africa and Asia—that provided the most visible and unambiguous signs that the Almighty had elected the nations of Iberia for his special work.[15]

Alejo Fernández's painting, *The Virgin of the Navigators* (ca. 1535), may be the fullest expression of the ideology that the Protestant polemicists of the later sixteenth century sought to counter with their inversive polemics (Figure 5.1). In Fernández's representation Columbus, Magellan, and the celebrated mariners who had embarked under the flag of Aragon and Castile-Leon congregate around an immense figure of the Madonna. While the shadowy figures of Amerindians gather near—brought from "pagan" darkness to the light of Christianity by the navigators who have set sail in her holy name—*Santa María* straddles the seas, uniting the continents. In the view of the Roman Church, it was the enlargement of Christendom through the conversion of millions of Indian souls that most glorified Spain. Gold, riches, and the expansion of the Empire's boundless New World dominions were but the earthly signs of the blessings gained through Iberia's propagation of *La Santa Fé*; the increase of the corporate body of Christ was seen to offset the loss of so many souls, first to Islam, and later to Protestant heresy.

My appeal to this Catholic theological ideal, the *immensum imperii corpus*, is not intended to revivify a "white," pro-Hispanic legend any more than I want to reinscribe the black one that has so colored Anglo-American historical thought.[16] Nor do I want to minimize the international complexity of the early modern colonial dynamic. As Pompa Banerjee suggests, far from revolving around a simple Anglo-Hispanic axis, European expansion in the

Figure 5.1. Alejo Fernández, *La Virgen de los Navegantes*, ca. 1535. Courtesy of El Ayuntamiento de Sevilla, copyright © Patrimonial Nacional.

Americas was part of a "vibrant triangulation of trade and exchanges along the Atlantic and Mediterranean linking Europe with the Ottoman Empire, North Africa, and America."[17] In this global commercial context, material gain was obviously a primary motive for the Spanish, just as it would be for the English colonial writers who preceded Smith in the New World—men like Sir Walter Ralegh, who had assured his superiors in 1595 that he had truly glimpsed "*El madre del oro* . . . the mother of golde," and that the "Empyre" he had discovered in Guiana would "suffice to inable her Majesty, and the whole kingdome, with no lesse quantities of treasure, then the king of Spayne hath in all the Indies, east and west."[18] Yet we should not fail to recall that the ideology of crusade would remain an important feature of the Roman Catholic mission well into the eighteenth century.

Writing of this "crusading impulse," Chilean historian Mario Góngora has noticed the "frequent occurrence in [Columbus's] writings . . . of the recuperation and rebuilding of the Holy House in Jerusalem."[19] Like the 1492 expulsion of the Iberian Jews, Columbus's discoveries were seen as yet another portent—which could be added to the even greater sign of the defeat of Islam in Granada that year—that Spain's Catholic kings were indeed acting by divine decree. It has long been a historical commonplace that the tremendous cultural energies of the reconquista were channeled almost immediately into Iberia's colonizing activities. But we should not underestimate the attractions of this narrative in the early modern period. "We are engaging in a just and good war, which will bring us fame," exhorted Cortéz to his men as they departed from Cuba to undertake the conquest of Mexico. "Almighty God, in whose name and faith it will be waged, will give us victory. . . . We have seen by experience how God has favored the Spanish nation in these parts, and how we have never lacked courage or strength, and never shall."[20] In the New World the Spanish battle cry remained *Santiago*—after their patron saint, St. James the Moor-killer—just as it had been down the long centuries of the Iberian reconquest.[21]

As the extent of the Spanish discoveries became known, this fundamentally eschatological crusading ideal became directed more and more to the New World.[22] Imperial zeal began to energize the Roman Church's evangelical orders. The Franciscans in particular—"enthusiastic over the prospect of the final conversion of the peoples of that New World, a process which some of them clearly considered to be a task appropriate to the 'end of the world'"—took to the Americas a potent strain of apocalyptic thought, much in the vein of the Joachimism that had inspired Columbus.[23] Even the devastation of the Amerindian population Bartolomé de Las Casas sought to expose found a ready place in this ideology. One of the most prominent friars among the first generation of Franciscans to evangelize in Mexico, Toribio de Benevente, better known as Motolinía (in Nahuatl, "the poor one"), spoke quite earnestly about the "ten plagues of Egypt and the 'grievous plagues' [of] deaths, epidemics, heavy labour in the mines" that the natives were forced to endure as retribution for the prior sins of their culture and a sign that the end-times were near. Motolinía was voicing the majority position when he attacked Las Casas and "wholeheartedly accepted the legitimacy of the Conquest."[24] And Jerónimo de Mendieta, another Franciscan, pushed the biblical analogy even further, comparing Hernán Cortéz with Moses as he argued that the conquistador had "opened for missionaries the doors to the new Christendom" in order to offset the loss the Church had suffered as a result of the Lutheran schism.[25] Witnessing that the colonies founded during the reign of the Catholic kings had been increased, first by Holy Roman Emperor Charles V, and later by his heirs, Philip II (1556–98) and Philip III (1598–1621), a significant number of European Catholics continued to be attracted to the idea of Spain's imperial "translation."[26] As late as the seventeenth century the Neapolitan political theorist Tommaso Campanella—like Las Casas, a Dominican—could still point prophetically and apocalyptically to the kingdom of "the Spains" as the last (and greatest) world Monarchy.[27] It is against the backdrop of Spain's international evangelical mission that we should set its ideological inverse, the Black Legend of Spanish cruelty.

The Mirror of Spanish Cruelty

Campanella's late enthusiasm notwithstanding, Spain's European rivals tended increasingly to turn a cynical eye on the universalist concerns of Spanish colonialism. By the mid-sixteenth century the astonishing depopulation of Spain's American viceroyalties had inspired a public reassessment of its colonial legacy. Scholastic disputations, such as those pitting Las Casas against Juan Ginés de Sepúlveda at Valladolid in 1550, openly raised questions concerning the morality and the legality of Iberian claims in the New World. Ironically, and *pace* Spain's reputation for absolutist tyranny, it was the comparative *openness* of Spanish society, a condition borne out by the fact that these colonial matters could be held up to public and institutional scrutiny, that unleashed the discursive raw material from which the Black Legend would be fashioned. For it was in this context that Las Casas penned his infamous *Brevissima relación de la destruyción se las indias* (Sevilla, 1552).

Once Europe's militant Protestant nationalists had begun to recognize the "educational" value of Las Casas's polemic—especially when it was used to amplify the more gruesomely triumphalist passages in the widely reprinted accounts of Cortéz and Gómara (which described the Mexican conquista), or León and Zárate (which recounted the conquest of Peru)— they never ceased exploiting it.[28] Certainly other texts were important to the dissemination of *La leyenda negra*: Girolamo Benzoni's *History of the New World* (Venice, 1565), *The discourse of the history of Florida, containing the trea-*

son of the Spaniards, against the subjects of the king, in the year 1565 (Dieppe, 1566), written by Nicolas Le Challeux, a survivor of the punitive attack on the Huguenot colony at Fort Caroline, and Gonsalvius Montanus's *Discovery and Playne Declaration of the sundry and subtill practices of the Holy Inquisition of Spayne* (which had appeared in English translation by 1568) were key contributors.[29] But it was the language and imagery of the *Brevissima relación*—which claimed that the American "destruction" had been "carried out with but one aim: to extract gold from the Indians"—in combination with the sheer numbers Las Casas reported in connection with the Amerindian genocide, that would portend anti-Spanish diatribes.[30]

The commanding figure in terms of the conversion of Las Casas's condemnation of his own nation's "more than Turkish cruelty" into highly effective anti-Hispanic propaganda had been William I of Orange, the Prince of Nassau.[31] Produced in the context of his dynastic struggle with Philip II, the widely circulated *Apology [or Defense] Against the Proclamation and Edict Published by the King of Spaine* (1580) drew upon the Dutch translations of Las Casas that had been published in 1578 and 1579. Like these two editions of the *Brevissima relación*, the latter of which had received the inflammatory new title, *The Mirror of Spanish Tyranny, in which are Told the Murderous, Scandalous, and Horrible Deeds Which the Spaniards Have Perpetrated in the Indies,* Orange's *Apology* made explicit a connection between Spanish colonizing practices in the New World and the atrocities his own subjects had been experiencing under the Hapsburg yoke.[32] Just as significantly, this text laid the foundations for a rhetorical strategy that explained the acts of cruelty experienced by his subjects as a function of the *ethnicity* of the Spanish perpetrators: "I will no more wonder," wrote the Dutch prince, "at that which all the worlde beleeveth, to witte, that the greatest parte of the Spanyardes, and especially those, that coounte themselves Noble men, are of the blood of the Moores and Jews, who also keepe this virtue of their Auncestors, who solde for readie money downe tolde, the life of our Saviour, which thing also, maketh me to take patientlie this injurie layde upon me."[33] The discursive shift Orange and his ghost-writers made from the matter of his own "injurie" (the Hapsburg rejection of his own "nation's" secession) into the mire of ethnic essentialization is easily observed: the "mixed blood" of Iberian culture became a sign of both religious and "racial" corruption.[34] Las Casas's critique of the *ethics* of the conquest had been recast as the "natural" consequence of America's having been colonized by a people of particular *ethnicity*.[35] According to this new calculus of lineage, of Europe's nations only Spain had been capable of such "devastation."

While much Black Legend discourse was motivated by Spanish military entanglement in the Netherlands, an additional context was also vital to its development. This was the Portuguese succession crisis of the early 1580s. Though the significance of the Iberian consolidation has tended to fade from view, largely as a result of our nation-centered historiographical biases, which disjoin "Spanish" history from "Portuguese" as surely as they disconnect the histories of Britain and Iberia, the unification of Las Hispanias may have been the most consequential political event of the second half of the sixteenth century. The appearance of the *Brevissima relación* in England as *The Spanish Colonie, or briefe chronicle of the acts and gestes of the Spaniardes* (1583), a full thirty years after its publication in Spain, coincided with the failure of the pretender, Dom Antonio, the Prior of Crato, to recover the Portuguese crown by enlisting the support of the northern European dynasties.[36] The Spanish victory over Dom Antonio seemed once more to evidence Spain's imperial election, even as it gave Roman Catholics throughout Europe hope that the revolt of the Protestant North might soon be quelled. At the same time, Philip's assumption of the Portuguese crown created the religiopolitical alignment that made the Armada inevitable, and, or so it was advertised, "invincible."[37]

The publication of the *Brevissima relación* in English translation during this moment of crisis marked a pivotal move in one of the most successful propaganda campaigns ever carried out. In the manner of Orange's Hispanophobic polemics, *The Spanish Colonie*'s preface implored those allied with the Low Countries to "beholde as it were in a picture or table, what they are like to be at, when through their reclessness, quarrels, controversies, and partialities themselves have opened the way to *such an enemie.*"[38] Thus Las Casas was mobilized not so much to encourage English colonial expansion in a mode that could displace the coercive methods of the Spanish (though Richard Hakluyt made use of him in this way), but to suggest that the destruction that had been exacted upon the natives of Spain's New World possessions was of the same stripe as that being felt in the many European dominions (read: "colonies") of the Spanish Hapsburgs.[39] Not only did the Black Legend polemicists imply that the Spanish were "devastating" the Low Countries in the same way they had the Indies, they also went so far as to construct the newly incorporated kingdom of Portugal as the latest in a long line of Spanish conquests and usurpations, rather than as the legitimate succession it was.[40] Nor did the propaganda surge abate with the failure of the "Enterprise" of 1588. Faced with continuing Spanish designs for the liberation of Ireland, the possibility of a new Spanish alliance with the Catholic faction in Scotland, and rumors of new Armadas in the making, as well as feeling the effects of increasing internal unrest brought on by agricultural famine and the succession crisis that Elizabeth I's advancing age made imminent, English polemicists turned out an astonishing number of Hispanophobic titles in an effort to turn public opinion against Spain and Roman Catholicism once and for all.[41] This propaganda deluge of the 1590s fixed in English public culture essentializing perspectives and prejudices that would have an exceedingly long shelf-life in the Anglo-American world. Whether invoked in England, the Low Countries,

Protestant Germany, or Huguenot France, the message of *La leyenda negra* was an unambiguous "it can happen here" (Figure 5.2).[42]

The Land Itself Would Wage War

With Anglo-Hispanic relations having grown so tense on the European front, we should not be surprised to find the Spanish specter pervading much of the early writing from Jamestown. In their first report from Virginia, the letter of June 22, 1607 (also signed by Smith), company principals Wingfield, Martin, Gosnold, Rattcliff, and Kendall wrote, "wee entreate your succors for our seconds with all expedition leaste that all-devouringe Spaniard lay his ravenous hands uppon theas gold showing mountaines, which if we be so enhabled he shall never dare to think on."[43] As in the passage from Smith with which this essay began, the epithets that attach to the Spanish in the company letter were calculated to move their audience. The Black Legend polemicists of the 1580s and 1590s had accomplished their cultural work; in seventeenth-century England it was common knowledge that the prospect of gold meant the Spanish could not be far away.

Ironies of the sort that become apparent when we hear English colonists clamoring to secure "gold showing mountains" in opposition to *Spanish* greed abound in English colonial discourse. Another profound irony is the fact that although the Chesapeake outpost had been conceived to serve as a base for privateering and warfare, Jamestown survived mainly because it took root during a time of peace. Earlier attempts to establish settlements on the Outer Banks had been short-circuited in 1585 and 1587, the first retreating to England after one winter, and the second abandoned when "the threat of the Spanish Armada caused the government to detain all ships."[44] It was the 1604 Treaty of London, which sealed Britain's participation in Philip III's *Pax Hispanica*, that allowed the Stuart regime the opportunity to extend its sphere of influence into the Atlantic world. With the international conflict momentarily in abeyance, the new Anglo-Scottish dynasty could now project its colonial activities beyond the Irish Sea in the manner the Elizabethans had imagined.[45]

But Spain still reserved its prewar monopoly on American trade, which kept the English in a difficult position.[46] Whereas Elizabethans like Hakluyt had seen western planting as a means to "annoy" or "bridle" the Spanish king, the commission of the Virginia Council included the "instruction (to avoide all danger of quarrell with the subjects of the King of Spaine) not to touch upon and of his dominions actually possessed, or rightly entituled unto."[47] What constituted actual possession or right entitlement remained a difficult question. As had Hakluyt before him (and as would Samuel Purchas during the more antagonistic political climate of the 1620s), Virginia colonist William Strachey declared that "the King of Spayne . . . hath no

Figure 5.2. Theodore de Bry's images meet Las Casas's text: *Narratio Regionum Indicarum per Hispanos Quosdam devastatarum verissima* (Oppenheim, 1614). Courtesy of the Folger Shakespeare Library.

more Title nor colour of title to this place ... which we by our industry and expenses have only made ours ... then hath any Christian Prince, (or then we, or any other Prynce, maye have to his Mexico, and Peru, or any dominions ells, of any free State or Kingdome:) how neere soever the West-Indies, and Florida, may ioyne thereunto, and lye under the same portion of Heaven."[48] Though many in Europe had long questioned the legitimacy of the Papal Donation of 1493, it would have been both imprudent and politically dangerous to utter such sentiments publicly, especially during a time of tenuous peace.[49]

Technically, Virginia did lie within the King of Spain's dominions. What is more, the Spanish had previously established a mission in the Chesapeake, though it was short-lived, at a site very near the Jamestown plantation. Earlier still they had picked up a Powhatan prince, who, baptized Luís de Velasco, had sailed to Spain, Havana, and Mexico City before he was bought back to rejoin to his people in September 1570. As a result of explorations in north Florida, however, the overextended Iberians seem to have recognized the limited value of the region for their colonial purposes.[50] "To maintain Florida is merely to incur expenses because it is and has been entirely unprofitable, nor can it sustain its own population" wrote Alonso Suárez de Toledo to Philip II in July of 1587: "What would happen to foreigners there who must bring their subsistence from a great distance to an inhospitable coast? The land itself would wage war on them."[51]

The strategy of disengagement Suárez suggested continued to make sense. Although some forty years earlier they had dealt with the French Huguenot plantation at Fort Caroline in the most severe way possible, in the early seventeenth century, with James I now a pensioner of Philip III, the Spanish chose not to police the Chesapeake with forces that could be better employed elsewhere.[52] The Virginia colony was on the verge of collapse throughout its early years after all, which the Spanish seem to have known. Extant documents confirm that Spanish officials, including the infamous ambassador, Don Diego Sarmiento de Acuña, the Count of Gondomar, were kept abreast of developments in the Chesapeake by Diego de Molina, who had been captured by (or planted among) the English in 1611. Informers also seem to have been enlisted from the English ranks.[53]

With the colony kept under such scrutiny, it is understandable that an atmosphere of deep mistrust prevailed in Jamestown. Accusations of foreign collusion, some of them warranted, were rife. As the Irish spy Francis Maguel reported in a deposition given to Fray Florencio Conryo at Madrid on July 1, 1610, "they have tried in that James-fort of theirs an English captain, a Catholic, called Captain Tindol, because they knew that he wanted to come to Spain to reveal to His Majesty what goes on in that land and many pretensions of the English which he knew."[54] Captain George Kendall (ca. 1570–1607), the "Tindol" to whom Maguel referred, was shot by a firing squad in Virginia, while the "hispanyolated Inglisheman Limbrecke [called Francisco Lembri in the Spanish sources]" was "hanged upp att the yardes Arme" before his case could be heard in London.⁵⁵ A number of reputations were irreparably impugned by accusations of double-dealing, including that of the first Company president, Edward Maria Wingfield, who by May 1608 had already returned to England to answer charges. "It is noysed that I Combyned with the Spanniards to the destruccion of the Collony," he wrote,

> That I ame an Atheist because I Carryed not a Bible, with me, and because I did forbid the preacher to preache, that I affected a Kin[g]dome: That I did hide of the Comon provision in the ground /
> I Confesse I have always admyred any noble vertue and prowesse as well in the Spanniards (as in other Nations) but naturally I have alwayes distrusted, and disliked their neighborhoode.⁵⁶

On the Spanish side, during the 1611 incursion that had landed Molina, Antonio Pérez (who died during his Virginia captivity), and Limbrecke in Jamestown, Virginia Company pilot John Clark (1573–1623) had been kidnapped and would be transported to Havana and then on to Seville for yet another interrogation before a prisoner exchange enabled him to return to Virginia in 1619.⁵⁷ Although Smith himself had left the colony prior to the appearance of Molina, Pérez, and Limbrecke, he was certainly involved in the "disgrace" of Wingfield and the discovery and judgment of the "dangerous conspiracy, for which Captaine Kendall as principal, was by a Jury condemned and shot to death."⁵⁸ As late as 1613, James I's ambassador John Digby wrote from Madrid that "[the Spanish] understood that our Plantation in Virginea is likely to sinke itselfe."⁵⁹ So at Jamestown the English lived in fear, having good reason to believe that a Spanish attack could wipe out them at any moment.⁶⁰ Years later Smith would recall that when his scouts reported the arrival of the company's third provisioning in 1609, "little dreaming of any such supply," he "supposed them Spaniards."⁶¹

Enlarging the Gospel

While Spain's militantly Catholic ethos has received endless commentary, the role of religion in England's colonial pretensions has been much more difficult to bring into focus.⁶² To get a sense of how indistinct English religious goals were by comparison, we need turn no further than Hakluyt's *Discourse of Western Planting* (1584). While the unpublished manifesto listed evangelism first among its twenty-one advertised goals, claiming "This westerne discoverie will be greately for thinlargement [sic] of the gospell of Christe," this priority yielded quickly to a long list of propositions "concerninge the greate necessitie and manifolde commodities that are like to growe to this realme of Englande by the westerne discoveries lately attempted."⁶³ Without an institutionalized culture of professional missionaries to undertake this proposed evangelization, English Protestants had no option but to theorize other means of spreading the Word.

Smith had comparatively little to say about the Virginia Colony's missionary potential, and would have known Hakluyt's published volumes rather than the *Discourse*. However, Thomas Hariot's early claim that the natives "may in short time be brought to civilitie, and the embracing of true religion"⁶⁴ squared wishfully with the Hakluyt master plan. In this spirit James I revisited the issue nearly twenty years later, inserting a clause into the Virginia Company Charter that emphasized the priority of evangelization. The instructions prepared for Governor Sir Thomas Gates on the occasion of his voyage insisted that the conversion of the Indians to Christianity was "the most noble and pious end" of the colony.⁶⁵

To discourage Indian collusion with Spain, the English of Virginia attempted to mobilize the Hispanophobic discourse that had proved so useful to the Protestant cause at home. As the Irishman Maguel disclosed, "messengers say that those who are in [West] India treat their natives very badly, and like slaves, and the English tell [the Powhatans] that those people are very cruel and wicked, meaning the Spaniards."⁶⁶ William Crashaw also alluded to the tyrannous example of the Spanish in defending the colony's actions, stating that "we will take nothing from the Savages by power nor pillage, by craft nor violence . . . (as some other Christian nations have done, to the dishonor of religion)."⁶⁷ Though their sovereign James had once proclaimed, "Lett us abhorre the bestlie Indians whose unworthie particulars made the way patent of their miserable subjection and slaverie to the Spaniard," the English argued that bringing the Indians to "civility" would glorify God while simultaneously doing a great service to humanity. Citing the influence of the Romans and later Christian disciples on English culture, Crashaw recalled "the time was when we were savage and uncivill, and worshipped the divell, then God sent some to make us civill, others to make us Christians."⁶⁸ This evangelical precedent was invoked by William Strachey as well, who went so far as to proclaim that the "'Angli' should play the part of 'Angells' in converting the Americans."⁶⁹

Contrary to the Iberians, who marshaled considerable resources in their attempts to enact comprehensive strategies for the instruction and conversion of the Amerindians, the English were at a bit of a loss as to how to carry out a Protestant mission. Once on the ground, the colonists found it more difficult to elicit the "fearful love" they claimed to be offering in contradistinction to Spanish cruelty.⁷⁰ A 1610 encounter narrated by George Percy is telling enough that it bears lengthy quotation:

draweinge my sowldiers into Battalio . . . we fell in upon them putt some fiftene or sixtene to the Sworde and Almoste all the reste to flyghte Whereupon . . . my Lieftenantt bringeinge wᵗʰ him the Quene and her Children and one Indyann prisoners for the wch I taxed him becawse he had Spared them his answer was thatt haveinge them now in my Custodie I mighte doe wth them whatt I pleased. Upon the same I cawsed the Indians heade to be cutt of[f]. And then di[sp]ersed my fyles Apointeinge my Sowldiers to burne their howses and to cutt downe their Corne groweinge aboutt the Towne, And after we marched wth the quene and her Children to our Boates againe, where beinge no sooner well shipped my sowldiers did begin to murmur becawse the quene and her Children were spared. So upon the same A Cowncell beinge called itt was Agreed upon to putt the Children to deathe the wch was effected by Throweinge them overboard and shoteinge owtt their Brayns in the water yett for all this Crewellty the Sowldiers weare nott well pleased And I had mutche to doe To save the quenes lyfe for that Time.[71]

Percy's is a story is as worthy of "discovery" as the incidents brought to light by Las Casas, all the more so as the "quene" was taken ashore and "putt . . . to the Sworde" during the return to Jamestown.[72] In an age of exemplary violence the English were as adept as any nation.

Still, as Hakluyt had recommended, "Godliness is great riches, and that if we first seek the kingdom of God, all other things will be given unto us."[73] True to this vocation, the English put most of their trust in trade. This notion of "civilizing through exchange" may have differentiated their colonial enterprise from Spain's conquests in the minds of many Englishmen, but it was also recognized that their largely mercantile approach had its limitations.[74] Thus more proactive strategies were also suggested. Among the original instructions issued to Gates was that the English should "procure from [the Amerindians] some convenient number of their children to be brought up in [the English] language, and manners."[75] Before the "Great Massacre of 1622" dramatically altered Anglo-Powhatan relations, a college was established at Henrico to aid this process. George Thorpe would arrive in 1620 with a commission to oversee the project, "which would allow Indian children to live among the English to be converted."[76] But with Thorpe's death in the troubles that ensued a scant two years later, the college died with him, as did the practice of "entertayninge [the Indians] in our howses, as if it were possible to Cohabitt with us."[77]

Economics and education were not the only civilizing avenues open to the English, who also brought with them more strongly coercive theories of assimilation. To overcome native resistance and speed evangelization "His Majesties Counsell" recommended, "seise into . . . custody half their corne and harvest and their Werowances and . . . known successors . . . and educate those which are younge . . . in your manners and religion, their people will easily obey you and become in time civill and Christian."[78] Even more radically, it was suggested that the colony might take all the Powhatan religious leaders prisoner in order to make this task easier. Gates was even authorized to kill these "murtherers of souls and sacrificers of gods Images to the Divell" for the sake of advancing the Christian cause.[79] These colonial policies bear an uncanny resemblance to the strategies reputed to have been used by the Spanish in Mexico and Peru. Fortunately, disinterest among the Powhatans, who seemed largely "uninterested in trading their faith for the English church," coupled with a "general lack of missionary zeal" among the colonists, seems to have precluded putting these measures into action.[80]

If the advancement of profit was as acceptable a way of increasing both God's glory and English honor, for most colonists the choice between the two was clear.[81] This is not to say that there were not some notable Protestant conversions in the early period of settlement. The English had christened the Croatoan Manteo within a week of their initial encounter with his people, and spoke of his having become "a most faithful English man."[82] But Manteo's presence in Roanoke did not avert the dissolution and disappearance of the colony. Indeed it helped to fuel the Roanoke mystery: did "CROATOAN" mean Manteo had betrayed the English, or could the colonists have wandered off to join his kinsmen? A far more exemplary conversion, of course, was that of Pocahontas, who according to Alexander Whitaker, "had openly renounced her country idolatry, confessed the faith of Jesus Christ, and was baptized—which thing Sir Thomas Dale had labored a long time to ground in her."[83]

The fullness of Indian conversion, however, was always deeply problematic. The Amerindians may have tended to incorporate whatever Christian cosmology they were offered into their own belief systems, and thus, as ethnohistorian Frederic Gleach has argued, could "accept the English God without giving up their own."[84] The problem of religious heterodoxy among "converts" would vex English observers for years to come, just as it did the Spanish in Latin America.[85] Spiritual and cultural retrogression were common patterns in the colonial world, and probably explain Don Luis de Velasco's abandonment of Spain's Chesapeake mission in the early 1570s.[86] As the Protestant faith practiced by the English lacked a principle of accommodation such as that developed by the Jesuits, it offered little room for either cultural difference or gradual assimilation to Christian culture and ideology.[87] Yet this did not inhibit them from declaring a primarily religious motivation in official colonial advertisements:

> The Principal and Maine Endes . . . were first to preach and baptize into Christian Religion, and by propagation of the Gospell . . . to endeavour the fulfilling, and accomplishment of the number of the elect, which shall be gathered from out all corners of the earth; and to add our myte to the Treasury of Heaven . . . to the ripening and consummation thereof.[88]

But while the salvation English Protestantism offered could be personal or national, it could never where the Indians were concerned be corporate. England's motivations were mercantile, and their faith was far too nationalistic to offer the Indians a substantial stake in either earthly fellowship or paradisiacal "Treasury." After the 1622 coup, Sir Francis Wyatt would declare, "Our first worke is expulsion of the salvages to gaine the free range of the countrey for encrease of Cattle, swine &c which will more then restore us, for it is infinitely better to have no heathen among us, who at best were but thornes in our sides, then to be at peace and league with them."[89] Even as they raised the specter of the Spanish conquests in order to justify their own Indian policy, the Council of Virginia addressed the problem in this way:

> to preach the Gospell to a nation conquered, and to set their soules at liberty, when we have brought their bodies to slaverie; It may be a matter sacred in the Preachers, but I know not how justifiable in the rulers. Who for mere ambition, doe set upon it the glosse of religion. Let the divines of Salamanca, discusse that question how the possessor of the west Indies first destroied, and then instructed.
>
> [It is honorable profit if we] by way of marchandizing and trade, doe buy of them the pearles of the earth and sell to them the pearles of heaven.[90]

Though well aware of Spain's public debates and theoretical projections concerning Indian rights, the English had little interest in such philosophical abstraction. Instead they preferred to define themselves mainly in opposition to Spanish practice (even when those practices differed very little from their own). While it could be argued by Spain and her Roman Catholic allies that the conquest had "opened for missionaries the doors to the new Christendom, offsetting the loss the Church had suffered as a result of the Protestant Reformation," England's national adventure would be a far more private (and privatized) errand into the wilderness.[91]

Indeed, the missionary calling was one the English could never completely embrace. While the importance of preaching God's word continued to be argued by many, there remained in the Chesapeake "relatively few clerics of any sort."[92] It was complained before Parliament of a "want of able and conscionable ministers . . . in Virginia," where clergymen were "more likely to turn heathen, than to turn others to the Christian faith."[93] Describing his countrymen as "making religion their color, when their aim was nothing but present profit, as most plainely appeared, by sending us so many Refiners, Gold-smiths, Jewellers, Lapidaries, Stone-cutters, Tobacco-pipe-makers, Imbroderers, Perfumers, Silke-men, with all their appurtenences," John Smith was among those who recognized this conflict of English interests.[94] "Religion above all things, should move us (especially the Clergie) if wee were religious, to shewe our faith by our workes," he wrote, once again finding the example of Spain apposite: "in converting those poor salvages, to the knowledge of God, see what paines the Spanyards take to bring them to their adulterated faith."[95] The mining, manufacturing, and agricultural enterprises of the English were unfocused and haphazard, but their missionary endeavors were even more so.

The Contemptible Trade of Fish

Any consideration of England's colonial errand must inevitably confront the tension between prophecy and profit. Throughout his career Richard

Hakluyt repeated in various ways the claim that "nothing more glorious or honorable can be handed doune to the future than to tame the barbarian, to bring back the savage and the pagan to the fellowship of civil existence and to induce reverence for the Holy Spirit into atheists and others distant from God."[96] But it was to the contraction of English overseas markets, along with an attendant speculation about what might be done to improve England's commercial situation, that Hakluyt gave the most ink. This is not to say that affairs of religion and commerce were not related; as D. W. Meinig has written, "the pressures of the Reformation progressively narrowed and compressed the area of free-ranging Atlantic outreach," in which "seafarers from half a dozen maritime districts from the Biscayan ports to the Bristol Channel [had] probed and gleaned the North American Coast during the early years of the [sixteenth] century."[97] What seems to have moved Hakluyt to write, as much as his Protestantism, was his deep sense that "englishe trades are growen beggarly or daungerous in all the kinge of Spayne his domynyons," and that "this western voyage will yelde unto us all the commodities of Europe, Affrica, and Asia as farr as wee were wonte to travell, and supplye the wantes of all our decayed trades."[98] One phrase deserves repeated emphasis: *in all the kinge of Spayne his domynyons*.

Although David Armitage has recently criticized our tendency to place Richard Hakluyt among England's "apocalypticists," what made Hakluyt the prophet of English profit—whether he saw England as entering the international struggle against antichrist or was more concerned with economics—was that he believed entry into the Atlantic world was vital to his nation's success in an increasingly international marketplace.[99] A longtime pensioner of the Clothworkers' Company, Hakluyt had come to see that England's economic well-being was to a large degree determined internationally.[100] The Iberian realignment of the early 1580s complicated an already difficult situation, and Hakluyt was clearly disturbed by England's worsening trade deficit, perceiving that "these eighteene yeres most cruell civill warres have . . . spoiled the traficque" with "all Flaunders and the lowe Contries [sic]."[101] His observations about England's difficult situation vis à vis an economic and ideological struggle grown increasingly global were astute. England's northern markets had worsened significantly even as participation in them had become more costly; dynastic changes in the south had resulted in stiffened competition worldwide, so that even England's former trade monopoly with Muscovy had been undermined. Since Iberia and the Netherlands had been linked commercially and dynastically for generations, their years of war with Spain had forced the Dutch to seek aggressively markets farther north, where they had shoved the English aside.[102] And with their long-time trading partner, Portugal, now centered within the Spanish Empire, the English found it more difficult to play the middlemen with their northern commercial affiliates. More than any of his English contemporaries, Hakluyt seems to have had a sense that

Europe had undergone a structural shift, and that if his nation did not respond creatively, the effects would soon be disastrous.

Unfortunately, there would be little in Virginia to improve deficits of trade or religion. Though a future of agricultural production might be speculated, and lists of potentially profitable commodities drawn up, entry into the Powhatan economy promised no immediate returns.[103] Timber, corn, and turkey did not an empire make, which helps to account for the persistence of the English search for precious metals. And even if gold or silver were to be discovered, the English were in no position to erect an infrastructure capable of mining, smelting, refining, transporting, and defending these resources.

Smith seems to have been of two minds about the prospect of large-scale trans-Atlantic settlement of the kind in which the Iberians were engaged. On the one hand, he argued that a Virginia plantation could help ameliorate his nation's overpopulation in the short run, which could eventually lead to the development of profitable agricultural commodities.[104] "Now he knows little," the Captain wrote in the *Description of New England* (1616), "that knowes not England may well spare many more people then Spaine."[105] To the end of his days he would draw attention to the fact that "here in Florida, Virginia, New-England, and Cannada [sic], is more land than all of the people in Christendome can manure, and yet more to spare than all the natives of those Countries can use and culturate."[106] But on the other, as Smith weighed the cost of the labor and resource intensive model as developed by Spain, versus the "empire of trade" the Netherlanders had begun to find so profitable, he observed: "What voiages and discoveries, East and West, North and South, yea about the world, make [the Dutch]? What an Army by Sea and Land have they long maintained, in despight of one of the greatest Princes in the world, and never could the Spaniard with all his Mines of Gold and Silver, pay his debts, his friends, and Army, half so truly as the Hollanders still have done by [their] contemptible Trade of Fish."[107] Smith recognized that conquest in the imperial mode might make a rapid colonial extension possible; but he also saw that it was the maintenance of empire that could be debilitating over the long haul.

Ruminations such as these have led Karen Ordahl Kupperman to see Smith as a forward-looking figure, whose "true radicalism" was to reject "the Elizabethan colonial tradition that focused on immense wealth won through exploits of great daring: raids on the Spanish treasure fleet or marches through hostile territory to discover mines."[108] Kupperman argues that "Smith's sympathies were all with the merchants because he saw [that] Colonial ventures were better run when merchants were in control, and [that] their activities would help build the nation's economy while they made their own fortunes."[109] But if Smith, as *The General Historie* indicates, came to see that England's colonial future, like that of "the warlike Hollanders," rested in a trade that could "afford as good gold as the Mines of Guiana or Potassie, with lesse hazard and charge, and more certainty and facility," he seems to have done so because he saw that the English lacked human resources and experience as much as material support.[110] He wrote in 1616 that

> it is not a work for everyone, to manage such an affaire as makes a discoverie, and plants a Colony: It requires all the best parts of Art, Judgement, Courage, Honesty, Constancy, Diligence and Industrie to doe but neere well. . . . Columbus, Cortez, Pitzara, Soto, Magellanes, and all the rest served more then a prentisship to learne how to begin their most memorable attempts in the West Indies.[111]

It was this "prentisship" that Smith saw the English lacking, an apprenticeship he believed the Dutch had gained in the fishing trade, even as the Iberians had similarly trained themselves in preparation for their great New World discoveries.[112]

If Smith would have the English emulate the hit and run tactics of the Dutch Sea Beggars—who from about 1580 had been exceedingly successful in their "global war" against Iberian interests—can we call this "true radicalism," or a rejection of "wealth won through exploits of great daring"?[113] Could a writer who as late as 1631 closed his *Advertisements* with an encomium "to the incomparable Sir Francis Drake, the renowned Captain Candish, Sir Richard Luson, Sir John Hawkins, Captaine Carlile, and Sir Martin Furbisher, etc."—going so far as to proclaim that it had been these English Sea Dogs who, "with many hundreds of brave English Souldiers, Captaines and Gentlemen" had "taught the Hollanders to do the like"—really have envisioned a brave new mercantilist world built upon a rejection of Elizabethan privateering values?[114] Indeed, the Dutch imperial vision Smith seems to favor may itself have been a kind of throwback. As Meinig has observed, "as an imperial type this Dutch creation was a maritime commercial system more like its older Mediterranean predecessors of Venice and Genoa than its Iberian rivals in the Atlantic."[115] By operating in an earlier, more "Mediterranean" imperial mode, the Dutch, like the Venetians and Genoans before them, had been able to maximize profits while minimizing investments. Forgoing large scale plantations and the subjection of native peoples in favor of isolated, easily defensible bases, they could funnel their resources into the construction of ships and the levying of mercenary soldiers and crewmen.[116] What must surely have made this older model attractive to a self-promoter like Smith were the possibilities it afforded for the advancement of experienced seafarers: witness the Genoan Christopher Columbus (upon whom Smith could not lavish too much praise), who in the service of Spain had risen from uncertain beginnings to Admiral of the Ocean Sea.

The specter of Spain thus haunted even the Dutch accomplishments Smith saw as so worthy of emulation. Having learned the seafaring trade and all that it entailed—which "Admirall" Smith, as he had begun to fashion himself, would detail in his works on seamanship—those who sailed under the flags of the Iberian kingdoms had been able to undertake "the wonder of all ages [which] successfully they effected, when many hundreds of others farre above them in the worlds opinion being instructed but by relation, came to shame and confusion in actions of small moment, who doubtlesse in other matters were both wise, discreet, generous and courageous."[117] Smith's indirection here may once again be politic; and though his precise referent is unclear, he seems to have been suggesting that his own nation, lacking experience in these matters, had been choosing colonists according to their ranks rather than their talents.[118]

Imperial Spain's "deductions of Colonies" and "attaining of conquests," which Hakluyt had written of so longingly in his Preface to the Second Edition of *The Principal Navigations* (1598)—alongside his erroneous speculation in the Second Edition's second volume (1599), that "the great & ample countrey of Virginia" was "so rich and abundant in silver mines"— would fuel expectations of easily acquired wealth among England's colonial promoters for decades to come.[119] Since, as Smith noted in the 1612 *Map of Virginia,* "many regions lying in the same latitude, afford mines very rich of diverse natures," it was understandable that English investors remained anxious to realize an immediate, Mexico-like profit.[120] Explaining the Company's failure to deliver the same in *The Proceedings of the English Colonie in Virginia* (1612), Smith wrote:

[our] temporall proceedings to some maie seeme too charitable to such a ... trecherous people: to others unpleasant that we washed not the ground with their blouds, nor shewed such strange inventions, in mangling, murdering, ransaking, and destroying (as did the Spaniards) the simple bodies of those ignorant soules; nor delightful because not stuffed with relations of heaps, and mines of gold and silver nor such rare commodities as the Portugals and Spaniards found in the East and West Indies. The want whereof hath begot us (that were the first undertakers) no lesse scorne and contempt, then their noble conquests and valiant adventures (beautified with it) praise and honor. Too much I confesse the world cannot attribute to their ever memorable merit.[121]

Clearly, Smith sees the conquista as so deserving of "praise and honor" that the world cannot ascribe "too much" of it to the Spaniards' "ever memorable merit." As he describes the "spoile and pillage" of Mexican plenty, and his own company's failure to produce the same, Smith acknowledges the "murdering, ransaking, and destroying" to which the Spanish had reputedly resorted. But rather than offering a condemnatory reinscription of Spain's more-than-Turkish cruelty in the Las Casas mode, Smith implies that had "Virginia bin [so] peopled" and "planted," the English would have both "done as much" and received equal "shame and infamy" as "recompense and reward."[122] At the same time, he recognizes that had the English been lucky enough to find themselves in a like situation, they might have behaved in an accordingly "Spanish" manner.

Let Your Poor Captain Speak

To the degree that Spain and Portugal have been "othered" by an Anglo-American historiographic tradition that venerates the national accomplishments of the Elizabethans and Jacobeans, many of the structural features of Atlantic society, especially its endemic racial problems, could be assigned Iberian roots—hadn't cruelty to the Indians and the African slave trade had origins in *them,* after all?[123] Among the things obscured by this tendency to accept the assumptions of *La leyenda negra* without examining the motivations behind its production and dissemination, is the degree to which the peoples of Britain and Iberia were among the co-participants in the development of the Atlantic world.[124]

And to the degree that we have seen the beginnings of England's colonial project as simultaneously an offshoot of the English "Renaissance" and a font of "Democratic" beginnings, we have tended to read the founding of Virginia in primarily Anglophilic terms. But let us not underestimate the degree to which Spain, even during the darkest days of Anglo-Hispanic conflict, remained as much England's model as its rival. Even as Richard Hakluyt had propagated Black Legend infamy in one breath, constructing "the Spaniard" as "the scourge of the world . . . Ravisher of virgins and wives," in another he appealed admiringly to the example of Isabella of Castile, who "laied her owne Jewells to gage for money to furnishe out Columbus . . . [which] the Princes of the [Protestant] Relligion (among which her majestie ys principall) oughte the rather to take in hande," a comparison clearly meant to inspire a similar devotion to colonial efforts in his own queen.[125]

Much in the manner of Hakluyt, John Smith visualized international linkages in the emerging Atlantic world. But unlike his more Hispanophobic contemporary, Smith seems to have seen the transoceanic dynamics in which he participated in terms that extended beyond the Us/Them binary we find in the militantly Protestant rhetoric that inhabits so much English colonial discourse. Thus we can glimpse in Smith's writing the pervasive Iberian cultural influence—technological, navigational, and economic as well as religiopolitical—that characterized the historical moment during which he wrote, an influence that he is much less ready to assign a strictly negative valence than many of his countrymen.

Smith's perspective on Iberia should also give us pause to consider how broadly the Spanish specter hovered over European culture at this early moment of transatlantic development. In his monumental study, *Civilization and Capitalism, 15th–18th Century,* Fernand Braudel offered what can serve as a partial corrective to our somewhat anachronistic Anglo-American enthusiasm. The early modern period was characterized by the "successive dominating influences" of European national styles, Braudel observed.[126] While the French style gradually came into favor during the course of the seventeenth century, "even in the Spanish territories," we should not fail to recall, that from the second half of the sixteenth century through the first two or three decades of the seventeenth, it was the Spanish fashion that had been most dominant, "a sign of the political preponderance of the Catholic King's 'world-wide" empire."[127]

Smith's English contemporary, the dramatist Ben Jonson (1573–1637), marked this broader Iberian cultural orientation in one of his most widely read plays, *The Alchemist* (ca. 1610), which provides a sense of the trend Braudel identified:

Aske from your courtier, to your innes of courtman,
To your mere millaner: they will tell you all,
Your *Spanish* jennet is the best horse. Your *Spanish*
Stoupe is the best garbe: Your *Spanish* beard
Is the best cut. Your *Spanish* ruffs are the best
Wear; your *Spanish* pavin the best dance;
Your *Spanish* titillation in a glove
The best perfume. And, for your *Spanish* pike,
And *Spanish* blade, let your poore Captain speak.[128]

Even granting Jonson's satirical slant, we can see Hispanophilia and Hispanophobia walking hand in hand in this passage, as they do at any number of moments in the corpus of England's colonial writing. While complicating the anti-Hispanism characteristic of so much contemporary religiopolitical discourse, Jonson's dramatization reveals how admiration and attraction could mix with resentment and fear, as the things that came by way of the Spains—the finest horses, articles of clothing, hair styles, entertainments and toiletries—were often judged to be of superior quality than their native counterparts and therefore became markers of status. Yet Jonson's comic lines assume a deadly serious tone when they turn suddenly to the technology of warfare, emblematized by the pikes and blades of which many a "poor [English] Captaine [could surely] speak."

Especially given the atmosphere of fear, intrigue, mistrust, and violence that hung about the Virginia operation, we might have reason to expect that Smith would have been gripped with far more of the Hispanophobia evident in the colonial writing of his English, Dutch, and French contemporaries than the Hispanophilia Jonson portrays.[129] While Smith often expressed nationalist sentiments, his discourse suggests that he stood at a remove from the xenophobic chauvinism that was so rampant at this moment in English history. Even when he writes of carrying out the nationalistic colonial projections theorized by writers like Hakluyt, Smith imagines himself as following in the New World footsteps of his Spanish predecessors. When we read Smith biographically—and everything about his writing suggests he begged to be read this way—it becomes clear that his narratives bespeak the values of martial heroism to which so many of Europe's early modern adventurers aspired. Indeed, as Pompa Banerjee's contribution to this volume shows, Smith's self-fashioning involved the internalization of European Romance narratives much in the manner of his Spanish heroes.[130] And unlike the English religiopolitical polemicists and propagandists who were his contemporaries, Smith never seems to evoke Hispanic typologies in order to discredit or delegitimize Spain's imperial accomplishments. When he *does* invoke them, it is in the spirit of constructing himself as the model *English* conquistador, on the one hand, and in an effort to persuade his English readers of his talents and self-importance, on the other. It is this intense Anglo-Hispanic identification which gives Smith's writing its odd refractory power, and a perspective on the Spanish specter seldom seen in the more partisan writings of his countrymen.

John Smith never ceased marveling at the magnitude of Spain's imperial success, including the military prowess and Machiavellian resourcefulness that had enabled it. Whereas Hakluyt had argued in the 1580s that it "would require more than one chapter" to discover Spain's New World atrocities,[131] John Smith preferred to praise Iberian accomplishments: "It would bee an historie of a large volume," he wrote in 1616, "to recite the adventures of the Spanyards, and Portugals, their affronts, and defeats, their dangers and miseries; which with such incomparable honor and constant resolution, so farre beyond beleefe, they have attempted and indured in their discoveries and plantations, as may well condemn us, of too much imbecillitie, sloth and negligence." In Smith's estimation the specter of this Spanish honor and resolution continued to humble the English. Far from seeing Spain lapsing into the "decadence" that would soon become an historiographic commonplace, nearly thirty years after the "inevitable" defeat of the Armada, Smith saw the Spanish imperial juggernaut rolling on. "Who seeth not what is the greatest good of the Spanyard," he wrote, "in searching those unknowne parts of this unknowne world?"[132]

The deference to Spain which surfaces in Smith's writing is not so far from the view that promoted the Spanish monarchy as divinely chosen to work in History. Smith may have glimpsed a future of trade and industry, but he did so more begrudgingly than prophetically. Whether on land or sea, Smith saw his profession above all else as a profession of arms. As such he stood in awe of the most inexplicable military accomplishment in the human record. And he never stopped trying to siphon off some this Spanish glory for himself. When, in *The Generall Historie,* we hear Smith begging his readership "peruse the Spanish Decades [of Richard Eden]" and "the Relations of Master Hackluit" to see "how many ever with such small means . . . did ever discover so many fayre and navigable Rivers, subject so many several Kings, people, and Nations, to obedience, and contribution, with so little bloodshed," we sense in his undeniably inflated estimation of the Virginia achievement a yearning, a wish that history, geography, and fortune had been kinder, and had offered England the possibility of conquest in the Spanish mode.[133]

To trace the Spanish specter through the layers of John Smith's discourse is to complicate the simplistic Us/Them antinomy around which the Black Legend was spun.[134] Indeed, in the rhetorical construction with which this essay began, Smith invoked a "Spanish" solution to the Virginia Company's difficulties. For when he drew attention to "his soldiers'" temptation "to abandon the country" and his own determination to "keep it," the English Captain placed himself on a par with the archetypal *conquistador* Cortéz: in Smith's words, the "worthy Ferdinando Courtus [who had] had scarce three hundred Spaniards to conquer the great Citie of Mexico."[135] At this moment, we catch Smith imagining himself the central figure in a foundational Jamestown moment quite unlike that which bore us representative democracy. His American dream has far more in common with that engineered by the Spanish Captain-General who had so legendarily founded New Spain, not only against all odds, but also against the judgment of his own less determined (and less heroic) countrymen, who would have preferred the possibility of a safe return to Cuba over the scuttling of their fleet at Vera Cruz. Its Black Legend reputation to the contrary, Spain remained at this early stage of English imperial aspiration not simply a measure of colonial excess, but a model for colonial success as well—as it would throughout the epoch of European expansion.

Chapter 6
The White Othello
Turkey and Virginia in John Smith's True Travels

POMPA BANERJEE

The Virginia Company was drawing up plans for a new colony in America when John Smith returned to England from his travels in the Ottoman Empire. It was 1605. Smith signed up, became a member of the council, and eventually went to Jamestown. The narrative of his Turkish adventures waited decades before it saw the light of print. Smith's account of his travels through the Ottoman Empire, *The True Travels, Adventures and Observations of Captaine John Smith, in Europe, Asia, Affrica, and America*, was finally published in 1630, decades after the events in Turkey, and long after Smith's experiences in Jamestown. Readers of *True Travels* often are perplexed by the long excerpts from the *Generall Historie of Virginia* and the seemingly irrelevant chapter on piracy that follow Smith's account of his Turkish travels. While the coupling of these two seemingly disparate narratives of Turkey and Virginia may be read as sloppy editing on Smith's part, the twinned narratives also point to the rhetorical function of Turkey as a resonant subtext to Smith's experiences in Virginia. By the end of the sixteenth century, Virginia was already part of the complex transactions in the Atlantic World, a vital site within the triangulated web of trade, slavery, and cultural exchanges that linked the New World, Africa, and Europe. However, we also need to take into account another space—Turkey—as a crucial site of exchange. In America, as Smith devoted himself to the survival of the fragile colony perched on the hostile eastern seaboard of a vast, alien continent, his experiences of another hostile geography, Turkey, bled into his narrative of Jamestown, commingling the stories of Virginia and Turkey into a single, multilayered narrative.

This essay highlights two aspects of Smith's adventures in the Ottoman Empire and their relevance to Jamestown with regard to trade, slavery, and colonization. The first section focuses on Smith's adventures in the Ottoman Empire, and his experiences as a sort of white Othello wandering over the Ottoman Empire, displaying fortitude and chivalry in situations fraught with peril and romance. This section of the essay also evaluates the lessons about miscegenation that Smith drew from his travels and from other colonial models. The second part of the essay centers on Smith's self-cultivation as an English gentleman in the Ottoman Empire, and his subsequent remodeling of that concept in Virginia. Smith's chapter on piracy appears as a plea to English pirates domiciled in the Ottoman Empire to renounce piracy, embrace versions of the new gentleman model, and become fruitfully engaged in the cultivation and seeding of the new Eden of Virginia.

Smith's text comes to us refracted through the lens of the larger mercantile, cultural, and imperial transactions of the English and other western Europeans who encountered the native tribes and the diverse cultures around the Mediterranean and the Atlantic. England's Atlantic ventures were intimately connected to English commerce and travels elsewhere. Travelers frequently traversed geographical boundaries, crossing from the center of their own spaces to the peripheries and margins of others as they negotiated the linked spaces of Ireland, North America, North Africa, and Turkey. Many Englishmen traveled in the East before coming to America. George Sandys traveled through Turkey, Palestine, Jerusalem, and North Africa before going to Jamestown in 1621 as the Virginia Company's resident treasurer. In 1563, the infamous mercenary Thomas Stukeley raised money in England to establish a colony in Florida but then used the ships and funds for piracy and freebooting on the Atlantic, eventually meeting his end fighting with Moroccan forces in the Battle of Alcazar.[1] Sir Anthony Sherley sailed through the West Indies before embarking on his more famous travels through the Levant and Persia. Sir Thomas Roe explored the Orinoco River with Sir Walter Ralegh before going to India in 1616 as James I's envoy to the Mughal emperor Jahangir. Nabil Matar notes, "Before John White drew Indians, he had drawn Turks and Levantines; before the Mayflower carried the so called 'Pilgrims' to Plymouth, it had traded in the Muslim Mediterranean." Furthermore, English colonists inscribed their Turkish experiences into the geography of the New World: Smith named Cape Ann as "Cape Tragabigzanda" after his mistress in the Ottoman Empire. He also named three islands close to Cape Cod "The Three Turkes heads."[2] Clearly, Smith's pairing of Turkey and Virginia in *The True Travels* reflected a conventional form of early modern crossover between diverse discourses.

By the time Smith published the account of his Turkish travels, extensive diplomatic and commercial ties existed between England and the Ottoman Empire. English trafficking in Turkey was officially sanctioned in the last three decades of the sixteenth century. In 1578 Sir William Harborne, Queen Elizabeth's envoy to the Turkish court, began diplomatic and commercial negotiations, and the Levant Company was founded in 1581. Yet in the 1580s the English had no colonies in Asia or America; in contrast, by the 1560s the Ottoman Empire was both powerful and fearful—in the words of Richard Knolles, the Elizabethan historian of the Turks, they were the "present Terrour of the World" and by the reign of Sultan Süleyman the Magnificent (1520–66), the empire was at its peak.³ The Turks controlled parts of North Africa and occupied the Holy Land, Greece, and the Balkans. In 1529 they crossed Hungary and threatened Vienna. The pervasive anxiety about Turks surfaced even in faraway Iceland, where Lutherans prayed to be saved from "the cunning of the Pope and the terror of the Turk." Bernard Lewis writes that this fear came true in 1627 when Barbary corsairs in Iceland carried several hundred captives to the slave markets of Algiers.⁴ Turkey's shadow also menaced Virginia: John Smith complained that the Turks had seized a ship sailing from Virginia to Spain. In 1625, William Bradford, the governor of Plymouth, recorded in his diary that Moroccan pirates had captured ships on their way to England to trade in beaver skins "almost within the sight of Plimoth."⁵

English representations of encounters with Turks and other Eastern peoples appear in early modern travelogues, English drama, captivity narratives, and texts such as John Smith's *True Travels*. Between 1581, the date of the establishment of the Levant Company, and the 1620s, several English plays dramatized the complex English responses to the Ottoman Empire. At times the Levant appeared as a submerged reference, as in *Macbeth* 1.3.7–8, which recalled the historic 1583 voyage of Ralph Fitch and Newberie to the Levant aboard the *Tiger*. More explicit treatments of the Turkish material appeared in English plays such as George Peele's The *Battle of Alcazar* (1588), Thomas Dekker's *Lusts Dominion* (1599), *The Famous History of the Life and Death of Captain Stukeley* (1605), and Philip Massinger's *The Renegado* (1624). Beyond the theater the English public also had access to the printed captivity narratives of several Englishmen who were captured in the Ottoman Empire; many of them chose to or were forced to "turn Turk."⁶

Taken together, the texts registered the Turks' formidable economic and military strength. Such recognitions often were based on the cross-cultural exchanges resulting from diplomatic ties between England and the Ottoman Empire, as well as increased English trafficking in vital Islamic commercial hubs such as Tunis, Algiers, and Tripoli. Predictably, many plays exoticized Turkish encounters and circulated rabidly anti-Ottoman cultural stereotypes, gradually constructing a generic anti-Islamic type that frequently conflated "Turk" and "Moor." Given the gap between Smith's Turkish adventures and their publication, the shadows of many such texts might lurk behind Smith's observations about Turkish customs and culture in the *True Travels*.

A White Othello

The True Travels was published in 1630 toward the end of Smith's life. The narrative recalls his youthful adventures, and hovers over the genres of travelogue, fiction, and secular autobiography. Smith did not offer a history in the manner of Richard Knolles's voluminous *The Generall Historie of the Turks* (London, 1603), an invaluable reference for diplomats, scholars, and travelers.[7] Yet Knolles never went to Turkey and did not have the language. Smith, on the other hand, did go to Turkey, although the confusion regarding names, places, and dates makes it difficult to separate fact from fiction. One scholar, for instance, notes Smith's "distinctly Falstaffian profile" and that "the cloth of truth has been patched out with colorful fabrications."[8] Others dismiss the entire text as fiction. Even as autobiography, its garbled names of places and people, confusing chronology, and notorious incoherence do not clarify details of Smith's lived experiences in Turkey. However, as Karen Kupperman observes, new evidence from ethnohistorians working on the Algonquians of eastern North America, as well as a more careful checking of sources, has revised the view of Smith the liar and braggart.[9] And Philip Barbour, the modern editor of Smith's text, notes there were not many models of secular autobiographies for Smith to follow, and most of his descriptions do match up with some of the complicated events on the ground at that time.[10] Establishing the status of Smith's text is beyond the scope of this essay, but whatever its status as a narrative—an outright work of fiction or an incredibly garbled version of some true experiences—Smith's text is worthy of sustained critical scrutiny. For Smith's Turkish adventures resonate beyond the Ottoman Empire and draw Jamestown into the web of the interconnected experiences that linked Europe with Africa, Asia, and America. As a colonist, and later as a historian of Jamestown, Smith himself put to many ideological uses his observations about his travels in the Ottoman Empire.

Smith's Turkish adventures seemed to have prepared him in many ways for his pivotal role in Virginia. After fighting alongside the Protestant Dutch against the Catholic Spanish army, Smith joined the Catholic Hapsburgs who were skirmishing with Turkish soldiers in Eastern Europe. According to Smith, his courage and magnificent exploits advanced him to the position of the commander of his regiment. He displayed extraordinary valor on and off the battlefield. One of his most significant achievements was a three-part single combat with three Turkish soldiers. As Smith tells it, during a temporary lull in the battle, the Turks and Christians were encamped side by side and the Turks derided the Christians who "grew fat for want of exercise."[11] The Turks sent a proposition to Smith's garrison to "delight the Ladies, who did long to see some court-like pastime." A Turk challenged the English to a single combat: whoever lost would lose his head. The Christians drew lots and it fell upon Smith to meet the challenge. He successively fought and beheaded three Turks—first Turbashaw, the Turkish lord, then the improbably named Grualgo, and finally, Bonny Mulgrow. With this chivalric triple feat, Smith was granted his own coat of arms featuring three Turks' heads (Figure 6.1).

Smith's story turned a corner when the Hapsburgs were defeated, and

The White Othello   139

Figure 6.1. "Three TURKS heads in a banner given him for Armes." John Smith, *True Travels* (London, 1630). Courtesy of the John Carter Brown Library, Brown University. This composite image shows a series of events that happened at different times. During the seige of a town in southern Transylvania in early 1602, Smith engaged in three public duels with Turkish officers (the first two were jousting matches). Each time, Smith won, cut off his opponent's head, and brought it back as a trophy for his general. Soon thereafter, the town fell to the Christian forces and Prince Zsigmond of Trannsylvania rewarded Smith with an insignia bearing three Turks' heads.

Smith was captured. Captivity and slavery followed: "at Axopolis they were all sold for slaves, like beasts in a market-place" (Figure 6.2). Smith was sold and sent to Constantinople, "to his faire Mistresse for a slave. By twentie and twentie chained by the neckes, they marched in file to this great Citie, where they were delivered to their severall Masters, and he to the young Charatza Tragabigzanda." Smith's dark mistress possibly feared her mother would sell him, or perhaps she planned for him to join the Turkish army; at any rate, she sent him for training to Tartaria, by her brother Tymor. There, the brutality of Smith's new master opened a new chapter in Smith's life: "All the hope he had ever to be delivered from this thraldome, was only the love of Tragabigzanda, who surely was ignorant of his

Figure 6.2. "Capt. SMITH led Captive to the BASHAW of NALBRITS in TARTARIA." John Smith, *True Travels* (London, 1630). Courtesy of the John Carter Brown Library, Brown University. During the "dismall battell" at Rottendon, Smith was wounded and left for dead on the battlefield. When he showed signs of life, he was enslaved, taken to Constantinople, and then sent across the Black Sea to Tartary. There he was stripped, his head and beard were shaved, and an iron collar was fitted around his neck. Eventually, Smith killed his master with a scythe and escaped.

bad usage." One day Smith "beat out the *Tymors* braines with his threshing bat." He put on his captor's clothes, hid the body under the straw, filled his knapsack with corn, shut the doors, mounted his horse, and "ranne into the desart at all adventure." With the iron collar still on, Smith traveled across the Ottoman Empire to a Muscovite garrison in Russia. Among the Russians, Smith experienced a fleeting romance and spiritual regeneration: "The governor after due examination of those his hard events, tooke off his irons, and so kindly used him, he thought himself new risen from death, and the good lady Callamata, largely supplied all his wants."[12] The good lady Callamata did not reappear in Smith's narrative, but Smith's sense of himself as "newly risen from death" remained as he made his way through Lithuania, Transylvania, the German lands, France, Spain, and

North Africa back to London, where he signed up to become a member of the Virginia Company council.

It is difficult to assess how much or in precisely what ways Smith's travels over the Levant, eastern Europe, and North Africa colored his Virginian experiences or shaped his handling of the infant colony in Jamestown. But the triangulation of the New World encounters indicates that Smith's travels in the Ottoman Empire cannot be radically dissociated from his subsequent American experiences: one encounter seeped into the other. Smith always maintained that his Eastern adventures qualified him for the job in Virginia. Before coming to America, before leading the Chesapeake explorations, and before Jamestown, Smith learned critical skills. Elsewhere, he noted that "The Warres in Europe, Asia, and Affrica taught me how to subdue the wilde Savages In Virginia and New-England, in America."[13] And even the sketchy details in *The True Travels* suggest that Smith drew key lessons from his experiences in the Middle East and Africa.

In particular, Smith studied the Portuguese colonial model carefully. He appeared to have learned from both the success and the failure of the Portuguese exploits in Africa. His "African" lessons echoed similar lessons learned by the English in Turkey and echoed as well English experiences in Virginia. First, Smith, like Hakluyt, was haunted by England's belated entry into the transoceanic scene and by the *imperial* and so far unrealized potential of aggressive trade. He noted that all over Asia and Africa, the Portuguese "have subjected many great Kingdomes, erected many Common-wealths, built many great and strong Cities." His ensuing question, "and where is it they have not beene by trade or force?" appears to be a prescient understanding of the vastly different English colonial models in America and Asia; that is, the imperial possibilities of aggressive trade—the case of India—and outright force—the case of America. Furthermore, before going to Virginia, Smith seemed to have grasped the central "flaw" in the Iberian colonial paradigm, a flaw that the English would strive not to replicate in Virginia.[14] Smith noted that despite their remarkable exploits, the Portuguese failed to prevail in their farflung outposts because they dissipated their energies, mingled with the local populations, and went native. The Portuguese were "scattered; living so amongst these Blacks, by time and cunning they seeme to bee naturalized amongst them."[15] The collapse of white European Portuguese colonists into "these Blacks" suggests that a model of colonization based on miscegenation and "mingling" would surely destroy a sense of Englishness and English identity in America.

Smith recognized that the Portuguese had fallen prey to the cultural perils of global exchange. Yet although the diverse cultural and racial spaces of the Atlantic and Mediterranean regions threatened to converge in the New World, Smith sought to preserve those distinctions in Jamestown. His recognition that going native damaged Portuguese racial and military superiority in Africa is also echoed in the experiences of the Jamestown colonists. Although Smith dispersed many Englishmen to live among the native tribes to learn survival skills in that environment, his key focus was the integrity and survival of the young colony. Apart from the runaways during the starving years, or the children and interpreters left with native tribes on purpose by the English, or the celebrated case of Pocahontas and John Rolfe, there were few cases of English colonists going native with the explicit blessings of the English.

Smith's countrymen had come to similar conclusions in the Ottoman Empire. English travelers such as Fynes Moryson emphasized that "mixture" bred degeneration. In 1596 Moryson noticed that the common tradesmen in Jerusalem were irrevocably debased, "in generall poore rascall people, mingled of the scumme of diuers Nations, partly Arabians, partly Moores, partly the basest inhabitants of neighbour Countries."[16] Cross-racial offspring, products of "mingling," Moryson suggested, made for poor tradesmen and poor citizens; they were "the scumme of diuers Nations." Such racial muddling collapsed differences between the English and their various others in distant settlements of the world. As we shall see, Smith's "lesson," drawn from the Portuguese African ventures, was affirmed by English travelers in the Ottoman Empire.

Other Europeans confirmed Smith's awareness of the cultural perils of miscegenation. English staging of cross-racial relationships was fraught with extreme anxiety. English drama reinforced the value of "undiluted" European blood that Smith had recognized in Portuguese colonial relations. *The Famous History of Captain Thomas Stukeley* (1605), an anonymous play, elevated the status of "pure" European soldiers over cross-racial peoples. When King Sebastian of Portugal received Spanish military aid for his African campaigns, he treasured the "gallant Spanish bloud" of men born "pure," not of "Indian or Base bastard Moore" (19: 2333–35).[17] In *Othello*, Shakespeare's hero assumed Turkish absolutism and tyranny. Consequently, Othello's murder of Desdemona as well as his suicide validated European stereotypes of the "malignant Turk" (5.2.351).[18] In Dekker's *Lusts Dominion* the Queen Mother frets about the impending birth of a child: "What shape will this prodigious womb bring forth, / Which groans with such strange labour?" (161)[19] A product of miscegenation between Eléazar the Moor and the Spanish Queen Mother, the child's monstrosity is inevitable.

The fear of the unknown, signaled by the impending birth of a misshapen prodigy, positioned Englishmen as especially vulnerable in sexual liaisons with their racial others. Yet cross-racial sexual encounters would inevitably muddle racial and cultural distinctions, thereby replicating the Portuguese colonial failures that Smith had studied. Contemporary English plays capitalized on this fear by highlighting the supposedly uncontrollable lust of Islamic women. Philip Massinger's *The Renegado* (1624) contrasted the chastity of the Christian Paulina with the sexual excesses of "Turkish dames" who were akin to chained "English mastiffs" that turned, when unleashed, to ferocious orgies of bloodlust (1.3.8–13). The analogy between degenerate Turkish women and untamed, vicious dogs worked because such references to mastiffs were familiar to English audiences.[20] But the reference to English mastiffs also uncannily inverted English experiences in the New World. In *The Renegado* the lustful Turkish ladies are compared to fierce mastiffs; yet, as we know, the Algonquians were terrified of the mastiffs that the English transported to Virginia. Virginia, then, becomes a subtext of both Massinger's play and of English experiences with Turkish women in the East.

Smith's *The True Travels* treads carefully around the issue of miscegenation. While the depiction of his enslavement by his female Turkish captor resonated with other English representations of miscegenation, Smith's encounter with his Turkish mistress appeared as well in strange correspondence to his Virginian experiences. Smith's account of Charatza Tragabigzanda may well have reminded readers of the manifold anxieties hovering around the experiences of Englishmen in racially different spaces such as Turkey or Virginia. As John Rolfe's letter to Sir Thomas Dale about his marriage to Pocahontas suggests, miscegenation was something to be feared in Virginia—as it was in Turkey. Rolfe's letter rested on an absolute denial of "unbridled desire of carnal affection," and his letter sought "any fit wholesome and apt applications to cure so dangerous an ulcer."[21] We do not know if in Turkey Smith himself had sought to cure such dangerous ulcers of his own. But Smith's account of Charatza Tragabigzanda allowed him to indulge in fantasies of cross-racial relationships even as he bypassed the perils of miscegenation.

In *The True Travels* Smith's Turkish lady appears in a brief interlude when Smith surfaces in his own narrative as a white Othello, a wanderer whose exotic tales find an enraptured female audience. The lady Charatza becomes Smith's tawny mistress in a sort of cross-cultural fantasy, a flirtation with miscegenation that did not entail the agonizing soul-searching evident in John Rolfe's letter about Pocahontas. The Turkish Charatza Tragabigzanda appeared as entranced by Smith's tales of adventures as Desdemona was with Othello: "This Noble Gentlewoman tooke sometime occasion to shew him to some friends, or rather to speake with him, because shee could speake Italian, would feigne her selfe sick when she should goe to the Banians, or weepe over the graves, to know how Bogoll tooke him prisoner." Smith's positioning of himself, like Othello, as a voyager to exotic climes, located his Turkish mistress as a tawny Desdemona enthralled with tales of dangerous feats, perilous journeys, and marvels such as "The Anthropophagi, and men whose heads / Do grow beneath their shoulders" (*Othello* 1.3.143–44). Asian, European, and American versions of the fictional Mediterranean lady Desdemona crowded Smith's narrative. Dedicating *The Generall Historie* to Frances, Duchess of Lennox, Smith recalled the kindness of other women:

> The beauteous Lady Tragabigzanda, when I was a slave to the Turkes, did all she could to secure me. When I overcame the Bashaw of Nalbrits in Tartaria, the charitable Lady Callamata supplyed my necessities. In the utmost of many extremities, that blessed Pocahontas, the great King's daughter of Virginia, oft saved my life. When I escaped the crueltie of Pirats and most furious stormes, a long time alone in a small Boat at Sea, and driven ashore in France, the good Lady Madam Chanoyes, bountifully assisted me.[22]

The beautiful, bounteous, and influential women who presided like benevolent deities on Smith's adventures passed in and out of Smith's narrative, one figure summoning up the other. Smith's sympathetic Turkish mistress Charatza Tragabigzanda appeared in *The True Travels*, but also evoked the figure of Pocahontas in Smith's Virginian narrative. In *The Generall Historie*, Smith noted that during his brief captivity in Virginia, he was brought before Powhatan, with his head placed on two large stones "and being ready with their clubs, to beate out his braines." Then "Pocahontas, the King's dearest daughter, when no intreaty could prevaile, got his head in her armes and laid her owne upon his to save him from death." We do not know whether Smith saw in the young Pocahontas a glimpse of his vanished Turkish mistress, but Pocahontas also appears to prefigure Smith's other female representations. The Muscovite Lady Callamata who supplied Smith's wants during his flight from captivity and slavery also recalls the generous Pocahontas who "brought him so much provision that saved many of their lives that els for all this had starved with hunger."[23]

Although Pocahontas reappeared several times in *The Generall Historie*, in *The True Travels* Smith's romantic Turkish imaginary remained incomplete; he did not flesh out the fantasy, and the lady Charatza Tragabigzanda remained a hazy prototype of Pocahontas and other patronesses. In this context, use of words such as "prefigure" and "prototype" indicates the tangled chronology at work: Smith supposedly encountered both Charatza and the lady Callamata long before he saw Pocahontas, but he wrote about the Turkish lady (as well as Callamata) long *after* he met Pocahontas. It is difficult to say with certainty who prefigured whom. The two ladies, Turkish and Algonquian, shadow each other much like Smith's twinned narratives of Turkey and Virginia.

Smith's linking of Turkey with Virginia in his *True Travels* also blurred the discourses that characterized the triangulated spaces under discussion. Turkey recalled Ireland; the Turks shadowed the Native Americans. In Dekker's play *Lusts Dominion*, Turks and Moors morphed into American Indians or perhaps those other Indians—from India. The lustful Moor Eléazar is a "slave of Barbary" (103), but he is simultaneously an "Indian slave" (142) who swears by "all our Indian gods" (164). English travelers frequently transposed one space onto another. In 1617, Fynes Moryson compared the lawlessness in some parts of the Ottoman Empire with the lawless wild Irish: "The Arabians are not unlike the wild Irish, for they are subject to the great Turke, yet being poore and farre distant from his imperiall seat, they cannot be brought to due obedience, much lesse to abstaine from robberies."[24] Henry Blount's *A Voyage into the Levant* (1636) also blurred geographical metaphors. Writing about his travels through North Africa and the Ottoman Empire, Blount relied upon Ireland to describe Turkey to his readers: "for through all *Turky*, especially in places *desert* there are many *Mountainers*, or *Outlawes*, like the wild *Irish* who live upon spoyle, and are not held members of the State, but enemies, and used accordingly."[25] For Englishman Thomas Herbert, African and Irish dialects bestially coupled in linguistic "miscegenation": African dialects were "apishly sounded" because they were "voyced like the Irish."[26] Smith himself negotiated the triangulated reality of the Atlantic world by relying on Ireland to illustrate Turkey and on Turkey to depict Virginia. Chronicling the Turkish manner of living, Smith invoked Ireland: Turkish houses were "much worse than your Irish."[27] However, in America, Virginian customs became more comprehensible when explained with reference to Turkey. Describing the social protocols of native households in Virginia, Smith noted "If any great commander arrive at the habitation of a Werowance, they spread a Mat as the Turkes doe a Carpet for him to sit upon."[28] Displaced into "mixed" analogies, anxieties about racial mingling recurrently surfaced in English drama and travelogues, linking the disparate spaces of America, Africa, Europe, and the Levant through similar metaphors for alterity.

Smith the Gentleman

As the English encountered the hazards of commercial and imperial transactions with various cultures around the Mediterranean and the Atlantic, ripples of those encounters reached the New World. Via Smith, Jamestown became the site where many of those anxieties were resolved or kept in abeyance. We have already seen the blurring of metaphors and discourses that connected diverse geographic spaces such as Turkey and Ireland to the New World. Significantly, Smith's *Turkish* experiences enabled him to cope with the cultural consequences of the clash of divergent cultures in America. Smith's compatriots already understood that while anxiety about cross-racial relationships was habitual, such relationships were inevitable. Early modern writers such as Samuel Purchas had long noted the liaison between trade and culture; sexual exchanges inevitably followed commercial ones. Kim Hall notes, "Associations between marriage, kinship, property, and economics become increasingly anxiety-ridden as traditional social structures (such as marriage) are extended when England develops commercial ties across the globe." As Hall further remarks, Purchas's assumption that English trade would "turn a world of difference into a world of Protestant similitude" left unspoken "the more threatening possibility: that English identity will be subsumed under foreign difference."[29]

Perhaps that is why many English narratives describing English encounters with cultural difference in Asia, Africa, and America insistently returned to issues of nationalisms and identities. Smith's *True Travels* engaged, in fascinating ways, with the discourses of emergent nationalisms, English nationhood, and identity. His comments on those issues drew on both Turkey and Virginia for their fullest expression. Concepts of nation and nationalism were, after all, contested affiliations for early modern Englishmen. Emerging nations called for complex cultural negotiations and did not follow according to simple binary oppositions between East/West and Islam/Christianity.[30] Furthermore, as Benedict Anderson has observed, nationalism is often an invisible bond, "an imagined political community—and imagined as both inherently limited and sovereign."[31] Nation is a cultural construct concurrently understood by those who imagine themselves as citizens of a particular space. Smith's *The True Travels* displays some of the complexities of these "national" paradigms on two levels. First, Smith's efforts to become an English gentleman through studied and artful self-cultivation commented on the notion of "Englishness." Smith's fashioning of the English gentleman in the proving grounds of the larger theaters of European mercantile and cultural exchanges in the East also emphasized the nascent flexibility of the notion of the English gentleman—it was possible for a yeoman's son to achieve upward mobility outside England. Second, Smith's revision of the traditional gentleman in response to the needs of the English colony in Virginia demonstrates that his model of the gentleman was fluid and dynamic. By allowing his Turkish experiences to adapt in new ways in Virginia, Smith responded to the peculiar contingencies of the new, vibrant triangulation in the Atlantic World.

As we learn from his *True Travels*, before going to Turkey, Smith occupied himself with a sort of literary fashioning of himself as an English gentleman, the inheritor of the culture and civilization of Troy and Rome. Smith, the son of a yeoman, fictionalized his youthful self as withdrawn in "a little wooddie pasture, a good way from any towne, invironed with many hundred Acres of other woods." Here the young Smith prepared to be a gentleman: "by a faire brook he built a Pavillion of boughes, where only in his cloaths he lay. His studie was Machiavills Art of warre and Marcus Aurelius; his exercise a good horse, with his lance and Ring; his food was thought to be more of venison than any thing else."[32] At the end of his life, the older Smith projected his younger self in an imaginary idyll akin to Shakespeare's forest of Arden, a green world of infinite romantic possibilities where one could remake oneself. Here, the young Smith studied Machiavelli and Marcus Aurelius to school himself to become a gentleman. The fusion of Machiavelli's artful self-fashioning to the Roman emperor's Stoic rumination extended the fantasy of the translation of empire, linking the English gentleman with Roman civilization. Perhaps because he was still on English soil, the journey to gentility remained incomplete; Smith achieved a literary makeover that allowed him to adopt the rhetoric of a gentleman without the possibly of extending it to gentlemanly conduct.

Smith's transformation to gentlemanly conduct pointedly took place outside England, in the Ottoman Empire. Perhaps Smith recalled the venerable tradition of young Christian gentlemen seeking their fortunes in knightly adventures involving romance and peril in the East. In any case, he used his travels in the Ottoman Empire as a setting for his maturation, not just in the gentleman's rhetorical garb, but also in deed. In his text, Smith's gentlemanly experiences included multiple subject positions. One might say that in his soldiering, first with the Protestant Dutch in their struggle for freedom from Catholic Spain and later with the Roman Catholic Hapsburgs against the Turks, Smith was enacting the role of a Christian knight. His subsequent Turkish adventures were intimately connected to Smith's clever production of himself as a gentleman. After his chivalrous deeds in the Ottoman Empire—the combat with the three Turks—Smith began to receive tokens of his status as gentleman; first, "a faire Horse richly furnished," exquisite weapons, a promotion to Sergeant major of his Regiment, and finally the grant of his coat of arms—the three Turks' heads.[33] This moment was prophesied by the incident of the younger Smith reading Machiavelli and Marcus Aurelius in an English idyll. In Turkey, Smith "proved" himself worthy of the Roman legacy of civility by moving from the rhetorical model of gentleman in England to a more active gentlemanly role in the Ottoman Empire.

Smith's transformation from yeoman's son to English gentleman appeared to have been complete. However, the model of the gentleman brought to maturity in the East was to undergo significant revision in the New World. When Smith went to Jamestown after his Turkish adventures, he thought about the young plantation in Virginia and was compelled to compare it to Rome. Virginia, Smith reflected, was not altogether inferior to Rome. In his *Generall Historie* Smith wrote that the Romans had a great part of Europe, Asia, and Africa, "but as for all the Northerne parts of Europe and Asia, the interior Southerne and Westerne parts of Affrica, all America, and Terra Incognita, they were all ignorant."[34] Even mighty Romans at the height of their power and influence were not absolutely powerful or omniscient, for they were "ignorant" of all the riches that lay in parts of Asia and Africa, and in all of America, just beyond the limits of their cognitive horizon. In contrast, English exploration and penetration into regions that were unknown to the Romans suggested that English gentlemen such as Smith had augmented their imperial legacy. Furthermore, Smith recognized that Roman achievements were the rewards of toil and industry, and the English could only hope to replicate Roman imperial successes "if their Land were cultured, planted, and manured by men of industry, judgement, and experience." Civility implied cultivation; cultivation demanded labor. The Roman example demonstrated that an imperial space, wrested from the wilderness by sheer industry, had the potential to relapse into wilderness through lack of industry: "those by their paines and vertues became Lords of the world, they by their ease and vices became slaves to their servants."[35] Through English cultivation and "planting," Virginia, though in its infancy, was already a contender for the laurels once due solely to imperial Rome, but those achievements had to be vigilantly sustained by labor.

Ideas such as the remaking of gentlemen in the context of the translation of empire from Rome to America, or reimagining a new kind of gentleman, were not unique to Smith. Other Englishmen also were imagining the "Virginian" gentleman as practical laborer. Samuel Purchas's panegyric appended to the *Generall Historie* explicitly recognized Smith's Virginia as "Smiths Forge," where "fetters are forged / For Silke-sotts, Milk-sops." Here, "base Sloth" is banished, and "Englands dregs" are made "To plant (supplant!) Virginia."[36] John Donne exploited the plantation's rich potential in a sermon preached before the Virginia Plantation on November 13, 1622. Entwining the metaphors of seeding and planting, Donne fused imperial and evangelical interests as he lauded the birth of a polity that would not "nourish an incompatibility betweene *Merchants* and *Gentlemen*." In Virginia, work would "redeem" the English shiftless and idle. Donne's vision of criminals and vagabonds performing socially redemptive roles in the service of empire had practical as well as spiritual implications, for Virginia was "already, not onely a *Spleene*, to draine the ill humors of the body, but a *Liver*, to breed good bloud."[37] Donne's Virginia was "a *Liver*," a purifying organ of the social body. The labor of the British idle in the service of the infant colony "cleansed" England; public salvation and toil went hand in hand.

Smith's own use of manual labor and industry in the service of the plantation was intimately related to his concept of the gentleman. Smith, one might say, learned through his Turkish travels and soldiering how to be a traditional gentleman, but the lesson of Rome as well as the chivalric code that had served Smith well in Turkey needed revision in America. In Virginia, Smith fashioned a new gentleman, one claiming Roman and courtly privilege, to be sure, but also a pragmatist uniquely trained to handle the contingencies of English colonial ventures in Virginia. In 1606 when the Virginia council was recruiting for the colony, Smith was selected for his experience in Turkey, not for his status as gentleman. As his famous biblical motto "he who shall not work shall not eat" suggested, in Virginia, a gentleman could not remain a dandified aristocrat; he needed to work and to cultivate the land and its resources.

The experience of the Atlantic world revised previous paradigms; circumstances in Jamestown shaped the way Smith modified the aristocratic model of gentleman he had acquired in Turkey through his single combat with the three Turks and the acquisition of his coat of arms. Smith and Virginia had no use for useless gentlemen. Smith wrote to the Virginia Company: "When you send againe, I intreat you rather send but thirty Carpenters, husbandsmen, gardiners, fishermen, blacksmiths, masons, and diggers-up of trees' roots, well provided; then a thousand of such as we have."[38] Effete gentlemen who could not actively raise a thriving colony from hostile Algonquian land were clearly "inferior" to carpenters, fishermen, and masons. The colony needed gentlemen with "management" skills to direct the men who would actually build the houses and farms of Jamestown. They also had to be willing to share in their labors when necessary. Not surprisingly, many scholars have seen the emergence of a new, secular, pragmatic American identity in Smith's modus vivendi.[39]

Smith's "gentleman" persona did not hold up outside Turkey or Virginia. When Smith was simply an Englishman among other Christians, he was no longer regarded as a "gentleman"; instead he was treated as an "Englishman," a word that suggested pirate rather than gentleman to many. Aboard a storm-tossed ship full of pilgrims going to Rome, for instance, his shipmates swore that the English nation was full of pirates. The passengers, "so vildly railed on his dread Soveraigne Queene Elizabeth," and were so fearful that it was Smith who was causing the storm that they threw Smith overboard. At this time English gentlemanliness did not connote imperial Roman legacy, but instead, connected Smith to more recent models of the "gentleman" found in the freebooting style and piracy of Englishmen such as Sir Walter Ralegh and John Ward. Ironically, among fellow Europeans, Smith was thrown overboard for being an English gentleman and trying to defend Queen Elizabeth whose name would be inscribed in the name of Virginia where Smith himself was to make a mark. Smith needed Virginia to fully become a gentleman.

The perception of Englishmen as pirates and renegades once again brought Turkey and Virginia into close relationship. The reference to pirates connected Smith's narrative to the actual English pirates and renegades that prospered under Muslim patronage in places such as Tunis and Algiers. At the end of *True Travels*, Smith extolled the virtues of Virginia in order to coax renegade seamen to renounce piracy and live like lords in America. Smith devoted an entire chapter to the subject, titled, "The bad life, the qualities and conditions of Pyrats and how they taught the Turks and Moores to become men of warre." In his roster of lawless Barbary pirates Smith mentioned Simon Danisker and John Ward, who "lived like a Bashaw in Barbary," but rather than emphasize their rich lifestyles, he wrote, "any wise man would rather live amongst wilde beasts, than them," because they were "the scumme of the world."[40] In the Atlantic world of the late sixteenth and early seventeenth century, the status of piracy was muddled, "a free-for-all whereby any intimidating ship or group of ships encountering a vulnerable ship flying under another flag could take advantage and plunder the less fortunate vessel."[41] Piracy was as profitable as it was dangerous, and in the Ottoman ports, the opulent and seemingly carefree lifestyles of "successful" pirates and renegades such as John Ward and Simon Danisker underscored the lure of piracy. Furthermore, Europeans converted to Islam in large numbers for various reasons.[42]

At the end of his *True Travels*, Smith invited pirates to come "home" to Virginia from Turkey. Just as he had made a journey from England to Turkey to Virginia and in the process made a journey from yeoman's son to gentleman, he invited pirates and renegades domiciled in the Ottoman Empire to find their personal redemptions in Virginia. Smith suggested that the heyday of piracy was over; indeed, piracy was tantamount to slavery. The pirates, he wrote, were now scattered, "disjoynted, disordered, debawched, and miserable that the Turks and Moores beganne to command them as slaves." Smith concluded *The True Travels* by entreating merchants to pay seamen well so they were not compelled by hardship to take to piracy. He also counseled seamen and soldiers to "endeavour rather to adventure to those faire plantations of our English nation." Addressing an audience of potential pirates, Smith noted that in Virginia they could get "more in one yeare, than you by Piracie in seven."[43] Virginia offered more lucrative futures than did Turkey. It was time to return to English polity and preside over the birth of the infant nation in Virginia. Smith's appeal to pirates to come to Virginia suggests that a Christianized Virginia redeemed from its former heathen darkness offered English renegades a profitable alternative to Islamic Turkey. Instead of a life given over to piracy and Islam, Virginia would nurture a Christian Paradise, planted with Christian and English redemptive values. Instead of English pirates plundering other Englishmen, they could fully realize—together—the potential of the vast, uncultivated Eden of Virginia.

Smith's *True Travels* urges us to reconsider the role of Turkey in the phenomena of Jamestown. Although his travels in the Ottoman Empire preceded his American ventures, Smith's encounters in the Ottoman Empire filtered into his experiences in the New World. As commercial and imperial ties brought the cultures of Africa, Europe, Asia, and America into a web of growing intricacy, they simultaneously ensured that no space was totally insulated from another, and no culture was completely inoculated from "contamination" from another. Virginia compellingly evoked Turkey, and Turkey Virginia. Smith's book about Turkey physically bound to his Virginian experiences signaled the *seepage* of one world into another. Smith took his knowledge from his soldiering days in the Ottoman Empire into his transatlantic crossing to the New World. There, as he and his compatriots attempted to "settle with the Indians," to use Karen Kupperman's phrase, they worked their own story into the already unfolding transactions of several cultures, Native American, West African, and European, on the Atlantic rim. As we unpack the story of Jamestown, we may want to recall that Turkey both preceded Virginia as well as followed it—that is, Smith went to Turkey before he went to Virginia, but Virginia may have mediated his account of Turkey published long after his passage to Virginia.

Chapter 7
England, Morocco, and Global Geopolitical Upheaval

SUSAN IWANISZIW

> *I wonder not the Moors so grac'd this nation,*
> *If all the English equal their virtues.*

Diplomatic relations between Christian and Islamic states in the sixteenth century were shaped by a network of official and covert policies covering the spectrum from open warfare and imperial engulfment to trade and alliance. Whether amities and conflicts arose from religious belief, familial relationships, dynastic instability, trade competition, or territorial acquisitiveness, all states trading across the Mediterranean region were forced to take into account the shifting balance of power between the hostile Ottoman and Hapsburg empires. Under pressure, amities across the Eastern Hemisphere were necessarily contingent, self-serving, and competitive, yet these included a longstanding cooperation between England and Morocco. The exchange of Moroccan saltpeter for English bullets and naval timber served military needs directly, while general trade and diplomatic contact also enhanced national security for both states. Morocco mitigated for England the threat posed by Spanish hostility and by a rebellious Ireland in league with papal and Spanish forces, while England mitigated for Morocco the threats posed by Spain's and Turkey's territorial ambitions.[1] Unlike historians, many literary scholars have neglected the diplomatic history of early modern European-African interchanges, focusing instead on racial tension, which surfaced rather later than recent criticism has implied.[2] But whatever racial tension was felt at this time was subsumed by England's interest in befriending powerful Moroccan kings, especially Ahmad al-Mansur, who reigned from 1578 to 1603.

English drama of the time underscores the mutuality of this alliance by its focus on the diplomatic interaction between Queen Elizabeth and Ahmad al-Mansur in the last decades of the 16th century. Two Elizabethan/

Jacobean dramas speaking to this alliance are *The Famous Historye of Captaine Thomas Stukelely*, printed in 1605 (an anonymous play whose multiple authorship probably includes Thomas Heywood), and *The Fair Maid of the West Part I*, ca. 1600 (by Thomas Heywood). *Famous History* is a fictionalized biography of the real-life adventurer Thomas Stukeley, whose quasi-comic peregrinations culminate in his death at Alcazar, Morocco in 1578. This battle involved Catholic forces allied with Muhammed al- Mutawakkil (a deposed king of Morocco) against the Muslim victors 'Abd al-Malik and Ahmad. *Fair Maid* is a fictional biography of Bess Bridges, whose sea voyages mirror those of Stukeley but culminate in her diplomatic bonding with Ahmad al-Mansur (or, as he is named in this play, Mullisheg). These plays expose the complexity of the international negotiations that led to the Spanish-English peace of 1604, which, in turn, preceded the Jacobean acquisition and exploitation of New World territories. Appearing on the stage at the very end of Elizabeth's reign, they decode public assumptions about the diplomatic strategy which sustained England's embryonic national identity at the eve of imperial ascendancy.

By their alliance, the minor states of England and Morocco resisted Habsburg or Ottoman hegemony to forge instead their own empires. Morocco's empire was established by its consolidation under one ruler in 1578 and funded, in large part, by the invasion and exploitation of the Songhay (from 1590). England's imperial growth was founded on the pacification of Ireland after 1603 and Spain's suspension of aggression by the Treaty of London in 1604 which opened up the New World to English exploitation: both of these advantages stemmed, indirectly to be sure, from England's unusual alliance with Morocco. English and Dutch colonial ventures (long stymied by the 1494 Treaty of Tordesillas between Spain and Portugal, which had divided the unexplored regions of the world between themselves) were encouraged by these peace agreements negotiated in 1604 and 1609.[3] With Spain's compliance, England acquired an option for territorial expansion in the New World, authorized by James I's patent issued in 1606 and renewed in 1609. Without Morocco's cooperation, Elizabethan England might well have succumbed to Catholic militarism and containment: James I's diplomatic rapprochement with Spain and continuing trade relations with Morocco (less powerful but still a potent ally after al-Mansur's death) ensured the degree of national stability essential for England's founding of Jamestown in 1607.

Famous History and *Fair Maid*, among other plays touching on English-Spanish-Moroccan involvement, served as both entertainment and a supplementary form of news reporting years before the regular publication of news corantos (1622).[4] With the aim of tracing the complexities of historical interaction encoded in dramatic works and, thus, their reflection of global geopolitical alignments, this essay first outlines diplomatic, military, and mercantile interactions among England, Morocco, and Spain from

1578 to 1614 and then examines the related plays written at the turn of the seventeenth century that illustrate England's dependence upon Moroccan friendship.[5]

Diplomacy and History

The alliance of Elizabethan England and Morocco in trade and national defense signals an instance of collaboration between governments possessing a more or less equal share of world power in the divided camps of Christianity and Islam. Mutual resistance to the imperial powers of Spain and Turkey bound the states to a fourfold diplomatic game in which the similarity in aims and practices, if not religious faith, was decisive. Fear, alienation, and anti-Muslim or anti-black xenophobia may well have circulated in popular culture by way of negative images culled from the fantastic treatises of classical authors and their early modern imitators, but racism proper emerged from British experience of black slavery institutionalized in New World colonies only long after Elizabeth's death.[6] The disdainful picture of Moroccans as racial *others* that modern commentators have construed as a perquisite of Elizabethan sensibility is an unlikely construction, in fact a bar to understanding African cosmopolitanism. Indeed, it helps to recall that racial identifications in these dramas are generally incidental (deriving from historical settings) rather than integral to the plays' central themes and concerns.

Whether Moors, Negroes, Arabs, or European renegades, Moroccans made no claim to social precedence by primogeniture or, indeed, by the accident of racial heritage. Phenotypic differences neither signified nor caused rigid social demarcation, and, generally, non-Muslim faith was tolerated except in cases of service to the sultan. Both Muhammed al-Mutawakkil, killed at Alcazar, and Muly Ismael, who reigned from 1672 to 1727, were black-complexioned Moroccan kings, both, presumably, the sons of Negro concubines, and, therefore, in European reckoning, illegitimate.[7] At the same time, English valuation of Moroccan kings in the Elizabethan era accrued, not from preconceptions about color, birth, or religious parity, but from cognizance of local power dynamics. Morocco was a world power and was acknowledged as such by ambassadors, travelers, and even stay-at-home playwrights.

The actual Battle of Alcazar in 1578 is the *terminus a quo* for these dramas, and its history the foundation of these plots. The historical record reveals that 'Abd Allah al-Ghalib unlawfully established his son Muhammed al-Mutawakkil on the Moroccan throne from which he was rapidly displaced by his uncles, the rightful heirs, 'Abd al-Malik and Ahmad. At the cost of his vassalage to Portugal, Muhammed al-Mutawakkil was successful in recruiting Don Sebastian to his aid and a crusading Catholic European army, supplemented by Muhammed al-Mutawakkil's supporters, attempted to take back Morocco at Alcazar. On the opposing side, 'Abd al-Malik had relied on Ottoman military assistance to win the battle, but he died during the fighting and his brother Ahmad al-Mansur rejected Ottoman dominion to rule as emperor of a unified Morocco.

Modern critics' sensitivity to the legacy of racism has often obscured the fact that English playwrights depicted the victorious Moroccan kings as fully deserving the crown of Morocco. In both George Peele's *Battel of Alcazar* (ca. 1589) and the anonymous *Famous History*, which is clearly an adaptation of Peele's play, the "Black King" Muhammed al-Mutawakkil (or Muly Mahamet) is represented as the criminal usurper and his Catholic allies as wrong to offer their support. Philip II in *Famous History* wonders about Don Sebastian's insistence on providing Muly Mahamet with military aid against the rightful king, 'Abd al-Malik (who was generally known in Spain as Muly Molocco): "The right is in Molucco: wherefore then / Would Prince Sebastian ayde the other part." At an early stage of Anglo-Moroccan cooperation, Peele depicts Muly Mahamet in racially charged language as the murderer of his father and younger brothers, but some ten or fifteen years later, when diplomatic relations were firmer, the author of *Famous History* barely alludes to racial difference, erases the charge of murder, and simply denounces him for cowardice.[8] Such a softening in characterization indicates a reduction in notions of Moroccan difference even with respect to a hostile figure. The anonymous playwright thus acknowledges England's strong bond of friendship with Ahmad al-Mansur. Some Moroccans were black-skinned and some deserved censure: indeed, the two characteristics were often linked. But this correlation is a function of the historical record rather than an instance of early modern racism.

The authority of the emperor Ahmad al-Mansur was never in dispute. His right to rule resulted in the first instance from his father's stipulation that his three sons inherit the crown sequentially, but secondarily from his survival at Alcazar where his brother 'Abd al-Malik died.[9] English-Moroccan diplomacy had been established some time before the Moroccans defeated Portugal in the Battle of Alcazar, the first agreement to trade Moroccan saltpeter (a component of gunpowder) for English bullets having been negotiated by Muhammed al-Mutawakkil before 'Abd al-Malik seized the crown.[10] After the accession of Ahmad, relations were strengthened by Elizabeth's grant of a twelve-year license to the Barbary Company (1585). Her favorite, the Earl of Leicester, who was already involved in many overseas trade ventures and in partnership with other members of the Barbary Company, thus acquired the monopoly to trade specifically in metals and saltpeter.[11] In spite of the continuing presence of the Spanish, who occupied a number of significant garrisons in Morocco, the sultan strove to maintain his independence from Iberian as well as adjacent Ottoman influence. If Ahmad al-Mansur rejected Turkish control and cleverly played English demands against Spanish blandishments during this tumultuous period, by the time these plays reached the stage at the turn of the century the balance weighed in England's favor.[12]

English-Moroccan amity during Elizabeth's reign was instrumental in the continued political independence of both states, and plans for cooperative military ventures prove delightful examples of a common grandiose ambition to outdo Spain and Turkey. This cooperative spirit is evident in the state papers and personal correspondence of Elizabeth and al-Mansur.[13] At the height of England's fear of an Irish/Papal /Spanish assault in 1578, Morocco dispatched a secret embassy to London. The merchant Jasper Thomson reported Ahmad al-Mansur's interest in England's assisting him to carry 20,000 soldiers and horses from Barbary to conquer Spain. Consul Henry Roberts was accompanied to England in 1589 by a Moroccan ambassador who offered to provide England with 100 ships and 150,000 ducats to facilitate the landing of Don Antonio in Portugal. In return, al-Mansur sought material and technological assistance for improving his galleys.[14] The Moroccan king was pressed hard by England to support Don Antonio, the pretender to the Portuguese throne which had passed to Philip II of Spain, but he was saved from having to commit himself (and alienating Spain) by Antonio's timely death. In 1600, al-Mansur dispatched a new embassy to England. The reports of this visit are instructive in two ways: first, they reveal an English shock (even outrage) that these ambassadors surreptitiously used their privileged diplomatic rank to enhance Morocco's trading status; secondly, they illuminate the scope of Moroccan prestige.[15] The Moroccans failed to be intimidated; instead, they intimidated the English.[16] Not awed by Elizabeth's court and English culture, and aided by the queen's participation in secret discussions, the Moroccan ambassadors simply accepted the warrant of their own authority embedded in a firm Anglo-Moroccan alliance.[17] With trade interests, colonial ambition, and prospective joint reprisals against Spain, England and Morocco found common cause that transcended racial and even religious difference.

Secret discussions and correspondence in 1600–1601 focused on Elizabeth's request for financial assistance to harry Spanish treasure ships in the West Indies and al-Mansur's proposal that England and Morocco combine forces in a joint colonization project.[18] Al-Mansur writes that he will act within two years: "For our intent is not onely to enter upon the land to sack it and leave it, but to possesse it and that it remayne under our dominion for ever, and—by the help of God—to joyne it to our estate and yours."[19] His favored locale appears to be Eastern, where other Muslims and Moors will support her claims, rather than West Indian, where Elizabeth set her sights; but his proposal went nowhere. His eldest son instigated a revolt in Morocco at about this time, and al-Mansur died immediately after he reconsolidated his empire. Elizabethan and early Jacobean dramas inspired by late sixteenth-century history appear fully accepting of Ahmad al-Mansur's friendship, notwithstanding his *outré* or "eastern" habits. If Moroccan military assistance for England's New World anti-Spanish activity was not ultimately forthcoming and treaties to refrain from dealing in captive Englishmen were not always upheld, English prestige in Ahmad al-Mansur's Morocco was high and the English privileged Moroccan practices over those of neighboring Muslim states even beyond 1603 when both Elizabeth and Ahmad died.

The Battle of Alcazar was the ground of this cooperative alliance, but a negative result for England was Spain's absorption of Portugal after the deaths of King Sebastian (1578) and his successor Cardinal Henry (1580). When Philip II claimed the entire Iberian Peninsula, he had access to virtually all the riches of the New World: American silver and gold funded Spanish militarism in Africa, in Europe, and in the New World over the course of the sixteenth and seventeenth centuries. Philip II had withheld support from Sebastian's crusade in Morocco—perhaps with his future acquisition of Portugal fully in mind—and, following Portugal's defeat, was content to maintain the status quo with Ahmad al-Mansur. Morocco's compact with England seems an unlikely obstacle to Spanish ambitions, but Morocco continued to serve as a friendly buffer state between Catholics and Muslims that Elizabeth was able to put to good use. Not only did she press for materials of war, she had no compunction about negotiating Ottoman aid to force al-Mansur's hand in the matter of placing Don Antonio on the Portuguese throne. And Spain was reluctant to alienate Morocco. Morocco was not simply an exotic dramatic location or a marginal player in international relations; it was of paramount importance in shaping seventeenth-century global foreign policy. Al-Mansur's conquest of the Songhay in 1590 and his control of the legendary Timbuktu provided vast wealth in the form of gold, salt, and slaves, all of which funded his program of unification and generated international prestige.

During al-Mansur's reign, the coastline of a unified Morocco stretched from the Atlantic to the Mediterranean, providing vital ports for shipping—both legitimate and pirate—en route to and from the Americas and the East. As Richard Hakluyt reminds us, Irish ports had initially been targeted to secure England-New World exploration and settlement, but Morocco's Atlantic ports proved equally valuable.[20] By 1600, al-Mansur's wealth and status in the international world were legendary, his hospitality invaluable to a nation contemplating westward expansion. When Spain acquired vast properties by its usurpation of Portugal and its New World dominions, Elizabeth and her diplomats courted the Moroccan emperor as a counterweight to Iberian hegemony.

However, while al-Mansur was busy consolidating his power locally, Spanish aggression against England continued. Measures were afoot before the Battle of Alcazar for a combined Catholic force to attack England from Irish strongholds. Ahmad al-Mansur was exotic and powerful, but the Irish were far more worrisome. Not only were the Irish openly Catholic, seemingly savage, and frighteningly hostile, they were supported in their resistance to English rule by Philip II and the pope.

Through his connections to Ireland and Catholic Europe, Thomas Stukeley acted a prominent part in this international melee. He was an adventurer born of a well-respected Devonshire family, though by repute an illegitimate son of Henry VIII.[21] His involvement in piracy, Irish military affairs, Spanish and papal plots against Protestantism, and, ultimately, his military participation at Alcazar render him, along with the rebels of Tyrone, an emblem of the Catholic threat. Piracy was rampant worldwide and not an unusual undertaking for the making of English fortunes and the creation of gentlemen.[22] Piracy was also a subterfuge, sanctioned by governments to intimidate enemies and steal their assets without an overt declaration of war. Piracy is, thus, an apt vehicle for examining the pragmatism that governed global trade and the maintenance of military power. State-sponsored piracy was a covert act of war that facilitated personal and national economic and territorial advancement; Spanish bullion frequently fell into English pirates' hands (with a portion then finding its way into the queen's coffers) just as English goods and men fell into the hands of Ottoman, North African, and European pirates. Depending on the target, Stukeley's piracies could have enhanced or diminished England's global stature, but Stukeley opted to act against the queen's interests in Ireland.

In 1578, with its multiple references to the whereabouts and activities of Stukeley, the *Acts of Privy Council* reveals England's unease with his suspected treason on behalf of Catholic enemies.[23] Stukeley was bribed or won over by papal title to numerous Irish estates and nominated the leader of Pope Gregory's expedition to establish a base in Ireland for the purpose of invading England. His death at Alcazar temporarily prevented the implementation of the plan. Stukeley's dramatic biography introduces him militarily in Shane O'Neill's second Ulster rebellion and the siege of Dundalk in 1566. His precise dealings with the Irish rebels and the English government during this time are not crystal clear.[24] Richard Simpson provides a lengthy if somewhat speculative and anodyne account. An anonymous text entitled "A Thankful Remembrance," which is pasted into William Stukeley's annotated copy of the play, provides a more or less contemporaneous version that corroborates the view of Stukeley's treasonous activities in Ireland presented in Raphael Holinshed's *Chronicles of England, Scotland and Ireland*. Although Stukeley became acquainted with Shane O'Neill when he appeared at Elizabeth's court to beg her pardon following his earlier rebellion, it is unlikely that Stukeley participated in O'Neill's 1566 revolt, wherein the Irish lord lost his head to a stake at the summit of Dublin Castle.[25] Between 1568 and 1578, however, the historical record shows a tense awareness of Catholic sponsorship of Stukeley's prospective invasion of Ireland. Stukeley was reported to have arrived out of Italie unto Cadis in Spaine, with certeine men, ships, and munitions assigned unto him by the pope. And being accompanied with certeine strangers attending upon him, he was come to the seas, to land upon some part of the realme of Ireland, in traitorous maner to invade the same, and to provoke the people to joine with him in rebellion.[26]

By 1578, the Lord Governor of Ireland, Sir Henry Sidney (the father of Sir Philip Sidney) was ready to leave his post, having restored "order and peace, being now delivered from inward and civill warre, and from the feare of Stukeleies invasion."[27]

Two years after Stukeley's death at Alcazar, Italians landed at Smerwick to foment further rebellion in Ireland. They were quickly overcome, but continental Catholics did not abandon their invasion plans. Of course, the troubles in Ireland stemmed from England's military and cultural interference over the course of several centuries, but inter- and intraclan rivalries jeopardized sustained resistance to English domination, and the pope was evidently no more adroit at negotiating with clan leaders than were the English.[28] Indeed, even the Spanish Armada (1588) was dispersed, and, following that invasion attempt and English reprisals, Philip III's last assault at Kinsale, in cooperation with Hugh O'Neill's Ulster forces, met with similar failure. Challenging English occupation, the rebellious lords led by the Earl of Tyrone, young Hugh O'Neill, had waged a nine-year war that devastated the countryside but resulted in no enduring victory for either side. After his continental allies were defeated in Kinsale in 1601, O'Neill surrendered at Mellifont in 1603. Philip III of Spain was then ready to make peace.

After James I was crowned in 1603, the Portuguese crusade in Morocco and the turmoil in Ireland prompted a global realignment of power that favored the English. Spain, juggling far too many international conflicts, began to decline as a global leader. Its failure to win over the Irish and invade England and its subsequent eviction of all Moriscos from Spain (1609) were significant spurs to new geopolitical configurations. Revising Queen Elizabeth's international policies, James exiled English and Irish pirates, many of whom settled in Morocco and swelled the ranks of the fearsome Sally Rovers, who were, for the most part, Moriscos exiled from Spain and especially hostile to Spanish shipping.[29] These new developments enhanced England's international status, depleted Spain's population, and swelled the ranks of Moroccan pirates.[30] On Morocco's side, a bloody period of internecine warfare followed Ahmad al-Mansur's death, which spurred piratical activity and put a brake upon Morocco's further expansion. Indeed, following the deaths of Elizabeth and al-Mansur, Elizabeth's former ambassador, Henry Roberts, proposed to James I that England attempt to colonize Morocco.[31] King James did not follow through with this suggestion, but rather continued to nurture Anglo-Moroccan cooperation.

Following James's peaceful succession, England was set fair to expand its dominions elsewhere. Of course, England's New World aspirations had taken shape some time before Spain's defeat in Ireland and the 1604 Treaty of London. It is probably coincidental that Humphrey Gilbert acquired a patent for the exploration and colonization of "Virginia" in 1578, the year of Portugal's defeat in the Battle of Alcazar, but his experience in colonizing Ireland was surely crucial.[32] Sir Walter Ralegh, too, was experienced in Irish affairs, and it was he to whom the subsequent patent was issued in 1584. These men of the "West Country" were instigators of the 1584, 1585, and 1587 voyages to the eastern Atlantic coast and the founding of the colony at Roanoke. That colony was quickly expunged, but the idea of settlement in Indian lands, couched in terms of civil interaction and conversion, remained an attractive alternative to Irish colonization that had proved so arduous and expensive an undertaking. Potential English colonies began to be valued as early as 1585 not only as sites for spreading "civilization" and Christianity to North America but also as bases of operation against Iberian fishing and treasure fleets, and as prospective marketplaces for manufactures.[33] England's successful parrying of Spanish assaults over the next decade and the treaty of 1604 renewed interest in these possibilities.

The settlement of Jamestown under the authority of James I began as yet another aristocratic colonial exploitation in line with the Iberian-American and Moroccan-Songhay models, but such venturing was stymied by the absence of treasure or discernible mineral resources.[34] Regularly emblematized in England as a virgin saved from Spanish lust, Virginia provided an imaginary Eden and an actual locus for the English fantasy of imperial aggrandizement.[35] Eventually, England's reliance on Moroccan products—especially sugar—was reduced by the establishment of New World plantations, and trade lessened in importance for both states. Initially, however, North American colonization was fostered by Moroccan-English resistance to Catholic, and especially Spanish, power in the circum-Atlantic arena and, perhaps most importantly, the material support of settlements was contingent upon England's continued access to secure Atlantic harbors in both Ireland and Morocco. Al-Mansur's immense value to England is recorded in John Smith's *True Travels, Adventures and Observations*: the writer—whether Smith or Henry Archer—observes that al-Mansur was "a most good and noble King, that governed well with peace and plentie . . . [in] everie way noble, kinde and friendly, verie rich and pompous in State and Majestie."[36] This backward look at Elizabeth's ally in a narrative by a prominent colonist in Jamestown suggests the extent of England's real debt to his friendship.

Drama in Context

When we approach England and Morocco as allies in both spirit and fact, we see that any anxiety occasioned by the dissimilarity of race slips beneath the greater anxiety about Spanish and Catholic aggression.[37] The ideological threads of England's self-fashioning as an independent Protestant state colluding politically and economically with Morocco, its primary analog not only in North Africa but, arguably, worldwide, are clearly marked in *Famous History* and *Fair Maid*, both of which celebrate this specific moment of relative stability and mutual empowerment. The two plays are linked by geography, time, and plot; their staging at the cusp of the new century and their concern with dynastic instability invoke a national awareness of the ramifications of global change. In this late Elizabethan era, playwrights looked outward in order to configure imaginative but not entirely fictitious histories of England's allies and enemies entering a new, but as yet unknowable world order.

Bess Bridges, heroine of *Fair Maid*, caps a serialization of Thomas Stukeley's treacherous history which had become the focus of popular ballads as well as several dramas (including Peele's *Alcazar* and lost plays entitled *Stewtly* or *Stucley*). The tensions evident in the dramatic constructions of Stukeley and Bridges graph the geopolitics by which England, in concert with Muslim Morocco, was able to buttress its independence. These two plays possess related structural and thematic elements, such as the anomalous chorus, but, more importantly, they validate Ahmad al-Mansur's authority. Instead of presenting Moors like Othello, Aaron, or Eleazar isolated within European culture, *Famous History* and *Fair Maid* show the African as king of his own people, forced to deal with the demands of intrusive Europeans desiring to fight with, trade with, or convert the Moors.

The plays represent international events that would remain topics of public interest well beyond the death of Queen Elizabeth. Acted in the 1590s but first published in 1605, *Famous History* fictionalizes Captain Thomas Stukeley's later career, its action set consecutively in England, Ireland, Spain, and Morocco at the time of the Battle of Alcazar. Stukeley's action in Shane O'Neill's rebellion in Ireland may well be apocryphal, but the susceptibility of Ireland to rebellion, especially in view of the assistance at hand from Rome and Spain, remained a concern of English Protestants until the Act of Union in 1801. Having quit Ireland to sail to Cadiz and present himself at Philip II's court, after some delay Stukeley is deployed as Philip's emissary to the pope. He returns to Spain with a contingent of Italian soldiers assigned to Ireland, but he chooses rather to assist King Sebastian and his Portuguese army in reinstalling the dispossessed king of Morocco, Muly Mahamet (Muhammed al-Mutawakkil). Their combined forces are defeated by the reigning monarch Abdelmeleck ('Abd al-Malik) and his brother Muly Hamet (Ahmad). The historical record of the battle and its aftermath is quite specific as to the fates of the major players, but the dramatic plot centered on Stukeley proceeds from the military defeat at Alcazar to the murder of the Englishmen, Stukeley and Vernon, by vengeful Italian soldiers.

Sebastian's success at Alcazar would have permitted the blossoming of Catholic power in North Africa. It was, if nothing else, expedient for England to support the reigning monarch 'Abd al-Malik when Sebastian took up Muhammed al-Mutawakkil's cause in his zeal for a crusade, especially since "the Black King" promised Morocco's future vassalage to Portugal. England thereafter took Portugal's part against Spain—in order, as William Monson argues, to profit from trade with Portugal's American colonies.[38] Nonetheless, the author of *Famous History* asserts the right of the Moorish kings Abdelmeleck and his brother Muly Hamet to reclaim the crown from their usurping nephew Muly Mahamet. The scene concluding the battle presents a civilized Muly Hamet, who listens to a recitation of the list of enemies killed and then enjoins his soldiers to

See that the Body of Sebastian,
Have Christian and kingly buriall,
After the country maner for in life,
A Braver sperit nere lived upon the [f]ame,
And let the christian bodies be interd,
For muly-mahamet: let his skin be flead,
From of the flesh; from foote unto the head,
And stuft within: and so be borne about,
Through all the partes of our Dominions,
To terefie the like that shall pursue,
To lift their swords against their soverayn.[39]

An anointed king, Sebastian is accorded the privileges of his rank; only with respect to Muly Mahamet's usurpation does Muly Mahamet slip into the rhetoric of debasement. Even so, the prospective offstage mutilation of Muly Mahamet constitutes a subdued version of European torture, far less horrific (since Muhammed al-Mutawakkil is already drowned) than the sentence passed on Sir Walter Ralegh (but never fully exacted) when he was found guilty of treason in 1603.[40] The usurper's or traitor's bloody fate was designed to frighten subjects rather than generate a sympathetic response: there was no sympathy extended to Muhammed al-Mutawakkil.

Even the ballad "The Life and Death of the Famous Thomas Stukeley" roundly condemns the forces allied against the legitimate Moroccan kings:

Heaven was so displeased
And would not be appeased,
But took us off Gods heavy wrath did show
That he was angry at this War,
He sent a fearful Blazing Star
Whereby ye Kings might their misfortunes know.[41]

Stukeley's challenge to legitimate Moroccan authority was incorporated into stage lore in George Peele's *Battel of Alcazar.* Peele sets Stukeley up as a self-righteous Catholic crusader: "No doubt the quarrell opened by the mouth / Of this young prince unpartially to us, / May animate and hearten all the hoast, / To fight against the devill for Lord Mahamet."[42] To a Protestant English sensibility, militant Catholicism was anathema. Peele was certainly aware that Stukeley posed a grave danger to Queen Elizabeth. In fact, the historical Stukeley had been imprisoned from time to time facing charges ranging from piracy to treason. Whether he genuinely subscribed to Catholicism or not, his acceptance of Philip's patronage at a time his queen feared a Spanish invasion leaves us in little doubt of his status in English political discourse. In Holinshed's *Chronicles,* he is depicted thus:

And out of Ireland ran awaie one Thomas Stukeleie, a defamed person almost thorough all Christendome, and a faithlesse beast rather than a man, fleeing first out of England for notable Pirasies, and out of Ireland for trecheries not pardonable.[43]

The popular record constituted by drama and ballads tends to obscure the official response to his treason and preserves his reputation as a warrior hero. Peele represents him ironically as one who did "glitter all in golde, / Mounted upon his Jennet white as snowe, / Shining as Phoebus in King Phillips Court," an image creating a fine stage show but a poor excuse, surely, for an Englishman. Ballads might occasionally have rendered a strict account of topical events, but more usually commented on them—their contents "chiefly emotional rather than literal."[44] Attributed to Richard Johnson (1573–1659), the ballad reflects on Stukeley's activities from a temporal and emotional distance and fails to indict him directly as a traitor or a recusant. The quintessential "English" bravery allowed to the popular representations of Stukeley, however, by no means justified his consorting with Sebastian, nor did his martial prowess in any way diminish Ahmad al-Mansur's legitimacy.[45]

Indeed, like Peele's *Alcazar, Famous History* shows Stukeley meeting death—not as a military hero in battle—but at the hands of papal soldiers disgruntled by his choice to deflect them from Ireland in order to join Sebastian's forces in Africa. In his last speech, Stukeley blames treason for his downfall:

England farewell: what fortune never yet,
Did crosse Tom Stukley in, to show her frowne,
By treason suffers him to be overthrowne.[46]

An English audience would surely have construed "treason" as his own involvement in Catholic invasion plans of Ireland rather than the actions of mutinous Italian soldiers. The ballad version of his death credits him with more repentance but provides little detail about his transgressions. Elided from popular discourse is any definitive articulation of his treasonous activities in Ireland, and Stukeley's most serious shortcomings remain elusive. But his reputation as a freewheeling adventurer and military hero is clearly tempered by hubris and moral ambivalence. The play reveals that he despises the Irish, yet he accepts the pope's commission to assist them in rebellion against the queen; he is generous to his soldiers and valiant in war, yet he glorifies Muly Mahamet and his illegitimate claim. On the other hand, perhaps he shows himself a "true" Englishman in keeping his word to the governor's wife in Cadiz while he breaks his oath to the pope.

Despite the cultural record's ambivalence about the precise nature of his crimes, I suggest that the dramatic Stukeley functioned as an exemplary (if somewhat shadowy) villain brought to his just end. Heywood's Bridges functions as his iconic foil. Tom Stukeley's collusion with continental Catholics and his wrong-headed support of Muly Mahamet is rectified in Bess Bridge's resolute constancy and her embrace of Mullisheg.

Heywood's *Fair Maid* excises moral ambiguity in its reconstruction of English adventuring and heroism. Bridges's voyages and good works are embedded in the same matrix of international affairs that provides the setting for *Famous History*, the plays teaching inverse lessons about expectations for the behavior of England's representatives in foreign lands.

The iconic opposition of Bridges and Stukeley in these plays celebrates England's friendship with Morocco. Stukeley actually fought in Morocco, but Bridges comprehends multiple influences historically grounded in the period between Henry VIII's French wars (in which Stukeley participated) and the end of Elizabeth's reign, but particularly in the period of Anglo-Moroccan cooperation from 1578 onward. These influences include Edmund Spenser's *Faerie Queene* as well as ballads and the chapbook histories of less elevated women than Britomart and Queen Elizabeth: specifically, Mary Ambree, Long Meg of Westminster (both of whom Bridges mentions), and Grace O'Malley (Grania ny Maille), the notorious Irish pirate.[47] A woman of low birth, Bess Bridges nevertheless upholds the chivalric idealism of the virginal Britomart, her attachment to the portrait of Spencer (whose name is an obvious homonym of Edmund Spenser) an emblem of Britomart's magical image of Artegall and symbol of Bridges's commendable chastity. All of her female precursors—both fictional and historical—are cross-dressing women warriors like Britomart. Moreover, Bridges's occupation is indebted both to Long Meg and to the tavern culture that fashioned Tom Stukeley. As in Long Meg's popular history, Bridges derives her strength from her exemplary constancy, honesty, and intelligence rather than the mere physical prowess and outrageous bravado of Stukeley. Owner of the Windmill tavern rather than a barmaid, Bridges falls in love with a soldier in line with Meg's template. His name is Spencer. When he kills a fellow Englishman in defense of his lover's honor, he flees abroad to join Sir Walter Ralegh's forces sacking Fayal and leaves Bridges his tavern in Foy (Cornwall), his possessions, and his portrait.[48] While in Fayal, he is wounded in a duel, and, anticipating death, he calls upon Goodlack to execute his will in England. Goodlack quits Fayal believing his friend to be mortally wounded, but he is saved by the skill of his physician while another man named Spencer happens to die. From this point on, the plots of the two plays run parallel.

Bridges uses her inheritance from Spencer to purchase a ship called the *Negro*—a "prize" brought to England by pirate or privateer—and sets out with her friends with the secret intention of reclaiming Spencer's body from territory retaken by the Spanish. Bridges's voyage through Spanish territory on her black ship illuminates English concerns in this geopolitical web. The *Negro*, her ship, transcends any simple binary opposition between black and white or the anticipation of England's engagement in African slave trading. In its first mission the ship emblematizes her neoplatonic commitment to Spencer, in its second mission it emblematizes the moderation of English pirates, and in its third mission it emblematizes the fruitfulness of English diplomacy. While we cannot entirely discount the equation of blackness and African subordination, in this figure black resonates more compellingly at other levels. First, it represents mourning, as befits the heroine's mood;[49] second, it represents religion, for Protestant ships were traditionally black; and thirdly, it represents piracy, for pirates often used black vessels in order to slip unnoticed past warships in the night.[50] Finally, it represents topical events. The impetus behind Heywood's choice of name may come from actual ships similarly named,[51] but, rather more likely, from those edicts issued by Elizabeth I in 1596 to deport slaves from England. One edict calls for the repatriation of ten "blackamores" whom Sir Thomas Baskerville brought from the New World to England; the other calls for the voluntary exchange of 89 black slaves resident in England (a question of their masters' compliance rather than their own) for 89 English subjects held as slaves in Spain and Portugal.[52] Universally cited by modern scholars as evidence of early English racism, these edicts reflect, instead, a domestic concern with the dire corn shortages at that time and a diplomatic negotiation for the redemption of English captives. Shortfalls in the harvest necessitated an aggressive policy of alms distribution to the unemployed and poor, the *Acts of Privy Council* in 1596 repeatedly enjoining well-provisioned subjects to curtail their own appetites in order to feed the hungry. The government justified the deportation of "those kinde of people," not on the grounds of black inferiority, but because their employment as slaves usurped the jobs of needy English men and women. Bridges's vessel, already a "prize" taken from enemy shipping and, therefore, not valued as English, represents those unfortunate Negroes to be deployed in the redemption of captive Englishmen. Alerting the audience to the despicable Spanish policy of enslaving freeborn Englishmen, she is prepared to risk the *Negro* and all aboard to retrieve Spencer's corpse from the Spaniards.

En route for Fayal and dressed as a sea captain, she captures Spanish fishermen who reveal that Spencer's corpse was disinterred from consecrated ground, reburied (aptly enough) in an infertile corn field, then exhumed again and burned. Her enduring commitment to love even after Spencer's death is a neoplatonic convention of the age, but her mission is rendered futile by Spanish desecrations. Thus, she fires on the Fayal church, which is once again in Spanish hands, her battery a symbol of Protestant England's religious and moral outrage against Spain's illicit treatment of fellow Christians. She goes on to rescue the English merchant vessel upon which the still living Spencer and his physician had taken passage. Circumstances are such that she fails to recognize her lover (she thinks him a ghost) or he her (she is dressed in male clothing) and he goes on his way to Mamorah. They meet again in the court of Mullisheg, the sultan. Not tempted by unearned wealth offered by the smitten Moroccan, Bridges completes her metamorphosis from tavern-keeper to warrior-pirate to diplomat.

Spencer (whose role reflects that of Vernon in *Famous History*) is also at court; his mission is to plead for the English merchant accused of cheating Mullisheg (or Ahmad al-Mansur/Muly Xeque) of his customs duties. When Bridges spots him, she offers Mullisheg all her wealth ("leave naught that's mine unrifled") to relieve him. Mullisheg graciously resists taking advantage of her self-sacrifice, conferring upon Spencer the dubious honor of chief eunuch. Her corrupt and foolish servant, Clem, steps in to accept the promotion, and Spencer, freed from the threat of castration, asks Mullisheg for Bridges's hand in marriage—a double transference of agency to which she willingly accedes, although, like Britomart's, her history is far from concluded.

Heywood made Anglo-Moroccan interactions something of his stock in trade. His play *If You Know Not Me, You Know Nobody* (1606) deals with English-Moroccan trade specifically; *Fair Maid Part I* speaks to late Elizabethan diplomatic cooperation; and *Fair Maid Part II* reflects England's declining dependence on Morocco. Domestic legal policy, diplomacy, and trade opportunities were then, as now, contingent components in international transactions. In Part I, Bridges acts as an ambassador who is called upon to mitigate Mullisheg's severity in dealing with foreign merchants and missionaries caught flouting his laws. All countries engaged in international trade imposed restrictions on imports, required payment of customs duties, and monitored the behaviors and rights of foreign sailors, England no less than any other state.[53] These rules were spelled out quite clearly in international treaties. There is no question that the European merchants represented in the play have transgressed Moroccan laws articulated by public edict. The French merchant has attempted to "deal in commodities forbid"; the Italian merchant has failed to monitor the "outrage" of his crew who have been sentenced to the Moroccan galleys; and the English merchant carrying Bridges's beloved Spencer has failed to pay customs duties.[54] The "quiddit" in Moroccan law that permits Mullisheg to confiscate both goods and ships when European merchants evade import or customs regulations, as in the case of Spencer's ship master, is more clearly a European trick than a Moroccan one. The historical record reveals the English as particularly prone to this draconian punishment of interlopers and smugglers. For example, England confiscated ships and goods from interlopers in the Barbary and Turkey trades.[55] Trade charters note the division of spoils from such infractions at the ratio of 50 percent to the queen and 50 percent to the company or patentees. Another telling example of England's greed for ships is to be found in the *Dolphin* incident when, in 1586, the English illegally captured the Spanish *Dolphin* and its cargo, returning the spoils only after the Spanish petitioned Ahmad al-Mansur for intervention in the return of their property.[56] In *Fair Maid Part I*, Ambassador Bridges convinces Mullisheg to forgive all transgressions, his sole reward a chaste kiss. Not a titillating kiss between a flirt and a king, this gesture simply mirrors those kisses she has previously bestowed upon her admirers in evidence of her exemplary chastity, her worth as Queen Elizabeth's representative. The sultan's heroic spirit, generosity, honor, and overall good humor are lauded by the English and the satisfied merchants, and his confirmation of Bridges as a "girl worth gold" points toward her perfection as well as to his own elevation over Philip II, who dressed Stukeley in tawdry "glitter." Untarnished by treason, inconstancy or greed, Bridges symbolizes the very best of English virtue. Concomitantly, the victor at Alcazar, while not so constant (he craves an intercultural harem) and not nearly so self-negating, represents the best of Moroccan virtue: he is a king actually worth gold and a man, a Moor, on almost equal terms with good Queen Bess. If the theatrical Bess Bridges is seen to "bosom" with a Moor following her voyage from England aboard the *Negro*, the image is not one of simple cross-racial titillation: rather, her embrace of Mullisheg reflects the queen's long-term history of diplomatic "bosoming" with her Moroccan ally. From this iconic voyage, part piratical and part diplomatic, Bridges is set to bring home freed English captives, Spanish booty, Moroccan gold, and international goodwill.

Bridges's history was not narrowly confined to Morocco. Like Stukeley's, her adventures take place in a global context. England's major threat was not Muslim difference but England's risk for absorption by European Catholics, and, especially, by Spain which had striven to invade England indirectly through Ireland and directly by sea. Morocco facilitated England's avoidance of imperial engulfment by trading materials of war and providing safe Mediterranean and Atlantic ports for commercial and military shipping; England performed a reciprocal service in providing Morocco with vital weapons and naval timber with which to withstand ongoing Ottoman and Iberian military pressure. In the plays that were written and performed at this precise juncture the final scenes set in Africa form only part of the international nexus: like Stukeley, Bridges proceeds from English to Spanish and then to Moroccan territory.

The representation of English-Spanish interaction in both plays would have incensed contemporaneous audiences. Playgoers surely realized that Stukeley mistakes the tyranny of his Spanish host for generosity when Philip, remarking on his overweening pride and reckless gullibility, boasts "If England have but fifty thousand such, / the power of Spain their coast shall touch." Stukeley is characterized as a dual liability to English security while Bridges is deliberately figured as both a commercial and a political asset. The desperate situations in which *Fair Maid*'s Spencer and his merchant companion find themselves, first in Spanish waters and then in Morocco, shadow the mistreatment of Thomas Stukeley and his rival Vernon when they arrive in Spain. Captain Stukeley is not himself a merchant; however, the governor of Cadiz accuses him of fraud in evading customs duties, seizes his ships and horses, and commits him to prison. In contradistinction to the historical record that attests to his piracies and tends to justify the governor's suspicion, Stukeley is not, on this occasion, engaged in common piracy—only treason. His detention highlights Spanish greed, breach of hospitality, and, perhaps, stupidity. Vernon, too, merely a traveler, acts as spokesperson for an English sea captain and merchant whose ship and goods have been seized by the Spanish. To Philip II, Vernon accuses the Spanish of "unchristian" behavior in enticing him and the captain ashore in order to declare the ship a wreck and, thus, subject to seizure.[57] Philip restores the ship and goods—but, of course, the merchant in this case is completely innocent of any malfeasance and is entitled by "natural law" to his possessions.[58] Treaties from this era tend to specify exactly the conditions of punishment for trade infractions, which suggests that infractions were frequent and often subject to dire retribution. The 1604 Spanish-English peace agreement stipulates precisely the limitations to official retaliation.[59] It goes without saying that treaties, even in times of peace, were frequently ignored. Muslims in North Africa were not untutored in diplomacy or warfare with European powers; they were self-interested and experienced traders accustomed to the cheats and impositions of their Christian counterparts and fully capable of reciprocal double-dealing. However, in these two plays, the Spanish and their collaborators epitomize the international malefactor.

Bess Bridges's diplomatic resolution at Mullisheg's court is comic and celebratory; in contrast, the episodes describing English encounters with the Spanish navy underscore English disgust with Spanish treachery. Undoubtedly buoyed by the rout of the Spanish Armada but chagrined by Ralegh's failure to retain the Azores or permanently impair Cadiz, Heywood embodies Spanish immorality in the figure of the Spanish captain. Having captured the merchant vessel on which Spencer and his physician travel to Morocco, the captain refuses to accept any ransom and enslaves the Englishmen, presumably for galley or New World labor. Although he grudgingly acknowledges English pluck, he nonetheless threatens Spencer with torture rather than welcoming him as a chivalric peer. Bridges defeats the captain in battle, and, measuring English behavior by his own and expecting to be enslaved, he submits. Yet she simply confiscates his goods and releases his captives. At this juncture, the Spaniard contritely modifies his tone to one of awed respect: "I know not whom you mean, but be't your queen, / Famous Elizabeth, I shall report / She and her subjects both are merciful."[60] Both Bridges and the queen illuminate by inversion the excesses occasioned by Spanish vice.

Apart from Queen Elizabeth, merchants, officials, and sovereigns depicted in these plays are intransigent, not only in terms of personal honor but also in commercial transactions even when treaties regulated such behavior. In this era of circum-Atlantic piracy and mutual coastal raiding, bullion and goods were not the only valuable commodities, and West African slaves were not the only human commodity. The Spanish enslaved Christians and Muslims; North African corsairs alone or in cooperation with their governments enslaved or ransomed Christians and Africans; and English naval officers and pirates often sold their captives to other European nations. But official English policy was different: neither Christians nor Muslims seized from foreign shipping were subject to enslavement— even if they were sometimes exchanged for Englishmen, imprisoned, or even hanged. The difference may seem minor to us now, but it underscores an official rejection of institutionalized slavery within England proper. Queen Elizabeth's willingness to deport slaves already in residence, her efforts to redeem European captives, her failure to authorize an official slave trade, and, perhaps, above all, Henry Roberts's proposition to colonize the slave-rich empire of Morocco immediately after her death all point to her intolerance for this trade in human beings, no matter their race or religion. This is not to suggest that Elizabeth, any more than other Englishmen and women, was an exemplar of tolerance. Extreme violence in colonizing Ireland and converting the Irish to Protestantism served her interests by protecting England's western flank from Catholic invasion, and potential force against the natives was envisioned by the West Country men intent on settling North America. In contrast to the Iberians, whose imperial imperative enjoined them to baptize heathens both in the New World and in Africa, Elizabeth and her subjects had no colonial ambition in Morocco. The English therefore felt little compulsion to attempt to sway the infidel from his faith or his slave-trading, so long as these did not impinge on English affairs. England's imperial hopes did not, at that time, include the usurpation of African territories; African slaves were traded primarily by the Portuguese and the Dutch, and other African commodities were available through regular diplomatic channels. In matters of both national security and trade, therefore, Englishmen and Moroccans shared similar objectives that were mutually promoted by frequent diplomatic interaction and an absence of territorial conflict.

Staged in the early years of the century but not published until 1631, *Fair Maid* reiterates *Famous History*'s view of Stukeley's role in international events. The later play counterposes Stukeley's treasonous, intemperate, and choleric character to Bridges's patriotism, equanimity, and valor. Bess functions as Stukeley's positive foil—her gender, youth, beauty, piety, constancy, and cross-dressed valor rehearsing those qualities possessed by chapbook heroines and replicating the virulently nationalist agenda of Edmund Spenser's Britomart who defeated the warlike and effeminizing *Irish* rebel Radigund in Book V of *The Faerie Queene.* Putting aside for now other telling details of the Stukeley-Bridges correspondence, a vital one is that Stukeley hails from the West Country and Bridges, of course, is similarly a West Country native. When we read the play in its geopolitical context, her western heritage points us toward the West Country explorers and to Grace O'Malley, pirate and, ultimately, patriot from the west of Ireland. Although the "west" identifies a discrete region in England, in Bridges's designation "Fair Maid of the West" the term serves to balance Elizabeth's "West" with Ahmad's "East" and gestures toward England's ambition for colonial expansion west, across Ireland and thence to the shores of the New World. Indeed, "West Country men" such as Drake, Grenville, Hawkins, Ralegh, and Gilbert were all implicated in Irish pacification before they turned their hands to Atlantic piracy or sponsorship of New World colonization.[61] (It is well to bear in mind that Stukeley was also involved in a scheme to exploit Florida.) "West" is a linguistic cornerstone bearing the full weight of English-Moroccan diplomacy in the actualization of England's pacification of Ireland and its prospective colonization of North America.

New World settlement overcame the Elizabethan antipathy to institutional slavery in part by colonists' imitation of Spanish and Portuguese conquest but primarily, after the Restoration, by Charles II's chartering of the English slave trade. Jamestown was established just a few years after Elizabeth's death on the foundation of English-Moroccan amity that had been fostered during a prolonged period of Spanish aggression. But the geopolitical world was undergoing radical shifts driven by new monarchies, revised government policies, and mass migrations: English men and women traveled to the New World and killed or displaced Native Americans, Spanish Moriscos were deported to North Africa; Europeans carried ever more African slaves to the Caribbean. During the entire course of the seventeenth century, plays with African and Muslim themes continued to depict or analogize the turbulence characterizing the Mediterranean/Atlantic region from the time of the Spanish reconquista.[62] Just as the characterization of Spaniards in contemporaneous drama reflected and perhaps shaped English imperial history, so too the characterization of

England, Morocco, and Global Geopolitical Upheaval   171

Moroccans reflected and shaped assumptions about England's relations with Morocco and with Africa in general. With its powerful king, long-term history of civil interaction, comprehensible laws, and enduring spirit of cooperation, Morocco inspired historically grounded characters for the English stage only slightly inferior to the self-congratulatory English. Indeed, in 1604 John Smith ranks Ahmad al-Mansur's Morocco high on an English workingman's scale of satisfaction:

so much [al-Mansur] delighted in the reformation of workmanship, hee allowed each of them ten shillings a day standing fee, linnen, woollen, silkes, and what they would for diet and apparell; and custome-free to transport, or import what they would.[63]

Had the colonial government of Jamestown offered so much, the English immigrants and Native Americans might have found reasons for cooperation.

The stage at the turn of the century served a utilitarian role in disseminating news about current events, and the plays central to this study, touching as they do on local and international affairs, supplemented the historical record and narratives of travelers. They constitute a brief dramatic historiography that reveals popular attitudes and opinions that helped chart the rise of England's empire, ideologically opposed to Spaniards and Catholicism yet tolerant of Moroccan Moors and their religious difference. In short, they establish the ideological and diplomatic context within which Jamestown became feasible. In the New World, in North Africa, or in Europe, the Spanish with their well-publicized array of vices and accessible, comprehensive history served as the preeminent foils for English practices and what the English preferred to consider their own domestic and colonial sobriety and moderation. To the English, infidels—whether Muslim, Moor, or Native American—were always envisioned, at least prospectively, as allied players in the geopolitical opposition to Spain and its Catholic network. Yet after Charles II acquired the Moroccan port of Tangier in 1662 and chartered the Atlantic slave trade, the theatrical representation of both Spaniards and Moroccans became ever more unhistorical and romanticized. It remains to be seen whether this change resulted from a proliferation of news periodicals, a dramatic trend premised on the availability of continental romances, or a new—but by no means improved—paradigm of England's global self-fashioning following upon its expropriation of vast tracts of North America and the institutionalization of chattel slavery.

Chapter 8
Irish Colonies and the Americas

ANDREW HADFIELD

> *By translating of colonies, the people conquered are drawen and intised by little and little, to embrace the manners, lawes, and government of the conqueror . . . the colonies being placed and dispersed abroade amongest the people, like Beacons doe foretell and disclose all conspiracies, and as a garrison also are wont to suppresse the mutinies of such as are desirous of alteration and change . . . lastly, they yeelde a yearely rent, profite, or service unto the crowne for ever[.]*

Epimenides's enthusiastic endorsement of colonies as a means of establishing order and government in Ireland in Richard Beacon's dialogue *Solon His Follie* (1594) neatly illustrates the varied and complex nature of the early modern colony. As the first of the three propositions illustrates, following the Roman model colonies are seen in terms of *translatio imperii*, the translation of authority and its culture from the conquering realm to the conquered, bringing in their wake manners, laws, and proper government.[1] The second reason in favor of colonization emphasizes the military and strategic importance of colonies which serve as military outposts able to root out conspiracies and so prevent and suppress rebellion. Beacon's recommendation of the military purpose of colonies/garrisons may well be received wisdom, but the victories of Lord Charles Mountjoy, which brought the Nine Years War to an end in the early 1600s, depended in part on his shrewd establishment of military outposts.[2] The pun on the author's name indicates how important the author felt the role of colonies was, and how they could shed light into areas of darkness, reclaiming them for civilization. The third reason, revenue for the crown, is clearly designed to assuage the fears of the queen—to whom *Solon His Follie* was dedicated—or any crown servant that extensive colonization would be a significant drain on crown finances. The expense of intervening in Ireland, as elsewhere, was often the cause of Elizabeth's cautious approach to problems that her more militant subjects felt could be solved through immediate military action.[3]

It is clear that in Beacon's text colonies were not only supposed to fulfill a variety of needs but were also envisaged in different, almost inevitably competing, ways. On the one hand colonies spread culture and government from the colonizer to the colonized; on the other, they helped to protect the colonizer from the hostility of the colonized, bringing to light any opposition and attempt to resist English rule in Ireland. While the first conception of the colony imagines the two peoples' integrating and mingling, the second sees them carefully kept apart.

Beacon's dual conception of the purpose of colonies expresses the divided nature of early modern colonialism, not just in Ireland, but further afield, most significantly in the Americas. In times of plenty, peace, and confidence colonizers would advocate that they could mingle with the peaceful but ignorant natives and so spread Christianity and civilization to a backward land. In times of dearth and mutual hostility arguments would center around the need to use colonies as garrisons to control a recalcitrant population. Indeed, as I will argue below, in some colonial propaganda the author attempts to argue the former case but has to admit that the latter is the reality. The debate which took place at Sir Thomas Smith's home, Hill House, Theydon Mount, in 1570–71, as a prelude to colonial activity in Ireland, saw the disputants argue over a passage in Livy. One side argued that the hard-line Marcellus was right to pursue unscrupulous and ruthless tactics in the pursuit of his military aims; the other sympathized with the more principled and moderate Fabius. The debate served as a prelude to Sir Thomas Smith's planned colonization of the Ards Peninsula.[4] The reality in colonial Ireland mirrored the theory. The Ulster Plantation was established in 1609 as a series of walled cities, precisely because the dispersed model of the Munster Plantation had rendered it especially vulnerable to a concerted attack and it was easily destroyed by Hugh O'Neill's forces, who could rely on considerable help from the local Irish in the fall of 1598.[5] In the Americas, as Bernard Sheehan has argued, representations of the natives as pliable, capable of reason, and good neighbors coincided with periods of peace and optimism; representations of them as savage, ineluctably hostile, and needing to be controlled with a rod of iron occurred when the two peoples were in conflict.[6]

In this essay I plan to explore this binary division in English colonial theory and practice in the years leading up to the establishment of the Jamestown colony in 1607. I want to show how colonialism and texts that explicitly argue for colonial ventures are not monolithic in purpose or style, indicating that we need to be very careful when generalizing about the phenomenon of colonialism, as a means of preserving rather than undermining its usefulness.[7] As Robert Young has pointed out, "Despite the heterogeneity of history, geography, and administrative models, from the point of view of the colonized society, colonization of all forms brought about similar disruptive consequences."[8] My concern here is the interrelationship between English colonial ventures in Ireland and in the Americas in the late sixteenth century, whether they can be seen as part of the same process, with the one leading to the other. I will specifically address the question of the impact of the example of Ireland on English attempts to colonize America.

Ideologies of Expansion

There undoubtedly was a relationship between English expansion in Ireland and America, a phenomenon that became known as the "Westward Enterprise."[9] Indeed, Ireland was the main area of colonial activity for the English. Colonies were established as early as the middle of the sixteenth century in Leix and Offaly in the center of Ireland; in the early 1570s in Ulster (although these were a disaster and were easily destroyed by the native Irish); in Munster in the 1580s, when huge numbers of English settlers occupied the lands of the defeated Earl of Desmond; and, when Ireland had finally been conquered after the Battle of Kinsale (1601), in Ulster in the early seventeenth century.[10] In fact, "For 80 years after 1560, Ireland attracted more English settlers than all American and Caribbean colonies combined. Only after 1641, when the Irish rose and killed thousands of English settlers, did the Western Hemisphere replace Ireland as a preferred site for English colonization."[11] Very few settlers returned from the Roanoke colonies established in the 1580s—apart from John White and Thomas Hariot.[12] When the Jamestown colony was established in 1607, colonial experience in Ireland formed the only serious precedent and means of making sense of the New World.

Many colonial pioneers had experience in both areas, notably Sir Walter Ralegh, who owned vast tracts of land in Munster, sponsored the Roanoke Voyages (even though he never actually went on them), and sailed to Guiana twice to locate the mythical golden city, El Dorado.[13] Equally significant was the experience of Ralegh's stepbrother, Sir Humphrey Gilbert, a soldier with a brutal reputation, who served in Ireland in the 1570s, before becoming interested in colonizing the Americas, and perished in the Azores on the way back from Newfoundland.[14] Furthermore, Ralph Lane, Thomas Hariot, and John White were all involved in the less than successful attempts to colonize Roanoke Island, and all ended up on the Munster Plantation, presumably remaining in the orbit of their master, Ralegh.[15]

Also of note are the Sidney family, Sir Henry and Sir Philip, who were prepared—although never actually undertook—to make the longest journey westward of the lot. The father started out as governor in England's first real colony, Wales, before moving to Ireland; the son was only prevented from traveling to the New World in the 1570s on the explicit orders of the queen.[16] Nicholas Canny suggests that the key figure in the development of English attitudes was Sir Henry Sidney, a man, according to Canny, deeply and carefully read in the literature of the New World—José de Acosta, Johan Boemus, and Peter Martyr d'Anghera.[17] It was Sidney who saw the possibilities of using colonies to subdue and conquer the Irish, encouraging the poorly thought out efforts of the earl of Essex senior and Sir Thomas Smith on the Ards Peninsula in the 1570s, "a major advance in English colonial practice."[18] Furthermore, Sidney's suggestion that a system of forts, built by the crown but financed by the lords involved, be used to establish colonies in Ulster was later adopted as the model for New World colonies.[19] The harsh treatment meted out to the native Americans was often a result of bitter experiences in Ireland, confirming suspicions that they must be like the bad natural savages who had been encountered nearer home, not the peaceful creatures represented elsewhere.

The Irish and the Americans were seen as similar peoples who needed to be colonized and so made civilized; proponents of colonization in Ireland were keen to learn from and copy Spanish precedents in the New World. Furthermore, models of colonial venture developed in Ireland were then exported back to the Americas when English colonization began in earnest, so that "The Elizabethan conquest of Ireland should therefore be viewed in the wider context of European expansion."[20] Englishmen who had no special advantages of birth—often second sons who would not inherit any land under the rules of primogeniture—could sometimes make substantial fortunes in Ireland. Settling in Ireland was a safer alternative to risking a voyage to the New World, which could be, as Gilbert's fate illustrates, hazardous in the extreme.[21] Despite the failures of colonies in Ireland in the 1570s, interest revived again in the 1580s when the Munster Plantation "renewed prospects of cheap Irish land" and, given that many of the surnames "associated with the early ventures in Ireland recurred in later plantations both in Ireland and Virginia," the early disasters nevertheless "contributed towards the establishment of a pattern of conquest."[22]

More recently, the direct and specific link between colonialism in Ireland and the Americas has been modified and questioned. Rather, it is argued, colonial theory and practice can be seen to come from the same series of classical and European sources and authorities: Livy, Herodotus, Tacitus, Justus Lipsius, and, most important, Machiavelli. Colonialism does not have to be read as a trans-Atlantic phenomenon based on first-hand experience in Ireland; it can be read, more comprehensively, as a European development, at once internal and external.[23] Machiavelli, after all, was not providing a blueprint for intercontinental expansion and domination, but explaining to governors how to rule peoples and territories adjacent to their principalities.[24] It was a commonplace that Ireland was at the same stage of development as England had been when conquered by the Romans, the invaders in each case providing much needed law, order, and civilization.[25] Such links suggest that the writings of the ancients—especially Tacitus's *Agricola* and *Germania*—were a further dimension that complicated notions of straightforward links between the natives of Ireland and the natives of the New World.[26]

As the debate at Hill House demonstrates, Sir Thomas Smith's project for colonizing the Ards peninsula grew out of a series of intellectual discussions of Livy at Smith's house. None of the participants in the debate seem to be making any close link between Ireland and the Americas, but seeing colonial theory and practice in terms of the wisdom of the ancients. More significantly still, substantial and sustained arguments produced in lengthy works analyzing the ways and means of controlling Ireland in the 1590s also turn to Latin and Greek examples rather than ones from the Americas. Sir William Herbert's *Croftus sive de Hibernia Liber* (ca. 1591), a work which its modern editors consider to be "the considered reaction of a cultivated but unimaginative gentleman to his Irish experiences," makes no mention of the Americas but turns time and again to the canon of classical authorities familiar to educated English readers in the Renaissance for support—Aristotle, Plato, Cicero, Tacitus, Boethius—as well as modern authors such as Machiavelli and Justus Lipsius.[27] Herbert includes an extensive discussion of colonization as a means of establishing control over Ireland derived from Tacitus, Plato, and Herodotus, emphasizing the dual purpose of colonization:

> In conducting and establishing colonies two things in particular must be avoided, first their dissolution, second their degeneration. . . . Tacitus mentions the first cause: when colonies are being conducted one should not simultaneously despatch separate and scattered individuals from different cities and regiments, but rather entire tribes and neighbouring tribes or regiments assembled together.
> Plato put it excellently: in conducting colonies the laws, location, land allotments and fortifications of the colony and also its method of government should be carefully delineated and protected.
> Herodotus says briefly and to good effect: a colony, if it is to be capable of protecting itself against the natives, must not be conducted into a foreign place at random but with prudence.[28]

Herbert's recommendations and concerns are roughly equivalent to the military, social and political issues raised by Richard Beacon's discussion of colonization cited at the start of this essay. Beacon, more so than Herbert, stresses the crucial role that colonies will play in establishing civilization and restructuring Irish society. Colonization is discussed and analyzed as the last and most effective solution to the problem of "declined commonweales" in the final chapter of *Solon His Follie*.[29] Neither author mentions the colonies established in the Americas, but frequently refers the reader to the discussions of colonization in Machiavelli, Cicero, Herodotus, Lipsius, and so on. The same is also true of Edmund Spenser's *A View of the Present State of Ireland* (ca. 1596), which contains an extensive discussion of garrisons but has little on colonies.[30] There are clearly dangers in equating the situations of English settlers in Ireland and those in the Americas.[31]

Furthermore, it needs also to be noted that Englishmen and women in Ireland did not view all the Irish as wild, uncivilized savages, even in times of crisis. Obviously they interacted with a variety of Irish men and women, from lowly servants to aristocrats, in the same ways that they would have done in English society.[32] There is a danger in assuming that arguments in pamphlets, treatises, and manuscript letters, explicitly designed to persuade government officials to intervene in Ireland, can be taken at face value when they have a vested interest in deliberately exaggerating the wild and unruly nature of the Irish in order to make their cases even stronger. Indeed, it is possible that few English writers actually believed exactly what they were arguing in public (although proving this would be difficult). Society in Dublin and the Pale (the surrounding area controlled and administered by the English) was heavily Anglicized, as it was in other areas such as Cork city; far less so the further one traveled into the north of Ulster (especially Donegal), or the west of Connacht.[33] English observers often reacted with shock when Irish lords chose to rebel against them, illustrating that they felt that such aristocrats were properly civilized and would therefore choose to be English. The reactions to Hugh O'Neill's rebellion in the 1590s are the most high profile case in point.[34] It is doubtful if native American society was seen in the same way.[35]

And one final point needs to be borne in mind, namely, how important and effective was propaganda and reasoned analysis anyway? Did people really take it seriously and make use of colonial theory and comparative government as Quinn and Canny claim? Might we not argue that if Gilbert, Lane, and Ralegh behaved in brutal ways in colonial situations it was simply because they were brutal men like Lord Grey, not because they had been persuaded by what they had read to behave in that manner?[36] Too much can be made of the link between an individual's presence in Ireland and in Virginia. Lane and Gilbert were soldiers who also served in the Low Countries and elsewhere, traveling wherever they were needed, and could occupy themselves with employment.[37] It is no surprise if people on the make gravitate toward areas where it has been claimed large fortunes can be made, as was generally claimed for Ireland and America. It is worth noting that the largest fortune acquired in the British Isles in the late sixteenth century was that of Richard Boyle, first earl of Cork (1566–1643), through his unscrupulous appropriation of land titles in Ireland.[38] Many literary figures—including Barnaby Googe, Edmund Spenser, Barnaby Rich, John Bale, and Walter Ralegh—spent time in Ireland, mainly because it was one of the areas where money could be made for those who did not inherit land and wealth themselves.[39] And, as Karen Kupperman has argued, we should not assume that those at home and those in the Americas read things in the same way, believed the same propaganda, or behaved identically. Professor Kupperman's point is that the Virginia colonists existed in relative harmony with the local natives until the 1622 Massacre, and we should ignore the more hostile representations of the Indians produced by those who never left England when assessing the actual interaction of natives and colonists and concentrate on the writings and records of those who knew what they were encountering.[40] Equally, one might suggest that those who behaved badly would have done so anyway, and wherever they were.

However, while issuing these series of cautions about making too direct a link between the two spheres of colonial activity, I think it would be a grave mistake to deny a series of links between the ways in which Englishmen represented Ireland and America, and the Irish and the Americans. No text should ever be reduced to one context, or placed within one discursive field. Historians of genre point out that no work can ever be said to belong to one genre and exist as a "pure" form of writing. In the same way, it is clear that connections were made between English experience in the Americas and Ireland, even if such links were denied or suppressed. A whole range of contexts and meanings must be considered, even if some are not obvious at first sight. Analysis should never be a simple question of either/or, but rather, both/and, as the evidence surveyed in the next section indicates.[41]

The Wild Irish

Some comments—almost asides—in various documents written in Ireland in the late sixteenth and early seventeenth centuries indicate that writers did think of the native—often referred to as "wild"—Irish in terms of the peoples of the Americas.[42] Sir John Dowdall, an army captain serving during the Nine Years War, wrote to Lord Burghley from the fort at Dungannon in 1596, describing the rebellious Irish as "these cannibals."[43] We know from the researches of Peter Hulme that the use of a word such as "cannibal"—"tempest" is another—connotes a New World context. "Cannibal" was the word used to describe the Caribs, natives of the Caribbean, who were held to have been man-eaters, an argument, which, as Hulme has demonstrated, inevitably becomes circular so that "cannibal" comes to mean "man-eating native of the Caribbean" rather then a term to describe the people who lived in the Caribbean.[44] It replaced the older term "anthropophagi," notably used in Shakespeare's *Othello*, which has an African as its protagonist, whereas *The Tempest*, partly based on accounts of the Americas, refers more obviously to "cannibal" in the name "Caliban," indicating that one writer certainly knew the implications of geographical location.[45]

But could Dowdall have made the same connections? We might ask a whole series of questions about the use of this one particular word. Was he indulging in a frenzied outburst, not really meaning what he was saying? Or did he really think that the Irish were like the nasty native Americans of popular report? And was he suggesting that they were like them, or did his usage indicate that he was indulging in the sort of postdiluvian racial theory commonly found in the works of writers such as Jean Bodin, Jacob Boemus, Stephen Batman, and others?[46] The context does not help us a great deal. Dowdall notes that the Irish rebels "have drawn the greatest part of their kerne to be musketeers, and their gallowglasses pikes, they want no fowling pieces, calivers, swords, grave murrions, powder and shot great store." The "cannibals" are surrounded by military technology which they "were unaccustomed to have in this measure." In other words, they are a people habitually without sophisticated means of warfare who are now dangerous because the gap between them and their more advanced enemies, the English, has been bridged. Is Dowdall pointing out a sharp contrast between their habitual state and their newly acquired hardware? Or, should we simply read the comment as a piece of undigested prejudice and file it as an insult that reveals little?

The word "cannibal" is used in other works and in other contexts. Another example is the usage made by Luke Gernon, writing around 1620—this time after the successful American colonies had been established and entered English consciousness far more clearly. Gernon's long letter to an unknown friend, later given the title "A Discourse of Ireland" by editors, shows the author trying to persuade his friend that "The Irishman is no Caniball to eate you up nor lowsy Jack to offend you."[47] Once again, it is not entirely clear whether this is an off the cuff remark of little consequence, a piece of sly humour in a familiar letter, or a real effort to counter some poisonous rumors circulating in England (one might compare the dark hints contained in Hariot's *Briefe and True Report*; see below) that criticism of the American colonies had reached quite serious levels, or the painful efforts of another Englishman in Ireland, Robert Payne, whose *Brief Description in Ireland*, printed in 1590, aimed to persuade his former neighbors in Nottinghamshire that it really was safe to move over the Irish Sea and settle in Elizabeth's other island.[48] However we choose to read it, the reference does suggest that some Englishmen were making the connection between the Irish and the natives of the Americas.

This point is made even more forcefully in one of Barnaby Rich's characteristically unguarded moments (Rich later commented that "thos wordes that in Englande would be brought wythin the compasse of treason, they are accounted wyth us in Ireland for ordynary table taulke," which was hardly surprising given what he was prepared to say in other circumstances and clearly just as well for him).[49] In a *New Description of Ireland* (1610) Rich stated that the "barbarous Irish" were worse than the Scythians or the cannibals in their cruelty and lawlessness.[50] Rich subsequently wrote a lengthy defense of his comments, *A True and Kinde Excuse written in defence of that booke, intitled A Newe Description of Ireland* (1612), clearly because his comments caused such offence. Rich referred to the "poysoned speares of slanderous tongues" and claimed that he had not criticized the Irish for their barbaric nature but simply their adherence to Catholicism.[51] He further claimed that he had only criticized some of the Irish for their barbarity, and that England also contained similar areas full of primitive people. There were, he added, many good Irish as well as bad ones. However, the evidence that some readers—Dubliners, according to Rich—took his comments at face value, does indicate that many people were making the comparisons between the two spheres of colonial activity, and either finding the juxtaposition instructive, or vehemently denying the connection.

One final example does provide evidence of the use of specific texts, namely, Robert Payne's *Brief Description of Ireland*. The title of Payne's short work must surely echo that of Thomas Hariot's important and well known *A Briefe and True Report of the New Found Land of Virginia*, published the previous year (and it should be noted that Hariot was in Munster in 1589, having returned from Virginia).[52] Payne—like Hariot—spends a lot of time telling his readers what fine produce, minerals, and wealth can be obtained in Ireland.[53] Payne also—like Hariot—is at pains to stress the friendly and pliable nature of the natives who are keen to surrender to English rule and cooperate with the colonists. Both emphasize that any reports to the contrary are to be ignored as aberrations and the propaganda of the disaffected.[54]

It is important to note that Payne makes a clear reference to Bartolomé de Las Casas's *The Spanish colonie, or briefe chronicle of the acts and gestes of the Spaniardes*, the most graphic and disturbing account of the atrocities committed by the Spaniards in the New World, which had been translated into English by the unknown M. M. S. in 1583 (does Payne's title allude to Las Casas's work?).[55] Payne argues that Las Casas's text has been widely circulated in Ireland among the Catholic Irish and has helped to turn them against their coreligionists:

Most of the better sort of the Irish haue read of their monsterous cruelties in the west Indies, where they most tiranously haue murthered many millions moe of those simple creaturs then now liue in Ireland, euen such as sought their fauours by offering unto them al that they had, neuer resisting nor offering them any harme. Wherefor I doubt not, that the Irish are so foolish to entertaine such proud guestes knowing their tyrannie, and hauing not so well deserued at their handes as those simple soules whom they so cruelly murdered.[56]

Las Casas, according to Payne, serves as a prophylactic for rebellion in Ireland, encouraging faith in the ruling colonial government of the English and distrust of the would-be liberators.[57] Moreover, Payne's comments reveal the extent to which Irish and American colonial ventures were part of the same struggle for the English, a means of protecting their Protestant identity against the aggression of the Catholic Antichrist, a message repeated time and again in the writings of the principal propagandist for empire, Richard Hakluyt.[58] This way of linking colonial spheres of activity should not be overlooked, indicating that it is false to see them as separate concerns because they were seen as part of a larger enterprise, namely the struggle between Protestantism and Catholicism. European concerns were never simply limited to Europe but subsumed wider enterprises too.[59]

The Americans and the Picts

The comments above were all made by men who resided in Ireland and never made it to the Americas—although it is hard to believe that they had not encountered some who had been, given the number of trans-Atlantic voyagers who were involved in Ireland. But more sustained links between the Irish and the native Americans were made by those who did travel there, most notably in Thomas Hariot's *Briefe and True Report of the New Found Land of Virginia*, a work the impact of which can hardly be underestimated.[60] The short report was first published in 1588, as a small quarto, which seems to have had some influence—as Payne's work suggests. It was clearly important enough—being the first published analysis of the Roanoke colonies—to have been included not only in Hakluyt's first volume of the *Principal Navigations* (1589), but also as the first part of Theodor De Bry's massive multinational and multilingual compendium of voyages, *America*.[61] Hariot's volume came out in a handsome folio edition in 1590, accompanied by a series of illustrations based on the drawings of John White, official artist and some time governor of the Roanoke colony and, to a lesser extent, Jacques Le Moyne de Morgues, a Huguenot refugee in England who had escaped from the French colony in Florida in 1564 when it was destroyed by the Spanish. De Bry's *America* continued in print long after his death—new editions appear in Latin as late as 1634, in German as late as 1655.[62]

The illustrations in the 1590 De Bry folio are of major significance and have occasioned much comment.[63] They conclude with a sequence of five plates representing "Som pictures of the Pictes which in the olde tyme dyd habite one part of the great Bretainne," obviously the least specifically American images in the volume (Figures 8.1, 8.2). The Picts are shown to be savage, violent, and uncivilized. The first picture shows a Pict with a naked tattooed torso, long hair and moustache, brandishing the severed head of an enemy, while another head rests in the foreground; the second shows a Pictish woman, also naked with flowing locks and a body similarly tattooed with patterns, suns, and stars, and, on her right shoulder, a wolf. She carries two spears in her right hand and one in her left. The third picture is of "a yonge dowgter of the Pictes" who stares at the reader with apparently aggressive intent. She is also naked, heavily tattooed, mainly with flowers, has long flowing locks and rests on a spear she is holding.[64] The last two images show the "neighbours unto the Picte," that is, the Bri-

Figure 8.1. "The truue picture of one Picte," engraving by Theodor de Bry after a drawing by John White. Hariot, *Briefe and True Report* (1590), part 5, pl. 1. Courtesy of the John Carter Brown Library, Brown University. After a series of plates representing the natives of the region around Roanoke, Hariot's *Report* includes a set of images representing ancient British peoples in order "to showe . . . that the Inhabitants of the great Bretannie have bin in times past as sauvage as those of Virginia."

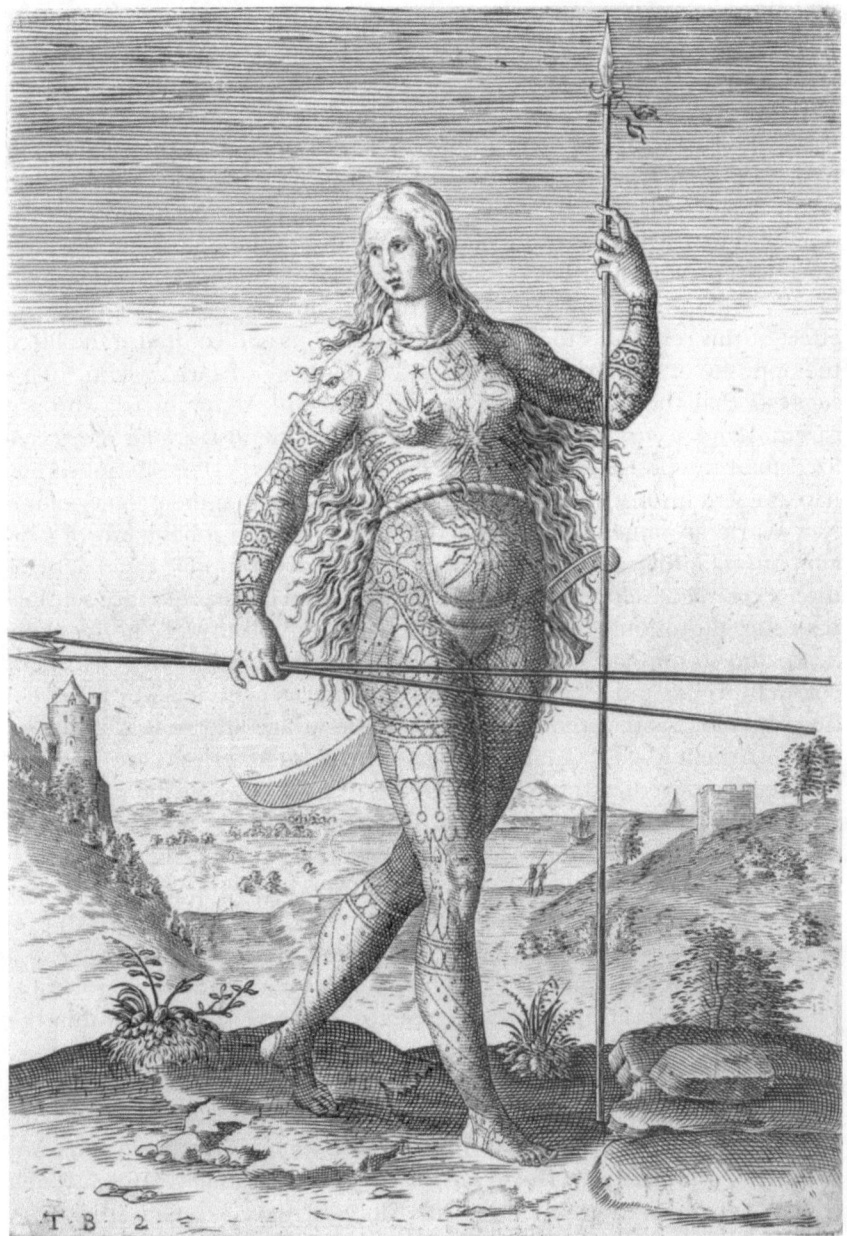

Figure 8.2. "The truue picture of a women Picte," engraving by Theodor de Bry after a drawing by John White. Hariot, *Briefe and True Report* (1590), part 5, pl. 2. Courtesy of the John Carter Brown Library, Brown University.

tons. They are significantly more civilized than the Picts, wearing clothes, sporting no tattoos or body art, although they also brandish spears and possess swords.

These five images form a disturbing sequence for a number of reasons. It is significant that the Picts are highlighted rather than the Britons, an unusual choice given the number of histories and chronicles which, often taking their cue from Geoffrey of Monmouth's *History of the Kings of Britain*, represent the Britons as the ancient inhabitants of the island and the Picts as savage marauding tribes of border raiders in Scotland.[65] It is clear that the "Neighbours to the Picts" are the Britons, but they are not named. The effect of this reversal is to marginalize the Britons and centralize the Picts, the opposite of the order usually found in histories of early Britain.[66] This suggests that the native Americans, the peaceful Algonquians, who are carefully and accurately observed by Hariot as a scientist, are far more civilized than the savage inhabitants of the British Isles.[67] Does Hariot simply have ancient history in mind? If so, is he suggesting that the peoples of the New World are much more civilized than the ancient inhabitants of Britain? After all, they are shown to build towns, have a sophisticated agriculture, a clearly developed system of law, and social order, eat more sensibly than the gluttonous English, look after their children well, honor their dead, and so on, hardly the traits of a primitive people. This is excellent colonial propaganda, because it works to alleviate the fears of potential English colonists that the Americans are the savage and violent creatures they fear them to be.[68] On the contrary, the native Americans are shown to be docile, civilized, and intelligent creatures in contrast to the savage and violent Picts. Furthermore, the pictures imply that if the Britons could triumph to rule over more dangerous people, then so can English colonists in the Americas, who only have to face a friendly people lacking proper religion, a problem that can easily be rectified because they are already predisposed to accept the truth of Christian belief.

But the images undoubtedly also have a more contemporary resonance. The terrifying Picts can perhaps be seen as the current savages within the realm who threaten the civil and social order of English civilization, i.e., the Irish. They appear naked, in contrast to their clothed, and hence more civilized, neighbors, just as the Irish invariably did. Fynes Moryson narrates an incident in his account of his travels throughout Europe, *An Itinerary Containing His Ten Yeeres Travell through the Twelve Dominions* (1617), which concludes with an epigram of Irish life. Moryson describes the terrible Irish diet and unseemly behaviour of Irish women before demonstrating their effects on a visitor:

> An Italian friar coming of old into Ireland, and seeing at Armach this their diet and nakednesse of the women . . . is said to have cried out,
> Civitas Armachana, Civitas vana,

Carnes crudae, mulieres nudae.
Vaine Armach City, I did thee pity,
Thy meates rawnes, and womens nakednesse.
 . . . To conclude, not onely in lodging passengers, not at all or most rudely, but even in their inhospitality towards them, these wild Irish are not much unlike to wild beasts, in whose caves a beast passing that way, might perhaps finde meate, but not without danger to be ill intertained, perhaps devoured of his insatiable Host.[69]

Moryson was a vociferous Protestant who served as Lord Mountjoy's secretary during the last years of the Nine Years War.[70] Therefore his point is made all the more forcefully because the observation is that of an Italian friar, showing that even the natural allies of the Irish are shocked by their lack of civilization.[71]

The Picts are represented as a bellicose people, brandishing weapons and aggressively confronting the civilized observer. The opening picture shows the Pictish man with one severed head in his hand and another resting by his feet: a resonant image. The accompanying note states, "And when they hath ouercomme some of their enemies, they did neuer felle to carye awe their heads with them." The landscape of severed heads might have reminded readers of the frequency with which heads on sticks were displayed in the woodcuts to John Derricke's *The Image of Irelande* (1581), one of the most impressive series of images to emerge from the Tudor period.[72] It might also be linked to descriptions such as that of Murrogh O'Brien's foster-mother drinking his blood after his execution in 1577, recounted in Spenser's *View*.[73] Spenser explicitly links the practice of blood drinking to the ancient Gauls, something that marks both peoples out as primitive and hostile to civilization. In general, similar social practices and rituals were seen to establish a link between peoples, who were then thought to have a common origin.[74] Hariot, I would suggest, is making use of precisely this type of logic to force readers to make the links that he wants them to make. In short, these naked, warlike Picts would have looked much more like the Irish than the American Indians to a late sixteenth-century reader.

If so, then it seems reasonable to claim that Hariot's *Report* has one eye on Ireland as it looks squarely at the New World, making the point that the greater distance and greater journey, if braved, might yield more hospitable and profitable results for those able to undertake the venture than attempts to colonize Ireland. The text itself ends with the famous and much-analyzed description of the deaths of the Indians from imported disease and their inability to explain events in terms of their own understanding of the world.[75] This may, of course, contain some unorthodox religious and political sentiments. But, equally, it suggests that the moment is ripe for the colonizing English to bring their religious, cultural, and technical superiority to Virginia and sort out the worthy but benighted natives once and for all.[76] Protestantism will explain why some live and some die better than the natives' own religion and belief in "invisible bullets." The frontispiece to the sequence of illustrations shows Adam and Eve about to pick the apple from the tree of knowledge, a clear indication that a key moment in world history has been inaugurated by the discovery of the Americas (Figure 8.3).[77] There are various possibilities. The English can colonize the natives effectively and well, enlarging God's (Protestant) empire. They can do it badly and cruelly, destroying the Edenic Paradise of the New World. Or, worst of all, they can leave the innocent Americans to become the prey of the Spanish, evil Catholics in the grip of the Antichrist. Colonialism was always conceived as an extension of the struggle in Europe for religious supremacy.[78] Ireland, as part of the ancient island cluster, in contrast, seems a more difficult proposition, perhaps because of opportunities missed, perhaps because the natives are more corrupt and less amenable than those in Virginia, more Pict than Algonquian. But we should note that Payne's *Description*, also a piece of colonial propaganda, makes the opposite case and tries to plug Ireland as a site for colonial settlement, possibly as a response to Hariot's.

Hariot's *Report*, in arguing that English and Americans can exist in mutual harmony, echoes a number of earlier English works on Ireland. One might point to Edmund Campion's *Historie of Ireland* (ca. 1570), an influential work by a Catholic martyr which formed the basis for Richard Stanihurst's work on Ireland in Holinshed's *Chronicles* (1577, 1587).[79] These works did represent the "wild" Irish in familiar stereotypical ways: as dirty, ignorant, violent, unable to form proper societies, etc., but argued that education would sort such problems out (the Irish were basically good and redeemable).[80] Clearly, representations of savages oscillate between images of good and bad savages, malleable or hostile, as numerous works on colonialism have argued.[81] Representations of Irish savages were no exception.

Furthermore, because the Campion/Stanihurst arguments appeared in Holinshed's influential and comprehensive chronicles, their approach entered the very mainstream and heart of English works on Ireland (although tempered in the 1587 edition by John Hooker's aggressive Protestant history and translation of Giraldus, illustrating the diverse nature of the work).[82] It is perhaps not surprising that many New English, English settlers who had come to Ireland in the sixteenth century, felt aggrieved at what they saw as their legitimate concern and right to govern as true Protestant Englishmen being undermined by the presence of the less severe solutions favored by the Old English, English settlers who had come to Ireland in the wake of the Norman conquest and who were mainly Catholic.[83] It is no accident that many New English, even in times of peace, tended to favor violent solutions to the Irish problem, ousting both "wild" Irish and Old English, and having no truck with any solution that failed to countenance

Figure 8.3. "Adam and Eve in Eden," engraving by Theodor de Bry. Hariot, *Briefe and True Report* (1590), p. 71. Courtesy of the John Carter Brown Library, Brown University.

drastic measures. Indeed, many New English targeted the Old English as more serious enemies than the "wild" Irish.[84]

The most sustained and carefully argued analysis of Ireland to make the case for the New English right to rule Ireland is Edmund Spenser's *A View of the Present State of Ireland*.[85] *A View*, unlike other works such as *Solon His Follie* and *Croftus*, does not recommend extensive colonization as a means of pacifying Ireland. This is principally because Spenser already lived on the largest and most successful English colony of the sixteenth century, the Munster Plantation (although he was writing just as it was about to be destroyed by Hugh O'Neill's forces in the Nine Years War). Spenser does refer to establishing garrisons in Ireland as a military means of controlling the rebellious populace. What is crucial to note about a *View* is that its violent solution to the Irish problem—sending out a huge army, victualed from England (an important point), granting surrender before a final conquest is organized, at which point Irish society can finally be rebuilt—comes in the teeth of the moderate suggestions and objections from Eudoxus, who cannot believe that Irenius can really be serious in his proposals.[86] Spenser is arguing the case that Irish society as it stands is inimical to reform. English and Irish cannot mix until English law has been properly established in Ireland, and this can only be done after a full military conquest. Readers are meant to complete the *View* won over to Irenius's proposals, however objectionable we might find them (most noticeably the famous Munster famine passage), convinced that the colonist in Ireland is right and metropolitan English objections misguided.[87]

A View, I would suggest, expresses in essence the colonists' dilemma. How were colonists to live in other cultures? Were they to become integrated and make use of native labor, treating natives as equals, servants, or slaves? This problem haunts English colonies in Ireland from the early efforts of the 1570s to the Londonderry Plantation, established alongside the Virginia Plantation.[88] In quiet times, attempts were made to integrate and cooperate with the natives, notably in the early plans for the colonies in the Ards, the Munster Plantation, and the Londonderry Plantation. In harsher times, strict separation was the order of the day, notably in the later plans for the Ards colonies and the Londonderry Plantation. *A View* is a treatise written at one of the worst times for English settlers and argues the worst possible case, indicating that we ought to read it alongside a desperate and aggressive treatise such as the anonymous "The Supplication for the blood of the English Most Lamentably Murdered in Ireland, Cryeng Out of the Yearth for Revenge" (1598), which also pleads for extensive military intervention to crush the rebellious Irish forces.[89] The extensive genealogical material aims to disabuse the Irish of their dreams of European/Spanish ancestry, with the claim that they are really of the barbarous race of the Scythians.[90] And Spenser is so afraid of Irish malice that he wants the invading army to be victualed from England, an extremely costly task.[91] In such times the colony becomes a fortress and colonization simply a military operation.

We need to pay attention to the specific moment when *A View* was actually written in order to understand its vicious and desperate language, descriptions, and proposals. It is instructive to contrast it to the work of Stanihurst and Campion written earlier and that of Sir John Davies written later (1612). In *A Discovery of the True Causes Why Ireland Was Never Entirely Subdued . . . until his Majesty's Happy Reign* (1612), Davies argues that previous attempts to reform Ireland failed because the English common law was not rigorously and impartially applied to Ireland as James was now attempting to do, a stark contrast to Spenser's recommendation that the common law be suspended as harmful until the time of conquest is over. Davies was writing at a time of optimism when many English colonists and administrators believed that Ireland was now properly subject to English rule and law, the Londonderry Plantation being a sign of future peace and prosperity (a rather neat historical irony given how frequently the Plantation is seen as the author of modern Ireland's divisions).[92]

Of course, as I have argued throughout this essay, there are larger patterns to be considered as well as specific contexts. Colonists in the Americas had similar experiences, sometimes integrating well with the natives, sometimes existing at war with the locals.[93] As Hariot's *Report* demonstrates, there was violence committed by his fellow countrymen, presumably the bellicose Ralph Lane, who, as Karen Kupperman has pointed out, was extremely successful as a military leader of the Roanoke colonies, but failed to make adequate provision for the social and economic growth of the community that was being established.[94] Lane ran Roanoke along strictly military lines, and it is no wonder that the lost colonists probably perished at the hands of Powhatan. But until the Massacre of 1622, relations can probably best be described as mixed.

Parallels and Continuities

What exactly was the relationship between Irish colonialism and the colonization of the Americas?[95] Parallels are easy to suggest, but a direct relationship is often harder to prove and can sometimes be an example of wishful thinking or ignorance of other possible sources and relationships between types of colonial theory and colonial practice. I will conclude with two series of observations relating English colonial experience in Ireland to that in North America. The first will record important empirical links which can be proved or disproved by research of the existing records. The second provides a series of the wider implications of the links between the two "contact zones" of colonial experience.[96]

In what specific ways can the experience of English colonial activity in Ireland be related to the establishment of American colonies? First, the joint-stock principle of colonial development was developed in Ireland and was later transferred to America, notably in the Virginia colonies after the establishment of the Virginia Company.[97] Second, the military experience and use of fortresses in Ireland undoubtedly influenced the form and development of colonies in America, especially given the overlap in figures involved. The same is also true of the development of colonial towns in both places.[98] Third, a related point, the anxiety of how closely to cooperate with the natives, was transferred from Ireland to the New World, and, to a lesser extent, back again. Fourth, some texts on Ireland appear to have been read by influential figures in American colonialism, just as texts on American colonialism were read by would-be colonists keen to establish settlements in Ireland.[99] Moreover, certain works such as Thomas Hariot's *Briefe and True Report* can be seen to be relevant to the colonial histories of Ireland and America, given the author's involvement in colonization in both places.

More generally, the following observations might be made. Colonial activity in both Ireland and America existed as part of a wider struggle perceived by colonial propagandists in particular as a religious conflict between the true Protestant church and the false Catholic Church of the Antichrist.[100] Such a clear perspective, I would argue, underlies a large collection of colonial and travel writing such as Richard Hakluyt's *Principal Navigations*, as well as Thomas Hariot's *Briefe and True Report*, a message made evident though the accompanying illustrations; specifically, the opening engraving of Adam and Eve.[101] Separating out the Americas from other aspects of English government at home or experience overseas gives us a false sense of how carefully different events and actions in diverse places were linked by contemporary Englishmen.

Second, the relationship between colonial thought in Ireland and the Americas was mutual and reciprocal. This occurred most obviously in the perception of the different peoples under scrutiny. As Hariot's *Report* and numerous works on Ireland demonstrate, Englishmen often saw one race in terms of the other, as comparison or contrast (Hariot's being a good example of contrast).

Third, discussions of colonial experience are often similar for different cases, making it easy to generalize and hard to point to specific influences. The examples of English colonies in Ireland in Ulster and Munster and those on Roanoke Island and Virginia are good examples of the ways in which policies and assumptions shuttle backwards and forwards from one extreme to another. Natives are cast as ignorant but redeemable when all is progressing well or the colonists are dependent on the indigenous population; they are cast as savage, violent, and implacable enemies when there is revolt or conflict. Colonies were accordingly designed to allow colonists and natives to intermingle, the natives acting as servants and laborers to the colonists; or as garrisons designed to control the natives, keeping them away from the dwellings of the colonists in order to protect the settlers.[102] The history of colonialism has to be written to take account of the overall picture without losing sight of the specific and individual cases. English colonialism in Ireland can neither be divorced from nor assimilated to colonialism in the Americas.

Part III
American Metamorphosis

Chapter 9
Hunger in Early Virginia
Indians and English Facing Off over Excess, Want, and Need

ROBERT APPELBAUM

About 15 percent of Thomas Hariot's *Brief and True Report*, whether in its 1588 or in its expanded and illustrated 1590 edition, is concerned with food and drink. That seems about right. In the first volume, Hariot is concerned with the "Marchantable Commodities" of Virginia (Part One) and "Such Commodities as Virginia is known to yield for victual and sustenance of man's life" (Part Two), as well as "Such Other Things" as would be useful for settlers to know (Part Three). In the second volume he is presenting "The True Pictures and Fashions of the People . . ."[1] From the point of view of the practicalities of colonization, food is obviously a primary concern, whether for trade or for daily sustenance. But from the point of ethnography, of knowing the "fashions" of the people, food is of primary interest too. Travel writing in Europe had already long since adopted the custom of reporting on the food practices of foreign peoples. If one wanted to understand the "customs" or "manners" of a people, one first of all needed to describe and decode what it was the people did to feed themselves, and how what they did was related to other social and economic practices. Even the fanciful *Utopia* is frequently preoccupied with explaining how the citizens of that fanciful land produced and consumed their food.

English ethnography in the New World beginning with Hariot was similarly preoccupied. Food practices could not tell the whole story of the peoples of the eastern seaboard, to be sure, especially given the obsessive interest of ethnographers in religion. But they articulated an important theme. Indeed, observations of food practices articulated a crucial demarcator of difference, which spoke not only to the fluid domain of habits and manners but to the deeper structures of social life. Food practices are not just a matter of table settings, as it were, a superficial arrangement for consuming goods whose deeper meaning lies elsewhere. They are invested in material life as such; they are intrinsic to the experience of ethnic identity and territorial community. And so when writers described the manners of

Native Americans, they turned to food practices as signs of who these people at bottom, materially, really were. But what the writers found was somewhat peculiar.

"They accustom themselves to no set Meals," Robert Beverley wrote of the Algonquian Indians of Virginia, "but eat night and day, when they have plenty of Provisions, or if they have got any thing that is a rarity." And conversely, "They are very patient of Hunger, when by any accident they happen to have nothing to eat; which they make more easy to them by girding up their Bellies, just as the wild Arabs are said to do, in their long marches; by which means they are less sensible of the impressions of Hunger."[2] The Indians are "very patient in fasting," Samuel Lee similarly reported of the Algonquians of New England, "and will gird in their bellies till they meet with food; but then none more gluttons or drunk on occasion, they'll eat 10 times in 24 hours, when they have a bear or a deer."[3] "At home," William Wood wrote, also of Indians in the north, "they will eat till their bellies stand forth, ready to split with fullness; it being their fashion to eat all at sometimes, and sometimes nothing at all in two or three days, wise Providence being a stranger to their wilder ways."[4]

As might be expected, there are exceptions. Roger Williams, for example, wrote that he "could never discern that excess of scandalous sins amongst them which Europe aboundeth with. Drunkenness and gluttony, generally they know not what sins they be."[5] The anonymous author of *A Relation of Maryland* made similar statements: "They have some things amongst them which may well become Christians to imitate, as their temperance in eating and drinking."[6] Thomas Hariot himself originally suggested that the Indians were "very moderate in their eating," or "very sober in their eating," and added "I would to god we would follow their example."[7] But even these last three writers subscribe to a common set of terms and values, a common perspective through which food practices among the Indians were to be assessed. In explaining the food practices of the natives, over and above the particulars of dietary choices, English ethnographers felt compelled to account for four things: whether or not the Indians overate (or overdrank); with what regularity they ate; with what "providence" the Indians arranged to feed themselves; and to what extent they experienced and tolerated hunger. The terms of analysis and the values behind them remain constant from Hariot's first report, published in 1588, to early eighteenth-century writers like Beverley. Temperance, decorum, providence, and, oddly, hunger—these were the fundamental categories though which English ethnography assessed the food practices of the natives. And, significantly, the majority of reports adopting these categories settled on the less favorable pattern. On the one hand, when the Indians eat, they eat improvidently and intemperately and without decorum, that is without regard for the niceties of time and place or self-restraint: "they accustom themselves to no set meals." On the other hand, "they are very patient of Hunger." "In keeping with their stoic nature," a modern historian writes, adopting the categories of early accounts for his own ends, natives "accepted [the] lean times as inevitable and rode them out without complaint."[8]

How shall we explain this? Part of the explanation must lie, of course, in what early ethnographers saw—a system of food practices common to most Algonquians of the eastern seaboard that included hunting and foraging expeditions as well as agricultural and aquacultural pursuits, and which seemed to provide a less steady supply of goods and less regular occasions for consumption than the ethnographers were familiar with in England. Indians seemed to respond more cavalierly to the need for food. They didn't follow the rules or betray the psychology of food that Europeans took for granted. But in some respects the observations ethnographers made were faulty, and their generalizations unwarranted, based as they were on limited evidence and constructed by uncertain methodologies.

The Indians of the eastern seaboard kept no livestock, it is true, and therefore relied on hunting and fishing for animal protein. And they had no salt, so that they could only preserve their animal products by smoking and drying them—a difficult feat to pull off while in the midst of hunting expeditions. According to a model developed by William Cronon for the Algonkian Indians north of Virginia and adapted by Timothy Silver for Virginia and parts south, moreover—a model based in large part on the ethnographic record—Indians practiced a seasonally mobile system of subsistence. Indians sought to "obtain their food wherever it was seasonally most concentrated," Cronon writes, and "Indian communities had learned to exploit the seasonal diversity of their environment by practicing mobility."[9] Periods of settlement in villages for sowing and harvesting products like corn, squash, and beans alternated with periods of dispersal, where smaller groups decamped, leaving the village to hunt or fish and forage in the forests for wild fruits, nuts, tubers, and greens. So far as Indians were "mobile," away from their villages, they may well have had to consume products quickly at the site of a kill, and they may well have had to alternate between eating grandly on freshly caught quarry and grazing modestly, between kills, on the vegetarian products of the forest.[10] They may also have allowed the rhythms of the chase and the successes of hunting and foraging to determine when and how food was consumed, so that at times they may well have eaten "night and day," as at other times they may well have had to delay eating or even do without for extended periods of time. But the seasonal mobility of the Indians may be exaggerated. Archaeological evidence suggests that many Algonquians were far more sedentary than ethnographic accounts would lead us to believe; Hariot's *Brief and True Report*, for one, especially through the illustrations by Theodor de Bry (based on paintings by John White), depicts a picture of a largely sedentary, village-bound people, who among other things dine in a formalized setting, largely on agricultural products (Figures 9.1 and 9.2).[11] And in any case, eyewitness reporting was relatively scanty. From author to author ethnographic legend and rhetorical conventions were pirated, reduplicated, and elaborated, so that by the time we get to "observers" like Beverley we are dealing as much with hearsay as anything else; even early observers like William Wood and the author of the *Relation of Maryland* shows signs of pirating some of their material from other accounts. And some of the piracies were based on earlier observations that were made during times of abnormal dearth. When Smith tells us of Indians in certain villages imparting to the white explorers "what little they had, with such complaints and tears from women and children," or when he similarly notes that "near three parts of the year, they only observe times and seasons, and live of what the Country naturally affordeth from hand to mouth," he may possibly be responding to conditions when groups he encountered were dispersed from their main villages and larger stores of grain, but he may also be observing people in the extremities of a famine, caused by a drought and an unusually severe cold spell.[12]

So the facts were various, and what early writers actually saw is problematic. And the explanation of the vision of Indian food practices that emerges must therefore lie not only in what the ethnographers saw but also in how ethnographers were seeing it. Attempting to represent who the Indians actually were, early ethnographers also inevitably betrayed who *they* were. Attempting to disclose the alimentary "fashions" of others, they relied on the categories they had absorbed from the fashions of their own alimentary culture. Yet the vision that emerges is not simply a one-sided account. What early writers composed with regard to food practices was what I shall call a "contact vision," constructed from within the domain of experience on the eastern seaboard and made of both the phenomena before the eyes of the observers and the biases, textual piracies, interests, and needs they brought to their observations. This vision could be quite superficial at times. "An idle, improvident, scattered people," they were, said one early observer in Virginia, "ignorant of the knowledge of gold, or silver, or any commodities; and careless of anything but from hand to mouth."[13] But even superficial accounts expressed something deeper. Writers were compelled to express a conception or intimation of what it meant for individuals to feed and otherwise provide for themselves. In the circumstances in which observers found themselves, in the course of "facing off," as Karen Kupperman puts it in the title of one of her books, traditional European notions like temperance and "providence" acquired new associations, and out of the preconscious or unconscious assumptions about social life a vision about the meaning of hunger emerged. As the biological *reality* of hunger soon emerged as a problem of unforeseen dimensions for early colonists, so did the *significance* of hunger: the meaning of hunger in the management of human affairs; the consequences of hunger as a symbolic and social as well as personal

Figure 9.1. Detail of "The Towne of Secotan," engraving by Theodor de Bry after a drawing by John White. Hariot, *Briefe and True Report* (1590), pl. 20. Courtesy of the Folger Shakespeare Library.

 Heir manner of feeding is in this wife. They lay a matt made of bents one the grownde and sett their meate on the mids therof, and then sit downe Rownde, the men vppon one side, and the woemen on the other. Their meate is Mayz sodden, in suche sorte as I described yt in the former treatise of verye good taste, deers flesche, or of some other beaste, and fishe. They are verye sober in their eatinge, and trinkinge, and consequentlye verye longe liued becaufe they doe not opprefs nature.

C

Figure 9.2. "Their sitting at meate," engraving by Theodor de Bry after a drawing by John White. Hariot, *Briefe and True Report* (1590), pl. 16. Courtesy of the Folger Shakespeare Library. On the Carolina coast, a native couple share what by European standards would be an appealing and adequate but nevertheless meatless "Lenten" meal, eaten with moderation.

experience; the accommodation of the need to eat by complex systems of economics, social structure, and "fashions."

* * *

The food system English travelers brought with them to America was not always so completely different from the system of the Indians as the former assumed, to be sure. The European diet as well was marked by seasonal variety and swings of excess and want. Grains and preserves were more staples of the winter months in Europe, for example, and fresh meat and vegetables of summer and fall. Moreover, ritualistic variation in England and elsewhere in Europe had far more in common with Indian practices than contemporary observers cared to admit. Alternating flesh days with fish days, abundant days with lean, feasting with fasting, ceremonial meals with more private and everyday affairs, Europeans too experienced both excess and want; on ceremonial and religious occasions they might even deliberately experience the avoidance of the rule of set meals for which they criticized the Indians.[14] However, the system as a whole was structured to minimize variation and maximize sumptuary regularity; the impetus toward regularity was what colonial writers had in mind when they reacted against Indian customs. Apart from feasts, which followed the liturgical calendar as well as the demands of secular ceremony (weddings, political events, etc.), and which were served out of the deliberate cultivation of surpluses, most Europeans kept to a sparingly monotonous diet, dominated by grain—wheat, barley, rye, and oats, depending on the region, prepared as coarse bread and gruel—supplemented in good times with fresh vegetables, herbs, or bits of meat or cheese or (on lean days) fish, the latter usually of the dried and salted variety.[15] Even the wealthiest members of society kept to a fairly monotonous regime, though with an emphasis on animal flesh rather than grain and on fresh rather than preserved fish. Sumptuary regularity was part and parcel of the immobility demanded by European notions of private property and the stasis necessary to a predominantly landed, agricultural economy.[16] Whether or not the European system was in place because it was the most efficient system for agricultural prosperity (as most writers of the time believed), the imposition of a static way of life for most Europeans, however well or ill it turned out for them, was nearly absolute, and the values of sumptuary regularity were embedded in the way Europeans managed their lands, livelihoods, and social relations.

When early observers took note of the variations in the Indian diet and its swings of excess and want, they were both condemning the Indians for adopting a form of behavior their own society sometimes encouraged and registering the fact that, despite the considerable actual variation in their food practices, the European system as a whole militated against variation, excess, and want. On the one hand, the European was highly rhythmic, and even in Protestant lands like England old customs like lean days and Lent, or indulgence carnivals like Shrovetide (when pork and sausages ruled) and Martinmas (when freshly slaughtered beef was consumed in abundance) guaranteed that the diet would be subject to considerable variation with respect to both the quantities of foodstuffs consumed and the nature of the foodstuffs themselves. On the other hand, a whole system of food practices had emerged by the late sixteenth and early seventeenth centuries, particularly in England, whose defining feature was its militant defense against extremes. However important the "war between Carnival and Lent" was to European experience, as the title of a famous painting by Breugel puts it, the defense against extremes, the rule of "not too much" and "not too little" dominated the discourse of food in early modern Europe. The rule determined as well the social relations by which food was produced, distributed, and prepared.

Food writers—and dietary guidebooks, known as "regimens of health," were extremely popular among the educated classes in the sixteenth and seventeenth centuries, as were conduct books and moral guides—were universal proponents of moderation, and cautioned specifically against the dangers of both overeating and undereating. Following the traditional strictures of Galenic medicine, which had long since entered into the mainstream of both popular and professional culture, dietary writers maintained that food intake was the primary contributing factor to health. Eating the wrong foods and eating any foods in a bad combination or in excess were the main causes of the humoral imbalances that were thought to constitute most forms of physical and mental illness. Similarly, not eating enough was also a cause of illness; although it would not be until the nineteenth century that the condition of anorexia nervosa would be an established diagnosis, anorexia in general—loss of appetite—was a condition known to physicians since the heyday of the Hippocratic writers, and was always thought to require prompt and thorough treatment. Although dietary writers warned again and again against "surfeit" or "repletion," they thus also commonly recommended foodstuffs, beverages, and exercises that could help "procure appetite." For "the wise man sayeth," as physician Andrew Boorde put it, "that surfeit do kill many men, and temperance doth prolonge the life."[17]

The moralists of the early modern period, especially in Protestant countries, by and large echoed the doctrines of the doctors. The sin of gluttony, accordingly, was even more often a target of homiletic writers than the sin of pride. "O gluttony, full of cursedness!" Chaucer's Pardoner exclaims, "O cause first of our confusion! / O original of our damnation!" "All kind of excess offendeth the Majesty of Almighty God," the Church of England's "Homily Against Gluttony and Excess" asserts. Popular images of notorious, kingly overeaters like Henry VIII and Louis XIV aside, the official moral code of early modern Europe dictated against consuming more than was enough to sustain a vigorous and muscular body. And taking advantage of medical lore, a tract like the "Homily Against Gluttony" could thus prove its point about the offensiveness of overindulgence by noting how "grievously [God] punisheth the immoderate abuse of those his creatures which he ordaineth to the maintenance of this our needy life, as meats, drinks, and apparel."[18] Although European thought by and large embraced the pleasures of the table, it tried to maintain a clear distinction between what was known, following Stoic traditions, as "right pleasure" (*honesta volupta*), deriving from "continence," and "the pleasure which the intemperate and libidinous derive from self-indulgence and a variety of foods and from the titillations of sexual interests."[19] On the one hand, wrote the influential Calvinist divine, William Perkins, "We may use these gifts of God [food and drink], with Christian liberty. . . . Not sparingly alone, and for mere necessity, to the satisfying of our hunger, and quenching of our thirst, but also freely and liberally, for Christian delight and pleasure." But on the other hand, "We must use our meat in Sobriety," sobriety being "a gift of God, whereby we keep a holy moderation in the use of our diet." Eat well, eat joyously, for the sake of the Lord and "*in* the Lord," as Perkins put it, but "be very careful and circumspect in taking thy food, bridle thine appetite, take heed thou dost not exceed measure."[20] It is in this spirit that Spenser's Guyon famously goes about temperately destroying the Bower of Bliss, that epitome of luxurious, Golden Age fantasies, declining to be seduced by the "life intemperate," and Guyon's companion the devout pilgrim remarks,

The dunghill kind
Delights in Filth and foule incontinence:
Let Grill be Grill, and have his hoggish mind,
But let us hence depart.[21]

One of the consequences of the dual, medical-moral imperative of temperance was inevitably the rise of controversy over just what constituted eating too little or too much. In England, which seems to have had one of the most abundant diets per capita in Europe during the early modern period, Puritan-leaning critics often complained about the excess of English tables, and what they took to be the new fashion for extravagance and refinement in English cooking. "Oh, what nicety is this," wrote the anti-theatrical Puritan Phillip Stubbes: "what vanity, excess, riot, and superfluity is here." In typical fashion combining the moral and the medical, Stubbes adds that "I cannot persuade myself otherwise, but that our niceness and curiousness in diet, hath altered our nature, distempered our bodies, and made us more subject to millions of . . . diseases, then ever were our forefathers subject unto, and consequently of shorter life than they."[22] By and large, English writers were proud of English abundance, sometimes finding it necessary to defend themselves against charges that they ate too much. As we have seen, despite the crankiness of Puritans like Stubbes, authorities like Perkins found no reason not to eat freely and joyfully, as long as one did so for the glory of God.

But lurking beneath educated attitudes toward food was a suspicion that English sumptuary habits were degenerate, overcivilized and overindulgent. Travelers to Italy were sometimes challenged by the example of the "thrifty" food habits of the Italians, for example, or by discussions favoring Spartan abstemiousness in a number of classical authors.[23] And again and again one finds English writers alluding to the Spartan virtues of their distant forebears, particularly in the north, as first expressed by the ancient historian Dio Cassius. After justifying the lavish hospitality of English tables, for example, William Harrison recalled with a nostalgia for culinary virtue that "In old time . . . North Britons did give themselves universally to great abstinence, and in time of wars their soldiers would often feed but once or twice at the most in two or three days. . . . In the woods, moreover, they lived with herbs and roots."[24] The source for Harrison's remarks goes even farther: The northern tribes of Britain, Dio wrote, shortly after the original Roman conquest of Britain,

> possess neither walls, cities, nor tilled fields, but live on their flocks, wild game, and certain fruits. . . . They can endure hunger and cold and any kind of hardship; for they plunge into the swamps and exist there for many days with only their heads above water, and in the forest they support themselves upon bark and roots, and for all emergencies they prepare a certain kind of food, the eating of a small portion of which, the size of a bean, prevents them from feeling either hunger or thirst.[25]

Obviously we are close here to the Picts or Scots whom Hariot compared to the Indians of Virginia, and close to the language used by many early observers of the Indians with respect to their sumptuary (and conjugal) habits, from Hariot all the way to Beverley. The Indians who could be so "patient of hunger" when necessary were the moral allies of the virtuous tribesmen who inhabited pre-Roman Britain.[26] This is the subtext of Hariot's remark, previously cited, that he "would to god we would follow the [Indians'] example." For if we did so, he goes on to say, "we should be free from many kinds of diseases which we fall into by sumptuous and unseasonable banquets, continually devising new sauces, and provocation of gluttony to satisfy our unsatiable appetite."[27]

Living in a land of relative plenty, the English were thus taught the values of abundance, conviviality, and pleasure on the one hand, and the virtues of thrift, stoic abstemiousness, and temperance on the other. If excess was censured, abundance was embraced; yet if abundance was embraced, frugality and temperance were embraced as well. And beneath it all there lurked a suspicion, rooted at once in Biblical injunctions and classical learning, that dietary prosperity in any form, however temperate or generous, however simple or refined, violated a pure code of virtue that advanced civilization had forgotten how to enforce or had become too degenerate to practice.[28]

This complex culture of food found an especially striking expression—something like a Freudian reaction formation—in the evolution of dining customs. Expressions of abundance—liberality, hospitality, what was in medieval language referred to as the "freedom" of a household—were highly valued in sixteenth- and seventeenth-century England, so much so that social critics repeatedly bewailed their decline and degeneration over the years.[29] In the locus classicus of English Renaissance hospitality, Ben Jonson extolls the "free provisions" of a manorial estate "from whose liberal board doth flow, / With all, that hospitality doth know." "Here no man tells my cups," Jonson goes on to say about the ideal manor at Penshurst; "nor, standing by, / A waiter, doth my gluttony envy."[30]

However, amidst the displays of abundance, however fictional they might be on occasion, the common meal was all the same a strictly hierarchical affair, a scene of discipline and stratification; and if individuals up and down the ranks were to eat and to eat their fill, Jonson's notorious and often mocked gluttony aside,[31] they were to do so temperately and modestly, taking what they took from platters going around, consuming their food and generally comporting themselves at the table in accordance with a system of manners that ratified differences of rank. From the perspective of our own more democratic and chaotic system of table manners, the result was striking, and became more and more so as the sixteenth century gave way to the seventeenth, and both stratification and politeness advanced (Figure 9.3). "I might here talk somewhat of the great silence that is used at the tables of the honorable and wiser sort, generally over all the realm," William Harrison notes; "likewise of the moderate eating and drinking that is daily seen, and finally of the regard that each one hath to keep himself from the note of surfeiting and drunkenness."[32] "When you be at Meat," one writer exhorts "the Young Gentlewoman at the Age of Six, or upward,"

> be not out of the Way, but attend the Grace, and then take the Place that is Appointed you: After having done your Reverence, see your Napkin be fastened about you to save your Clothes, and Thankfully take what is given without Craving; nor is it seemly for you to Speak at the Table, unless you are asked a Question, or there be some great Occasion. Cut your Meat Handsomely, and be not over desirous of Sauce, nor of another sort of Meat, before you have disposed of what is on your Plate. Put not both your Hands to your mouth at once, nor eat too Greedily.[33]

Norbert Elias, following the lead of Alfred Franklin, made the "civilizing" effect of table manners a commonplace of cultural history; but both Elias and Franklin underemphasized what might be called their subornation effect, their contribution to the enforcement of deference, by which self-restraint was joined at once to good conduct and to one's unambiguous submission to others.[34] Certainly, they underemphasized what it felt like to a subaltern at a communal dinner table. "When any thing is given you," Woolley writes for the female apprentice, "be sure to bow to those who carve it to you; and if your Mistress doth you that favor, you must shew the more respect. Talk not at all at Table, for that is unseemly, unless it be to answer your Mistress when she asks you a question."[35] Not too much

Figure 9.3. "Europeans at Table," engraving from Georg Phillip Harsdoerffer, *Vollstaendig vermehrtes Trincir-Buch handlend* (Nornberg, 1640. A waiter (right, with napkin draped over his hand) stands at the ready, perhaps while the lady of the house issues orders for the next course. Courtesy Folger Shakespeare Library.

food, not too much pleasure, not too much conversation, not too much conviviality, not too much assertiveness, all in the interest of deference— such was the general rule of table manners among those whom Harrison called the "wiser sort," and who increasingly included the middling sort of people as well as aristocrats and their household guests. Certainly there were exceptions; not all dinners were formal affairs and not all diners would be described as "the wiser sort." Harrison himself complains about the unruly boisterousness of "the meaner sort of husbandmen and country inhabitants," and there must have been a number of people, in or out of the cities, rich or poor, who took pleasure in flouting the rules. Intensely ceremonial occasions, such as weddings and court masques, also featuring feasts, are known to have frequently dissipated into unruly affairs under the inspiration of alcohol. But as medical and religious writers extolled an adequate but temperate diet, so dining customs, generally understood, superimposed upon displays of abundance, dictated adequate but temperate consumption, practiced in an atmosphere of deference and self-restraint, and the tendency over the centuries was for more and more deference and more and more self-restraint.

For all the celebrations of moderated abundance, to be sure, the early modern period was not an age in which food supplies were as secure as they might have been. Dearth was a serious threat throughout the period—especially in the 1590s, the decade just before the *Susan Constant*, the *Godspeed*, and the *Discovery* set sail in the direction of the Chesapeake Bay, soon to establish a colony in Jamestown.[36] The distribution of foodstuffs was highly uneven. It has been surmised that while the wealthy classes compromised their health by eating what now may be seen to be excessive amounts of meat and fish, and the poor majority of the people compromised their health by consuming too little of anything but grain, only the middling sort, who could not afford to keep up with the gentry's excessive meat-eating but could afford to avoid the monotony and impoverishment of peasant fare, regularly consumed a nutritionally balanced diet.[37] But however inadequate the English system may have been, on the account of foreign visitors and modern statisticians it was more successful than most European systems in providing for its people, second perhaps only to the Dutch.[38]

In the more urbanized areas of the country, the English economy was already highly capitalized, its agricultural practices often oriented toward the market, the market itself becoming increasingly national and international in scope, and food products becoming highly commodified.[39] This convergence of economic procedures—capitalization, marketing, and commodification—reached even into the daily life of peasants in the hinterlands, so far as their subsistence practices had to make way for the sheep-herding or cattle-raising of larger landowners, or so far as their ceremonial Lenten diet came to depend on salted or smoked herring caught and processed by the state-sanctioned fishing industry in port towns like Yarmouth, or by way of the enormous fish trade based in Holland or the international cod fisheries working the waters off Newfoundland and Labrador.[40] The colonial experiment indeed depended on prior conditions, such as the capitalization of food production and the commodification of food products. And the "ventures" of emigration required that the nutrition be rendered as an abstractly quantifiable operation organized in advance of use and with an eye toward exchange values rather than sustenance. We thus hear from one of the most interesting food writers of seventeenth-century England, the traveler Richard Ligon, describing how prospective settlers in Barbados should consider, among their capital expenses, "the feeding of our servants and slaves, over and above the provisions which the Plantations bear." "That will be no great matter," Ligon goes on to say,

for they are not often fed with bone-meat. But we will allow to the Christian servants, (which are not above thirty in number) four barrels of Beef, and as much

Pork yearly, with two barrels of salt Fish, and 500 poor-Johns, which we have from New England, four barrels of Turtle, and as many of pickled Mackerels, and two of Herrings, for the Negroes; all of which I have computed, and find they will amount unto 100 l., or thereabouts; besides the freight, which will be no great matter; for you must be sure to have a Factor, both at New England and Virginia, to provide you of all the Commodities those places afford, that are useful to your Plantation; or else your charge will be treble.[41]

Himself formerly a professional chef and always a gourmand, repeatedly adverting to the delights of gastronomic experience, Ligon can nevertheless pause to consider food supplies from the perspective of the commodities (a word taking on its modern usage at the time Ligon is writing) needed to feed a labor force and fuel a commercial enterprise. The separation of the population in Barbados (far more simply and dramatically than would be the case back home, or for that matter in Virginia) into a managerial class on the one hand and a laboring class of servants and slaves on the other is one of the chief conditions not only for the commodification of foodstuffs on a grand scale for the many, but for the sustenance of gastronomy on a grand scale for the few.[42]

An even more striking an example of the commodification of food, and the inequalities it helped to enforce, is to be found in a story from Maryland repeated by Timothy Silver, where both English settlers and Indian hosts engage in disturbing reifications. George Alsop, an indentured servant, in Silver's words,

observed in 1666 that "the extreme glut and plenty" of deer "daily killed by the Indians and brought in to the English" made venison "the common provision the Inhabitants feed on." Indeed, the man to whom he was indentured (who regularly traveled with the natives) once had some eighty deer cured and stored to feed his family and servants. According to Alsop, "before this Venison was brought to a period by eating, it so nauseated our appetites and stomachs, that plain bread was rather courted and desired than it."[43]

The commodification Alsop was subjected to, based on an English predilection for salting and preserving animal products rather than eating them fresh, on the spot, could veer the pleasure of eating meat into the unpleasure of being monotonously force-fed on it, and it could even encourage doubtful social policies of economic specialization. "Though the Jamestown people had easy access to some 3,000 square miles of inland tidal water and were only a little way from the open sea," we are told by a historian of fisheries, "they never developed their marine riches." Instead, "though surrounded all the while by their own huge marine resources," the Virginia colonists soon learned to "subsist on salt fish from the North."[44] Sheer commercial calculations may have been responsible for this development. The financial logic of monoculture is a feature of world capitalism. Yet one suspects that a number of other kinds of forces are at work in such situations. The choice for monoculturalists in English America was a choice in the first place in favor of a certain form of expediency, and in the second place in favor of the cultural and social consequences that followed from it.

Sidney Mintz, ethnohistorian of the West Indian sugar industry, has spoken eloquently about "a newly emerging world in which working people produced less and less of what they themselves consumed; in which they filled most of their needs by selling their labor for wages and buying what they consumed in an impersonal market."[45] Mintz was mainly referring to West Indian laborers and British laborer-consumers beginning in the late seventeenth and early eighteenth centuries, but the disjunction of production and consumption and desire and need was no doubt established much earlier among many Europeans. It was part and parcel of the surge of large-scale urban life beginning in Italy and elsewhere in the late Middle Ages. Laborers and no doubt many landowners too in early Virginia, bent on producing tobacco for European markets, were forcing themselves to subsist not on what they raised but on venison and fish got in trade from Indian hunters and New England merchants. This was "providence," providence enlivened (and reified) by the spirit of capitalism, leading to a disjunction between the givens of physicality and sensuality on the one hand and the means of administering to them on the other: a disjunction that would mar much of Anglophone culture throughout modernity (people like the French and the Dutch would make separate sorts of peace between capitalism and gustatory need), but that would nevertheless guarantee that whether at home or abroad British culture would operate officially—"officially," which is to say ideally, and in principle, whatever the reality at any given time—as a society without hunger.

Not too much, not too little, and the two together making for a society officially prohibited from knowing hunger: the society without hunger that England assumed itself to be was aware of the possibility of hunger and of the idea of societies where hunger could be experienced—even practiced—as a virtue. It was (usually) aware of the great mustering of resources needed to sustain itself as a society without hunger, as well as the self-restraint required to attune consumption with supplies. But hunger itself in this society was always considered an anomaly. It was an exception, a disruption, a corruption. It was not to be borne with patience. It was believed to be caused by anomalous events. And both the toleration of conditions of hunger and the actual experience of it were regarded as something as a taboo. "Why, how have I done this forty years?" a sanguine, elderly merchant named Merrythought proclaims on the English stage at just about the same time as the first fleet arrived in Jamestown, "I never came into my dining room, but at eleven and six o'clock I found excellent meat and drink o'th'table; my clothes were never worn out, but next morning a tailor brought me a new suit; and without question it will be so ever.

Use makes perfectness."[46] As the upper class were encouraged to exercise hospitality, representatives of the middling sort like Merrythought were exhorted to practice the self-restraint of thrift, but for both classes sumptuary prosperity was ideally and even ethically the norm. And by contrast, in one of the clearest indications of dominance of the idea, in a garrulous and relatively literate society, the observer cannot help but note the absence of discussions about hunger. Appetite, yes. And during periods of dearth, it was true, references to hunger in printed material and public discussion multiply. Thus we find documents like the pamphlet issued by the erstwhile cookbook writer Hugh Plat, *Sundrie New and Artificall Remedies Against Famine*, recommending "new and artificial discoveries of strange bread, drink and food, in matter and preparation so full of rarity to work some alteration and change in this great and dangerous dearth," including such preparations as making bread from chestnuts and applying a clod of earth to one's stomach to allay cravings.[47] But as historian John Walter has noted, unlike the continent, there was no Hansel and Gretel story or analogue thereof circulating in early modern England; there was little folkloric testimony to the realities of starvation.[48]

Texts like Plat's *Remedies Against Famine*, anticipating modern economic theory, consider the main problem to be distribution, not production. Commoners went hungry, according most observers, because of the greed of landowners. Shortages of grain meant not that there was no grain to be had, but that the price of grain was too steep for too many people, and that the basic resources of agricultural production were too unevenly and unjustly distributed.[49] This was a position writers could sustain even in a decade like the 1590s, which suffered the worst harvests per capita in early modern English history.[50] And if problems arose from the failure of harvests, such failures were themselves to be explained theologically, and accounted for as God's own anomalous responses to the repeated sins of his people. Famine "is a judgment," wrote the minister William Gouge, "a fearful judgment." What is not acknowledged, indeed so far as I know *never* acknowledged, is the idea that inadequate food supplies might ever result simply from a concurrence of natural events and human error, or that starvation might ever be among humans a normal condition. Gouge is speaking representatively when he says that, given God's fearful judgment, His occasional bringing of famine to his people, "it will be our wisdom to do what in us lieth to prevent it, or to moderate, or remove it." And indeed the process for preventing, moderating, or removing famine, according to Gouge, is both secular and religious, both technological and theological, as Max Weber might have predicted it to be:

For preventing Famine, we must
1. Observe such duties as procure plenty.
2. Avoid such sins as cause famine.

For procuring and continuing plenty, Walk worthy of the Lord, unto all well pleasing: being fruitful in every good work.[51]

Even when John Smith considers the causes of deprivation in the first years of the Virginia colony, he makes assumptions about the inevitable bountifulness of the world, if only one has the opportunity to work in good season.[52]

Under these circumstances, it is easy to see how evidence of sumptuary regularity, and the doctrines and practices sustaining it, could have been one of the first things that ethnographic observers were looking for among the natives of America. Such evidence was first of all a sign as to whether the Indians too lived in a society without hunger, and thus, by the same token, lived in conformity with European standards of civility. It is in light of the normativity of the society without hunger that we should read the comments of English observers like the wary John Smith or the romantic Robert Beverley, for what they are claiming, in effect, is that contrary to their own ideals about these things, the Indians are *always hungry*. They are hungry under conditions of abundance, eating "night and day, when they have plenty of Provisions," "gorging themselves." They are hungry when they have nothing, "girding up their Bellies." Hunger, according to such observers, is an ever-present condition of Indian experience, even if Indians also show themselves to be quite successful at acquiring food and sustaining themselves nutritionally and, when necessary, enduring hunger with patience. For writers like Smith, indeed, it is not just a token of their savagery, it is savagery itself; and similarly, for writers like Beverley, it is token of something like noble savagery, an innocent ignorance of civilized manners that is also a virtue. Nor are observations about the hunger of the Indians restricted to writers wishing to belittle or romanticize them.

For an observer in New England like Roger Williams, with a rather different agenda in mind, the relation of Indians to hunger serves as an equally noteworthy sign of their amenability to education, both human and divine. Williams's Indians never really *suffer* hunger, though their appetites are healthy, and this in spite of the fact that their *society*, given its primitive economic arrangements, *ought* to make them suffer hunger all the time:

Course bread and water's most their fare [Williams poeticizes],
O England's diet fine

* * *

Sometimes God gives them Fish or Flesh,
Yet they're content without;
And what comes in, they part to friends
and strangers all about.
God's providence is rich to his.[53]

"Content without," lacking a "diet fine," not relying on a "plenteous store," but always generous with what they have, Williams's Indians lack both the wisdom of European society and the corruption that gave rise to it. Living in a society *with* hunger, they have no appetite; living in a society lacking surpluses, they nevertheless share generously with all comers.

We do not know enough about Indian life in the contact period to determine precisely what kinds of structures and values they attached to eating and drinking, or to determine much about differences between different groups in different areas.[54] Hospitality was widely practiced up and down the eastern seaboard; feasts were a part of life, but so were non-feasting periods; and from what we know about their time-consuming cookery—the seething of stews, the pounding of maize, the baking of maize-cakes, the rending of oils, the broiling of fish and game—eating and drinking must certainly have followed according to set schedules, though by what schedules they were set, or how, we do not know. Most early Europeans visitors, after all, observed dining customs from the position of a guest, for whom special arrangements were made. And as natives provided for and prepared their food under conditions of cooperative behavior, men fishing together for example, or villagers sowing and harvesting together, so we must imagine them to have observed their own forms of "table" manners and other food-related codes of conduct. Henry Spelman paints a picture of formal dinner customs among the Powhatans, probably on the occasion of a special ritual, which emphasizes a rigid, ritualistic separation of men from women, rich from poor, and individual from individual, and where the same general silence and deference the English valued is strictly observed.[55] John Lawson provides a picture of village life in the Carolinas which, for all its exotica, corresponds to village life in England, among whom a plenteous variety of food is both exchanged as a commodity and shared as a token of communal values.[56] Robert Byrd tells us a story (several times) about what for him seems to be an unnecessary and somewhat primitive but otherwise European-like food taboo, where an Indian guide protested against "cooking beasts of the field and birds of the air together in one vessel."[57] Eating for the Indians, no less than for the English, was obviously a *meaningful* activity, with rules and regulations, with laws and values, with totems and taboos. Only, the meanings were different, as was also, therefore, the relation of eating to hunger.

Historians have debated the actual facts of hunger, starvation, and mortality among the English in early Virginia, some suggesting that accounts of starvation or assessments of the affect of starvation on mortality are exaggerated.[58] But the horror of hunger that early colonists experienced was very real—that is, the *horror* was real, real enough indeed to play a significant role in the subsequent development of colonial policy.[59] It is only an expression of the nature of horror and the conditions giving rise to it that it should be experienced and communicated in the context of a complex cultural apparatus. Ideas about food and its values were inscribed in the social order that the European invaders, to use Jennings's term, brought along with them as they set foot in early Virginia; so by the same token were ideas about what it would mean to do without both food and the values it embodied. "WE ARE STARVED! WE ARE STARVED!" George Percy reports the men at Jamestown crying through the streets during the infamous Starving Time: "Many through extreme hunger have run out of their naked beds, being so lean that they looked anatomies."[60] The genuine horror, the bare anxiety and dismay, is unmistakable, yet so is the fact that from the outset Percy's representation couples the horror with cultural conventions that mediate and define the experience. Even if Percy and others erred in ascribing most of the deaths to starvation, they did so in accordance with their understanding of the nature of disease, the demands of diet, and psychic economy corresponding to the society without hunger in which they had been accustomed to live. And even if Percy and others set about their work as reporters with the barest journalistic veracity as their primary goal (although that was indeed often the case), what they report is not only colored but even structured by the cultural apparatus of the food system to which they were accustomed. As Percy describes the sequence of events during the starving time, he delineates the regressive behavior of the settlers as they feed themselves first from the valued surpluses, which were to guarantee the condition of alimentary civility they had taken for granted, and then go down the scale and consume less and less edible products, until they are forced to violate the food taboos underlying their nutritional system. The regressive sequence seems plausible, and yet it follows the logic and even the language of those accounts of uncivilized yet virtuous practices reported by writers like Dio.

> Now all of us at James Town beginning to feel the sharp prick of hunger, which no man truly describe but he which hath tasted the bitterness thereof, a world of miseries ensued, as the sequel will express unto you, insomuch that some, to satisfy their hunger, have robbed the store, for the which I caused them to be executed. Then having fed upon horses and other beasts as long as they lasted, we were glad to make shift with vermin, as dogs, cats, rats, and mice. All was fish that came to net to satisfy cruel hunger, as to eat boots, shoes, or any other leather some could come by. And those being spent and devoured, some were enforced to search the woods and to feed upon serpents and snakes and to dig the earth for wild and unknown roots.[61]

Similar sequences, which amounted to something of a "topos," can be found in stories that had been circulating throughout the European world since Flavius Josephus's account of the conquest of Jerusalem by the Romans in 70 A.D.[62] Such sequences had resonated in legends throughout the Middle Ages. Boistaurau's well-known account of the Great Famine in France of 1528–33 and the poet Edmund Spenser's chilling description of the starvation of Irish soldiers and civilians during a victorious siege waged against them by the English were only two recent, high humanist, Protestant examples.[63] The end of the sequence, frequent in ancient and medieval redactions though only hinted at by Boistaurau and Spenser, and repeated again and again in early accounts of the Starving Time, is the experience of cannibalism:

> And now famine beginning to look ghastly and pale in every face that nothing was spared to maintain life and to do those things which seem incredible, as to dig up dead corpses out of graves and to eat them, and some have licked up the blood which hath fallen from their weak fellows. And amongst the rest, this was most lamentable that one of ours, Collines, murdered his wife, ripped the child out of her wound and threw it into the river, and after chopped the mother in pieces and salted her for his food.[64]

Repeated time and again in the literature of early Virginia, the story of Collines and cannibalism served as a symbol of absolute extremity—the end not only of the natural means of human subsistence but of the natural restraint on human impulses that would several centuries later be discussed so compellingly in Conrad's *Heart of Darkness*.[65] Yet interestingly, it does not depict an absolute reversion to savagery, for like any good Englishman (and many other figures of cannibalistic legend in Europe) Collines is made in this story to halt before certain taboos, to practice "providence," and indeed to commodify his diet: as most English people were trained to be, he is disposed to eat meat from a mature rather than an immature animal (like a typical subject preferring beef over veal or mutton over lamb, he throws away the baby) and programmed to "salt" his meat, to put it in storage, and resign himself to eating it again and again whether he has an appetite for it or not. Even when practicing cannibalism, the Englishman attempts to reproduce the conditions of a society without hunger. Indeed, in refusing to gorge himself at the site of his kill, he practiced not only providence but moderation. Since he seems to have eaten alone, however, it is unclear what kind of table manners he practiced, although it may be conjectured that he comported himself with the quiet dignity of "the wiser sort."

* * *

The contact vision I have been examining is a vision of the English colonists with respect to both themselves and the Indians they encountered. It leaves certain aspects of Indian customs opaque, but it calls attention very strongly to the fundamentals of the conflict between English and Indian culture. Whatever else their needs and wants may have been, and even in spite of sporadic crises and food riots, the English understood themselves to inhabit a world without hunger, a world where the very experience of hunger—of what could be taken as real, morbid famishment as opposed to a healthy appetite—had the status of a taboo. And yet hunger was the first terror the early settlers encountered, especially at Jamestown. They encountered their own hunger; they encountered what they took to be a hunger that the Indians experienced night and day. Moreover, it was with respect to hunger that European and Indian society in the first instance most emphatically differed. They expected hunger to be as missing from the Americas as it was from Britain. If anything, they expected more plentiful supplies of foodstuffs in the Americas than at home, such that as many gentle travelers would continue to live as sumptuously as they were accustomed to at home, so members of lower classes would actually improve their standard of living.[66] And instead, again, they found hunger everywhere they went; they found hunger to be the normative condition of life in North America, whether among themselves, struggling to survive, or among the Indians, who prospered, paradoxically, in a condition of perpetual hunger.

Obviously, as we critically reexamine the texts of early English colonialism in North America, we assure ourselves that Indian life was only partly what they English took it to be, and take note of how much in early accounts was conditioned by expectations and values based on food practices established on the other side of the Atlantic. We take note, too, of how culturally marked even the most desperate of encounters with hunger among the English really were. Collines kills his wife, according to legend, in order to practice providence and provide himself with salt meat. The notorious famished indentured servant Richard Frethorne pleads to his agent either to free him "out of this Egypt" or else "to send over some beef and some Cheese and butter, or any eating victual will be good trading"—placing his own circumstances metaphorically in a biblical context but still, in his hunger, sticking at once to habitual English preferences and to a commodified relation to food, which includes keeping an eye out for making a quick profit.[67] He continues in this vein in the course of his still more desperate pleading to his parents: "since I am out of the ship, I never ate anything but pease, and loblolly (that is water gruel); as for deer or venison I never saw any; [we servants] must Work hard both early and late for a mess of water gruel, and a mouthful of bread, and beef; a mouthful of bread for a penny loaf must serve for four men, which is most pitiful if you did know as much as I." "I am not half a quarter as strong as I was in England, and all is for want of victuals, for I do protest unto you, that I have eaten more in [a] day at home than I have allowed me here for a Week. You have given more than my day's allowance to a beggar at the door." "For God's sake get a gathering or entreat some good folks to lay out some little Sum of money, in meal, and Cheese and butter, and beef, any eating meat will yield a great profit, oil and vinegar is very good."[68] Whatever the real purpose of Frethorne's letter, our servant blithely rushes from the pathetic pathology of suffering from hunger—sure to evoke outrage and pity—to a realm of commodification where pathetic need slides into a calculated demand for the wherewithal to sell quantities of excess goods at a handsome profit.[69]

Food practice was one of the first lines of contact and conflict between the English and the Indians. The English came to depend on Indians economically, especially when it came to food, so that the conflict between the two groups was modified by necessity, tempered by the terms of an uneasy relation of symbiosis.[70] But the conflict was fundamentally unresolvable on the level of culture and custom because, over and above differences with respect to religion, language, trade, and the like, the Indians and the English constructed their societies according to different systems for ministering to the needs of the body, beginning with the need for food. Symbiosis and assimilation could only be carried so far between societies with such incompatible home economies, social protocols, and attitudes toward the needs of the body. Surely, as most European observers found the Indians to be either always hungry or always in a condition where they ought to be hungry, so the Indians must often have found their visitors from Europe constantly hungry too, for it was food that they were constantly requesting, trading for, and demanding. And if the English imagined that Indians could remain content with their hunger, at least so long as they remained uncivilized, which is to say unassimilated to the English way of life, so the Indians must have seen eventually that the English would never be content with their hunger, that their hunger could not be allayed, that they would always be demanding more, that there would always be more meat to procured and salted, always more grain to dry and put aside, and following behind the preserved commodities, more English bellies to practice temperance upon them.

Chapter 10
Between "Plain Wilderness" and "Goodly Corn Fields"
Representing Land Use in Early Virginia

JESS EDWARDS

In 1612 John Smith published *A Map of Virginia*, a text that juxtaposes a cartographic map with a narrative "description" of the region incorporating the infant English colony of Jamestown. It is often remarked of colonial maps that they desocialize the terrain they represent, privileging the abstract rationale of mathematical measurement over details of past and present occupation and use and thereby simplifying the act of appropriation.[1] This may well be true in one respect of Smith's map, whose giant compasses noisily draw attention to its mathematical frame of reference. Yet the map also acknowledges, even insists upon the Indian presence in Virginia. Aesthetically, the Indians pictured might be dismissed as iconologically marginal. They are on the map rather than in it. However the map is also full of Indian place names. And at its borders John Smith even acknowledges his dependence on local help and narrative testimony in the making of it. His key reads: "to the crosses hath been discovered; what beyond is by relation." The narrative "description" which accompanies Smith's map acknowledges specifically that the help Smith had came from Indians.[2]

Smith's verbal geography of Virginia vacillates, as his cartography might be said to do, between generalizing declarations of the land's emptiness and availability for colonial exploitation, and detailed observations of its current native use. Smith describes terrain "all overgrowne with trees and weedes being a plaine wildernes as God first made it," and comments that "heaven and earth never agreed better to frame a place for mans habitation being of our constitutions, were it fully manured and inhabited by industrious people."[3] Lacking the significant details of English cultivation, the "plainness" of this well-framed space seems indeed to suggest the inviting emptiness of cartographic geometry. Yet Smith also maps what must seem to the modern reader like the perfectly industrious practices of Indian agriculture, in passages such as the following:

The greatest labour they take, is in planting their corne, for the country naturally is overgrowne with wood. To prepare the ground, they bruise the barke of the trees neare the root, then do they scortch the roots with fire that they grow no more. The next yeare with a crooked peece of wood, they beat up the woodes by the rootes, and in that moulds they plant their corne. Their manner is this. . . . Their women and children do continually keepe it with weeding, and when it is growne midle high, they hill it about like a hop-yard. They plant also pease.[4]

Moreover, these details of native use bring with them—as the Indian contributions to Smith's cartography suggest they should—details of native knowledge: another kind of intimacy with the land. While they have no writing, records Smith, the Indians enjoy their rights "by customes," and "all knowe their severall landes, and habitations, and limits."[5] Far from being empty, Smith's Virginia would appear to be worked, known, and owned.

This is not the first time that the ambivalence of John Smith's Virginian geography has been commented upon. Lisa Blansett's essay in the present volume notes Smith's incorporation within his map of elements that elude the epistemology of reason and mathematical design, and explores the map as a product of the colonial "contact zone" between native and European cosmologies. Karen Ordahl Kupperman's 1980 study of the colonial encounter *Settling with the Indians* notes the acute contrast between "the rhetorical flourishes which occur in general statements" in which Smith deems Virginia empty, or at least "'little planted, laboured and manured,'" and specific observations of the detail of Indian agriculture.[6] In fact, she insists, "no writer who actually went to America ever denied that the Indians lived in organized civil communities, and that they therefore had the minimum attributes of human life."[7]

If Kupperman's corrective argument about the acknowledgement of Indian Virginia was necessary in 1980, I think it is all the more necessary now. The presumption that colonial representation works to reinforce lines of racial demarcation through aggregating distinctions between civilized and savage cultural practices, including those of habitation and land use, has been reinforced through the accumulating hegemony of postcolonial politics and theory. One of the characteristics of colonial representations of America most widely recognized both in now-canonical older and in recent studies is their tendency to evacuate it: to deem it—at most—empty of significant habitation, and—at least—empty of appropriate use.[8] This theoretical projection of colonial ideologies and representations structured around binary oppositions has been modified in recent years, as Lisa Blansett notes, by Mary Louise Pratt's suggestion that we think of the colonial encounter in terms more of hybrid contact zones than of frontiers. However, it is not only explicitly "theorized" studies which tend to overemphasize the dismissive aspect of early colonial representation. There is a general consensus even in recent work which distances itself from theoretical abstraction that whatever the experiences of early colonizers, English colonial representation is extensively determined by a stable ideology of legitimate appropriation through the "improvement" of empty land.[9] Where this narrative has been troubled, as in recent work by Anthony Pagden and David Armitage, it has been most convincingly with an attention to the complexities of international law. Law which presents colonial propagandists with the difficulties of reconciling legitimate conquest, or "imperium" (requiring a subject people to subject themselves to one rather than another imperial power) with legitimate dominion, or property rights and sovereignty, allowed empty land, as "res nullius," to be appropriated and "improved."[10]

This chapter will acknowledge that the ambivalence of John Smith's geography can be explained, as Kupperman and Blansett explain it, partly in terms of specifically colonial experiences: the experiences of the contact zone. It will also, however, try to explain this ambivalence in terms of more general early modern English ideas and practices regarding land, its proper use, and representation. I want to argue one case strongly, and to suggest a second. My first case is that the ambivalence of Virginian geography is not just the product of ambivalent colonial experiences. Neither, however, is it only the product of conflicting legal arguments specifically applied to colonization: arguments for conquest and dominion. It is also the product of ambivalent domestic discourses regarding the right use and representation of land, discourses which were only beginning to be able to disparage and discount customary, common practice in favor of capitalist land use. I think that we cannot separate eye-witness description from distant, "armchair" rhetoric as easily as Kupperman suggests, since domestic discourse on land was just as conflicted in the early seventeenth century as its colonial counterpart. My second case, more tentatively made, is that colonial America may well have provided English geography with material for thinking its way through this conflict.

Just as the quantifying, dehistoricizing perspective of the mathematical map has been associated with colonial ideology, it has also been associated with the enclosure movement and the capitalization of early modern agriculture. The mathematical map, it is suggested, helps the agrarian capitalist overlook the complex web of customary rights that overwrote the post-feudal English landscape, and to re-present it instead in terms of calculations of quality, quantity, and profit. It may have been possible in the later seventeenth century to discount the customary uses of land occupied and used in common, and to designate such land "empty" and available for appropriation, and indeed later in this essay I shall demonstrate that this was the case. Things, however, were not really so simple when Virginia was first colonized. To borrow the language of Michael McKeon, in *The Origins of the English Novel*, different things were still "virtuous" and different things were still "true." Or, to translate into terms which will be useful to the present discussion, different forms of land use from just private property were still regarded as legitimate, and codes from just the abstract measurements of mathematical surveying still counted as true representation of land. These issues of truth and legitimacy are intimately related. What counted as legitimate land use, up to and including a great deal of the seventeenth century, was customary land use, and what counted in a landscape, and therefore what must feature in true representation, was therefore to a predominant extent its social identity, as a nexus of various customary practices.[11]

Truth and Legitimacy

We can trace these precapitalist standards of truth and legitimacy in land representation in surveying manuals produced in the period: texts designed to teach the professional practitioner what counted in the representation of land. "Surveie consisteth," explains Edward Worsop in 1582,

> upon three principal parts: that is to say the Mathematicall, the Legall, and the Judiciall. Unto the Mathematical part belongeth true measuring, which is Geometrie; true calculation of the thing measured, which is Arithmetike: and true platting, and setting forth of the same to the eye, in proportion and symetrie, which is Perspective. To the Legall part belongeth the knowledge of keeping courts of surveie, of the diversities of tenures, rents, and services, likewise how to make terrors, rentals . . . & also how to engrosse books, with many other things appertaining to ye part. . . . The Judicial part consisteth upon the consideration, and knowledge of the fertilitie, vesture, situation for vent, healthsomeness, commodiousnesse, discommodiousnesse, and such like of every kinde of ground, building, and encrease, in his owne nature, & kind.[12]

The earliest treatises to tackle the subject of surveying focus principally on what Worsop identifies as the "legal" and the "judicial." John Fitzherbert's *Boke of Surveynge and Improvementes* (1523), the first surveying text printed in English, only devotes a small portion of its whole to land measuring. The same is broadly true of Valentine Leigh's *Surveying of Landes* (1577). John Norden's fictional surveyor in his *Surveyor's Dialogue* (1607), although the treatise contains guidance in some advanced mathematical techniques and instructs in the making of a map, is still in many respects the older type, concerned more with an understanding of the "diversities" and "particulars" of law and custom than with universal science; more with empirical judgments about the singular "nature"; the propriety of "every kinde of ground" than with the geometric constants of "proportion and symmetrie"; more with the words of records, books, interviews, and courts than with the new surveyor's cartographic mathematics.

Norden's treatise reminds us that his era was witnessing only a gradual separation of the role of surveying from that of day-to-day manorial stewardship, and places the work of stewardship within the context of distinctly precapitalist values regarding land use. Its introductory dedication to Robert Cecil, first earl of Salisbury, and James I's lord treasurer from 1608, depicts the surveyor maintaining and defending the customary social order connecting king to commoner through the land. "There is none," warns Norden, "but well considereth, that how great or powerful soever he be in land revenues, it is brought in unto him by the labours of inferiour tenants: yea the king consisteth by the field that is tilled."[13] "Dominion and Lordship," he writes, "principally grow . . . by Honors, Mannors, Lands and Tenants." The surveyor can and should enhance the landlord's revenues, grants Norden, but only so that such revenues may be "the meanes to enable the Honorable, to shelter the virtuous distressed, and to cherish such, as by desert may challenge regard."[14] The surveyor must help his employer balance his right to benefit from his land with his responsibilities to those who must share its use and benefits, seeking the lord's "uttermost lawfull profite . . . disswading him yet from distastefull Avarice."[15] Where Norden compares the surveyor to "Magistrates and Officers," in their responsibility to "see into, informe, punish and reforme," the reformation that he has in mind involves the restoration of customary forms of land use, rather than their revision, and their deterioration might, in theory at least, be blamed on either end of the social spectrum.[16]

In performing his conservative work of stewardship, Norden's surveyor cannot merely be a mathematician. On a precapitalist manor the identity of the land and the revenue of its owner are determined not just by the nature of the property, its quality and quantity, but also by the nature of its use: by whom it is used, and under what conditions. The legal limits of each individual's usage must be ascertained and recorded as they correspond to the physical terrain: a process known as butting and bounding. As with the steward's regular surveillance duties, accounts of the boundaries of tenure are dependent on verbal report for their information. Where the surveyor might found quantitative/qualitative assessments of land purely or at least fundamentally on the basis of his own inspection, for the latter, more specific material he must turn either to written records, to the testimony of the users themselves, or, for comparison, to a combination of the two.[17] "These are the two pillars," states Norden, "upon which a Surveyor must of force build his worke, information and record."[18]

In precisely the year that the colony of Jamestown was established, the year that John Smith began exploring the territory of Virginia, John Norden's *Surveyor's Dialogue* defines for us both the political values and the epistemology of contemporary local geography. These may leave room for profit and the abstract calculations of mathematics, but not to the exclusion of the customary, social usages of land, defined in the concrete particularities of verbal testimony and written law. Late sixteenth- and early seventeenth-century "how-to" manuals which promote mathematics more enthusiastically than Norden's as the defining factor in the surveyor's authority also tend to retain a marginal role for stewardly discretion and local knowledge.[19] At the margins of the surveyor's map, in verbal supplements to its tidy mathematical forms, still stand local lists, descriptions, and interviews with tenants. It may have been possible to represent land without any reference to its social nature in the early seventeenth century, but not to secure consensus in the truth of such a representation. These distinctly precapitalist standards of truth and legitimacy help explain John Smith's apparent ambivalence in representing Virginia. Smith does not just measure up the proportions of a "plain" space and estimate its capacity to yield profit to the "industrious." Foreign empire, like domestic "dominion," must principally grow not just by revenues, but by the colonial equivalent of Norden's "Honors, Mannors, Lands and Tenants." Like any steward butting and bounding a manor, Smith accordingly pays attention to native customary uses of the land and to native testimony on these uses. This dependence may well not have been a comfortable one, and certainly we can understand such discomfort as part of the unsettling experience of the colonial "contact zone." But we also need to understand such an uncomfortable dependence as an inherent element in contemporary domestic geography. In the preface to a survey undertaken for the crown, the same John Norden who insists upon tenant information as the "pillar" of true survey complains that the "verball" evidence of manorial tenants is "for the moste parte forged untruthes."[20]

The Ralegh Circle

Norden's frustration reminds us once again of the precarious rhetorical balance of his treatise. It cautiously advances the interests of the landlord's "profit," but still within a reassuringly conservative vision of social order, accommodating both the rights and the voices of peasant land users, however mendacious. This balance of predominant conservatism, flavored by a capitalist impulse, is fairly representative of contemporary politics regarding land use. In 1597 and 1601, when two "tillage" bills intended to stem the tide of capitalist enclosure were debated in parliament, what Andrew McRae calls "divergent representations of agrarian order" were already distinctly evident.[21] Statesmen such as Francis Bacon and Robert Cecil, dedicatee of Norden's *Surveyor's Dialogue*, drew in these debates on a conservative rhetorical tradition of complaint against covetousness and social change. Sir Walter Ralegh, among others, sought to turn the legislative tide. In 1601, and in another contemporary and related parliamentary debate, Ralegh sought to dismantle the model of a static, regionally diverse, and self-sufficient social order, arguing for regional specialization, freer trade, and the "liberty" of each man to do what he wished, unhindered, with his land. In McRae's words, Ralegh "struck the keynote of English capitalism, which would reverberate through the centuries to come."[22] And it is clear that while Ralegh regarded freer trade and private property as a desirable goal for England, he had already looked to America for the immediate creation of "a more complex, more varied economy than England itself possessed."[23] He had looked to America, in part, for a desocialized conception of land.

The efforts of Ralegh and his circle of associates at Roanoke in the 1580s generated the first properly colonial English geographies of Virginia.[24] Like Smith's two decades later, these geographies are evidence of a vigorous capitalist impulse to make the land available for profitable exploitation. But like Smith's geographies too, they also accommodate native, customary use. For Richard Hakluyt the younger, in the now famous *Discourse of Western Planting* which he circulated privately to canvass government support for colonization, the America of future English "planting" is presently a "waste firm."[25] This "waste firm," like Smith's "plaine wildernes," represents unrealized potential: a blank accounting sheet and cartographic template available for artful filling in. And art is what England currently abounds in, to the point of surplus. "Nowe," warns Hakluyt, "there are of every arte and science so many, that they can hardly lyve one by another."[26] The remedy to this "inconvenience" is to set this surplus skill to work. This done, writes Thomas Hariot, sent by Ralegh as surveyor and historian to the Roanoke colony, Virginia promises

> commodities there already found or to be raised, which will not onely serve the ordinary turnes of you which are and shall bee the planters and inhabitants, but such an overplus sufficiently to bee yeelded or by men of skill to bee provided as by way of traffick and exchaunge with our owne nation of England, will enrich your selves the providers.[27]

Although Hariot, like Hakluyt, wants his reader to imagine a virgin land responsive to the novel addresses of English skill, the either/or formulations of his *A Briefe and True Report of the New Found Land of Virginia* also point the way to something other than an artless, empty Virginia. Some of Hariot's American commodities want no English skill to bring them forth. They are already present, and if they lack anything, it is not the physical intervention of "arte," but only the new legal frame of English ownership. A similar ambivalence characterizes the account written for Ralegh by the governor of the first colony established at Roanoke, Sir Ralph Lane, and edited and published by Hakluyt. Lane's account certainly makes ample claim for the general underexploitation of Virginia, and we may guess that Hakluyt's editing did nothing to tone down such a claim. But in his geographic description of the specific "peculiarities" of this territory, Lane acknowledges a landscape dense with Indian polities and "goodly corne field[s]."[28] And indeed Hakluyt's *Discourse* itself, like Hariot's *Briefe and True Report*, is preoccupied not just with the artful filling of a void, but also with the reframing of Virginia's already fruitful content. Hakluyt asserts not just that Virginia soil "may be made to yelde," but that it already "yeldeth all the severall commodities of Europe."[29] Moreover, while he certainly claims that American commodities are little labored over and little used, he also acknowledges the human presence in Virginia that must be framed along with its commodities. He is confident, at this early stage, that Virginia's natives will "yelde themselves" to English "gouvernement."[30] Such government can only be achieved when the English are strongly seated in America, and thereby able "to have full knowledge of the language manners and custommes of the people of those Regions."[31] And such knowledgeable government is necessary, Hakluyt insists, as the precondition for both Christian conversion and trade—the first and second priorities of the English western venture.

Thomas Hariot's work at Roanoke can be interpreted as an extensive attempt to bring a frame of intellectual government to bear on Virginia, in the disciplinary forms not just of botany, but also of mathematical cartography, philology, and ethnography, in preparation for the political government and transatlantic trade that Hakluyt projects. One of the most influential readings of the *Briefe and True Report* of the last two decades, Stephen Greenblatt's "Invisible Bullets," reads it as an exemplary exercise in the definition and containment of difference. Hariot is certainly well known as a scientist so seduced by the all-encompassing potency of mathematics that he sought to reduce even the most humdrum of English domestic problems to its form.[32] But he was also the man who spent hours with two Indians brought back to England in a bid to make himself conversant with the detail of their language, and thereby the detail of their customs, their manners, and their home, precisely as Hakluyt had urged.[33] And if it is an attempt at the dissipation of American "otherness," Hariot's *Report* conspicuously fails, leaving native knowledge, use, and ownership of Virginia persistently in excess of its English circumscription.[34]

Like Smith's, Hariot's surveying work may aspire to produce abstract, exchangeable commodities, but it also leaves customary Indian knowledge and use of Virginia and its products substantially intact. In this qualification of abstract frame with local custom, these geographers typify the more conservative aspect of contemporary English attitudes to the use and representation of land. The difference appears to be that whereas in English geographies conservative, post-feudal truths and values are still dominant, and capitalist ones only just emergent, American geographies push capitalist truths and values to the fore.

The Age of the Improver

If the English presence in America was established in a period when customary, native use and knowledge of land still enjoyed considerable legitimacy, their first century of life would see substantial changes in these values. H. C. Darby calls the period between 1600 and 1800 "The Age of the Improver." Sixteenth- and early seventeenth-century topographers such as John Leland and William Camden distinguish between the "champaign," or open regions of England, broadly the midland counties; the wooded parts; and counties such as Essex, Kent, and Devon, whose open land had already undergone a form of modification: the separation into individually husbanded tracts of private property which historians conventionally indicate by the term "enclosure." This distinction began to break down in the later seventeenth century, as both forest and champaign gave way to enclosure increasingly viewed more as a national program than a local feature.[35]

While earlier governmental responses to enclosure had sought to suppress a phenomenon perceived as detrimental to the national interest,[36] and to this end set up commissions of inquiry in 1607, 1630, 1632, 1635, and 1636 to look into depopulating enclosures,[37] the last parliamentary proposals to deal with enclosure as a "problem" were rejected in the 1650s as a threat to "property." When, in 1660, an act was passed abolishing feudal tenures, it failed to safeguard the rights of copyholders, leaving them subject to eviction. By the last few decades of the century the tide had definitively turned: the new government of landlords ensconced at the Restoration passed no anti-enclosure legislation, and the Hanoverian era saw the majority of enclosures licensed by parliamentary statute.[38]

The period between the Tudor enclosures spearheaded by much vilified individual lords, and the sweeping parliamentary enclosures of the eighteenth century, is chiefly that of "enclosure by agreement": the process whereby freeholders contracted to extinguish common rights and reallocate their holdings as consolidated enclosures, under the supervision of a commission of arbitrators whose decisions were ratified by courts of Chancery or Exchequer.[39] This means of going about the business of enclosure, cooperative at least as far as the freeholding tenantry were concerned, is one among five legal routes by which enclosure was achieved over the long history of early modern agrarian reform. The others include the parliamentary enclosure typical of a later period, and the following avenues more characteristic of an earlier: the "extinction of common" which might be licensed by the law, for instance where a population of common users had dwindled; "withdrawal from common by sufferance," where common users would theoretically be in some way compensated, and "approvement."[40] The principle of enclosure by "approvement" is of particular importance here.

At the beginning of the seventeenth century, the primary language for defining what was legitimate in the usage of land, and thereby what counted in any representation of it, was the language of the common law: not a rationalist language of absolute, inherent rights, such as the right to property, but a "procedural" language, as P. G. McHugh puts it, designed to protect and restore "diversity, community, immemoriality, custom."[41] This language was not immediately replaced by one of rights, but evolved and was redefined to incorporate it. The period in which we are interested—the early seventeenth century—is the beginning of this evolution. It is, in McHugh's words again, a "transitional" period in the language of English law.[42] During this transitional period, the legitimacy of customary land use vies with the legitimacy of the absolute right of property, not just across English culture, and between conservative court/peasant and progressive, whiggish interests, but within the ideas and discourses of individuals representing and debating land. In an important sense this contest of values was waged over the principle and meanings of "improvement."

"Approvement," or "improvement"—the terms are to a degree interchangeable—denotes, in its legal sense, some kind of appropriation from the devolved use of others, to the owner's direct use and profit: a reframing of that which is currently dispersed. "Approvement" is the word used in medieval and early modern law, for instance, to indicate the king's direct appropriation of state levies otherwise "farmed" out to others.[43] In these legal terms, approvement could be either a legitimate appropriation of resources, or an illegitimate one. The legal resort of enclosure by approvement appealed to the landowner's customary right, enshrined in common law by thirteenth-century statutes made at Merton and Westminster and confirmed again in the seventeenth century,[44] to make whatever use of his own land he wished, so long as this use did not hamper "the legitimate claims of others to share in any part of its profits."[45] The case for enclosure, within the terms of these statutes, had then to turn on an understanding of what constituted such a legitimate claim.

While the minutiae of subfreeholder customary uses were upheld in the nation's law, the right to improve could only involve the absence or deterioration of customary uses in the land involved: its condition of being, in the language of the statutes, "waste." Improvement on grounds less than such waste-ness could be denounced, at least until the sixteenth century, as an assault on the social order which a network of customary uses constituted. But as the rights of the nonfreeholding tenantry began to be contested, ultimately to lose the protection of law towards the latter half of the seventeenth century, the language defining legitimate use and legitimate improvement came under pressure. Progressive writing of the period works to characterize nonfreehold, and especially common land use as "illegitimate," in some absolute sense that begs, even if it might lack the recognition of law. Keeping within the terms of the established statutes, such writing even works to characterize such land as somehow fitting the old category of "waste."

Within law, a waste is the sufferance or deliberate causation of change to the substance of a tenement by its tenant. A genuine or "actual" waste, states the early seventeenth-century jurist Sir Edward Coke, a crucial actor in the promotion of a rights, rather than custom-protecting common law, is one the tenant has effected "voluntarily": covertly, or without permission.[46] Another kind of waste, not so properly so named, thinks Coke, is that which he has been "permitted" to make. In both instances, the term waste defines a legal state of affairs, rather than the physical condition of the land involved. The kind of "waste" that legitimates improvement, within the remit of the Merton statute, is the kind John Norden's surveyor is employed to remedy: the alteration or decay of customary, social use.

The potential always resides in the term waste, however, for another, more absolute meaning, defining the condition not of a legal contract, but of the land involved in it. Waste land can simply be empty land, even if, as with the wasted human body, the etymology of this term (from the Latin vasto "to devastate") still recalls a previous use destroyed or abandoned, rather than a state of pristine virginity. Where legitimacy comes to be judged by increasingly capitalist standards of productive use in the later seventeenth century, the physical condition of the land comes increasingly to determine its condition of waste-ness, and hence the legitimacy of its improvement.

The second of John Locke's 1690 *Two Treatises of Government* defines waste as "Land that is left wholly to Nature, that hath no improvement of Pasturage, Tillage, or Planting."[47] Improvement of such land as Locke describes must, in an unqualified, absolute sense, be ameliorative, since such land utterly lacks the supplement of use, and any benefit taken from it cannot detract from the benefit of anyone else. In so far as use—the mixing of one's labor with a resource, and in the case of land, cultivation—depends upon and defines "appropriation," or "property," states Locke, and marks the limit of common ownership, no consent is needed to appropriate and thus create property, since property can only be created out of that which is unused.[48] Such a definition of the legitimate appropriation of "waste" land sweeps away the problem of prior usage, and makes it possible for the customary, civil right of improvement to be perceived not as limited by specific contextual conditions, but as absolute. For Locke, this absolute right even takes precedence over the natural right of men to use the earth in common.[49]

For Locke, then, it is possible simply to observe the quality of land to deem it fit subject for improvement. There is no need to inquire into its legal condition, since whether or not it has any legal identity as waste, common, or even petty-tenanted land, and whether indeed the legal conditions that define this identity have been contravened, has no bearing on its physical condition of waste-ness. For Locke, common land can be as waste as waste land legally so defined, as long as it can be judged devoid of the signs of significant usage. And, crucially, this absence of use can be a relative quality. Poor or unproductive use, can, in the later seventeenth century, be judged a waste. Abstracted from its specific, contextual, social meanings, waste comes to enjoy an absolute value as the negative complement to and justification for improvement. Waste is no longer a specific historical condition of declined or absent custom, but a generalized physical condition of inefficiency.

As the meanings of "waste" evolve during the seventeenth century, so do the meanings of "improvement." The primary, "ancient" meaning of "improve" is given in the Oxford English Dictionary as "avail oneself (of) by using to one's profit."[50] Closely related to this primary meaning, however, is that of increasing the profitability/value of something, frequently land: of "turning" it to profit. This second meaning bears originally on the usefulness of a resource, its fertility, or capacity to yield, and is closely related to that of "husbandry." The OED illustrates it with a phrase from Skelton, written in 1529, which praises Chaucer's English for being "wel ... enprowed, For ... There is no English voyd." It is possible, then, to understand in uses of the term improvement two different means by which the improvers might benefit themselves and/or the land. Skelton's phrase serves in fact to illustrate either equally well. Chaucer might be regarded as making a profit of common verbal resources either by appropriating them as if by enclosure, or by making them yield—husbanding them artfully, and turning void to fullness, waste to good use. There is also, of course, a possibility that he does both.

Neither appropriation nor husbandry is necessarily of any absolute positive or negative value within the complex social scenario of feudalism and post-feudalism or within the procedural discourse of the classical common law. Both the pasture enclosures of greedy feudal lords and the illicit husbandry of peasants encroaching on legally designated "forest" might be defined within this scenario in specific legal terms as illegitimate, where they violated custom. However, by the late seventeenth century, the OED notes, improvement had acquired the meaning of absolute betterment which it bears today: a meaning which has been only lately and "gradually separable" from the ancient, legal senses. This integration of a positive, absolute meaning with the variably determined legal denotations of improvement must clearly represent the discursive victory of the seventeenth-century agrarian capitalist seeking unqualified legitimacy for his cause, as recognized in accumulating discourses of rights and productivity. It meant that improvement—the private appropriation of a common resource—could always be seen as an improvement: a contribution to the general good.

Andrew McRae suggests that a "mature legal conception" of private property, and an understanding of private property as a source of universal benefit, does not emerge until the late seventeenth century, but that this conception and this equation are the product of arguments for absolute individual property rights waged throughout the sixteenth and seventeenth centuries.[51] While the legal process of enclosure in the seventeenth century was largely one of "enclosure by agreement," then, the principle of an absolute right to "improve" which overruled the claims of those who "disagreed" was paramount in justifying this process and in constituting the consensus upon which it depended. A discourse of "improvement," which can be traced in numerous polemic treatises from the early to mid seventeenth century, was essential to the articulation of this principle. Thus, while he discounts the legal significance of "approvement" as a means of enclosure, E. C. K. Gonner acknowledges the importance of what he calls its "literary" role.[52] This literary work is characteristically the work of ambiguity. While it may be possible for Locke to depict common land use as in some absolute, physical sense a waste, and enclosure as, in some absolute, physical sense an improvement, for much of the seventeenth century this judgment remains contentious. The commons cannot yet seem empty, nor—until they lose the protection of residual anti-enclosure law—can they be deemed illegitimate. What we tend to find in literature promoting English agrarian reform is a blurring of the boundaries between waste and common land: a strategic vagueness which associates the legal condition of a common resource demanding reframing with the physical condition of an empty one, demanding artful husbandry. As with the colonial American geographies of a half-century before, it is often unclear whether the common land of Commonwealth enclosure propaganda is empty and devoid of art, or full of an undisciplined and frameless content, and correspondingly whether the improvement proposed by the reformer is one of artful husbandry, or simply capitalist appropriation.

The Commons

The commons, suggests Adam Moore, writing in 1653, are as a "common prostitute," through which medium the commoner is "cuckolded by Forreigners and strangers."[53] "Your Common," he mocks, is "used before your face, even as commonly as by yourselves." Moore evidently puns here on one subsidiary meaning of common: the public woman, available to every man. Moreover, he extends the correspondence of land and woman in this pun beyond the basic alternatives of devolved or private use. Commons are ascribed linked physical qualities of ugliness and barrenness conventionally associated in contemporary discourse with the prostitute.[54] They are the void-ness of the empty womb: they are "gulfes of want and penury in a deformed visage"; they are "fruitless, naked and desolate"; they are, "(as nature in defect) . . . delivered of nothing but Monsters."[55] Here, as is usual in such literature, the social, legal, textual excess of common, rather than private property, is registered as physical lack. The commons lack the proper supplement of "husbandry," where husbandry is understood as physical tending, or—in the more general, physical and modern sense—"improvement" of the soil. Nature in defect is Nature undressed, un-husbanded, left waste. At the same time, however, within the terms through which waste and common use are discursively coimplicated, nature in defect is nature raped; laid waste; used in illegitimate fashion; improperly supplemented, and made to yield not properly but monstrously.

The disorderly social and sexual commerce of the commons in reformist discourse such as Moore's adds up to a negative aesthetic which paradoxically fuses the excessive fullness and the excessive emptiness of gluttonous, idle drunkenness; of the prostitute's overfilled yet barren womb; of common wastes whose cacophony of customary uses leaves them excessively written, yet also beyond rational representation. This empty/full aesthetic is encapsulated in the figure of boundlessness: a figure which expresses in its purest form and seeks to legitimate the improver's desire not just to husband virgin land, but to husband to himself—to bridle in; to yoke—the shoreless resources of other people's land and labor. Those social levellers, writes Joseph Lee in 1656, who see common rights as the basis of the "liberty of conscience" which they seek, desire

> to live as the [sic] list and sin cum privelegio; the golden reins of discipline please not, this yoke they cannot bear, but cast off this, and then they may swear, and lie and rob, and rifle, and swill, and swagger, riot and revell in a shorelesse excesse.... The very same spirit of disorder in the very same persons, and upon the same grounds doth decry Inclosure because it would put a bridle upon their licentious lusts.[56]

The remedy for such a boundless, lawless, wasted common yield in improvement discourse is naturally to subject it to the economic and mathematical discipline of enclosure. In a letter to the reformer Samuel Hartlib, Cressey Dymock presents a farm design which achieves "the better casting out" of land "in point of Forme, and doth in no way remedy this, but as it contracts your businesse into a close order."[57] Dymock's abstract geometric plan presents the private farm "all bound together as with a girdle," and thus, with all "inconvenient passages" stopped, secure in its expectation of a natural, rather than the prostituted common's monstrous birth.[58]

To anyone familiar with early modern writing on America this gendered discourse on land may well sound familiar. In "The Work of Gender in the Discourse of Discovery" Louis Montrose has explored gendered iconography and language that, from the 1570s on, often characterized America as a virgin bride willingly and productively yielding to an English husband. Such sexual metaphors dismissed the native inhabitants of America as impotent suitors, or, like Moore on the prostituted English commons, as sires of an unlawful issue. The colonial chronicler and propagandist Samuel Purchas responded to Indian resistance in the 1620s by declaring Virginia so "violently ravished by her owne ruder Natives, yea her Virgin cheekes dyed with the bloud of three Colonies" that she "is ready to spue out her Inhabitants."[59] In *Colonial Encounters*, Peter Hulme identifies the Indian "massacre" of 1622 as the point at which it became possible, for the first time, to discount native rights to American soil. This might appear to accord with Anthony Pagden's suggestion that colonists used the "res nullius," or empty land, justification for dominion over American soil from the 1620s on.[60] Indeed Hulme identifies English colonial discourse, including John Smith's, very closely with an individualist, capitalist, even "Lockeian" discourse of American waste-ness and legitimate colonial improvement.[61] And yet what writers such as Purchas are claiming, according to the distinctions made by Pagden and Armitage, is not simply dominion over a land devoid of significant use: they are claiming empire over a land obtained through conquest. Such writers still take the Indians seriously as owners of their land. The verbal battle to discount such ownership, waged with the same blunt weapons soon to be used against the English commoner, is far from achieving Lockeian closure.

Conquest and the Ideology of the Land

Hulme ends his chapter on John Smith's Jamestown with a quotation from another chronicle of 1622, in which Edward Waterhouse describes with ugly relish the violence that colonists may now allow themselves to visit on the Indians in revenge. Indeed Jamestown paid the Powhatan Indians liberally in kind. A passage that Hulme does not quote, however, indicates clearly the legal rationale for such aggression. It is a rationale that claims Indian land enthusiastically by conquest, or "imperium," and in doing so seems to concede the failure of the argument for general dominium over American waste. Waste for Waterhouse, in fact, is not an entire continent left virgin by its nomadic inhabitants, but, as in England under the terms of the Merton statute, the disregarded surplus of an agrarian economy.

> We, who hitherto have had possession of no more ground than their waste, and our purchase . . . may now by right of Warre, and law of Nations, invade the Country, and destroy them who sought to destroy us: whereby wee shall enjoy their cultivated places, turning the laborious Mattocke into the victorious Sword (wherein there is more both ease, benefit, and glory). Now their cleared grounds in all their villages (which are situate in the fruitfullest places of the land) shall be inhabited by us, whereas heretofore the grubbing of woods was the greatest labour.[62]

Recent accounts of colonial ideology have tended to look at the way in which ideas about land use established at "home" were exported to America, and indeed this approach has a lot to tell us. And yet there may also be a sense, to some extent counter-intuitive, in which America preceded England in the formulation of discourses of possession, not only because it offered new experiences—colonists could hardly be said to have experienced a virgin land—but also because it provided conceptual space for the articulation of new ideas. English agrarian reformers such as Adam Moore and Joseph Lee might have sought to discredit existing, customary use, but they were neither politically nor conceptually able to ignore it. Their ambiguous metaphorical work registers a political and conceptual struggle between the post-feudal obligation to define and acknowledge the prior use and benefit of the resource they desire, within a residually social understanding of the nature of land, and the capitalist drive to overlook such historical specificities. These writers are waging a battle, as the violence of their language makes abundantly evident. What early writing on Virginia suggests is that this battle had already been going on for half a century, and that some of its important early skirmishes were fought over America.

"In the beginning," writes Locke in his 1680 essay "Of Property," "all the world was America."[63] This formula has as much to say about seventeenth-century conceptions of America as it does about "the world." Locke implies that America, as its first European explorers and colonizers saw it, was empty, virgin, or if inhabited, inhabited by a race of men whose relation to the land was naïve, Adamic, and incommensurable with "civil" standards of property and agriculture. The American Indian helps Locke imagine the progress of European socioeconomic history. America helps him imagine the opposite of, and the basis for imposing, civil practices of land use. Thinkers such as Locke, at the vanguard of a shift of values in favor of enclosure, could depict both peasant use of the English "commons" and native use of American land as practically no use at all: at best a prelapsarian anachronism in a postlapsarian world; at worst an element of residual savagery in a civil society; and in any case a de jure justification for appropriation and "improvement" by a private owner. "Of Property" functions equally well as a colonial ideology of appropriation and as a history of the general progress of mankind from primitive commonality to civil private property, in an era when this "progress" was beginning to be widely acknowledged as such. It clears both American and English land as cleanly as the mathematical map is sometimes said to do.

And indeed as it became increasingly possible in the seventeenth century to think and speak of common and indeed petty tenanted land as "waste" or empty, it became less necessary to recognize its particularities in representation. Where patterns of communal land use on the feudal manor were marked and maintained through the discrete verbal judgments and negotiations of an experienced local steward, the boundaries of seventeenth-century private property were increasingly ruled by the surveyor's absolute and universalizing geometry.

The serviceability of mathematical surveying to the argument for private property is easily explained. Well before the predominance of private ownership as an economic reality, surveying had begun to make both local inhabitants and the local features of the land they tenanted appear secondary to a universal form signifying the landlord's direct relationship with his property. Though still verbally recorded in the surveyor/steward's fieldbook, histories of land use were practically silenced, pushed to the margins of the map, by mathematics.[64] A sample of surveying treatises from the end of the seventeenth century demonstrates how much has changed since John Norden's *Surveyor's Dialogue*. By the time of John Love's *Geodaesia: or the Art of Surveying and Measuring of Land Made Easie* (1688), the legal element in Worsop's tripartite conception of the truth and legitimacy of land has all but disappeared. The "how-to" situations hypothesized by Love include, rather than being more or less contained by, the physical scenario of the manor.

Published two years before Locke's *Two Treatises of Government*, John Love's *Geodaesia* also faces both ways across the Atlantic. Like Locke, Love defines a moment when the specificities of local custom in English land use can be represented as marginal to the universal form of mathematics and private property. And like Locke also, Love looks to America to help him "forget" these specificities, and imagine the identity of land in absolute terms. Love's *Geodaesia*, we are told on its title page, is intended to show "How to Lay-out New Lands in America." The relationship between geometry and America in this treatise seems reciprocal. The colonist needs geometry: "How," asks Love, "could Men set down to Plant, without knowing some Distinction and Bounds of their Land?"[65] In America, Love reminds his reader, geometry will allow the colonist to "inclose" the wildest, most indefinite land "in the thick woods of Jamaica, Carolina, &c.," where otherwise he might not proceed except with "exceeding great trouble."[66] But if the colonist needs geometry, the geometrician also needs America, as the blank sheet for his abstract designs. In America, the surveyor is allowed full scope to try, uncompromised, such techniques as "How to lay out a parallelogram that shall be 4, 5, 6, or 7, etc. times longer than it is broad." "In Carolina," Love notes, "all Lands lying by the sides of Rivers . . . are (or ought, by order of the Lord's Proprietors to be) thus laid out."[67] Indeed Love, concluding a surveying treatise in which America has allowed him space to explore the full range of planimetric possibilities, assures his reader complacently: "so will you have a fair Map . . . better done, I think, than in any place of the World yet, except for the Harbours of Eutopia."[68]

We are accustomed to thinking of colonial representations of America in precisely these abstract, utopian terms, perhaps largely because we are used to looking backwards at America through the spectacles of the Lockean Enlightenment, with its taste for mathematicity and absolute property rights. But such absolute conceptions of land and its proper usages were only a horizon in the first half of the seventeenth century even for the radical wing of English Commonwealth reformism—the vanguard of a proto-Lockean conception of land in a pre-Lockean age. They were almost impossible to imagine or articulate without supplementation, contradiction, and an aggressively "literary" rhetoric, whose metaphors forced and fudged the case. Customary use still enjoyed a residual value in any discourse concerned with legitimacy, and in any true representation of land. Mid-seventeenth-century English propagandists for enclosure wrote accordingly as much to re-frame a landscape dense with customary rights and usages as they did to bring art to an empty, waste one, and English cartographers working in this period were as much stewards managing a landscape of customary use as they were surveyors of the blank, abstracted spaces of capitalism. Similarly in early seventeenth-century America, by necessity as much as choice. If English representations seem often to acknowledge and even sometimes to legitimate Indian geography and the customary uses of Virginia, we don't necessarily have to attribute this to openness and fairness of mind. English ideas, discourses, and representations of land use in this period presented the most ardent colonial propagandist with a problematic set of representational and ideological tools. To represent American land truly, those who mapped it—whether in verbal or cartographic form—were still obliged to describe not just its physical quantities and qualities but also its social form. For several decades, at least, this social form was necessarily a principally Indian one. And in their constant, anxious consideration of the proper use of American land, these same colonial geographers were still obliged to take into account its customary uses, even if, like their counterparts at home, they came increasingly to denigrate them.

As Karen Kupperman abundantly demonstrates, the early part of the seventeenth century was a period of intense ambivalence about social and economic change. Such ambivalence could permeate an organization such as the Virginia Company,[69] a project such as the colonization of Virginia,[70] and the attitudes and texts of individuals such as John Smith.[71] Kupperman's own distinction between the true geographies of eyewitness travelers to and settlers in early America, and the false rhetorical flourishes of armchair propagandists, does not fully accommodate the uncertainty of both groups about the proper use of land. The same uneasiness that unsettles contemporary legal debate over the proper foundation for statehood and empire unsettles a local geography caught between lordship over political subjects and dominion over empty land. Where Kupperman and other recent scholars regard the hybridity of early colonial geography principally as an embodiment of the experiential contact zone, I also see evidence of a growing domestic conflict between the capitalist truths and values of productivity and property, and the post-feudal ones of customary, social use.[72]

Much has been made, for quite some time, of the importance to colonists and colonial discourse of designating American land "waste," and thereby overlooking its prior, native use in favor of private ownership and capitalist exploitation. This essay has demonstrated that such a narrative of waste land and improvement was slow to develop and was compromised in application in the early seventeenth century. At most Virginian geographies made possible an early representational compromise between post-feudal values and languages and those of Lockean capitalism: a compromise to be found in both maps and literary rhetoric. Just as the discourse and cartography of Commonwealth improvement would struggle both to acknowledge and yet to discount the customary land use of the English commoner and petty tenant, so colonial geographies of Virginia flicker rather earlier between goodly corn fields and plain wilderness.

Chapter 11
Settling with Slavery
Human Bondage in the Early Anglo-Atlantic World

MICHAEL J. GUASCO

Did the arrival of "20. and Odd Negroes" in the fledgling English colony of Virginia in 1619 mark the beginning of slavery in America? United States historians have long thought so, but in recent years this assumption has been challenged on both factual and conceptual grounds. For one thing, it now appears that there may have been as many as thirty-three African men and women in Virginia before 1619, and historians have begun to recognize the relevance of other "firsts" in the Anglo-Atlantic world, such as the arrival of at least one African man in Bermuda in 1616. More fundamentally, American historians are becoming more sensitive to the place of the early English colonies in the context of much broader and far-reaching Atlantic developments.[1] The history of slavery is perhaps the most obvious example of the large-scale dynamics that shaped the history of English colonial ventures: West Africans, the Portuguese, and the Spanish had set in motion the enslavement and forced migration of huge numbers of people and established an enduring model of colonial plantations long before English leaders began to think seriously about establishing a foothold in North America. But slavery nevertheless played a role in English culture, both in theory and in practice. Long before the Jamestown settlement, a number of English writers thought seriously about slavery; a surprising number of English people actually experienced slavery; and many more feared the threat of enslavement.

Few English thinkers contemplating opportunities for wealth and glory in the emerging Atlantic world considered the institution of slavery either necessary or even desirable. And as slavery in various forms, involving a variety of different peoples, was common throughout Africa, the Mediterranean, southern Europe, and, increasingly, the Iberian colonies in the Americas, few sixteenth-century English people—unlike their later descendants—thought about slavery in terms that had anything to do with ideologies of race, or for that matter with the peoples of sub-Saharan West Africa.[2] To be sure, the expanding transatlantic slave trade was familiar to many English merchants, ship captains, and sailors, and interest in establishing a trading relationship with Africa dated back to the 1480s when John Tintam and William Fabian proposed an expedition during the reign of Edward IV. Numerous Englishmen also recognized the correlation between blackness and slavery in coastal West Africa. Still, with the notable exception of three expeditions under the command of Sir John Hawkins and another commanded by John Lovell during the 1560s, few Englishmen went to Africa to participate in the transatlantic slave trade before the mid-seventeenth century.[3] Instead, most English merchants in Africa sought gold, ivory, and pepper, and therefore regularly came in contact with African peoples who stood out more as power brokers than potential slaves.[4] While the occasional English visitor to coastal West Africa may have dwelled on images suggesting a belief that sub-Saharan Africans were inferior or abnormal, most Englishmen before the mid-seventeenth century seem to have been comfortable with the notion that Africans in Africa were, in Richard Jobson's words, "gentle and loving," or "very friendly and tractable."[5]

If English people did not immediately think of Africans as slaves or slavish characters, they did associate themselves with liberty.[6] In stark contrast with much of the rest of the known world, the practice of slavery had become uncommon in England—and historians, political leaders, legal theorists, and Protestant theologians were all proud of that distinction. Human bondage, particularly in its most extreme form, may have been almost entirely absent from England in the sixteenth century. But late Tudor and early Stuart sources are nevertheless frequently concerned with bondage as an idea bearing upon English social life in a variety of ways, and use the terms associated with it in a variety of important if not always commensurate senses.

Some of the meanings early modern English people associated with slavery are apparent in the records of early Jamestown. In fact, before either African peoples or tobacco plantations began to redefine colonial American society, at least three forms of slavery were already manifest in Virginia, and the written record reflects that. First, in judicial proceedings, slavery was a punishment inflicted on criminals by the government. In 1617 and 1618, company records indicate that a Virginia settler could be sentenced to "slavery" for anywhere from a week to three years for crimes ranging from failing to attend church to failing to adhere to strict price controls. Second, in private correspondence and political writings, slavery was a metaphor used to protest either harsh treatment or the commodification of human beings. John Rolfe had the latter in mind in 1619 when he complained of the practice of "buying and selling men and bois," a practice that was held to be "most intolerable" in England and was, in Virginia, already the subject of numerous complaints. From 1622 to 1624 , other early Virginians like Richard Frethorne, Thomas Best, and Jane Dickinson similarly used references to slavery in letters home begging to be "freed out of this Egipt" and complaining that they had been sold from one master to another "like a damnd slave." And third, in all sorts of early colonial discourse slavery was an important political metaphor. In 1622 John Bargrave, for example, accused the former secretary of the Virginia Company, Sir Thomas Smith, of "having contrary to the patent and royal instructions caused a certain book to be printed of tyrannical government in Virginia, whereby many lost their lives, and were brought into slavery."[7] Nor were the Virginians alone in their concerns and confusions. Similar references to slavery, in all three senses, appeared in New England, Bermuda, and elsewhere in the English-speaking world during the first half of the seventeenth century.[8]

Even as the English established their settlement at Jamestown, they were wrestling with the meanings of slavery at home. Some political thinkers worried that slavery might actually be on the rise in England, and slavery remained alive in legal theory and religious thought, as well as in government efforts to control the poor and punish criminals. In addition, given its weighty historical grounding in classical sources, some English writers exploited the idea of slavery as a metaphorical or conceptual platform from which to celebrate their inherent national liberties. Meanwhile, other "freeborn" Englishmen imagined that a redoubled domestic institution of slavery could be a means for curing a variety of social ills. But most prominently, and perhaps surprisingly, slavery was an actual experience: a fate suffered by thousands of Englishmen throughout the Atlantic world, especially in North Africa among the dreaded Moors. On the one hand, speeches, sermons, royal proclamations, and published texts thus decried the enslavement of Christian Englishmen by infidel Moors, outraged at slavery's inhumanity. But on the other hand, English settlers in North America were beginning to think about how large-scale slavery—particularly of Indian war captives—might serve as an instrument of colonial power and profit.

Slavery in Early Modern England

Slavery was a word that thus immediately resonated in the imagination of sixteenth-century English men and women. Although the institution ceased to exist as a viable labor system soon after the Norman Conquest, the *idea* of slavery was alive in Tudor religious and intellectual life. Indeed, it would have been difficult to avoid the issue, if only because slavery and the image of human bondage pervaded the nation's most ubiquitous text, the Christian Bible. It was also prominent in Roman law, medieval theology, and local historical legend. In some ways the emerging myth that the

English were distinctly free, especially vis-à-vis other European peoples, was buttressed by what they took to be their conscious rejection of slavery as either a justifiable practice or a legitimate condition.

The Bible was filled with references to slaves and slavery and established human bondage as an apt metaphor, particularly in sermons, for the complete submission of mankind and particular individuals to God. Throughout the book of Exodus, one could read of the children of Israel who "sighed for the[ir] bondage and cryed" in an Egypt so miserable and cruel that when Moses told them that Yahweh would free them of their burdens and lead them to a better place they could not listen, "for anguish of spirit & for cruel bondage." The entire Old Testament, in fact, granted tacit justification for the legality of human bondage, provided it conformed to certain religious precepts. The book of Leviticus made it clear that slaves should come from foreign nations and that "ye shal take them as inheritance for your children after you, to possesse them by inheritance, ye shal use their labours for ever: but over your brethren the children of Israel ye shal not rule one over another with crueltie."[9] Similarly, the New Testament, particularly the letters of Paul, reveals a certain recognition of slavery as a legitimate human institution and contain sentiments that upheld the status quo, such as that slaves must "counte their masters worthie of all honour, that the Name of God, and *his* doctrine be not evil spoken of."[10] Subsequent Christian writers continued to endorse the legitimacy of slavery. As St. Augustine argued in his *City of God* (translated into English early in the seventeenth century), slavery had been normalized by God's punishment of Cham.[11] Therefore, although slavery was not part of God's original intent, Augustine maintained that slavery "as a punishment" was "ordained by that law which enjoins the preservation of the order of nature, and forbids its disturbance." In an important sense, slavery had become a natural part of the Fallen World and masters and slaves alike were obligated to respect their condition in order to ensure peace and harmony.[12]

For educated Englishmen, however, impressions about legal and political slavery were also informed by the Latin sources many of them had encountered in their university or grammar school education.[13] In particular, the Roman *Digest* spoke directly to the early modern English conception of slavery, as well as the idea of freedom. Indeed, it might be argued that the idea that human beings could, and should, be free only became meaningful in relation to the degree that they fully understood its historical opposite, slavery. Thus, according to Roman law, "Manumission means sending out of one's hand, that is, granting freedom. For whereas one who is in slavery is subjected to the hand (*manus*) and power of another, on being sent out of hand he is freed of that power. All of which originated from the *jus gentium*, since, of course, everyone would be born free by the natural law, and manumission would not be known when slavery was unknown."[14] Following Roman conventions, legally minded Englishmen subscribed to the notion that there were three classes of men: "free men, and set against those slaves and the third class, freedmen, that is, those who had stopped being slaves."[15] Moreover, this simple pronouncement easily translated into political rhetoric, particularly the notion that the absence of political liberty, among either individuals or nations, was tantamount to slavery. And, as Quentin Skinner has argued, classical Roman writers and, especially, the *Digest*, were central to the developing "neo-Roman" discourse of slavery in early Stuart England. Thus, educated Englishmen determined that the essence of slavery involved being *in potestate domini*, in the possession of another. It was this concept, which had nothing to do with physical treatment, race, or labor, that made the idea of slavery such a powerful weapon in the verbal condemnation of tyrannical rule during the reign of Charles I.

These religious, legal, and political conceptions of slavery were all the more significant in the early modern era because they blended seamlessly with emerging historical notions of English national identity. Sixteenth-century Englishmen believed they were uniquely free and some writers even maintained that the English would sooner die than submit to slavery. According to the boastful rhetoric of Sir Thomas Smith during the 1560s, the "nature of our nation is free, stout, haultaine, prodigall of life and bloud: [but] contumelie, beatings, servitude and servile torment and punishment it will not abide." William Harrison echoed Smith by claiming that Englishmen cherished freedom to such a degree that they would sooner suffer death than "yield our bodies unto such servile halings and tearings as are used in other countries." For this reason, Harrison claimed, "our condemned prisoners [go] cheerfully to their deaths, for our nation . . . cannot in any wise digest to be used as villeins and slaves, in suffering continually beating, servitude, and servile torments."[16]

The pious declaration that Englishmen were *exceptionally* free was buttressed during the late Tudor and early Stuart eras by national mythologizers who propounded that the English and British past was centered around the struggle for liberty, including efforts to resist enslavement by foreign powers. This idea was prominently featured in the increasing importance placed on the writings of Tacitus and other authors who traced the English past to Germanic roots. Writers like William Camden and Richard Verstegan vigorously promoted the idea that modern English people were the heirs of Germanic Anglo-Saxon invaders. Employing the writings of Tacitus, then, Englishmen could ignore the ugly fact that the Roman period witnessed the virtual enslavement of the British to the Romans by celebrating the fact that their true forebears, the Germans, "had shaken off the yoke of obedience." The Anglo-Saxon heritage of Tudor-Stuart England promised great rewards for those in search of an honorable and *free* past. Unlike the ancient Britons, Germans "were never subdued by any, for albeit the Romans with exceedingly great cost, losse & long trooble, might come to bee the comaunders of some part thereof; yet of the whole never."[17]

Slavery was a recurring theme in religious, legal, political, and historical arenas. These separate strands came together to inform elite notions about what bondage meant to both individuals and societies. Intellectual sources, however, could only inform popular conceptions of human bondage to a limited degree. Although England may have been in the midst of an "education revolution" during the late Tudor and early Stuart era, only a small percentage of English society benefited substantively from the elementary and grammar schools, much less the two universities or the Inns of Court.[18] Therefore, *how* people might have developed thoughts about slavery, including both what it meant to be a slave and what slavery entailed for a society as a whole, must be conceptualized beyond the significant, but decidedly limited confines of religious and intellectual traditions.

Domestic Slaves? Human Bondage in Early Modern England

Whatever rhetoric existed about the sacrosanct freedoms of Englishmen, there was a remarkable disjunction between the patriotic proclamations made for public and transnational consumption and social practice in the countryside. In 1567, for example, the Star Chamber recorded that one Cartwright "brought a slave from Russia . . . for which he was questioned; and it was resolved that England was too pure an air for slaves to breathe in." England was hardly unique in asserting its "free air," but the case did demonstrate the belief among jurists that everyone under common law was free. In Jonathan Bush's apt words, freedom was "positive, normal, and English" while slavery meant "tyranny at home and foreign despotism threatening from abroad." At the same time, the notion that the English nation was free did not necessarily mean that human bondage was entirely unacceptable. Freedom, in the late sixteenth century, had more to do with the ability to own property, to defend that property within the common law tradition, and to be part of a political community. As future proslavery arguments would bear out in colonial America and the United States, freedom could even imply the right to own another human being.[19]

The mythical freeborn Englishman actually inhabited a society where several forms of unfreedom, including slavery, not only were practiced, but might even be imagined as progressive measures. Many interdependent relationships in early modern England, like indentures and apprenticeship, were contractual arrangements that involved a measure of temporary bondage.[20] In other situations the distinctions between servitude and slavery were even less clear. Villeinage, a decayed manorial institution akin to serfdom, involved a perpetual and inheritable servile status that still applied to a small number of Englishmen.[21] Slavery was also legislated into existence during the mid-sixteenth century as a punitive measure to control vagrancy in the countryside, attack political prisoners, and deal with military deserters. The existence of these forms of human bondage suggests that while slavery may have been rhetorically distasteful and inconsistent with the national self-image, government officials were willing to use perpetual bondage or penal slavery to control English subjects.

Villeinage was a medieval agrarian institution whereby bondmen were attached, according to Sir Thomas Smith, "to the manor or place, and did followe him who had the manors." Villeins were not slaves, but many of those who remained in the archaic condition seem to have believed there was little in their status to distinguish them from that lowliest of conditions. This may have been due, in part, to abuses that bondmen, or their sympathizers, attributed to the problem of reconciling the rights of freeborn Englishmen with the rights of English lords over their human property. John Fitzherbert even commented in 1523 that "there be many freman taken as bondmen, and their lands and goodes taken from them so that they shal nat be able to sue for remedy, to prove them selfe fre of blode." Fortunately, for sixteenth-century bondmen, Tudor monarchs generally sympathized with villeins and several blanket manumissions were issued during the era as the crown sought to clear the landscape of the remnants of a system of perpetual and inheritable bondage.[22]

Englishmen were also able to witness and experience slavery as a penal institution during the sixteenth century. Penal slavery, however, differed from villeinage in a number of regards. Unlike villeins, penal slaves were not born into unfreedom; rather they were reduced to slavery as a form of punishment. Penal slavery was also envisaged, in some circles, as a progressive form of individual improvement and social control. The idea of penal slavery as a positive, virtue-instilling institution was most clearly advocated in the publication of Thomas More's *Utopia* (1516). More's carefully crafted, ideal society was made up of both slaves and freemen, yet Utopian slaves were convicted criminals whose enslavement reformed the flawed individual through "mild and practicable" punishment in order "to destroy vices and save men." If slaves accepted their punishment "in the spirit of obedience and patience" then they might expect to be reintegrated back into free Utopian society.[23]

This conception of slavery as a mechanism by which degenerate individuals could be salvaged was echoed in 1547 when Parliament passed its most extreme penal measure, possibly authored by Sir Thomas Smith, to attack "idle beggars and sturdy vagabonds." This short-lived act imposed slavery on recalcitrant individuals who refused to work—any competent man "not applying them self to some honest and allowed arte, Scyence, service or Labour" could be taken for a vagabond and enslaved for two years. The master would have absolute control over the diet of his bondmen, and could "cawse the saide Slave to work by beating, cheyninge or otherwise in such worke and Labor how vyle so ever it be." The slave could also be leased, sold, or bequeathed, as "any other of the master's movable goodes or Catelles." Nonetheless, the tacit recognition that slavery was neither permanent nor heritable, as well as the idea that slavery could instill a sense of virtue and hard work in otherwise idle men, distinguished this conception of slavery from the subsequent New World model.[24]

Another form of penal slavery was more draconian: galley slavery. Bondage in the galleys was a harsh, though infrequently employed, reality in Tudor England. In 1548, the city of London punished Edmund Grymeston for "writing an infamous libel full of reproach" by cutting off his ears at the pillory and sentencing him "to serve in the galleys as a slave." In 1586, Francis Walsingham pressed Queen Elizabeth's solicitor general to make plans to condemn the most vile criminals, "being repryved from execution," to the galleys, which would "both terrify ill disposed persons from offending, and make thos that shall hasard them selves to offend in some sorte proffitable to the common wealthe." Of course, galley slavery never amounted to much in Britain. In 1589, Sir John Hawkins issued a memorandum on the sea charges of the *Galley Bonavolia*, noting that the ship would require 150 slaves to fill its 50 banks. Hawkins, however, did not even feel equipped to provide a budget for food expenditures for the slaves, since "we are not yett in the experyence of yt."[25] And, in truth, on the few occasions when an English galley took to the sea, it was typically powered by free oarsmen. Thus, although numerous individuals were sentenced to galley slavery and several royal proclamations were issued by Tudor monarchs setting aside the galleys for particular crimes, the practice remained uncommon.[26]

The lingering presence of villeinage and the practice of penal slavery for criminals, deserters, idlers, or political prisoners in the sixteenth century demonstrate the viability of human bondage as a practical, even pragmatic, institution within England.[27] Although slavery ultimately affected few individuals, government officials were willing to condone it and many early modern English people could see its basic tenets laid out before them from the pulpit, in print, and even on stage. How surprised, for example, would an English audience have been during a production of William Shakespeare's *Merchant of Venice* when Shylock, pressed by the court to forgive Antonio the pound of flesh he owes him for defaulting on a loan, sneers:

What judgement shall I dread, doing no wrong?
You have among you many a purchased slave,
Which, like your asses and your dogs and mules,
You use in abject and in slavish parts,
Because you bought them. Shall I say to you,
'Let them be free, marry them to your heirs?
Why sweat they under burthens? Let their beds
Be made as soft as yours and let their palates

Be season'd with such viands.' You will answer
'The slaves are ours.' So do I answer you:
The pound of flesh, which I demand of him,
Is dearly bought: 'tis mine, and I will have it.[28]

Freedom may have been a defining element of English national identity on the eve of the founding of Jamestown, but that did not mean that the law protected all Englishmen from being forced to work. Indeed, if penal slavery and vagrancy legislation demonstrate anything, they reveal the readiness of Tudor authorities to compel the lower orders to labor—not for labor's sake, but for that of society as a whole. Slavery earned the disdain and scorn of many commentators, particularly when it appeared to result from arbitrary circumstances, but Tudor elites also accepted that slavery was reasonable if individuals brought it upon themselves, if the practice served a social purpose, or if it was directed toward stabilizing and preserving, paradoxically, the idea of freedom in England. As Philip Massinger wrote in the popular seventeenth-century play, *The Bondman*, "Such as have made forfeit of themselves, By vicious courses, and their birthright lost, 'Tis not injustice they are marked for slaves."[29]

The Fear of Slavery

While *ideas of slavery* were clearly shaped by England's religious and intellectual heritage, and domestic social practice, broad-based English cultural conceptions about *what it meant to be enslaved* were powerfully conditioned by the sensational accounts of slavery beyond the nation's borders. In most places throughout the early modern world very few Englishmen were personally threatened by thralldom. This was not the case in the Mediterranean, particularly in North Africa, however, a place that Samuel Purchas comfortably referred to as the "Stinke of Slavery."[30] Few English ships plied their trade in this region before the sixteenth century, but during the final decades of the sixteenth century narratives penned by English merchants and sailors about their experiences—often as slaves—began to circulate more widely. These narratives reveal how early modern English men and women imagined slavery and helped turn the plight of English captives in North Africa into a cause celebre around the turn of the century. Royal proclamations were issued to publicize the plight of Englishmen held in bondage. Public lotteries were organized to gather funds to redeem Christian captives out of the hands of irascible and piratical Moors. Ministers cooperated in this endeavor as they incorporated the image of slavery and the language of published narratives into their weekly sermons. Dramatists even staged productions featuring Islamic characters and English slaves. Taken together, the distribution and circulation of information about enslaved Englishmen added to the intensity with which early modern

Englishmen characterized slavery and celebrated their own inherent freedom.

Englishmen believed that bondage had always plagued the peoples of the Levant, Palestine, and North Africa. As Christians, they accepted that God had allowed slavery to flourish and even those people that the Lord had blessed with greatness in the past were not exempt from lapsing into a state of "extreame bondage" in later eras. With a great appreciation of the vicissitudes of time, William Davies warned his fellow Englishmen that if the Jews, "being a Nation [God] had once selected himselfe from all the Nations of the earth," and the Greeks, who were once the "Monarches of the Earth," could fall into a condition of "extreame thraldome and punishment," there certainly was no guarantee that an unduly humble or unrepentant English nation might not suffer the same fate in the future. This was a key Christian doctrine, a lesson to be found throughout the Bible, where slavery often appeared as a just and divinely ordained fate for portions of humankind.[31]

English merchants and sailors, who began to traverse the Mediterranean sea routes in greater numbers during the Elizabethan era, understood the risks involved in sailing into foreign waters. Few Tudor Englishmen were surprised that many of their countrymen fell into the hands of the feared Algerian pirates, or others, who easily incorporated the newly arrived northern Europeans into the same slave system that accommodated so many southern Europeans.[32] Over the course of subsequent centuries, tens of thousands of Englishmen found themselves enslaved in Mediterranean galleys, where many suffered quick deaths.[33] Others survived, however, and produced exotic tales and fanciful renderings of their dramatic exploits in the form of "slave narratives" for a receptive audience in their native England. These narratives conformed to a fairly reliable pattern, dramatizing for the English public the nature of the capture, the conditions of enslavement, the types of work performed, and the recovery of English freedom. Religion served as a central point of contention throughout, whether between Christians and Muslims or Protestants and Catholics, as enslaved Englishmen struggled to maintain their identity within their forlorn condition.[34]

English slave narratives began with innocent Englishmen exercising their self-professed prerogative to trade in the Mediterranean. At some point the ill-fated seamen would either encounter an overwhelming force of Turkish or Algerian pirates or find themselves incapacitated by some misfortune, such as shipwreck or subterfuge. Subsequently, captives endured practical and symbolic assertions of subjection at the hands of their captors. The "first villany and indignitie that was done unto them, was the shaving off of all the hayre both head and beard." Soon after Thomas Sanders and the crew of the *Jesus* were condemned as "slaves perpetually unto the great Turke" in 1584 they were "forceably and most violently shaven, head and beard." The shorn head of the slaves was common in early modern slave societies and the Mediterranean world was no different.[35] In the case of Mediterranean galleys, the act tended to be partly associated with hygiene, but shaving a newly enslaved individual's head was also highly symbolic. According to Anthony Munday, the act robbed "them of those ornaments which all Christians make much of, because they best become them." Likewise, by taking a man's hair, his captor began the symbolic process of stripping the individual of his manliness and freedom.[36]

Newly enslaved Englishmen were also stripped of their clothing and personal possessions. After the *Tobie* was taken off the coast of Morocco in 1593, the crewmen were stripped naked as part of the search for hidden valuables, but the stripping and "reclothing" of new bondmen was also part of the process of breaking the man and making the slave. Richard Hakluyt retold the popular story of John Fox late in the sixteenth century, detailing that no sooner were the Christian captives sent to the galleys than "their garments were pulled over their eares, and torne from their backes, and they set to the oares." Once Fox and the other men were enslaved their hardships were increased by their miserable apparel, which amounted to "thin and course canvas, their stockings and shooes, heavie bolts and cold Irons." Others simply went naked, "onely a short linnen paire of breeches to cover their privities." William Davies, who spent nearly nine years as a slave in the galleys of the duke of Florence, reported that every man was stripped naked and placed in irons in the galleys and only after they had been shaven were they given "a red coate, and a red cap, telling of us that the Duke had made us all slaves."[37]

Naked and poorly clothed slaves were regularly taken to public markets for sale, "whereat . . . certaine Moores and Officers attended either to beate you forward, or thrust you into the sides with Goades [because] this was the manner of the selling of Slaves." By all accounts, the sale of slaves in the marketplace was a degrading and dehumanizing experience. The men were taken "like dogs" to the market, and "whereas men sell Hacknies in England, we were tossed up and down to see who would give most for us." Emmanuel D'Aranda, whose experiences as a slave were translated into English in 1666, reported that after he was captured in the Atlantic in 1640 he was taken to an Algerian market where prospective buyers questioned him and examined his hands to see if they were "hard and brawny by working, and they caus'd me to open my mouth, to see whether my teeth were able to overcome Bisket in the Galleys." The physical examination of captives and their sale at market consistently reminded Englishmen of the way they sold draft animals in their homeland.[38]

In spite of their condition, Christian slaves might bear few physical burdens if they found himself in a benevolent household. A slave might also continue to be locked up in a private *baño*, or be consigned to accommodations that amounted to no more than "the bare boords, with a very simple cape to cover us" or, possibly, merely "cold earth." Many slaves were simply sent to the galleys, "chained three and three to an oare," where food and water were often in such short supply that they would "pawne their soules" for a drop of water. Galley slaves were subjected to harsh treatment. According to one former slave, while they rowed the boatswain and his mate hovered above "eche of them a bulls pissell dried in their hands, and when their divelish choller rose, they would strike the Christians for no cause." Indeed, the standard slave narrative lamented the misery of the galley slave who was "at the pleasure of the prowd and dogged Turke for the least fault, nay for none at all, but onely to feed his humor, to receive a hundred bastinadoes on the rim of the bellie with a bulls dried peezle, at one time, and within a day after two hundred stripes on the backe."[39]

Whatever physical hardships captive slaves may have endured, the most pointed moment in the majority of the narratives occurred when the enslaved Englishman was compelled to "turn Turk." For many English, the apostasy of Christians who converted to the Muslim faith was an issue of apocalyptic proportions, prompting King James I to express concern that "most of the youthfuller sort are of late forced and compelled by intolerable and insufferable punishments and torments, to deny their Saviour, and turne to the Mahumetan Religion." Charles Fitz-Geffrey was clearly disgusted in 1636 when he told his audience that conversion rites included "the abomnable *circumcision* in their flesh." Some ministers had little sympathy for Englishmen who went through the conversion process no matter how they were punished or tortured. Edward Kellet told an Englishman who returned to England and desired to reconvert to Christianity that his sin "weigheth more, than the sinne of *Caine* . . . or of the Jewes, which murthered Christ." Henry Byam lamented the "intolerable servitude" of Christian captives, but suggested that anyone who sailed into the Mediterranean should have been aware of the danger from "That *African* monster, to which so many poore soules have been made a prey; The Turke, (which God forbid) may bring you under his Lee."[40]

English slave narratives imparted an image of slavery that was characterized by brutality, dehumanization, unbearable labor, the loss of control over one's own life, and potential death. Slave narratives therefore offered the most detailed, threatening, and immediate touchstone for the mass of English society when they imagined the implications of actual enslavement. Slavery threatened what it meant to be English, and its menace prompted the Tudor government to secure the freedom of Englishmen. One avenue to this end was diplomatic, including the conclusion of treaties of amity with several of the ruling powers of North Africa. Much to the dismay of other Christian nations who were in perpetual conflict with their southern foes, England even reached a trade agreement with the Ottoman Turks in 1580. This thirty-five-point agreement with the "great Turk" determined that any English slave in Turkish dominions would be immediately released. Subsequently, England concluded a similar treaty with Morocco in an effort to ensure that Mediterranean trade would remain safe for English merchants and sailors. Furthermore, as a measure of good faith, the English government even went to some lengths to return the "100 Turkes brought by Sir Francis Drake out of the West Indyes (where they served as slaves in the Spanish Galleyes)" to their homeland. This benevolent gesture, it was hoped, might also lead to "the release of some of the captives of the English nation there."[41]

The significance and impact of these narratives was enhanced in dramatic ways through other methods of distribution to a wider audience. Where treaties and other high-level international affairs failed to settle the issue of Englishmen held in bondage, the English public stepped in with funds to pay the ransoms demanded by the Barbary states. As early as 1567 Elizabeth's government received requests for licenses to collect ransom funds to redeem Englishmen out of Algiers. In the last two decades of the sixteenth century, frequent collections were recorded at the parish level to redeem Englishmen and others who had been "kept bond and thrall in most cruell slaverie and Bondage" in the Mediterranean.[42]

The use of public charities to redeem enslaved Englishmen reveals how thoroughly the information contained in slave narratives disseminated throughout society. Perhaps the most systematic expression of the relationship among public charity, redemption, and ideas of slavery occurred at the annual Easter week sermons preached at the Hospital of St. Mary or St. Mary Spital. Once one of the five main hospitals in London, by the late sixteenth century St. Mary Spital had ceased to care for the sick, but continued to be famous for the elaborate and well-attended sermons that took place on special occasions in the churchyard. As John Stow recounted in his *Survey of London*, "the Maior, with his brethren the Aldermen were accustomed to bee present . . . in their Scarlets at the Spittle in the Holidayes." There the local dignitaries heard "some especiall learned man . . . preach on the forenoones at the sayde Spittle, to perswade the Article of Christs resurrection." The diarist Samuel Pepys attended in 1662, noting what a "fine sight of charity it is," before he and his wife went to the theater to see *The Bondman*, which "we had seen . . . so often, yet I never liked it better than today."[43]

Though it dates from a slightly later era, Pepys's *Diary* is a reminder that information about the enslavement of Englishmen could filter through society informally. In February 1661, Pepys recounted that he "met with sea-commanders: and among others, Captain Cuttle, and Curtis and Mootham; and I went to the Fleece tavern to drink and there we spent till 4 a-clock telling stories of Algier and the manner of the life of slaves there." This proved to be a particularly compelling conversation because Mootham and Mr. Dawes, who was also in attendance, "have both been slaves there." Mootham and Dawes regaled their friends with stories about how "they eat nothing but bread and water" and how "they are beat upon the soles of their feet and bellies at the Liberty of their *Padron*. How they are all at night called into their master's Bagnard (*baño*)." Similar conversations surely occurred in other taverns; former English slaves were not hard to come by in seventeenth-century England.[44]

This growing problem prompted the Elizabethan Privy Council to divert charitable funds to the cause of redeeming Englishmen out of slavery. In a typical entry, the council ordered the Bishop of London "to geve order unto the preachers at the Spittal in their Sermons these Easter Holy Daies . . . to move the people" to redeem "their countrymen from thraldom and miserie." The Privy Council could be even more specific, as when it specified that "Thomas Lowe, gentleman . . . deserved [to be reimbursed] for his great paynes taken in redeeming . . . poore captives out of Barbary." The Council therefore requested the Lord Mayor and Aldermen of London "to take some course that he may receive some good receite by the collections which are accostomed to be made at the spittle sermons is kynde [so] that his good endeavors . . . may not turne to his ruyne and others be discouraged by his example to undertake the lyke."[45]

In subsequent decades the English government continued to be concerned about the thousands of Englishmen who continued to fall into slavery in the Mediterranean. On several occasions the Stuarts issued proclamations to raise funds for redemptions. Like the licenses issued during the Tudor era, Stuart royal proclamations were typically issued for the benefit of one or two specific individuals. Occasionally, however, the declarations were more sweeping, as in 1624 when James I took notice of the case of "fifteen hundred of our loving Subjects, English men, remaining in miserable servitude and subjection in *Argier, Tunis, Sally,* [and] *Tituane.*" According to the proclamation, Turkish pirates had surprised 150 English ships at sea and had taken the men into "miserable slavery" where they were "sold from party to party, and kept in chaines of Iron, their food, bread and water to their extreme grief." Many Englishmen were also "compelled by intollerable and insufferable punishments . . . to deny their Saviour, and turne to the Mahumetan Religion, and to deny their King and Country." Proclamations like this one also ordered ministers "to stirre up the charity of their Parishioners," to raise the necessary funds to rescue their countrymen who were compelled to labor "in a bestiall manner like horses, for to get some foode to preserve their wretched lives, with infinite miseries." To that end, Charles Fitz-Geffrey reminded his Plymouth audience in 1636 that although their brethren were suffering from back-breaking labor and senseless beatings, the "want of liberty is sufficient to make up misery." Fitz-Geffrey castigated Turks who sunk so low as to "make marchandize of *men*," which resulted in Englishmen being "sold in markets like beasts, by creatures more brutish than beasts, stigmatized, branded when they are bought by circumcised *monsters, miscreant Mahumetans.*"[46]

Sermons, royal proclamations, and public collections appeared in late Tudor and early Stuart England as both cause and consequence of an increasingly well-informed public's knowledge of the enslavement of fellow Englishmen. These sources also reveal a certain level of collective fear. Englishmen did not have to be literate or even particularly worldly in order to encounter the prevalence of slavery in the world around them. Redeemed slaves lived in England. Some Englishmen traveled to Persia or Egypt and returned to tell their tales. The travails of Englishmen were vocalized in parish churches or in other public places when it came time to collect funds to redeem countrymen. Actors played slaves in obscure stage productions set in exotic locales—more than fifty history plays featuring the Mediterranean world appeared on London stages in the half-century after 1579. Ballads were sung about unfortunate Englishmen who were taken and enslaved in the Mediterranean. None of this would have been possible without the information and themes provided by English slave narratives. Indeed, so important were these developments that we should not be surprised that many early seventeenth-century Englishmen possessed some firm ideas, based on the experience of their own countryman, about the nature of human bondage in the early modern Mediterranean and Atlantic worlds.[47]

Settling Slavery in Early America

As the English sailed to Jamestown, they carried slavery with them as part of their political heritage, as a legal tool for controlling unruly people, and as a powerful image against which they could imagine themselves as distinctly free in an otherwise unfree Atlantic world. Slavery was not, at this time, understood primarily as a labor institution or as grounded in racial ideologies. During the previous century and a half, the Portuguese and Spanish had created vast plantation economies based on the labor of enslaved Africans, but early English settlers were not initially focused on reproducing this model of colonialism. Many people in early modern England and the broader Anglo-Atlantic world had dealt with Africans in one manner or another since the mid-sixteenth century.[48] Yet, no long-lived institutions, wide-reaching popular associations, or well-articulated historical and religious ideas informed the enslavement of African peoples in the Atlantic world; the enslavement of African peoples in the Atlantic was really only a vague notion among the English.[49] Certainly, English colonists accepted the enslavement of Africans without pause, since enslaved Africans were integrated in Anglo-American settlements with little dissent from the 1610s. But if the English were inclined to view slavery as normative for Africans in the Atlantic world and even if they viewed the practice as both legitimate and useful, it was not their initial intention to create plantation societies populated by displaced Africans.[50]

Indians, however, were another matter. With several notable exceptions, colonial promoters and English leaders had avoided enslaving Indians during the initial years of overseas settlement. To be sure, tens of thousands of Indians, like hundreds of thousands of Africans, were vilified in highly charged language and subjected to grueling plantation labor regimes during the colonial era. Nonetheless, Indians remained more useful as trading partners and military allies than as potential slaves. And some settlers, wishing to hold themselves above the Spanish, sought to create an inclusive—though clearly English—colonial community that would eventually assimilate Indians within its ranks.[51] These considerations, ironically, promoted the notion that Indians *could* be enslaved but, unlike Africans, only for reasons that might legitimately be applied to the English themselves. In other words, it was the presumed *similarity* between English and Indian peoples, originally espoused to encourage overseas settlement and deflect concerns about what might happen to English bodies in the New World, that allowed for the development of the idea that natives might be justifiably enslaved. It was even imagined in some circles that the enslavement of Indians might be not only punitive, but also redemptive.[52]

A less rosy view of Indian slavery developed as local Indians demonstrated an unwillingness to cooperate with English plans to appropriate both their land and their labor. English impressions of Indians were transformed after March 1622, when nearly 350 Englishmen lost their lives. The surprise attack "of that perfidious and inhumane people" condemned Indians in the minds of many people. Edward Waterhouse epitomized the change when he characterized natives as those "naked, tanned, deformed Savages." He hoped, in particular, that the English would soon begin to exact revenge by "force, by surprize, by famine in burning their Corne, by destroying their Boats, Canoes, and Houses," and, as the Spanish had done before them, "by pursuing and chasing them with our horses, and blood-Hounds to draw after them, and Mastives to seaze them." This proposal agreed with the sentiments of the Virginia Council, which ordered the colonists "to roote out from being any longer a people, so cursed a nation, ungratefull to all benefitts, and uncapable of all goodnesse." As a reward for service, colonists could expect to acquire "men for slaves" from among the defeated natives.[53]

The language employed by the English after 1622 reveals a more concerted effort to deal with the Indians in a manner resembling the Spanish conquest. Indeed, two conflicting justifications for Indian removal and slavery were articulated during these years. First, since many writers had argued that Indians in mainland North America were essentially similar to the English (or at least their forebears), justification for Indian slavery was premised on European conceptions of just war and the enslavement of prisoners of war. Indians, according to Waterhouse, "may now most justly be compelled to servitude and drudgery" in Virginia, including "digging in the mynes" or being "sent for the service of the Sommer Islands." John Martin wrote that the Indians were "fitt to rowe in Gallies & friggetts and many other pregnant uses too tedious to sett downe."[54]

Second, some observers began to emphasize the legality of enslaving Indians because they were fundamentally *dissimilar*, and therefore could be treated with the same kind of impunity increasingly applied to African peoples in the Atlantic world. Samuel Purchas printed a text in 1625 that was particularly direct: "that bloudy Massacre . . . requires that servile natures be serviley used; that future dangers be prevented by the extirpation of the most dangerous, and commodities also raised out of the servileness and serviceablenesse of the rest." The Powhatan Uprising apparently revealed, in the words of John Morton, that "natives are apter for worke then yet o[ur] English are." Perhaps even more dramatically, the Virginia Company of London took a giant step away from its avowed intention of "converting . . . the Infidells," declaring that "itt was an attempt impossible they being descended of ye cursed race of Cham." This was no idle assessment. Just seven years later the author of *The Planters Plea* felt compelled to answer an objection to settlement and proselytization based on the idea that "some conceive the Inhabitants of *New-England* to be *Chams* posterity, and consequently shut out from grace by *Noahs* curse." This was an exceptional notion, even among the generally ethnocentric English, but it revealed the growing tendency to find other explanations for the basic nature of Indians in the wake of their violent resistance to English efforts to introduce their own notions of civility in North America. And by connecting Indians to the so-called "Curse of Ham," at least a few Englishmen revealed a willingness to racialize Indian identity.[55]

The developing perception of racial difference, then, helps explain why Indians could not so easily be integrated into an older system of slavery as the seventeenth century wore on. Indeed, just as an emerging racial consciousness was integral to the development of plantation slavery in colonial America, it precipitated the destabilization of the older idea and models of slavery Englishmen initially possessed when they settled Jamestown. The association between blackness, or African peoples, and abject slavery became particularly pronounced as the English colonies gradually developed into large-scale agricultural plantations fueled by the labor of bondmen. When the practice became widespread, the association between African peoples and human bondage overshadowed all other forms of slavery that had been present from the settlement era.

Perhaps the best example of the tensions created by the increasingly crucial link between race and slavery appeared during the late 1650s when Parliament received two petitions on behalf of more than seventy Englishmen claiming that they were "freeborn people of this nation now in slavery" in Barbados. In response, Parliament conducted a brief debate, although some people protested that the petitions had been introduced through irregular channels. Those who were directly implicated by name or as property holders in Barbados were particularly defensive. Martin Noel of Staffordshire noted that he traded into those parts and to the best of his knowledge the work was indeed hard, "but none are sent without their consent" and those who went "were civilly used, and had horses to ride on." Besides, Noel added, they were commonly contracted for five years and did not work as hard as the petition claimed since "the work is mostly carried on by the Negroes." Other parliamentarians, however, were not so certain that the grievances were false. Hugh Boscawen of Cornwall, in particular, made a compelling argument when he warned that if Englishmen lost the right to a trial or to petition Parliament "our lives will be as cheap as those negroes. They look upon them as their goods, horses, &c., and rack them only to make their time out of them, and cherish them to perform their work." For that reason alone, Boscawen "would have [Parliament] consider the trade of buying and selling men."[56] Parliament, however, was apparently content to leave the matter alone.

It was no simple matter to determine who was a slave, who could be enslaved, and what that slavery meant in the early modern Anglo-Atlantic world. Although the notion that Africans were, by nature, slaves was clearly ascendant, Old World notions of human bondage were meaningful to early Americans (even if they meant something different to separate groups of colonists). We might even suppose that these older notions of slavery could have survived their Atlantic crossing were it not for the fact that they were rooted in conflicting ideologies that had been managed successfully in a domestic English context. Enslaving Englishmen was one thing when there were few African or Indian slaves (as in England); it was quite another when the meaning of slavery was blurred by the simultaneous existence of multiple social practices and separate racial groups. In the long run, of course, the notion that English men and women were (or should be) distinguished by their access to freedom and protection from bondage would be even more pronounced. During the late Tudor and early Stuart years, however, slavery was more complex and its existence played an important role in the articulation of the early Anglo-Atlantic world.

Chapter 12
"We All Smoke Here"
Behn's The Widdow Ranter *and the Invention of American Identity*

PETER C. HERMAN

When does a colony become a country? When does an inherited culture develop into a new one? In particular, when did the inhabitants of Jamestown stop considering themselves as English, but as natives of Virginia? And when did the English realize that their colony had metamorphosed into something unprecedented and new? In her neglected last play, *The Widdow Ranter, or, The History of Bacon in Virginia* (written ca. 1688, performed in 1689, published in 1690),[1] Aphra Behn addresses precisely these questions. In this chapter I will examine *The Widdow Ranter*'s relationship to the Atlantic World along with Behn's contribution to the development of a distinct identity for Virginia.

Richard S. Dunn proposed more than forty years ago that "the historical writings on English America during the seventeenth century are our best guide to the emerging awareness by Englishmen at home that they held a large empire, and contrariwise, to the colonials' increasingly self-conscious identification with their new land."[2] While subsequent critics have substantiated and qualified both aspects of Dunn's findings, they continue to show how European writers used the newfound lands as a screen for projecting "their homeland and its imperial ambitions,"[3] and they continue to examine how colonial texts nurtured, as Dunn puts it, a sense of difference between themselves and England. Yet the development of this sense of cultural difference in *English* writing has been the object of much less analysis (if any at all), and that is where Behn's *The Widdow Ranter* may intervene.[4] Behn's play complicates the standard model by producing on the English stage, not the English awareness of empire or English self-referentiality,[5] but a view of Virginia as a separate cultural space, different from and possibly superior to England. Rather than using the New World as a screen to project Old World ideologies and concerns, Behn transforms Virginia's culture into something rich and strange for her English audience.[6]

To be sure, *The Widdow Ranter* does not always represent what actually went on in the colony. While Behn accurately portrays much of Virginia culture, other aspects, such as the Widow Ranter's complaint about the lack of marriageable men in the colony, derive more from fiction than fact.[7] Yet in terms of the development of a distinct identity, Behn is eerily accurate in portraying how American national consciousness may have been more an *English* than a homegrown concept. As John M. Murrin has argued, "British North America became more European, more English in the eighteenth century [and in the years just before]. The growth of cities, the spread of printing and newspapers, the rise of the professions, and the emulation of British political culture all encouraged this trend."[8] But as the colonists embraced and copied English political culture, in the eighteenth century "British writers almost took it for granted that one day the American colonies would demand and get their independence. . . . In a word, America was Britain's idea. Maybe it was even Britain's dream."[9] Behn's drama thus participates in the English development of "America" as a separate political entity.[10] Indeed, Behn may have begun the process, as the play's treatment of Virginia and its relationship to England is, so far as I can tell, unprecedented.

Yet Behn is not entirely sure how to interpret what she considers a new culture's birth, and she compounds the play's difficulties by coupling her depiction of a culturally different Virginia with a rewriting of Bacon's Rebellion that turns Nathaniel Bacon, previously associated with parliamentary leader and regicide Oliver Cromwell, into a romantic, chivalric hero. The transformation is remarkable because previously Behn was a loyal royalist who virulently detested the regicides, but by the time Behn writes her play, the Stuart dynasty had declined into political ineptitude. Behn's ambivalence over her construction of Virginia, which includes a blunt recognition of the injustice with which the native Americans were treated, both stems from and reflects her ambivalence over England's domestic political situation in 1688.

Idealized Virginia

As one might expect, books published in England from the earlier seventeenth century onward concerning Virginia always assume that the colony's inhabitants are English subjects who just happen to live across the Atlantic Ocean. Robert Johnson, for example, in *The New Life of Virginea* (1612) encourages "the Colonie" to "arme your selves therefore against all impediments, to effect those honorable ends that were first intended to be put upon *our* King, upon *our* nation, and Christian religion, by that plantation" (my emphasis), James VI/I being king of both England and Virginia.[11] The same sentiments show up in texts originating in the colonies. An anonymous pamphlet, *A New Description of Virginia* (1649), which the title page declares was "sent from Virginia at the request of a Gentleman . . . who desired to know the true State of Virginia," notes "That some English about a thousand are seated upon the Acamake-shore by Cape Charles," and describes the conflict between the colonists and the natives as one between Indians and the English: "Some of them [Indians] confessed, that their great King was by some *English* Informed, that all was under the Sword in *England*."[12]

While the authors of *The Present State of Virginia, and the College* (written in 1697 but published in 1727), Henry Hartwell, James Blair, and Edward Chilton—three royal officials in Virginia—allow for the existence of "Virginians," they do not mean that such people belong to a different political, social, or economic entity other than England. Hence they urge the English king to establish "some common Standard of Money . . . over the *English* Plantations of *America*," note the "Governor represents the King, in granting lands," and they begin by designating Virginia "the first and eldest of all the English plantations in *America*.[13] The literature concerning Virginia unanimously thought of the colony as "*English* ground in *America*," as one visitor wrote in 1649.[14] When occasional differences between Virginian and English practices do arise, as in Hartwell and his coauthors' recognition of how Virginia's legal system departs from England's, they are faults to be remedied as quickly as possible.[15]

Historians and literary critics generally agree that the first person to demonstrate a "self-conscious identification with their new land"[16] is Robert Beverley, who, at the start of his *History and Present State of Virginia* (1705), declares "I am an *Indian*, and don't pretend to be exact in my Language." By "Indian," Beverley means that he is *not* English, that he is as much a native Virginian as the aboriginal tribes he will describe in the third part of his *History*. While Beverley grants that Virginia is run by "the *English* form of Government," he makes a distinction made by neither Jones, Hartwell et al., nor the anonymous Virginia gentleman who authored *A Perfect Description*: "I have every-where made it my chief Business, to avoid *partiality*; and therefore have fairly expos'd the Inconveniencies, as well as proclam'd the Excellencies *of my Country* (emphasis in the original)."[17] Whereas everyone before Beverley considered his "Country" England, and Virginia a plantation or colony of England, Beverley recognizes the birth of a new country, a new place of origin, one dependent upon England but nonetheless separate and distinct from the mother country.[18] But while there are some indications that the process of national individuation exemplified by Beverley seems to have started earlier in New England, Beverley dates from the very early *eighteenth* century.[19]

However, in the *The Widdow Ranter*, Aphra Behn does not construct Virginia as an outpost of England, as so many did before and after. Instead, Behn puts forward the novel concept that Virginia is both different from and culturally superior to England. Behn indicates that Virginia constitutes a very different place from Europe at the start of the play, when Hazard tells his acquaintance from the Old World, Friendly, the reasons for his coming to Virginia. When Hazard says that he had "lost all" and therefore his elder brother "sent me hither with a small Cargo to seek my fortune" (1.1.42, 44), Friendly responds: "And begin the world withall" (1.1.46). At first, it would seem that Friendly is rather mundanely referring to the colony as a place where wastrels can restore their fortunes, but it quickly becomes clear that much more is at stake, that Virginia represents an entirely new *world*, with new rules, new possibilities, and even a new language. (When the Boy, who is newly arrived also, tries to deliver a message to Ranter, she speaks in such a way that he exclaims: "I don't understand this Country-Language forsooth, yet" [1.3.12]).

The comparison between England and Virginia becomes even more stark when Friendly informs Hazard that Madame Surelove would be a ripe target for his amorous/financial attentions since her husband "is Old and Sick, and now gone into *England* for the Recovery of his health, where he'l e'en give up the Ghost" (1.1.60). While Virginia is the place for fresh beginnings, England is where the old go to die. Consequently, when Surelove teases her would-be suitor, Hazard, by accusing him of writing "Some letter to dispatch to *English* Ladies you have left behind," to which Hazard responds, "I own I much admire the *English* Beauties, but never yet have put their Fetters on" (2.2.6–9), the implications go beyond simple geographical identification. Hazard (for his own reasons, of course) seems to prefer the "Ladies" of the new, vital land over the "Beauties" of England, who may have the charms, but nonetheless belong to a culture on the descent.

Significantly, Behn focuses on both class mobility and self-fashioning. After Friendly tells Hazard that one "Madam Flirt" will direct him to Surelove's house, Hazard notes "You are full of your Madams here," to which Friendly replies: "Oh! 'tis the greatest affront imaginable, to call a woman Mistriss, tho' but a retale Brandy-munger" (1.1.143–44). As Janet Todd notes in her gloss on these lines, the distinction between "Mistriss" and "Madame" concerned class difference, since "'Madame' was used as a matter of courtesy to a woman of some social standing, whether married or not. 'Mistris' implied a lower social status."[20] Since the bulk of Virginia's population at this time came from the lower orders of society, the fact that all the women desire to be Madames and are offended if called "Mistriss" suggests the degree of social mobility in this new land.

Of course, the context of this conversation implies that Behn wants to make fun of these pretensions, and she intensifies her mockery when three members of the ruling council, the appropriately named Dullman, Timerous, and Boozer, enter and proceed to discuss each other's origins. These characters demonstrate the same pride in Virginia that Beverley will show. Concerning the liquor they drank last night to get "damnable drunk," Dullman declares his aversion to "your *English French* wine, I wonder how the Gentlemen do to drink it" (1.1.161–62). The conflation of "English French" suggests that what is really at stake here is Europe versus Virginia, the Old World versus the New, and Timerous takes up exactly this theme in his answer to Dullman's lines: "Ay so do I, 'tis for want of a little *Virginia* Breeding: how much more like a Gentleman 'tis, to drink as we do, brave Edifying Punch and Brandy" (1.1.162–63). For these characters, punch and brandy not only afford a better drink than "English French wine," but the superiority of Virginia liquor matches the superiority of the Virginians in matters of class: the English gentlemen, according to Dullman, are not *really* gentlemen, for they lack "a little Virginia Breeding."

Behn returns to this theme in 2.2, when Timerous and Dullman expand on the statement in 1.1 that the old return to England to die by explicitly declaring that England itself is dying and decrepit, and that England should look to Virginia for political guidance (due to the passage's importance, I quote it in full):

TIMEROUS: But if these fears were laid and *Bacon* were hang'd, I look upon *Virginia* to be the happiest part of the world, gads Zoors,—why there's *England*—'tis nothing to't—I was in *England* about 6 years ago, & was shew'd the Court of Aldermen, some were nodding, some waying nothing, and others very little to purpose, but could it be otherwise, for they had neither Bowle of Punch, Bottles of wine or Tobacco before 'em to put Life & Soule into 'em as we have here: then for the young Gentlemen—Their farthest Travels is to *France* or *Italy*, they never come hither.
DULLMAN: The more's the Pitty by my troth,
TIMEROUS: Where they learn to Sear Mor-blew, Mor-Dee:
FRIENDLY: And tell you how much bigger the *Louvre* is than *White-Hall*; buy a sute A-la-mode, get a swinging Clap of some *French* Marquis, spend all their money and return just as they went.
DULLMAN: For the old fellows, their bus'ness is Usury, Extortion, and undermining young Heirs.
TIMEROUS: Then for young Merchants, their Exchange is the Tavern, their Warehouse the Play-house, and their Bills of Exchange Billet Doux, where to sup with their wenches at the other end of the Town,—now Judge you what a Condition poor *England* is in: for my part I look upon't as a lost Nation gads zoors.
DULLMAN: I have consider'd it, and have found a way to save all yet:
TIMEROUS: As how I pray[?]
DULLMAN: As thus, we have men here of great Experience and Ability—now I would have as many sent into *England* as would supply all places, and Offices, both Civill and Military, d'e see, their young Gentry should all Travell hither for breeding, and to learn the misteries of State. (2.2.71–96)

In these lines, Behn is not simply repeating conventional satires on English travelers, justice, and contemporary politics. Rather, Behn pairs the condemnation of England as provincial and corrupt with her presentation of Virginia as the antidote to England's problems. Again, very much unlike other writers on Virginia, Behn distinguishes between English and Virginian culture, and her characters posit Virginia as culturally and morally superior to England: so much so that in place of England sending its refuse to the colonies Dullman proposes that England should send its "young Gentry . . . hither for breeding and to learn the misteries of State." Finally, toward the end of the play, two other comic characters, Whiff and Whimsey, invert the relationship between Virginia and the mother country by proposing that Whimsey, for his cowardice, should be transported back to England (4.2.101–2).

One imagines that Behn hoped to induce gales of laughter from the spectacle of colonials having the unmitigated gall to pass judgment on the "lost nation" of "poor England," proposing that England send its youth to Virginia for political education ("the misteries of state") and—perhaps most ridiculous of all!—Virginia sending its criminals to England![21] Certainly, 2.2. would have served to further illustrate the foolishness of Timerous and Dullman and to prove the backwardness of Virginia's inhabitants, an interpretation that receives considerable backing from 3.1, in which Behn undercuts Timerous's criticism of the English court of Aldermen with her portrayal of the absurdly incompetent workings of Virginia's court.[22] Yet Dullman's proposal that Virginia should replace the continent as a source for political education cannot be simply dismissed, for Behn does not altogether disapprove the notion that Virginia is not only culturally different, but even superior to the Old World.

This passage, for example, recognizes the existence of Virginian cultural independence even as it seems to mock it. While Timerous may be a coward and a fool, when he says, "there's *England*—'tis nothing to't—I was in *England* about 6 years ago," he clearly conceives of England as a foreign country, not his homeland. In other words, Timerous's comparison of England and Virginia may be less important than his understanding of England as fundamentally *different.* There is no sense in this passage of remorse at how his mother country has declined in his absence, and that is because Timerous identifies Jamestown, not London, as his home. The contributions to this scene of Friendly, who is neither a coward nor a fool, also suggest that Behn wants the audience to take these sentiments as more than just evidence of Dullman's and Timerous's idiocy.

Ranter's reply to Hazard's refusal of her offer of tobacco supplies an especially resonant example of Behn's conception of Virginian identity: "Oh fy upon't you must learn then, we all smoke here, 'tis a part of good breeding" (1.2.75–76). Ranter's response seems to place her in line with other bawdy, brassy women who appropriate male privileges in early modern literature, in particular, e.g., Ursula, the Pig Woman of Ben Jonson's *Bartholomew Fair.*[23] To be sure, there is some evidence that women in this period were enjoined against smoking. For example, Henry Neville's satire, *Newes from the New Exchange, Or the Commonwealth of Ladies* (1650) begins by stating "There was a time, when men *wore the breeches,* and debar'd women of their *Liberty*. . . . [Women then could not] be acquainted with the *mode* of Drinke, *Dice*, and *Tobacco*."[24]

Yet the question of gender in this particular instance may be less vexed than one might think. While many writers condemned the plant, only a small minority included smoking by women among the abuses of tobacco.[25] Smoking, however, seems to have been associated more with the upper crust of society. For instance, *The Melancholy Cavalier* (1654), by one J. C., begins: "View here the Picture of a Cavalier, / Tobacco being all his Table-cheer," and the title page shows us a smoking cavalier with a broken sword on the table, suggesting a connection between his fondness for tobacco and losing the Civil War (note the crown by his foot; Figure 12.1). Thomas Brewer's equally satiric *A Knot of Fools* (1658) includes on its title page an illustration of, among others, a smoking cavalier.[26] When, therefore, Ranter states that "we all smoke here," she is not so much addressing the problem of gender as matters of class and cultural identity.

To take the latter first, when Ranter asserts that "we all smoke," she underscores the ubiquity of this local custom. Furthermore, this phrase signals the difference Behn perceives in class structure between Virginia and England. It is not accidental that she characterizes smoking as "a part of good breeding," a phrase which echoes what Timerous earlier called "*Virginia* breeding" (1.1.163). Ranter's characterization of tobacco as common and a sign of "good breeding" therefore recalls Friendly's earlier sense of Virginia as a place marked by a leveling of class distinctions ("Oh! 'tis the greatest affront imaginable, to call a woman Mistriss" [1.1.145]).

The contradictory relationship between English associations of smoking with the higher reaches of society and Ranter's (or Behn's) sense that smoking no longer constitutes an exclusionary practice, because everyone in Virginia smokes and thus can claim membership in the upper classes (there are no mistresses here, only madames), suggests that Behn intends to illustrate Virginia's looser social structure, which allows the low to rise, if not to great heights, then certainly to the position of a landowner and holder of political office, something the earlier promotional literature of the period repeatedly emphasized. In 1650, for example, one "E.W." concluded his advertisement for Virginia with an extraordinary prophetic image of successful immigrants:[27]

> Sated with the beauty of their Cornefield, they shall retire into their Groves checkered with Vines, Olives, Mirtles, from thence dilate themselves in their Walkes covered in a manner, paved with Orenges and Lemmons, whence surfeited with variety, they incline to repose in their Gardens upon nothing lesse perfumed than Roses and Gilly-flowers.

To be sure, the reality had become increasingly different as the century progressed. Yet something approximating this fantasy had previously come true often enough in the early seventeenth century to fuel the considerable

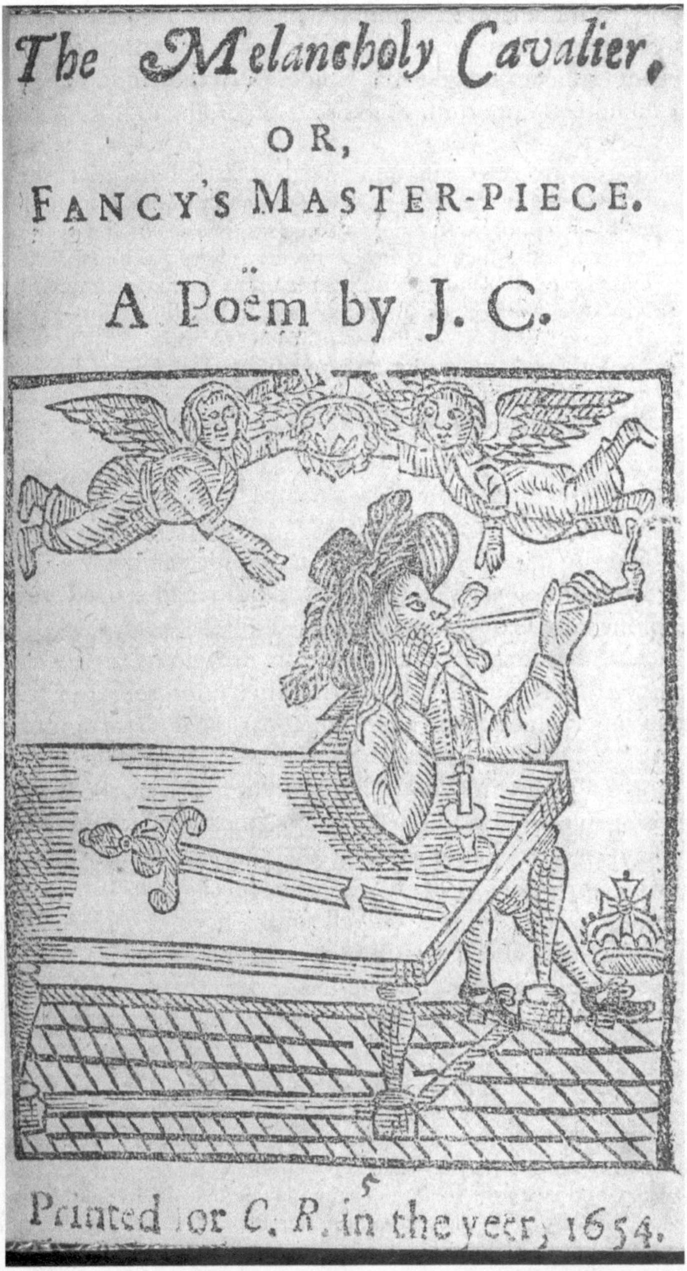

Figure 12.1. *The Melancholy Cavalier, or, Fancy's Master-piece. A Poem by J. C.* (1654). Courtesy of the New York Public Library. The smoking cavalier is posed with a broken sword on the table and a crown by his foot—suggesting a connection between his fondness for tobacco and the king's defeat during the English Civil War.

emigration from England to Virginia. While earlier historians emphasized the lack of success among indentured servants emigrating to the colonies, more recent estimates suggest that emigrants to the colonies before 1660 enjoyed "abundant opportunity" to rise.[28] According to Russell R. Menard:

> Former servants participated in the government of Maryland as jurors, minor office holders, justices of the peace, sheriffs, burgesses, and officers in the militia. Many also attended the Assembly as freemen at those sessions at which they were permitted. The frequency with which responsible positions were given to ex-servants testifies to the impressive status mobility they achieved in the mid-seventeenth century. Seventy five or seventy-six of the survivors—just under 50 percent—sat on a jury, attended an Assembly session, or filled an office in Maryland. . . . [The same mobility obtained in Virginia, for four servants who left Maryland for this colony] became justices of the peace in Virginia, while two others . . . served as militia officer and clerk of a county court respectively.[29]

Smith also cites seven men who were servants in 1624 and yet "were sitting in the assembly of 1629 as burgesses."[30] Even criminals, he reluctantly admits, could rise to positions of wealth and respectability.[31]

By the later seventeenth century, this fluidity had started to ossify on account of increased emigration, depressed tobacco prices, and longer life expectancies.[32] Furthermore, as the century drew to its close, Chesapeake society moved more and more toward patterning itself after traditional English society (helped along in no small part by the reaction to Bacon's Rebellion).[33] Yet it seems that reality had not yet affected the popular conception (or at least, Behn's conception) of Virginia as marked by the possibility of rising in the world. All of the council members, for example, either fled England or were transported for their various petty crimes, and yet they now occupy positions of power and respectability. In the scene just before Ranter's assertion that "we all smoke here" (1.1.168–207), Flirt, Dullman, Timerous, and Boozer reveal each other's origins, and while all do their best to bury their not so illustrious past, they all in fact have risen considerably in the world since their arrival on Virginia's shores:

> FLIRT: Your Honours are pleas'd—but me-thinks Doctor *Dunce* is a very Edifying Person, and a Gentleman, and I pretend to know a Gentleman,—For I my self am a Gentlewoman; my Father was a Barronet, but undone in the late Rebellion—and I am fain to keep an Ordinary now Heaven help me.
> TIMEROUS: Good lack, why see how Virtue may be bely'd—we heard your Father was a Taylor, but trusting for old *Olivers* Funerall, Broke [i.e. went broke, bankrupt], and so came hither to hide his head,—but my Service to you; what, you are never the worse?
> FLIRT: Your Honour knows this is a Scandalous place, for they say your Honour was but a broken Excise man, who spent the Kings money to buy your Wife fine Petticoats, and at last not worth a Groat, you came over a poor Servant, though now a Justice of Peace, and of the Honourable Council. (1.1.185–98)

When, therefore, Ranter says "we all smoke here," her statement encapsulates the possibility in Virginia of everyone, regardless of origin, achieving some status in the world.

To be sure, Behn always qualifies her recognition of Virginian cultural difference with mockery. In the exchange between Flirt and Timerous over their origins, for example, Behn puts assertions of Virginian nationalism in the mouths of highly suspect characters. Yet at the same time, those who speak for England's superiority are equally compromised. At the start of the play, Friendly informs his newly arrived friend, Hazard, that

This country wants nothing but to be People'd with a well-born Race to make it one of the best Collonies in the World, but for want of a Governour we are Ruled by a Councill, some of which have been perhaps transported Criminals, who having Acquired great Estates are now become your Honour, and Right Worshipfull, and Possess all Places of Authority; there are amongst'em some honest Gentlemen who now begin to take upon'em, and Manage Affairs as they ought to be. (1.1.105–11)

Certainly, the next scene, which reveals Flirt as a social climber and Timerous as a petty embezzler, seems to justify Friendly's contempt for Virginia's social mobility. Yet Behn also carefully undermines the credibility of the spokesmen for royal and English privilege.

After Friendly describes Bacon and the unfair treatment he received—"he took the opportunity, and led them forth to fight, and vanquishing brought the Enemy to fair terms, but now instead of receiving him as a Conquerour, we treat him as a Traytor" (1.1.129–31), Hazard rightly notes that "it seems all the Crime this brave fellow has committed, is serving his Country without Authority" (1.1.132). Friendly *agrees* with his companion's assessment, but decides that he stands to gain more by siding with royal authority: "'Tis so, and however I admire the Man, I am resolv'd to be of the Contrary Party, that I may make an Interest in our new Governour" (1.1.134–35). I will return in a moment to the problem of Bacon's Rebellion. Right now, I want to emphasize how the calculus of Friendly's decision to oppose Bacon—his measuring Bacon's support and determining that despite the merits of his case, Bacon stands no chance against royally appointed authority—does not encourage an unthinking acceptance of his political judgments, which are obviously grounded in self-aggrandizement.

As for Hazard, his contempt for Timerous and the others is hypocritical, since the cause of his emigration—he "lost all" at gambling, and his elder brother "mollified by perswasions and the hopes of being for ever rid of me, sent me hither with a small Cargo to seek my fortune" (1.1.42, 44–45)—is no different from that of Flirt or Timerous. Moreover, Behn wastes no time in establishing the unattractive side of his personality. When the newly arrived Englishman first enters the local tavern, Boozer, Dullman, and the other members of the council invite the stranger to their table.

DULLMAN: Please you Sir to tast of our Liquor—My service to you: I see you are a Stranger and alone, please you to come to our Table?
FLIRT: Come Sir, pray sit down here, these are very Honourable Persons I assure. (1.1.215–18)

The Virginians then ask Hazard what he intends to do in Jamestown, and Hazard responds to their hospitality with churlishness. In answer to Timerous's polite offer, "What have you brought over any Cargo Sir, I'le be your Customer," Hazard responds: "I was not bred to Merchandizing Sir, nor do intend to follow the drudgery of trading" (1.1.223, 225–26). The others understandably take offense, but Hazard only exacerbates matters:

DULLMAN: Men of Fortune seldom travell hither Sir to see fashions.
TIMEROUS: Why Brother, it may be the Gentleman has a mind to be a Planter, will you hire yourself to make a Crop of Tobacco this year?
HAZARD: I was not born to work Sir.
TIMEROUS: Not work Sir, zoors, your betters have workt! I have workt my self Sir, both set and stript Tobacco, for all I am of the Honourable Councill, not work quoth a—I suppose Sir you wear your fortune upon your Back Sir?
HAZARD: Is it your Custom here Sir to affront Strangers? I shall expect satisfaction. (1.1.227–36)

Hazard cannot answer a civil question civilly, and while he may have in mind his widow-hunting (not the most dignified of professions, to be sure), his assertion that labor is beneath him and his quickness to take offense in the face of Dullman's and Timerous's hospitality offer also puts into question his political judgment. Moreover, his assertion, "I was not born to work," while possibly echoing earlier conceptions of America as a land of ease and plenty, contradicted both official English attitudes toward the necessity of labor (in 1649, one Peter Chamberlen argued that "It is certain that employment and competencies do civilize all men"[34]) and the reality of life in Virginia. Immigrants from the higher regions of England's social structure may not have stooped to manual labor, yet they still had to work, either as planter-merchants or by taking "on a variety of roles: managing their plantations or engaging in trade, money-lending, land speculation, or any other kind of entrepreneurial activity."[35] The scene concludes, appropriately, with Timerous (rather generously, given the provocations), seeking to excuse Hazard's behavior on the by now expected grounds of Virginian gentility and English crudity: "Let him alone, let him alone Brother, how should he learn manners, he never was in *Virginia* before" (1.1.244–45), with the additional implication that he will learn soon enough how he must work if he wants to eat, now that he is in Virginia.

Behn concludes the play with another assertion of Virginia's cultural superiority to England, only this time she puts it in the mouth of Colonel Wellman, one of the few indisputably "good" characters. Therefore, his words are untouched by irony or satire:

Come, my brave Youths, let all our Forces meet,
To make this Country happy, rich and great;
Let Scanted Europe see that we enjoy
Safer Repose, and larger Worlds, than they. (5.5. 398–401; my emphasis)

Wellman begins by urging unity, as perhaps one might expect after defeating a rebellion. But then, his speech goes against expectation. First, the purpose of political unity is "To make *this Country* happy, rich and great." Wellman's phrase thus echoes the assertions peppered throughout of Virginia constituting "here" and England "there." Next, he calls for unity ("Let all our Forces meet") to prove the general superiority of "this country" over not just England, but all of "Scanted Europe."

What exactly does Behn mean by the adjective, "Scanted"? According to the *Oxford English Dictionary*, "scanted" means "to make small, stinted, diminished, restricted," and as one would expect, the definitions of "scant" all have to do with limitations, be they physical, spatial, or moral. To call Europe "scanted," therefore, means drawing attention to Europe's overcrowding, but even more to the general state of diminishment and the limits on opportunity. Europe is no longer the source of authority, but a place where both physical and immaterial "things, actions, qualities" exist in an "inadequate or barely sufficient amount, quantity, or degree" (definition A.1). Jamestown, on the other hand, is not only "safer" (a significant contradiction to the widespread perception of the colonies as highly dangerous places due to disease, poor food, difficult farming, and hostile natives) but enjoys greater freedom of movement, both physical and cultural ("larger Worlds"), than Europe. The play concludes, in other words, with Wellman *confirming* the earlier assertions by Ranter, Timerous, Whiff, and Whimsey, among others, of Virginia's difference and superiority to England, only this time, one cannot doubt the speaker's credibility.

Behn's treatment of Virginia's cultural autonomy is almost perfectly balanced. The play begins with foolish characters asserting Virginian identity, and ostensibly credible characters as the spokesmen for English imperialism. But as the play progresses, the evaluation of both positions switches: Behn substantiates the views of the foolish characters, and she shows the representatives of "England" as venal and calculating. Behn is thus literally ambivalent about Virginia's new cultural independence. To find out why Behn would react in such a complex fashion, I will now turn to her treatment of Bacon's Rebellion, which reflects her sense that Virginia's rise is not a purely happy event, that it is accompanied by, perhaps even caused by, England's senescence and decay.

Idealized Rebellion

Bacon's Rebellion (1675–76),[36] a complex fight among friendly and hostile Indians, Bacon's followers, and the colonial administration of Sir William

Berkeley, lies behind Behn's sense of Virginia's nascent cultural difference. Initially, the conflict between Berkeley and Bacon arose from Bacon's defiance of the governor's refusal to allow retaliatory raids on the Indians (possibly because of Berkeley's profitable ties with these tribes), but the dispute quickly moved from the narrow issue of whether Bacon had permission to retaliate to a broad-based armed rebellion against Berkeley's government that was fueled by economic hardship (English trade laws forbade foreign competition for Virginian tobacco, a policy that impoverished farmers) and Berkeley's arbitrary government. Berkeley prevailed, although at the cost of his authority (the royal commissioners appointed to investigate the matter were appalled at his misgovernment) and the burning of Jamestown.[37] Bacon died of a fever in 1676 and his body was never found, much to the simultaneous satisfaction and frustration of his enemies, who would have preferred to see the rebel hang, or failing that, to have the corpse publicly displayed and humiliated.[38] It took another ten years for the revolt to be finally snuffed out.

While Bacon's Rebellion did not have much of an impact in England, Behn could have learned about the Rebellion in various ways. Two news pamphlets appeared in 1677, *Strange News from Virginia* and *More News from Virginia*, and her court connections may also have allowed her access to the report of Charles's commissioners as well as other documents.[39] Yet whatever the source, virtually all contemporary discussions of Bacon's Rebellion interpret the event in light of the English Revolution. The anonymous author of *Strange News from Virginia* notes that Bacon could not resist continuing "his opposition against that prudent and established Government, ordered by his Majesty of *Great Britain* to be duly observed in that Continent," implying that Bacon's target was not so much Berkeleyan incompetence but royal authority itself. In *More News from Virginia*, the author makes this position explicit.[40] The second person to be executed "was one *Farlow* (a Chip of the old block of Rebellion) one of *Cromwell's* Souldiers." and the others are all condemned as enemies of the king.[41] The author calls Bacon "the Grand Opposer of the *Royall Party* in *Virginia*," and continues to harp on how Bacon's followers were "executed for their Opposition or Rebellion against His Majesties Establisht—Laws and Government," how "one . . . *Page*, a Carpenter . . . [for his] remarkable violence against the *Royall Party*, [was] made *Collonel*," and how a third person "was thought guilty of death for trayterously shooting to death an Eminent Person of the *Royall Party*."[42]

Had Behn read the report of the royal commissioners, she would have seen language emphasizing the Cromwellian overtones of Bacon's Rebellion. Like Charles I's opponents, Bacon saw himself as protecting the lives, estates, and, most importantly, "Libertyes" of the people.[43] Bacon was, according to the commissioners, the "Darling" or the "hopes of the People," and he "turn'd the sword of a civil warr into the heart and bowels of the country."[44] His government also degenerated (albeit much more quickly) into a military dictatorship: "Bacon now begins to show a more merciless severity and absolute authority than formerly, Plundering and imprisoning many and condemning some of power of martial law."[45]

Other contemporary documents attest to how both Bacon and his contemporaries interpreted his rebellion in terms of the most threatening elements of the English Revolution, and while Cromwell was not a radical in comparison with such groups as the Levellers, the Ranters, and the Diggers, this distinction was lost on the witnesses to Bacon's Rebellion. For example, one William Sherwood, writing in 1676 to Sir Joseph Williamson, the Secretary of State, warned that Bacon aimed at the "subvercon of the Laws & to Levell all," a clear allusion to the more radical elements of the Revolution.[46] After Bacon entered the House of Burgesses with his armed escort, an act that by itself called to mind Pride's Purge (1648), one of Berkeley's supporters called him "Oliver Bacon" to his face,[47] and the revolutionary convention, which met August 3, 1676, ordered that every civil authority take "Bacon's Oath." The new government would constitute a revolutionary "Association," which, as Webb notes, was itself a concept "borrowed from the English revolutionaries of the 1640s."[48] Echoing the Levellers, Bacon allegedly "insinuates into and possess the people with lyberty and free[dom] . . . from Bondage," and what is more, he promised to rid Virginia of social hierarchy: "he would make the meanest of them equall with, or in better condition than those that Ruled over them."[49]

Bacon and his followers took their rhetorical cue from such Leveller tracts as "An Agreement of the People" (1647), which constituted England's "people" as the ultimate source of political authority (e.g., "that the power of this and all future representatives of this nation is inferior only to their who choose them"), by also claiming that they act for "the people."[50] In 1676, Bacon issued a proclamation entitled "The Declaration of the People," accusing Berkeley of, inter alia, "having with only the privacy of some few favourites without acquainting the People, only the Alteration of a Figure forged a Commission by wee know not what hand, not only without but against the Consent of the People, for raising and effecting of Civill Wars," and signed by "NATH BACON, Gen'l., By the Consent of ye People."[51] Sherwood quotes Bacon as telling Berkeley that "he came for redress of ye peoples grievances," and when Berkeley's followers predicted that the rebellion "would fall like the rebellion in England," the Baconians responded by defending the English Revolution: "the people of England had some reason for some of theire rebellion."[52]

After their defeat, the rebels' trials revealed again the Baconians' allegiance to Interregnum-style radicalism. One Anthony Arnold declared to the royal judges that "hee had no Kindnesse for Kings, and that they had Noe Right but what they gott by Conquest and the Sword," adding that "hee that could by power of the sword deprive them thereof had as good &

just a Title to it, as the King himselfe: and that if the King should Deny to do him right . . . he would make noe more to sheath his sword in His heart or Bowells than in his owne mortall Enemyes."[53]

Now, Behn herself was a Royalist, possibly a fanatical one, for most of her life,[54] and only a few years earlier, she wrote a play satirizing the revolutionaries, *The Roundheads, Or, The Good Old Cause* (1681–82), which concerns the power struggles following Oliver Cromwell's death leading up to the Restoration. In her dedicatory letter, she presents this play to her potential patron to show "how the Royal Interest thrives," and the prologue, spoken by "the ghost of Hewson [a commander under Cromwell and a member of the House] ascending from Hell," not only damns the Revolution, but asserts that Cromwellians are worse than even the Jesuits:[55]

I am the Ghost of him who was a true Son
Of the late GOOD OLD CAUSE, Ecliped, *Hewson*,
Roud'd by strange scandal, from th'eternal flame
With noise of plotts, of wonderous birth and name
Whilst the sly Jesuit robs us of our fame.
Can all their Conclave, tho' with Hell th'agree
Act mischief equal to Presbittery?

There is, in sum, no reason to assume that Behn would have treated Bacon's Rebellion with any sympathy whatsoever. The event was universally regarded as an aftershock of the English Revolution. Bacon himself used the language of the Revolutionaries, and his contemporaries frequently and explicitly associated him with Cromwell. Bacon and his Rebellion, therefore, represented a political viewpoint that Behn openly and unreservedly despised. And yet, instead of writing a version of *The Roundheads* set in Virginia, Behn goes entirely against expectation and transforms the "Oliverian" Bacon into a chivalric hero whose virtues everyone, including if not especially his enemies, recognizes.

In his opening summary of Virginia's state, Friendly describes Bacon as "A man above the Common Rank, by Nature Generous; Brave, Resolv'd, and Daring" (1.1.113–14). He then recounts how Bacon has not only attacked the Indians, but "brought the Enemy to fair terms," and the newly arrived Hazard exclaims that the supposed villain of the play, the rebel against royal authority, has been treated with monstrous pettiness: "it seems all the Crime this brave Fellow has committed, is serving his Country without Authority" (1.1.130, 133). Friendly agrees with this assessment, although he nonetheless decides to oppose Bacon out of pure self-interest, the "new Governour" presumably being in a better position to do him good than Bacon (a fact which works against his credibility, not Bacon's, as we have already noted). And slightly later, Friendly repeats his admiration for Bacon despite his status as a rebel: "And faith it goes against my Conscience to lift my Sword against him, for he is truly brave, and what he has done, a Service to the Country, had it but been by authority" (1.3.121–23).

Significantly, Behn depicts both Bacon and Cavarnio as not just morally superior to everyone else in the play, but as embodying the antique, highly anachronistic virtues of English chivalry, an ideology already exhausted by the early 1600s.[56] Bacon's key characteristic, everyone in this play seems to agree, is his chivalric nobility. The Indian king, Cavarnio, regrets the necessity of battle on exactly these grounds: "For your part, Sir, you've been so Noble, that I repent the Fatall differences that makes us meet in Arms" (2.1.1–10). Behn also invests the Indian king with equally chivalric qualities. After the initial exchange, he pointedly treats Bacon with magnanimity: "Come Sir, let this ungratefull Theme alone, which is better disputed in the Field" (2.1.20–21), and diplomatically allows Bacon privacy to deal with his council: "I've leave you till you have dispatch'd the Messenger, and then expect your presence in the Royal Tent" (2.1.48–49).

As the scene continues, Bacon extends his nobility to everyone. When Dunce brings the letter "inviting" Bacon to a meeting with the council (the invitation is a trap), Bacon refuses to believe that anyone would act duplicitously because such acts are beneath the chivalric code, and he answers Dareing's suspicions thus: "You wrong me when you but suspect for me, let him that acts dishonourably fear" (2.1.76–77). In this scene, Bacon also meets the Indian queen, Semernia, with whom he immediately falls in love, and he woos her with the language of courtly love: "Beauty has still a power over great Souls, And from the moment I beheld your eyes, my stubborn heart melted to compliance, and from a nature rough and turbulent, grew Soft and Gentle as the God of Love" (2.1.127–29). Semernia responds in kind, recognizing her passion but refusing to give in to such a dishonorable act as adultery: "I'll talk no more our words exchange our Souls, and every look fades all my blooming honour, like Sun beams, on unguarded Roses.—Take all our Kingdoms—make our People Slaves, and let me fall beneath your Conquering Sword. But never let me hear you talk again or gaze upon your Eyes" (2.1.145–49).[57]

Behn further emphasizes Bacon's association with chivalric honor through his refusal to treat women with anything other than the utmost courtesy. When Fearless asks for Colonel Downright's daughter, who is a prisoner of Bacon's forces, in order to rape her ("I would fain be Plundering for a Trifle call'd a Maiden-head" [3.2.197–98]), Bacon explicitly forbids treating women thus: "On pain of Death treat them with all respect; assure them of the safety of their Honour" (3.2.199–200).

Bacon consistently treats his enemies in the same fashion. When he meets the Indian king for their final confrontation, Bacon does not kill his enemy at the first opportunity, but rather, transforms the fight into a chivalric duel: "Abandon'd as thou art I scorn to take thee basely, you shall have Souldiers chance Sir for your Life" (4.2.25–26). The king responds by recognizing the ideology behind the act: "That's Nobly said" (4.2.30), and after Bacon mortally wounds Cavarnio, he does not gloat, but instead, treats him as a chivalric opponent should: "Command my surgions,—instantly—make haste Honour returns and Love all bleeding's fled" (4.2.56–57).[58]

Bacon's chivalric qualities might be compromised by the two major charges against him, rebellion and ambition, yet he defends himself against both on the grounds that he, like Sir Gawain in his confrontation with the Green Knight, has "not offended Honour nor Religion" (3.4.83). Concerning the crime of taking up arms without a commission, Bacon responds:

Shou'd I stand by and see my Country ruin'd, my King dishonour'd, and his Subjects Murder'd, hear the sad Crys of widdows and of Orphans. You heard it, Lowd, but gave no pitying care to't. And till the war and Massacre was brought to my own door, my Flocks, and Herds surpriz'd, I bore it all with Patience. Is it unlawfull to defend my self against a Thief that breaks into my doors? (2.4.85–90)

As for ambition, after Bacon's death, Dareing asserts that Bacon "cou'd have conquer'd all *America*" (5.4.314), and at the play's start, Friendly claims that he often heard Bacon say, "Why cannot I Conquer the Universe as well as *Alexander*? Or like another *Romulus* form a new *Rome*, and make my self Ador'd?" (1.1.117–19). Yet not only do we never hear Bacon himself say such words, but he specifically disclaims any such ambition. In answer to Downright's statement "'Tis fear'd Sir, under this pretence you aim to Government," Bacon states flatly that such is not the case: "I scorn to answer to so base an accusation, the height of my ambition is, to be an honest Subject" (2.4.103–5).[59] Given his refusal to grant that the council might try to trick him because honorable people just do not act that way ("Away, you wrong the Council, who of themselves are Honourable Gentlemen, but the base Coward fear of some of them, puts the rest on tricks that suit not with their nature" [2.1.63–65]), we have to assume that lying to Downright suits not with *his* nature.

The question is, why would Behn treat Bacon and his Indian enemy so sympathetically? Why would she turn a figure universally associated with Oliver Cromwell into an admirable, if flawed, tragic hero who might be more at home in Sir Philip Sidney's *Arcadia* and involve him in a romantic triangle which echoes Chaucer's "noble" *Knight's Tale*? Part of the answer to this problem lies in the mutually reinforcing relationship between Behn's increasing pessimism concerning England's future resulting from the shifting political circumstances in the years following *The Roundheads* and her sense that Virginia represents a rising culture destined to replace "poor England."

The "lunatic anti-popery"[60] in the wake of the fictional Popish Plot, the real, if failed, Rye House Plot, and the Exclusion Crisis certainly did nothing to confirm Behn's earlier faith in the Stuart dynasty, but so long as Charles II remained alive, she could still equate royalism with virtue, as she does in *The Roundheads*. But starting with the ascension of the determinedly Catholic (and politically maladroit) James II in 1685, Behn's skepticism started intensifying, as did her sense that an era was about to end.[61] While, as Todd points out, she continued to write royalist panegyrics and odes, her fictions started to embrace doubts and ambiguities about her previous political allegiances.[62] The astoundingly complex and duplicitous plots and gyrations of her patron, the Earl of Sunderland, undercut her belief that "aristocrats were the bulwark of the monarchy," while the monarchy worked hard to destroy its own credibility.[63] James' politically obtuse Catholicism alienated almost all of his English followers, as did his increasing reliance upon royal prerogative, his hated Scots allies, and the law courts at the expense of Parliament.[64] On November 5, 1688, William of Orange landed in England at the invitation of the nobility, and James II, the last of the Stuart line, fled England with his wife and son. The "Glorious Revolution" succeeded because of the highly inglorious flight of the monarch, the queen, and the heir. The political certainties that guided Behn's life, in other words, were quickly fading, and they were replaced by what Robert Appelbaum terms the "new uncertainties" of a new age.[65]

Behn's *The Widdow Ranter* reflects precisely these uncertainties. The standard view of Nathaniel Bacon, as we have seen, was that he represented a noxious repeat of Oliver Cromwell, but rather than lampooning him as she does Lambert et al. in *The Roundheads*, she creates a representative of antique, English virtue, a virtue firmly rooted in England's long gone past, who rebels against an incompetent council. Prompted by her disillusionment with the Stuarts and the coming end of their dynasty, Behn uses this play to reevaluate her earlier opposition to the anti-monarchic forces of the Revolution, transforming them from fools into avatars of ancient English chivalry.[66] The decline of the Stuarts, in other words, leads Behn to invest their enemies with precisely the virtues she originally thought the monarchy and their followers embodied.

Behn balances her reevaluation of the "Oliverian" Nathaniel Bacon with a similarly politically charged reevaluation of Cavarnio, the Indian king. In the first meeting between the two, Behn clearly depicts their conflict as generally representing the problem of the New World:

CAVARNIO: Yet tho I'm young I'm sensible of Injuries; And oft have heard my Grandsire say—That we were Monarchs once of all this spacious World; Till you an unknown People landing here, Distress'd and ruin'd by destructive storms, Abusing all our Charitable Hospitality, Usurp'd our Right, and made your Friends your slaves.
BACON: I will not justify the Ingratitude of my fore-fathers, but finding here my Inheritance, I am resolv'd still to maintain it so, and By my sword which first cut out my Portion, Defend each inch of Land with my last drop of Bloud. (2.1.10–18)

This exchange obviously refers to the morality of colonialism, and as Margaret Ferguson nicely puts it, the scene "allows considerably more room for interrogating the morality of the colonial enterprise than many contemporary texts do."[67] Bacon's insistence on defending "each inch of Land with my last drop of Bloud" equally reveals the "particularly intense dream of possession" which Stephen J. Greenblatt asserts shaped "the whole experience of Europeans in America."[68] As such, this passage accords with Behn's complex treatment of colonialism in *Oroonoko* (which she wrote in 1688, about the same time as *The Widdow Ranter*).

Yet the conflict between Bacon and Cavarnio also sets in motion echoes of the English Civil War. The phrase, "Usurp'd our Right," recalls the Royalist charges against Cromwell, and Behn consistently refers to their clash as a fight between "the general" and "the king" (e.g., "BACON: 'The King!' KING: 'The General here, by all the Powers betray'd by my own men" [4.2.23–24]), appellations that, in all likelihood, reminded the audience of a clash between another general and king: Lieutenant-General Cromwell and King Charles I. Furthermore, just as "the mangl'd King" Oroonoko partly refigures Charles I, Cavarnio also partly represents Charles.[69] Granted, he may not be "mangl'd," but Cavarnio is certainly a king unrightfully deposed and betrayed by those closest to him. Yet unlike *Oroonoko*, Behn registers no outrage at the killing of this king. One could account for her approval of Cavarnio's demise by seeing a fundamental approval of English colonialism. But at the same time, her suggestive parallel between Charles I and Cavarnio implies that like the Indians, the monarchy too belongs to the past. Whereas Cavarnio harps on past injustices, Bacon's response signals something in addition to "breezy pragmatic cynicism,"[70] because he puts his response in terms of the *present*: "I *will not justify* the Ingratitude of my fore-fathers, but *finding here* my Inheritance, I *am resolv'd* still to maintain it so" (my emphasis).

The exhaustion of monarchic authority represented by the conflict between Cavarnio and Bacon also finds representation in the "absent presence," as it were, of the governor in this play. While it could be argued that Behn altered the historical record in order to parallel the council's rule with the Interregnum government[71] (making Bacon, oddly, a representative of the Royalist forces), there is another way of interpreting the matter. Behn's characters regularly emphasize not only the governor's absence, but his expected return. Friendly, for example, makes explicit the temporary nature of Downright's authority: "I'le present you to the two Collonels, *Wellman* and *Downright*, the Men that manage all till the Arrival of the Governour" (2.1.68–69), and at the play's conclusion, Wellman asserts that "The Governour when he comes shall find the Country in better hands than he expects to find it" (5.5.390–91). Yet anyone in Behn's audience familiar with Virginia history would know that the English governors of Virginia from Berkeley onward were disasters.

Berkeley, as we have seen, was roundly criticized by the royal commissioners, and according to one narrative, "a report was Whisper'd about, that the King did Say 'That old fool has hang'd more men in that naked Country, than he had done for the Murther of his Father.'"[72] His successors did not improve the situation, with the exception of Colonel Herbert Jeffreys, who died almost immediately upon being appointed. Sir Henry Chicheley was too "old, sickly and crazy" to govern effectively, and the eighteen months of his administration were marked by "ill blood" and continuing factionalism.[73] Then came Thomas Lord Culpeper, a man "insensible of any obligation to guard the welfare of the people of Virginia."[74] As Robert Beverley put it: "This Noble Lord was skilful in all the Ways of getting Money, and never let slip any Opportunity of doing it."[75] If Culpeper threatened everyone's wallets, Lord Howard Effingham, his successor (and the last governor before Behn composed *The Widdow Ranter*), threatened the very foundations of government. As Wertenbaker describes him, he was "unscrupulous, deceitful, overbearing, resentful, persistent; he proved a dangerous foe to the representative institutions of the colony, and an able defender of royal prerogative."[76] Beverley reported that his government was so despotic that the "People look'd upon their Acts of Assembly, to be of no more Force, than the Laws of an *Ottoman* province, which are liable to be suspended or repeal'd, at the Pleasure of the *Bashaw.*"[77] Those in Behn's audience aware of these developments would have recognized that the hopes of her Virginians were misplaced, to say the least. Not only would the return of the governor not perfect the colony, as Friendly hopes, but it would make matters considerably worse.

The absence of royal authority in this play, then, may very well recall the Interregnum period, but it would have also emphasized the continuing absence of competent royal authority in Virginia, and by implication, in contemporary England. Even further, the disappointment that the historical Virginians would suffer once the governor and his forces returned to the colony refigures Behn's disappointment in James's failure to act in a politically sane manner. Behn's point, it seems, is that Virginians would be better off relying not on "the governor," but on *themselves*.

Old exhausted England will cause them nothing but further grief, and Virginia, as I noted in the first part of this essay, now constitutes a separate, new culture. Consequently, at the play's conclusion, Wellman seeks to subsume the rebellion's animosities in a recognition of Virginia's independence of England. On the one hand, the play's ending resembles the conclusion of the original (not Nahum Tate's) *King Lear* in that there is nobody with the grandeur of Bacon, Cavarnio, or Semernia to take over. Political authority, it seems, has devolved to lesser figures. And yet, while the sense of diminution arises from Behn's sense that the Old World ideologies represented by Bacon, Semernia, and Cavarnio have had their day, Virginia's future does not lie in the antique virtues embodied by these three characters or in confirming royalism. Instead, the future is represented in the marriage of Ranter, the unconventional woman who breaks gender rules through her cross-dressing and sexual forwardness, and Dareing, the rebel against English authority whose attraction to Ranter seems to be predicated upon recognizing his own unconventional sexuality ("I never lik'd thee half so well in Petticoats" (4.3.281).

Virginia thus represents for Behn both an ending and a beginning. Prompted by the decline of the Stuarts, Behn uses Bacon's Rebellion to reevaluate her royalism and her antipathy toward the republicans, and so she recreates Nathaniel Bacon, investing him with a chivalric ideology associated with England's glorious but dead past. His English enemies are no longer old royalists who fought for the king, but an incompetent council populated by such aptly named characters as Boozer, Dunce, and Dullman. Royal authority, as in England, is degraded and scandalous. His other enemy, the Indian king, is, ironically, a better embodiment of monarchic ideals than any of the English, yet he too dies, and with the deaths of the protagonists (including Semerina) one senses the fading of an ancient order.

Yet there is hope, and Behn locates that hope not in "poor England," but in Virginia, a place that affords the political, sexual, and social freedoms denied in the mother country. Throughout the play, Behn keeps pointing out how Virginia is not just England over the sea, but a different place with different social customs. Behn thus constructs Virginia for her audience as a place of *possibilities*, of *beginnings*, and the play concludes with Wellman—however much he does not measure up to Bacon's chivalric grandeur—calling for unity on the grounds of Virginia's difference from England. Recalling once again the distinction between Virginia as a place for youth and England for the old and the dying, he exhorts the "brave youths" to demonstrate this newly born country's superiority to "scanted Europe." Ironically, Behn constructs for her English audience a culturally independent Virginia long before the colonists themselves articulated their political and social differences from the mother country. Perhaps a better subtitle for *The Widdow Ranter* would have been "The Virginian."

Conclusion
Jamestown and Its North Atlantic World

CONSTANCE JORDAN

Landfall: April 26th, 1607. After eighteen weeks at sea, the captain of the *Susan Constant*, Sir Christopher Newport, saw the land that he and his crew had been commissioned to settle in behalf of the investors of the Virginia Company in London. The task to which they and those on their sister ships, the *Godspeed* and the *Discovery*, had looked forward probably seemed not a little dreadful. Spanish, Dutch, and French merchant ships were actively competing for resources from Florida, already settled by the Spanish, to Nouvelle France in what is now Nova Scotia and the northern coast of Maine. English settlements on the North Atlantic coast had not prospered. Sir Walter Ralegh's colony at Roanoke had vanished without a trace. The Spanish, notwithstanding the peace negotiated by James I with Philip II and concluded in 1604, continued to challenge the English presence in the North Atlantic. It was inevitable that the two nations should continue to be rivals on both sea and land; each hoped to dominate the traffic to, trade with, and colonization of the peoples of the Americas.

A year before the Jamestown landfall, on April 10, 1606, the Company had issued Letters Patent to the men charged with managing its Virginian investment, a grandiose swath of this new world: "lying and being all along the sea Coastes betweene fower and Thirtie degrees of northerly latitude from the equinoctiall lyne and Five and Fortie degrees of the same latitude ... and the Ilandes thereunto adiacente."[1] Many perhaps understood these terms were deserved, considering that the first duty of the settlers was to ensure the salvation of the natives of Virginia by the "propagating of the Christian religion to suche people as yet live in darkenesse and miserable ignorance of the true knowledge and worshippe," and to bring them "to humane civilitie and to a settled and quiet govermente." As time would show, however, it was trade that was really uppermost in the minds of the company's investors—trade and gold, and indeed their complementary roles. The settlers were to mine for metal but also to mint coin with which to buy goods and raw materials from the natives. Other provisions of these Letters, now known as the first Charter, guaranteed the settlers the civil status they would have had as English subjects at home: they were allowed a right of self-defense, "all the liberties, Franchises, and Immunities" due English subjects, and the land they secured for themselves was to be held in "free and Common Soccage onelie and not in Capite." In other words, Virginia was not to support a feudal society. By November of that year, the London Council of the Virginia Company, assigned the supervision of the enterprise at Jamestown, had issued a specific set of "Instructions . . . by way of Advice" which further specified what the prospective colonists should do. They were to settle where the "natural people of the Country" were; they were to "find out a Safe port in the Entrance of some navigable River"; to get "Country [that is, native] Corn" before "the naturals" could perceive that the settlers "meant to plant among them." Finally, the settlers were not to "advertise the killing of any of [their] men that the Country people may know it if they perceive they are but Common men."[2]

What actually happened to the settlers that first year is recorded in the various accounts by such men as John Smith, Gabriel Archer, and George Percy, and represented in part in the essays in this collection. What they thought they were doing, the contexts in which they placed their mission in order to give it a historical character and dimension, and the justification they sought for it in law, both civil and natural, are questions whose answers can help us today to place Jamestown in the large currents of cultural history. Commentary charged with the freight of religious, political, and social opinion, references to settings and contexts that rendered novelty more or less strange, and accounts of how the land was cleared, farmed, and made productive—these are the discourses that will help us learn how the experience of Jamestown was understood by those who lived it.

The North Atlantic was both a place and a concept. The place, the vast ocean separating Europe and the New World, was in the process of being mapped, its shorelines surveyed, its waters charted. The scene of competitive privateering during the reign of Elizabeth, it was increasingly recognized as a nexus of trade between distant peoples after England's peace with Spain in 1604. The concept, formulated following the discoveries of Columbus and the Papal Donation of Alexander VI (1493) which gave the better part of the New World to the Spanish and Portuguese, was shocking in itself, challenging as it did the ancient assumption that the world and its various peoples had been demarcated and identified in scripture. Jesus had told his apostles: "ye shall be witnesses to me . . . unto the uttermost part of the earth."[3] Probably few in Newport's company reflected on how their mission might fit into a larger scheme of things, ordered by a Providence presumed to favor Protestant and especially English enterprise, and dominated by a progress of *imperium* or rule—the imposition of civility on barbarous peoples, always to the west of a center of authority and prosperity. But such a scheme was much in evidence in the work of those who wrote epic and history. Accounts of westering conquest included those produced by the Spanish in Peru, Mexico, and the Caribbean; by the Ottomans in Africa; and even those pursued inconclusively by the English in Ireland. Rome, of course, provided the ultimate model.

Rome was both the beneficiary of the first and mythical exportation of rule or *translatio imperii*, and the legendary origin of all other later historical migrations that went west to the British Isles, east to Asia Minor, north to Europe, and south to Africa. The cultural meaning of such translation was brilliantly recorded in Virgil's *Aeneid*, the master text for Europeans seeking to justify their imperial legacies and future conquests. Important for those who made the voyage from Troy to Rome, and for their later imitators, was that such translations entailed both a remembering and a forgetting: Aeneas succeeded in bringing his household gods from Troy but he lost his father Anchises before he reached Latium. Nor could the new Troy replicate the old. Aeneas knew not to settle in Buthrotum, the diminutive replica of Troy founded by Helenus and Andromache in the Aegean. The translation Virgil proposed demanded an action less memorial and more creative. Aeneas and his Trojans were to cull from the past the seeds with which the alien ground of Latium could be made to produce its own particular growth in the future.[4]

English historians were fascinated by the origin of their own people as an event in the history of such imperial translation: William Camden asserted that the Romans under Julius Caesar colonized the barbarous Britons. Reflecting on England's status as a civilized nation, Samuel Purchas scribbled in the margins of his edition of *Purchas Pilgrims*, in which he had published William Strachey's "A True Reportory of a Wreck": "The Roman swords were the best teachers of civility to this and other countries near us."[5] And in 1609, William Strachey, imagining that he was on his way to extending English *imperium*, saw himself as a second Aeneas, sailing up the James River "as Virgil writeth Aeneas did, arriving in the region of Italy called Latium, upon the banks of the River Tiber."[6] On Virgil's account, the splendor illuminating the Trojan invaders as they navigated the Tiber excited the wonder of the natural world: "the waves wonder; the woods . . . wonder" (*mirantur et undae/Miratur nemus*).[7] The English at Jamestown were not so obviously celebrated; as we shall see, the land they settled and the people they dispossessed responded to them in quite different ways.

Actual encounters between the English colonists and their native counterparts revealed the contradictions between mythic expectations on the one hand and lived experience on the other: the land is ours, it is theirs; the land is wilderness, it is worked and made productive; food is from nature and seasonal, it is from labor and cultural. Recourse to these figures was linked to English claims to rights to colonize: if the land in Virginia was uncultivated (or, in the language of the time, "waste"), its people could be categorized as uncivil and their property possessed. To sustain such claims to a right to colonize required a certain blindness, however: it was clear to all colonists that the natives of Virginia were fully possessed of their land and were organized as a people in a civil order. The land they worked was highly productive; it was clearly the object of agricultural endeavor. Awareness of these contradictions forced the processes of translation to yield to those of invention.

First Years

During the first years in the settlement at Jamestown, relations between the colonists and Indians stood at a kind of equilibrium. The English sought to make subjects or "vassals" of the Powhatans, while the Indians believed they could make the English their tribal allies, governed by English leaders or werowances who would remain subject to Powhatan. These mutually illusory visions of coexistence lasted until the Indians devastated Jamestown in 1622; at that point, the English assumed a more aggressive role under the leadership of Sir Ralph Lane, and became committed to pushing the Indians west, and to claiming and clearing more Indian land.

The instances of early cooperation, which so conspicuously favored the English settlers in the long run, tell us much about the settlers' frame of mind at the outset of colonization. Their dependence on the Indians was remarkable. The Indian guide Navirans, introducing the settlers to the region, showed them its physical features; gifts were exchanged; rituals were performed, supposedly in order to confer ownership, tribal identity, and to institute mutual friendships.[8] Powhatan, the chief of the local tribes, wearing a "great payre of buckes hornes fastened to hys forehead not knowinge what esteem we make of men so marked," came to discuss matters with Captain Newport; the English, doubtless reading their own meanings in the figure, must have laughed among themselves.[9]

Indications of cultural difference were evident from the outset. Smith's account of the Indians' reaction to the gift of his compass to Opechancanough, Powhatan's half-brother, features Smith's wit and implies Indian gullibility. The instrument is extravagantly played up. Smith represents it as a means not only to measure and navigate the globe, but also to reveal "the diversitie of Nations, varietie of complexions, and how we were to them Antipodes." By comparison with Smith's world-embracing compass, which he declares made the Indians admire him "more then they did their owne Quiyouckosucks" or demigods, the map Powhatan later drew on Virginian soil to indicate the extent of Indian lands seems both futile and pathetic.[10] As Smith reports, Powhatan intended and probably believed that his map would show Smith the extent of the Powhatan empire and convince him that the English had no rights to it. Created on the occasion of his "coronation," Powhatan's map detailed the extent of his lands and those of other tribes, setting practically no westward limits to them. In

Smith's words, Powhatan denied that there was "any salt water beyond the mountains," and to illustrate his title, "he began to draw plots upon the ground (according to his discourse) of all those Regions."[11] But Powhatan's map was fixed in the soil in which it was drawn; it was uncommunicable in other than local terms. Its status meant that Wahunsonocock's *dominium* would never gain formal recognition in London.

As an expression of an ideology, the business of translation imitated the terms of its foundational myth; traffic went in one direction only, from east to west. In reality, Virginia proved inhospitable to some of its colonists, and in the first years of settlement many returned to England. From time to time, they brought a few Indians with them. The fate and influence of the Indians so transported from west to east fashion a sad history, one characterized by an overwhelming sense of bewilderment and betrayal.

Jamestown's Indians went to England because Powhatan wanted to learn more about the English and to be represented in London. John Smith's account of the visit in 1616 of Tomocomo or Uttamattomakin, Powhatan's brother-in-law, reveals the futility of Powhatan's enterprise. Coming from Plymouth to London, Tomocomo was overwhelmed by the sheer numbers of people he saw en route (he gave up counting them), and also at "the sight of so much Corne & Trees." He must have recognized then that this wealth in people and resources could fuel a prodigious engine of conquest. Soon also he must have realized that his people were already undone by English disdain for their ways and their status. The usual marks of favor were withheld from him. He told Smith that while Smith had given Powhatan a token of respect and friendship from James I, "a white dog, which Powhatan fed as himselfe," Tomocomo, Powhatan's envoy to James I, had been given "nothing"—"and I am better than your white Dog."[12] Tomocomo's complaint seems to come to this: while Powhatan had elevated the king's gift to a level of dignity comparable to his own, the king had ignored Powhatan's dignitary as he might have any casual stray. Had Pocahontas not died in 1617 after one brief year in England as the wife of John Rolfe, relations between the two people might have been more auspicious; conversion and even intermarriage seem to have been in view. The Spanish had predicated much of their colonizing efforts on intermarriage between Spanish and Indian. But events on the ground in Jamestown already pointed to a different outcome.

John Smith's important *Map of Virginia* (1624) conveys how such events on the ground could be represented. Like most maps of the period, it shows a territory as the technical expertise invested in the calculation of latitude and longitude could render it: divided by a grid. Upon this grid is superimposed yet a second representation of space, this time according to a succession of bird's eye views showing such topographical features as mountains and forests. Finally, embellished by representations of historical moments, Smith's map is also a kind of narrative. Smith's captivity and the huge Indian warrior depicted on the margins of the map point to the mapmaker's belief in the eventual triumph of the English colony: Smith survived; in time, the Indian was forced west. This was powerful propaganda.

A comparable literariness, though of a more conventional kind, is apparent in Richard Frethorne's letter, which reports other kinds of events on the ground. True, what the letter says to us and to the naïve reader generally may not be all it was intended to say to those to whom it was sent. Long read as a cry for help, Frethorne's letter to his mother and father in England details the hardship that he encountered routinely as he traveled from the plantation to the port of Jamestown and back. But the letter was perhaps also a factor in a conflict between two rival factions within the Virginia Company, one led by Sir Edwin Sandys and the Earl of Southampton, and a second led by Henry Rich, Earl of Warwick. At issue was the management of the company itself. Eventually, Warwick triumphed. It's important to recognize that Frethorne was not the usual sort of Jamestown servant: he was literate, could write, and despite his admitted destitution, had pen, paper, and ink at hand. None of these conditions suggests that he had parents who would have packed him off to servitude in Virginia. But even assuming he was no more than a factor for the interests of the Warwick party, he paints a telling picture of Jamestown. To investors, the colony seemed a source of immense wealth; to those who labored to secure this wealth, it could well have appeared as a pit of privation.

Global Rivalries

The settlement of the English at Jamestown was a relatively minor event in the larger picture of global rivalries; retrospectively, it has acquired meanings that were not at all contemplated in 1607. Competition for resources remained a European affair, much of it centered on the Mediterranean and involving the powers invested in the Ottoman Empire as well as in Morocco. The Channel and the Irish Sea continued to demarcate zones of endeavor. English ships took English "undertakers" to their plantations in Ireland to subdue both the natives and those of the Old English who resisted the rule from London. Farther afield the English vied with the Dutch for what John Smith would call "the contemptible Trade of Fish" in the waters off the northern portions of "Virginia," and contended with the French for furs and timber in the regions around the St. Lawrence. England's chief preoccupation during this period was with Spain.

It was the hope of finding gold that most closely identified English ambitions with those of their Spanish competitors. The lure of a quick return on their Virginia investment appears never to have been far from English imaginations. A letter from the Council in Virginia to the Council for Virginia in London, dated June 22, 1607, begs for help "least that all devouringe Spaniard lay his ravenous hands upon theas gold showing mountains, which if we be so enhabled he shall never dare to think on."¹³ This gold was utterly chimerical (or alchemical), of course; on August 12, Sir Walter Cope wrote to Lord Salisbury that he expected the local ore to yield "2000 at the Least in the Tonn" (110), but on the very next day, playing the role of Jonson's Sir Epicure Mammon as it were, he confessed that this local ore could not "return . . . so much as Copper . . . . In the ende all turned to vapore."¹⁴ John Smith, ever the realist, deplored these efforts. His description of colonists' grubbing for gold in 1607 illustrates his contempt for their preoccupations: "there was no talke, no hope, no worke, but dig gold, wash gold, refine gold, loade gold, such a bruit of gold, that one mad fellow desired to be buried in the sands least they should by their art make gold of his bones." Smith derisively reports that Newport's "drunken" ship was loaded with supposed ore, in fact "so much guilded durt."¹⁵

Smith was fascinated by Spanish colonialism. In this respect, he differed from most of his compatriots, for whom Hispanophobia was almost instinctive. The so-called Black Legend, featured in most explanations of Spain's dominance in Mexico and the Caribbean regions to which English adventurers traveled regularly, went unchallenged by its counterpart, a "white legend" asserting the providential nature of Spain's American conquests to redeem the heathen. English and more generally Protestant condemnation of Spain gained considerable leverage through the immensely popular translation of Bartholome de Las Casas's *De regia potestate*, 1554 (as *The Spanish Colonie*, 1583), which outlined Spain's mistreatment of the Indians in the Caribbean in an effort to change Spanish colonial policy in that region. To the English, however, it appeared to justify the plans for conversion proposed earlier by Hakluyt and others. By 1610, in its polemical "A True Declaration of the estate of the colony in Virginia," the Council of Virginia was able to invoke the Spanish example with a deep irony: "Let the divines of Salamanca discuss that question how the possessor of the West Indies first destroyed and then instructed," in other words, a dead native is not a candidate for conversion.¹⁶ By contrast, once having expressed their pious purposes, the English saw themselves as converting the natives to and by trade: as had Hakluyt stated, they sought to "civilize through exchange."

Against these prevailing notions of Spanish duplicity Smith was in a sense a holdout. Admiring Spain's dexterous use of resources deployed across the vastness of the North *and* South Atlantic, he entertained twinned reactions to her conquests. His contribution to this discourse is the very clarity of his descriptions of English behavior, which lets us see that the English resembled the Spanish in both their aspirations and their practices. Were the English to have settled in Mexico and the Spanish to have remained in Virginia, Smith states that their fates would have been exchanged: the English would have "done as much as by their examples might bee expected from us," that is, gained as much as had the Spanish by following

Spanish tactics.[17] Smith may well have envied the Spanish conquest; in any case, he does not seem to have felt much scorn for the means by which they had achieved it.

Second to Spain in the English consciousness of lands beyond their shores was Ireland. Did English attempts to colonize Ireland shape English experiments in settling Jamestown? Certainly numbers of parallels can be made: the imposition of Protestantism upon a population whether Catholic or heathen; the construction of fortresses to protect colonial populations from the natives, whether Irish or Indian; and the investment in plantations by joint-stock companies. That to English eyes neither Irish nor Indian practiced the true faith went without saying: at times, both peoples were condemned for being cannibals. Resistance to English settlements, disputes over English appropriation of land and how it was planted, and fear of what was perceived as native nomadism argued for the presence of garrison-like structures in each of these regions. Finally, both Irish and Virginian colonies were supposed to yield profits to investors. Thus, despite English reliance on humanist texts for legitimation of their colonizing efforts (notably the works of Herodotus, Livy, and Tacitus), England could be said to have served a practical and quite specific apprenticeship in the arts and strategy of colonization between 1565 and 1576, when their initial efforts to occupy Ireland in behalf of the crown occurred.

Yet these parallels are also fault lines illustrating how the two colonies differed. First and perhaps foremost: it was not clear that the Indians were not an autonomous people. Robert Gray's question and its answer are worth reconsidering. In 1609 in a treatise entitled *A Good Speed to Virginia*, he asks: "by what right or warrant we can enter into the lands of savages, take away their rightful inheritance from them, and plant ourselves in their places, being unwronged or unprovoked by them?" His answer was that the English disturbed no rights because the Indians had "offered" their land to English colonists "on reasonable conditions."[18] What these "conditions" were he does not say; had they entailed a transfer of sovereignty, they would have been recognized in a treaty. William Symonds asked a similar question: "The country [Virginia] they say is possessed by owners that rule and govern it in their owne right; then with what conscience and equitie can we offer to thrust them with violence out of their inheritances?" His answer also elides legality: Scripture, he declares, justifies conquest by the sword;[19] and England is overcrowded and needs room for her people.[20] By contrast, English assertions that Ireland was an extension of their rule, although unsupported by the law of nations, at least had the patina of age; almost time out of mind, the English had declared that the Irish lacked civility and were not a sovereign people.

Of course, civility, with its foundation in the institutions of commerce and religion, was not considered to be a property of Europeans only. Neither Morocco in north Africa nor the Ottoman empire in the eastern Mediterranean was considered in the same light as the Irish and the Indians. England and Morocco behaved toward each other as cultural equals, their differences in appearance, modes of dress, familial relations, and practices of servitude notwithstanding. By contrast, the Ottoman empire earned another kind of English respect by overtly threatening English interests. Turkish conquests were regarded as fearsome; as Fynes Morison claimed, they were "the present Terrour of the World." John Smith's *The True Travels*, an account of his military service for the Hapsburgs well before his voyage to Virginia but included in *The General Historie* as a kind of afterword, is designed in part to remind readers of the confluence of trade and culture between Europe, the New World, and the near East. But more particularly, its purpose is rhetorical. Smith's high and deliberate style, his elaborate diction replete with figures and images reminiscent of the epics of Ariosto and Tasso, removes *The True Travels* from the sphere and concerns of history and places it in the genre of romance. Its treatment of the beloved enemy, especially the lady Tragabigzanda who returned Smith's affections and helped him escape, tropes on the ambiguous careers of such infidel heroines as Ludovico Ariosto's Marfisa in the *Orlando Furioso*, and Torquato Tasso's Clorinda in the *Gerusalemme Liberata (Jerusalem Delivered)*. By the bravura colors of his self-portrait as a Christian knight combating retrograde heathen, the John Smith of *The True Travels* eclipses altogether his representation in *The General Historie*, which shows him managing the practical affairs of daily life essential for the welfare of the colony. Whether the later text casts its account of earlier events in light of those that were to follow is, of course, pure speculation. But Smith's troubled view of miscegenation in *The True Travels* may reflect his attitude toward relations between English and Indian, especially after the marriage of Pocahontas and John Rolfe had no sequels. By the second decade of the seventeenth century, the language of alterity emphasized comparisons of Indians with "the wild Irish," whom Turks and Africans were also said to resemble.

The stylistic difference between *The True Travels* and *The General Historie* raises the central question posed of westward enterprise: what to take to the new country; what to leave behind in the old. In this case, Smith's decision is pointed though perhaps also unintentional and even unconscious. Untranslated were to remain the textured memories of the Europe of romance, of combat with an infidel alien to the East, a peril at least as old as that posed by the Persians to the Hellenes in Herodotus's *Histories*. Smith's emplotment allows us to see how the English in Virginia thought they might plan for and enjoy a particular dispensation: the West was to move west, to recast all human history in another mode, while the East was to remain fixed in an antique and memorialized world. It may not be an exaggeration to say that Smith's account of his travels created an alien East in order better to evoke a familiar West.

The Traffic in Culture

Europeans adventuring in the North Atlantic and certainly the English settling along the shores of Virginia doubtless clung to the belief that the cultural traffic they engaged in was chiefly one way, from east to west. To discern a traffic in the opposite direction and gauge the impact of Indian culture on the settlers in Jamestown requires careful reading between the lines, more particularly because the lines that have survived are almost all by English hands. Reports of how the settlers negotiated the most basic needs, food, shelter, property, labor, and a social order, illustrate how the English in Virginia fashioned a way of life that became progressively more independent of Old World habits and practices. Their differences may be attributed to those factors in the new environment that impinged on the consciousness of settlers.

The first accounts of Virginia reported such an abundance of food to be had for the mere gathering of it that hunger and starvation must have been unimaginable. Prints decorating John Smith's *Map of Virginia* show him dwarfed by his Indian counterparts—an indication that they were better fed than he.[21] In time, of course, seasons of plenty were matched by seasons of dearth, and while the English marveled at the Indians' huge appetites when food was readily available, they were awed by the Indians' toleration of hunger when food was scarce. In any case, however, the English imposed a cultural interpretation upon Indian practices. Indians ate what was at hand; their diet was strictly seasonal. By contrast, the English ate regularly. Unlike Indian fare, the fruits of the English table were transseasonal and its consumption, largely independent of climatic differences in nature, was determined for the most part by factors indicating their civility: the feasts and fasts of the liturgical year, the vestigial pagan holidays associated with the solstices, and the particular rituals of family life: birth, marriage, and death. To be oblivious to the strictures enforced and privileges allowed by the Christian calendar, as were the Indians, meant also to be characteristically intemperate, unpredictable, and dangerous. Such an account of Indian diet finally supported English claims to property rights in the New World. Interested in pursuing argument for possession from "waste," the English overlooked the methodical nature of Indian agriculture, their treatment of forest and shoreland, and the extent to which the Indians lived not from nature but as careful developers of her resources.

Evidence in the early version of John Smith's *Map of Virginia* (1612) reveals how the colonists at Jamestown regarded the land they claimed and sought to occupy. Their reasons were as we have already stated: land that was "waste firm" in Hakluyt's terms, or, as Smith would say later a "plaine wildernesse," was proof that it was in no one's possession. Denoting an emptiness yet to be filled by human art, these terms hark back to the ancient legal doctrine of *res nullius*, or a thing which is void and therefore able to be possessed and rightfully claimed by one who demonstrates that he is using it. Uncultivated land could be regarded as no more than common property in the sense that Locke would later define: it was God's gift to the human race as a whole.[22] Early reports of Indian reaction to English planting suggest that the English feared that they might be seen as appropriating Indian property: "The people used our men [the English] well until they found they began to plant & fortefye. Then they fell to skirmishing & kylled 3 of our people."[23] The belief in possession by cultivation or use could produce very self-serving claims, as it did in George Percy's *Observations*, dated 1608 but describing events in 1607: "The savages murmured at our planting in the countrie, whereupon this Werowance (of Paspahegh) made answere againe very wisely of a Savage, why should you bee offended with them as long as they hurt you not, nor take anything away by force, they take but a little waste ground, which doth you nor any of us any good."[24] While we may doubt that the werowance said any such thing, his words could have been understood to justify English appropriation of Indian land. The anonymous writer of "A Description of the River and Country" summed up the situation: "the commodities of this country, what they are in Esse, is not much to be regarded, the inhabitantes having no comerce with any nation, no respect of profitt, neither is there scarce that we call meum et tuum among them save only the kinges know their owne teritoryes & the people their severall gardens."[25] In other words, a claim to possess property in land is dependent on its being used, a notion that English apologists for colonial expansion invoked from Hakluyt on. Colonial argument coupled the doctrine of use, as in acts or cultivation, which conferred possession or *dominium*, with a commitment to promoting a universal civility, which promised rule or *imperium*. The doctrine implied that if there was no evidence of Indian use or cultivation or, more probably, if it could be plausibly ignored, English claims to possession might be pursued without qualification. Rule or *imperium* tended to follow from possession or *dominium*.

Improving a "waste" was not, of course, a concept exclusively relevant to English arguments for possession of land in Virginia. It accounted for much of the reasoning supporting enclosures in England from the early sixteenth century on. It meant that the common rights to land that had been honored time out of mind could be superseded by the civil rights owed to one who was using what had been a "waste." This reasoning allowed the law governing possession of land in England an easy translation to Virginia.

But the process also reflected a tortured perception: the kinds of use to which common land was usually put—as a locale for grazing cattle, fishing, hunting, gathering food and fuel—had to be considered "non-uses" in order for the land to be characterized as "waste." With the exception of grazing, such "non-uses" were regular features of Indian economy; thus they could be adduced as evidence supporting English freehold rights. What could not be assimilated into the category of "waste" was the land the Indians farmed. Their agriculture was a demonstrable fact, perhaps the more arresting because the first colonists had depended so utterly on Indian corn for their very livelihood.

The issue of Indian status with respect to their English counterparts, especially with respect to what work each people did, was not easily resolved. It became complicated by the arrival of Africans, called "Negroes," in Jamestown in 1619, two years after Tomocomo had told Smith of his humiliation in London. Virginia was to become a site in which peoples from three continents were to gather, to live and work. By what human calculus were they to be distinguished?

The determination of status inevitably involved acknowledging kinds of difference, of gender and also of rank, which was registered in terms of authority and subordination. The epithet "slave" was used across social categories to denote conditions of abuse, and its actual reference could vary quite broadly depending upon contexts. Wives could complain of being slaves to exacting husbands; in 1610, some members of the Commons declared that the king's impositions had made them slaves; and prisoners of war, like Smith, could write of their enslavement by the enemy. Men and boys who arrived in Virginia as indentured servants were bought and sold for a term of service; and servants throughout the colony could declare that their treatment had been like that of a slave, meaning simply that it was very bad. These conditions, however horrible, were unlike those that obtained later, when men, women, and children became chattels to be traded in labor markets.

Sir Thomas More's model of a society which permitted slavery, described in his fictive state of Utopia, proved prescriptive in one important respect: in *Utopia*, slavery was neither permanent nor heritable, but rather a punishment for crime. Sir Thomas Dale's *Lawes Divine, Morall and Martial*, 1611, which sentenced criminals to terms of slavery, follows More's model; Virginians convicted even of petty crimes risked servitude in the "Gallies."[26] Ideology supporting a racialized slavery became apparent in Virginia after the Indian attack on Jamestown in 1622, when the Virginia Company condemned the Indians as the "cursed race of Cham" and implicitly invoked the notion of slavery as it appears in scripture.[27] The position of Africans in this period was ambiguous: they were bought and sold like indentured servants; they were freed only by an act of manumission like slaves.

The rather muddled history of slavery and the dominance of indentured servitude in early Virginia becomes especially interesting in light of the professions of liberty that were coming to characterize English political discourse. In England, those who could claim "freedom" were typically property holders; those who had no means of supporting themselves other than the labor they could sell were considered "unfree." As property was generally inherited, "freedom" remained a privilege of a recognizable class, typically "gentle." In Virginia, where very considerable real property could be acquired quickly, a new and hybrid class of "free" person was created: in that sense, American freedom was from its inception different from anything in England. Free Virginians routinely performed some kind of work; they acted as their own stewards, bailiffs, and overseers on the plantations they owned. The English gentleman Hazard, a prominent character in Aphra Behn's *The Widdow Ranter*, is prospectively very un-American: he aspires to getting property through marriage with a Virginian widow, yet he asserts that he does no work and the audience presumes he will not want to change his ways once a married man.

The Widdow Ranter returns us to the questions that began this introduction and which find restatement in many of the essays in this collection: in what ways do Jamestown and nearby settlements express a vision of life that embraces new and different vistas from those found in the English landscape? By the last quarter of the seventeenth century, Virginian culture had severed its most important connections to English ways, practices, and attitudes. Socially it expressed an egalitarianism created by the circumstances in which Virginians lived: unlike Hazard, Virginians worked; like Ranter, they smoked. Distinctions as to rank and status existed, but they tended to express differences created in the New World rather than inherited in England. By dramatizing the rebellion of Nathaniel Bacon, Behn provides some of the terms by which we can assess an American identity in seventeenth-century Virginia.

Bacon's grounds for rebellion were twofold, but what they implied set them strangely at odds. Bacon asserted that the governor of the colony, William Berkeley, was unfit to rule, first, because he and his cohorts were disreputable (an argument from natural law and an elitist view of class); and second, because they had misspent the property and resources of those they had been appointed to govern and preserve (an argument from positive law and the liberties of the subject).[28] Behn follows history in sending Bacon to defeat, but her interpretation of events gives his demise and his cause a fascinating twist. She represents Bacon as a chivalric hero, his Indian ally Cavarnio as an illicitly deposed monarch, and their rebellion as sympathetic. She does not illustrate it as a cause to which right adheres; on her account, Bacon is a rebel, however noble, and Berkeley is to retain the power and authority of governor appointed to his post by the crown despite his vulgarity. Behn's vision of the alignment of social and political power in Virginia shows a degradation of legitimacy and the office of governor. It also shows that this degradation is not much minded, that the people so governed follow prudent policy, connive at malfeasance, and are generally genial citizens who look forward to wealth and gains in social rank.

Can one assume that Behn, a professed royalist, would have sympathized with Bacon's open criticism of the governor's party, and like Bacon, deplored the "sudden Rise" of those of "vile extractions"?[29] Can one guess that she also deplored Bacon's rebelliousness, evoking, as it did, memories of Cromwell? Finally, can one imagine that such disparate attitudes might cohere in a comprehensive acceptance of a new American style in which abuse by the higher powers is tolerated because it is hedged by apparently endless abundance and opportunity? So it would seem. If Behn is critical of her Americans, she mitigates much of her scorn: if unscrupulous, they are amiable; if ill-informed, they are open-minded; if keen to exploit ignorance of American ways, they are hospitable to strangers. Behn constructs the tragedies of Bacon and Cavernio so that they can be subsumed in the cheerfully comic effects of Ranter and her friends, to whom she sees that the future in Virginia belongs.

The editors of this volume have suggested that a vision of the Jamestown enterprise is implied by George Sandys's preoccupation with Ovid's *Metamorphoses*. On this account, the colony is featured as the site of a succession of sea-changes, if not random then at least continuous. Absent from this vision is, of course, what Strachey had responded to in the first years of the colony's settlement: Virgil's massively constructed sense of purpose, his concretization of a vast mythical history, his promise of a beneficent future for the new world he illustrated. From Ovid and Sandys we get a different and arguably paler vision. Less determined and positive, it outlines the terms not of translation but of endless change. It obscures the idea of a westward and civilizing movement (from Troy to Rome, from London to Jamestown) and rather attests to the fragility of civilization itself, always already old even as it is created anew. "There are always new things" (*nova sunt semper*) the poet declares, but in reality they are the things of the past: Time's "whole round of motion is gone through again (and again)" (*fitque, quod haut fuerat, momentaque cuncta novantur*).[30] We tend to read these words and the final book of the *Metamorphoses* in which they appear as Ovid's repudiation of epic. Correctly, I think. But we need to consider that Sandys may have understood them as paradox, as referring the familiar kind of novelty created by the new world English. Aware of what had gone and wary of what was to come, he saw that the world to which his fellows were committed was neither new nor old but both at once.

Notes

Foreword

1. John Pory to Sir Dudley Carleton, Sept. 30, 1619, in Virginia Company, *Records*, 3: 219–222, quote 220.
2. Pory, *Africa*.
3. Sluiter, "The '20. and Odd Negroes,'" 395–98.
4. See Striker, "Smith's Hungary and Transylvania," app. 1, and Striker and Smith, "Rehabilitation of Captain John Smith," 474–81.
5. *True Travels*, in Smith, *Complete Works*, 3: 156–57.
6. Potter, *Commoners, Tribute, and Chiefs*, chap. 4; Turner, "Protohistoric Interactions"; Rountree, "Summary and Implications," in *Powhattan Foreign Relations*, 206–28; Gleach, *Powhatan's World*, chap. 1. For similar findings in New England see Bragdon, *Native People*.
7. This interpretation was first suggested by Philip L. Barbour in *Pocahontas*, 23–26. For the events see Smith, *Generall Historie*, in *Complete Works*, 2: 150–51, 260–61; see also the marginal note about Smith's adoption in Samuel Purchas, *Purchas His Pilgrimes*, 2nd ed. (London, 1614), 757.
8. For recent studies of the Little Ice Age see Grove, *Little Ice Age*; Schwartz, "Little Ice Age"; Gribbin and Lamb, "Climatic Change," esp. 74; and Bryson and Murray, *Climates of Hunger*, 24–43.
9. Stahle, et al., "Jamestown Droughts," 564–67; Blanton, "Drought as a Factor," 74–81; Smith, *Proceedings* in *Complete Works*, 1: 246, 256.
10. This discussion draws on the unpublished work of Jean Howard and on Vitkus, ed., *Three Turk Plays*, quote from *The Renegado*, 256; Matar, *Turks, Moors, and Englishmen*; Squier, *John Fletcher*, 81–85; Hoenselaars, *Englishmen and Foreigners*, 174–78.

Introduction: Sea Changes

This chapter was written in close collaboration with Robert Appelbaum. We would like to thank Constance Jordan, Jerry Passanante, Dan Richter, and James Robertson for carefully reading drafts and offering suggestions and insights; their help greatly improved this essay.

1. Ovid, *Ovid's Metamorphosis Englished by G. S.* (1626), John Carter Brown Library, Providence, R.I.
2. Sandys apparently published the first five books of the translation in 1621, before he left for Virginia. After the publication of the complete translation in 1626, Sandys published a slightly emended, illustrated, and heavily annotated edition in 1632, which has become the standard version of this work. Davis, "Early Editions of George Sandys's 'Ovid.'" For a broader study of Sandys, see Ellison,

George Sandys. Rubin, *Ovid's Metamorphosis Englished,* focuses on Sandys's prosody and the sources for his 1632 annotations.

3. Quint, *Epic and Empire.* For a recent attempt to grapple with the relationship between humanist thought and the Virginia venture, see Fitzmaurice, *Humanism and America.*

4. Kupperman, Introduction, "Texts of Imagination and Empire," http://www.folger.edu/institute/jamestown/intro.htm.

5. See the essays in Rountree, ed., *Powhatan Foreign Relations.*

6. Smith, *A True Report* . . . (London, 1608), in *Complete Works,* 1: 53.

7. Virginia Company of London, Instructions Given by Way of Advice, Nov. 1606, in Barbour, *Jamestown Voyages,* 1: 49–54.

8. A useful summary of Native-European interactions in the seventeenth century is Gleach, *Powhatan's World,* 88–105. On the Jesuit mission, see also Hoffman, *New Andalucia,* 245, 262–65; he gives Don Luis's Algonquian name as Paquinquineo (184), and traces his Atlantic travels. Lewis and Loomie, *The Spanish Jesuit Mission in Virginia,* 44–49.

9. Kupperman, *Roanoke,* 122–24, 136–38.

10. On Smith's departure: Vaughan, *American Genesis,* 65. On the Pocahontas story, see Barbour's "Rescension of the Narratives of Smith's Captivity," in *Complete Works,* 1: 9–15, and his comments, 1: 416, and 2: 31. Barbour unpersuasively suggests that the story was suppressed in 1612 because it might have frightened off prospective settlers. Smith, *New England Trials* (1622): "God made Pocahontas the Kings daughter the meanes to deliver me," C2v (*Complete Works,* 1: 432). The story is only elaborated in the *Generall Historie,* 49 (*Complete Works,* 2: 151).

11. Gleach, *Powhatan's World,* 18, 106–22. Richter, *Facing East from Indian Country,* 69–78, 108–9. Perdue, "Columbus Meets Pocahontas."

12. Jackson et al., "Historical Overfishing and the Recent Collapse of Coastal Ecosystems."

13. Vaughan, *Genesis,* 29.

14. Ransome, "The Neck of Land in the 1620s," 365–66.

15. *Good Newes from Virginia, Sent from James his Towne this present moneth of March, 1623, by a Gentleman of that Country.*

16. Gordon Connell-Smith's study of English trade with Spain in the early Tudor period, *Forerunners of Drake,* suggests an intriguing alternative to the combative strategy of raiding Spanish colonial treasure fleets promoted by Drake and others.

17. On the Hakluyts, a basic reference is Quinn, ed., *The Hakluyt Handbook.* On Samuel Purchas, the Hakluyt's equally industrious, though less meticulous, successor, see Pennington, ed., *The Purchas Handbook.*

18. Canny, "Origins of Empire: An Introduction," in Canny, ed., *Origins of Empire,* 4.

19. Between 1585 and 1641, some 30,000 Scots and 70,000 Welsh and English migrants went to Ireland; while only about 6,000 British migrants went to New England by 1636, and about 8,000 to Virginia by 1640; Ohlmeyer, "Colonization Within Britain and Ireland," in Canny and Low, eds., *Origins of Empire,* 139–40. See also Games, *Migration,* and MacCarthy-Morrogh, *The Munster Plantation.*

20. Smith, Advertisements for the Unexperienced Planters (1631), 1, in *Complete Works,* 3: 269.

21. Ralegh, *Guiana,* ed. Whitehead, 127.

22. Lorimer, *English and Irish Settlement on the River Amazon.*

23. Murrin, "Beneficiaries of Catastrophe"; Diamond, *Guns, Germs, and Steel.*

24. Smith, *True Travels,* in *Complete Works,* 3: 156–57.

25. For an argument that James I was less open than Elizabeth to diplomatic rela-

tions with Morocco, see Croft, "New Light on Bates's Case." On later representations of North Africa, see Colley, "Barbary, Sex, and Power."

26. Indeed, a number of Romans themselves tempered this triumphalism with a sense of ambivalence: The "last of the free" speech that Tacitus puts into the mouth of Agricola, for instance, recognized that empire could also be the enemy of liberty.

27. For a discussion of one prominent English critic of this imperial vision, see Armitage, "John Milton: Poet Against Empire."

28. Strachey, *The True Repertory of the Wreck...*" in Purchas, *Pilgrimes*, 19: 62, margin. Canny, "England's New World and the Old," 154.

29. Shakespeare, *The Tempest*, Act I, Scene II. *OED*, s.v. "Sea," 23a.

30. Crosby, *Ecological Imperialism*.

31. Shakespeare, *Tempest*, Act I, Sc. 2.

32. Gray, *A Good Speed to Virginia* (1609), ed. Craven, C3v.

33. "Letter of Sir Francis Wyatt, Governor of Virginia, 1621–1626," *WMQ*, 2nd ser. 6 (1926): 118–19.

34. Horn, *English Society*, 175–76.

35. For summaries of Spanish efforts, see Emmer and Carrera Damas, eds., *Caribbean in the Long Sixteenth Century*. Thornton, "The African Experience of the '20. and Odd Negroes.'"

36. Ovid, *Ovid's Metamorphosis*, Englished by G. S., 3r, 325, JCB copy.

37. Ovid, *Ovid's Metamorphosis, Englished, Mythologized, and Represented in Figures* (1632), ed. Hulley and Vandersall, 649. Davis, "America in George Sandys' Ovid," 297–304.

Chapter 1. The Conquest of Eden: Possession and Dominion in Early Virginia

Epigraphs: Smith, *True Relation*; Johnson, *Nova Britannia*.

1. Quinn, *New American World*, 3: 34–59; Juricek, "Territorial Claims," 12; Andrews, *Trade, Plunder, and Settlement*, 141.

2. Quinn, *Explorers and Colonies*, 207–23; French, *John Dee*, 180, 197; Armitage, *Ideological Origins*, 105–8; Hakluyt and Hakluyt, *Writings* 2: 211, 2: 327–35, 347; Quinn, *New American World*, 3: 85, 89.

3. On this subject also see Blansett, "Virginia Mapped," this volume.

4. On European justifications for possessing America (and dispossessing its peoples) see Seed, *Ceremonies of Possession*, Green and Dickason, *Law of Nations*, and Muldoon, *Justification for Conquest*. Good summaries of English-Indian relations in early Virginia can be found in Fausz, "Aggression and Accommodation," 225–55, Axtell, *After Columbus*, 182–221, Gleach, *Powhatan's World*, 106–58, and Oberg, *Dominion and Civility*, 48–80; more generally, see Kupperman, *Indians and English*.

5. Quinn, *Roanoke Voyages*, 1: 82. Muldoon, "Alexander VI's *Inter Caetera*," 168–84. Differences between the languages of papal bulls and letters patent are explored in Seed, "Taking Possession," 200–205. The best short account of the Roanoke colonies is Kupperman, *Roanoke*.

6. Quinn, *Roanoke Voyages*, 1: 94, 96–97, 108.

7. Quinn, *Roanoke Voyages*, 1: 98–99, 112; Hariot, *Briefe and True Report*, intro. Hulton, 24–25.

8. Quinn, *Roanoke Voyages*, 1: 260–61, 266; Hariot, *Briefe and True Report*, intro. Hulton, 28–29.

9. Quinn, *Roanoke Voyages*, 1: 266–67; 2: 549–52; Kupperman, "Perceptions of Treachery," 263–87.

10. Andrews, *Trade, Plunder, and Settlement*, 245–55, 280–97.

11. Quinn, *Discovery of America*, 311–36. For narratives of the New England voyages of 1602, 1603, and 1605, see Quinn, *New American World*, 3: 345–91.
12. Barbour, *Jamestown Voyages*, 1: 13–21, 24–34.
13. See the "Instructions" issued by the London Company "by way of Advice" shortly before the expedition set out, Barbour, *Jamestown Voyages*, 1: 49–54.
14. Barbour, *Jamestown Voyages*, 1: 133–37. Descriptions of Powhatan culture can be found in Rountree, *Powhatan Indians* and Gleach, *Powhatan's World*, 22–60.
15. Barbour, *Jamestown Voyages*, 1: 80–81. The "Laake mentyoned by others" and "Mountaynes Apalatsi" (Appalachian Mountains) derive from Le Moyne's *Floridae Americae* and De Bry's *Collectiones Peregrinationum*.
16. Smith, *Complete Works*, 2: 138; Barbour, *Jamestown Voyages*, 1: 80–95, 98–102, 141. The textual complexity of early English descriptions of Virginia and native peoples encountered is considered by Fuller, *Voyages in Print*, 103–40; Hulme, *Colonial Encounters*, 137–73; and Mackenthun, *Metaphors of Dispossession*, 193–264.
17. Barbour, *Jamestown Voyages*, 1: 88.
18. Barbour, *Jamestown Voyages*, 1: 95–96.
19. Barbour, *Jamestown Voyages*, 1: 101–2.
20. Smith, *Complete Works*, 1: 29.
21. Earle, "Environment, Disease, and Mortality," 96–125; Barbour, *Jamestown Voyages*, 1: 143–45; Smith, *Complete Works*, 1: 33, 210.
22. Smith, *Complete Works*, 1: 33–57.
23. Smith, *Complete Works*, 2: 150–51.
24. Smith, *Complete Works*, 1: 224–29.
25. Smith, *Complete Works*, 2: 170–80.
26. Smith, *Complete Works*, 1: 226–27; 2: 207. The "Spanish Decades" refers to Richard Eden's translation of Anghiera, *Decades of the newe worlde* and "the Relations of Master Hackluit" to Hakluyt's *Principal Navigations*, (1598–1600).
27. Smith, *Complete Works*, 1: 232; 2: 172.
28. Smith, *Complete Works*, 2: 129, 168, 176–78.
29. Smith, *Complete Works*, 1: 143–77 (quote from 150–51).
30. Smith, *Complete Works*, 2: 206–7.
31. Quinn, *Roanoke Voyages*, 1: 279; 2: 531. John White reported, "our Savage Manteo, by the commandement of Sir Walter Ralegh, was christened in Roanoak, and called Lord thereof, and of Dasamongueponke, in reward of his faithfull service." Evidently, conversion to Anglicanism was not considered a necessary precondition for Wahunsonacock's coronation. For Irish precedents in the form of surrender and regrant arrangements with Gaelic chieftains conducted by the English in the 1540s, see Canny, "England's New World," 156–57.
32. Smith, *Complete Works*, 1: 236–37.
33. Smith, *Complete Works*, 1: 234. Some recent critics have argued that Wahunsonacock's speeches were merely a rhetorical device on the part of Smith to underline his opposition to Newport. "The discourse about European encounters with nonliterate peoples," writes Mackenthun, "was almost by definition monological, however dialogical it at times pretends to be by giving a voice to the natives," *Metaphors of Dispossession*, 206. On the other hand, Joyce Chaplin argues it "would be foolish to expect to recover transparent meaning from these texts, but it is equally damaging to give up on them entirely," *Subject Matter*, 27. See also Jehlen, "Smith's Unfinished Symphony," 676–92.
34. Smith, *Complete Works*, 1: 246.
35. Johnson, *Nova Britannia*; Gray, *Virginia*. For a review of the sermon literature of this period, see Parker, "Religion and the Virginia Colony," 245–70.
36. Barbour, *Jamestown Voyages*, 2: 265–66.

37. Virginia Company, *Records*, 3: 12–24.

38. Percy, "Trewe Relacyon," 266–67. And see Appelbaum, "Hunger," this volume.

39. Percy, "Trewe Relacyon," 269; Purchas, *Hakluytus Posthumus* (1905–7 ed.), 19: 44–45, 53–54.

40. The best account of the war is Fausz, "Abundance of Blood," 3–56; quotes from Percy, "Trewe Relacyon," 272, 276.

41. Hamor, *True Discourse*, 11–16; *Briefe Declaration*, 5.

42. On the importance of the "Massacre" in terms of the construction of English narratives of early Virginia, see Hulme, *Colonial Encounters*, 172. Gleach argues it was not the intention of the Powhatans to wipe out the English, or even to force them to abandon Virginia, but rather to restrict the spread of settlement. *Powhatan's World*, 158.

43. See Vaughan, "Expulsion of the Salvages," 57–84. Purchas, "Virginia's Verger," 157–64, 229–31.

44. Three studies that have stressed issues of trade, tribute, reciprocity, and cultural exchange in relation to early Anglo-Powhatan relations are Hulme, *Colonial Encounters*,137–73, Potter, "Virginia Algonquian Exchange," 151–72, and Quitt, "Trade and Acculturation," 227–58. For an emphasis on English aggression and violence, see Vaughan, "Expulsion of the Salvages," 57–84.

45. Smith, *Complete Works*, 1: 249.

Chapter 2. Powhatans Abroad: Virginia Indians in England

1. The term for Powhatan's territory first appears in William Strachey, *Virginia Britania*, 37. The tentative translation of "Tsenacommacah," its boundaries and approximate population, are discussed in Gleach, *Powhatan's World*, 22–28. In Gleach's geographical classification, the Rappahannocks—from whom the canoeists probably came—were on the edge of Tsenacommacah and "at a relatively late date" came under Powhatan's authority (24). This chapter includes them in Tsenacommacah. This generalization excludes English explorers who had briefly probed the Chesapeake Bay area before 1603 and limits the geographical context to tidewater Virginia. There had been earlier human exchanges in the Roanoke Island region, of course, where many English men and a few women settled for a year or more, and from where several Indians journeyed to England for a comparable time.

2. Any of three English expeditions on which little information survives could have seized Indians from the Chesapeake Bay area. The possibilities are discussed in Quinn, "'Virginians' on the Thames," 7–14, and Quinn, *Discovery of America*, 427–28.

3. "September 2, 1603. Virginia Indians in the Thames," in Quinn, *New American World*, 5: 166. After England's sphere of interest was named Virginia in 1584, the term Virginians applied almost exclusively to natives rather than colonists until the mid-eighteenth century.

4. English motives for luring Indians to England did not, of course, preclude distinct Indian motives. Indians may have wanted, for example, to observe a foreign country and culture or to gather information about potential colonial friends or enemies.

5. Manteo's and Wanchese's involvement with the Roanoke colonies and their trips to England are documented in Quinn, *Roanoke Voyages*. I discuss the four natives of the Roanoke region who went to England in Vaughan, "Ralegh's Indian Interpreters," 345–57. Manteo's role is perceptively assessed in Oberg, "Early Anglo-Indian Exchange."

6. "The names of all the men, women, and Children, which safely arrived in Virginia . . . 1587, in Hakluyt, *Principall Navigations*, 770–71; "Entries in Bideford Parish Register," in Quinn, *Roanoke Voyages*, 1: 495.

7. Keymis, *Guiana*, sigs. B2r, E2r, E3r; Harcourt, *Guiana*, 5–6, 13; and Vaughan, "Ralegh's Indian Interpreters," 358–75.

8. Quinn, *Discovery of America*, 421–22.

9. Rosier, *Prosperous Voyage*, sig. [E4r]; John Stoneman, "*The Voyage of M.* Henry Challons *intended for the North Plantation of* Virginia, 1606," in Purchas, *Haklytus Posthumus*, 4: 1832–37; Strachey, *Virginia Britania*, 164–73; Gorges, *America*, 8–9.

10. Hamor, *True Discourse*, 38.

11. Various versions of the exchange are in Smith, *True Relation*, sigs. D1v, [D4r]; Smith, *Proceedings of Virginia*, 19; Smith, *Generall Historie*, 52.

12. On Thomas Savage, see Smith, *True Relation*, sig. [D1v]; Smith, *Proceedings of Virginia*, 19, 27; Smith, *Generall Historie*, 52, 55, 115, 141–42; Hamor, *True Discourse*, 37; Strachey, *Virginia Britania*, 86; and minor references scattered through other documents on early Virginia. An undocumented sketch of Savage's life is Stiles, "Hostage to the Indians."

13. Smith, *Generall Historie*, 52–53.

14. Zorzi Giustinian to the Doge and Senate (4 June 1608) in UK, PRO, *CSP, Venice*, 137; Pedro de Zuniga to Philip III (26 June 1608) in Barbour, *Jamestown Voyages*, 1: 163. See also Emanuel van Meteren, *Commentarien*, in Barbour, *Jamestown Voyages*, 2: 274, where Namontack is referred to as a "hostage."

15. Jonson, *Works*, 5: 251.

16. Van Meteren, *Commentarien*, in Barbour, *Jamestown Voyages*, 2: 274; Smith, *Proceedings of Virginia*, 16.

17. Smith, *Proceedings of Virginia*, 45; Smith, *Generall Historie*, 68.

18. "Francis Magnel's Relation of the First Voyage and the Beginnings of the Jamestown Colony," in Barbour, *Jamestown Voyages*, 1: 154.

19. Smith, *Proceedings of Virginia*, 46–51; Smith, *Generall Historie*, 68–70.

20. Hamor, *True Discourse*, 37–38.

21. Smith, *Generall Historie*, 175. The attribution of authorship to this section of *Generall Historie* is on 174. Assuming for the moment that Smith's report was accurate, perhaps Matchumps kept the murder a secret in Bermuda to avoid execution there, whereas in Tsenacommacah he would more likely have provided retribution to Namontack's kin—a punishment in accord with American Indian emphasis on liability rather than culpability.

22. Purchas, *Hakluytus Posthumus*, 4: 1771. Purchas almost certainly got his information from Smith, whose works he often quoted or cited and on whose recollections he often relied.

23. See the table of ship arrivals and departures in Barbour, *Jamestown Voyages*, 1: xxiv.

24. Strachey's "A true reportory of the wracke, and redemption of Sir Thomas Gates Knight; upon, and from the Ilands of the Bermudas . . ." arrived in England in the early autumn of 1610 and circulated in manuscript, probably several copies, until published in 1625 in Purchas, *Hakluytus Posthumus*, 4: 1734–56. Strachey's history of early English colonization in America, complied in 1611–12, survives in three MS copies but remained unpublished until the nineteenth century. See Culliford, *Wiliam Strachey*, 151–91. Strachey's references to Matchumps and Namontack are in *Virginia Britania*, 34, 61–2, 98, 131.

25. Either Manteo or Wanchese, or both, may have been sent to England by his superiors and thus been intended to be an envoy and fact-finder. If Manteo was intended for such a role, his subsequent close alliance with the Roanoke colonists suggests that he no longer directly served his tribe.

26. Strachey, "True Reportory," in Purchas, *Hakluytus Posthumus*, 4: 1756; Strachey, *Virginia Britania*, 61.

27. First Charter of Virginia (10 April 1606), in Barbour, *Jamestown Voyages*, 1: 25; Gray, *Virginia*, sig. C2; Robinson, "Missions in Colonial Virginia," 152–59.

28. "Instructions . . . to Sir Thomas Gates" (May 1609), in Virginia Company, *Records*, 3: 14; "Instructions . . . [to] Sir Thomas West" (1609/10?), in Virginia Company, *Records*, 3: 27.

29. White, *Planters Plea*, 53–54. For conflations of Nanawack with Namontack, see, for example, Foreman, *Indians Abroad*, 18; and of Nanawack with Kainta, see Brown, *First Republic*, 134.

30. Virginia, Journals of the House of Burgesses, 10; Brinsley, Consolation for Our Schooles, 3, 15.

31. Purchas, *Pilgrimage*, 947; Chester, *Saynte De'nis*, 212.

32. The broadside has been rendered a number of times, most conveniently (though much reduced and reset) in Brown, *Genesis*, 2: following 760. A full-sized facsimile was published by the John Carter Brown Library in 1907. For the poem's broader context, see Vaughan, *Roots of American Racism*, 44–49.

33. Feest, "Virginia Indians in Pictures," 6–13; Feest, "Virginia Indian Miscellany," 3–5 (a reproduction of the van Meer painting faces p. 4). The translations of the captions into English are by Charles T. Gehring.

34. Purchas, *Pilgrimage*, 955; Lord Carew to Thomas Roe (20 June 1616) in Brown, *First Republic*, 234.

35. John Chamberlain to Dudley Carleton (22 June 1616), in Chamberlain, *Letters*, 2: 12; George Thorpe and others to George Yeardley (18 Feb. 1619), in Virginia Company, *Records*, 3: 136–37. Evidence on the two male Virginians is in Chester, *Saynte De'nis*, 213; and Mason, *St. Martin in the Fields*, 56, 180. Matachanna's presence in England is not documented in the sources; that Thomas's anonymous attendants were ill is attested in Rolfe to Sandys (June 8, 1617) in Virginia Company, *Records*, 3: 71.

36. Court Records for May 11, 1620, in Virginia Company, *Records*, 1: 338–39.

37. Court Records for May 11, 1620, in Virginia Company, *Records*, 1: 338–39; "Mony disbursede for Marye the virginian Mayd . . . ," and "To the Right Honourable the Earle of Southampton . . . ," in Ferrar Papers, reel 2, frame 282; "Att a Quarter Courte" (November 15, 1620), in Virginia Company, *Records*, 1: 427–28; "A Praeparative Court" (June 21, 1621), in Virginia Company, *Records*, 1: 485; "Att a Great and Generall Quarter Courte" (13 June 1621), in Virginia Company, *Records*, 1: 496.

38. "Moneys layd out for the two virginian mayds . . . ," in Ferrar Papers, reel 2, frame 292; Butler, *Bermudaes*, 271–72; Smith, *Generall Historie*, 197.

39. Butler, *Bermudaes*, 271, 284.

40. The nature of Pocahontas's experiences in England—her impressions of the place and the people, her true feelings about the sudden reacquaintance with John Smith, her expectations for future Powhatan-English relations—require more attention than can be given in this essay. Recent assessments include Rountree, *Pocahontas's People*, 62–64 and several discursive notes on 299–300; Faery, *Cartographies of Desire*, 16–17, 126–41; Strong, *Captive Selves*, 65–71; and Kupperman, *Indians and English*, 196–203. The fullest treatment of the Pocahontas legend is Tilton, *Pocahontas*.

41. Barbour, *Pocahontas*, 159, suggests that the "Bell" may have come from the sign of a bell, used perhaps in the inn's early days, or as a corruption of "bail" because the inn was close to the boundary (bail) of the district. The name "Belle Sauvage Inn," with its implied derivation from Pocahontas, was a later contrivance.

42. Purchas, *Hakluytus Posthumus*, 4: 1774; Smith to Queen Anne (early June 1616) in Smith, *Generall Historie*, 122.

43. Warrant of Edwin Sandys and John Wrothe to Thomas Smythe (10 Mar. 1617), in Ransome, "Pocahontas," 94.

44. Purchas, *Hakluytus Posthumus*, 4: 1774; "At a Quarter Court Held for Virginia" (30 Jan. 1622), in Virginia Compnay, *Records*, 1: 589.

45. Purchas, *Pilgrimage*, 954–56; Purchas, *Hakluytus Posthumus*, 4: 1774.

46. Smith, *Generall Historie*, 123.

47. Purchas, *Pilgrimage*, 954–55; Purchas, *Hakluytus Posthumus*, 4: 1774.

48. Purchas, *Hakluytus Posthumus*, 4: 1774.

49. Samuel Argall to Council for Virginia (?) (9 June 1617), in Virginia Company, *Records*, 3: 73–74.

50. The refutations of Tomocomo's criticisms of England could have come from colonists rather than Indians, but it seems unlikely that Opechancanough would have taken the foreigners' word over Tomocomo's without corroboration by one or more Powhatans with first-hand knowledge.

51. Purchas, *Hakluytus Posthumus*, 4: 1774; Smith, *Generall Historie*, 206.

52. Crashaw, *Sermon*, sig. E2.

53. Crashaw, *Sermon*, sigs. C3r-[C3v]. Implications that English observers gained respect for Indians they met, whether in America or England, is found, for example, in Rosier, *Prosperous Voyage*, E2v-E3 (five captives in 1605); and Purchas, *Hakluytus Posthumus*, 4: 1774 (Pocahontas).

54. Rosier, *Prosperous Voyage*, sigs. [E2r]-[E3v]; Gorges, *America*, 4.

55. Smith, *True Relation*, sig. [D4r]; Purchas, *Pilgrimage*, 954.

56. Hamor, *True Discourse*, 42.

Chapter 3. John Smith Maps Virginia: Knowledge, Rhetoric, and Politics

1. See Smith's *True Travels*.

2. Barbour, "Earliest Reconnaissance," 21.

3. For more information on the history of engraving, see Eisenstein, *Printing Press*.

4. See Eames, *Bibliography of John Smith*.

5. Approaches to the history of geography have changed enormously in the last two decades to resituate maps in terms of social and cultural matrices. See, for example, J. B. Harley, "Texts and Contexts in the Interpretation of Early Maps." Among Harley's most transformative (and often referenced) essays are: 'Deconstructing the map' and "Rereading the Maps of the Columbian Encounter" (Harley also contributed enormously to a "History of Cartography" project, a multivolume collection conceived with his friend and colleague David Woodward). See also Boelhower, "Inventing America"; Brotton, *Trading Territories*; Buisseret, *From Sea Charts to Satellite Images*; Edney, "Theory and the History of Cartography"; Helgerson, *Forms of Nationhood*; Lestringant, *Mapping the Renaissance World*; Mignolo, "Local Histories/Global Designs" and "Putting the Americas on the Map"; Schmidt, "Mapping an Empire"; Traub, "Mapping the Global Body"; and Woodward, "The Study of the History of Cartography."

6. "Map" had two meanings when Smith was working, one of which designated the verbal description of lands—particularly the description of an estate compiled and written by a surveyor, estate manager, or even the estate "husbandman." The text was generally comprised of an inventory of livestock, farm implements, and other "moveables"; the state of structures on site including cottages let to laborers. It was a general accounting of the estate much as an annual report might serve

investors today. A graphic map of the property was sometimes included, sometimes not, and was almost always a roughly measured, hand-sketched depiction of the topographical features from "wild" to "meadow" to "common" to "house."

7. The choice of Hole would hardly seem random as he had also engraved some of Christopher Saxton's chorographic maps.

8. See Williams, *Keywords*.

9. Williams, "Culture," 87.

10. See Haile, *Jamestown Narratives*, 157.

11. McCrary, *John Smith's Map*, 1.

12. McCrary, *John Smith's Map*, 1. For discussion of the search for the sea Newport was charged with, see Smith, *Complete Works*, 2:184.

13. As a measurement, fathoms are based on the generalized length of a man's outstretched arms—about six feet. Such standards reveal a residual embodiment of space, in which the sensual experience is transformed into a visual representation. Compare the more abstract mathematical measurements of geography that would eventually take precedence over the embodied human measure.

14. Archer, "A Relation," in Haile, *Jamestown Narratives*, 103.

15. Smith, *Complete Works*, 1:25.

16. Percy, "Discourse," in Haile, *Jamestown Narratives*, 96–97.

17. See Seed, "Taking Possession," 206–7.

18. Patricia Seed compares the subtle Spanish, Portuguese, and English religious and social agendas that infiltrate colonial claim and control in "Taking Possession," 183–209.

19. See McCrary, *John Smith's Map*, 3.

20. Smith complained that the Virginia Company sent settlers who expected "downe pillows, Tavernes and Alehouses" *Complete Works*, 2:128.

21. See Smith, *Complete Works*, 2:323–332. For a study of Smith's commonwealth model, see Canny, "To Establish a Common Wealthe."

22. For a complete analysis of the commodification of nature, see Mrozowski, "Colonization and Commodification" and Taylor, "Base Commoditie."

23. Smith, *Complete Works*, 2:212–13.

24. Smith, *Complete Works*, 1:343ff.

25. See Edwards, "Between 'Plain Wilderness,'" this volume.

26. The striking similarities of social structure described by Thomas Hariot (and engraved by de Bry) serve to invoke both identification and difference in the hearts of Englishman. *The Brief and True Report* depicts several Picts and compares them to Native Americans. The Picts had been overrun by the Anglo-Saxons, who saw the Picts as even more barbarous than themselves or the Celts, their other target. Thus, the Picts do not so much serve as a cheerful comparison of early Englishman to sixteenth-century American, as an allegorical measure of the English triumphs over their local barbarians. Another analysis of the relationships between early English ethnic groups and Native Americans depicted in Hariot is found in Hadfield, "Bruited Abroad."

27. See Spenser, *FQ*, 5.1.7; in which "She cause him to make experience upon wilde beasts" as quoted in OED, "experience."

28. OED, s.v. "Experience," definitions 2, 3, 6, 7a.

29. The less than charitable characterization of Smith's background comes from Barbour, "The Earliest Reconnaissance," 22. Barbour compares Strachey's formal education at Oxford and diplomatic career to Smith's ad hoc instruction in somewhat less refined situations.

30. Smith, *Complete Works*, 1:136.

31. Smith, *Complete Works*, 1:151.

32. For a full account of Smith's modest background as the son of a Lincolnshire "husbandman," see Beckwith, "Yeoman Background."

33. The title shifts from husbandman to steward to surveyor over the course of the sixteenth century with "surveyor" becoming dominant by the seventeenth century; the use of overseer was generally reserved for colonial plantations, where the primary function was managing investment—property—in labor (i.e., slaves, in practice) rather than landed property.

34. Taylor, "The Surveyor," 122.

35. Taylor, "The Surveyor," 122

36. As Edwards points out (Edwards, "Between 'Plain Wilderness,'" this volume), Smith's descriptions in the *Map of Virginia* highlight the land's fecundity, the ample irrigation sources, and space rendered in apparently precise figures of acreage (See *Complete Works*, 143–45). Smith's descriptions of "naturall inhabitants," often promoted as being proto-ethnographic, can also be situated in a long history of describing the people found on expeditions. See Hogden, *Early Anthropology*. Three years before Smith published the *Generall Historie*, Peter Heylyn's *Microcosmus . . . A treatise, historicall, geographicall, politicall, theological*, was published at Oxford.

37. See Helgerson, *Forms of Nationhood*, for a complete analysis of early modern chorographic maps in England.

38. The fourth state would have been made for the first run of Smith's *Generall Historie* (McCrary, *John Smith's Map*, 6).

39. Smith carried several navigational texts with him, some of which featured the most up-to-date revisions to older texts. Wright's *Errors of Navigation*, for example, placed mathematical emendations to old-fashioned reckoning on tables for quick reference. The person navigating would thus observe the position of the North Star and read a latitudinal position from it. Smith's compass, discussed below, may well have been a type of compendium dial that incorporated small navigational instruments and spheres inside a fold compass.

40. As Barbour suggests, "no name should be taken literally in its written or printed form unless we think we know (1) that the Indian who supplied it spoke distinctly, (2) that the Englishman who recorded it heard it correctly, and (3) what the phonetic value of the transcription is, three almost unsolvable problems." Barbour, "Smith's Chickahominy Voyages," 219.

41. Dee, Preface to *Euclid*, a.iiij.

42. Gregory, *Geographical Imaginations*, 389.

43. On the history and use of these nautical charts, see Pfederer,"Portolan Charts."

44. Samuel, *Island Stories*, 16.

45. Smith, *Complete Works*, 1. The *Generall Historie* contains a much abbreviated summary of this incident, in which Powhatan "more like a devill then [sic] a man with some two undrend more as blacke as himself, came unto him [Smith] and told him now they were friends," *Complete Works*, 2: 152.

46. Elsewhere, I have developed a reading of the interplay of Renaissance portraits of gentlemen (who strike the same pose and have a glistening sword rather than a bow and arrow), as well as suggested a connection with the Ditchley portrait of Queen Elizabeth, I, in which the monarch stands on a map. Blansett, "The Man in the Mirror," unpublished MS.

47. See Traub, "Mapping the Global Body." Her illustrations of maps of territories that include classified bodies include Champlain's map in *Les Voyages de la Nouvelle France Occidental*, 1612; Petrus Plancius, *World Map*, 1594; Pieter van den Keere, wall map of world, 1611; Jodocus Hondius, wall map of world, 1624; Willem Blaeu, *Le Theatre du monde, or Nouvel Atlas*, 1635; and several from Englishman John

Speed's analogical depiction of provincial and metropolitan English in his *Theatre of the Empire of Great Britain*, 1611.

48. "Contact zone," is Mary Louise Pratt's useful term to characterize the relationships between Western colonists and the people they encountered. She defines her use of "contact zone" as "an attempt to invoke the spatial and temporal copresence of subjects previously separated by geographic and historical disjunctures, and whose trajectories now intersect." Pratt, *Imperial Eyes*, 7.

49. See Hayes, "Defining the Ideal Colonist" for an analysis of elaborations and revisions to Smith's stories.

50. In the *Map of Virginia*, Smith resides with Powhatan for about three weeks; in the *General Historie* that time is doubled.

51. Smith, *Complete Works*, 2:147.

52. The compass dial is an encased directional compass, while a compass globe, also referred to as a compendium dial, includes a number of miniaturized navigation instruments and representations of the spheres in a small case (the compact collection being rather like a cookie-shaped version of our more familiar Swiss Army knives.)

53. Smith, *Complete Works*, 2:147.

54. As Read points out, Smith's cosmography owes more to Ptolemy than to Copernicus. See Read, "Colonialism and Coherence," 434 n. 12.

55. Smith, *Complete Works*, 2:147.

56. Smith, *Complete Works*, 2:147.

57. Myra Jehlen's discussion of Native American influences can be found in "History before the Fact." Peter Hulme's cogent response (and Jehlen's counter-response) also offer interesting discussions of recent postcolonial approaches to colonial texts.

Chapter 4. The Politics of Pathos: Richard Frethorne's Letters Home

The author would like to thank James Marrow, Ted Rabb, John Murrin, and the editors for comments on early drafts of this chapter; I am also grateful to Karen Kupperman and participants at a history department seminar at New York University, where I benefited from useful discussion.

1. Frethorne to Father and Mother, 1623, first published in its entirety by Kingsbury in 1935 from a manuscript then on deposit at the Public Record Office. In 1970, the manuscript was sold at auction and I have been unable to ascertain its current whereabouts; Parke-Bernet Galleries, "Papers of Nathaniel Rich," lot 21.

2. Brown, *First Republic*; Brown, *Genesis*; Brown, *English Politics*; Wertenbaker, "Patrician and Plebeian"; Wertenbaker, Virginia.

3. Andrews, *Colonial Period*, 131n.

4. Bailyn, *Peopling*; Morgan, *American Slavery*.

5. Powell, *Pory*, 50. Pory was a good example of "an emerging class of semi-professional journalists who ranged from well connected men of affairs, such as John Chamberlain, to the sort of anonymous hack caricatured in Ben Jonson's 1620 play "News from the World." Cust, "News and Politics", 135.

6. Undated, unsigned PRO document ca. 1621, cited in Powell, *Pory*, 52.

7. Sir George Yeardley to Sir Edwin Sandys, June 7, 1620, Virginia Company, *Records*, 3: 298.

8. Letter writers in London first mention the attack in mid-July. The official company response to the bad news was sent to the colony Aug. 1, and a commemorative poem was issued Sept 11.

9. Noël Hume and Noël Hume, *Archaeology*, 1: 32.

10. Games, *Migration*, 42.

11. Bristol was an important port of embarkation, but debate continues over the enthusiasm of Bristol merchants for the Virginia colony. McGrath, "Bristol and America."

12. Canny, "Permissive Frontier," 25.

13. Gethyn-Jones, *George Thorpe*, analyzes their joint venture based on the "Smyth of Nibley Papers."

14. Broadway, "John Smyth."

15. Elrington, "Church Livings," 94. It was so small that church officials concluded it should be merged with the neighboring parish of Saul.

16. Franklin, "Malaria."

17. Elrington, "Church Livings," and Herbert, *Gloucester*, 10: 169.

18. Bigland, *Gloucester*, 625 is the source for the information on Frethorne in this paragraph. Elrington, in the new *VCH Gloucester*, p. 160, corrects Bigland and traces the descent of the manor from a Clifford to Baily in 1655.

19. Elrington, *Gloucester*, 163 is the source for the information in this paragraph.

20. See Edwards, "Plain Wilderness," this volume.

21. The introduction of tobacco by London merchants and investors in 1619 is traced in Thirsk, "Mutual Aid in Tewkesbury."

22. The King had announced "A Proclamation to restraine the planting of tobacco in England and Wales" on December 30, 1619 but held it in abeyance until the shareholders approved the additional tax of 9p. per pound which the company voted at a special meeting on January 8, 1620. He issued "A Proclamation for restraint of the disordered trading for Tobacco" on June 29, 1620, the day after the annual meeting of the company confirmed this payment. See Larkin and Hughes, *Proclamations of James I*, 1: 457, 479.

23. *Harry Hangman's Honour* (London, c. 1655) made a plea that the government cease its interference with the tobacco planters in Gloucestershire in order to protect the colonies; a plea repeated by Reynell Carew, in *The True English Interest* (London, 1674), cited in Arents, et al., *Tobacco*.

24. UK, PRO, CSP Domestic, James I, 103, no. 42.

25. Council in Virginia to the Virginia Company of London, April, 1622, Virginia Company, *Records*, 3: 615.

26. Supple, *Commercial Crisis*, 56.

27. Supple, *Commercial Crisis*, 56.

28. Noël Hume and Noël Hume, *Archaeology*, 1: 33 conclude that because Frethorne spelled badly ("Harrod" for Harwood) he did not know the head of Martin's Hundred very well and wrote home to inform his parents of the name of his master. It should be noted that the extant evidence of Frethorne's letter is a contemporary copy, not an autograph manuscript. We therefore cannot be sure how he spelled his master's name.

29. Noël Hume, *Discoveries*, 12.

30. Berkeley Hundred, by contrast, had 8,000 acres.

31. The middle-aged lawyer and poet Richard Martin (1570–1618) signed documents for Virginia in 1610 and 1616, both before and after his notable defense of the company in the 1614 Parliament which was standing room only.

32. Wolstenholme was a member of the Virginia Council, a founder of the Northwest Passage Company, a supporter of Henry Hudson's voyage to find a northwest passage in 1610, and a member of the East India Company. Both he and Richard Martin were early investors in the Bermuda Company.

33. Wolstenholme's daughter was to marry the nephew of Sir Thomas Smith, Sandys's predecessor as head of the company. Smith's son married Warwick's

daughter, his daughter married Alderman Johnson. Wolstenholme had stood against Edwin Sandys in the election of 1619 when Smith declined to run again; Alderman Johnson, Smith's son-in-law, lost the deputyship to John Ferrar.

34. John Wolstenholme and his associates received a new charter from the company in January 1622 when some of the early investors in Martin's Hundred did not want to proceed.

35. Noël Hume and Noël Hume, *Archaeology*, fig. 89, nos. 40/40A.

36. Noël Hume, *Discoveries*, 31.

37. Noël Hume, *Discoveries*, 3. Noël Hume and Noël Hume, *Archaeology*, 356–57, fig. 42.

38. George Thorpe to John Smyth, Dec. 19, 1620, "Smyth of Nibley Papers," 33. Virginia Company, *Records*, 3: 417.

39. Peter Arundell to John Smyth, Jan. 1622, "Smyth of Nibley papers," 37, Virginia Company, *Records*, 3: 589. See Cust, *News*, cited in note 5 above.

40. Thorpe to Smyth, December 19, 1620.

41. Earle, "Environment, Disease, and Mortality," blames salt poisoning for the high mortality.

42. McCartney, *People Associated with Jamestown*.

43. Sluiter, "'20. And Odd Negroes'" and Thornton, "African Experience."

44. Noël Hume, *Discoveries*, 52, and Noël Hume, *Martin's Hundred*. She was dubbed "granny" because she had lost her molars.

45. Archaeologists have just begun to dig on the site of the Popham colony: it has been undisturbed since the colonists left in 1608.

46. New York Public Library, Arents collection, MSS. Add. 6550, signed autograph letter of George Calvert, Lord Baltimore, Newfoundland August 18, 1629 announcing his intention of leaving Newfoundland and going to Virginia to raise tobacco.

47. Robert Bennett to Edward Bennett, June 9, 1623, Virginia Company, *Records*, 4: 221.

48. Stith, *Settlement of Virginia*, 305.

49. Virginia Company, *Records*, 4: 41; List of Adventurers, 1618?, Virginia Company, *Records*, 3: 80, 319. Bateman invested £25 (two shares).

50. The King repeatedly indicated that he wanted merchants to replace the Sandys, Southampton, and Ferrar administration elected by the shareholders.

51. Virginia Company, *Records*, 4: 80.

52. Brown, *Genesis*, 2: 826.

53. Rich, *Papers*, 43. The colonists had high standards for gunsmiths; at Martin's Hundred they used the work of the royal gunner to Charles I.

54. Noël Hume and Noël Hume, *Archaeology*, 1: 34.

55. Chamberlain to Carleton, June 19, 1623, Chamberlain, *Letters*, 2: 502.

56. Sir Edwin Sandys had been the chief executive of the Virginia Company ("treasurer") until the king demanded he not be reelected in 1622. His good friend Henry Wriosthely, the Earl of Southampton, then took over the nominal leadership with Sandys playing an active but unofficial role as the two men continued to work closely together continuing the earlier policies.

57. *Good News from Virginia* (London, 1623). A copy was kept with the Manchester papers along with Frethorne's letters; the copy reproduced in a facsimile edition by the University of Virginia Library in 1971 was formerly owned by Sir Nathaniel Rich.

58. In the nineteenth century these groups were identified as the "patriot" and "crown" parties, but that is misleading and the terms are no longer used.

59. "Notes of Letters from Virginia," May–June 1623, Virginia Company, *Records*, 4: 161.

60. Butler left Bermuda without permission eight days before the arrival of the new governor, because of questions over his treatment of a Spanish wreck. In February 1623 the Somers Island Company officials in London reported to the Privy Council that they had not known about Butler's departure and that he did not go in a company boat.

61. Stith, *Settlement*, 310–11.

62. Discourse of the Old Company, April, 1625, Virginia Company, *Records*, 4: 536–37.

63. John Smyth to Mr. Berkeley, June 1, 1620, "Smyth of Nibley Papers" 15, Virginia Company, *Records*, 4: 293.

64. Alsop, *Maryland*, 99.

65. Hotten, *Original Lists*.

66. Carter's Grove, now under the auspices of the National Parks Service, is open to the public and is the site of ongoing archaeological excavations.

67. Kupperman, "Apathy and Death."

Chapter 5. The Specter of Spain is John Smith's Colonial Writing

1. Smith, *General History*, ed. Barbour, 2: 145. All Smith Quotations are from *Complete Works*, ed. Barbour, 3 vols.

2. See Meinig, *Shaping of America*, especially 3–244.

3. See Geertz, *Interpretation of Cultures*: "Cultural acts, the construction, apprehension, and utilization of symbolic forms, are social events like any other; they are as public as marriage and as observable as agriculture," 91.

4. See Hadfield, *Literature, Travel, and Colonization*, 85–104; Powell, *Tree of Hate*; Maltby, *Black Legend*; Fernández Retamar, "Black Legend"; Juderías, *Leyenda negra*.

5. See Geertz, *Interpretation of Cultures*, "Culture is public because meaning is," 12.

6. On "Hispanophobia's" relation to the Black Legend, see Weber, *Spanish Frontier*, 336.

7. Although the French had been active in the St. Lawrence Valley on and off since the 1530s, and had attempted to found colonies in Brazil (1555) and Florida (1562), their first permanent settlement at Quebec (1608) was virtually contemporaneous with Jamestown. See Baumgartner, *France*, 277–80. Portuguese plantation in Brazil had begun as early as the 1530s. See Fausto, *Brazil*, 9–13. Significant English and Dutch colonial activity awaited the seventeenth century.

8. Hakluyt, "Preface to the Second Edition, 1598," in *Principle Navigations* (1598–1600), xl.

9. See Hart, *Representing the New World*, 5, and passim; see also Scanlan, *Colonial Writing*, 38–67.

10. After Geertz, *Interpretation of Cultures*, 5, 12.

11. Quoted in Lange, "Unsettling Discoveries," 77. For typical restatements of the topos see Nöel Hume, *Virginia Adventure*, 358; and Billings, *Old Dominion*, vii.

12. On the "White Legend," see Gibson, *Black Legend*, 3–27; see also, Hart, *Representing the New World*, 5, 279.

13. See Schmidt, *Innocence Abroad*, 17–23.

14. Anghiera [Peter Martyr], *Decades of the Newe World*, 50. See also Hart, *Representing the New World*, 62.

15. See Schmidt, *Innocence Abroad*, 71; Pagden, *Ideologies of Empire*, 74–75.

16. The Latin phrase is from Tacitus. See Pagden, *Ideologies of Empire*, 13.

17. See Banerjee, "The White Othello," this volume.

18. See Ralegh, *Guiana*, 125–28.

19. Góngora, *Spanish America*, 207.
20. Gómara, *Cortés*, 24–25. Gómara's history appeared in English as early as *The Pleasant Historie of the East India, Now Called New Spayne*, trans. T. Nicholas (London, 1578).
21. See Griffin, "Un-sainting James," 58–99.
22. Góngora, *Spanish America*, 209.
23. Góngora, *Spanish America*, 209–10.
24. Góngora, *Spanish America*, 210. See also Baudott, "Amerindian Image," 375–400; Cervantes, *Devil*, 5–33.
25. Quoted in Góngora, *Spanish America*, 210–11.
26. See Allen, *Admonition*, xlv–xlix. See also Pagden, *Ideologies of Empire*, 13.
27. See Headley, "Campanella," 245. See also Hilgarth, *Mirror of Spain*, 304–7; Tanner, *Last Descendant of Aeneas*, 145.
28. See Schmidt, *Innocence Abroad*, 25–30.
29. On Benzoni, see Elliott, *Old World*, 95–96; Gibson, *Black Legend*, 78–89. See also Montanus, *Holy Inquisition*. For commentary, see Hilgarth, *Mirror of Spain*, 233, and Schmidt, *Innocence Abroad* 79. On Le Challeaux, see Schmidt, *Innocence Abroad*, 43–6, and Hart, *Representing the New World*, 70–82.
30. See Las Casas, *Devastation of the Indies*, 125.
31. On the propaganda campaign of William of Orange, see Schmidt, *Innocence Abroad*, 86–88; Hilgarth, *Mirror of Spain*, 311–17.
32. On Dutch and German uses of Las Casas, see Schmidt, *Innocence Abroad*, 96–99, 115–22; Keen, *Aztec Image*, 162–66.
33. William I, *Apology*, O2 (probably written by the Huguenot Pierre Loyseleur). According to Schmidt, *Innocence Abroad*, 84–86, and Hilgarth, *Mirror of Spain*, 313–15, this argument from ethnicity was first engineered by the Calvinist nobleman Philip Marnix of Saint-Aldegonde (1540–98). On Spain in the Dutch public mind, see Schama, *Embarrassment of Riches*, 83–93; Schmidt, *Innocence Abroad*, passim.
34. On English miscegenation obsessions, see Banerjee, "The White Othello," this volume. See also Griffin, "Ethos to Ethnos," 69–116. For French contributions to this discourse, see Parmellee, *Good Newes from Fraunce*, passim.
35. After Walker Connor, I conceptualize "nationality" as the tendency toward self- identification, whereas "ethnicity" suggests the construction of "others." See "Nation Is a Nation," 45–46. There is evidence that early moderns used the term "ethnicke" in this way. See Montanus, *Holy Inquisition*, Aij.
36. On the Anglo-Spanish-Portuguese context, see Griffin, "Thomas Kyd," 202–22.
37. See Parker, *Grand Strategy of Philip II*, 170–71.
38. Las Casas, *Spanish Colonie*, q2a (my italics).
39. See Hakluyt, *Western Planting*, ed. Taylor, especially 257–65.
40. See Parker, *Strategy of Philip III*, 166. See also Van Langan, *Prince Anthonie*.
41. See Neale, *Elizabeth and Her Parliaments*, especially 298–302, for various invasion threats, and 335–51, for famine and other economic troubles. On the Elizabethan propaganda onslaught, see Woodfield, *Surrepititious Printing*, and Parmellee, *Good Newes from Fraunce*, passim.
42. On allegory in the Le Moyne/De Bry illustrations, see Scanlan, *Colonial Writing*, 52–67. See also Conley, "De Bry's Las Casas," 103–31.
43. See Virginia, Council, "Council in Va. To Council of Va., 22 June 1607," 79–80.
44. See Kupperman, *Indians and English*, 12.
45. As many as 50,000 English troops saw action on the continent between 1585 and 1597. See Appleby, "Colonization" 56, 66.

46. On access to the Indies during these negotiations, see Allen, *Philip III*, 134–36.
47. Virginia, Council, *Declaration of Purpose*, 343.
48. Strachey, *Virginia Britania*, 9.
49. See Kupperman, *Indians and English*, 203.
50. See Quinn, *Roanoke Voyages*, 717–838.
51. Quoted in Hoffman, *Roanoke Voyages*, 34.
52. See Gradie, "Powhatans." For James I's Spanish pension, see Akrigg, *Jacobean Pageant*, 65.
53. Molina remained in Jamestown for three years. For his correspondence of July 8, 1613, April 30, 1614, and June 14, 1614, see Brown, *Genesis*, 652–54, 740–43, 743–45.
54. Maguel, "Report," 156. The Irishman Francis Maguel is also referred as "Magnel," "Maguer," or "Maguire" in various sources.
55. Percy, *Trewe Relacyon*, 279. On the Elizabethan coining, "to Hispaniolize," and its variants, see Griffin, "Ethos to Ethnos," 71.
56. Wingfield, "Discourse," 229.
57. On the capture and release of John Clark, see Haile, *Jamestown Narratives*, 44–45; see also "Report of the Voyage to Virginia," in Brown, *Genesis*, 511–22 and the "Declaration of the Englishman [John Clark] from Virginia," Haile, *Jamestown Narratives*, 542–48.
58. On Wingfield's "disgrace," see Smith, *General History*, 3: 2, 145. For the execution of Kendall, see Smith, *True Relation*, 1: 41.
59. Quoted in Gleach, *Powhatan's World*, 76.
60. On the exemplary punishment of the French in 1564 at Fort Caroline, Florida, see Weber, *Spanish Frontier*, 68–69; see also Meinig, *Shaping of America*, 27.
61. Smith, *General History*, 3: 12, 219.
62. See Griffin, "Burden of Comedy." See also, Boxer, *Church Militant*, especially 39–48.
63. Hakluyt, *Western Planting*, ed. Taylor, 211.
64. Hariot, *Brief and True Report*, ed. Hulton, 25.
65. Council of Va. "Instructions to Thomas Gates," in Quinn, *Extension of Settlement*, 213. See also Gleach, *Powhatan's World*, 69.
66. See Maguel, "Report," 154.
67. Crashaw, *Sermon Preached in London*, D4.
68. Quoted in Williamson, "Scots, Indians, and Empire" 63; Crashaw, *Sermon Preached in London*, C6.
69. Strachey, *Virginia Britania*, 6.
70. See Scanlan, *Colonial Writing*, 53–58.
71. Percy, *Trewe Relacyon*, 271–72.
72. Percy, *Trewe Relacyon*, 273.
73. Hakluyt, *Divers Voyages*, ed. Taylor, 178.
74. Gleach, *Powhatan's World*, 67–68.
75. Virginia, Council, "Instructions to Thomas Gates," 213.
76. See Gleach, *Powhatan's World*, 144.
77. "Council in Virginia to the Virginia Company, January 20, 1623," quoted in Kupperman, *Indians and English*, 224. On the end of Thorpe's educational efforts and the Great Massacre of 1622, see Gleach, *Powhatan's World*, 147–58.
78. Virginia, Council, "Instructions to Thomas Gates," 215.
79. See "Master Stockhams relation," in Smith, *General History*, 2: 285–86; see also Kupperman, *Indians and English*, 139.
80. See Gleach, *Powhatan's World*, 70.

81. See Gleach, *Powhatan's World*, 69.
82. On the conversion of Manteo, see Kupperman, *Indians and English*, 188, and Gleach, *Powhatan's World*, 103.
83. Whitaker to Gouge, 59–60. On Pocahontas's conversion, see Gleach, *Powhatan's World*, 134–35, and Kupperman, *Indians and English*, 196–203.
84. See Gleach, *Powhatan's World*, 56, passim.
85. See Gleach, *Powhatan's World*, 55–56.
86. For a thick description of what has commonly been thought of as Don Luis's "betrayal," see Gleach, *Powhatan's World*, 90–97.
87. See Axtell, *European and the Indian*, especially 43–86. On "accommodation," see O'Malley, *First Jesuits*, 111–12 and passim.
88. De la Ware et al., "Declaration of Purpose," 339.
89. "Letter of Sir Francis Wyatt, Governor of Virginia, 1621–26," quoted in Horn, "Tobacco Colonies," 175–76.
90. Virginia, Council, *True Declaration*, 6.
91. Góngora, *Spanish America*, 210–11.
92. Gleach, *Powhatan's World*, 64–5.
93. Gleach, *Powhatan's World*, 65.
94. Smith, *To Erect a Plantation*, 3: 272.
95. Smith, *Description of New England*, 1: 350.
96. Hakluyt ed., *De Orbe Novo Peter Martyris* (Paris, 1587), quoted in Armitage, *Ideological Origins*, 76.
97. Meinig, *Atlantic America*, 46; Sacks, *Widening Gate*, 15, 19.
98. Hakluyt, *Western Planting*, ed. Taylor, 218, 222.
99. While Armitage, *Ideological Origins*, rejects the possibility of Hakluyt's apocalypticism by placing him in a tradition of "Protestant scholasticism," 74, I would argue that profit and prophecy were not mutually exclusive, and that many "puritans" retained much scholastic method and authority. Thus classicism and national election often merged, as in the writing of Edmund Spenser and Thomas Kyd, for example. See Griffin, "Thomas Kyd," 196–208.
100. See Armitage, *Ideological Origins*, 71.
101. Hakluyt, *Western Planting*, ed. Taylor, 219–20.
102. See Braudel, *Perspective of the World*, 441–42.
103. When the English began to cultivate tobacco, they found that Spain also had the advantage in this area. See Gleach, *Powhatan's World*, 139, and Horn, "Tobacco Colonies," 176.
104. Though many contemporaries sensed that England had grown overpopulated, Chaplin, *Subject Matter*, has pointed to probable population *decrease* as a result of the recurrence of the plague (117–30). Armitage, *Ideological Origins*, restates the traditional view: "The necessity of colonization arose from simultaneous overpopulation at home, and the contraction of English markets abroad," 74. Concurring are Braudel, *Everyday Life*, 33; Lloyd, *British Empire*, 17–19; Neale, *Elizabeth and Her Parliaments*, 337–40.
105. Smith, *Description of New England*, 1: 350.
106. Smith, *Advertisements*, in *Works*, 3: 277.
107. On the fishing and shipbuilding industries in the United Provinces, see Braudel, *Perspective of the World*, 188–93. On the opposition of English fishing interests to permanent colonial settlement, as well as the insufficiency of trade in raw materials, see Solow, "Slavery and Colonization," 25–27.
108. See Kupperman, Introduction, Smith, Captain John Smith, 21.
109. Kupperman, Introduction, 21.
110. Smith, *General History*, 2: 474.

111. Smith, *Description of New England*, in *Works*, 1: 327.

112. On Iberia's early lead in the emerging Atlantic world, see Phillips, Jr., "Background of Slavery," 43–61.

113. For the Dutch "world war" against Spain and Portugal, see Emmer, "Second Atlantic System," 75–88. On the Dutch SeaBeggars (Watergeuzen or Gueux de Mer), see Parker, *Dutch Revolt*, 121–22, 128–37; Geyl, *Netherlands*, 113–18; and Schmidt, *Innocence Abroad*, passim.

114. Smith, *Advertisments*, in *Works*, 3: 301.

115. Meinig could be describing Jamestown: "Small islands lying off a productive mainland were the ideal geographic base for such a system: secured by a natural moat, easily defended by a small garrison yet readily accessible alike to river, coastal, and ocean vessels; a natural compound for slave and indentured labor; an obvious unit for separate political administration. It was a geographic type of empire that was therefore fragmentary, shallow in continental impact, irregular in territorial hierarchy. Because a large share of Europeans came as sojourners rather than settlers, assigned for a tour of duty or attracted by the hope of profit, it was a system that tended to foster spatial and class segregation rather than the integration of local peoples . . . and there was little hope of or desire to invest in the comprehensive control of all islands or coasts as the Spanish had attempted" (Meinig, *Shaping of America*, 62).

116. See Geyl, *Netherlands*, 234.

117. Smith, *Description of New England*, 1: 327.

118. See Smith, *Description of New England*, 1: 328.

119. Hakluyt, *Principal Navigations* (1598–1600), xl, lxvi. On the expectation of mineral wealth, see Smith, *Captain John Smith*, 20.

120. Smith, *Map of Virginia*, 1: 156.

121. Smith, *Proceedings of Virginia*, in *Works*, 1: 257.

122. Smith, *Proceedings of Virginia*, in *Works*, 1: 257.

123. This perspective was common among the nineteenth-century advocates of Manifest Destiny and slavery apologists. See, for example, Davis, "Naval Appropriation Bill," 4: 523, 71. See also Sweet, "Iberian Roots," 143–66.

124. For a more internationalist approach, see Howe, *American History*, 1–8. See also Griffin, "Burden of Comedy."

125. Hakluyt, *Western Planting*, ed. Taylor, 264, 217.

126. Braudel, *Everyday Life*, 318.

127. Braudel, *Everyday Life*, 317.

128. Ben Jonson, *Alchemist* 4.4.7–15.

129. On Spain in Ralegh's colonial writing, see Montrose, "Work of Gender," 194.

130. See Leonard, *Books of the Brave*, especially 25–35.

131. Hakluyt, *Western Planting*, ed. Taylor, 257.

132. Smith, *Description*, 1: 343, 1: 349. The fullest realization of this historiographic commonplace is probably James Anthony Froude, *History of England*.

133. Smith, *General History*, 2: 207.

134. Eriksen, *Ethnicity and Nationalism*, distinguishes processes of "complementarisation," which recognize difference as "an asset" in order to produce a "shared field" for "We-You" relationships, from the process of "dichotomisation," which "essentially expresses an Us-Them kind of relationship," 26–28.

135. Smith, *General History*, 2: 315.

Chapter 6. The White Othello: Turkey and Virginia in John Smith's True Travels

1. The English play (London, 1605) bearing his name stages many aspects of Stukeley's life. See below. See also Canny, *Kingdom and Colony*, 1; Quinn, *North*

America, 244–45; and Iwanisziw, "Diplomacy and Drama," this volume. Quinn's work highlights figures such as Walter Ralegh, Humphrey Gilbert, Ralph Lane, and Thomas White; their lives impinged on Irish and American colonization. See Quinn, ed., *Voyages . . . of . . . Gilbert*; and Quinn, ed., *Roanoke Voyages*.

2. Matar, *Turks, Moors, and Englishmen*, 97–98.

3. Knolles, *Historie of the Turkes*; Lewis, *Muslim Discovery*, 32; Parker, "Introduction" to *Tales of the Orient*, 1–35.

4. Lewis, *Muslim Discovery*, 32. On Anglo-Ottoman relations, see Chew, *Crescent and the Rose*; Matar, "Mediterranean Captivity," 1–52. Barbary pirates also raided English coastal towns, while in 1617 a Turkish pirate ship was captured in the Thames estuary. See Vitkus, "Introduction" to the *Three Turk Plays*, 3–4.

5. Matar, *Turks, Moors, and Englishmen*, 94.

6. Captivity narratives by John Fox (1589), Richard Hasleton (1595), John Rawlins (1622), William Okeley (1875), Thomas Phelps (1685), and Joseph Pitts (1704) popularized this genre. See the recent compilation of captivity narratives in Vitkus, ed., *Piracy, Slavery, and Redemption*.

7. Reissued in 1610, 1621, 1631, 1638, and 1687, Knolles's lavishly produced folio of over 1150 pages was grand but not the only chronicle of the Turks. Knolles profited from earlier compilations such as Newton's *Saracens* (London, 1575).

8. Seelye, *Prophetic Waters*, 60.

9. Kupperman, "Introduction" to *Captain John Smith*, 3; and Kupperman, Foreword, this volume.

10. Barbour, "Introduction" to *The True Travels*, 3: 125–36. For details of the conflicts in the region, see Braudel, *Mediterranean World*.

11. Smith, *True Travels*, 3: 172.

12. Smith, *True Travels*, 186, 200–201. Other Englishmen endured similar captivity and escape from slavery. Edward Webbe was one of the many Christian slaves freed through the intervention of Sir William Harborne, Queen Elizabeth's envoy to the Ottoman Empire. See Chew, *Crescent and the Rose*, 155–56.

13. Smith, *To Erect a Plantation*, 3: 269; also Seelye, *Prophetic Waters*, 63.

14. On Smith's response to the Spanish, see Eric Griffin, "Specter of Spain," this volume.

15. Smith, *True Travels*, 208–9.

16. Moryson, *Itinerary*, (1907–8) 1: 219.

17. On the *Famous History* in this context, see Iwanisziw, "Diplomacy and Drama," this volume.

18. See Vitkus, "Introduction" to *Three Turk Plays*, 2.

19. Quotations from *Lust's Dominion* are cited by page numbers. See also Tamora's cross-racial offspring, "A joyless, dismal, black and sorrowful issue!" a child "as loathsome as a toad / Amongst the fair-fac'd breeders of our clime" in *Titus Andronicus* (4.2.66–68).

20. See the "unmatchable courage" and wildness of mastiffs in Shakespeare, *Henry V* 3.7.141, and restrained women like "English mastiffs, that grow fierce with tying" in Webster, *Duchess of Malfi* 4.1.12–15.

21. Rolfe to Dale, 63–64.

22. Smith, *General Historie*, ed. Barbour, 2: 41–42, 151–52.

23. Moryson, *Itinerary*, 1: 216. See also Matar, *Turks, Moors, and Englishmen*, 99.

24. Blount, *Levant*, 13.

25. Herbert, *Travels*, 18.

26. Smith, *True Travels*, 190.

27. Smith, *General Historie*, ed. Barbour, 2: 120.

28. Hall, *Things of Darkness*, 123–24.

29. Helgerson, *Forms of Nationhood*.
30. Anderson, *Imagined Communities*, 6.
31. Smith, *True Travels*, 3: 155–56. Smith was possibly reading Machiavelli's *The Art of War* (trans. Peter Whitehorne) and one of two translations of Aurelius: Antonio de Guevara's *Dial of Princes*, or *The Book of Marcus Aurelius*. See Barbour, *Three Worlds*, 14.
32. Smith, *True Travels*, 3: 174–75.
33. Smith, *General Historie*, ed. Barbour, 2: 226.
34. Smith, *General Historie*, ed. Barbour, 2: 411, 421. See also Seelye, *Prophetic Waters*, 62.
35. Smith, *General Historie*, ed. Barbour, 2: 47.
36. Donne, *Sermons*, 269, 277, 272.
37. Smith, *General Historie*, ed. Barbour, 189–90.
38. Lemay, "John Smith," 3–16; and Seelye, *Prophetic Waters*, 57–95.
39. Smith, *True Travels*, 3: 240.
40. Vitkus, "Introduction" to *Three Turk Plays*, 4, 29–30.
41. Matar, "Mediterranean Captivity," 2.
42. Smith, *True Travels*, 3: 240–41.

Chapter 7. England, Morocco, and Global Geopolitical Upheaval

Epigraph quoted from Heywood, *Fair Maid of the West Part II* (5.4.179–80). *Part II* was published with *Part I* in 1635 but written some 25 or 30 years after the first part, which dates from the turn of the century.

1. The studies of Moroccan-English history to which I refer include: Castries, *Histoire du Maroc;* Abun-Nasr, *Maghrib;* Julien, *North Africa;* D'Amico, *Moor;* Hakluyt, *Principal Navigations (1598–1600)*, vols. 5 and 6; Willan, *Elizabethan Foreign Trade;* Matar, *Turks, Moors, and Englishmen;* Barbour, "Northwest Africa" and *Morocco;* Holinshed, *Chronicles*, vol. 4; and Smith, *Complete Works*, Part 3. For English-Irish history, I refer to Holinshed, *Chronicles*, vol. 6; Lennon, *Sixteenth-Century Ireland;* Simpson, *School of Shakespeare*, vol. 1; Quinn and Ryan, *England's Sea Empire;* Fallon, *Armada in Ireland;* Reynolds, *Navies;* Izon; *Stuckley;* Stukeley, Annotations in *Famous History;* and Monson, *Wars with Spain*.
2. In particular, I contest interpretations of the first part of *Fair Maid of the West* in Howard, "An English Lass;" Sebek, "'Strange Outlandish Wealth;'" and Crupi, "Bess Bridges."
3. Reynolds, *Navies* 35–44. See "Article V," *England-Articles of the Peace*, Sig. B-3, and Hakluyt's notes on Grotius's *Mare Liberum* (1609) in Hakluyt and Hakluyt, *Writings*, 497–9.
4. See Shaaber, *Forerunners of the Newspaper in England* and Voss, *News Pamphlets*.
5. For a basic outline of global/imperial theory as it pertains to England, see Jay, "Beyond Discipline" and Hopkins, "Viewpoint: Back to the Future."
6. On the ubiquity of slavery even in a supposedly "free" England, see Michael Guasco's essay "Settling with Slavery," this volume.
7. Accusations of bastardy, for example, bedeviled Muhammed al-Muttawakkil and his uncle Ahmad al-Mansur. In her essay "The White Othello" in this volume, Pompa Banerjee shows that such accusations were frequent— though they seem to have been less important to Africans and Ottomans than to European writers emphasizing these people's exoticism and alterity. See, for example, Ro. C.'s account of Muley Zeydan's spurious claim to inherit the Moroccan crown on the basis of his mother's marriage to Ahmad al-Mansur and European notions of legitimate royal descent (Castries, *Histoire du Maroc*, 1.3.2: 333).
8. *Famous History*, 14.1569–70, 14.1600–6.

9. Julien, *North Africa*, 235–36. Some historians note that the Saadian dynasty was founded on this fraternal form of inheritance, others claim it a peculiar wish of Muhammed al-Sheikh. For the former, see Castries, *Histoire du Maroc*, 1.1: 346–49; for the latter, see Mayerne, *Spaine*, 1195.

10. Willan, *Elizabethan Foreign Trade*, 118.

11. Willan, *Elizabethan Foreign Trade*, 240–65; Hakluyt, *Principal Navigations (1598–1600)*, 6:426–34.

12. D'Amico, *Moor*, 33; Abun-Nasr, *Maghrib*, 215.

13. A useful compilation of these records is Castries, *Histoire du Maroc*.

14. D'Amico, *Moor*, 37; Willan, *Elizabethan Foreign Trade*, 305–7.

15. For a particularly virulent account of the Moroccan embassy, see Harris, "A Portrait of a Moor." See also Castries, *Histoire du Maroc* 1.3.2: 177–209.

16. While English responses about this visit tend to demean the Moroccan visitors and their failure to follow local customs, English diplomats at the Moroccan courts often report excellent entertainment and courtesy. See Hakluyt, *Principal Navigations (1598–1600)*, esp. vol. 6.

17. D'Amico, *Moor* 34–38; Barbour, *Morocco*, 110–11.

18. D'Amico, *Moor*, 38; Julien, *North Africa*, 235–36.

19. Castries, *Histoire du Maroc*, 1.3.2: 206–9.

20. See "Discourse of Western Planting" in Hakluyt and Hakluyt, *Writings* 265.

21. Izon, *Stuckley* 34, 56; Simpson, *School of Shakespeare* 1: 28, 33–34.

22. See Banerjee, "White Othello," this volume.

23. UK, Privy Council, *Acts*, vol. 10.

24. I thank Vincent Carey of SUNY Plattsburgh for his advice on Irish history. In addition, I thank Peter Parolin of the University of Wyoming, Robert Appelbaum, and Travis Combs for their advice on composition and clarity.

25. Holinshed, *Chronicles*, 6: 329–38.

26. Holinshed, *Chronicles*, 6: 398.

27. Holinshed, *Chronicles*, 6: 399

28. Lennon, *Sixteenth-Century Ireland*, 222–26; Fallon, *Armada in Ireland*, 4, 10.

29. See Bookin-Weiner, "The 'Sallee Rovers,'" 316–17. After 1603, some 2000 English and Irish pirates congregated in Mamora and then in Rabat-Sale, an entrepot which operated independently of the Moroccan government. Aware of the value to England of piracy against Spain, which was intent on holding the Moroccan city of Larache, in 1610 Francis Cottingham gloated at the "evyll successes" of the pirates who prevented Spain from monopolizing trade through the port (Castries, *Histoire du Maroc* 1.3.2.451).

30. Histories that deal with Spain's international standing include Stradling, *Spain's Struggle*; Parker, *Strategy of Philip II*; Kamen, *Inquisition*; and Mayerne, *Spaine*.

31. Castries, *Histoire du Maroc*, 1.3.2.222–28.

32. But see Andrew Hadfield's essay, "Irish Colonies and the Americas," this volume.

33. See Wallace, *Raleigh*, in which he notes that one such pamphlet appears to fuse the ideas of Ralegh and Hakluyt, 37. Two pamphlets attributed to Hakluyt are printed in Hakluyt and Hakluyt, *Writings*, 2: 327–43.

34. Wallace, *Raleigh*, 42; Abun-Nasr, *Maghrib*, 217; Barbour, "Northwest Africa." See also Skidmore and Smith, *Latin America*, 15–19. This brief summary of New World exploration is selected from the studies of Skidmore and Wallace as well as the following texts: DeVoto, *Course of Empire*; Milton, *Elizabeth*; Neill, *Virginia Company*; and Queseda, "Spain."

35. Brown, *Good Wives*, 14; Adler, *Discovering a New World*, 32–35.

36. Smith, *Complete Works*, 3: 205.

37. John Smith is at pains to point out that King Mully Hamet (Ahmad al-Mansur) was "tawnie, as are the most of his subjects" and not "blacke" (*Complete Works*, 3: 205).

38. Monson, *Wars with Spain*, 15; Smith, *Complete Works*, 3: 205.

39. *Famous History*, 28.2898–908.

40. Milton, *Elizabeth*, 292.

41. Peele, *Battel of Alcazar*, sig. E.

42. Holinshed, *Chronicles*, 4.516.

43. Peele, *Battel of Alcazar*, sig. F. Shaaber, *Forerunners of the Newspaper in England*, 194.

44. UK, Privy Council, *Acts* of 1578 makes no mention of Moroccan affairs but records Stukeley's papal commission to infiltrate Ireland and instigate rebellion against English authority.

45. *Famous History*, 29.2980–2.

46. See "Mary Ambree"; "The Whole Life of Long Meg"; and Druett, *She Captains*.

47. See Turner's account of Fayal in *Fair Maid*, 198–99.

48. D'Amico, *Moor*, 87.

49. Manuel Bouyssou in an e-mail correspondence to Susan Iwanisziw, 27 August 2001.

50. This name was not unique. Stukeley at one point in his piratical ventures seized a vessel named the *Ethiope* (Izon, *Stuckley*, 2); the Spanish Armada included a supply vessel named the *Castillo Negro*, which was wrecked near Ireland (Fallon, *Armada in Ireland*, 127–28).

51. UK, Privy Council, *Acts*, vol. 26.

52. See Sebek, "'Strange Outlandish Wealth'" and Howard, "An English Lass" for less positive views of Moroccan trade and cultural practices.

53. *Fair Maid*, 4.3.15–19; 5.1.143–44; 5.2.142–43, 13.1413–15, 5.2.55.

54. Willan, *Elizabethan Foreign Trade*, 194; Skilliter, *Trade with Turkey*, 180.

55. D'Amico, *Moor*, 28.

56. *Famous History*, 16.2160–7, 18.2314–5, 16.2067–83.

57. Richard Hakluyt is particularly concerned with a nation's right to "freedom of the seas" in Hakluyt and Hakluyt, *Writings*, 424, 468, 497.

58. England and Wales, *Articles of Peace*, Article V, Sig. E.

59. *Fair Maid*, 4.1.12–3, 22–26, 4.4.121–23. Monson describes and deplores his own forced labor in Spanish galleys and the policy of redeeming such Englishmen by an exchange of captives (*Wars with Spain*, 31, 43–49). His narrative asserts that while the Spanish forced even chivalric men of honor, such as himself, into service in the galleys (he does not use the word slavery), when subsequently freed he treated his Spanish prisoners with respect.

60. Taylor, *American Colonies*, 119.

61. See Orr, *Empire on the English Stage*.

62. Smith, *Complete Works*, 3: 205.

Chapter 8. Irish Colonies and the Americas

Earlier versions of this essay were given as talks for the NEH Summer Institute, "Texts of Imagination and Empire: The Founding of Jamestown in its Atlantic Context" and the Department of English, University College. The author would like to thank the audiences on both occasions for their helpful questions, points, and corrections which improved this essay tremendously. The epigraph quote is from Beacon, *Solon*, 139–40.

1. On "Translatio Imperii," see Coleman, *Political Thought*, 18–19. See also Cheyfitz, *Poetics of Imperialism*; Fuchs, 'Conquering Islands,' 47.
2. See Hayes-McCoy, "Tudor Conquest," at 129–36. See also Ellis, "Modern Irish State."
3. See Ellis, *Tudor Ireland*, passim. More generally see Neale, *Queen Elizabeth*, 284–90; Wilson, *Queen Elizabeth*, 128, 155.
4. Jardine, "Encountering Ireland," 63–65. The colonial ventures which followed did adopt opposite models of organization vis-à-vis the native Irish; for details see Quinn, "Sir Thomas Smith"; Morgan, "Sir Thomas Smith."
5. Moody, *Londonderry Plantation*, 32; MacCarthy-Morrogh, *Munster Plantation*, ch. 4; Sheehan, "Plantation of Munster."
6. Sheehan, *Savagism and Civility*. See also Porter, *Inconstant Savage*. Comparison should also be made with the Spanish colonial experience: see Pagden, *European Encounters*.
7. For incisive comment see Boehmer, *Literature*, ch. 2; Said, *Culture and Imperialism*, ch. 1.
8. Young, *Postcolonialism*, 24.
9. For discussion of the relationship between England, Ireland, and America, see Quinn, *Elizabethans and the Irish*; Canny, *Conquest of Ireland*. See also Quinn, "Ireland"; Quinn, *Discovery of America*; Andrews et al., *Westward Enterprise*; Canny and Pagden, *Colonial Identity*; Canny, "Marginal Kingdom"; Miller, *Raleigh Circle*, ch. 2.
10. For details, see Morgan, "Sir Thomas Smith."; MacCarthy-Morrogh, *Munster Plantation*; Moody, *Londonderry Plantation*.
11. Murrin, et al., *Liberty, Equality, Power*, 54.
12. See Kuppermann, *Roanoke*.
13. See also Lacey, *Raleigh*.
14. For further information see Gosling, *Gilbert*.
15. See Shirley, "Raleigh and Harriot,"; Fuchs, 'Conquering Islands', 50–51.
16. Duncan-Jones, *Sidney*, 230, 273–74, passim.
17. Canny, *Elizabethan Conquest*, ch. 3.
18. Canny, *Elizabethan Conquest*, 76.
19. Canny, *Elizabethan Conquest*, 62–65.
20. Canny, "English Colonization," 586; Canny, *Elizabethan Conquest*, chs. 2–4.
21. For an account of the largest fortune made, see Canny, *Upstart Earl*.
22. Canny, *Elizabethan Conquest*, 92.
23. See Finley, "Colonies"; Quinn, "Renaissance Influences"; Armitage, "Literature and Empire"; Armitage, *Theories of Empire*; Armitage, *Ideological Origins*.
24. Machiavelli, *Prince*, passim; Machiavelli, *Discourses*, Bk. 2, 6–10.
25. See, for example, Elyot, *Book Named the Governor*, fo. 40.
26. Tacitus, *On Britain and Germany*.
27. Herbert, *Croftus Sive*, xli.
28. Herbert, *Croftus*, 77–79.
29. Beacon, *Solon His Follie*, 143.
30. Spenser, *Ireland*, 128–29, passim.
31. See also Morgan, "Mid-Atlantic Blues"; Hadfield, "Rocking the Boat."
32. See, for example, Butlin, "Land and People"; Lennon, *Lords of Dublin*; Hadfield, *Strangers to That Land*, ch. 3.
33. Brendan Bradshaw has pointed out how urgently a geographical analysis of the forms of the Old English in Ireland is required; "Keating." See also Cunningham, *Keating*.
34. See Hadfield, *Strangers to That Land*, ch. 7.
35. But see Peter Hulme's analysis of the Pocahontas story, in which he argues that her aristocratic status can be seen to offset her race; *Colonial Encounters*, ch. 4.

36. See Canny, *Elizabethan Conquest*, ch. 6. On Grey, see McCabe, "Fate of Irena"; Brady, *Chief Governors*, epilogue.
37. See the respective *DNB* entries; Gosling, *Gilbert*, ch. 6.
38. Canny, *Upstart Earl*; Ranger, "Richard Boyle."
39. See Hadfield and Maley, "Irish Representations."
40. See Kupperman, *Settling with the Indians*.
41. For further reflections on this question see my "Crossing the Borders."
42. On the "wild" Irish see Foster, *Modern Ireland*, ch. 1; Hadfield., *Strangers to That Land*, ch. 3.
43. Sir John Dowdall to Lord Burghley, 9 March 1596, UK, Calendar of State Papers of the Reign of Elizabeth, Ireland, Oct. 1592–June 1596, 486.
44. Hulme, *Colonial Encounters*, chs. 1–2; Quinn, "New Geographical Horizons." See also the discussion in Klein, *Maps*, 178–87.
45. For further discussion see Hadfield, *Literature, Travel, and Colonial Writing*, ch. 4.
46. See Hogden, *Early Anthropology*, passim; Bodin, Easy Comprehension of History.
47. Reprinted in Falkiner, *Irish History*, 345–62.
48. Payne, *Ireland*. For comment see Hadfield, *Spenser's Irish Experience*, 33–37.
49. Hinton, "Rich's 'Anatomy of Ireland," 91.
50. Rich, *Description of Ireland*, 18.
51. Rich, *Defence*, 1, 5. Subsequent references in parentheses in the text.
52. See Shirley, "Raleigh and Harriot," 20, 22.
53. Payne, *Ireland*, 6–8; Hariot, *Briefe and True Report*, ed. Hulton, 7–21.
54. Payne, *Ireland*, 3, 6; Hariot, *Briefe and True Report*, ed. Hulton, 5–6, 30.
55. For comment see Hadfield, *Literature, Travel, and Colonial Writing*, 91–7; Maltby, *Black Legend*, ch. 2.
56. Payne, *Ireland*, 6.
57. On English fears of the dangers of Spanish aid to the Irish and Irish contact with Spain in the 1590s see Morgan, *Tyrone's Rebellion*, passim: Silke, "Irish Appeal of 1593."
58. See Hadfield, *Literature, Travel, and Colonial Writing*, ch. 2.
59. See Hadfield, "Black Legend."
60. For an indication of Hariot's influence see Quinn and Shirley, "Harriot References." I have concentrated on this work in this essay; analysis of works by authors such as John Smith, George Percy, Sir Walter Raleigh, William Strachey, and others, would repay further analysis.
61. Quinn, *Hakluyt Handbook*, 112, 246–47.
62. See the discussion in Hadfield, *Literature, Travel, and Colonial Writing*, 112–26. See also Fuller, *Voyages in Print*, 40–54; Miller, *Ralegh Circle*, ch.4.
63. See, for example, John White, *American Drawings*; Hulton, "Images of the New World"; Bucher, *Icon and Conquest*; Sokol, "Assessing Harriot"; Albanese, *New Science*, 24–29; Fleming, "Renaissance Tattoo"; Hadfield, "Bruited Abroad." For further response to these images as versions of primitivism, see Appelbaum, "Hunger in Virginia," this volume.
64. For comment, see Fleming, "Renaissance Tattoo."
65. See Kendrick, *British Antiquity*; Kidd, *British Identities*, part 1.
66. See, for example, Holinshed, *Chronicles*, 1–26.
67. See Sokol, "Assessing Harriot."
68. See Sheehan, *Savagism and Civility*, ch. 2; Porter, *Inconstant Savage*, passim.
69. Moryson, *Itinerary*, 1907 ed., 4: 202–3.
70. On Moryson's life in Ireland, see Kew, *Moryson's Unpublished Itinerary*.

71. Compare the comments of Barnaby Rich, who argues that the Irish are more uncivil and superstitious than Rome itself: *Description of Ireland*, "To the Reader." See also *Short Survey of Ireland*, passim.
72. See Derricke, *Ireland*, which contains extensive discussion of the woodcuts.
73. Spenser, *Ireland*, 66.
74. Hogden, *Early Anthropology*, 59. See also Hadfield, *Spenser's Irish Experience*, 102–8.
75. The best known discussion of Hariot's last chapters is Greenblatt, "Invisible Bullets."
76. See Hadfield, "Writing the New World."
77. Hadfield, *Literature, Travel, and Colonial Writing*, 115–16.
78. For comment see Hadfield, "The *Revelation*."
79. Campion, *Ireland*; Lennon, *Stanihurst*.
80. Campion, *Ireland*, 144–46, passim; Holinshed, *Chronicles*, 6: 83, passim.
81. See Sheehan, *Savagism and Civility*; Porter, *Inconstant Savage*; Pagden, Fall of Natural Man.
82. For discussion see Patterson, *Holinshed's Chronicles*, 9–15, passim.
83. See the discussion in Moody et al., eds., *New History of Ireland*, 3: xlii–xlviii.
84. See Canny, "Spenser."
85. See Brady, "Spenser's Irish Crisis."
86. See Brady, "Spenser's Irish Crisis," 34–36; Hadfield, *Spenser's Irish Experience*, ch. 2. Victualling the army from England was designed to prevent reliance on the native Irish; but, as Brady points out, it had been tried in the past and had (not surprisingly) proved impossible to organize.
87. For the Munster famine passage see Spenser, *Ireland*, 101–2. For a different reading of the text see Patricia Coughlan, "'Some scourge."
88. See Calder, *Revolutionary Empire*, part 1. It was especially acute when colonists were dependent on natives for their food: see Kupperman, *Roanoke*.
89. "Supplication," ed. Maley.
90. Spenser, *View*, 54–57, 61–66.
91. Brady, "Spenser's Irish Crisis," 34–35.
92. For historical analysis see Gillespie, *Colonial Ulster*; Canny, *Making Ireland British*, ch. 4.
93. Kupperman, *Settling with the Indians*, passim.
94. Kupperman, *Roanoke*; Quinn, *Roanoke Voyages*, passim.
95. For other explorations see McLeod, *Geography of Empire*; Scanlan, *Colonial Writing*.
96. On "contact zones" see Pratt, *Imperial Eye*, 6–7.
97. Canny, *Conquest of Ireland*, 86–87; Calder, *Revolutionary Empire*, 136–43.
98. McLeod, *Geography of Empire*, 103, 174.
99. For one rather speculative example see Hadfield, "Percy Copy."
100. For the general overview see Maltby, *Black Legend*; Weiner, "Beleagured Isle"; Wernham, *After the Armada*.
101. Hadfield, *Literature, Travel, and Colonial Writing*, ch. 2.
102. See Finley, "Colonies"; Quinn, "Renaissance Influences"; Morgan, "Thomas Smith."

Chapter 9. Hunger in Early Virginia: Indians and English Facing Off over Excess, Want, and Need

1. Hariot, *Brief and True Report*, ed. Hulton. For all citations I have modernized spelling but retained punctuation and capitalization.

2. Beverley, *Virginia*,181-82.
3. Cited in Cronon, *Changes in the Land*, 47.
4. Wood, *New England's Prospect*, 87.
5. Williams, *Key into the Language of America*, 135.
6. *Relation of Maryland*, 30.
7. Hariot, *Brief and True Report*, ed. Hulton,60-61.
8. Silver, *New Face on the Countryside*, 64-65.
9. Cronon, *Changes in the Land*, 37.
10. Beverley also claims that Indians "eat Grub, the Nymphaea of Wasps, some kinds of Scaraboei, Cicadae, &c.," which he excuses because of legends that ancient people ate them too. The claim cannot be rejected out of hand. A great passage in Lévi-Strauss, *Tristes Tropiques*, 160, discusses grub-eating among the Caduveo Indians of Brazil, and praises the taste of grubs as having "the consistency and delicacy of butter, and the flavor of coconut milk."
11. Bragdon, *Native Peoples of Southern New England*; Rountree and Davidson, *Eastern Shore Indians of Virginia and Maryland*, 33-37.
12. Smith, *Complete Works*,1: 256, 1: 159. On Smith's practical response, see Gleach, *Powhatan's World*, 187. On weather conditions see Kupperman, *Indians and English*, 160-64 and Kupperman, Foreword, this volume, note 8. Unusually severe weather conditions were also experienced in England during the 1590s and early 1600s.
13. Simmonds, *Proceedings*, 27.
14. For England, see Bristol, *Carnival and Theater*, and compare the account of the Netherlands in Schama, *Embarrassment of Riches*.
15. Montanari, *Culture of Food*.
16. Wrightson, *Earthly Necessities*; and see Edwards, "Between 'Plain Wilderness,'" this volume.
17. Boorde, *Compendyous Regyment*, 250.
18. *Certain Sermons*, 2: 176. And see Miller, "Gluttony," esp. 95-99.
19. Platina, *Right Pleasure*, 101.
20. Perkins, *Workes*, 2: 131-32.
21. Spenser, *Fairie Queene*, 2.12.87. On Guyon and the meaning of temperance compare Greenblatt, *Renaissance Self-Fashioning*, and Schoenfeldt, *Bodies and Selves*. "Grill" was the companion of Ulysses, who surrendered to the allure of Circe, and was turned into a hog. The secondary meaning of the line is, "let Grill be grilled."
22. Stubbes, *Anatomie*, G3 v4.
23. Moryson, *Itinerary*, 4: 173. Nashe, *Works*, 1: 200, 2: 122.
24. Harrison, *Description of England*, 125
25. Cassius, *Roman History*, 3: 263-65.
26. See related remarks in Kupperman, *Indians and English*, 23-27.
27. Hariot, *Report*, 60.
28. See, for example, Shakespeare's *Antony and Cleopatra*, 1: 4.62-67.
29. Heal, *Hospitality*.
30. Jonson, "To Penshurst," *Poetry*.
31. Boehrer, *Men's Gullets*.
32. Harrison, *Description of England*, 132.
33. J. S., *Closet of Rarities* 170-71.
34. Franklin, *Vie priveé*; Elias, *Civilizing Process*.
35. Woolley, *Guide to Ladies*, 40.
36. Appleby, *Famine*.
37. Sim, *Food and Feast*.
38. Schama, *Embarrassment of Riches*. Also see Rose, *Sensible Cook*.

39. Thirsk, *Policy and Projects*; Agnew, *Worlds Apart*; Archer, *Pursuit of Stability*; Brenner, *Merchants and Revolution*.
40. Nashe, *Lenten Stuffe*, in *Works*; Kurlansky, *Cod*.
41. Ligon, *Barbadoes*, 113.
42. Goody, *Cuisine and Class*. Also see Mintz, *Sweetness and Power*.
43. Silver, *Countryside*, 90, citing Alsop, *Character of the Province of Maryland*, 36.
44. Wharton, *Fishing in Colonial Virginia*, 13–14.
45. Mintz, "Changing Roles of Food," 267.
46. Beaumont, *Knight of the Burning Pestle*, 1.1.362–66.
47. Plat, *Sundrie Remedies*, A3v.
48. Walter, "Social Economy of Dearth." However, Walter may have overlooked the story "Molly Whuppie."
49. Tilly, "Food Entitlement." Tilly bases her argument on Amartya Sen's notion of "entitlement relationships." But the theory is already anticipated in early modern works like Arthur Standish, *The Commons Complaint*.
50. Slack, *Poverty and Policy*.
51. Gouge, *Gods Three Arrowes*, 138.
52. See Smith, *Complete Works*, 1: 211.
53. Williams, *Key to the Language*, 17.
54. Rountree, "Powhatans as Travelers," 39–41.
55. Spelman, *Relation of Virginia*, 493.
56. Lawson, *Carolina*, 178–84.
57. Byrd, *Works*, 243–44.
58. For example, Earle, "Environment, Disease, and Mortality."
59. Gleach, *Powhatan's World*, esp. 127, 265.
60. Percy, *True Relation*, 507.
61. Percy, 505.
62. Pleij, "The Topos of Hunger," in *Dreaming of Cockaigne*, 107–17.
63. Boistaurau, *Theatrum Mundi*, 154–58; Spenser, *Ireland*, 102.
64. Percy, *True Relation*, 508–9.
65. On the meaning of cannibalism in the colonial context see Hulme, *Colonial Encounters*, and Barker et al., *Cannibalism and the Colonial World*.
66. Horn, *Adapting to a New World*.
67. Frethorne, Letter to Mr. Bateman, 4: 41.
68. Frethorne, Letter to His Father and Mother, 4: 58–60.
69. See Emily Rose, "Politics of Pathos," this volume.
70. Kupperman, *Indians and English*, 213–14.

Chapter 10. Between "Plain Wilderness" and "Goodly Corn Fields": Representing Land Use in Early Virginia

1. For one of the earlier and more definitive statements of this case see Harley, "Maps, Knowledge, and Power." For a recent exploration of it see Klein, *Maps*.
2. Smith, *Map of Virginia*, 1: 151.
3. Smith, *Map of Virginia*, 1: 144, 145.
4. Smith, *Map of Virginia*, 1: 157.
5. Smith, *Map of Virginia*, 1: 174.
6. Kupperman, *Settling with the Indians*, 80–81.
7. Kupperman, *Settling with the Indians*, 5.
8. See Slotkin, *Regeneration Through Violence*, 48–49; Jennings, *Invasion of America*,

71–76; Hulme, "Hurricanes in the Caribees," 69; Seed, "Caliban and Native Title," 206.

9. See for instance Seed, *Ceremonies of Possession* and Mackenthun, *Metaphors of Dispossession*.

10. See Pagden, *Ideologies of Empire* and Armitage, *Ideological Origins*.

11. In *God Speed the Plough* McRae comments on the long transition from a Tudor to a capitalist notion of land (41). The former identifies it in terms of an absolute and inextricably social value, that individualist exploitation could only corrupt; the latter regards it as an almost infinitely enhanceable material resource.

12. Worsop, *Discoverie of Sundry Errours*, sig. I3v.

13. Norden, *Surveyor's Dialogue*, sig. B2r.

14. Norden, *Surveyor's Dialogue*, sig. A3v

15. Norden, *Surveyor's Dialogue*, sig. B2v

16. Norden, *Surveyor's Dialogue*, 4.

17. Richeson, *English Land Measuring*, 94.

18. Norden, *Surveyor's Dialogue*, 23.

19. See, for instance, Lucar, *Lucarsolace* and Rathborne, *Surveyor*.

20. Norden, *Prince Charles's Manors*, f.15.

21. McRae, *God Speed the Plough*, 8.

22. McRae, *God Speed the Plough*, 12.

23. Morgan, *American Slavery*, 85.

24. See Miller, *Raleigh Circle*, for an account of the relationships and textual productions of the Ralegh group.

25. Hakluyt, *Discourse*, 115.

26. Hakluyt, *Discourse*, 28.

27. Hariot, *Brief and True Report*, Dover edition, 6.

28. Lane, "Account," 8: 321–22.

29. Hakluyt, *Discourse*, 115.

30. Hakluyt, *Discourse*, 119.

31. Hakluyt, *Discourse*, 72.

32. Clucas, "Thomas Hariot," 111–12.

33. Quinn, "Thomas Hariot," 14.

34. As with Smith's, there are a variety of critical explanations for Hariot's ambivalence. In her 1995 *Voyages in Print* Mary C. Fuller associates Hariot's unstable containment of his Indian subject matter with a more general colonial masochism. In *Metaphors of Dispossession* Gesa Mackenthun regards it as characteristic of a state of transition half way towards the denarrativized scientific classicism which Michel Foucault has described.

35. Darby, "Age of the Improver," 27.

36. Hill, *Century of Revolution*, 13.

37. Darby, "Age," 21.

38. Hill, *Century of Revolution*, 127–28.

39. Butlin, "Enclosure," 66, 68, 76; Hill, *Century of Revolution*, 37.

40. Butlin, "Enclosure," 66.

41. McHugh, "Tribal Encounter," 119.

42. McHugh, "Tribal Encounter," 126.

43. *OED*, s.v. "improvement."

44. Gonner, *Common Land*, 49–51.

45. Gonner, *Common Land*, 55.

46. *OED*, s.v. "waste."

47. Locke, *Treatises of Government*, 297.

48. Locke, *Treatises of Government*, 286–91.

49. Locke, *Treatises of Government*, 286.
50. In *Landscape Terms*, I. H. Adams defines "improvement" as "an encroachment on common land, thus improving its value."
51. McRae, "Husbandry Manuals," 49–50.
52. Gonner, *Common Land and Enclosure*, 51.
53. Moore, *Bread for the Poor*, sig. A2ʳ.
54. Lacqueur, *Making Sex*, 230.
55. Moore, *Bread for the Poor*, 17; sig. B1v; 20.
56. Lee, *Vindication*, 22–30.
57. Dymock, "New Divisions," 5.
58. Dymock, "New Divisions," 10, 4.
59. Purchas, "Virginia's Verger," 19: 220.
60. Pagden, *Ideologies of Empire*, 77.
61. Hulme, *Colonial Encounters*, 155, 158.
62. Waterhouse, *Colony in Virginia*, 24.
63. Locke, *Treatises of Government*, 301.
64. See McRae, *God Speed the Plough*, for definitive comment on landownership "figured as reducible to facts and figures" (178).
65. Love, *Geodaesia*, title page.
66. Love, *Geodaesia*, 59.
67. Love, *Geodaesia*, 133.
68. Love, *Geodaesia*, 194.
69. Kupperman points out aristocratic involvement and precedence in what we might generalize as the "modern" institution of the joint-stock company, and characterizes the Virginia Company as "an uneasy alliance between powerful merchants and members of the gentry," noting uncertainty even amongst the gentry over which element should dominate (Kupperman, *Indians and English*, 11, 151).
70. As well as noting the differing social ideals of the different social classes who traveled to Virginia, Kupperman comments that even "the field representatives of the new capitalism" can express a paradoxical nostalgia for feudal values of cooperation and hospitality (Kupperman, *Indians and English*, 9, 141). These writers, she points out, who sometimes hold Indian life up as a foil to an England corrupted by individualistic covetousness, are causing the very changes they deplore.
71. Kupperman, *Indians and English*, observes ambivalence not only in Smith's attitude to Indian land use, but also in his attitude to the social politics of the Jamestown project (148). In one breath Smith, a rare representative of the yeoman class in early colonial government, is a champion of the social fluidity to which America would ultimately give scope, ridiculing the inappropriateness of courtly virtues in a situation demanding practical skill and hard work. In another he praises precisely these virtues as the bulwark of the colony. See Banerjee, "White Othello," this volume.
72. See, for instance, Chaplin, *Subject Matter*.

Chapter 11. Settling with Slavery: Human Bondage in the Early Afro-Atlantic World

1. Thorndale, "Virginia Census of 1619," 155–70; Sluiter, "'20. and Odd Negroes'," 395–98; Thornton, "African Experience," 421–34. On Bermuda, see Bernhard, *Slaves and Slaveholders*. On slavery and Anglo-African interaction before 1619 see Jordan, *White over Black*. But see also Fryer, *Staying Power*, esp. 1–13, and Blackburn, *New World Slavery*, 39–41, 46–48, 56–61, 72–76. Two works that have helped reframe the study of early modern slavery are Thornton, *Africa and Africans*, and Berlin, *Many Thousands Gone*.

2. Phillips, *Slavery from Roman Times*, esp. 43–113; Lewis, *Race and Slavery*; Segal, *Islam's Black Slaves*; Lovejoy, *Transformations*; Manning, *Slavery and African Life*, esp. 1–26. See Patterson, *Slavery and Social Death* on shared characteristics of all the world's slave systems.

3. Blake, *Europeans in West Africa*, 2: 295–99; Hair and Law, "The English in Western Africa to 1700," Scammell, "The English in the Atlantic Islands," 310; Appleby, "A Guinea Venture," 84–87; Appleby, "'A Business of Much Difficulty'," 3–14.

4. This interpretation stands in contrast to that of scholars, following Winthrop Jordan, who have argued that Englishmen were profoundly shocked by the blackness of Africans from the moment of first contact. Jordan, *White over Black*, 4–20. See also Vaughan and Vaughan, "Before *Othello*," 45–64.

5. Jobson, *Golden Trade*, 116–17; Hakluyt, *Principal Navigations* (1598–1600), 6: 457, 7: 93. Thornton, *Africa and Africans*, 43–71; Hair, "Attitudes to Africans," 43–68; Andrews, *Trade, Plunder, and Settlement*, 41–63, 101–15.

6. Jordan, *White over Black*, esp. 3–43. See also Hall, *Things of Darkness*.

7. Virginia Company, *Records*, 3: 69, 93 (2); 4: 41, 58, 61, 235, 473; Smith, *Complete Works*, 2: 268; UK, PRO, *CSP Colonial*, 2: 28–9 (12 April 1622).

8. Massachusetts, *Records of the Governor*, 1: 246, 269, 284, 297, 300, and 2: 21, and *Records of the Court of Assistants*, 2: 78–9 (3), 86, 87, 90, 94, 97, 118 (2); Massachusetts, *General Laws*, 4. On Bermuda, see especially Lefroy, *Memorials*, 1: 127.

9. Exodus 2: 23, 6: 1–9; Leviticus 25: 44–46. All biblical citations taken from *Geneva Bible*. The translators of the Geneva Bible invariably use the words "servant," "servitude," and "bondage," though the context and marginal notations leave little room for doubt when they mean "slavery."

10. 1 Timothy 6: 1; see also Titus 2: 9–10. Davis, *Problem of Slavery*, 63–66.

11. According to Genesis 9: 21–27 Noah became intoxicated on the ark and "was uncovered in ye middes of his tent. And when Ham the father of Canaan sawe the nakednes of his father, he tolde his two brethren without. Then toke Shem and Japeth a garment and put it upon bothe their shulders and went backward, and covered the nakednes of their father." When Noah awoke "from his wine, and knewe what his yonger sonne had done unto him" he said "Cursed *be* Canaan: servant of servantes shall he be unto his brethren. He said moreover, Blessed *be* the Lord God of Shem, and let Canaan be his servant." The marginal notation attached to the phrase "servant of servantes" reads: "That is, a moste vile slave." See also Evans, "Sons of Ham," 15–43; Braude, "Sons of Noah,"103–43.

12. Augustine, *City of God*, 874–75 [Book 19, ch. 15]. On St. Augustine see Garnsey, *Ideas of Slavery*, 206–19; Jablonski, "Ham's Vicious Race," 173–90.

13. Livy, *Romane Historie*, Tacitus, *Germanie* and *Agricola*.

14. Justinian, *Digest*, 1: 2 (Bk. 1, pt. 1, no. 4); Patterson, *Freedom*.

15. Justinian, *Digest*, 1: 2 (Bk. 1, pt. 1, no. 4); Skinner, *Liberty Before Liberalism*, 36–57; Armitage, *Ideological Origins*; Watson, "Seventeenth-Century Jurists," 1343–54.

16. Smith, *Republica Anglorum*, Bk. 2, Ch. 24, 118; Harrison, *Description of England*, 147.

17. Camden, *Britain*, 49–50; Verstegan, *Decayed Intelligence*, 43; MacDougall, *Racial Myth*, esp. 7–27. On the slippery meaning of words like "freedom" and "liberty" in early modern England, see Hill, *Liberty Against the Law*, 242–51.

18. Stone, "Educational Revolution," 41–81; Simon, *Education and Society*, esp. 369–403; Wrightson, *English Society*, 183–99; Palliser, *The Age of Elizabeth*, 411–28.

19. "Cartwright's Case" cited in Bush, "The First Slave," 610, 614. I thank Robert Appelbaum for raising this subtle, though important, distinction.

20. Kussmaul, *Servants in Husbandry*; P. J. P. Goldberg, "What Was a Servant," 1–20.

21. Chris Given-Wilson, "Service, Serfdom, and English Labour Legislation, 1350–1500," in Curry and Matthew, *Service*, 21–37.
22. Smith, *Republica Anglorum*, Bk. 3, ch. 8, 135–36; Fitzherbert, *Surveying*, 26–27. MacCulloch, "Bondmen Under the Tudors," in Cross, et al., *Law and Government*.
23. More, *Utopia*, 16, 7.
24. Davies, "Protector Somerset," 533–49; Armitage, *Ideological Origins*, 51
25. Dyer, *Lost Notebooks*, 1: 135; Collier, *Egerton Papers*, 116–17. Hawkins's memorandum is published as an appendix to J. E. G. Bennell, "English Oared Vessels," 185. Adair, "English Galleys," 497–512.
26. Hughes and Larkin, *Tudor Proclamations*, 1: 326–27, 352, 456, and 3: 86–92.
27. Rozbicki, "To Save Them from Themselves," 29–50.
28. William Shakespeare, *The Merchant of Venice*, 4: 1. See Vaughan and Vaughan, "Before *Othello*," and Bartels, "*Othello* and Africa."
29. Massinger, *Bondman*, 1: 3.
30. Purchas, *Hakluytus Posthumus*, 1905–7 ed., 6: 108.
31. Davies, *True Relation*, E4; Davis, *Problem of Slavery*, 63–66.
32. Purchas, *Hakluytus Posthumus*, 1905–7 ed., 6: 114, 123–24. On piracy and English trade, see Braudel, *Mediterranean World*, 1: 612–29; Andrews, *Trade, Plunder, and Settlement*, 87–100; Lloyd, *English Corsairs*; and Matar, *Turks, Moors, and Englishmen*.
33. According to Clowes, *Royal Navy*, at least 466 English ships with perhaps 5,600 Englishmen were taken between 1609 and 1616 (2: 22). Hebb, *Piracy*, estimates that more than 400 ships and 8,800 Englishmen were taken by Barbary pirates between 1616 and 1642 (139–40). Colley, "Britain and Islam," offers the more conservative estimate that there may have been 15,000 "British captives" between 1600 and 1800 (5). For a comprehensive effort to determine the total number of Christian captives in North Africa, see Davis, "European Slaves."
34. For an argument that these narratives *should not* be equated with later American slave narratives, see Baepler, "Barbary Captivity" and *White Slaves*.
35. See, for example, Sir William Monson, *Naval Tracts*, 4: 107–9.
36. Hakluyt, *Principal Navigations* (1598–1600), 5: 62; Munday, *Admirable Deliverance*, B2.
37. Hakluyt, *Principal Navigations* (1598–1600), 7: 126–7, 5: 155; Munday, *Admirable Deliverance*, B2; Knight, *Slaverie*, 28; Davies, *True Relation*, C1.
38. Purchas, *Haklutus Posthumus*, 1905–07 ed., 6: 155; D'Aranda, *Algiers*, 9; and Thomas, *Man and the Natural World*, 41–50.
39. Munday, *Admirable Deliverance*, B3; Friedman, "Christian Captives," 624–6; Knight, *Slaverie*, 28; Hakluyt, *Principal Navigations* (1598–1600), 5: 301.
40. James I, *Proclamation* (London, 1624) [STC (2nd ed.) 8729]; Fitz-Geffrey, *Compassion towards Captives*, 35; Byam and Kellet, *Returne*, 16–17, 65, 76–77. More recently, see Colley, *Captives*.
41. Hakluyt, *Principal Navigations* (1598–1600), 5: 187–88, 6: 40, 429; UK, Privy Council, *Acts*, 14: 205–6 (August 1586).
42. UK, PRO, *CSP Domestic*, 1: 295. The reference to "most cruel slavery" comes from the daybook of Thomas Harridance, clerk of St. Botolph Aldgate, 1583–1600, reprinted in Knutson, "Foreign History Plays," 75–110.
43. Stow, *London*, 167–68. O'Mara, *Middle English Sermons*, 32–38. See also Machyn, *Diary*, 33, 131–32, 192, 231, 254, 299, 304–5. Pepys, *Diary*, 3: 58.
44. Pepys, *Diary*, 3: 33–4.
45. UK, Privy Council, *Acts*, 18: 375 (April 1, 1582), 21: 281 (July 13, 1591), 31: 270–1 (April 7, 1601).
46. James I, *Proclamation* (London, 1624) [STC (2nd ed.) 8729]; Fitz-Geffrey,

Compassion towards Captives, 4, 11, 17. See also Hebb, *Piracy*, 77–104, 237–65, and Aylmer, "Slavery Under Charles II," 378–88.

47. Knutson, "Foreign History Plays," 94–101. Specific plays include Robert Daborne's *A Christian Turnd Turk* (1615) and Philip Massinger's *The Renegado* (1624). For a ballad see "An Admirable New Northern Story."

48. Hair and Law, "The English in West Africa to 1700."

49. See also Guasco, "Human Bondage," 231–405.

50. As Alden Vaughan has pointed out, even under the best of circumstances during the first half century of colonization, at least 70 percent of Africans were enslaved. Vaughan, "The Origins Debate: Slavery and Racism in Seventeenth-Century Virginia," in *Roots of American Racism*, 156–57, 309 n.50, 309 n.84.

51. Even John Smith sounded a regretful tone when he recalled that Thomas Hunt had "abused the Salvages . . . and betrayed twenty seaven of these poore innocent soules, which he sould in Spaine for slaves." Smith, "A Description of New England," in *Complete Works*, 1: 352. Morgan, *American Slavery*, 6–9.

52. For an argument that Indians were neither necessarily scorned nor conceptualized as natural slaves by the first generation of settlers see Kupperman, *Indians and English*, and Chaplin, *Subject Matter*.

53. Virginia Company, *Records*, 3: 557–58, 672. Waterhouse's characterization of Indians as "deformed Savages" brings to mind Shakespeare's Caliban in *The Tempest* whose physical appearance signifies rather than explains his bondage. Vaughan and Vaughan, *Shakespeare's Caliban*, 7–15.

54. Virginia Company, *Records*, 3: 558–59, 672, 706.

55. Purchas, *Hakluytus Posthumus*, 1905–7 ed., 19: 246; Virginia Company, *Records*, 3: 706, 2: 397; "The Planters Plea, Or the Grounds of Plantations Examined, And usuall Objections answered" (London, 1630), in Force, *Tracts*, vol. 2.

56. Burton, *Diary*, 4: 255, 260–62, 268.

Chapter 12. "We All Smoke Here": Behn's The Widdow Ranter *and the Invention of American Identity*

The author would like to thank Robert Appelbaum and Edith Frampton for their essential help with this essay.

1. All references are to *The Widdow Ranter* will be to Behn, *Works* (1996), 7: 285–354. On the play's stage history, *Works* (1915), 4: 219–20. The two most substantial articles are Ferguson, "News," and Hendricks, "Widow Ranter."

2. Dunn, "English Historians," 195.

3. Bach, *Colonial Transformations*, 113. See also Armitage, "New World," 52–78. See also Greenblatt, *Marvelous Possessions*; Todorov, *Conquest of America*; and the essays by Montrose, Clendennin, and Pagden in Greenblatt, *Encounters*.

4. Witmer and Freehafer also note that Behn "praises the 'Old Dominion' at the expense of Europe," ("Behn's Strange News," 9).

5. See Kupperman, "Introduction" to *European Consciousness*, 6.

6. See Hendricks, who argues that Behn's play carries forward England's colonial project.

7. In fact, significantly fewer women than men emigrated to the Chesapeake. See Carr and Walsh, "Planter's Wife," 550. Nonetheless, on the predominance of patriarchy in the colony, see Brown, *Good Wives*.

8. Murrin, "Roof Without Walls," 339.

9. Murrin, "Roof Without Walls," 339.

10. Earlier studies of "American" identity concentrated almost exclusively on works produced by eighteenth-century writers living in the colonies, ignoring what

was happening across the Atlantic. See, for example, Martin, *Interpreting Colonial America*, 443–95.

11. Johnson, *New Life of Virginea*, sig. D3r.
12. *New Description of Virginia*, 11.
13. Hartwell et al., *Virginia*, 14, 16, 21, 9.
14. Norwood, *Virginia*, 47.
15. "The Forms of Proceeding in this Court are, almost in every Thing, disagreeable to the Laws of *England*, and very irregular" (Hartwell et al., *Virginia*, 47).
16. Dunn, "English Historians," 195.
17. Beverley, *Virginia*, 9, 11.
18. According to the *Oxford English Dictionary*, the definition of "country" as indicating "the territory or land of a nation; usually of an independent state" (def. 3) was well established by the early seventeenth century.
19. For New England, Dunn finds the development of a "sense of distinction from the mother country" starting in John Winthrop's *Journal* (1630–49) ("English Historians," 205). On the different paths of New England and the Middle Colonies, see Vaughan, "Virginia History"; Ward, "American Identity"; and Bonomi, "Middle Colonies."
20. Todd, "Notes," in Behn, *Works* (1996), 452.
21. Alas, the play flopped "owing to the slipshod and slovenly way in which it was put on . . ." (Summers, "Theatrical History," in Behn, *Works* [1915], 219).
22. This scene "was expunged in its entirety" from the play's first production (Behn, *Works* [1915], 219).
23. See Rustici, "Smoking Girl."
24. Sig. A2, cited in Arents et al., *Tobacco*, 2: 290.
25. Some evidence exists for the acceptance of smoking by women. In *Epistolae Ho-Elianae* (1650), a collection of familiar letters, the author, James Howell, testifies that "one shall commonly see the serving maid upon the washing block, and the Swain upon the plowshare when they are tir'd with labour, take out their boxes of smutchin and draw it into their nostrills with a quill, and it will beget new spirits in them with a fresh vigour to fall to their work again" (cited in Arents et al., *Tobacco*, 2: 287).
26. Sig. A1^r, cited in Arents et al., *Tobacco*, 2: 305–6, and 2: 325–26.
27. E. W. *Virginia*, in Force, *Tracts*, 3: 11, 50.
28. Smith, *Colonists in Bondage*, 299–300.
29. Menard, "From Servant to Freeholder," 42.
30. Smith, *Colonists in Bondage*, 297.
31. Smith, *Colonists in Bondage*, 303.
32. See Morgan, *American Slavery*, 213–92.
33. See Greene, *Pursuits of Happiness*, 81, 93, and Brown, *Good Wives*, 3.
34. Quoted in Horn, *Adapting to a New World*, 255.
35. Horn, *Adapting to a New World*, 282.
36. Bacon's Rebellion has elicited varying interpretations over the years. Wertenbaker, (*Torchbearer of the Revolution*) sees Bacon as a symbol of liberty, whereas Washburn, writing at the height of the Cold War, has much less use for rebels against established authority, and so, in *The Governor and the Rebel*, he is very sympathetic to Berkeley. The most recent treatment is by Webb (*1676*), who regards Bacon's Rebellion as the progenitor of the American Revolution.
37. Webb, *1676*, 155. See generally the "True Narrative of the Late Rebellion."
38. According to Thomas Mathew (who wrote his narrative some thirty years after the event), "Bacon's Body was so made away, as his Bones were never found to be Exposed on a Gibbet as was purposed" (Mathew, "Bacon's Rebellion," 39).

39. While it seems evident that Behn would have read the pamphlets, Batten ("Source") and Witmer and Freehafer ("Behn's Strange News") both argue that she also read the reports. Ferguson, however, doubts this doubts this possibility ("News," 154 n.6).

40. *Strange News*, 16.

41. *More News from Virginia*, 23.

42. *More News from Virginia*, 21, 24–25.

43. "True Narrative," 111.

44. "True Narrative," 20, 121.

45. "True Narrative," 137–38.

46. Sherwood, "Account," 169. Given Behn's intimacy with the court, it is at least possible that she read these letters.

47. Cited in Webb, *1676*, 36.

48. Webb, *1676*, 48.

49. Webb, *1676*, 145.

50. "Agreement of the People," 284.

51. Bacon, "Proclamation," 59–61.

52. Sherwood, "Account," 172, 49.

53. Sherwood, "Account," 150.

54. Mendelson, *Stuart Women*, 120.

55. Behn, *The Roundheads: Or, The Good Old Cause*, in *Works* (1996), 361, 365.

56. See, for example, Herman, "Is this Winning?"

57. On the problem of potential miscegenation, see Ferguson ("News," 164–65) and Hendricks ("Widow Ranter," 235).

58. Also, Bacon is the only character in the play consistently paralleled with classical heroes. After the Indian king dies, Bacon says that "now like *Caesar* I cou'd weep over the Hero I my self destroy'd" (4.2.61–62); he chooses to die by poison because that is how Hannibal committed suicide (5.4.287); and Dareing asserts, after Bacon leaves this vale of tears: "So fell the Roman *Cassius* (5.4.310), eulogizing him as "that great Soul'd Man, no private Body e're contain'd a Nobler" (5.4.313).

59. While Behn takes considerable liberties with history (inventing the romantic subplot with the Indian queen Semirana, for instance), both the historical Bacon and his literary counterpart insist upon their loyalty to the crown. In the oath that Bacon had his followers swear, the first item is: "You are to oppose what Forces shall be sent out of England by his Majesty against mee, till such tyme I have acquainted the King with the state of this country, and have had an answer" ("Narrative of the Commissioners," 122).

60. Todd, *Aphra Behn*, 265.

61. Todd, *Aphra Behn*, 386.

62. Todd, *Aphra Behn*, 387.

63. Todd, *Aphra Behn*, 390.

64. The legal system was much less cooperative than his father and grandfather found it. When in 1688 James put on trial the Archbishop of Canterbury and his bishops for refusing to read the Declaration of Indulgence, which suspended the laws against dissenters and recusants, they were acquitted.

65. Private conversation.

66. On republicanism in the 1680s generally, see Worden, "English Republicanism."

67. Ferguson, "News," 168.

68. Greenblatt, *Marvelous Possessions*, 121.

69. Behn, *Oroonoko*, 65.

70. Ferguson, "News," 168.
71. Ferguson, "News," 153 n. 5.
72. Mathew, "Bacon's Rebellion," 40.
73. Wertenbaker, *Virginia*, 221.
74. Wertenbaker, *Virginia*, 239.
75. Beverley, *Virginia*, 89.
76. Wertenbaker, *Virginia*, 240.
77. Beverley, *Virginia*, 91.

Conclusion: Jamestown and Its North Atlantic World

1. Barbour, *Jamestown Voyages*, 24, 25, 28, 29, 31, 33.
2. Barbour, *Jamestown Voyages*, 49, 52 This counsel may hark back to Hariot's observation that the Indians at Roanoke took the English as "not mortall but . . . of an old generation many yeeres past then risen againe to immortalitie," because they were generally immune from the diseases that were killing the Indians. Hariot, *True Report*, sig. D.
3. Acts 1.8.
4. For a study of this topic, see Quint, *Epic*, 50–96.
5. Strachey, *Reportory*, 89, n. 116.
6. Strachey, *Reportory*, 78.
7. Virgil, *Aeneid*, 8. 90–93.
8. Barbour, *Jamestown Voyages*, 80–98.
9. Barbour, *Jamestown Voyages*, 110.
10. Smith, *General Historie*, 146–47.
11. Smith, *General Historie*, 110.
12. Smith, *General Historie*, 261.
13. Barbour, *Jamestown Voyages*, 79, 80.
14. Barbour, *Jamestown Voyages*, 110, 111.
15. Smith, *General Historie*, 157–58.
16. Force, *Tracts* 3, 6.
17. Smith, *Proceedings of Virginia*, 257.
18. Brown, *Genesis* 1, 293–302; 299.
19. Isaiah 45: 1–4.
20. Symonds, "Sermon," 10.
21. On the ethics of size, see the Castiglione's claim that a small stature in men denotes superior intelligence. Castiglione, *Courtier*, Book One, Ch. 20, 39.
22. Locke stated that the land is God's and given to all mankind in common as "waste" to be used and possessed. The user acquires a property in the land he uses. As James Tully notes: "Locke calls [property] the 'appropriation of any parcel of Land by improving it.'" Tully, *Property*, 119.
23. Barbour, *Jamestown Voyages*, 110.
24. Barbour, *Jamestown Voyages*, 141.
25. Barbour, *Jamestown Voyages*, 101.
26. Billings, *Old Dominion*, 30.
27. Leviticus states that the Israelites may "possess in Perpetuity" and pass on as inheritance persons who are "heathen" as well as their children (Lev. 25.45).
28. These were specifically guaranteed under the First Charter; see above.
29. These are the epithets to which Bacon resorts in his "Manifesto"; see Billings, *Old Dominion*, 278.
30. Ovid, *Metamorphoses*, 15. 184.

Bibliography

Abbreviations

PMLA   *Proceedings of the Modern Language Association*
PRO   Public Record Office
VMHB   *Virginia Magazine of History and Biography*
WMQ   *William and Mary Quarterly* 3rd series

Primary Texts

"An Agreement of the People." In *Divine Right and Democracy: An Anthology of Political Writing in Stuart England*, ed. David Wootton, 283–85. New York: Penguin, 1986.
"An Admirable New Northern Story." In *The Euing Collection of English Broadside Ballads*, 10. Glasgow: University of Glasgow Publications, 1971.
Allen, William. *An Admonition to the Nobility and People of England and Ireland*. Antwerp, 1588.
Alsop, George, *A Character of the Province of Maryland*. . . . London: Printed by T[homas]. J[efferson]. for Peter Dring, 1666. Ed. Newton D. Mereness. Cleveland: Burrows Brothers, 1902.
Andrews, Charles M., ed. *Narratives of the Insurrections, 1675–1690*. New York: Charles Scribner's Sons, 1915. Reprint New York: Barnes and Noble, 1952.
Anghiera, Pietro Martire. *The Decades of the newe worlde or west India by Pietro Martire d'Anghiera*. Trans. Richard Eden. London, 1555.
———. *The Decades of the New Worlde of West India*. Ed. and trans. Richard Eden. London, 1555. In *The First Three English Books on America*, ed. Edward Arber. Birmingham, 1885.
Augustine. *Concerning the City of God Against the Pagans*. Trans. Henry Betterson. Harmondsworth: Penguin, 1972.
Bacon, Nathaniel. "Proclamation of Nathaniel Bacon." *VMHB* 1 (1893–94): 59–61.
Barbour, Philip L. *The Jamestown Voyages Under the First Charter, 1606–1609*. 2 vols. Hakluyt Society Works 2nd ser. 136–37. Cambridge: Cambridge University Press, 1969.
Beacon, Richard. *Solon His Follie, or, a Politique Discourse Touching the Reformation of Common-Weales Conquered, Declined or Corrupted*. 1594. Ed. Clare Carroll and Vincent Carey. Binghamton, N.Y.: Medieval and Renaissance Texts and Studies, 1996.
Beaumont, Francis. *The Knight of the Burning Pestle*. Ed. Michael Hattaway. New York: Norton, 1969.
Behn, Aphra. *Oroonoko: A Norton Critical Edition*. Ed. Joanna Lipking. New York: Norton, 1997.

———. *The Works of Aphra Behn*. Ed. Janet Todd. 7 vols. Columbus: Ohio State University Press, 1992.

———. *The Works of Aphra Behn*. Ed. Montague Summers. London: W. Heinemann, 1915. Reprint New York: Benjamin Blom, 1967.

Beverley, Robert. *The History and Present State of Virginia*. 1705. Ed. Louis B. Wright. Chapel Hill: University of North Carolina Press, 1947.

Billings, Warren H., ed. *The Old Dominion in the Seventeenth Century: A Documentary History of Virginia, 1606–1689*. Chapel Hill: University of North Carolina Press, 1975.

Blake, John William, ed. *Europeans in West Africa, 1450–1560*. 2 vols. London: Hakluyt Society, 1942.

Blount, Henry. *A Voyage into the Levant. A Breife Relation of a Journey, lately performed by Master H. B. Gentleman, from England by way of Venice*. London: Andrew Crooke, 1636.

Bodin, Jean. *Method for the Easy Comprehension of History*. Trans. Beatrice Reynolds. New York: Columbia University Press, 1945.

Boistaurau, Jean. *Theatrum Mundi: The Theatre or Rule of the World*. Trans. John Alday. London, 1581.

Boorde, Andrew. *The fyrst boke of the introduction of knowledge made by Andrew Borde, of physycke doctor. A Compendyous Regyment: Or, a Dyetary of Helth Made in Mountpyllier*. 1640–63. Ed. F. J. Furnivall. London: Early English Text Society, 1870.

A Briefe Declaration of the Present State of Things in Virginia. London, 1616.

[Brinsley, John]. *A Consolation for Our Grammar Schooles; More Specially for . . . Ireland, Virginia, and the Sommer Ilands*. London: Richard Field for Thomas Man, 1622.

Brooks, Jerome E. *Tobacco: Its History Illustrated by the Books, Manuscripts, and Engravings in the Library of George Arents, Jr.* New York: Rosenbach, 1938.

Brown, Alexander. *The Genesis of the United States: . . . Set Forth through a Series of Historical Manuscripts Now First Printed, Together with a Reissue of Rare Contemporaneous Tracts*. 2 vols. Boston: Houghton Mifflin; London: W. Heineman, 1890.

Burton, Thomas. *Diary, of Thomas Burton, Esq. Member in the Parliaments of Oliver and Richard Cromwell from 1656–59 . . . With An . . . Account of the Parliament of 1654; from the Journal of Guibon Goddard*. 4 vols. London: H. Colburn, 1828.

[Butler, Nathaniel]. *The Historye of the Bermudaes or Summer Islands*. Ed. Henry J. Lefroy. Hakluyt Society Works 1st ser. 65. London: Hakluyt Society, 1882.

[Byam, Henry and Edward Kellet.] *A Returne from Argier*. London, 1628.

Byrd, William. *The Prose Works of William Byrd of Westover*. Ed. Louis B. Wright. Cambridge, Mass.: Harvard University Press, 1966.

Camden, William. *Britain, or a Chorographicall Description of the most flourishing Kingdomes, England, Scotland, and Ireland*. Trans. Philemon Holland. London, 1610.

———. *Remaines Concerning Britain*. 1605. London: J.R. Smith, 1870.

Campion, Edmund. *Two Bokes of the Histories of Ireland*. Ca.1570. Ed. A. F. Vossen. Assen, Netherlands: Van Gorcum, 1963.

Cassius, Dio. *Roman History*. Trans. Earnest Cary. 9 vols. Cambridge, Mass: Harvard University Press, 1927.

Castries, Henry, Comte de, ed. *Les Sources inédites de l'histoire du Maroc de 1530 à 1845*. Book 1, *Dynastie saadienne*, Part 1, *Archives et bibliothèques de France*. Vols. 1–3. Paris: Ernest Leroux, 1905. Part 2, *Archives et bibliothèques d'Angleterre*. Vol. 2. Paris: Paul Geuthner; London: Luzac et Cie, 1925.

Certain Sermons or Homilies Appointed to be Read in Churches in the Time of Queene Elizabeth. 2 vols. London, 1683.

Chamberlain, John. *The Letters of John Chamberlain*. Ed. Norman Egbert McClure. 2 vols. Philadelphia: American Philosophical Society, 1939.

Chester, Joseph Lemuel, ed. *The Reiester Booke of Saynte De'nis Backchurch Parishe.* Harleian Society Publications 3. London: Harleian Society, 1878.

Collier, John Payne, ed. *The Egerton papers: A collection of public and private documents, chiefly illustrative of the times of Elizabeth and James I, from the original manuscripts, the property of the Right Hon. Lord Francis Egerton.* London: Camden Society, 1840.

Cooke, Ebenezer. "The History of Bacon's Rebellion." In *The Maryland Muse.* Reprinted in *Proceedings of the American Antiquarian Society* n.s. 44 (1934): 311–26.

Cortes, Martin. *The Art of Navigation.* Trans. Richard Eden. London, 1561.

Crashaw, William *A Sermon Preached in London Before the Right Honorable Lord Lawarre, Lord Governour and Captaine Generall of Virginea.* 1610. Facsimile reprint Boston: Massachusetts Historical Society, 1937.

D'Aranda, Emmanuel. *The History of Algiers and it's Slavery with Many Remarkable Particularities of Africk.* Trans. John Davies. London, 1666.

Davies, William. *True Relation of the Travailes and most miserable Captivitie of William Davies, Barber-Surgion of London.* London, 1614.

De Bry, Theodore. *Collectiones Peregrinationum in Indiam Orientales ("Petits Voyages") et Indiam Occidentalem ("Grand Voyages").* Part 2. Frankfurt: De Bry, 1591.

Dee, John. Preface. *The Elements of Geometrie of the Most Auncient Philosopher Euclide of Megara.* Trans. H. Billindsley. London, 1570.

Dekker, Thomas. *Lust's Dominion; or, the Lascivious Queen.* In *A Select Collection of Old Plays Originally Published by Robert Dodsely in the Year 1744.* Rev. 4th ed. Ed. W. Carew Hazlitt. New York: Benjamin Blom, 1874–76.

De la Ware, Thomas, Lord, et al. *A True and Sincere Declaration of the Purpose and Ends of the Plantation begun in Virginia.* In Billings, *Old Dominion,* 14–15.

Derricke, John. *The Image of Ireland.* 1581. Ed. David Beers Quinn. Belfast: Blackstaff, 1985.

Donne, John. *The Sermons of John Donne.* Ed. George R. Potter. Berkeley: University of California Press, 1959.

Dowdall, Sir John, to Lord Burghley, 9 March 1596. In *Calendar of State Papers, Relating to Ireland in the Reigns of Henry VIII, the Reign of Elizabeth, Ireland.* 11 vols. London: Longman, 1860–1912. 5: 486.

Drayton, Michael. *The Works of Michael Drayton.* Ed. J. William Hebel. Oxford: Blackwell, 1933.

Dyer, Sir James. *Report from the Lost Notebooks of Sir James Dyer.* Ed. John Hamilton Baker. 2 vols. London: Selden Society, 1994.

Dymock, Cressey. "A Discovery for New Divisions: Or Setting out of Lands, as to the Best Forme: Imparted in a Letter to Samuel Hartlib." In Samuel Hartlib, *A Discoverie For Division Or Setting out of Land, as to the Best Form . . . Whereunto are Added Some Other Choice Secrets or Experiments of Husbandry.* London, 1653.

Elyot, Thomas. *The Book Named the Governor.* London, 1531.

The Famous History of Captain Thomas Stukeley. London: Thomas Pavier, 1605. Ed. Judith C. Levinson. Malone Society Reprints. Oxford: Oxford University Press, 1975.

The Ferrar Papers, 1590–1790. Magdalene College, Cambridge. Microfilm ed., 14 reels. Introduction and Finding List by David R. Ransome. East Ardsley, England: Microform Academic Publishing, 1992.

Finestone, Harry, ed. *Bacon's Rebellion: The Contemporary News Sheets.* Charlottesville: University of Virginia Press, 1956.

Fitz-Geffrey, Charles. *Compassion towards Captives, chiefly Towards our Brethren and Country-men who are in miserable bondage in Barbarie.* Oxford, 1637.

Fitzherbert, John. *The Boke of Surveying and Improvements.* London, 1523.

Force, Peter, ed. *Tracts and Other Papers Relating Principally to the Origin, Settlement,* and *Progress of the Colonies in North America*. 4 vols. Washington, D.C., 1836. See http://hdl.loc.gov/loc.gdc/lhbcb.7018a, b, c, d.

Frethorne, Richard. Letter to His Father and Mother, Mar. 20, Apr. 2 and 3, 1623. In Virginia Company, *Records*, 458–62.

———. Letter to Mr. Bateman, Mar. 5, 1622/23. In Virginia Company, *Records*, 4: 41–42.

The Geneva Bible: A Facsimile of the 1560 Edition. Madison: University of Wisconsin Press, 1969.

Gómara, Francisco López de. *Cortés: The Life of the Conqueror by His Secretary*. Trans. and ed. Leslie Byrd Simpson. Berkeley: University of California Press, 1964.

Good Newes from Virginia, Sent from James His Towne This Present Moneth of March, 1623, by a Gentleman of That Country. To the Tune of All Those That Be Good Fellows. London: Printed at London for John Trundle, [1623]. Facsimile ed. Charlottesville: University of Virginia Library, 1971.

Gorges, Ferdinando. *A Briefe Narration of the Originall Undertakings to . . . America*. London: Nathaniel Brook, 1658.

Gouge, William. *Gods Three Arrowes: Plagues, Famine, and Sword*. London, 1631.

Gray, Robert. *A Good Speed to Virginia*. London: William Welbie, 1609.

———. *A Good Speed to Virginia*. Ed. Wesley Frank Craven. New York: Scholars' Facsimiles and Reprints, 1937.

England and Wales: Articles of the Peace, Entercourse, and Commerce. The English Experience, Its Record in Early Printed Books Published in Facsimile, No. 378. Amsterdam: Theatrum Orbis Terrarum; and New York, Da Capo Press, 1971. Article V (1605).

Haile, Edward Wright, ed. *Jamestown Narratives: Eyewitness Accounts of the Virginia Colony*. Champlain, Va.: Roundhouse, 1998.

Hakluyt, Richard. *Discourse of Western Planting*. 1584. In Hakluyt and Hakluyt, *Original Writings*.

———. *Divers voyages touching the discoverie of America*. London, 1582.

———. *Divers Voyages Touching the Discoverie of America*. 1582. In Hakluyt and Hakluyt, *Original Writings*, vol. 1.

———. *A Particuler Discourse Concerninge the Greate Necessitie and Manifolde Commodyties that are Like to Growe to this Realme of Englande by the Westerne Discoveries Lately Attempted. Known as Discourse of Western Planting*. 1584. Ed. David B. Quinn and Alison M. Quinn. Hakluyt Society Extra Series 45. London: Hakluyt Society, 1993.

———. *The Principall Navigations, Voiages and Discoveries of the English Nation*. London: George Bishop and Ralph Newberie, 1589.

———. *Principal Navigations Voyages Traffiques and Discoveries of the English Nation*. 3 vols. London: Printed by George Bishop et al., 1598–1600. 12 vols. Glasgow: James Maclehose and Sons, 1903–1905. Also reprint New York: AMS Press, 1965.

Hakluyt, Richard and Richard Hakluyt. *The Original Writings and Correspondence of the Two Richard Haykluyts*. Ed. E. G. R. Taylor. 2 vols. London: Hakluyt Society, 1935.

Hamor, Ralph. *A True Discourse of the Present Estate of Virginia*. London: William Welby, 1615. In Haile, *Jamestown Narratives*, 850–56.

Harcourt, Robert. *A Relation of a Voyage to Guiana*. London: W. Welby, 1613.

Hariot, John. *A Briefe and True Report of the New Found Land of Virginia*. Frankfurt, 1590.

Hariot, Thomas. *A Briefe and True Report of the New Found Land of Virginia. The Complete 1590 Theodor de Bry Edition*. Intro. by Paul Hulton. New York: Dover, 1972.

Harrison, William. *The Description of England in Shakespeare's Youth*. 1870–71. Ed.

Georges Edelen. Folger Documents of Tudor and Stuart Civilization. Ithaca, N.Y.: Cornell University Press for the Folger Shakespeare Library, 1968. Reprint New York: Dover, 1994.

Harry Hangman's Honour: Or, Glocester-Shire Hangman's Request to the Smoakers or Tobacconists in London. London, 1655.

Hartwell, Henry, James Blair, and Edward Chilton. *The Present State of Virginia.* 1697. Ed. Hunter Dickinson Farish. Williamsburg, Va.: Colonial Williamsburg, 1940.

Herbert, Thomas. *Some Yeares Travels into Africa & Asia the Great. Especially describing the Famous Empires of Persia and Industan. As also Divers other Kingdoms in the Orientall Indies, and I'les Adjacent.* London, 1638.

Herbert, Sir William. *Croftus Sive De Hibernia Liber.* Ed. Arthur Keaveney and John A. Madden. Dublin: Irish Manuscripts Commission, 1992.

Heywood, Thomas. *Fair Maid of the West, Parts I and II.* Ed. Robert K. Turner, Jr. Lincoln: University of Nebraska Press, 1967.

"The History of Bacon's and Ingram's Rebellion." In Andrews, *Narratives of the Insurrections,* 47–98.

Holinshed, Raphael. *Chronicles of England, Scotland and Ireland.* 1587. With a new introduction by Vernon Snow. 6 vols. Reprint of the London, 1807–8 ed. New York: AMS Press, 1965.

Hotten, John Camden, comp. *The Original Lists of Persons of Quality, Emigrants, Religious Exiles, Political Rebels, Serving Men Sold for a Term of Years, Apprentices, Children Stolen, Maidens Pressed, and Others, Who Went from Great Britain to the American Plantations, 1600–1700.* London and New York, 1874. Reprint Baltimore: Genealogical Publishing Co., 1986.

Hughes, Paul L. and James Francis Larkin, eds. *Tudor Royal Proclamations.* 3 vols. New Haven, Conn.: Yale University Press, 1964–69.

Jobson, Richard. *The Golden Trade, or A Discovery of the River Gambra, and the Golden Trade of the Aethiopians.* London, 1623.

Johnson, Robert. *Nova Britannia.* London, 1609.

———. *The New Life of Virginea.* London, 1612.

Jonson, Ben. *The Alchemist.* In *Ben Jonson's Plays and Masques.* Ed. Robert M. Adams. New York: W.W. Norton, 1979.

———. *Complete Poetry of Ben Jonson.* Ed. William B. Hunter, Jr. New York: Norton, 1968.

———. *Works.* Ed. C. H. Herford, Percy Simpson, and Evelyn Simpson. 10 vols. Oxford: Clarendon Press, 1925–30.

Justinian. *The Digest of Justinian.* Ed. Theodor Mommsen and Alan Watson. 4 vols. Philadelphia: University of Pennsylvania Press, 1985.

Keymis, Lawrence. *A Relation of the Second Voyage to Guiana.* London: Thomas Dawson, 1595.

Knight, Francis. *A Relation of Seven Yeares Slaverie under the Turkes of Argiere, suffered by an English Captive Merchant.* London, 1640.

Knolles, Richard. *The Generall Historie of the Turkes, from the first beginning of that Nation to the rising of the Ottoman Familie: with all the notable expeditions of the Christian Princes against them. Together with the lives and conquests of the Othoman Kings and Emperours, Faithfullie collected out of the best Histories, both auncient and moderne, and digested into one continual Historie untill this present yeare 1603.* London: Adam Islip, 1603.

Lambarde, William. *A Perambulation of Kent: Conteining the Description, Hystorie, and Customes of that Shire.* 1576. Reprint of 1826 edition. Bath: Adams and Dart, 1970.

Lane, Ralph. "An account of the particularities of the imployments of the English men left in Virginia by Sir Richard Greenevill under the charge of Master Ralph

Lane Generall of the same, from the 17. of August 1585. until the 18. of June 1586. at which time they departed the Countrey: sent and directed to Sir Walter Ralegh." In Hakluyt, *Principal Navigations* (1598–1600; Glasgow ed.), 8: 319–45.

———. "Ralph Lane's Report to Sir Walter Raleigh." In Lorant, ed., *The New World*, 135–50.

Larkin, James Francis and Paul L. Hughes, eds. *Royal Proclamations of King James I, 1603–1625*. Oxford: Clarendon Press, 1973.

Las Casas, Bartolomé de. *The Devastation of the Indies: A Short Account*. Trans. Herma Briffault. Baltimore: Johns Hopkins University Press, 1992.

———. *The Spanish Colonie, or the Brief Chronicle of the Acts and Gestes of the Spaniardes in the West Indies*. Trans. M. M. S. London: William Brome, 1583.

Lawson, John. *A New Voyage to Carolina*. 1709. Ed. Hugh Talmage Lefler. Chapel Hill: University of North Carolina Press, 1967.

Le Moyne, Jacques. *Brevis Narratio Eorum Quae in Florida Americae Provincia Gallis Acciderunt*. Ed. Theodor de Bry. *America, Part 2*. Frankfurt, 1591.

Lederer, John. *The Discoveries of John Lederer*. 1672. Ed. Willliam P. Cumming. Charlottesville: University of Virginia Press, 1958.

Lee, Joseph. *A Vindication of a Regulated Inclosure*. London, 1656.

Lefroy, J. H., ed. *Memorials of the Discovery and Early Settlement of the Bermudas or Somers Islands, 1515–1685*. 2 vols. Toronto: University of Toronto Press, 1981.

Leigh, Valentine. *The Most Profitable and Commendable Science, of Surveying of Landes*. London, 1577.

Ligon, Richard. *A True and Exact History of the Island of Barbadoes*. London, 1673.

Livy. *The Romane Historie Written by T. Livius of Padua*. Trans. Philemon Holland. London, 1600.

Locke, John. *Two Treatises of Government*. Ed. Peter Laslett. 3rd ed. Cambridge: Cambridge University Press, 1988.

Lorant, Stefan. *The New World: The First Pictures of America made by John White and Jacques Le Moyne and engraved by Theodore de Bry*. New York: Duell, Sloane and Pearce, 1946. Reprint 1965.

Love, John. *Geodaesia: or the Art of Surveying and Measuring of Land Made Easie*. London, 1688.

Lucar, Cyprian. *A treatise named Lucarsolace*. London, 1590.

Machiavelli, Niccolò. *The Discourses*. Ed. Bernard Crick, trans. Leslie J. Walker. Harmondsworth: Penguin, 1970.

———. *The Prince*. Trans. George Bull. Harmondsworth: Penguin, 1961.

Machyn, Henry. *The Diary of Henry Machyn*. Ed. J. G. Nichols. London: Camden Society, 1847.

Maguel, Francis. "Report of What Francisco Maguel, an Irishman, Learned in the State of Virginia during the Eight Months that He was There, July 1, 1610." In Brown, *Genesis*, 393ff.

Manchester Papers. In Historical Manuscripts Commission, *Report VIII*, App. 2. 1881.

"Mary Ambree." In *Oxford Book of Ballads*, ed Arthur Quiller-Crouch. Oxford: Clarendon Press, 1910. 829–31.

Mason, Thomas, ed. *A Register of Baptisms, Marriages, and Burials in St. Martin in the Fields . . . 1550 to 1619*. Harleian Society Registers, 25. London: Harleian Society, 1898.

Massachusetts. *The Book of the General Lawes and Libertyes Concerning the Inhabitants of the Massachusetts: Reproduced in Facsimile from the Unique 1648 Edition in the Huntington Library*. Ed. Thomas Barden Barnes. San Marino, Calif.: Huntington Library, 1975.

———. *Records of the Court of Assistants of the Colony of Massachusetts Bay, 1630–1692*.

Ed. John Noble and John F. Cronin. 3 vols. Boston: Published by the County of Suffolk, 1901-28.

———. *Records of the Governor and Company of the Massachusetts Bay in New England.* Ed. Nathaniel B. Shurtleff. 5 vols. Boston: W. White printer to the Commonwealth, 1853-54.

Massinger, Thomas. *The Bondman.* London, 1624.

Mathew, Thomas. "The Beginning, Progress, and Conclusion of Bacon's Rebellion, 1675-1676 (1705)." In Andrews, *Narratives of the Insurrections,* 15-41.

Mayerne, Louis Turquet de. *The Generall History of Spaine.* Trans. Sir Edward Grimeson. London: A. Islip and G. Eld, 1612.

Monson, Sir William. *The Naval Tracts of Sir William Monson.* Ed. M. Oppenheim. 4 vols. London: Naval Records Society, 1913.

———. *A True and Exact Account of the Wars with Spain, in the Reign of Q. Elizabeth.* London: W. Crooke, 1682.

Montanus, Gonsalvius. *A Discovery and Playne Declaration of the Sundry and Subtill Practices of the Holy Inquisition of Spayne.* London, 1568.

Moore, Adam. *Bread for the Poor and Advancement of the English Nation Promised by Enclosure of the Wastes and Common Grounds of England.* London, 1653.

More News from Virginia. London: for William Harris, 1677. In Finestone, *Bacon's Rebellion,* 19-27.

More, Thomas. *Utopia.* Trans. and ed. Robert M. Adams. New York: Norton, 1992.

Moryson, Fynes. *An Itinerary written by Fynes Moryson, Gent. First in the Latine Tongue, and then Translated by him into English Containing His Ten Yeeres Travell through the Twelve Dominions of Germany, Bohmerland, Switzerland, Netherland, Denmarke, Poland, Italy, Turky, France, England, Scotland, and Ireland.* London: John Beale, 1617.

Moryson, Fynes. *An Itinerary . . . Containing His Ten Yeeres Travell through the Twelve Dominions.* 1617. 4 vols. New York and Glasgow: Macmillan, 1907-8.

[Munday, Anthony]. *The Admirable Deliverance of 266. Christians by John Reynard.* London, 1602.

Nashe, Thomas. *The Works of Thomas Nashe.* Ed. Ronald B. McKerrow. 5 vols. London, 1904. Reprint Oxford: Blackwell, 1958.

A New Description of Virginia. London: 1649. In Force, *Tracts,* vol. 2, item V8, 1-20.

Newton, Thomas. *A Notable Historie of the Saracens. Briefly and faithfully describing the originall beginning, continuance and successe as well of the Saracens, as also of Turkes, Souldans, Mamalukes, Assasines, Tartarians and Sophians.* London, 1575.

Norden, John. *Survey of Prince Charles's Manors* Additional ms. 6027. British Museum, London.

———. *Surveyor's Dialogue.* London, 1607.

Norwood, Colonel Henry. *A Voyage to Virginia.* 1649. In Force, *Tracts,* vol. 3, item X, 1-52.

Ovid. *Ovid's Metamorphosis Englished by G.S. Imprinted at London Mdcxxvi Cum Privilgio.* Trans. George Sandys. London, 1626. John Carter Brown Library copy.

———. *Ovid's Metamorphosis Englished, Mythologized, and Represented in Figures.* Trans. George Sandys. (1632 ed.) Ed. Karl K. Hulley and Stanley T. Vandersall. Lincoln: University of Nebraska Press, 1970.

Parke-Bernet Galleries. "The American Papers of Sir Nathaniel Rich, Property of His Grace the Tenth Duke of Manchester." May 5, 1970.

Payne, Robert. *A Brief Description of Ireland.* 1590. Ed. Aquila Smith. Dublin: Irish Archaeological Society, 1841.

Peckham, Sir George. "A True Report of the late discoveries and possessions, taken in the right of the Crowne of Englande, of the New-founde Landes . . . [1583]." In Quinn, *New American World,* 3: 34-59.

Peele, George. *Battel of Alcazar.* London: Edward Allde for Richard Bankworth, 1984.
Pepys, Samuel. *The Diary of Samuel Pepys.* Ed. Robert Latham and William Matthews. 11 vols. Berkeley: University of California Press, 1970–83.
Percy, George. "A Trewe Relacyon of the Procedeinges and Occurrentes of Moment which have hapned in Virginia." 1609–12. *Tylers Quarterly Magazine* 3 (1922): 266–67.
Perkins, William. *Workes.* 2 vols. London, 1631.
Plat, Hugh. *Sundrie New and Artificiall Remedies Against Famine.* London, 1596.
Platina, Bartolomeo. *On Right Pleasure and Good Health: A critical edition and translation of De honesta voluptate et valetudine.* Trans. and ed. Mary Ella Milham. Tempe, Ariz.: Medieval and Renaissance Texts and Studies, 1998.
Pory, John. *A Geographical Historie of Africa.* London, 1600.
Powell, William Stevens. *John Pory, 1572–1636: The Life and Letters of a Man of Many Parts.* Microfiche Supplement. Chapel Hill: University of North Carolina Press, 1977.
Purchas, Samuel. *Hakluytus Posthumus, or Purchas His Pilgrimes.* 1625. 20 vols. Glasgow: James MacLehose and Sons, 1905–7.
———. *Purchas His Pilgrimage, or Relations of the World.* 3rd ed. London: Henry Fetherstone, 1617.
———. *Purchas His Pilgrimes.* 4 vols. London: Henry Fetherstone, 1625.
———. "Virginia's Verger." In Purchas, *Hakluytus Posthumus,* 1905–7 ed., 19: 218–67.
Quinn, David B., ed. *New American World: A Documentary History of North America to 1612.* 5 vols. New York: Arno Press and Hector Bye, 1979.
———, ed. *The Roanoke Voyages, 1584–1590: Documents to Illustrate the English Voyages to North America Under the Patent Granted to Walter Raleigh in 1584.* 2 vols. Hakluyt Society Works 2nd ser. 104–5. London: Hakluyt Society, 1955. Reprint New York: Dover Publications, 1990.
———, ed. *The Voyages and Colonising Enterprises of Sir Humphrey Gilbert.* London: Hakluyt Society, 1940.
Ralegh, Sir Walter. *The Discoverie of the Large, Rich and Bewtiful Empyre of Guiana.* Ed. Neil L. Whitehead. Norman: University of Oklahoma Press, 1997.
Rathborne, Aaron. *The Surveyor in Foure bookes.* London, 1616.
A Relation of Maryland, together, vvith a map of the countrey, the conditions of the plantation, his Majesties charter to the Lord Baltemore. London, 1635.
Rich, Barnaby. *A New Description of Ireland.* London, 1610.
———. *A Short Survey of Ireland.* London, 1609.
———. *A True and Kinde Excuse written in defence of that booke, intitled A Newe Description of Ireland.* London, 1612.
Rich, Nathaniel. *The Rich Papers: Letters from Bermuda, 1615–1646.* Ed. Vernon A. Ives. Toronto: University of Toronto Press for Bermuda National Trust, 1984.
Rolfe, John. "The Copy of the Gentleman's Letters to Sir Thomas Dale." Ed. Ralph Hamor. *A True Discourse of the present estate of Virginia.* 1615. In Haile, *Jamestown Narratives,* 850–56.
Rosier, James. *A True Relation of the Most Prosperous Voyage Made this Present Yeere . . .* London: George Bishop, 1605.
S., J. *The Accomplished Ladies Rich Closet of Rarities: Or, The Ingenious Gentlewoman and Servant-Maids Delightful Companion.* 1687. 7th ed. London, 1715.
Shakespeare, William. *Norton Shakespeare.* Ed. Stephen Greenblatt. New York: Norton, 1996.
Sherwood, William. "William Sherwood's Account." *VMHB* 1 (1893–94).

Simmonds, William. *Proceedings of the English Colonie in Virginia Since their first beginning from England in the Yeare of Our Lord, 1606, till this present 1612.* In Billings, *Old Dominion*, 26–27.
Smith, John. *An Accidence or The Path-way to Experience. Necessary for All Young Sea-man, or Those that are Desirous to Goe to Sea. . . .* 1626. In Smith, *Complete Works*, 3: 5–40.
———. *Advertisements for the Unexperienced Planters of New England, or Any Where.* 1631. In Smith, *Complete Works*, 3: 253–312.
———. *Captain John Smith: A Select Edition of His Writings.* Ed. Karen Ordahl Kupperman. Chapel Hill: University of North Carolina Press, 1988.
———. *The Complete Works of Captain John Smith (1580–1631).* Ed. Philip L. Barbour. 3 vols. Chapel Hill: University of North Carolina Press, 1986.
———. *A Description of New England: or the Observations and Discoveries, of Captain John Smith (Admirall of that Country) in the North of America, in the Year of Our Lord 1614.* 1616. In Smith, *Complete Works*, 1: 387–414.
———. *The Generall Historie of Virginia, New-England, and the Summer Isles.* London: Michael Sparkes, 1624.
———. *The Generall Historie of Virginia, New England, and the Summer Isles.* 1624. In Smith, *Complete Works*, 2: 27–488.
———. *A Map of Virginia. With a Description of the Countrey, the Commodities, People, Government and Religion.* 1612. In Smith, *Complete Works*, 1: 121–290.
———. *The Proceedings of the English Colonie in Virginia [1606–1612].* London: Joseph Barnes, 1612. Also published as part two of *A Map of Virginia.*
———. *A Sea Grammar.* 1627. In Smith, *Complete Works*, 3: 41–122.
———. *A True Relation of Such Occurences and Accidents of Note, as Hath Hapned Since the First Planting of that Colony, Which is Now Resident in the South Part Thereof, Till the Last Returne.* London: John Tappe, 1608. In Smith, *Complete Works*, 1: 5–118.
———. *The True Travels, Adventures, and Observations of Captaine John Smith.* 1630. In Smith, *Complete Works*, 3: 125–252.
Smith, Sir Thomas. *De Republica Anglorum.* Ed. Mary Dewar. Cambridge: Cambridge University Press, 1982.
"The Smyth of Nibley Papers, 1613–1674." *New York Public Library Bulletin* (July 1897): 186–90.
Spelman, Henry. *Relation of Virginia.* London, 1609.
Spenser, Edmund. *The Faerie Queene.* Ed. A. C. Hamilton. Harlowe: Longman, 1977.
———. *A View of the State of Ireland.* Ed. Andrew Hadfield and Willy Maley. Oxford: Blackwell, 1997.
Standish, Arthur. *The Commons Complaint.* London, 1612.
Stith, William. *The History of the First Discovery and Settlement of Virginia.* Williamsburg, 1747. Reissue, London, 1753. Facsimile of 1747 edition. New York, 1865, Spartanburg, S.C.: Reprint Co., 1965.
Stow, John. *A Survey of London.* Oxford: Clarendon Press, 1908.
Strachey, William. *The Historie of Travell into Virginia Britania.* 1612. Ed. Louis B. Wright and Virginia Freund. Hakluyt Society Works 2nd ser. 103. London: Hakluyt Society, 1953.
———. *The True Reportory of the Wreck and Redemption of Sir Thomas Gates, Knight, upon and from the Islands of the Bermudas.* Ed. Louis B. Wright. Charlottesville: University Press of Virginia, 1964.
Strange News from Virginia. London, 1677. In Finestone, *Bacon's Rebellion,* 5–18.
Stubbes, Phillip. *The Anatomie of Abuses.* 1583. Reprint New York: Garland, 1973.
Stukeley, Thomas. *The Famous Historye of Captaine Thomas Stukeley.* Ed. Judith C. Levinson. Oxford: Oxford University Press, 1975.
Stukeley, William. Manuscript annotations, 1720, in Folger copy of *The Famous Historye of the life and death of Captaine Thomas Stukeley.* London: Thomas Pavyer, 1605.

Supple, Barry. *Commercial Crisis and Change in England, 1600–1642: A Study in the Instability of a Mercantile Economy*, Cambridge Studies in Economic History. 1959. Reprint Cambridge: Cambridge University Press, 1964.

"A Supplication of the blood of the English most lamentably murdered in Ireland, Cryeng out of the yearth for revenge." 1598. Ed. Willy Maley. *Analecta Hibernica* 36 (1994): 1–90.

Symonds, William. *A Sermon Preached at White Chappel*. London, 1609.

Tacitus, Cornelius. *The Agricola*. Trans. Henry Savile. London, 1598.

———. *On Britain and Germany*. Trans. H. Mattingly. Harmondsworth: Penguin, 1948.

———. *The Description of Germanie: and Customes of the People*. Trans. Richard Greneway. London, 1598.

Thorpe, Francis Newton, ed. *The Federal and State Constitutions, Colonial Charters, and Other Organic Laws.* . . . 7 vols. Washington, D.C.: Government Printing Office, 1909.

"A True Narrative of the Late Rebellion in Virginia, By the Royal Commissioners, 1677." In Andrews, *Narratives of the Insurrections*, 105–41.

United Kingdom Privy Council. *Acts of the Privy Council of England . . . New Series, 1542–1604.* 32 vols. Ed. John Roche Dasent. London: HMSO, 1890–1907.

United Kingdom Public Records Office. *Calendar of State Papers and Manuscripts*. Vol. 11, Venice. Ed. Horatio F. Brown. London: HMSO, 1904.

———. *Calendar of State Papers: Colonial Series*. Ed. William N. Sainsbury et al. 40 vols. London: HMSO, 1860–1939.

———. *Calendar of State Papers: Domestic Series, of the reigns of Edward VI, Mary, Elizabeth, and James I (1547–1625)*. Ed. Robert Lemon and Mary Anne Everett Green. 12 vols. London: HMSO, 1856–72.

Van Langan, I. *Explanation of the True and Lawfull Right and Tytle, of the Moste Excellente Prince Anthonie the First of that Name, King of Portugall, Concerning His Warres, Against Phillip King of Castile* . . . Leyden, 1585.

Verstegan, Richard. *A Restitution of Decayed Intelligence*. Antwerp, 1605.

Virginia Company of London. *The Records of the Virginia Company of London*. Ed. Susan Myra Kingsbury. 4 vols. Washington, D.C.: Government Printing Office, 1906–35. See also http://memory.loc.gov/ammem/mtjhtml/mtjser8.html#pub.

Virginia, Council in. "Letter to the Council of Virginia, 22 June 1607." In Brown, *American Genesis*, 1: 106–8.

———. "Instruccions, Orders and Constitucions by Way of Advice Sett Downe, Declared and Propounded to Sir Thomas Gates Knight Governor of Virginia and of the Colonie There Planted . . ." 1609. In *The Extension of Settlement in Florida, Virginia, and the Spanish Southwest*, ed. David B. Quinn. New York: Arno Press, 1979.

———. *A True Declaration of the Estate of the Colony in Virginia, With a Confutation of Such Scandalous Reports as Have Tended to the Disgrace of So Worthy an Enterprise*. London, 1610.

Virginia, General Assembly. *Journals of the House of Burgesses of Virginia, 1619–1658/59*. Ed. H. R. McIlwaine. Richmond: Virginia State Library, 1915.

Vitkus, Daniel J., ed. *Piracy, Slavery, and Redemption: Barbary Captivity Narratives from Early Modern England*. New York: Columbia University Press, 2001.

———, ed. *Three Turk Plays from Early Modern England*. New York: Columbia University Press, 2000.

W., E. *Virginia: More Especially the South part thereof, Richly and Truly ValuEd*. London, 1650. In Force, *Tracts*, vol. 3, no. 11, 1–64.

Waterhouse, Edward. *A Declaration of the State of the Colony in Virginia*. London, 1622.

Webbe, Edward. *The Rare and most wonderfull thinges.* London, 1610.
Whitaker, Alexander. Letter "To My Very Dear and Loving Cousin M[aster]-G[ouge], Minister of the B[lack] F[riars] in London," 18 June 1614.
White, John. *America 1585: The Complete Drawings of John White.* Ed. Paul Hulton. Chapel Hill: University of North Carolina Press, 1984.
―――. *The American Drawings of John White, 1577–1590.* Ed. Paul Hulton and David B. Quinn. 2 vols. London: British Museum, 1964.
[―――]. *The Planters Plea.* London: William Jones, 1630.
"The Whole Life and Death of Long Meg of Westminster." In *Amusing Prose Chapbooks,* ed. Robert Hays Cunningtham. London: Hamilton Adams, 1889, 299–309.
William I of Orange. *An Apology or Defense of My Lord the Prince of Orange . . . Against the Proclamation and Edict Published by the King of Spaine.* Delft, 1581.
Williams, Roger. *A Key into the Language of America.* London: Gregory Dexter, 1643. Facsimile reprint Menston: Scolar Press, 1971.
Wingfield, Edward Maria. "A Discourse per Edward Maria Wingfield." 1608. Lambeth Palace Library, MSS 250, 383–96. In Barbour, *Jamestown Voyages,* 213–34.
Wood, William. *New England's Prospect.* 2nd ed., 1635. Ed. Alden T. Vaughan. Amherst: University of Massachusetts Press, 1977.
Woolley, Hannah. *A Guide to Ladies, Gentlewomen and Maids.* London, 1668.
Worsop, Edward. *A Discoverie of Sundry Errours and Faults Daily Committed by Landemeaters.* London, 1582

Secondary Sources

Abun-Nasr, Jamil M. *A History of the Maghrib.* Cambridge: Cambridge University Press, 1971.
Adair, E. R. "English Galleys in the Sixteenth Century." *English Historical Review* 35 (1920): 497–512.
Adams, I. H. *Agrarian Landscape Terms: A Glossary for Historical Geography.* London: Institute of British Geographers, 1976.
Adler, Mortimer J. *Annals of America.* Vol. 1, *1493–1754: Discovering a New World.* Chicago: Encyclopedia Britannica, 1976.
Agnew, Jean-Christophe. *Worlds Apart: The Market and the Theater in Anglo-American Thought, 1550–1750.* Cambridge: Cambridge University Press, 1986.
Ahmad, Aijaz. "Jameson's Rhetoric of Otherness and the National Allegory." In *Theory: Classes, Nations, Literatures.* London: Verso: 1992.
Akrigg, G. P. V. *Jacobean Pageant: Or, The Court of King James I.* Cambridge, Mass.: Harvard University Press, 1962.
Albanese, Denise. *New Science, New World.* Durham, N.C.: Duke University Press, 1996.
Allen, Paul C. *Philip III and the Pax Hispanica, 1598–1621: The Failure of Grand Strategy.* New Haven, Conn.: Yale University Press, 2000.
Anderson, Benedict. *Imagined Communities: Reflections on the Origin and Spread of Nationalism.* London: Verso, 1990.
Andrews, Charles M. *The Colonial Period of American History.* 4 vols. New Haven, Conn.: Yale University Press, 1934. Reprint, with a foreword by Leonard W. Larrabee, 1964.
Andrews, Kenneth R. *Trade, Plunder and Settlement: Maritime Enterprise and the Genesis of the British Empire, 1480–1630.* Cambridge: Cambridge University Press, 1984.
Andrews, Kenneth R., Nicholas. P. Canny, and P. E. H. Hair, eds. *The Westward Enterprise, English Activities in Ireland, the Atlantic, and America, 1480–1650.* Liverpool: Liverpool University Press, 1978.

Appleby, Andrew. *Famine in Tudor and Stuart England.* Stanford, Calif.: Stanford University Press, 1978.
Appleby, John C. "'A Business of Much Difficulty': A London Slaving Venture, 1651–54." *Mariner's Mirror* 81, 1 (February 1995): 3–14.
———. "A Guinea Venture, c. 1657: A Note on the Early English Slave Trade." *Mariner's Mirror* 79, 1 (February 1993): 84–87.
———. "War, Politics, and Colonization, 1558–1625." In Canny, *Origins of Empire*, 55–78.
Archer, Ian W. *The Pursuit of Stability: Social Relations in Elizabethan London.* Cambridge: Cambridge University Press, 1991.
Arents, George, Jerome E. Brooks, and Alice Hollister Lerch. *Books, Manuscripts, and Drawings Relating to Tobacco from the Collection of George Arents, Jr., on Exhibition at the Library of Congress, Washington, D.C., April 1938.* Washington, D.C.: Government Printing Office, 1938.
Armitage, David. *The Ideological Origins of the British Empire.* Ideas in Context 59. Cambridge: Cambridge University Press, 1998.
———. "John Milton: Poet Against Empire." In *Milton and Republicanism, Ideas in Context,* ed. David Armitage, Armand Himy, and Quentin Skinner, 206–25. New York: Cambridge University Press, 1995.
———. "Literature and Empire." In Canny, *Origins of Empire*, 99–123.
———. "The New World and British Historical Thought: From Richard Hakluyt to William Robertson." In Kupperman, *America in European Consciousness*, 52–78.
———. *Theories of Empire.* Aldershot: Ashgate, 1998.
Ashcroft, Bill. *Post-Colonial Transformation.* London: Routledge, 2001.
Axtell, James. *After Columbus: Essays in the Ethnohistory of Colonial North America.* Oxford: Oxford University Press, 1988.
———. *The European and the Indian: Essays in the Ethnohistory of Colonial North America.* Oxford: Oxford University Press, 1981.
Aylmer, G. E. "Slavery Under Charles II: The Mediterranean and Tangier." *English Historical Review* 114 (April 1999): 378–88.
Bach, Rebecca A. *Colonial Transformations: The Cultural Production of the New Atlantic World, 1580–1640.* New York: Palgrave, 2000.
Baepler, Paul. "The Barbary Captivity Narrative in Early America." *Early American Literature* 30 (1995): 95–120.
———, ed. *White Slaves, African Masters: An Anthology of American Barbary Captivity Narratives.* Chicago: University of Chicago Press, 1999.
Bailyn, Bernard. *The Peopling of British North America: An Introduction.* New York: Knopf, 1986. Reprint New York: Vintage, 1988.
Barbour, Nevill. *Morocco.* New York: Walker, 1965.
———. "Northwest Africa from the 15th to 19th Centuries." In *The Last Great Muslim Empires—The Muslim World: Historical Survey,* ed. Hans J. Kissling, Bertold Spuler, et al., 97–147. Princeton, N.J.: Markus Weiner, 1969.
Barbour, Philip L. "The Earliest Reconnaisance of the Chesapeake Bay: Captain John Smith's Map and Indian Vocabulary." *VMHB* 80 (1972): 21–51.
———. "Introduction." In Smith, *True Travels,* 125–36.
———. *Pocahontas and Her World.* Boston: Houghton Mifflin, 1970.
———. *The Three Worlds of Captain John Smith.* Boston: Houghton Mifflin, 1964.
Barker, Francis, Peter Hulme, and Margaret Iversen, eds. *Cannibalism and the Colonial World.* Cambridge: Cambridge University Press, 1998.
Bartels, Emily C. "*Othello* and Africa: Postcolonialism Reconsidered." *WMQ* 54, 1 (January 1997): 45–64.
Batten, Charles L., Jr. "The Source of Aphra Behn's *The Widow Ranter*." *Restoration and 18th Century Theatre Research* 13 (1974): 12–18.

Baudott, Georges. "Amerindian Image and Utopian Project: Montolinía and Millenarian Discourse." In *Amerindian Images and the Legacy of Columbus*, ed. René Jara and Nicholas Spadaccini, 375–400. Minneapolis: University of Minnesota Press, 1992.
Baumgartner, Frederic J. *France in the Sixteenth Century*. New York: St. Martin's Press, 1995.
Beckwith, Ian. "Captain John Smith, the Yeoman Background." *History Today* 26, 7 (1976): 444–51.
Beer, George Louis. *The Origins of the British Colonial System, 1578–1660*. New York: Macmillan, 1908.
Bennell, J. E. G. "English Oared Vessels of the Sixteenth Century." *Mariner's Mirror* 60 (1974): 9–26, 169–85.
Berlin, Ira. *Many Thousands Gone: The First Two Centuries of Slavery in North America*. Cambridge, Mass.: Belknap Press of Harvard University Press, 1998.
Bernhard, Virginia. *Slaves and Slaveholders in Bermuda, 1616–1782*. Columbia: University of Missouri Press, 1999.
Bigland, Ralph. *Historical, Monumental and Genealogical Collections Relative to the County of Gloucester*. Ed. Brian Frith. Gloucester: Bristol and Gloucestershire Archeological Society, 1989.
Blackburn, Robin. *The Making of New World Slavery: From the Baroque to the Modern, 1492–1800*. London: Verso, 1997.
Blakemore, Michael. "From Way-Finding to Map-Making: The Spatial Information Fields of Aboriginal Peoples." *Progress in Human Geography* 5 (1981): 1–24.
Blanton, Dennis B. "Drought as a Factor in the Jamestown Colony, 1607–1612." *Historical Archaeology* 34 (2000): 74–81.
Boehmer, Elleke. *Colonial and Postcolonial Literature*. Oxford: Oxford University Press, 1995.
Boehrer, Bruce Thomas. *The Fury of Men's Gullets: Ben Jonson and the Digestive Canal*. Philadelphia: University of Pennsylvania Press, 1997.
Boelhower, William. "Inventing America: A Model of Cartographic Semiosis." *Word & Image* 4 (1988): 475–97.
Bonomi, Patricia U. "The Middle Colonies: Embryo of the New Political Order." In Vaugan and Billias, *Perspectives*, 63–94.
Bookin-Weiner, Jerome. "The 'Sallee Rovers': Morocco and Its Corsairs in the Seventeenth Century." In *The Middle East and North Africa: Essays in Honor of J. C. Hurewitz*, ed. Reeva S. Simon, 307–31. New York: Columbia University Press, 1990.
Boxer, C. R. *The Church Militant and Iberian Expansion, 1440–1770*. Baltimore: Johns Hopkins University Press, 1978.
Bradshaw, Brendan. "Geoffrey Keating: Apologist of Irish Ireland." In Bradshaw et al., *Representing Ireland*, 166–90.
Bradshaw, Brendan, Andrew Hadfield, and Willy Maley, *Representing Ireland: Literature and the Origins of Conflict, 1534–1660*. Cambridge: Cambridge University Press, 1993.
Brady, Ciaran. *The Chief Governors: The Rise and Fall of Reform Government in Tudor Ireland, 1536–1588*. Cambridge: Cambridge University Press, 1994.
———. "Spenser's Irish Crisis: Humanism and Experience in the 1590s." *Past and Present* 111 (May 1986): 17–49.
Bragdon, Kathleen J. *Native Peoples of Southern New England 1500–1650*. Norman: University of Oklahoma Press, 1996.
Braude, Benjamin. "The Sons of Noah and the Construction of Ethnic and Geographical Identities in the Medieval and Early Modern Periods." *WMQ* 54, 1 (January 1997): 103–43.

Braudel, Fernand. *The Mediterranean and the Mediterranean World in the Age of Philip II.* Trans. Siân Reynolds. 2 vols. New York: Harper and Row, 1972.

———. *The Perspective of the World.* Vol. 3 of *Civilization and Capitalism, 15th–18th Century.* Trans. Siân Reynolds. Berkeley: University of California Press, 1992.

———. *The Structures of Everyday Life: The Limits of the Possible.* Vol. 1 of *Civilization and Capitalism, 15th–18th Century.* Trans. Siân Reynolds. Berkeley: University of California Press, 1992.

Breen, T. H. and Stephen Innes. *"Myne Owne Ground": Race and Freedom on Virginia's Eastern Shore, 1640–1676.* New York: Oxford University Press, 1980.

Brenner, Robert. *Merchants and Revolution: Commercial Change, Political Conflict, and London's Overseas Traders, 1550–1653.* Princeton, N.J.: Princeton University Press, 1993.

Bridenbaugh, Carl. *Vexed and Troubled Englishmen, 1590–1642.* New York: Oxford University Press, 1968.

Bristol, Michael D. *Carnival and Theater: Plebeian Culture and the Structure of Authority in Renaissance England.* New York: Methuen, 1985.

Broadway, Jan. "John Smyth of Nibley: A Jacobean Man-of-Business and His Service to the Berkeley Family." *Midland History* 24 (1999): 79–97.

Brotton, Jerry. *Trading Territories: Mapping the Early Modern World.* Ithaca, N.Y.: Cornell University Press, 1997.

Brown, Alexander. *English Politics in Early Virginia History.* Boston: Houghton Mifflin, 1901. Reprint New York: Russell and Russell, 1968.

———. *The First Republic in America: An Account of the Origin of This Nation.* Boston: Houghton Mifflin, 1898.

Brown, Kathleen M. *Good Wives, Nasty Wenches, and Anxious Patriarchs: Gender, Race, and Power in Colonial Virginia.* Chapel Hill: University of North Carolina Press, 1996.

Bryson, Reid A. and Thomas J. Murray. *Climates of Hunger: Mankind and the World's Changing Weather.* Madison: University of Wisconsin Press, 1977.

Bucher, Bernadette. *Icon and Conquest: A Structural Analysis of the Illustrations of De Bry's Great Voyages.* Trans. Basia Miller Gulati. Chicago: University of Chicago Press, 1981.

Buisseret, David, ed. *From Sea Charts to Satellite Images:Interpreting North American History Through Maps.* Chicago: University of Chicago Press, 1990.

Bush, Jonathan A. "The First Slave (and why he matters)." *Cardozo Law Review* 18 (November 1996): 599–629.

Butlin, R. A. "The Enclosure of Open Fields and Extinction of Common Rights in England, Circa 1600–1750: A Review." In *Change in the Countryside: Essays on Rural England, 1500–1900,* ed. H. S. A Fox and R. A Butlin, 65–82. Institute of British Geographers Special Publication 10. London: Institute of British Geographers, 1979.

———. "Land and People, c.1600." In Moody et al. *A New History of Ireland,* 3: 142–67.

Calder, Angus. *Revolutionary Empire: The Rise of the English-Speaking Empires From the Fifteenth Century to the 1780s.* London: Cape, 1981.

Canny, Nicholas P. "Edmund Spenser and the Development of an Anglo-Irish Identity." *Yearbook of English Studies* 13 (1983): 1–19.

———. *The Elizabethan Conquest of Ireland: A Pattern Established, 1565–76.* Hassocks: Harvester, 1976.

———. "England's New World and the Old, 1480s–1530s." In Canny, *Origins of Empire,* 156–57.

———. "The Ideology of English Colonization: From Ireland to America." *WMQ* 30 (1973): 575–98.

———. *Kingdom and Colony: Ireland in the Atlantic World, 1560–1800.* Baltimore: Johns Hopkins University Press, 1988.

———. *Making Ireland British, 1580–1650.* Oxford: Oxford University Press, 2001.

———. "The Marginal Kingdom: Ireland as a Problem in the First British Empire." In *Strangers Within the Realm: Cultural Margins of the First British Empire*, ed. Bernard Baylin and Philip D. Morgan, 35–65. Chapel Hill: University of North Carolina Press, 1991.

———, ed. *The Origins of Empire: British Overseas Expansion to the Close of the Seventeenth Century.* Vol. 1 of *The Oxford History of the British Empire.* Oxford: Oxford University Press, 1998.

———. "The Permissive Frontier: Social Control in English Settlements in Ireland and Virginia, 1550–1650." In *The Westward Enterprise, English Activities in Ireland, the Atlantic, and America, 1480–1650*, ed. K. R. Andrews, Nicholas P. Canny, and P. E. H. Hair, 17–44. Liverpool: Liverpool University Press, 1978.

———. "'To Establish a Common Wealthe": Captain John Smith as New World Colonist." *VMHB* 92, 2 (1988): 213–22.

———. *The Upstart Earl: A Study of the Social and Mental World of Richard Boyle, First Earl of Cork, 1566–1643.* Cambridge: Cambridge University Press, 1982.

Canny, Nicholas P. and Anthony Pagden, eds. *Colonial Identity in the Atlantic World.* Princeton, N.J.: Princeton University Press, 1987.

Carr, Lois G. and Lorena S. Walsh, "The Planter's Wife: The Experience of White Women in Seventeenth-Century Maryland." *WMQ* 34 (1977): 542–71.

Cervantes, Fernando. *The Devil in the New World: The Impact of Diabolism in New Spain.* New Haven, Conn.: Yale University Press, 1994.

Chaplin, Joyce E. *Subject Matter: Technology, the Body, and Science on the Anglo-American Frontier, 1500–1676.* Cambridge, Mass.: Harvard University Press, 2001.

Chew, Samuel C. *The Crescent and the Rose: Islam and England During the Renaissance.* New York: Octagon Books, 1965.

Cheyfitz, Eric. *The Poetics of Imperialism: Translation and Colonisation from* The Tempest *to* Tarzan. Oxford: Oxford University Press, 1991. Reprint Philadelphia: University of Pennsylvania Press, 1997.

Clendinnen, Inga. "'Fierce and Unnatural Cruelty': Cortés and the Conquest of Mexico." In Greenblatt, *New World Encounters*, 12–47.

Clowes, W. Laird. *The Royal Navy: A History from the Earliest Times to the Present.* 7 vols. London: Low, Marston, 1897–1903.

Clucas, Stephen. "Thomas Harriot and the Field of Knowledge in the English Renaissance." In *Thomas Harriot: An Elizabethan Man of Science*, ed. Robert Fox, 93–136. Aldershot: Ashgate, 2000.

Cohen, Mark Nathan. "History, Diet, and Hunter-Gatherers." In *The Cambridge World History of Food*, ed. Kenneth F. Kile and Kriemhild Cornelas. 2 vols. Cambridge: Cambridge University Press, 2000.

Coleman, Janet. *A History of Political Thought: From the Middle Ages to the Renaissance.* Oxford: Blackwell, 2000.

Colley, Linda. "Britain and Islam, 1600–1800." *Yale Review* (October 2000): 2–20.

———. *Captives.* New York: Pantheon Books, 2003.

———. "The Narrative of Elizabeth Marsh: Barbary, Sex and Power." In Nussbaum, *Global Eighteenth Century*, 138–50.

Conley, Tom. "De Bry's Las Casas." In *Amerindian Images and the Legacy of Columbus*, ed. René Jara and Nicholas Spadaccini, 103–31. Minneapolis: University of Minnesota Press, 1992.

Connell-Smith, Gordon. *Forerunners of Drake: A Study of English Trade with Spain in the Early Tudor Period.* New York: Longmans Green for the Royal Empire Society, 1954.

Connor, Walker. "A Nation Is a Nation, Is a State, Is an Ethnic Group, Is a . . ." *Ethnic and Racial Studies* 1, 4 (1978): 377–97.
Cosgrove, Dennis. *Apollo's Eye: A Cartographic Genealogy of the Earth in the Western Imagination*. Baltimore: Johns Hopkins University Press, 2001.
Coughlan, Patricia. "'Some secret scourge which shall by her come unto England': Ireland and Incivility in Spenser." In *Spenser and Ireland: An Interdisciplinary Perspective*, ed. Patricia Coughlan, 46–74. Cork: Cork University Press, 1989.
Croft, Pauline. "New Light on Bates's Case." *Historical Journal* 30, 3 (1987): 523–39.
Cronon, William. *Changes in the Land: Indians, Colonists, and the Ecology of New England*. New York: Hill and Wang, 1983.
Crosby, Alfred W. *Ecological Imperialism: The Biological Expansion of Europe, 900–1900*. 2nd ed. New York: Cambridge University Press, 2004.
Cross, Claire, David Loades, and J. J. Scarisbrick, eds. *Law and Government Under the Tudors*. Cambridge: Cambridge University Press, 1998.
Crupi, Charles. "Subduing Bess Bridges: Ideological Shift in the Two Parts of *The Fair Maid of the West*. *Cahiers Élisabéthains* 54 (October 1998): 75–87.
Culliford, S. G. *William Strachey, 1572–1621*. Charlottesville: University of Virginia Press, 1965.
Cunningham, Bernadette. *The World of Geoffrey Keating: History, Myth and Religion in Seventeenth-Century Ireland*. Dublin: Four Courts Press, 2000.
Curry, Anne and Elizabeth Matthew, eds. *Concepts and Patterns of Service in the Later Middle Ages*. Woodbridge: Boydell, 2000.
Cust, Richard. "News and Politics in Early Seventeenth Century England." In *The English Civil War*, ed. Richard Cust and Ann Hughes, 233–60. London: Arnold, 1997.
Cust, Richard and Ann Hughes, eds. *The English Civil War*. Arnold Readers in History. London: Arnold, 1997.
D'Amico, Jack. *The Moor in English Renaissance Drama*. Tampa: University of South Florida Press, 1991.
Darby, H. C. "The Age of the Improver: 1600–1800." In *A New Historical Geography of England After 1600*, ed. H. C. Darby, 1–88. Cambridge: Cambridge University Press, 1973.
Davies, C. S. L. "Slavery and Protector Somerset: The Vagrancy Act of 1547." *Economic History Review* 2nd ser. 9 (1966): 533–49.
Davis, David Brion. *The Problem of Slavery in Western Culture*. Ithaca, N.Y.: Cornell University Press, 1966.
Davis, Jefferson. "Remarks on the Naval Appropriation Bill. June 18, 1860," and "Speech Before the Democratic State Convention at Jackson, Miss., July 6, 1859." In *Jefferson Davis, Constitutionalist: His Letters, Papers and Speeches*, ed. Dunbar Rowland. Jackson: Mississippi Department of Archives and History, 1923.
Davis, Richard Beale. "America in George Sandys' Ovid." *WMQ* 4 (1947): 297–304.
———. "Early Editions of George Sandys's 'Ovid': The Circumstances of Production." *Papers of the Bibliographical Society of America* 35 (4th quarter 1941): 255–76.
Davis, Robert C. "Counting European Slaves on the Barbary Coast." *Past and Present* 172 (August 2001): 87–124.
De Voto, Bernard. *The Course of Empire*. 1952. Boston: Houghton Mifflin, 1980.
Deal, Joseph Douglas. *Race and Class in Colonial Virginia: Indians, Englishmen, and Africans on the Eastern Shore During the Seventeenth Century*. New York: Garland, 1993.
Diamond, Jared M. *Guns, Germs, and Steel: The Fates of Human Societies*. New York: Norton, 1997.
Druett, John. *She Captains: Heroines and Hellions of the Sea*. New York: Simon and Schuster, 2000.

Duncan-Jones, Katherine. *Sir Philip Sidney: Courtier Poet.* New Haven, Conn.: Yale University Press, 1991.
Dunn, Richard S. "Seventeenth-Century English Historians of America." In *Seventeenth-Century America: Essays in Colonial History*, ed. James M. Smith, 195–225. Chapel Hill: University of North Carolina Press, 1959.
Eames, Wilberforce. *A Bibliography of Captain John Smith.* New York, 1927.
Earle, Carville V. "Environment, Disease, and Mortality in Early Virginia." In *The Chesapeake in the Seventeenth Century: Essays on Anglo-American Society*, ed. Thad W. Tate and David L. Ammerman, 96–125. Chapel Hill: University of North Carolina Press, 1979.
Edgerton, Samuel. *The Renaissance Rediscovery of Linear Perspective.* New York: Basic Books, 1975.
Edney, Matthew. "Theory and the History of Cartography." *Imago Mundi* 48 (1996): 185–91.
Eisenstein, Elizabeth L. *The Printing Press as an Agent of Change.* Cambridge: Cambridge University Press, 1982.
Elias, Norbert. *The Civilizing Process.* Trans. Edmund Jephcott. Oxford: Blackwell, 1994.
Elliott, J. H. *The Old World and the New, 1492–1650.* Cambridge: Cambridge University Press, 1970.
Ellis, Steven G. *Tudor Ireland: Crown, Community and the Conflict of Cultures, 1470–1603.* London: Longman, 1985.
———. "The Tudors and the Origins of the Modern Irish State: A Standing Army." In *A Military History of Ireland*, ed. Thomas Bartlett and Keith Jeffrey, 116–35. Cambridge: Cambridge University Press, 1996.
Ellison, James. *George Sandys: Travel, Colonialism, and Tolerance in the Seventeenth Century.* Studies in Renaissance Literature 8. Cambridge: D.S. Brewer, 2002.
Elrington, C. R. "Survey of Church Livings in Gloucestershire, 1650." *Transactions of the Bristol and Gloucestershire Archeological Society for 1964* (1965): 85–98.
Elrington, C. R. and N. M. Herbert, eds. *A History of the County of Gloucester.* London: Oxford University Press for the Institute of Historical Research, 1972.
Eltis, David. *The Rise of African Slavery in the Americas.* Cambridge: Cambridge University Press, 2000.
Emmer, P. C. "The Dutch and the Making of the Second Atlantic System." In *Slavery and the Rise of the Atlantic System*, ed. Barbara L. Solow, 75–88. Cambridge: Cambridge University Press, 1991.
Emmer, Pieter C. and Germán Carrera Damas. *General History of the Caribbean.* Vol. 2, *New Societies: The Caribbean in the Long Sixteenth Century.* London: UNESCO, 1999.
Eriksen, Thomas Hylland. *Ethnicity and Nationalism: Anthropological Perspectives.* London: Pluto Press, 1993.
Evans, William McKee. "From the Land of Canaan to the Land of Guinea: The Strange Odyssey of the 'Sons of Ham'." *American Historical Review* 85, 1 (February 1980): 15–43.
Faery, Rebecca Blevins. *Cartographies of Desire: Captivity, Race, and Sex in the Shaping of an American Nation.* Norman: University of Oklahoma Press, 1999.
Falkiner, C. Litton. *Illustrations of Irish History and Topography Mainly of the Seventeenth Century.* London: Longman, 1904.
Fallon, Niall. *The Armada in Ireland.* London: Stanford Maritime, 1978.
Fausto, Boris. *A Concise History of Brazil.* Trans. Arthur Brakel. Cambridge: Cambridge University Press, 1999.
Fausz, J. Frederick. "An 'Abundance of Blood Shed on Both Sides': England's First Indian War, 1609–1614." *VMHB* 98 (1990): 3–56.

———. "Patterns of Anglo-Indian Aggression and Accommodation Along the Mid-Atlantic Coast, 1584–1634." In *Cultures in Contact: The Impact of European Contacts on Native American Cultural Institutions, A.D. 1000–1800*, ed. William W. Fitzhugh, 225–55. Washington, D.C.: Smithsonian Institution Press, 1985.

Feest, Christian F. "The Virginia Indian in Pictures, 1612–1624." *Smithsonian Journal of History* 2 (1967): 1–30.

———. "Virginian Indian Miscellany III." *Archiv feur Vëolkerkunde* 26 (1972): 1–14.

Ferguson, Margaret. "News from the New World: Miscegenous Romance in Aphra Behn's *Oroonoko* and *The Widow Ranter*." In *The Production of English Renaissance Culture*, ed. David Lee Miller et al., 151–89. Ithaca, N.Y.: Cornell University Press, 1994.

Fernández Retamar, Roberto. "Against the Black Legend." In *Caliban and Other Essays*. Minneapolis: University of Minnesota Press, 1989.

Finley, M. I. "Colonies: An Attempt at Typology." *Transactions of the Royal Historical Society* 26 (1976): 167–88.

Fitzmaurice, Andrew. *Humanism and America: An Intellectual History of English Colonisation, 1500–1625*. Ideas in Context 67. New York: Cambridge University Press, 2003.

Fleming, Juliet. "The Renaissance Tattoo." *Review of Ethnographic Studies* 31 (1997): 35–52.

Foreman, Carolyn Thomas. *Indians Abroad, 1493–1938*. Norman: University of Oklahoma Press, 1943.

Foster, R. F. *Modern Ireland, 1600–1972*. London: Penguin, 1988.

Franklin, Alfred. *La Vie priveé d'autrefois: Arts et métiers, modes, moeurs*. 23 vols. Paris: Plon, 1887–1901.

Franklin, Peter. "Malaria in Medieval Gloucestershire: An Essay in Epidemiology." *Transactions of the Bristol and Gloucestershire Archeological Society for 1983* 101 (1984): 111–22.

Frantz, John B., ed. *Bacon's Rebellion: Prologue to the Revolution?* Lexington, Mass.: Heath, 1969.

French, Peter J. *John Dee: The World of an Elizabethan Magus*. London, 1972.

Friedman, Ellen G. "Christian Captives at 'Hard Labor' in Algiers, 16th–18th Centuries." *International Journal of African Historical Studies* 13, 4 (1980): 616–32.

Froude, James Anthony. *History of England from the Fall of Wolsey to the Defeat of the Spanish Armada*. 12 vols. New York: Scribner, Armstrong, 1873. Reprint New York: AMS Press, 1969.

Fryer, Peter. *Staying Power: The History of Black People in Britain*. London: Pluto Press, 1984.

Fuchs, Barbara. "Conquering Islands: Contextualizing *The Tempest*." *Shakespeare Quarterly* 48 (1997): 45–62.

Fuller, Mary C. *Voyages in Print: English Travel to America, 1576–1624*. Cambridge: Cambridge University Press, 1995.

Games, Alison. *Migration and the Origins of the English Atlantic World*. Cambridge, Mass.: Harvard University Press, 1999.

Garnsey, Peter. *Ideas of Slavery from Aristotle to Augustine*. Cambridge: Cambridge University Press, 1996.

Geertz, Clifford. *The Interpretation of Cultures*. New York: Basic Books, 1973.

Gethyn-Jones, J. Eric. "Berkeley Plantation, Virginia." Presidential Address, 1975. *Transactions of the Bristol and Gloucestershire Archeological Society for 1976* 94 (1977): 5–17.

———. *George Thorpe and the Berkeley Company: A Gloucestershire Enterprise in Virginia*. Gloucester: Alan Sutton, 1982.

Geyl, Pieter. *The Revolt of the Netherlands, 1555–1609.* 2nd ed. London: Ernest Benn, 1958.
Gibson, Charles. *The Black Legend of Spain: Anti-Spanish Attitudes in the Old World and the New.* New York: Knopf, 1971.
Gillespie, Raymond. *Colonial Ulster: The Settlement of East Ulster, 1600–41.* Cork: Cork University Press, 1985.
Gleach, Frederic W. *Powhatan's World and Colonial Virginia: A Conflict of Cultures.* Lincoln: University of Nebraska Press, 1997.
Goldberg, P. J. P. "What Was a Servant." In Curry and Matthew, *Concepts and Patterns of Service in the Later Middle Ages,* 21–37.
Góngora, Mario. *Studies in the Colonial History of Spanish America.* Trans. Richard Southern. Cambridge: Cambridge University Press, 1975.
Gonner, E. C. K. *Common Land and Enclosure.* London: Macmillan, 1912.
Goody, Jack. *Cooking, Cuisine and Class: A Study in Comparative Sociology.* Cambridge: Cambridge University Press, 1982.
Gosling, William Gilbert. *The Life of Sir Humphrey Gilbert: England's First Empire Builder.* 1911. Reprint Westport, Conn.: Greenwood Press, 1970.
Gradie, Charlotte M. "The Powhatans in the Context of the Spanish Empire." In *Powhatan Foreign Relations, 1500–1722,* ed. Helen C. Rountree, 154–72. Charlottesville: University of Virginia Press, 1993.
Green, L. C. and Olive P. Dickason. *The Law of Nations and the New World.* Edmonton: University of Alberta Press, 1988.
Greenblatt, Stephen. "Invisible Bullets: Renaissance Authority and Its Subversion, *Henry IV* and *Henry V.*" 1985. In *Shakespearean Negotiations: The Circulation of Social Energy in Renaissance England,* 21–65. Oxford: Clarendon Press, 1988.
———. *Marvellous Possessions: The Wonder of the New World.* Chicago: University of Chicago Press, 1991.
———, ed. *New World Encounters.* Berkeley: University of California Press, 1993.
———. *Renaissance Self-Fashioning.* Chicago: University of Chicago Press, 1980.
Greene, Jack P. *Pursuits of Happiness: The Social Development of Early Modern British Colonies and the Formation of American Culture.* Chapel Hill: University of North Carolina Press, 1988.
Greenfield, Matthew A. "Fragments of Nationalisms in *Troilus and Cressida.*" *Shakespeare Quarterly* 51, 2 (2000): 181–200.
Gregory, Derek. *Geographical Imaginations.* Cambridge, Mass.: Blackwell, 1994.
Gribbin, John and H. H. Lamb. "Climatic Change in Historical Times." In *Climatic Change,* ed. John Gribbin, 68–82. Cambridge: Cambridge University Press. 1978.
Griffin, Eric. "The Burden of Comedy: Ethno-poetics and the Whig Inheritance of Early Modern Literary Studies." *Diaspora: A Journal of Transnational Studies* (2003), in press.
———. "Ethos, Empire, and the Valiant Acts of Thomas Kyd's Tragedy of 'the Spains.'" *English Literary Renaissance* 31, 2 (Spring 2001): 202–22.
———. "From Ethos to Ethnos: Hispanizing 'the Spaniard' in the Old World and the New." In *CR: The New Centennial Review* 2, 1 (Spring 2002): 69–116.
———. "Un-sainting James: *Othello* and the 'Spanish Spirits' of Shakespeare's Globe." *Representations* 62 (Spring 1998): 58–99.
Grove, Jean M. *The Little Ice Age.* London: Methuen, 1988.
Guasco, Michael J. "Encounters, Identities, and Human Bondage: The Foundations of Racial Slavery in the Anglo-Atlantic World." Ph.D. dissertation, College of William and Mary, 2000.
Hadfield, Andrew. "Bruited Abroad: John White and Thomas Harriot's Colonial Representations of Ancient Britain." In *British Identities and English Renaissance*

Literature, ed. David Baker and Willy Maley. Cambridge: Cambridge University Press, 2002.

———. "Crossing the Borders: Ireland and the Irish between England and America," *Journal of Early Modern History: Contacts, Comparisons, Contrasts* 3, 2 (May 1999): 135–52.

———. *Literature, Travel and Colonial Writing in the English Renaissance, 1540–1625.* Oxford: Clarendon Press, 1998.

———. "A Percy Copy of Spenser's *View of the Present State of Ireland?*" *Notes and Queries* 242 (December 1997): 480–82.

———. "Rethinking the Black Legend: Sixteenth-Century English Identity and the Spanish Colonial Antichrist." *Reformation* 3 (1998): 303–22.

———. "The *Revelation* and early English Colonial Ventures." In *The Bible as Book: The Reformation*, ed. Orlaith O'Sullivan, 145–56. London: British Library, 2000.

———. "Rocking the Boat: A Response to Hiram Morgan," *Irish Review* 14 (Autumn 1993): 15–19.

———. *Spenser's Irish Experience: Wilde Fruyt and Salvage Soyl.* Oxford: Clarendon Press, 1997.

———. "Writing the New World: More 'Invisible Bullets.'" *Literature and History* 2nd ser. 2, 2 (Autumn 1991): 3–19.

Hadfield, Andrew and Willy Maley. "Introduction: Irish Representations and English Alternatives." In Bradshaw et al., *Representing Ireland*, 1–23.

Hadfield, Andrew and John McVeagh, eds. *Strangers to That Land: British Perceptions of Ireland from the Reformation to the Famine.* Gerald's Cross: Colin Smythe, 1994.

Hair, P. E. H. "Attitudes to Africans in English Primary Sources on Guinea up to 1650." *History in Africa* 26 (1999): 43–68.

Hair, P. E. H. and Robin Law. "The English in Western Africa to 1700." In Canny, *Origins of Empire*, 241–63.

Hall, Kim F. *Things of Darkness: Economies of Race and Gender in Early Modern England.* Ithaca, N.Y.: Cornell University Press, 1995.

Harley, J. B. "Deconstructing the Map." *Cartographica* 26, 2 (1989): 1–20.

———. "The Evaluation of Early Maps: Towards a Methodology." *Imago Mundi* 22 (1968): 62–74.

———. "The Map and the Development of the History of Cartography." In *The History of Cartography*, vol. 1, *Cartography in Prehistoric, Ancient, and Medieval Europe and the Mediterranean*, ed. J. B. Harley and David Woodward, 1–42. University of Chicago Press, 1987.

———. "Maps, Knowledge, and Power." In *The Iconography of Landscape: Essays on the Symbolic Representation, Design, and Use of Past Environments*, ed. Denis Cosgrove and Stephen Daniels. Cambridge: Cambridge University Press, 1988.

———. *The New Nature of Maps: Essays in the History of Cartography.* Ed. Paul Laxton. Baltimore: Johns Hopkins University Press, 2001.

———. "Rereading the Maps of the Columbian Encounter." *Annals of the Association of American Geographers* 82, 3 (1992): 522–36.

———. "Texts and Contexts in the Interpretation of Early Maps." In *Sea Charts to Satellite Images: Interpreting North American History through Maps*, ed. David Buissert, 3–19. Chicago: University of Chicago Press, 1990.

Harris, Bernard. "A Portrait of a Moor." In *Shakespeare Survey 11: The Last Plays*, ed. Allardyce Nicoll, 89–97. London: Cambridge University Press, 1958.

Hart, Jonathan. *Representing the New World: The English and French Uses of the Example of Spain.* New York: Palgrave, 2000.

Hayes, Kevin J. "Defining the Ideal Colonist: Captain John Smith's Revisions from *A True Relation* to the *Proceedings* to the Third Book of the *General Historie.*" *VMHB* 99, 2 (1991): 123–44.

Hayes-McCoy, G. A. "The Completion of the Tudor Conquest and the Advance of the Counter-Reformation, 1571–1603." In Moody et al., *A New History of Ireland*, 3: 94–141.

Headley, John M. "Campanella, America, and World Evangelization." In Kupperman, *European Consciousness*, 243–71.

Heal, Felicity. *Hospitality in Early Modern England*. Oxford: Oxford University Press, 1990.

Hebb, David Delison. *Piracy and the English Government, 1616–1642*. Aldershot: Scolar Press, 1994.

Helgerson, Richard. *Forms of Nationhood: The Elizabethan Writing of England*. Chicago: University of Chicago Press, 1992.

Hendricks, Margo. "Civility, Barbarism, and Aphra Behn's *The Widow Ranter*." In *Women, "Race," and Writing in the Early Modern Period*, ed. Margo Hendricks and Patricia Parker, 225–42. New York: Routledge, 1994.

Herman, Peter C. "'Is This Winning?' Prince Henry's Death and the Problem of Chivalry in *The Two Noble Kinsmen*." *South Atlantic Review* 62, 1 (1997): 1–31.

Hilgarth, J. N. *The Mirror of Spain, 1500–1700: The Formation of a Myth*. Ann Arbor: University of Michigan Press, 2000.

Hill, Christopher. *The Century of Revolution, 1603–1714*. 2nd ed. Walton-on-Thames: Nelson, 1980.

———. *Liberty Against the Law: Some Seventeenth-Century Controversies*. London: Penguin, 1996.

Hinton, E. M. "Rich's 'Anatomy of Ireland,' with an Account of the Author." *PMLA* 55 (1940): 73–101.

Hoenselaars, A. J. *Images of Englishmen and Foreigners in the drama of Shakespeare and His Contemporaries: A Study of Stage Characters and National Identity in English Renaissance Drama, 1558–1642*. Rutherford, N.J., Fairleigh Dickinson University Press, 1992.

Hoffman, Paul E. *A New Andalucia and a Way to the Orient: The American Southeast During the Sixteenth Century*. Baton Rouge: Louisiana State University Press, 1990.

———. *Spain and the Roanoke Voyages*. Raleigh: North Carolina Department of Resources and History, 1987.

Hogden, Margaret T. *Early Anthropology in the Sixteenth and Seventeenth Centuries*. Philadelphia: University of Pennsylvania Press, 1964.

Hopkins, A. G. "Viewpoint: Back to the Future: From National History to Imperial History." *Past and Present* 164 (1999): 198–243.

Horn, James. *Adapting to a New World: English Society in the Seventeenth-Century Chesapeake*. Chapel Hill: University of North Carolina Press, 1994.

———. "Tobacco Colonies: The Shaping of English Society in the Chesapeake." In Canny, *Origins of Empire*, 170–92.

Howard, Jean. "An English Lass Amid the Moors." In *Women, "Race," and Writing in the Early Modern Period*, ed. Margo Hendricks and Patricia Parker, 101–17. London: Routledge, 1994.

Howe, Daniel W. *American History in an Atlantic Context*. Oxford: Oxford University Press, 1993.

Hulme, Peter. *Colonial Encounters: Europe and the Native Caribbean, 1492–1797*. London: Methuen, 1986.

———. "Critical Response to Myra Jehlen." *Critical Inquiry* 20 (1993): 180–86.

———. "Hurricanes in the Caribbees: The Constitution of the Discourse of English Colonialism." In *1642: Literature and Power in the Seventeenth Century*, ed. Francis Barker et al., 55–83. Colchester: University of Essex, 1981.

Hulton, Paul. "Images of the New World: Jacques Le Moyne De Morgues and John White." In Andrews et al., *Westward Enterprise*, 195–214.

Huss-Ashmore, Rebecca and Susan L. Johnston. "Wild Plants as Famine Foods: Food Choice Under Conditions of Scarcity." In *Food Preferences and Taste: Continuity and Change*, ed. Helen Macbeth, 83–100. Providence, R.I.: Berghan Books, 1997.

Izon, John. *Sir Thomas Stuckley c. 1526–1578: Traitor Extraordinary*. London: Andrew Melrose, 1956.

Jablonski, Stephen. "Ham's Vicious Race: Slavery and John Milton." *Studies in English Literature, 1500–1900* 37, 1 (Winter 1997): 173–90.

Jackson, Jeremy B. C. et al. "Historical Overfishing and the Recent Collapse of Coastal Ecosystems." *Science* July 27, 2001.

Jardine, Lisa. "Encountering Ireland: Gabriel Harvey, Edmund Spenser, and English colonial ventures." In Bradshaw et al., *Representing Ireland*, 60–75. Cambridge: Cambridge University Press, 1993.

Jay, Paul. "Beyond Discipline?: Globalization and the Future of English." *PMLA* 116, 1 (January 2001): 32–47.

Jehlen, Myra. "Critical Response to Peter Hulme." *Critical Inquiry* 20 (1993), 187–91.

———. "History Before the Fact; Or, Captain John Smith's Unfinished Symphony." *Critical Inquiry* 19 (1993): 676–92.

Jennings, Francis. *The Invasion of America: Indians, Colonialism, and the Cant of Conquest*. Chapel Hill: University of North Carolina Press, 1975.

Jordan, Winthrop D. *White over Black: American Attitudes Toward the Negro, 1550–1812*. Chapel Hill: University of North Carolina Press, 1968.

Juderías, Julián. *La Leyenda negra: Estudios acerca del concepto de España en el extranjero*. 1914. Reprint Barcelona: Casa Editorial Araluce, 1929.

Julien, Charles Andre. *History of North Africa*. Trans. John Petrie, ed. C. C. Stewart. London: Routledge, 1970.

Juricek, John T. "English Territorial Claims in North America Under Elizabeth and the Early Stuarts," *Terrae Firma* 7 (1976): 12.

Kamen, Henry. *The Spanish Inquisition*. London: Folio Society, 1998.

Keen, Benjamin. *The Aztec Image in Western Thought*. New Brunswick, N.J.: Rutgers University Press, 1971.

Kendrick, T. D. *British Antiquity*. London: Methuen, 1950.

Keuning, Johannes. "The History of Geographical Map Projections Until 1600." *Imago Mundi* 12 (1955): 1–24.

Kew, Graham, ed. *The Irish Sections of Fynes Moryson's Unpublished Itinerary*. Dublin: Irish Manuscripts Commission, 1998.

Kidd, Colin. *British Identities Before Nationalism: Ethnicity and Nationhood in the Atlantic World, 1600–1800*. Cambridge: Cambridge University Press, 1999.

Klein, Bernhard. *Maps and the Writing of Space in Early Modern England and Ireland*. London: Palgrave, 2001.

Knutson, Roslyn. "Elizabethan Documents, Captivity Narratives, and the Market for Foreign History Plays." *English Literary Renaissance* 26, 1 (Winter 1996): 75–110.

Kolodny, Annette. *The Lay of the Land: Metaphor as Experience and History in American Life and Letters*. Chapel Hill: University of North Carolina Press, 1975.

Konig, David Thomas. "Dale's Law and the Non-Common Law Origins of Criminal Justice in Virginia." *American Journal of Legal History* 26, 4 (October 1982): 354–75.

Kupperman, Karen Orhahl, ed. *America in European Consciousness, 1493–1750*. Chapel Hill: University of North Carolina Press, 1995.

———. "Apathy and Death in Early Jamestown." *Journal of American History* 66 (1979): 24–40.

———. "English Perceptions of Treachery, 1583–1640: The Case of American 'Savages.'" *Historical Journal* 20 (1977): 263–87.
———. *Indians and English: Facing Off in Early America.* Ithaca, N.Y.: Cornell University Press, 2000.
———. "Introduction." In John Smith, *Captain John Smith: A Select Edition of His Writings.*
———. "Introduction." In Kupperman, *European Consciousness,* 1–32.
———. *Roanoke: The Abandoned Colony.* Totowa, N.J.: Rowman and Littlefield, 1984.
———. *Settling with the Indians: The Meeting of English and Indian Cultures in America, 1580–1640.* London: Dent, 1980.
Kurlansky, Mark. *Cod: A Biography of the Fish That Changed the World.* New York: Walker and Company, 1997.
Kussmaul, Ann. *Servants in Husbandry in Early Modern England.* Cambridge: Cambridge University Press, 1981.
Kwamena-Poh, M. A., John Tosh, Richard Waller, and Michael Tidy. *African History in Maps.* Harlow, Essex: Longman Group, 1982.
Lacey, Robert. *Sir Walter Ralegh.* London: Sphere, 1975.
Lacqueur, Thomas. *Making Sex: Body and Gender from the Greeks to Freud.* Cambridge, Mass.: Harvard University Press, 1990.
Lange, Karen E. "Unsettling Discoveries at Jamestown: Suffering and Surviving in 17th-Century Virginia." *National Geographic* 201, 6 (June 2002): 74–81.
Lemay, J. A. Leo. "Captain John Smith: American?" *University of Mississippi Studies in English* n.s. 5 (1984–7): 3–16.
Lennon, Colm. *The Lords of Dublin in the Age of Reformation.* Dublin: Irish Academic Press, 1989.
———. *Richard Stanihurst, the Dubliner, 1547–1618.* Dublin: Irish Academic Press, 1981.
———. *Sixteenth-Century Ireland: The Incomplete Conquest.* New York: St. Martin's Press, 1995.
Laxton, Paul, ed. *The New Nature of Maps: Essays in the History of Cartography.* Baltimore: Johns Hopkins University Press, 2001.
Leonard, Irving A. *Books of the Brave: Being an Account of Books and of Men in the Spanish Conquest and Settlement of the Sixteenth-Century New World.* 1949. Reprint with a new introduction by Rolena Adorno. Berkeley: University of California Press, 1992.
Lestringant, Frank. *Mapping the Renaissance World: The Geographical Imagination in the Age of Discovery.* Trans. David Fausett. Berkeley: University of California Press, 1994.
Lévi-Strauss, Claude. *Tristes Tropiques.* Trans. John Weightman and Doreen Weightman. New York: Atheneum, 1984.
Lewis, Bernard. *The Muslim Discovery of Europe.* New York: W.W. Norton, 1982.
———. *Race and Slavery in the Middle East: An Historical Inquiry.* New York: Oxford University Press, 1990.
Lewis, Clifford Merle, Albert J. Loomie, and Virginia Historical Society. *The Spanish Jesuit Mission in Virginia, 1570–1572.* Chapel Hill: University of North Carolina Press for the Virginia Historical Society, 1953.
Lewis, G. Malcolm. "The Indigenous Maps and Mapping of North American Indians." *Map Collector* 9 (1979): 25–32.
Lloyd, Christopher. *English Corsairs on the Barbary Coast.* London: Collins, 1981.
Lloyd, T. O. *The British Empire, 1558–1995.* 2nd ed. Oxford: Oxford University Press, 1996.
Lorimer, Joyce. *English and Irish Settlement on the River Amazon, 1550–1646.* Works Issued by the Hakluyt Society 2nd ser. 171. London: Hakluyt Society, 1989.

Lovejoy, Paul E. *Transformations in Slavery: A History of Slavery in Africa.* New York: Cambridge University Press, 1983.
MacCarthy-Morrogh, Michael. *The Munster Plantation: English migration to southern Ireland, 1583–1641.* Oxford: Clarendon Press, 1986.
MacDougall, Hugh A. *Racial Myth in English History: Trojans, Teutons, and Anglo-Saxons.* Montreal: Harvest House, 1982.
Mackenthun, Gesa. *Metaphors of Dispossession: American Beginnings and the Translation of Empire, 1492–1637.* Norman: University of Oklahoma Press, 1997.
Maltby, William S. *The Black Legend in England: The Development of Anti-Spanish Sentiment, 1558–1660.* Durham, N.C.: Duke University Press, 1971.
Manning, Patrick. *Slavery and African Life: Occidental, Oriental, and African Slave Trades.* New York: Cambridge University Press, 1990.
Martin, James Kirby, ed. *Interpreting Colonial America: Selected Readings.* 2nd ed. New York: Harper and Row, 1978.
Matar, Nabil. "Introduction: England and Mediterranean Captivity, 1577–1704." In *Piracy, Slavery, and Redemption: Barbary Captivity Narratives from Early Modern England*, ed. Daniel J. Vitkus, 1–52. New York: Columbia University Press, 2001.
———. *Turks, Moors, and Englishmen in the Age of Discovery.* New York: Columbia University Press, 1999.
McCabe, Richard A., "The Fate of Irena: Spenser and Political Violence." In *Spenser and Ireland: An Interdisciplinary Perspective*, ed. Patricia Coughlan, 109–25. Cork: Cork University Press, 1989.
McCartney, Martha W. *Biographical Sketches: People Associated with Jamestown Island.* An Archeological Assessment of Jamestown, Virginia Technical Report 5th ser. 3. Williamsburg: Prepared for Colonial National Historic Park, National Park Service, 1998.
McCary, Ben C. *John Smith's Map of Virginia.* Williamsburg: Virginia 350th Anniversary Celebration Corporation, 1957.
McGrath, Patrick. "Bristol and America 1480–1631." In Andrews et al., *Westward Enterprise*, 81–102.
McHugh, P. G. "A Tribal Encounter: The Presence and Properties of Common Law Language in the Discourse of Colonisation in the Early-Modern Period." In *Voyages and Beaches: Pacific Encounters, 1769–1840*, ed. Alex Calder, Jonathan Lamb and Bridget Orr, 114–31. Honolulu: University of Hawai'i Press, 1999.
McKeon, Michael. *The Origins of the English Novel, 1600–1740.* Baltimore: Johns Hopkins University Press, 1987.
McLeod, Bruce, *The Geography of Empire in English Literature, 1580–1745.* Cambridge: Cambridge University Press, 1999.
McRae, Andrew. *God Speed the Plough: The Representation of Agrarian England, 1500–1660.* Cambridge: Cambridge University Press, 1996.
———. "Husbandry Manuals and the Language of Agricultural Improvement." In *Culture and Cultivation in Early Modern England: Writing and the Land*, ed. Michael Leslie and Timothy Raylor, 35–62. Leicester: Leicester University Press, 1992.
Meinig, D. W. *The Shaping of America: A Geographical Perspective on 500 Years of History.* Vol. 1, *Atlantic America, 1492–1800.* New Haven, Conn.: Yale University Press, 1986.
Menard, Russell. "From Servant to Freeholder: Status Mobility and Property Accumulation in Seventeenth-Century Maryland." *WMQ* 30, 1 (1973): 37–64.
Mendelson, Sara Heller. *The Mental World of Stuart Women: Three Studies.* Brighton: Harvester Press, 1987.
Mignolo, Walter. "Local Histories/Global Designs." In *Latin America and Postmodernity*, ed. Pedro Lange-Churion and Eduardo Mendieta, 177–209. New York: Prometheus, 2001.

———. "Putting the Americas on the Map: Cartography and the Colonization of Space." In *The Darker Side of the Renaissance: Literacy, Territoriality, and Colonization*, 259–313. Ann Arbor: University of Michigan Press, 1995.

Miller, Shannon. *Invested with Meaning: The Raleigh Circle in the New World*. Philadelphia: University of Pennsylvania Press, 1998.

Miller, William Ian. "Gluttony." *Representations* 60 (1997): 92–112.

Milton, Giles. *Big Chief Elizabeth: How England's Adventurers Gambled and Won the New World*. London: Hodder and Stoughton, 2000.

Mintz, Sidney W. "The Changing Roles of Food in the Study of Consumption." In *Consumption and the World of Goods*, ed. John Brewer and Roy Porter, 261–73. London: Routledge, 1993.

———. *Sweetness and Power: The Place of Sugar in Modern History*. New York: Viking, 1985.

Mohanty, Satya P. "Colonial Legacies, Multicultural Futures: Relativism, Objectivity, and the Challenge of Otherness." *PMLA* 110, 1 (January 1995): 108–18.

Montanari, Massimo. *The Culture of Food*. Trans. Carl Ipsen. Oxford: Blackwell, 1994.

Montrose, Louis. "The Work of Gender in the Discourse of Discovery." In Greenblatt, *New World Encounters*, 177–217.

Moody, T. W. *The Londonderry Plantation, 1609–41*. Belfast: W. Mullan and Son, 1939.

Moody, T. W., F. X. Martin, and F. J. Byrne, eds. *New History of Ireland*. Vol. 3, *Early Modern Ireland, 1534–1691*. Oxford: Clarendon Press, 1976.

Morgan, Edmund S. *American Slavery, American Freedom: The Ordeal of Colonial Virginia*. New York: W.W. Norton, 1975.

Morgan, Hiram. "The Colonial Venture of Sir Thomas Smith in Ulster, 1571–1575." *Historical Journal* 28 (1985): 261–78.

———. "Mid-Atlantic Blues." *Irish Review* 11 (Winter 1991/1992): 50–55.

———. *Tyrone's Rebellion: The Outbreak of the Nine Years War in Tudor Ireland*. Woodbridge: Royal Historical Society, 1993.

Mossiker, Frances. *Pocahontas: The Life and Legend*. New York: Knopf, 1976.

Mrozowski, Stephen A. "Colonization and the Commodification of Nature." *International Journal of Historical Archeology* 3 (1999): 153–66.

Muldoon, James. *The Americas in the Spanish World Order: The Justification for Conquest in the Seventeenth Century*. Philadelphia, 1994.

———. "Papal Responsibility for the Infidel: Another Look at Alexander VI's *Inter Caetera*." *Catholic Historical Review* 64 (1978): 168–84.

Murrin, John M. "A Roof Without Walls: The Dilemma of American National Identity." In *Beyond Confederation: Origins of the Constitution and American National Identity*, ed. Richard Beeman, Stephen Botein, and Edward C. Carter II, 333–48. Chapel Hill: University of North Carolina Press, 1987.

Murrin, John M. et al. *Liberty, Equality, Power: A History of the American People*. 2nd ed. Fort Worth: Harcourt Brace, 1999.

Neale, J. E. *Elizabeth and Her Parliaments, 1584–1601*. New York: St. Martin's Press, 1957.

———. *Queen Elizabeth*. London: Cape, 1934.

Neill, Edward D. *The History of the Virginia Company of London*. New York: Burt Franklin, 1869.

Noël Hume, Ivor. *Discoveries in Martin's Hundred*. Williamsburg Archeological Series 10. Williamsburg: Colonial Williamsburg Foundation, 1983.

———. *Martin's Hundred*. Rev. ed. Charlottesville: University Press of Virginia, 1991.

———. *The Virginia Adventure, Roanoke to James Towne: An Archaeological and Historical Odyssey*. New York: Knopf, 1994.

Noël Hume, Ivor and Audrey Noël Hume. *The Archaeology of Martin's Hundred.* 2 vols. Philadelphia: University of Pennsylvania Museum of Archaeology and Anthropology, and Williamsburg: Colonial Williamsburg Foundation, 2001.

Nugent, Nell Marion. *Cavaliers and Pioneers: Abstracts of Virginia Land Patents and Grants, 1623–1800.* Richmond, Va.: Dietz, 1934.

Nussbaum, Felicity, ed. *The Global Eighteenth Century.* Baltimore: Johns Hopkins University Press, 2003.

O'Malley, John W. *The First Jesuits.* Cambridge, Mass.: Harvard University Press, 1993.

O'Mara, V. M. *A Study and Edition of Selected Middle English Sermons.* Leeds: University of Leeds, 1994.

Oberg, Michael Leroy. "Between 'Savage Man' and 'Most Faithful Englishman': Manteo and the Early Anglo-Indian Exchange, 1584–1590." *Itinerario* 24 (2000): 146–69.

———. *Dominion and Civility: English Imperialism and Native America, 1585–1685.* Ithaca, N.Y.: Cornell University Press, 1999.

Obrist, Barbara. "Wind Diagrams and Medieval Cosmology." *Speculum* 72 (1977): 33–84.

Ohlmeyer, Jane H. "Colonization Within Britain and Ireland." In Canny, ed., *Origins of Empire*, 124–47.

Orr, Bridget. *Empire on the English Stage 1660–1714.* Cambridge: Cambridge University Press, 2001.

Paar, Karen. "The European Presence on the Chesapeake Bay Before Jamestown." Texts of Imagination and Empire, Folger Institute website: www.folger.edu/institute/jamestown/c_parr.htm, accessed 28 February 2004.

Pagden, Anthony. *European Encounters with the New World.* New Haven, Conn.: Yale University Press, 1994.

———. *The Fall of Natural Man: the American Indian and the Origins of Comparative Ethnology.* Cambridge: Cambridge University Press, 1982.

———. "*Ius et Factum*: Text and Experience in the Writings of Bartolomé de Las Casas." In Greenblatt, *New World Encounters*, 85–100.

———. *Lords of all the World: Ideologies of Empire in Spain, Britain and France c.1500–c.1800.* New Haven, Conn.: Yale University Press, 1995.

Palliser, D. M. *The Age of Elizabeth: England Under the later Tudors, 1547–1603.* 2nd ed. London: Longman, 1992.

Parker, Geoffrey. *The Dutch Revolt.* Ithaca, N.Y.: Cornell University Press, 1977.

———. *The Grand Strategy of Philip II.* New Haven, Conn.: Yale University Press, 1998.

Parker, John. "Religion and the Virginia Colony, 1609–1610." In *The Westward Enterprise: English Activities in Ireland, the Atlantic, and America, 1480–1650*, ed. K. R. Andrews, Nicholas P. Canny, and P. E. H. Hair. Liverpool, Liverpool University Press, 1978.

Parker, Kenneth. "Introduction." In *Early Modern Tales of the Orient: A Critical Anthology*, ed. Kenneth Parker, 1–35. London: Routledge, 1999.

Parmellee, Lisa Ferraro. *Good Newes from Fraunce: French Anti-League Propaganda in Elizabethan England.* Rochester, N.Y.: University of Rochester Press, 1996.

Patterson, Annabel. *Reading Holinshed's Chronicles.* Chicago: University of Chicago Press, 1994.

Patterson, Orlando. *Freedom in the Making of Western Culture.* New York: Basic Books, 1991.

———. *Slavery and Social Death: A Comparative Study.* Cambridge, Mass.: Harvard University Press, 1982.

Pennington, Loren, ed. *The Purchas Handbook: Studies of the Life, Times and Writings of Samuel Purchas 1577–1626, with Bibliographies of His Books and of Works About Him*. London: Hakluyt Society, 1997.

Penrose, Boies. *Travel and Discovery in the Renaissance, 1420–1620*. Cambridge, Mass.: Harvard University Press, 1952.

Perdue, Theda. "Columbus Meets Pocahontas in the American South." *Southern Cultures* 3 (1997): 4–20.

Pfederer, Richard. "Portolan Charts: Vital Tool of the Age of Discovery." *History Today* 52 (2002): 20–27.

Phillips, William D., Jr. *Slavery from Roman Times to the Early Transatlantic Trade*. Minneapolis: University of Minnesota Press, 1985.

———. "The Old World Background of Slavery." In *Slavery and the Rise of the Atlantic System*, ed. Barbara L. Solow, 43–61. Cambridge: Cambridge University Press, 1991.

Pitcher, Donald Edgar. *An Historical Geography of the Ottoman Empire from Earliest Times to the End of the Sixteenth Century*. Leiden: Brill, 1973.

Pleij, Herman. *Dreaming of Cockaigne: Medieval Fantasies of the Perfect Life*. Trans. Diane Webb. New York: Columbia University Press, 1997.

Porter, H. C. *The Inconstant Savage: England and the North American Indian, 1500–1660*. London: Duckworth, 1979.

Potter, Stephen R. *Commoners, Tribute, and Chiefs: The Development of Algonquian Culture in the Potomac Valley*. Charlottesville: University of Virginia Press, 1993.

Potter, Stephen R. "Early English Effects on Virginia Algonquian Exchange and Tribute in the Tidewater Potomac." In Wood et al., *Powhatan's Mantle*, 151–72.

Powell, Philip Wayne. *Tree of Hate: Propaganda Affecting United States Relations with the Hispanic World*. New York: Basic Books, 1971.

Prager, Carolyn. "'Turkish' and Turkish Slavery: English Renaissance Perceptions of Levantine Bondage." *Centerpoint* (Fall 1976): 57–64.

Pratt, Mary Louise. *Imperial Eye: Travel Writing and Transculturation*. London: Routledge, 1992.

Quesada, Miguel Angel Ladero. "Spain, Circa 1492: Social Values and Structures." In *Implicit Understandings: Observing, Reporting, and Reflecting on the Encounters Between Europeans and Other Peoples in the Early Modern Era*, ed. Stuart B. Schwartz, 96–133. Cambridge: Cambridge University Press, 1994.

Quinn, David B. *The Elizabethans and the Irish*. Ithaca, N.Y.: Folger Monographs on Tudor and Stuart Culture, 1966.

———. *England and the Discovery of America, 1481–1620*. London: Allen and Unwin, 1974.

———. *Explorers and Colonies: America, 1500–1625*. London, 1990.

———, ed. *The Extension of Settlement in Florida, Virginia, and the Spanish Southwest*. New York: Arno Press, 1979.

———, ed. *The Hakluyt Handbook*. 2 vols. London: Hakluyt Society, 1974.

———. "Ireland and Sixteenth-Century European Expansion." *Historical Studies* 1 (1958), 20–32.

———. "New Geographical Horizons: Literature." In *First Images of America: The Impact of the New World on the Old*, ed. Fredi Chiappelli, 635–58. Berkeley: University of California Press, 1976.

———. *North America from the Earliest Discovery to First Settlements*. New York: Harper and Row, 1977.

———. *Ralegh and the British Empire*. New York: Macmillan, 1949.

———. "Renaissance Influences in English Colonisation," *Transactions of the Royal Historical Society* 5th ser. 26 (1976): 73–93.

———. "Sir Thomas Smith (1513–1577) and the Beginnings of English Colonial Theory." *Proceedings of the American Philosophical Society* 89 (1945), 543–60.

———. "Thomas Harriot and the Problem of America." In *Thomas Harriot: An Elizabethan Man of Science*, ed. Robert Fox, 9–27. Aldershot: Ashgate, 2000.

———. "'Virginians' on the Thames in 1603," *Terrae Incognitae*, 2 (1970): 7–14.

———, ed. *The Voyages and Colonising Enterprises of Sir Humphrey Gilbert.* London: Hakluyt Society, 1940.

Quinn, David B. and A. N. Ryan. *England's Sea Empire.* London: Allen and Unwin, 1983.

Quinn, David B. and John W. Shirley. "A Contemporary List of Harriot References." *Renaissance Quarterly* 22 (1969): 9–26.

Quint, David. *Epic and Empire: Politics and Generic Form from Virgil to Milton.* Princeton, N.J.: Princeton University Press, 1993.

Quitt, Martin H. "Trade and Acculturation at Jamestown, 1607–1609: The Limits of Understanding," *WMQ* 52 (1995): 227–58.

Ranger, Terence O. "Richard Boyle and the Making of an Irish Fortune, 1588–1641." *Irish Historical Studies* 10 (1957): 257–97.

Ransome, David R. "Pocahontas and the Mission to the Indians." *VMHB* 99 (1991): 81–94.

———. "Village Tensions in Early Virginia: Sex, Land, and Status and the Neck of Land in the 1620s." *Historical Journal* 43, 2 (2000): 365–85.

Read, David. "Colonialism and Coherence: The Case of Captain John Smith's *Generall Historie of Virginia.*" *Modern Philology* (1993): 428–48.

Reynolds, Clark. *Navies in History.* Annapolis, Md.: Naval Institute Press, 1998.

Richeson, A. W. *English Land Measuring to 1800: Instruments and Practices.* Cambridge, Mass.: Society for the History of Technology, 1966.

Richter, Daniel K. *Facing East from Indian Country: A Native History of Early America.* Cambridge, Mass.: Harvard University Press, 2001.

Robinson, W. Stitt. "Indian Education and Missions in Colonial Virginia." *Journal of Southern History* 18 (1952): 152–68.

Rose, Peter G., trans. and ed. *The Sensible Cook: Dutch Foodways in the Old and New World.* Syracuse, N.Y.: Syracuse University Press, 1989.

Rountree, Helen C. *Pocahontas's People: The Powhatan Indians of Virginia through Four Centuries.* Norman: University of Oklahoma Press, 1990.

———, ed. *Powhatan Foreign Relations, 1500–1722.* Charlottesville: University Press of Virginia, 1993.

———. *The Powhatan Indians of Virginia: Their Traditonal Culture.* Norman: University of Oklahoma Press, 1989.

———. "Powhatans and Other Woodland Indians as Travelers." In Rountree, *Powhatan Foreign Relations,* 21–52.

Rountree, Helen C. and Thomas E. Davidson. *Eastern Shore Indians of Virginia and Maryland.* Charlottesville: University Press of Virginia, 1997.

Rozbicki, Michal J. "To Save Them from Themselves: Proposals to Enslave the British Poor, 1698–1755." *Slavery and Abolition* 22, 2 (August 2001): 29–50.

Rubin, Deborah. *Ovid's Metamorphoses Englished: George Sandys as Translator and Mythographer.* New York: Garland, 1985.

Rustici, Craig. "The Smoking Girl: Tobacco and the Representation of Mary Frith." *Studies in Philology* 96, 2 (1999): 159–79.

Sacks, David Harris. *The Widening Gate: Bristol and the Atlantic Economy, 1450–1700.* Berkeley: University of California Press, 1991. See also http://ark.cdlib.org/ark:/13030/ft3f59n8d1/

Said, Edward W. *Culture and Imperialism.* New York: Knopf, 1993.

———. *Orientalism*. London: Penguin, 1985.
Samual, Raphael. *Island Stories: Unravelling Britain*. Ed. Alison Light with Sally Alexander and Gareth Stedman Jones. London: Verso, 1998.
Scammell, G. V. "The English in the Atlantic Islands, c. 1450–1650." *Mariner's Mirror* 72, 3 (August 1986): 295–317.
Scanlan, Thomas. *Colonial Writing in the New World, 1583–1671: Allegories of Desire*. Cambridge: Cambridge University Press, 1999.
Schama, Simon. *The Embarrassment of Riches: An Interpretation of Dutch Culture in the Golden Age*. Berkeley: University of California Press, 1988.
Schmidt, Benjamin. *Innocence Abroad: The Dutch Imagination and the New World, 1570–1670*. Cambridge: Cambridge University Press, 2001.
———. "Mapping an Empire: Cartographic and Colonial Rivalry in Seventeenth-Century Dutch and English North America." *WMQ* 54, 3 (1997): 549–78.
Schoenfeldt, Michael. *Bodies and Selves in Early Modern England*. Cambridge: Cambridge University Press, 1999.
Schwartz, Serena Ann. "An Interdisciplinary Approach to the Little Ice Age and Its Implications for Global Change Research." PhD dissertation, University of Michigan, 1994.
Sebek, Barbara. "'Strange Outlandish Wealth': Transglobal Commerce in *The Merchant Mappe of Commerce* and *The Fair Maid of the West, Parts I and I*." In *Playing the Globe: Genre and Geography in English Renaissance Drama*, ed. John Gillies and Virginia Mason Vaughan, 176–202. Madison, N.J.: Fairleigh Dickinson University Press, 1998.
Seed, Patricia. "Caliban and Native Title: 'This Island's Mine.'" In *"The Tempest" and Its Travels*, ed. Peter Hulme and William H. Sherman, 202–11. Philadelphia: University of Pennsylvania Press, 2000.
———. *Ceremonies of Possession: Europe's Conquest of the New World, 1492–1640*. Cambridge: Cambridge University Press, 1995.
———. "Taking Possession and Reading Texts: Establishing the Authority of Overseas Empires." *WMQ* 49 (1992): 183–92.
Seelye, John. *Prophetic Waters: The River in Early American Life and Literature*. New York: Oxford University Press, 1977.
Segal, Ronald. *Islam's Black Slaves: The Other Black Diaspora*. New York: Farrar, Straus, and Giroux, 2001.
Shaaber, Matthias A. *Some Forerunners of the Newspaper in England, 1476–1622*. Philadelphia: University of Pennsylvania Press, 1929.
Sheehan, A. J. "The Overthrow of the Plantation of Munster in October 1598." *Irish Sword* 15 (1982–83): 11–22.
Sheehan, Bernard W. *Savagism and Civility: Indians and Englishmen in Colonial Virginia*. Cambridge: Cambridge University Press, 1980.
Shirley, John W. "Sir Walter Raleigh and Thomas Harriot." In *Thomas Harriot: Renaissance Scientist*, ed. John W. Shirley, 16–35. Oxford: Oxford University Press, 1974.
Silke, J. J. "The Irish Appeal of 1593 to Spain: Some Light on the Genesis of the Nine Years War," *Irish Ecclesiastical Record* 5th ser. 92 (1959): 279–90.
Silver, Timothy. *A New Face on the Countryside: Indians, Colonists, and Slaves in South Atlantic Forests, 1500–1800*. Cambridge: Cambridge University Press, 1990.
Sim, Alison. *Food and Feast in Tudor England*. New York: St. Martin's Press, 1997.
Simon, Joan. *Education and Society in Tudor England*. Cambridge: Cambridge University Press, 1966.
Simpson, Richard. *The School of Shakespeare*. 2 vols. New York: J.W. Bouton, 1878.
Skidmore, Thomas E. and Peter H. Smith. *Modern Latin America*. New York: Oxford University Press, 2001.

Skilliter, S. A. *William Harbonne and the Trade with Turkey.* London: British Academy, Oxford University Press, 1977.
Skinner, Quentin. *Liberty Before Liberalism.* Cambridge: Cambridge University Press, 1998.
Slack, Paul. *Poverty and Policy in Tudor and Stuart England.* London: Longman, 1988.
Slotkin, Richard. *Regeneration Through Violence: The Mythology of the American Frontier, 1600–1860.* Middletown, Conn.: Wesleyan University Press, 1973.
Sluiter, Engel. "New Light on the '20. and Odd Negroes' Arriving in Virginia, August 1619." *WMQ* 54, 2 (April 1997): 395–98.
Smith, Abbott. *Colonists in Bondage: White Servitude and Convict Labor in America, 1607–1776.* Reprint Gloucester, Mass.: Peter Smith, 1965.
Sokol, B. J. "The Problem of Assessing Thomas Harriot's *A briefe and true report* of His Discoveries in North America." *Annals of Science* 51 (1994): 1–16.
Solow, Barbara L. "Slavery and Colonization." In *Slavery and the Rise of the Atlantic System,* ed., Barbara L. Solow, 21–42. Cambridge: Cambridge University Press, 1991.
Squier, Charles L. *John Fletcher.* Boston, 1986.
Stahle, David W. et al. "The Lost Colony and Jamestown Droughts." *Science* 280 (1998): 564–67.
Stiles, Martha Bennett. "Hostage to the Indians." *Virginia Cavalcade* 12 (Summer 1962): 5–11.
Stone, Lawrence. "The Educational Revolution in England, 1560–1640." *Past and Present* 28 (1964): 41–81.
Stradling, R. A. *Spain's Struggle for Europe 1598–1668.* London: Hambledon Press, 1994.
Striker, Laura Polanyi. "Captain John Smith's Hungary and Transylvania." In Bradford Smith, *Captain John Smith: His Life and Legend,* 311–42. Philadelphia: Lippincott, 1953.
Striker, Laura Polanyi and Bradford Smith. "The Rehabilitation of Captain John Smith." *Journal of Southern History* 28 (1962): 474–81.
Strong, Pauline Turner. *Captive Selves, Captivating Others: The Politics and Poetics of Colonial American Captivity Narratives.* Boulder, Colo.: Westview Press, 1999.
Sweet, James H. "The Iberian Roots of American Racist Thought." *WMQ* 54, 1 (January 1997): 143–66.
Sweet, John Wood. *Bodies Politic: Negotiating Race in the American North, 1730–1830.* Baltimore: Johns Hopkins University Press, 2003.
Tanner, Marie. *The Last Descendant of Aeneas: The Hapsburgs and the Mythic Image of the Emperor.* New Haven, Conn.: Yale University Press, 1993.
Tate, Thad W. and David L. Ammerman, eds. *The Chesapeake in the Seventeenth Century: Essays on Anglo-American Society.* Chapel Hill: University of North Carolina Press for the Institute of Early American History and Culture, 1979.
Taylor, Alan. *American Colonies.* New York: Viking, 2001.
Taylor, E. G. R. "The Agrarian Contribution to Surveying in England." *Geographical Journal* 82, 6 (1933): 529–35.
———. "The Surveyor." *Economic History Review* 17, 2 (1947): 121–33.
Taylor, James David. "'Base Commoditie': Natural Resource and Natural History in Smith's *The General Historie.*" *Environmental History Review* 7 (1993): 73–89.
Thirsk, Joan. *Economic Policy and Projects: The Development of a Consumer Society in Early Modern England.* Oxford: Clarendon Press, 1978.
———. "Projects for Gentlemen, Jobs for the Poor, Mutual Aid in the Vale of Tewkesbury 1600–1630." In *Essays in Bristol and Gloucestershire History: The Centenary Volume of the Bristol and Gloucestershire Archeological Society,* ed. Patrick McGrath

and John Cannon, 147–69. Bristol: Bristol and Gloucestershire Archeological Society, 1976.
Thomas, Keith. *Man and the Natural World: Changing Attitudes in England, 1500–1800.* New York: Oxford University Press, 1983.
Thorndale, William. "The Virginia Census of 1619." *Magazine of Virginia Genealogy* 13, 3 (Summer 1995): 155–70.
Thornton, John. *Africa and Africans in the Making of the Atlantic World, 1400–1800.* 2nd ed. Cambridge: Cambridge University Press, 1998.
———. "The African Experience of the '20. and Odd Negroes' Arriving in Virginia in 1619." *WMQ* 55, 3 (1998): 421–34.
Tilly, Louise A. "Food Entitlement, Famine, and Conflict." In *Hunger and History: The Impact of Changing Food Production and Consumption Patterns of Society,* ed. Robert Rothberg, Theodore K. Raab, and Ester Boserup, 135–68. Cambridge: Cambridge University Press, 1983.
Tilton, Robert S. *Pocahontas: The Evolution of an American Narrative.* Cambridge: Cambridge University Press, 1994.
Todd, Janet. *The Secret Life of Aphra Behn.* New Brunswick, N.J.: Rutgers University Press, 1997.
Todorov, Tzvetan. *The Conquest of America: The Question of the Other.* Trans. Richard Howard. New York: Harper and Row, 1984.
Traub, Valerie. "Mapping the Global Body." In *Early Modern Visual Culture: Representation, Race, and Empire in Renaissance England,* ed. Peter Erickson and Clark Hulse, 44–97. Philadelphia: University of Pennsylvania Press, 2000.
Tully, James. *A Discourse on Property: John Locke and His Adversaries.* Cambridge: Cambridge University Press, 1980.
Turner, E. Randolph. "Native American Protohistoric Interactions in the Powhatan Core Area." In Rountree, *Powhatan Foreign Relations,* 76–93.
Vaughan, Alden T. *American Genesis: Captain John Smith and the Founding of Virginia.* boston: Little, Brown, 1975.
———. "The Evolution of Virginia History: Early Historians of the First Colony." In Vaughan and Billias, *Perspectives,* 9–39.
———. "'Expulsion of the Salvages': English Policy and the Virginia Massacre of 1622." *WMQ* 35 (1978): 57–84.
———. *Roots of American Racism: Essays on the Colonial Experience.* Oxford: Oxford University Press, 1995.
———. "Sir Walter Ralegh's Indian Interpreters, 1584–1618." *WMQ* 59 (2002): 341–76.
Vaughan, Alden T. and George A. Billias, eds. *Perspectives on Early American History: Essays in Honor of Richard B. Morris.* New York: Harper and Row, 1973.
Vaughan, Alden T. and Virginia Mason Vaughan. "Before *Othello*: Elizabethan Representations of Sub-Saharan Africans." *WMQ* 54, 1 (January 1997): 19–44.
———. *Shakespeare's Caliban: A Cultural History.* Cambridge: Cambridge University Press, 1991.
Vitkus, Daniel J. "Introduction." In *Three Turk Plays,* 1–53.
Voss, Paul J. *Elizabethan News Pamphlets.* Pittsburgh: Duquesne University Press, 2001.
Walker, John. "The Social Economy of Dearth in Early Modern England." In *Famine, Disease, and the Social Order,* ed. John Walter and Roger Schofield, 75–128. Cambridge: Cambridge University Press, 1989.
Wallace, Willard M. *Sir Walter Raleigh.* Princeton, N.J.: Princeton University Press, 1959.
Ward, Harry M. "The Search for American Identity: Early Historians of New England." In Vaughan and Billias, *Perspectives,* 40–62.

Washburn, Wilcomb E. *The Governor and the Rebel: A History of Bacon's Rebellion in Virginia*. Chapel Hill: University of North Carolina Press, 1957.

Watson, Alan. "Seventeenth-Century Jurists, Roman Law, and the Law of Slavery." *Chicago-Kent Law Review* 68 (1993): 1343–54.

Webb, Stephen Saunders. *1676: The End of American Independence*. New York: Knopf, 1984.

Weber, Daniel J. *The Spanish Frontier in North America*. New Haven, Conn.: Yale University Press, 1992.

Weiner, Carol Z. "The Beleagured Isle: A study of Elizabethan and Early Jacobean Anti-Catholicism," *Past and Present* 51 (1971): 27–62.

Wernham, R. B. *After the Armada: Elizabethan England and the Struggle for Western Europe*. Oxford: Clarendon Press, 1984.

Wertenbaker, Thomas Jefferson. *Patrician and Plebeian in Virginia; or, the Origin and Development of the Social Classes of the Old Dominion*. Charlottesville, Va.: Michie Co., 1910.

———. *Torchbearer of the Revolution: The Story of Bacon's Rebellion and Its Leader*. Princeton, N.J.: Princeton University Press, 1940. Reprint Gloucester, Mass.: Peter Smith, 1965.

———. *Virginia Under the Stuarts, 1607–1688*. Princeton, N.J.: Princeton University Press, 1914. Reprint New York: Russell and Russell, 1959.

Wharton, James. *The Bounty of the Chesapeake: Fishing in Colonial Virginia*. Williamsburg: Anniversary Corporation, 1957.

Willan, T. S. *Studies in Elizabethan Foreign Trade*. Manchester: Manchester University Press, 1959.

Williams, Raymond. "Culture." In *Keywords: A Vocabulary of Culture and Society*. New York: Oxford University Press, 1983.

Williamson, Arthur H. "Scots, Indians and Empire: The Scottish Politics of Civilization." *Past and Present* 150 (1996): 46–83.

Wilson, Charles. *Queen Elizabeth and the Revolt of the Netherlands*. London: Macmillan, 1970.

Witmer, Anne and John Freehafer. "Aphra Behn's Strange News from Virginia." *Library Chronicle* 34, 1 (1968): 7–23.

Wood, Peter H., Gregory A. Waselkov, and M. Thomas Hatley, eds. *Powhatan's Mantle: Indians in the Colonial Southeast*. Lincoln: University of Nebraska Press, 1989.

Woodfield, Denis B. *Surreptitious Printing in England, 1550–1640*. New York: Bibliographical Society of America, 1973.

Woodward, David. "The Study of the History of Cartography: A Suggested Framework." *American Congress on Surveying and Mapping* 1 (1974): 101–15.

Worden, Blair. "English Republicanism." In *The Cambridge History of Political Thought 1450–1700*, ed J. H. Burns with Mark Goldie, 458–61. Cambridge: Cambridge University Press, 1991.

Wrightson, Keith. *Earthly Necessities: Economic Lives in Early Modern Britain*. New Haven, Conn.: Yale University Press, 2000.

Wrightson, Keith. *English Society, 1580–1680*. New Brunswick, N.J.: Rutgers University Press, 1982.

Young, Robert J. C. *Postcolonialism: An Historical Introduction*. Oxford: Blackwell, 2001.

Contributors

Robert Appelbaum, Lecturer in Renaissance Studies, Lancaster University, Lancaster, England, is the author of *Literature and Utopian Politics in Seventeenth-Century England* and numerous articles. He is currently at work on a study of literature, culture, and food in Europe, 1470–1700.

Pompa Banerjee, Associate Professor of English at the University of Colorado, Denver, is the author of *Burning Women: Widows, Witches, and Early Modern European Travelers* as well as numerous essays on early modern international relations.

Lisa Blansett directs the writing program at Wheelock College. She is completing three manuscripts: *Atlas of the Imagination; Cartographies: British Fiction and Mapping, 1700–1817;* and *Janet Schaw's Journal of a Lady of Quality: Travels in the Caribbean with Historical and Critical Appendices.*

Jess Edwards lectures in Early Modern English literature at London Metropolitan University. He is the author of the forthcoming *Geometry, Writing, and Space in Seventeenth-Century England and America.*

Eric Griffin, Associate Professor of English and Interdisciplinary Studies, Millsaps College, is the author of several articles on Anglo-Hispanic literary relations, and is currently completing a manuscript entitled *Ethno-Poetics and Empire.*

Michael J. Guasco, who teaches history at Davidson College, received his Ph.D. in 2000 from the College of William and Mary. His current research focuses on the development of slavery in Anglo-America.

Andrew Hadfield, Professor of English at the University of Sussex, is the author of three books on Ireland and English colonialism: *Literature, Politics and National Identity: Reformation to Renaissance; Spenser's Irish Experience: Wilde Fruit and Salvage Soyl;* and *Literature, Travel and Colonial Writing in the English Renaissance, 1545–1625.*

Peter C. Herman, Professor of English at San Diego State University, is the author of *Squitter-Wits and Muse-Haters: Sidney, Spenser, Milton, and Renaissance Antipoetic Sentiment* and the editor of five recent anthologies of essays.

Contributors

James Horn, Director of the John D. Rockefeller Jr. Library, Colonial Williamsburg Foundation, is the author of *Adapting to a New World: English Society in the Seventeenth-Century Chesapeake*.

Susan Iwanisziw received a Ph.D. in English from the University of Pennsylvania. She is the editor of *Troping "Oroonoko" from Behn to Bandele* and coeditor, with Jessica Munns, of *"Oroonoko": Adaptations and Offshoots*, forthcoming.

Constance Jordan, Professor Emeritus of English, Claremont Graduate University, is the author of two books, *Renaissance Feminism* and *Shakespeare's Monarchies*, as well as numerous articles. She is also the coeditor of *The Longman Anthology of British Literature* and editor of a new edition of *Hamlet*.

Karen Ordahl Kupperman, Silver Professor of History, New York University, is the award-winning author of a number of books on early colonial experience in America, including *Indians and English: Facing Off in Early America*; *Major Problems in American Colonial History*; and *Providence Island, 1630–1641: The Other Puritan Colony*. She is also editor of *America in European Consciousness, 1493–1750*.

Emily Rose, Senior Research Associate at the City University of New York, currently holds visiting fellowships at New Hall College, Cambridge University and the McNeil Center for Early American Studies at the University of Pennsylvania. She is at work on a monograph entitled *Company Colony, Court: The Triangular Politics of Virginia, 1619–1625*.

John Wood Sweet, who teaches history at the University of North Carolina, Chapel Hill, is the author of *Bodies Politic: Negotiating Race in the American North, 1730–1830*.

Alden T. Vaughan is Professor Emeritus of History at Columbia University. Among his publications are *New England Frontier: Puritans and Indians, 1620–1675*; *American Genesis: Captain John Smith and the Founding of Virginia*; and *Roots of American Racism: Essays on the Colonial Experience*. With Virginia Mason Vaughan he wrote *Shakespeare's Caliban: A Cultural History* and edited the new Arden Shakespeare edition of *The Tempest*.

Index

Abenaki Indians, 66
Abigail, 95, 102
Adam and Eve, 186, 190
Africa, xi, xii, 141, 244–50. *See also* Barbary
Africans, 14, 165, 237, 250–53; Black Africans, 165; West Africans, xi, 236, 237
Africanus, Leo, xi
agrarian reform, 229
"An Agreement of the People," 267
Alcazar, Battle of, 136, 154, 157, 159, 162, 167. *See also* Peele, George, *Battel of Alcazar*
Alexander VI (pope), 27
Algiers, 246, 248
Algonquian Indians, xiii, 138, 184; food and culture, 196–217; language, 33, 52
al-Malik, 'Abd ("Muly Molocco"), 153–55, 161–62
al-Mansur, Ahmad ("Mullisheg"), 152–57, 160–61, 163–64, 166–67, 171, 308 n. 7
al-Mutawakkil, Muhammed ("Muly Mahamet"), 153–55, 161–62, 164, 308 n. 7
Alsop, George, 107, 208
Amadas, Philip, 28
Amazon River, 30
Ambree, Mary, 164
America: as a continent, xiii, 30; as an idea, 231–32, 255; as a "wilderness," 18, 231–32
Amherst Island, 30
Andrews, Charles, 92–93
Anglicization of the landscape, 33
Anglo-American world, 118
Anglo-Moroccan relations, 152–71
Anne of Denmark, queen of England, 62
Antichrist, 180–81, 186, 190
Antonio, Don, 156
Appelbaum, Robert, 5, 16
approvement, 226. *See also* improvement
Arabs, 154
Arcadia, 28
archaeology, xiv
Archer, Gabriel, 32, 74
Ards Peninsula, 175–76

Argall, Samuel, 63, 65, 95
Ariosto, Lodovico, *Orlando Furioso*, 283
Armitage, David, 127, 219, 231, 205 nn. 99, 104
Arnold, Anthony, 267
Arundell, Peter, 100
Asia, 3
Atlantic Ocean, 28
Atlantic world, xi, 67, 100, 127, 131, 136, 141, 149, 276; as "frame" or context for historiography, xi–xv, 3, 30; "triangulated," 145; slavery in, 236–38, 250, 252
Avalon colony, 101

Bacon, Sir Francis, 222
Bacon, Nathaniel, 255, 262, 266–74, 287–88
Bacon's Rebellion, 6, 17, 21, 255, 262, 265–74, 321 n. 36
Bailyn, Bernard, 93
Balboa, Vasco Nuñez de, 113
Bale, John, 177
Baltimore, Calvert, Lord
Banerjee, Pompa, 14, 113, 133, 308 n. 7
Barbados, 207–8, 253
Barbary Coast, xi, 248–49; Barbary pirates, xi, 137, 149. *See also* Algiers; Morocco
Barbary Company, 155
Barbour, Philip, 138, 295 n. 41, 297 n. 29
Bargrave, John, 238
Barlowe, Arthur, 28–29
Basque (people), 30
Bateman, Robert, 103, 108
Batman, Stephen, 179
Beacon, Richard, *Solon His Follie*, 172–73, 176, 188
beer, 100–101
Behn, Aphra, 17; *The Roundheads*, 268, 271; *The Widdow Ranter*, 255–74, 287
Benevente, Toribio de. *See* Motolinía
Benzoni, Girolamo, *History of the New World*, 116
Beowulf, 86

Berkeley Hundred, 96
Berkeley, Sir William, 265–66, 272–73, 287
Bermuda, 15, 44, 54
Best, Thomas, 238
Beverley, Robert, 196, 198, 211, 256, 273, 314 n. 10
Bible, 238–39, 245, 318 n. 11
Black Legend, xi, 14,111–12, 116–19, 131, 134, 281
blackamores, 165
Blair, James, 256
Blansett, Lisa, 8, 218–9
Blount, Henry, *A Voyage into the Levant*, 145
Bodin, Jean, 179
Boemus, Jacob, 179
Boethius, 176
Boistaurau, Jean, 213–14
Boorde, Andrew, 202
Boscawen, Hugh, 253
Bourchier, Sir John, 106
Boyle, Richard, earl of Cork, 177
Bradford, William, 137
Braudel, Fernand, *Civilization and Capitalism*, 131–32
Brewer, Thomas, *A Knot of Fools*, 260
Bridges, Bess, 153, 161, 164–70
Brinsley, John, 56
Bristol, 96
Britain: ancient, 204; Anglo-Saxon, 15
Britomart, 164, 166, 170
Britons, 184, 204, 240–41
Bush, Jonathan, 241
Butler, Nathaniel, 59–60; *Unmasking of Virginia*, 106, 302 n.60
Byam, Henry, 247
Byrd, Robert, 212

Cabot, John 12, 26, 27
Cabot, Sebastian, 26
Cadiz, 168
Caesar, Augustus, 20
Caesar, Julius, 20, 277
Caliban, 178
Camden, William, 225, 240
Campanella, Tommaso, 116
Campion, Edmund, *Historie of Ireland*, 186, 189
cannibalism, 178, 214
Canny, Nicholas, 174–75, 177
Cape Ann, 136
Cape Breton, 26
Cape Cod, 30, 136

Cape Fear, 30
Cape Henry, 31
capitalism, 209–10, 222–23, 228
Carib Indians, 30, 178
Caribbean Sea, 27, 30. *See also* West Indies
Carleill, Christopher, 26
Carter's Grove, 108
cartography, 68–91, 217–20
Cassius, Dio, 204, 213
Castiglione, Baldassar, 323, n. 21
Catholics (Roman) and Catholicism, 12, 13, 113, 118, 157, 163, 174, 180; Catholic Antichrist, 180–81, 186, 190; Catholic Europe, 157–58, 167
Cecil, Sir Robert, 50–51, 221–22
Chamberlen, Peter, 264
Chaplin, Joyce, 292 n. 33, 305 n. 104
Charles I, 240, 266, 272
Charles II, 271
Charles V, Holy Roman Emperor, 116
Chaucer, Gregory, 202, 228, 270
Chawanoc Indians, 29
Chesapeake (region), xiv, 3, 30–31, 40–41
Chesapeake Bay, 3–4, 31, 74–75, 8
Chesapeake Indians, 34, 40
Chicheley, Sir Henry, 272
Chickahominie Indians, 46
Chilton, Edward, 256
chivalry, 148
Christianity, xiv, 154, 173; conversion to, 3, 49, 115, 123, 125. *See also* evangelization
Cicero, 176
civility, civilization, 173, 282; "civilizing" the natives, 124, 127; as *imperium*, 276. *See also* evangelization
Clark, John, 122
classrooms, modern, 92–93
Clifford family, 97
Coke, Sir Edward, 226–27
Cole, Humphrey, Compendium Dial, 88 (fig. 3.4)
colonialism: discourse of, 231; doctrine of, 172–73, 186, 219; ideology of, 231–35; Irish and American, 189–91
colonists: conception of natives, 8–9, 142, 277–78; English, 2–3, 16–17, 25–48; Roanoke, 4, 26–28; second and third waves (1610–11), 45; Spanish, 14
colonization, 29, 195, 234
Columbus, Christopher, 3, 11, 16, 113, 115, 129, 131
commodities, commodification, 195, 207–8, 215, 224

commons, 229–31
compass dial, 299 n.52
conflict, Anglo-Indian, 9, 25–48; armed, 9, 16, 34; cultural, 195–216; slaughter of Indians at celebration of peace treaty, 102. *See also* "Massacre" of 1622
Connacht, 177
Connell-Smith, Gordon, 290 n. 16
Connor, Walker, 303 n. 35
conquest, meaning of, 47
Constantinople, 139
"contact vision," 198, 214–15
"contact zone," 87, 218, 234, 299 n. 4
Cope, Sir Walter, 50–51, 281
Cork, 177
Cortéz, Hernán, 14, 113, 115–16, 134
Coup of 1622. *See* "Massacre of 1622"
Crashaw, William, 65–66
Cromwell, Oliver, 255, 266–67, 270–72, 288
Cronon, William, 197
Croatan Island, 50
Culpeper, Thomas, Lord, 273
cultural conflict. *See* conflict
culture, idea of, 71–73

D'Aranda, Emmanuel, 246
Daborne, Richard, *A Christian Turn'd Turke*, xv
Dale, Sir Thomas, 43, 58–59, 63, 65, 67, 125, 143; *Lawes Divine, Moral and Martiall*, 286
Danisker, Simon, 149
Darby, H. C., 225
Davies, Sir John, 189
Davies, William, 245–46
de Bry, Theodore, 81, 120 (fig. 5.2); engravings for Hariot, *Briefe and True Report*, 83–85 (figs.3.2, 3.3), 87, 181–87 (figs. 8.1, 8.2, 8.3), 197–200 (figs. 9.1, 9.2)
De La Warr, Thomas West, Lord, 43, 56; arrives in James River, 44
Dee, John, 26–27; *Elements of Euclid*, 82
Dekker, Thomas, *Lusts Dominion*, 137, 142, 144
dendrochronology, xiv
Derricke, John, *The Image of Ireland with a Discoverie of Woodkarne*, 185
"A Description of the River and Country," 285
Desdemona, 143
Desmond, earl of, 174
Dickinson, Jane, 238
diet books, 202

Digby, John, 122
Digest of Justinian, 239–40
disease, at Jamestown, 34–35, 101–2
Dolphin, 167
Dominican Order, 115–16
Donegal, 177
Donne, John, 148
Dowdall, Sir John, 178–79
Drake, Sir Francis, 29, 88, 129, 248
drama, English, 137, 156, 161
drought conditions, xiv, 198
Dublin, 177
Dundalk, siege of, 158
Dunn, Richard S., 255
Dutch (people and nation), xiii, 127–29; Dutch Sea Beggars, 129. *See also* Low Countries
Dymock, Cressy, 230

East, idea of the, 170
Eastern Shore, 38, 46
Eden, Garden of, 28, 186, 187 (fig. 8.3)
Eden, Richard, 113, 133
Edwards, Jess, 18, 298 n. 36
Effingham, Howard, Lord, 273
Eiakintomino, 57, 58 (fig. 2.1)
El Dorado, 30
Elias, Norbert, 205
Elizabeth I, 25, 27, 97, 136, 149, 152, 155–57, 163, 167, 169, 172
enclosure, 225, 229, 234
England, 12, 26, 30; attitudes toward slavery and freedom, 236–53; Church of, 202; economy, 207–8; "exhausted," in comparison to Virginia, 273–74; global aspirations of, 160; Powhatan embassies to, 49–67; Revolution, 267
English (people), 12, 13, 20; dominance over Ireland, 158–59, 179; empire, 171; English slaves, 238, 241–50; "Englishness," 146, 149; food practices, 200–210; intended by Powhatan to be absorbed into his dominions, 37; New and Old in Ireland, 188; policy toward foreign interlopers, 167; privateers, 29, 129
engraving, process of, 71
ethnography, 195–217
ethnohistorians, xiv
Europe, southern, 31
evangelization, 124, 125. *See also* Christianity, conversion to
exploration, 33

Fabian, William, 237
Fair Maid of the West. See Heywood, Thomas
Falls (of James River), 32
famine, 34, 45, 103, 165, 198, 207, 213, 284; in England, 99, 210–11; response at Jamestown under Smith, 44
Famous History of the Life and Death of Thomas Stukeley, xv, 135, 142, 153, 155, 161–64, 170
Fayal, 164–66
Ferguson, Margaret, 272
Fernandes, Simon, 27–28
Fernández, Alejo, *La Virgen de los Navagentes* 113, 114 (fig. 5.1)
Ferrar family, 107; Mrs. John, 106; Nicholas, 106
feudalism, 228, 232, 276
fish, 207–8
Fitz-Geffrey, Charles, 247, 249
Fitzherbert, John, 79, 242; *Boke of Surveyenge,* 220
Florida, 4, 26, 30, 121
food, foodstuffs, xiv, 16–17, 195–216, 284; food practices, 195–96
Fort Caroline, 121
Fox, John, 246
France, 26
Franciscan Order, 115–16
Franklin, Alfred, 205
French (people), 30
Frethorne, Richard, 11, 92–108, 215, 238, 280
Frobisher, Martin, 26, 129
Fuller, Mary C., 316 n.34

Galley Bonavolia, 243
Gates, Sir Thomas, 43–45, 56, 123–24
Gauls, 185
Geertz, Clifford, 302 nn. 3, 5
Genesis, 318 n. 11
Genoa, 129
geography, 217–35
Germans, ancient, 240–41
Gilbert, Sir Humphrey, 26, 27, 160, 174–75, 177
Gilbert, Sir John, 51
Giraldus, 186
Gleach, Frederic, 125, 292 n. 1
Glorious Revolution, 271
Gloucester, 95

Gloucestershire, 96–98
gluttony, 196, 202, 205
Godspeed, 31
gold, search for, 26, 30, 115,119
Gondomar, Diego Sarmiento de Acuña, Count, 121
Góngora, Mario, 115
Gonner, E. C. K., 229
Googe, Barnaby, 177
Gorges, Sir Ferdinando, 66
Gouge, William, 210–11
Gray, Robert, *A Good Speed to Virginia,* 18, 44, 282
Greenblatt, Stephen, 224, 272
Gregory (pope), 158–59
Grenville, Sir Richard, 25–26, 50
Grey, Lord, 177
Griffin, Eric, 14
Grymeston, Edmund, 243
Guasco, Michael J., 20
Guiana, 13, 30, 51, 115
Gulf of Mexico, 4
Gulstone, Theodore, 64

Hadfield, Andrew, 13, 15
Hakluyt, Richard (the elder), 12
Hakluyt, Richard (the younger), xi, 12, 26, 29, 112, 119, 126–27, 131–33, 141, 157, 181, 246, 281, 284; *Discourse of Western Planting,* 122–24, 223–24; *Principall Navigations,* 130, 181
Hall, Kim, 142–43
Hamor, Ralph, 53, 67
Handlin, Oscar, 93
Hansel and Gretel, 210
Hapsburg Empire, xiii, 152. *See also* Spain, Spanish Empire; Charles V
Harborne, Sir William, 136
Hariot, Thomas, 28–29, 32, 50, 79, 81, 123; *A Briefe and True Report of the New Found Land of Virginia,* 83, 180–90, 195–200, 223–24, 297 n.26
Harrison, William, 204–6, 240
Hartlib, Samuel, 230
Hartwell, Henry, 256
Harwood, William, 99–100, 102–3
Hatarask Island, 28
Hawkins, Sir John, 237, 243
Hebb, David, 319 n.33
Henry VII, 26, 27
Henry VIII, 158, 202
Henry, Cardinal, 157

Herbert, Thomas, 145
Herbert, Sir William, *Croftus sive de Hibernia Liber*, 176, 188
Herman, Peter, 17
Herodotus, 175–76, 283
Heywood, Thomas: *The Fair Maid of the West Part I*, 153, 161–70; *Part II*, 166; *If You Know Not Me, You Know Nobody*, 166
Hippocratic writers, 202
Hispanophilia, 132
Hispanophobia, 111, 132, 281
historians, 2; in contrast to literary critics, 6
Hole, William, 69, 71, 81, 83, 297 n. 7
Holinshed, Raphael, *Chronicles of England, Scotland, and Ireland*, 158, 163, 186
Holy Roman Empire, 13
Hooker, John, 186
Horn, James, 9
Howard, Jean, xv
Howell, James, 321 n.25
Hulme, Peter, 178, 231
Hungary, xiii, 137
hunger, 16–17, 196–217; horror of, 212–13

Iberia, as political unit, 118
Iceland, 137
ideology, 2, 219; American expansionist, 77; English, 161; imperial, 113–15. *See also* Spain, "specter of"
Imperium britannicum, 26, 277
improvement, 226, 228–29
indentured servants, 19, 104
"Indian College," 55–60, 124
Indians, North American, xiv, 28, 70, 286; agency in European texts, 90–91, 218; Caribbean, 14; compared to Picts, 181–86; education of by English, 55–60; food practices, 195–217; generalized image of, 81, 190, 232; presumed racial identity, 65, 251; representations of, 173, 178, 184, 217; as slaves, 251–53; treated like Irish, 175. *See also* Christianity, conversion to; individual groups
Ireland, xi, 12–13, 15, 118, 157–58, 161, 163, 167, 172–91, 282
Irish (people), 15, 29, 56, 164, 177; "wild Irish," 145, 178–80, 184–85, 188
Irish colonies, 13, 172–91
Isabella of Castile, 131
Islam, 150, 154, 247, 249
Islamic states, 152
Italy, 203, 209,
Iwaniszíw, Susan, 14

Jackson, Goodman, 103–4
Jahangir, emperor of Mughal, 136
James I, 5, 30–31, 64–65, 123, 153, 159–60, 221, 247, 249, 255, 301 n.50
James II, 271
James River, 32, 40, 74, 277
Jamestown: achieves prosperity, 100; conditions in, 99–102; founding, xi, 29–35, 160, 170, 278–80; General Assembly of 1619, 100; ideological and diplomatic context, 171; siege of (1609–10), 44; site, 34, 41; slaughter of Indians at celebration of peace treaty, 102; "starving time," 44–45, 103, 213–14; study of, xi–viv, 2–5; and tobacco trade, 21
Jeffreys, Herbert, Colonel, 273
Jennings, Francis, 212
Jerusalem, 115
Jesuits, 4, 125
Jews, expulsion of, 115
Jobson, Richard, 237
Johnson, Richard, "Life and Death of the Famous Thomas Stukeley," 162–63
Johnson, Robert, 107; *The New Life of Virginea*, 255; *Nova Britannia*, 25, 44
Jonson, Ben: *The Alchemist*, 132, 281; *Bartholomew Fair*, 259; *Epicoene*, 53
Jordan, Constance, 21
Josephus, Flavius, 213

Kainta, 55–56
Kecoughtan Indians, 32
Kellet, Edward, 247
Kelso, William, 112
Kendall, George, Captain, 121
King, Dr. John, 62
Kinsale, 159; Battle of, 174
Knolles, Richard, 136; *Generall Historie of the Turks*, 138
Kupperman, Karen, 2, 128, 136, 150–51, 177, 189, 198, 218–19, 234, 317 nn.69–71

labor, 148
Lambeth Palace, 62
Lane, Ralph, 29, 174, 177, 189, 223, 278
Las Casas, Bartolomé de, 115–16; *Brevissima relación de la destruyción de las indias*, 116–18, 180, 281; translated as *The Spanish Colonie*, 117
Lawson, John, 212
Le Challeux, Nicolas, *The discourse of the history of Florida*, 116–17
le Moyne de Morgues, Jacques, 66, 181

364 Index

Lee, Joseph, 230, 232
Lee, Samuel, 196
Leigh, Valentine, *The Most Profitable and Commendable Science, of Surveying of Landes*, 220
Leland, John, 225
Lembri, Francis ("Limbrecke"), 121–22
Levant Company, xi
Lévi-Strauss, Claude, 314 n.10
Lewis, Bernard, 137
Leyenda negra. See Black Legend
"The Life and Death of the Famous Thomas Stukeley," 162–63
Ligon, Richard, 207–8
Lipsius, Justus, 175–76
literary critics, in contrast to historians, 6
Little Gidding, 107
Little Ice Age, xiv
liturgical calendar, 201–2
Livy, 173, 176
Locke, John, 18, 229, 285; Lockean paradigm, 77, 231, 233; "Of Property," 232; *Two Treatises*, 227–28, 233
London Company. *See* Virginia Company
London, xiii, xv, 30–31
Londonderry Plantation, 188–89
Long Meg of Westminster, 164
Louis XIV, 202
Love, John, *Geodaesia*, 233
Lovell, John, 237
Low Countries, xi, 118, 127. *See also* Dutch
Lowe, Thomas, 249
Lusts Dominion. See Dekker, Thomas
Lutherans, 137

Machiavelli, 146–47, 175–76
Mackenthun, Gesa, 292, n.33
Madonna, 113
Magdalen Islands, 30
Magellan, Ferdinand 113
Maguel, Francis, 121
Maine, 30, 66
Maltese Cross, on Smith's *Map*, 75
Manchester Papers, 94, 105
Mannahoacs, 38, 40–41
Manoa, 30
Manteo, 50, 125, 293 n. 5, 294, n. 25
maps, meaning of, 296 n. 6
Marcus Aurelius, 146–47
Martin, John, 252
Martin, Richard, 99
Martin's Hundred, 95, 99, 108
"Massacre" of 1622, 1, 10–11, 18, 46, 95, 124, 125, 177, 189, 231, 251–52, 278, 286

Massawomek Indians, 38
Massinger, Philip: *The Bondman*, 244, 248; *The Renegado*, xv, 137, 142–43
mastiffs, 143
Matachanna, 59
Matahan, 57, 58 (fig. 2.1)
Matar, Nabil, 136
Matchumps, 53–54, 294 n.21
mathematics, 221–22
McHugh, P. G., 225–26
McKeon, Michael, 219
McRae, Andrew, 222, 228–29, 316 n.11
Mediterranean world, 136, 141; slavery in, 244–50
Meinig, D. W., 306 n.115
Melancholy Cavalier, 260, 261 (fig. 12.1)
Mellifont, 159
Menard, Russell R., 262
Menatonon, 29
Mendieta, Jerónimo, 116
Merton statute, 226–27, 231
Mexico, 30, 125
Mintz, Sidney, 209
miscegenation, 142
Molina, Diego de, 121–22
Monacan Indians, 32, 38
Monson, William, 162, 310 n. 59
Montanus, Gonsalvius, *A Discovery and Playne Declaration*, 117
Montrose, Louis, 230
Moore, Adam, 229–30, 232
Moors, 154, 161; as ethnic/racial category, 137
More News from Virginia, 266
More, Sir Thomas, *Utopia*, 195, 233, 242, 286
Morgan, Edmund, 93
Morocco, 13, 14, 136, 152–71, 248, 280, 282–83; kings, 152
Moryson, Fynes, 142, 145, 185, 282; description of the Irish, 184–85
Motollinía, 115–16
Mountjoy, Charles, Lord, 172, 185
Mullisheg. *See* al-Mansur, Ahmed
Muly Mahamet. *See* al-Mutawakkil, Muhammed
Muly Molocco. *See* al-Malik, 'Abd
Munday, Anthony, 246
Munster, 174, 190; Munster Plantation, 173–74, 188
Murrin, John S., 255
Muscovy, 127

Namontack, 51–54; in London, 52–53, 66–67; mentioned in Jonson's *Epicoene*, 53; reported murdered, 54
Nanawack, 56–57
Nansemond Indians, 40
Narragansett Bay, 30
nations and nationalism, 146, 255
Native Americans. *See* Indians
Naurians, 32
Navirans, 278
Negro (ship), 165, 167, 310 n.50
Negroes, 154, 236, 286
Netherlands. *See* Low Countries
Neville, Henry, *News from the New Exchange*, 259–60
A New Description of Virginia, 255
New England, 30–31, 76–77, 209, 211, 256
New World, 26–27, 115, 150, 287; bounty of, 31–32, 34; "problem" of, 271. *See also* America
New York Public Library, 96
Newfoundland, 26, 30
Newport, Christopher, 31, 33–34, 40, 42–43, 51–52, 74, 275–76, 278, 281
Nine Years War, 172, 178, 185, 188
Noël Hume, Ivor and Audrey, 300 n.28
Noel, Martin, 253
Norden, John, *Surveyor's Dialogue*, 220–21, 227, 233
Nova Scotia, 30
Nuce, Sir William, 96

O'Brien, Murrogh, 185
O'Malley, Grace, 164, 170
O'Neill, Hugh, earl of Tyrone, 159, 173, 188
O'Neill, Shane, 161
Okee (Powhatan god), 64
Old World, 26
Opechancanough (Pawmunkey chief), 10, 35, 36 (fig. 1.1), 46, 65, 67, 88–89, 278
Opitchapam, 67
Orinoco River, 30, 49, 136
Othello, xv. *See also* Shakespeare, William
Ottoman Empire, xi, 13, 135–36, 142–47, 152, 155, 245–47, 273, 280–82. *See also* Turkey
Outer Banks, 28. *See also* Roanoke
Ovid, 56, *Metamorphoses*, 1–2, 6, 20–21, 288
Oxford, 68, 79

Pagden, Anthony, 219, 231
Pale, the, 177
Pamunkey Indians, 32, 90

papacy, 25–27, 158; Donation of 1493, 121, 276
Parliament (England), 11, 225, 252–53, 271
Paspahegh Indians, 32, 34
Payne, Robert, *Brief Description of Ireland*, 180–81, 186
Peckham, Sir George, 25–26
Peele, George, *The Battel of Alcazar*, 137, 155, 161–63
Penobscot Bay, 30
Pepys, Samuel, 248
Percy, George, 31–32, 35, 44, 75, 123–24, 213; *Observations Gathered out of a Discourse of the Plantation of the Southerne Colonie in Virginia by the English, 1606*, 285
Pérez, Antonio, 122
Perfect Description of Virginia, 256
Perkins, William, 203
Peter Martyr, 28; *De Orbe Novo Decades*, 113
Peru, 30, 125
Philip II, 116, 121, 156–58, 168
Philip III, 116, 119, 121, 159
Picts, 181–86, 204, 297 n.26
Pilgrims (New England), xi
pirates, piracy, 137, 149–50, 158–59, 165, 168–70, 309 n.29, 319 n.33. *See also* English (people), privateers
Pizarro, Francisco, 14, 113
Plat, Hugh, 210
The Planter's Plea, 252
Plato, 176
Plymouth Colony, xi, 31, 137
Plymouth Company, 102
Pocahontas, xiii–xv, 35, 142, 279; in England, 58–66, 295 n.40; evoked by Smith's Turkish mistress, 144; "Lady Rebecca Rolfe," 65; portrait, 61 (fig. 2.2); "saves" life of Smith, marries Rolfe, 46
Portugal, 26, 127, 131, 156; ambitions, 81; absorption into Spain, 118; empire, 75; involvement in slave trade, 236; as model of colonialist policy, 141–42; succession crisis, 117. *See also* Iberia
Pory, John, xi, 93, 99, 105–6, 299 n.5
Potomac River, 38
Powhatan (Wahunsonacock), xiv, 3, 7, 9, 25, 29, 32, 35, 37, 44, 47, 49, 52–53, 55, 67, 87, 144, 278–79; accedes to English occupation, 46; "coronation" by English, 42–43, 53; dispatches Namontack to England, 51; as figure and name on John Smith's Map, 70, 77, 81

366   Index

Powhatan Confederation, 29, 92
Powhatan Indians, 9, 16, 17, 33–34, 48, 49–67, 124–25, 278; religious leaders, 124, 231
Pratt, Marie Louise, 218
The Present State of Virginia, and the College, 256
Price, Hugh, 45
privateers, 29, 129
Privy Council, 98–99, 106, 249; *Acts of Privy Council*, 158, 165
property, private, 220, 225, 232, 284–86, 287
Protestantism, 12, 126–27, 158, 180, 185, 190, 282; English, 125; militant, 116. *See also* England, Church of
providence, 198, 209
Provost, John, 51
Purchas, Samuel, 46, 54–55, 58, 62, 66–67, 69, 119, 145, 148, 230–31, 244, 252; *Purchas His Pilgrimmes*, 71, 277; tries to convert Tomocomo, 64
Puritans, 30

Quebec, xiii
Quinn, David B., 177

race, 154–55, 165; and slavery, 250–53
Ralegh, Sir Walter xi, 4, 13, 27, 30, 50–51, 79, 115, 136, 149, 160, 162, 164, 174, 176–77, 222–23, 275; *Discoverie of Guiana*, 13
Rapahanna Indians, 32, 41, 293 n.1
Rappahannock River, 38, 40
A Relation of Maryland, 196
renegades, 149–50
The Renegado. See Massinger, Philip
Requierimento, 75. *See also* rituals of possession
Rich, Barnaby, 177; *New Description of Ireland*, 179; *True and Kind Excuse*, 179–80
Rich, Henry, earl of Warwick, 94, 103, 105–8, 280
Rich, Nathaniel, 105, 107–8
rituals of possession, 27, 32, 75
Roanoke, xi, 4, 27–29, 32–33, 41–42, 101–2, 119, 125, 160, 174, 189–90, 223, 275, 293 n. 1
Roberts, Henry, 156, 159, 169
Rolfe, John, 7, 46, 63, 142, 143, 279
Rome, ancient, 1–2, 5, 21, 146–49; institution of slavery, 240; model of imperialism, 172, 277. *See also translatio imperii*
Rose, Emily, 11
Royal African Company, 19
Russia, 140

Sagadahoc colony, 51, 101–2
St. Augustine (Florida), xi, 4
St. Augustine, *City of God*, 239
St. Lawrence Seaway, 4, 30
St. Mary Spital, 248
St. Nevis Island, 74
Sanders, Thomas, 245
Sandys, Sir Edwin, 10, 63, 65, 105–6, 280, 301 n.56
Sandys, George, xi, 1–2, 6, 11, 20, 105, 136; *Metamorphoses*, 1, 20, 288; *Relation of Journey*, xi
Sandys, Margaret, Lady Wyatt, 108
Santa Fe, xiii
Savage, Thomas, 52–53
savagery, 211
Scotland, 118
Scots, 15. *See also* Picts
Sea Venture, 53–56
Sebastian, king of Portugal, 157, 161–63
Secotan Indians, 28–29
Sepúlveda, Juan Ginés de, 116
Severn River, 96
Shakespeare, William 5, 146; *King Lear*, 273; *Merchant of Venice*, 243–44; *Othello*, 142, 178; *The Tempest*, 15–19, 178, 320 n.53
Sheehan, Bernard, 173
Sherley, Sir Anthony, 136
Sherwood, William, 267
Sidney, Sir Henry, 159, 174–75
Sidney, Sir Philip, 174, *Arcadia*, 270
Silver, Timothy, 197, 208
Simpson, Richard, 158
Skelton, John, 228
Skinner, Quentin, 240
slave trade, xi, 19, 165, 169–70
slavery, 19–20, 154, 165, 169, 236–53, 286; plantation, 19; black, 154, 165; chattel, 171; slave narratives, 244–50
Smith, John, xi, xiv, 6–7, 10, 14, 25, 34, 47–48, 51, 60, 62, 66–67, 98, 122–23, 171, 211, 231, 278–81, 286, 297 n. 29, 298 n.39, 320 n. 51; attitude toward Spanish, 111–12, 126–34, 281–22; and "coronation" of Powhatan, 42–43; criticizes idle gentlemen, 78; experience in Turkey, 14, 135–51; explores and maps the Chesapeake, 8–9, 35–40, 68–91; first meeting with Powhatan, 35, 37; joins Catholic Hapsburg army, 138; life story, xiii–xv, 78, 135–51; motto, *Vincere est Vivere*, 80; remodels himself as a "gentleman,"

147–49; returns Namontack to Powhatan, 53; "saved" by Pocahontas, 6–7, 12–13, 37; and Tomocomo in London, 63–64
Smith, John, works: *Advertisements for the Unexperienced Planters of New England*, 129; *A Description of New England*, 128; *The Generall Historie of Virginia, New-England, and the Summer Isles*, xiv, 36 (fig. 1.1), 53–54, 69, 71, 87–88, 89 (fig. 3.5), 128–29, 133–35, 144, 147–49, 217–19, 283; *A Map of Virginia*, 8, 38, 39 (fig. 1.2), 41–42, 69–91, 217–22, 279, 284; *The Proceedings of the English Colonie in Virginia*, 130; *A True Relation of Such Occurences and Accidents of Note*, 3, 35–37, 69, 75, 87; *The True Travels, Adventures, and Relations of Captaine John Smith*, xiii, xv, 135–51, 160, 283
Smith, Sir Thomas, 57, 59, 63, 99, 100, 107, 173–74, 176, 238, 240, 242
Smyth, John, of Nibley, 96, 107
Somers, Sir George, 44, 54
Songhay, 157
South Carolina, 30
Southhampton, earl of. *See* Wriosthely, Henry
Spain, xi, 12, 14, 25–26; aggression, 170; decline of global power, 159; empire, 3–4, 41, 75, 111–12, 115–16, 251, 281; English responses to, 111–35, 155–57; establishes Chesapeake outpost, 121; ethnicity, 117; eviction of Moriscos, 159; imperial ambitions, 81, 113–16, 152, 157; "providential election" as world leader, 112–15; relations with Morocco, 155–57, 168; relations with Portugal, 118, 153; and slave trade, 236; Spanish Armada, 4, 159, 168; Spanish Fleet, 29–30; Spanish Main, 27, 29–30, 42; "specter" of, 111–35
Spartan virtues, 204
Spelman, Henry, 212
Spenser, Edmund, 177; *The Faerie Queene*, 77, 164, 170, 203; *View of the Present State of Ireland*, 176, 185, 188–89, 213–14. *See also* Britomart
Squanto, xiii
Stanihurst, Richard, 186, 189
Star Chamber, 241
Stow, John, 248
Strachey, William, 15, 45, 54–55, 119–20, 123, 277, 288, 297 n. 29; *Historie of Travell into Virginia Britania*, 54; "A True Reportory," 294, n.24

Strange News from Virginia, 266
Stuart regime, 119
Stubbes, Phillip, 203
Stukeley, Thomas, 136, 158–59, 161, 310 n.50. *See also Famous History*
Suárez de Toledo, Alonso, 121
sugar industry, 209
Süleyman the Magnificent, sultan, 137
sumptuary laws, 100
Sunderland, earl of, 271
surveying, land, 33, 220, 233
Susan Constant, Godspeed, Discovery (first ships of Jamestown colonists), 31, 51, 207, 275
Susquehannock Indians, 38; Bowman on Smith's *Map*, 70–72, 73 (fig. 3.1), 74, 81–82, 85
Susquehannock River, 40
Symonds, William, 282

Tacitus, 175–76, 240
Tasso, Torquato, *Gerusalamme Liberata*, 283
temperance, 196, 203, 206, 216
tenure, leasehold, and copyhold, 97
Thames River, 49
Thomson, Jasper, 156
Thorpe, George, 59, 100, 108
Tiger, 137
Tindol, Captain. *See* Kendall, George
Tintam, John, 237
tobacco, xiii, 10, 21, 30, 98, 209, 237, 260
Todd, Janet, 271
Tomocomo, 58, 63–65, 67, 279; encounter with John Smith in London, 63–64, 286
Towaye, 50
Tracy, William, 96
Tragbigzanda, Charatza, 139, 143
translatio imperii, 15–16, 19, 21, 148, 172, 277; Spanish version, 116. *See also Imperium brittanicum*
Transylvania, xiii
Traub, Valerie, 86
travel writing, 195
treason, 163, 168
Treaty of London (1604), 119, 153, 168
Treaty of Tordesillas (1494), 153
Troy, 146, 277
Tsenacommacah, territory of Powhatans, 60, 62
Turkey, 13, 135–36, 149–51. *See also* Ottoman Empire
Turks, xiii, 137, 150, 245–49; "Turk" as ethnic category, 137; "turning Turk," xv, 137, 247; Turkish slaves, 248

Tymor, brother of Charatza Tragbigzanda, 139–40; murdered by John Smith, 140

Ulster Rebellion, Second, 158
Ulster, 174–75, 190; Ulster Plantation, 173
Uprising of 1622. *See* "Massacre" of 1622
Utopia. See More, Thomas

Vale of Berkeley, 96
van Meer, Michael, 58
Vaughan, Alden 9, 320 n. 50
Vaughan, Robert, 90
Velasco, Don Luís (Paquiquineo), xiii, 4, 121, 125
Venice, 129
Verstegan, Richard, 240
Vienna, 137
villeinage, 241–42
Virgil, *Aeneid*, 21, 277, 288
Virginia: compared to ancient Rome, 147–48; as constructed idea, 148, 150–51, 160; as constructed territory, 70, 136; mapped, 68–91, 217–22; as "separate cultural space," 255–74
Virginia Assembly, xi
Virginia Colony, xi, 1–2, 10, 12, 19–20, 49, 190; founding of, 27–35; early settlement, 119–21. *See also* Jamestown; Chesapeake region
Virginia Company, xi, 1, 5, 7, 10, 31, 33–35, 43–44, 49, 56, 59, 63, 76, 94–95, 106, 134, 135, 148–49, 234, 238, 275–76, 280; Charter revised by James I, 123; initial instructions for colony, 276; promotes lottery, 57, 58 (fig. 2.1); use of propaganda, 98; repopulates colony after 1622, 102
Virginia Council, 100, 119, 125, 251, 280–81, "A True Declaration," 281

Wahunsonacock. *See* Powhatan
Wales, 174
Walsingham, Francis, 243

Walter, John, 210
Wanchese, 50, 293 n. 5, 294 n.25
Ward, John, 149–50
warfare (Anglo-Indian). *See* conflict
Warwick, earl of. *See* Rich, Henry
waste, 223, 226, 228, 231, 284–86
Waterhouse, Edward, 46, 231, 251
Webb, Stephen, 267, 321 n.36
Weber, Max, 210
Werowocomoco, 35
Wertenbaker, 273, 321 n.36
West Country, 30–31, 160, 170
West Indies, 13; 29–30, 156, 248
West, idea of the, 170
"Westward Enterprise," 174
whiskey, corn, 100
Whitaker, Alexander, 125
White, John, 32, 41, 57, 136, 174, 182–83, 197, 199–200
Whittakers, Mrs., 106
Wild Coast, 30
William I of Orange, 117, *Apology Against . . . the King of Spaine*, 117
William III of Orange, 271
Williams, Roger, 196, 211–12
Williamson, Joseph, 267
Wingfield, Edward Maria, 122
Wingina, 28
Wolstenholme, John, 99, 103, 300 n.32
Wood, William, 196
Woolley, Hannah, 205
Worsop, Edward, 220
Wriosthely, Henry, earl of Southhampton, 106–7, 280, 301 n.56
Wyatt, Sir Francis, 18, 46–47, 106, 108, 125–26

Yeardley, George, 95–96
York River, 32, 37
Young, Robert, 173

Zuniga, Pedro de, 52

Acknowledgments

The editors wish to thank the staff and all the participants of the NEH Folger Institute Summer Seminar, "Texts of Imagination and Power," conducted by Karen Ordahl Kupperman in 2000, which was the inspiration for this collection.

We should especially like to thank Kathleen Lynch, Carol Brobeck, and Richard Kuhta of the Folger, Pompa Banerjee (the seminar participant who first came up with the idea for this volume), Alden and Virginia Vaughan, and Karen Ordahl Kupperman. Funds and other institutional support for the editors have been provided by the Folger Shakespeare Library, the National Endowment for the Humanities, the Newberry Library, the John Carter Brown Library, and the Center for the Humanities, Wesleyan University.

For help with illustrations, we wish to acknowledge Michael Scott of the Folger Shakespeare Library, Richard Hurley of the John Carter Brown Library, and Elizabeth Fuller of the Rosenbach Library. For advice and direction in putting together this book, we wish to express our gratitude to our editor at the University of Pennsylvania Press, Robert Lockhart, along with Dan Richter, our series editor, and the anonymous readers for the press who were very thoughtful and helpful.

www.ingramcontent.com/pod-product-compliance
Lightning Source LLC
Chambersburg PA
CBHW020634230426
43665CB00008B/166